Advance Praise for
The Political Speechwriter's Companion, Second Edition

"*The Political Speechwriter's Companion* is the first book on speechwriting I ever read, and it's the first one I recommend to anyone seriously interested in speechwriting as a craft. If you work in political communications (or really any type of communications) this edition belongs in your office."

—David Litt, Former Speechwriter for President Obama,
Best-selling author of *Thanks, Obama: My Hopey, Changey White House Years*

"Helpful research, more examples, and a great teaching tool! Politicians, preachers, corporate, academic, and nonprofit leaders need this book. Indispensable for both speechwriters and speechgivers."

—Robert Mallett, President, Africare
Former VP, Pfizer, Inc.,
Former Deputy Secretary of the U.S. Department of Commerce

"*The Political Speechwriter's Companion* is a must-have guide to good writing for those in politics, journalism and beyond. Stuffed with useful tips, examples and how-to advice, this book has it all."

—Lynn Sweet,
Washington Bureau Chief, *Chicago Sun-Times*

"Unique! Invaluable! I've learned from it for years, and have learned even more from this new edition."

—Ann Brown,
Former Chair U.S. Consumer Product Safety Commission

"Only a very few people can both write speeches and teach you how. Of those few, absolutely no one is more talented and dedicated than Robert Lehrman and Eric Schnure. As Strunk & White has been a timeless classic for writers, *The Political Speechwriter's Companion* will be a dog-eared desk-mate for speechwriters, forever."

—David Murray, Executive Director,
Professional Speechwriters Association
Editor & Publisher, *Vital Speeches of the Day*

Praise for the First Edition

". . . a gift from one of the country's most gifted speechwriters."

—The Honorable William Cohen,
U.S. Senator (R-ME, 1979–1997)
U.S. Secretary of Defense (1997–2001)

"Speechwriting is an art and a skill. Bob's new book will help readers develop their skills into an art."

—The Honorable James R. Sasser,
U.S. Senator (D-TN, 1977–1995)
Ambassador to China (1996–1999)

". . . a cookbook with all of the delicious ingredients for good speeches. The basics from soup to nuts are all here, as well as the sweeteners that make for great public presentations."

—Juan Williams,
Emmy Award–winning NPR commentator (1999–2010)
Author, *Eyes on the Prize* and *Thurgood Marshall: American Revolutionary*

"I keep Bob's book on my shelf, next to *Bartlett's*."

—Alex Castellanos, Partner, National Media Inc.
CNN Commentator, Advisor to Mitt Romney's
2008 Presidential Campaign

"The elements of good speech writing are all here—structure, clarity, delivery, persuasion, humor, and leaving your audience with a memorable close. Bob wrote speeches for me when I was the Majority Whip in the U.S. House of Representatives. He made me a far better speaker. My audiences were happier and so was I."

—David Bonior,
U.S. Representative (D-MI, 1976–2003)

"Bob Lehrman has packed a career's worth of oratorical knowledge into this indispensable guidebook."

—Terry Edmonds,
Chief Speechwriter for
President Bill Clinton (1998–2001)

The Political Speechwriter's Companion
Second Edition

To Susan, Eric, and Michael, with admiration, love, and gratitude.
Robert A. Lehrman

To Nancy for her love, support, and, yes, patience. Lots of it. And to Benjamin and Daniel, who constantly test my power of persuasion yet were convinced I could write a book about it. Love you all.
Eric Schnure

Sara Miller McCune founded SAGE Publishing in 1965 to support the dissemination of usable knowledge and educate a global community. SAGE publishes more than 1000 journals and over 800 new books each year, spanning a wide range of subject areas. Our growing selection of library products includes archives, data, case studies and video. SAGE remains majority owned by our founder and after her lifetime will become owned by a charitable trust that secures the company's continued independence.

Los Angeles | London | New Delhi | Singapore | Washington DC | Melbourne

The Political Speechwriter's Companion

A Guide for Writers and Speakers

Second Edition

Robert A. Lehrman
American University

Eric Schnure
American University

SAGE | CQPRESS

SAGE | CQ PRESS

FOR INFORMATION:

CQ Press
An imprint of SAGE Publications, Inc.
2455 Teller Road
Thousand Oaks, California 91320
E-mail: order@sagepub.com

SAGE Publications Ltd.
1 Oliver's Yard
55 City Road
London EC1Y 1SP
United Kingdom

SAGE Publications India Pvt. Ltd.
B 1/I 1 Mohan Cooperative Industrial Area
Mathura Road, New Delhi 110 044
India

SAGE Publications Asia-Pacific Pte. Ltd.
18 Cross Street #10-10/11/12
China Square Central
Singapore 048423

Copyright © 2020 by CQ Press, an imprint of SAGE. CQ Press is a registered trademark of Congressional Quarterly Inc.

All rights reserved. Except as permitted by U.S. copyright law, no part of this work may be reproduced or distributed in any form or by any means, or stored in a database or retrieval system, without permission in writing from the publisher.

All third party trademarks referenced or depicted herein are included solely for the purpose of illustration and are the property of their respective owners. Reference to these trademarks in no way indicates any relationship with, or endorsement by, the trademark owner.

Printed in the United States of America.

Library of Congress Cataloging-in-Publication Data

Names: Lehrman, Robert A., author. | Schnure, Eric, author.

Title: The political speechwriter's companion : a guide for writers and speakers / Robert A. Lehrman, Eric Schnure.

Description: Second edition. | Washington, D.C. : CQ Press, a Division of Sage, 2020. | Includes bibliographical references and index.

Identifiers: LCCN 2018061300 | ISBN 9781506387741 (pbk. : alk. paper)

Subjects: LCSH: Speechwriting. | Political oratory. | Public speaking. | English language—Rhetoric.

Classification: LCC PN4142 .L44 2020 | DDC 808.5/1—dc23
LC record available at https://lccn.loc.gov/2018061300

Acquisitions Editor: Lily Norton
Editorial Assistant: Sarah Wilson
Production Editor: Bennie Clark Allen
Copy Editor: Melinda Masson
Typesetter: C&M Digitals (P) Ltd.
Proofreader: Sue Schon
Indexer: Jeanne Busemeyer
Cover Designer: Glenn Vogel
Marketing Manager: Staci Wittek

19 20 21 22 23 10 9 8 7 6 5 4 3 2 1

Brief Contents

Preface	xv
Foreword	xxi
Senator Lamar Alexander	
Introduction: Why Speechwriting Matters	1

PART I: LAYING THE FOUNDATION   7

1	The Political Speech	9
2	Persuasion	21
3	Audiences	39
4	Research	53

PART II: HOW TO DO IT   71

5	Structure	73
6	Language People Understand	93
7	Language People Remember	111
8	Anecdote	133
9	Wit	151
10	Support	173

PART III: APPLICATIONS 201

11 Beginnings 203

12 Problems 227

13 Solutions 251

14 Writing Conclusions 273

15 Delivery 295

16 Ethics 319

17 The Uneasy Partnership: Advice for Speakers and Writers 345

18 Final, Final Words 365

Appendix: A Speech for *Almost* Every Occasion 369

Notes 449

Bibliography 463

Index 473

Index of Speakers 505

About the Authors 509

Contents

Preface xv

Foreword xxi
   Senator Lamar Alexander

Introduction: Why Speechwriting Matters 1
Does Speechwriting Matter? 3
Why This Book? 5
Why Focus Only on Political Life? 5

PART I: LAYING THE FOUNDATION   7

1 | The Political Speech   9

Politicians Must Speak More 10
Politicians Must Persuade 13
Politicians Must Be Liked 14
Politicians Must Stay Upbeat 15
Politicians Must Speak to Average Folks 16
Politicians Must Get Quoted 18
Final Words 19

2 | Persuasion   21

Persuasion: The Questions 22
Persuasion: The Modes 26
Appealing to Reason 31
Appealing to Emotion 32
Appealing through Characterization 35
Final Words 37
   The Speechwriter's Checklist: Persuasion 38

3 | Audiences   39

Who Are Your Audiences?   40
What Makes Each Audience Unique?   41
What Do Audiences Feel about the Speaker?   45
   Behind the Scenes: The President Tweets   49
Final Words   50
   The Speechwriter's Checklist: Audiences   50

4 | Research   53

Researching the Event   54
Researching the Ideas   57
   Behind the Scenes: Wyatt Tee Walker   62
Researching the Poetry   62
Final Words   67
   The Speechwriter's Checklist: Research   70

PART II: HOW TO DO IT   71

5 | Structure   73

Why Monroe Works Well in Politics   76
Other Structures   83
Monroe Plus   84
Monroe in Practice: Four Tips   86
Final Words   87
   The Speechwriter's Checklist: Structure   92

6 | Language People Understand   93

Writing for Clarity   94
Reading versus Hearing   94
   Experts Talk: Elvin Lim   104

Final Words	109
The Speechwriter's Checklist: Language People Understand	110

7 | Language People Remember — 111

Making Language Vivid	112
Making Language Rhythmic	118
Final Words	132
The Speechwriter's Checklist: Language People Remember	132

8 | Anecdote — 133

Relevant, Remembered, Ready to Act	135
Types and Tips	138
Experts Talk: Sarah Hurwitz	143
Final Words	149
The Speechwriter's Checklist: Anecdote	149

9 | Wit — 151

Writing to Make Them Laugh	153
How to Do It	157
Formulas	160
Types and Tips	162
Experts Talk: Jeff Nussbaum	164
Final Words	171
The Speechwriter's Checklist: Wit	172

10 | Support — 173

Using Evidence	174
Types of Evidence	175
Making Evidence Memorable	186
Arguing Responsibly	190
Fallacies	190
Final Words	198
The Speechwriter's Checklist: Support	198

PART III: APPLICATIONS — 201

11 | Beginnings — 203

Attention — 207
Praise, Thanks, Acknowledgments — 212
   Behind the Scenes: The Howdahell — 214
Getting Serious and Stating the Purpose — 220
Final Words — 225
   The Speechwriter's Checklist: Beginnings — 225

12 | Problems — 227

Structure — 229
Language — 233
Anecdote — 238
Wit — 240
Support — 242
Final Words — 246
   The Speechwriter's Checklist: Presenting the Problem — 249

13 | Solutions — 251

Inspire Solutions with Language — 255
Inspire Solutions through Ethos — 258
The Three Ps: Proposal, Persuasion, Punch Line — 263
Final Words — 269
   The Speechwriter's Checklist: Solutions — 271

14 | Writing Conclusions — 273

Four-Part Close: The Steps — 274
   Behind the Scenes: The Lenny Skutnik Story — 281
Four-Part Close: Strategy — 282
Final Words — 289
   The Speechwriter's Checklist: Writing Conclusions — 293

15 | Delivery — 295

Elements of Delivery — 296
Delivery's Best Practice: Practice — 309
Expanding Your Horizons — 314
Final Words — 316
    The Speechwriter's Checklist: Delivery — 317

16 | Ethics — 319

Plagiarism — 322
Misleading Listeners — 326
Lying — 333
    Experts Talk: Clark Judge — 334
Speechwriting: Unethical by Definition? — 337
Final Words — 343
    The Speechwriter's Checklist: Ethics — 344

17 | The Uneasy Partnership: Advice for Speakers and Writers — 345

For Speakers: What Speechwriters Need from You — 348
    Experts Talk: Rick Shapiro — 353
For Speechwriters: What Speakers Need from You — 355
Final Words — 362
    The Speechwriter's Checklist: The Uneasy Partnership—Advice for Speakers and Writers — 362

18 | Final, Final Words — 365

Appendix. A Speech for *Almost* Every Occasion — 369
Notes — 449
Bibliography — 463
Index — 473
Index of Speakers — 505
About the Authors — 509

Preface

*U*pdate.
 The term implies taking a project on its way to irrelevance and making it timely once more.

In this second edition of *The Political Speechwriter's Companion*, written a decade after the original version, there is much of that.

One obvious example: In the first edition, none of the almost 200 examples could come from later than 2009. Of the 244 examples in this edition, more than half are.

The reason we include so many recent ones: This book is a hybrid, written in part for both students and those in the business of politics. We don't discard every wonderful example from the long history of modern political speech. But each year our readers—especially students—get a bit younger. A speech from 1998 resonates less with students born that year than one they've heard.

Still, we've done more than update. This edition differs from the first in more ways than dates.

A lot of those differences stem from the fact that while Bob wrote the first edition, this one results from the partnership between him and his longtime colleague, coworker, and friend, speechwriter Eric Schnure.

In a preface written together, it is awkward for us to laud each other. Suffice to say we both feel working together has been a joy. Whether brainstorming, trading drafts back and forth, or wrestling with how to expand the section on ethics, we wound up gratified by the experience—and with a better book.

One improvement comes because we expanded its scope. The first edition was basically a "how-to." What kinds of speeches do politicians need? How can you write and deliver them effectively? This edition still focuses on those two questions.

We do that because we both believe in the value of political speeches done right. Of course, many political speeches are awful. But at its best a political speech doesn't just convey information or argue a point. It can be a dramatic monologue built around ideas, able to move, excite, entertain, and inspire. Even in the bitter 2016 election Americans saw skillful, moving, and thoughtful speeches from people in both parties.

Those speeches weren't typical, though, and the reasons are no mystery. Political speeches are usually written at breakneck speed, sometimes by committee, by young writers with little training, or by people whose main interest is policy, not language. Few books exist to help.

So our aim remains what it was in 2009: filling that gap. And not just for American politicians. Speechwriters and politicians use this book in Canada, Europe, Asia, and South America. We know that because they write us and send samples. Google Translate—thanks!

But while much of the book is about technique, there are six areas that are new and very different.

The Age of Trump: The first edition treated speeches from both parties the same. We pride ourselves on keeping what its reviewers called its "evenhanded approach." But especially since 2016, the amount of falsehoods and—frankly—lies in political life has made us expand the discussion of ethics, and not just in Chapter 16.

Technology: Much of the technology that influences speech today existed in 2009. But the ease of researching, the reach speeches now have, and the existence of not just new websites but new avenues to communicate—of which the tweet is just one—influence much of the way politicians use speeches. That changes what we suggest in many chapters.

Political Life: Writing speeches doesn't appear in a vacuum. Influencing it are the ways politicians live their lives, and the dynamics of an office. Readers will see more attention to those influences. Readers will also see a more anecdotal approach this time, with chapters laced with stories from our own lives and others. We want readers to see not just the language of speeches but the life that influences them.

Humor: We take advantage of Eric's experience. Called by one reporter one of the "go-to guys" for political humor in Washington, he has worked on dozens of the roasts that are part of Washington life. We expand the chapter on wit, but also expand how we treat it in various segments of the speeches we describe.

Persuasion: Bob was reluctant to offer much detail about the theories of and research into persuasion, in 2009. We have expanded our discussion of those elements here, in part influenced by the interest from readers, but also because in a field dominated by persuasive speech, understanding what theory and research make possible changes what writers create.

Other Views: The authors make our views clear. We believe in simple language, use of story, a variety of ways to persuade, and other ideas. Not everyone agrees, so we have expanded the book, for example, to include a long interview with the distinguished author of *The Anti-intellectual Presidency*, Elvin Lim, who agrees with us on very little except the importance of political speech. We want readers to examine his ideas unfiltered by our biases. And we offer a more nuanced view about other issues in the rest of the book.

Can you really learn to write speeches?

In a field where writers have traditionally learned on the job, it's not surprising that there are those who question the value of our systematic approach. It is the same question writers have asked about books on writing plays or short stories.

Systematic teaching seems to help most people, whether they're learning tennis, piano, or screenwriting. After teaching hundreds of students and seeing the results, we have no doubt. It does. As two people who have played and coached sports most of our lives—soccer and hockey—we try to teach speechwriting the way coaches operate. We could give soccer players a lecture on how to kick or trap. But as coaches, we take players onto the field and let them do a million touches. You will see this approach throughout the book, whether we cover the LAWS of speechwriting (language, anecdote, wit, and support) or the ways to apply those elements in the speeches most common in political life.

THE IMPORTANCE OF EXAMPLES

In virtually no sport is it enough to just play—or even practice. You have to watch others. A coach can tell you what to incorporate into your game. Examples *show* you. And because political speech is in the public domain, meaning we neither have to seek permission nor pay royalties for using them, this book is laced with examples of what others have done. You can't steal their language. But you can imitate their approaches.

Which is what all writers do.

Whether you are in class or in the White House, we want you to see what's worked. In our speechwriting course at American University, we see, semester after semester, that this makes a difference. You should read through and think about each example in the chapters that follow.

In the first few chapters, you will see us often draw from the speeches of Hillary Clinton and Donald Trump. For while media attention focused on their differences, political speechwriters should also see the similarities in rhetoric. But this book is not about just presidential speech. We draw our almost 250 examples from well over 200 speakers.

Because we learn not just from success but failure, some chapters use examples of speeches that did not work. But since the odds are that someone who writes a good opening is more likely to have closed well, and because by following one speech through we can examine how things planted in an opening recur later, you will see some speeches come back again and again:

Michelle Obama's 2016 Democratic National Convention speech, for example, or Mary Fisher's "Shroud of Silence" speech from the Republican National Convention in 1992.

To help readers learn, we have included a number of features. We're grateful first to CQ Press and now to SAGE for suggesting, encouraging, and in some cases insisting on them.

FEATURES

- *ANNOTATED SPEECHES:* In each chapter, we examine a variety of techniques in isolation. But in real life, speeches use them in combination. To show how that works, we have worked with skillful designers to annotate excerpts so you can see how each one works without destroying your ability to read on.

- *INTERVIEWS:* We don't have a monopoly on wisdom. So, in this edition, we have interviewed experts, including Professor Lim. Other interviews let readers see how some of the best speechwriters in the country go about their work, as well as the views of one of the leading consultants on political management.

- *BEHIND THE SCENES:* We don't have a monopoly on experiences either. So this edition includes historic insights.

- *EXERCISES:* Over the years, we have found a number of exercises that allow students not just to read what we suggest but also to experiment to see if our advice works for them.

- *THE SPEECHWRITER'S CHECKLIST:* Most chapters are full of suggestions, but you don't have to take notes. At the end of those chapters, you will find a checklist of the things you need to remember most as you are thinking, creating, and drafting speeches.

- *AS DELIVERED:* If this book were being published ten years ago, we would have to include a long section of speeches to study. The internet and YouTube have made that unnecessary. You can read, listen to, and watch online most of the speeches mentioned or excerpted in the chapters that follow. Each "As Delivered" box includes either an audio file or a video of each speech.

So far, we've examined what kinds of things we offer in the book. Of course, we would be happy if you read the book straight through and committed large swatches of it to memory. Not every reader has the same needs, though. Some of you may want to turn right to the chapter on delivery; others may be more interested in structure, or the research on what makes arguments persuasive. That's fine with us. We've tried to make the book easy to navigate so that you can dip in and out of the text to quickly find the advice you need.

For those who do want to read it all, we have organized it so each section prepares you for the next. But there's a reason the word *companion* is in the title. Like we do with lifetime friends, you may want to spend time with this book, drop it for a while, then pick it up again. Readers have told us that is true for the first edition. We hope that will be the case in the decade ahead.

Whether you read from beginning to end or skip around, please don't forget the way this preface opened: Technique is important but not everything. As you read about antithesis, or analogy, or Monroe's Motivated Sequence, remember: A gift for language and passion for issues will contribute more to a speech than technique alone ever can.

And this book results from contributions made by many people other than the authors.

ACKNOWLEDGMENTS

Faithful readers, in both the first and second editions of this book, you see us urge the absolute minimum number of acknowledgments you can get away with. But that's in speeches. This book is different. We owe too many people too much.

It is the custom with second editions to eliminate much of the editorial work valuable the first time around. That would have been a disaster with this one because there was so much new. We are grateful to Executive Editor Monica Eckman for seeing why for this book we needed an exception and grateful to the one she found, Lily Norton, for navigating us through the process; and to Sarah Wilson for making sure we met our deadlines, which we mostly did. We are grateful, too, for the work by former journalism professor and now editor Jane Harrigan. As she did with the first edition, she threw herself into not just what we wrote but what we thought in every chapter. We both relished and dreaded her long emails, along with comments and suggestions we ignored at our peril. Thank you also to Production Editor Bennie Clark Allen, Copy Editor Melinda Masson, Marketing Manager Staci Wittek, and Cover Designer Glenn Vogel.

We are grateful to five people known for the expertise who let us interview them so we could broaden the perspectives offered in this book: Sarah Hurwitz, Clark Judge, Elvin Lim, Jeff Nussbaum, and Rick Shapiro.

We are also grateful to the many speechwriters, friends, and academics who got right to work producing the stingingly honest critiques we wanted when we finished the first draft. Thanks to Brian Agler, Russ Block, Elizabeth

Gibson, Dan Gottleib, David Lehrman, Ryan Myers, Mintaro Oba, Mary Robbins, Genevieve Rozansky, and Desson Thomson.

We are also thankful for the perspective of two top-notch journalists, Clark Hoyt and Doyle McManus. They offered a different perspective from other reviewers, and the book is better for it. We are grateful as well to David Murray, not just editor of *Vital Speeches*, the only magazine that reprints speeches that would otherwise escape notice, but also the founder of a vital resource and network for speechwriters: the Professional Speechwriters Association.

Naturally, we didn't just learn from those critiquing this book. We learned a lot from the brilliant strategist and media person, and now friend, the communications director for Vice President Gore, Marla Romash, and her successor, the equally talented Lorraine Voles. We learned from colleagues like Dan Pink, who writes so accessibly, and Ginny Terzano, who reminds us to get to the point. We've learned from the writings of others, especially the textbook of Stephen Lucas. In fact, readers should frequently visit www.americanrhetoric.com, the website created by the indefatigable Lucas, author of *The Art of Public Speaking*. And of course, Alan Monroe. When Bob was hired to teach speech as a grad student, he used *Principles of Speech* (fifth edition) by Monroe and Ehninger. The ideas it contained shape Chapter 5 and our teaching. We have been involved with politics for much of our lives. This book is informed by every campaign and every political office we ever joined.

Do students understand that teachers learn from them? There hasn't been a class where we haven't learned from students not just how to be better teachers, but how to be better writers. When we look back, we take pride in knowing that alums of the class have been speechwriters for at least eight senators, Democrats and Republicans; governors; dozens of members of the House of Representatives; corporate CEOs; and university presidents, as well as officials in other countries. You will study some of their work in this new edition—and profit from their critiques as we wrote.

Finally, we are grateful to our families, Nancy (Epstein) Schnure, and Benjamin and Daniel Schnure; and Michael and Eric Lehrman and Susan Thaul. Every trip to California, hockey practice, or quiet dinner at home missed so we could spend time on this book came with a profound measure of guilt— and gratitude. And to Nancy and Susan: Your views have influenced everything we write. We two book partners are lucky to have found partners willing to share their lives with us—and tolerant of the times this book has kept us away.

We can't emphasize how grateful we are to Senator Lamar Alexander, who not only agreed to write the Foreword, but who turned in a witty piece of writing that enriches the book.

Thank you all.

Foreword

Senator Lamar Alexander

I once spoke to an audience that included "Roots" author Alex Haley, who was a marvelous storyteller. Afterward he politely suggested, "If when you begin talking, you would say, 'Instead of making a speech, let me tell you a story,' someone might actually listen to what you have to say." Ever since, I have tried to begin any speech with a story, often *that* story. As Robert Lehrman and Eric Schnure recommend: "Begin with some wit—and leave them eager to hear what comes next."

It helps if the opening story defines your purpose. When introducing myself to Republican audiences in Iowa during the 1996 presidential campaign, I began with: *"The New York Times* once wrote that 'Mr. Alexander grew up in a lower middle class family in the mountains of Tennessee.' When I called home that weekend, my mother was reading Thessalonians to deal with what she considered to be a slur on the family. 'Son, we never thought about ourselves that way,' she said. 'You had a library card from the day you were three and music lessons from the day you were four. You had everything you needed that was important.'"

If my purpose was to define a problem at a United States Senate hearing: "Last month, Becky Savage broke our hearts when she testified about the opioid crisis. One night her two high-school age sons returned home after graduation for a party in their basement. The next morning, she found both sons dead. Someone had brought opioid pills to the party and mixed them with alcohol. "My boys were not alcoholics," Becky said, "They were not drug addicts. They were the victims of this terrible public health epidemic that is affecting nearly every community."

Or, if I was arguing that bipartisan cooperation in Washington, D.C., still was possible: "In the Fall of 2016, I telephoned Vice President Joe Biden. "Joe," I said, "Our '21st-Century Cures' bill is stuck. I've got President Obama's precision medicine provision in it. Your cancer moonshot is in it. Mitch McConnell's regenerative medicine is in it. Paul Ryan has found a way to pay for it. But I can't get the White House's attention. I feel like the butler standing outside the Oval Office with a silver platter, and no one will open the door and take the order." Biden replied, "If you want to feel like the butler, try being vice president." Then we went to work together and, a few months later, President Obama signed what Senator McConnell called "the most important piece of legislation of this Congress."

After defining the problem comes the solution. When I was elected governor, John Seigenthaler, editor of *The Tennessean*, gave me "The Twilight of the Presidency," a book by President Johnson's press secretary, George Reedy. In it Reedy says the president's job is to (1) See an urgent need, (2) Develop a strategy to meet that need, and (3) Persuade at least half the people you are right.

At least since Aristotle, the speaker's job has been to persuade. This is easier if the listener understands who you are and what you are talking about. I have been surprised at how many visitors to my Senate office never properly introduce themselves or tell me exactly what they want and why. I am also surprised by the number of staff members who are unable to write jargon-free sentences describing who my visitors are, what their problem is and what I should do about it. Staffers able to write clearly move up quickly. Lehrman and Schnure call such writing "human English."

Fewer words encourage clarity. In 1967, after he spoke for 45 minutes in his maiden speech to the U.S. Senate, Senator Howard Baker Jr. asked his father-in-law, Senator Everett Dirksen, "How did I do?" Dirksen replied, "Howard, occasionally you might enjoy the luxury of an unexpressed thought." I once overheard President George H. W. Bush ask his wife, "Bar, what should I talk about?" "About five minutes, George," she replied. David's encounter with Goliath is told in 327 words. It only took President Lincoln three minutes to define the Civil War in the Gettysburg Address. Lehrman and Schnure: "Length guarantees neither clarity nor nuance."

The authors stress the importance of delivery. Unfortunately, in my experience, practice does not always make delivery perfect. In my second try for the presidency, I would say, "We need less from Washington, and more of ourselves." My phrase resonated so poorly that I was out of the race almost before it started. A few months later, I heard Margaret Thatcher use the same phrase. The audience was thrilled. Delivery matters. As Marshall McLuhan said about television, the medium is the message.

There are ways to work around the challenges of delivery. In 1992, I was invited to address the Gridiron Dinner, a Washington, D.C., gathering of national media and other big shots. Texas Governor Ann Richards was to be the Democrat speaker. I knew immediately that I was in trouble. Governor Richards could light up the house with her speeches. So instead of speaking, I wrote funny lyrics to country music tunes and sang them while I played the piano. The audience applauded both her speech and my music.

Lehrman and Schnure discuss the "uneasy partnership between speakers and writers." For a while, I was Senator Baker's speechwriter. The senator never criticized my work, but he also never delivered what I had written. "Senator," I said, "We have a problem." "No we don't," he said. "You write what you want to write, and I'll say what I want to say." While Senator Baker and I got along swimmingly after that discussion, my staff has learned to avoid that dilemma. They read what I have written, listen to what I have said and then regurgitate it in a better-organized form. From that I am usually able to compose a good speech.

When asked to write a column for *The Washington Post*, Ruth Marcus sought advice from David Broder, the Pulitzer Prize winning reporter. "One idea per column," Broder said – which is also good advice for a speech.

Then there is the eulogy. After witnessing one senator memorialize another in the U.S. Capitol Rotunda, I added this rule to "Lamar Alexander's Little Plaid Book:" "When asked to speak at a funeral, remember to mention the deceased as often as yourself." For a near perfect eulogy, devoid of the personal pronoun despite their intimate relationship, read Jon Meacham's tribute to President George H. W. Bush.

Speeches are like music. The speaker experiments with words and phrases and delivery and then adjusts based upon what resonates with the audience. No one precisely understands this mystery. After World War II, Pee Wee King and Redd Stewart wrote lyrics to an everyday melody, "The No Name Waltz," and delivered their song to the Nashville publisher, Wesley Rose. Rose changed one phrase: "Oh, the Tennessee Waltz, the Tennessee Waltz" became "I remember the night and the Tennessee Waltz." Did that simple change of phrase help the song sell 5 million copies and become the anthem of country music?

In this handbook, Lehrman and Schnure offer a handy framework of suggestions for all those who are, in Bill Moyer's phrase, "fooling with words" to create political speeches that capture the audience, present a problem and solution, and persuade at least half their audience that they are right. All of us who write and speak and try to help others do so should be grateful.

Senator Lamar Alexander
Maryville, Tennessee
February 1, 2019

Introduction

Why Speechwriting Matters

On July 21, 2016, during a presidential campaign reporters regularly called "poisonous," Donald Trump took to the stage in Cleveland's Quicken Loans Arena against a backdrop of American flags, smiling the close-lipped smile that has been his signature, and accepted the Republican Party's nomination for president.

Exactly a week later, in Philadelphia's Wells Fargo Center, Hillary Clinton walked onto the stage, kissed her daughter, and waved to the delegates before accepting the Democratic Party's nomination for president.

If anyone expected the bitter atmosphere that dominated the 2016 primaries to evaporate after those conventions, they kept it to themselves. Even now, neither author of this book sees anything approaching unity in American politics.

But on those two nights, while Trump and Clinton spoke harshly about each other, they and their writers were united about one thing: the techniques that largely form the subject of this book.

Both used modified versions of Monroe's Motivated Sequence, the five-step problem–solution structure, ending with a call to action often offering choice.

> **TRUMP:** We must break free from the petty politics of the past. We must choose to believe in America.
>
> **CLINTON:** America's destiny is ours to choose. So let's be stronger together.

Both used the approach to language favored by politicians in both parties: short words and sentences easy for average folks to understand. The readability gauges we explain later show Trump speaking at a ninth-grade reading level. While journalists have criticized him for "dumbing down" rhetoric, Clinton's speech actually registered below sixth grade.

Both made liberal use of repetition, like alliteration—a succession of words beginning with the same sounds . . .

> **TRUMP:** If you want to hear the corporate spin, the carefully crafted lies, and the media myths . . .
>
> **CLINTON:** Enough with the bigotry and the bombast.

... and especially anaphora or epistrophe in what some politicians call "litany"—the series of sentences beginning or ending the same way, allowing speakers to build in power.

> **TRUMP:** This administration has failed America's inner cities. It's failed them on education. It's failed them on jobs. It's failed them on crime. It's failed them at every level.
>
> **CLINTON:** If you believe that companies should share profits with their workers, not pad executive bonuses, join us.
>
> If you believe the minimum wage should be a living wage ... and no one working full time should have to raise their children in poverty ... join us.
>
> If you believe that every man, woman, and child in America has the right to affordable health care ... join us.
>
> If you believe that we should say "no" to unfair trade deals ... that we should stand up to China ... that we should support our steelworkers and autoworkers and homegrown manufacturers ... join us.
>
> If you believe we should expand Social Security and protect a woman's right to make her own health care decisions ... join us.
>
> And yes, if you believe that your working mother, wife, sister, or daughter deserves equal pay ... join us ...
>
> Let's make sure this economy works for everyone, not just those at the top.

Both used their families to reassure listeners that they share their values.

> **TRUMP:** My dad, Fred Trump, was the smartest and hardest-working man I have ever known ... It's because of him that I learned from my youngest age to respect the dignity of work ...
>
> **CLINTON:** I've had to pick myself up and get back in the game. Like so much else, I got this from my mother.

And that just scratches the surface.

This second edition, like its predecessor, aims at showing speakers and speechwriters on both sides of the aisle how to write convincing, substantive, exciting, inspiring, evocative, and effective speeches. Even in today's polarized political climate, most techniques politicians use are largely the same as they were in 2009.

But this edition involves many changes from the first.

As it should. We would be pretty disappointed if we learned nothing from another decade spent working together.

One change stems from new experiences. Before 2009, we taught only Americans. Since then, we have led workshops in Asia, Europe, and Canada. With years spent testing how students and politicians around the world use *The Political Speechwriter's Companion*, we are both excited about putting what we've learned to use.

Meanwhile, readers who have used the first edition will see a second change.

While the first edition focused almost exclusively on technique, it would be naive—myopic—to do that this time. Political speech involves ethics. In 2016, the changes in what characterizes responsible political speech went far beyond the idea that a president can communicate in a tweet. We saw a staggering amount of misleading or false passages and, in many cases, sheer lies.

Telling the truth also involves technique. What constitutes credible sources? How do writers avoid the ad hominem attacks, hasty generalizations, unsupported assertions, and other fallacies that dominated the campaigns in 2016? How should a campaign respond when what its candidate says turns out to be wrong?

We cover these often disheartening issues because students, journalists, and people in political life bombard us with questions about them. "Is this what you did?" they ask. We have expanded this edition to include more discussion about the way ethics and technique merge.

We do our best to do that without taking sides, though. Yes, we both started in Democratic politics. But we are resolutely nonpartisan when we teach, and the same goes for this book. Naturally, questions about ethics aren't the only ones we try to answer. And we start with one with an answer readers may think obvious.

DOES SPEECHWRITING MATTER?

Former Bill Clinton speechwriter Jeff Shesol once wrote about the time after one of Clinton's speeches when Clinton threw an arm around him and said, "Here's the guy who typed my speech." For those who believe speechwriters are glorified stenographers, the speechwriter's role might not matter. And for those who believe politicians are often empty vessels—actors—it might only matter as one more example of sleight of hand, written by those who couldn't care less about truth.

The authors have a different view. We see political speechwriters, including those whose views we detest, almost uniformly working for people they believe communicate truths that matter and making sacrifices to do it. They write about the biggest policy debates of the day. Out of their printers come the arguments that support or oppose a war, universal health care, or a $700 billion economic "stimulus." They help articulate the passionate debate about everything from abortion to, well, the value of wooden baseball bats, as Senator Dick Durbin did for one speech. They give voice to our emotions at events important to us all. When the two of us worked in the White House for Vice President Gore, we wrote his speech commemorating the fiftieth anniversary of D-Day, the twenty-fifth anniversary of the moon landing, and the inauguration of Nelson Mandela.

We wrote eulogies for firefighters who died in action. On Bob's fiftieth birthday, he spent the entire day at the White House writing a speech on the value of fatherhood. He missed the party his family was putting on for him, yet still found it worth doing. Once you accept the legitimacy of the idea that someone else should write what politicians say—more on that later—these are not trivial assignments.

And they require both skill and art—something speakers are not always willing to admit.

In 1988, when one of us (Bob) wrote Ed Muskie's tribute to Jimmy Carter for the 1988 Democratic National Convention, Muskie walked to the podium carrying Bob's speech.

Before starting, he turned to Texas governor Ann Richards, who had introduced him. "Madame Chairperson," he said, "as you know, I like to do things my own way. So I will complete this assignment reading from my own handwritten notes."

He then read from the 20-point text Bob had handed him.

At other times, it's the writer who feels uncomfortable revealing the truth. Eric remembers the first speech he wrote for Al Gore. He didn't know how to react when, at the event, he started getting compliments. He asked the communications director, Lorraine Voles. Her answer: "Take the credit. God knows you're going to get blamed a lot."

We understand both sides. Staffers want to protect the boss. And for speakers, performing what others have written can make them uneasy. They think the crowd would be disappointed to know the truth, as if they were claiming credit for eloquence they don't have. Later in this book, we will pay more attention to the view that, as Professor Elvin Lim argues in his book *The Anti-intellectual Presidency*, speechwriters write memorably at the expense of substance. Presidents, he suggests, might "temper the scholarly animus towards the rhetorical presidency" if they spoke "more like Washington and Jefferson with greater frequency and less like Ford and Carter with equal frequency."[1]

There are plenty of weaknesses in political speech. But—like Aristotle—we think it's possible to entertain, excite, move, and persuade listeners in a responsible way about issues that matter. And because the issues matter, so does the work.

WHY THIS BOOK?

Do a search. Go to the day's *Congressional Record* and scroll down through the House and Senate speeches. A distressing number begin with mind-numbing and fatuous acknowledgments, outline ideas in generalities, and finish with a flurry of clichés. To watch members debate in the House of Representatives too often means enduring an endless succession of platitudes uttered in a monotone by speakers of both parties—neither has an edge when it comes to terrible rhetoric.

And there exists very little about how to write them. On Amazon, you'll find anthologies, textbooks on public speaking, "how-to" books aimed at people in corporate life, books about how to be a great high school debater or how to give a TED Talk or sermon, and memoirs by political speechwriters. But when it comes to how one writes a political speech, the first edition of this book has stood almost alone.

And that is true of this edition. Much of the book covers subjects you will find in a public speaking text. But it is still alone in examining how they suit the unique demands of political life.

Those demands affect more people than you would think. When we include those running for, say, city or township office, it rises to well above five hundred thousand.

That doesn't include the hundreds of thousands who work for them. While we hope this book is useful for anyone interested in rhetoric, it is specifically for the students taking speech, communications, and political science courses and for those in public life: state representatives and state senators, governors, senators and members of Congress, cabinet officials, mayors, and city council members.

It is a book for an eighty-year-old senator who's decided to be more compelling—and for the twenty-year-old running for state assembly. While we often speak directly to speechwriters, the book is aimed equally at politicians who write speeches themselves, or just want to see what they can demand from their staff. Which leads to a third question.

WHY FOCUS ONLY ON POLITICAL LIFE?

The simple answer: We want to write about something important—and important to do well.

Americans often look at politics with contempt. "That's just politics," they say. The word is an insult, sometimes understandably. Over the last ten years, only 26 percent of Democrats and 11 percent of Republicans answered yes when asked if they "trust government."

Politicians don't always deserve the insults. The two authors hang around lots of them. They are complex, nuanced people; often surprisingly introspective; and passionate about issues. They chafe at the limits politics imposes on their freedom to express what they think, to be both substantive and inspirational—and win reelection.

And while they've chosen a heady occupation, they pay a price: a bifurcated routine in which their families live hundreds of miles away while they rent tiny apartments in state capitals or Washington, staying for days they are in session; in which weekends mean rushing back to the district to race from pancake breakfasts to ribbon-cuttings to fundraisers as part of the perpetual campaign of political life; in which a small battalion of aides schedule their days, transport them to and fro, write their letters, and sign their names while leaving no time for them to go to their daughter's lacrosse game or read something besides a stack of memos.

In the White House, we used to be amazed by the briefing book aides handed Al Gore each night, dividing the next day into fifteen-minute segments from the moment he stepped into his limo ("7:30 a.m.: CIA briefing") to the moment, often near midnight, when he returned to the residence. Once one of us asked him how he got the time to explore any of the issues he dealt with.

"You spend the intellectual capital you come here with," Gore said, in his careful way.

How to change political life is beyond the scope of this book. How to make speeches better so they reflect that intellectual capital is not.

But we'll examine that question in practical ways—ways useful for people learning on the job. To be useful means sacrificing depth. It means seeming to suggest formulas rather than encouraging originality. And it may seem like we ignore the large issues that dominate a politician's day to focus on technique. We don't mean to. Even Mozart needed to practice scales.

What are the scales and arpeggios of political speech? Let's begin by looking at the kinds of speeches politicians give; how their needs differ from, say, those of the Exxon CEO or the Harvard University president; and what skills they and their writers must have before opening their laptops and writing the first word.

PART I

LAYING THE FOUNDATION

1

The Political Speech

Denver. November 1994.

The motorcade heads downtown past snowbanks while police cars with flashers on hold back traffic. Al Gore, then vice president of the United States, is on his way to speak to the Council of Jewish Federations. The speech is one of four on his schedule that day, all written by both Bob and Eric, calculated to get the Clinton administration out of trouble. Republicans won control of Congress in the disastrous elections two weeks earlier, prompting speculation that Bill Clinton would abandon principle and move to the right.

The other day in Jakarta, Indonesia, someone asked Clinton about a Republican proposal for a constitutional amendment allowing prayer in schools. The president said he would "not rule anything out."[1] The *Washington Post* reported this response on its front page, outraging Jewish groups, and we've hastily scheduled this speech to reassure them. Much of the speech will do that, but right now Bob worries about the opening.

A heel injury has forced Gore to limp toward the podium before speeches, supporting himself with a flamboyantly orange cane. Since the accident, he likes to start speeches with a string of heel jokes. We wanted to find a Jewish one, but nothing seemed appropriate until our intern, Julie Fanburg, came down from the library with a brilliant discovery.

That week's Torah portion was about Jacob, who was born grasping the heel of his twin brother, Esau. Jacob—*Ya'akov*, in Hebrew—actually means "heel"! Perfect! Eric writes an opening.

Now in Denver, Bob's not sure. These are mostly secular Jews. Will they find it too arcane? Inside the auditorium, Gore asks if the crowd will get it. Bob decides to take a chance. They should, he says. Gore gives him the wordless stare that means he'd better be right.

At the podium, though, Gore starts out tentatively. "This may be a stretch," he says. Uh-oh.

But now he's locked into the joke. "I'm told there's a special biblical significance to my appearance this morning, given my heel injury," he says, overexplaining because he's unsure. "The Torah—."

The audience explodes with laughter. Bob is startled. So is Gore. But he isn't too taken aback to improvise. "I hadn't *realized*," he says, pretending absolute incredulity, "so many of you *read* the— . . ."

More laughter. "Jacob was born grasping—I say this for those *few* who have not read— . . ."

Now everybody's roaring. Staffers are high-fiving Bob. *You guys wrote that? Great!* Finally, he's relaxed.

Can one, somewhat serendipitous remark really matter as much as Gore's policy points? Of course not; but for politicians, speeches are about both policy *and* personality. Is the politician smart? Funny? Compassionate? Voters care about these questions, so politicians must. A joke can mean a lot.

Gore's four speeches that day took him from Washington to Denver, where in addition to the Jewish Council he talked to a Native American convention. Then he flew down to Orlando for a meeting of Florida Democratic Party chairs, then to New York for another Democratic group meeting before heading back to Andrews Air Force Base. Not many people other than those in the White House—or running for it—go racing around the country to speak, living large chunks of their lives at thirty thousand feet.

Beyond the high-flying life and the national profile, though, Gore's speaking needs mirrored the needs of every candidate and public servant from Congress to state legislatures to local school boards. In fact, those needs make political speech unique.

POLITICIANS MUST SPEAK MORE

In national politics, four speeches in a day constitute a moderate load. Even first-term House members often speak more: at a prayer breakfast, at the caucus, on the floor, on the steps of the Capitol for off-the-cuff remarks to visiting school groups—and, after adjournment, maybe at a meeting of shop stewards or in a nearby restaurant for a fundraiser.

It is a routine both authors have lived, and it's unique to politics. We know because while we specialize in political speech, we have also worked full time for and consulted with some of the biggest corporations in the world—among them, General Electric, Google, Pfizer, Texaco, American Express, Marriott, and Airbus. Many corporate CEOs believe speaking once a week is a lot. While writing this chapter, we looked back at the White House index covering our years together. In two years, Al Gore spoke 556 times, largely from texts that we'd written. And those were just the prepared texts; politicians often speak using only a few talking points, or nothing at all.

Their lives weren't always like this. In his book *The Rhetorical Presidency*, Jeffrey K. Tulis calculates that from George Washington through William McKinley, American presidents spoke in public about ten times a year—and almost never about policy.[2] In 2017, especially during campaigns, even a state senator might talk ten times a day.

Speaking so often creates special needs. First, politicians need material they can recycle. Everybody knows that's true during a campaign, but these are the days of perpetual campaigns. Senators and their writers cannot possibly generate enough speech drafts to cover every appearance. They wouldn't want to even if they could. What politician with half a brain would have a formal text folded inside a jacket pocket for an intimate audience of a dozen well-heeled supporters at a fundraiser? The solution: a "stump," a set of remarks politicians deliver so often they can perform them without notes.

Sometimes politicians resent that option. In 2008, a reporter asked Michelle Obama if she got bored giving the same speech over and over again.[3] "Yeah, absolutely," she said.

But she did it. Most politicians eventually see that the sheer amount of day-in, day-out speaking makes recycling necessary.

This is true even at the highest levels, with politicians who have not just a speechwriter but a speechwriting team. So, for example, on July 14, 2017, Vice President Mike Pence opened a speech to the Retail Advocates Summit this way:

> And I bring greetings this morning from a friend of mine, who's a businessman who knows just a little bit about retail, who's fighting every single day to unleash a new era of American opportunity and prosperity. I bring greetings from the forty-fifth president of the United States of America, President Donald Trump.

Later that day, he opened this way, talking to the National Governors Association:

> And I bring greetings today from my friend, a champion of federalism who is fighting every single day to restore power to the states and to the people, the forty-fifth president of the United States of America, President Donald Trump. (Applause.)

In the same speech, Pence mentioned the major issue for that week: health care.

> Every day Obamacare survives is another day the American economy and American families struggle. We all remember the broken promises that made it possible for Obamacare to get passed. You remember them? They said if you like your doctor you could keep them—not true. They said if you like your health insurance you could keep it—not true. We were told that health insurance costs would go down. That one wasn't true either.

Three days later, he talked at a Healthcare Roundtable. Here's what he said:

> We all remember the broken promises of Obamacare. I have Dr. Price here. He and I were both members of Congress when the debate over Obamacare happened in the Congress seven years ago. I can still hear those promises ringing in my ears, can't you? If you like your doctor, you can keep them—not true. If you like your health insurance, you can keep it—not true. The cost of health insurance would go down if Obamacare passed—not true.

Does this kind of repetition seem unimaginative? Lazy? It's not. It allows speakers to use an effective bit more than once and, like actors in a play, to become fluent at it. Recycling material is smart.

That heavy, never-ending speech load leads to a second necessity: Politicians must rely on material prepared by others. Clearly, people delivering hundreds of speeches a year can't write them all. That's true even for skillful writers, like Gore. That day in Denver and Orlando, how could he have mastered the nuances of Middle East issues, biblical names, church and state questions, Native American concerns, and the volatile disputes of Democratic Party politics?

He couldn't. He had to rely on two speeches and on talking points from staffers like us who had the time to think about them.

"Politicians should write their own speeches," a reporter once told one of us. Often they wish they could. When Barack Obama made Jon Favreau his chief speechwriter, Favreau asked Obama's communications director, "Why? He's a great writer."

"He also has to be president," Robert Gibbs said.

Obama generally had a staff of senior writers. During his two terms, they churned out about four thousand speeches, all with the one overarching goal we discuss next.

POLITICIANS MUST PERSUADE

During our years of corporate writing, neither of us produced a speech in which the speaker sounded angry, raised a voice, or pounded a lectern. In politics, all these things happen regularly. They help make political speechwriting fun. Luckily, emotions don't often reach the level they did in 1849, when a speech by Massachusetts abolitionist congressman Charles Sumner, so incensed a Southern colleague that he attacked Sumner at his desk, beating him unconscious with his gutta-percha cane. But when politicians sound furious, it's usually not an act.

That's not surprising. We argue at home about what's for dinner, or whether the kids can play video games before finishing their homework. Why shouldn't politicians get mad when they disagree about how to pay for cancer treatments, a company closing a factory or outsourcing jobs, or a president declaring war?

The contentiousness of political life means politicians need little of something that takes up a lot of space in public speaking textbooks: *informative speech*, the speech that should, as one text puts it, "convey knowledge or understanding."[4] There's room for informative speech in politics; just listen to a campaign organizer explaining a phone canvass to volunteers. But speeches by elected politicians almost always involve *persuasion*, the "process of creating, reinforcing, or changing people's actions."[5]

On the stump, politicians persuade people to vote for them. On the floor, they persuade people to support or oppose a bill. At a funeral, they persuade mourners that a dead friend lived a worthwhile life. Persuasive speeches, all. Moreover, they mostly use one kind. In Chapter 2, we examine three different types of questions central to persuasion: questions of fact (*Does North Korea have nuclear weapons?*), value (*Is that good or bad?*), and policy (*How should we handle it?*). In politics, politicians deal with the first two mostly to help answer the third.

Voters want politicians to solve problems. The solutions may be political (*Change the president!*) or based on issues (*Cut more taxes!*). Either way, speakers are urging—advocating—action, or *policy*.

Realizing that fact, values, and policy are *what* we argue about leaves open the question of *how* we argue. Aristotle identified the answer to how with his three modes of persuasion: *logos* (reasoning), *pathos* (emotion), and *ethos* (the speaker's character).

Persuasion is vital in political life; after all, politicians run for office because they have strong beliefs. To further those beliefs, it only makes sense to use every persuasive tool, even when you might think they have no reason to do so. Floor speeches rarely change a single vote, but reporters—and thus their readers and listeners—would look askance at a party that abandoned the effort to make a case for its position. Politicians take floor speeches seriously.

They persuade even when speaking to the friendly audiences that make up the bulk of their speaking schedule. Even friends need to hear evidence reinforcing their own beliefs. That's what makes them walk a precinct, write a check, or turn out on Election Day.

But in no way does this mean that persuasion alone is enough. Politicians have other needs.

POLITICIANS MUST BE LIKED

Late in September 2012, Mitt Romney felt hopeful about his chances in November. One thing worried longtime Republican strategist Stuart Spencer.

"It's the likability factor," Spencer said. "Many people think that Obama hasn't delivered, but they still like him. I'd rather have a beer with him than Romney. Wouldn't you?"[6]

At a time when politicians argue about health care, war in Syria, and investigations into whether Russia "hacked" American elections, do voters really care about who passes the beer test? Yes. Politicians measure likability by what pollsters call "favorability" ratings. Gallup's favorability ratings that month showed Obama ahead of Romney 53–45.

These days, when people see video of a damning mistake online even before the speaker has finished, speeches can instantly win or lose votes. And while political races principally turn on issues, *personality* influences voters, too. Voters usually want their politicians likable: humble, appreciative, energetic, moral, exciting, witty, and compassionate.

Being liked doesn't necessarily mean saying only what the audience wants to hear. It does, however, often mean downplaying the views a particular audience isn't likely to favor and highlighting those it likes. And there are other factors, as well.

Four years after Romney's loss, it was Hillary Clinton's turn to worry about likability.

"Presidential politics tends to be dominated by personality," wrote a *Washington Post* reporter, saying Clinton "may be hard pressed to win a traditional presidential election in which likability matters most."[7] Other reporters said something similar, sometimes quoting the beer test. And in her case, they mentioned the "mountain of evidence" making her unique. Much of that evidence was about one indisputable fact. Hillary Clinton is a woman.

Colleen Ammerman, director of Harvard Business School's Gender Initiative, saw here an old frustrating story. Women with strong ambitions and opinions "typically take a likability hit," she told *HuffPost*, which reported that "most people" expect women to be "feminine—quiet, supportive, nurturing and definitely not ambitious."[8]

Neither the beer test nor gender alone usually decides an election. But it can. It is still a fact that in the United States, about 8 percent of Republicans, 6 percent of Independents, and 3 percent of Democrats tell pollsters they would not vote for a qualified woman from their own party for president. In January 2019, no sooner had Elizabeth Warren declared her intention to run for president than reporters focused on this issue. "I'll say it," wrote defiant *Daily Beast* columnist Matt Lewis, "Elizabeth Warren isn't likeable."[9] Influencing likability—unfortunately—is one quality vital to effective political speech.

Now we look at one more political need.

POLITICIANS MUST STAY UPBEAT

In 1979, Jimmy Carter used an energy speech to deliver a sermon. His pollster, Pat Caddell, had persuaded Carter that Americans needed not optimism but candor.

Speaking from the Oval Office, Carter warned Americans that their "erosion of confidence in the future" was "threatening to destroy the social and the political fabric of America." He not only blamed voters for their problems but promised no solution.

The result: Historians call it Carter's "malaise" speech, using a word that the president never spoke but did appear in Caddell's original memo. Patrick Anderson, Carter's campaign speechwriter, later wrote that the president had "embraced Pat Caddell's mumbo jumbo about a national crisis of spirit."[10]

"No one ever took his speeches seriously again," Anderson wrote.[11]

Really, the speech wasn't so bleak, and of course many voters continued to trust Carter. But the controversy that speech inspired shows how unusual *any* measure of pessimism is in politics. Voters find it hard to hear that they are at fault, or that there may be no solutions. Partisans want to know they *can* win the election, though the polls say no; that government *can* and *will* help; that a bill *will* pass.

In a sense, they want speeches to resemble a well-made Hollywood feature, raising serious issues, like corruption, but providing a happy ending by the closing credits. "We chose hope over fear," Barack Obama said in his inaugural address, echoing his campaign theme. There are ways to be optimistic without sounding mindless. But the relentless need to promise success imposes sharp limits on the complexity of political debate.

Here again, we do not argue from anecdotal evidence alone. The classic research on this issue comes from two University of Pennsylvania professors, Harold Zullow and Martin Seligman. Beginning with the 1900 election

(McKinley v. Bryan), they analyzed the nomination acceptance speeches for every race through 1984.[12] Their question: Was there a correlation between optimism and outcome?

Candidates whose speeches were "sunnier" won eighteen of twenty-two elections. Three of the four exceptions involved Franklin Delano Roosevelt, which might mean that Americans will listen to pessimists if the situation is dire. But even FDR leavened his message with hope. "We have nothing to fear," he argued, "but fear itself." Similarly, Donald Trump appealed to the anger and frustration of the forgotten American. But he also told Americans they could be great again.

If the need for optimism can limit a speech's complexity, so too can another reality of political life.

POLITICIANS MUST SPEAK TO AVERAGE FOLKS

In 2008, Professor Elvin Lim, mentioned in the Introduction and who expresses his views in more detail later, analyzed every single American presidential inaugural speech, using one gauge of complex language: the Flesch-Kincaid reading level assessment.[13] The results distressed him. He found that in the nineteenth century, inaugural speeches were written for college graduates and averaged sixty-word sentences—three times longer than the average today.

BOX 1.1

THE FLESCH-KINCAID READABILITY TEST

He created it in 1948. Except for a little revision from John Kincaid, nobody has needed to change much about educator Rudolf Flesch's invention. Now called the Flesch-Kincaid Readability Test, its simple yet effective formula can tell you how many Americans are likely to understand what you've written.

For those of you using Microsoft Word, it's the little box that pops up after Spelling and Grammar Check. It looks like the image on the right. Note the elements besides grade level. Checking sentence length and percentage of passive verbs can really help speechwriters.

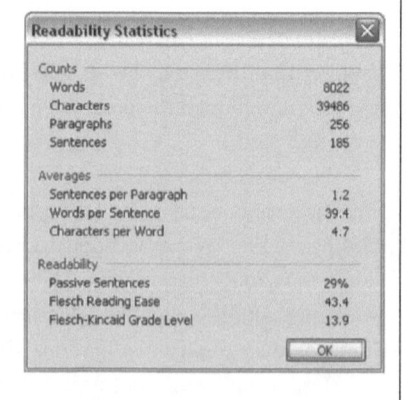

Readability Statistics	
Counts	
Words	8022
Characters	39486
Paragraphs	256
Sentences	185
Averages	
Sentences per Paragraph	1.2
Words per Sentence	39.4
Characters per Word	4.7
Readability	
Passive Sentences	29%
Flesch Reading Ease	43.4
Flesch-Kincaid Grade Level	13.9

For most people in politics, the change makes perfect sense. Rhetoric has become simpler as the country has become more democratic. Thomas Jefferson, for instance, wrote his inaugural for a tiny educated elite—not backwoods farmers in Virginia, or most women, or slaves forbidden to learn reading. Modern presidents draw a television audience on Inauguration Day almost ten times the entire population in Jefferson's America.

In 2017, Americans averaged a seventh-grade reading level. Forty percent of Americans struggled with language written for fourth graders. Op-eds can confuse even skillful readers. They can start over. Those listening to a speech don't have that option.

Luckily, writers can express a lot with short sentences and simple words— like the one who thought up, "I come to bury Caesar, not to praise him." Because power in speech depends so much on concrete detail and repetition, simplicity precludes neither profundity nor power. We see this in one of 1988 presidential candidate Jesse Jackson's most effective moments from that year's "Keep Hope Alive" Democratic National Convention speech:

Most poor people are not on welfare. They work hard every day. . . . They catch the early bus. They work every day. They raise other people's children. They work every day. They clean the streets. They work every day. They drive vans and cabs. They work every day. They change the beds you slept in at these hotels last night and can't get a union contract. They work every day.

Why is this passage so effective after almost three decades? The reasons include Jackson's use of repetition and his ability to pick examples that create a shock of recognition in the audience, both elements we will examine later in the book.

But look, too, at how easy his language is for average Americans to understand. Jackson uses fifty-six one-syllable words out of seventy-one, and of the fifteen words that have two syllables, the word *every* accounts for six. Naturally, simple doesn't mean simple-minded. Though the Flesch-Kincaid test measures Jackson's excerpt at a little below fourth-grade level, it made people with doctorates weep.

In order to write so that voters understand, speechwriters should be comfortable using sentence fragments and other modes of expression that wouldn't work in a formal essay or grant application. In speaking, it's fine to begin a sentence with "But" or "And." To be more conversational, you will have to ignore the wavy lines underneath your words indicating you need a spelling check. But you can do it.

We also suggest keeping most speeches short. Politicians often get requests to speak for a half-hour. Surveys show, however, that after twenty minutes, the attention of an audience is virtually zero. Even the authors have a hard time staying riveted during a State of the Union speech without a trip to raid the refrigerator.

Of course, the live audience is not the politician's only concern. Unlike most speakers, politicians have at least two sets of listeners: the people sitting in front of them and the secondary audiences reading news stories or watching snips on TV or YouTube. Speeches can influence listeners long after they end, which leads to a final point.

POLITICIANS MUST GET QUOTED

Sound bite. The term appears as early as 1980 in a *Washington Post* piece quoting former White House aide Bill Rhatican. "Any editor watching needs a concise 30-second sound bite. Any more than that, you're losing them."[14]

Now in the Twitter age, we count the number of characters, not just seconds. But the concept of a *sound bite* remains the same—a brief phrase memorably summing up an important idea or the point in a speech.

To some, that represents everything wrong with politics. Only about eight seconds of the average speech now make news. That's not much time to capture the complexity of an issue. But those are eight important seconds. Politicians need memorable lines. Reporters may not quote more. TV producers may not run much more. Still, sound bites uttered by a politician that run on even one TV talk show can reach millions of people. Moreover, they are neither new nor meaningless. Take these:

Give me liberty or give me death.

It's morning in America.

Yes we can.

Make America great again.

All four implied significant messages, easily understood by those who heard them. Despite their denials, speechwriters do work to provide sound bites. We know because we have. While later we write more about how to use them, right now we want readers at least to imagine that there might be some justification for phrases that sum up an idea in a way hard to forget. For if you can't make your point succinct and interesting, how can you be sure you have one?

Let's sum up. Usually, politicians must speak a lot. Their speeches need to accomplish five things. They must help the speaker be

- persuasive—about problems and solutions,
- likable,
- upbeat,
- understood by average folks, and
- quotable.

FINAL WORDS

This chapter has described what politicians need, not what we—or they—hope. Political speech has many flaws. We believe politicians should move and inspire listeners while they build a substantive case for ideas. They should be frank about the uncertainties surrounding proposals, seek out chances to debate in public with those on the other side, and seize every opportunity to promote candor.

These qualities are not absent from politics. The need for them has changed as America has changed. We hear them in committee meetings, in small groups, and in other ways when the cameras are not on.

In 1917, when President Woodrow Wilson came before Congress and asked it to declare war on Germany, not a single American heard him other than those in the hall. There was no YouTube, television, or radio. While newspapers widely reprinted Wilson's speech, relatively few Americans read it. The speech would have been way too hard for them anyway. It was written at a college junior's level when fewer than one out of ten Americans had gotten past eighth grade.

But one thing did make it through to most Americans: a quote. They knew Wilson wanted to "make the world safe for democracy." That one sentence was enough to help galvanize much of the country.

In the hundred years since Wilson's speech, radio, television, cable, and the internet have combined with the rise in the ability of Americans to read. In fact, getting quoted these days is almost too easy.

Whether it be Hillary Clinton's "basket of deplorables" in 2016, or Donald Trump's "there is blame on both sides" after the Charlottesville rally a year later, each found a home online. The two-edged sword of such permanence is not lost on politicians. They need to speak vividly. But even the most outspoken politicians must think twice about candor.

Perhaps as a result, Americans see less of an institution they saw regularly during much of the last fifty years: presidential press conferences. John F. Kennedy held about two a month. Trump held only one in his entire first year in office. Instead, presidents send press secretaries out to brief reporters. While they travel around the country, they play favorites—either states where they are popular or the battleground states.

"In his first term," reports Stanford University's Shanto Iyengar in his book, *Media Politics: A Citizen's Guide*, "more than half of [Barack Obama's] domestic travel went to the thirteen battleground states."[15] This practice is not likely to change.

Technology has dramatically increased Americans' ability to get informed—or misinformed. Websites offer substantive discussions of virtually any issue with policy implications, and listeners need sophistication to recognize bias. Yet speeches remain vitally important.

They remain the staple not just for presidents but for any politician, because they satisfy the special needs politicians have. Through those speeches they discuss policy, pay tribute, comment on national events, or urge action. They communicate views, characterize themselves, and persuade listeners. And they do that in real time, in front of an audience, "eyeball to eyeball." No other form of communication can do all of that.

Wouldn't it be nice, then, if one format existed that could work to meet all those needs? Actually, it does. Surprisingly, you can learn a single structure that's appropriate for almost every political occasion, especially when enlivened with what we have called the LAWS of persuasive speechwriting: language, anecdote, wit, and support.

Before you learn that structure, let's set the stage. How will you go about persuading, whom will you persuade, and where will you find what you need to get the job done? We explore answers to those questions in the next three chapters.

2

Persuasion

"Have you ever heard of Plato? Aristotle? Socrates?" asks the winningly evil Vizzini, played by Wallace Shawn in William Goldman's classic movie, *The Princess Bride*. "Morons!"[1]

Vizzini wants to impress Westley, dressed as the Dread Pirate Roberts, with his intellect. It's a sign of how much we still respect the Greeks that, 2,300 years after the morons died, Goldman still makes them Vizzini's yardstick for brilliance.

A lot has changed about speeches since Aristotle sat in the garden of his villa, transcribing student notes from his lectures into what became *Ars Rhetorica*. How could he still have anything useful to say? The man lived before Snapchat! But the human psyche remains consistent. Few political speakers may ever read Aristotle, but his insights form the foundation of every effective speech they deliver. So we start with him.

"Rhetorical study in its strict sense," he wrote, "is concerned with the modes of persuasion."[2]

Certainly, politicians aim to persuade. Chapter 1 defined a persuasive speech as one that attempts to *change or reinforce values, beliefs, or action*. That contrasts with an informative speech: a speech that attempts to *convey knowledge and understanding*.

The distinction can seem artificial because both types often cover the same ground. We know that when a speaker says "We should deport undocumented immigrants," we hear an attempt to persuade.

The key word is *should*. If the same speaker says "Here's why *the administration believes* we should deport undocumented immigrants," that becomes informative. The speaker has conveyed factual information about a view without endorsing it.

Political speech can be informative—but almost always to persuade listeners. In this chapter, we cover the questions, modes, and strategies politicians use to persuade.

PERSUASION: THE QUESTIONS

Questions, that is, of fact, value, and policy.

Political rhetoric usually includes all three, especially since influential eighteenth-century philosopher David Hume saw people making decisions they believed resulted from answers to questions of fact. Really, Home argued, those questions were about values.

Today, politicians establish the *facts*, remind listeners of the *values* they hold, then propose the *policies* they want listeners to embrace.

Let's look closely at each question, using two speeches with vastly different views—one by Barack Obama from 2014, and the other from Donald Trump in 2017. Both cover one of the bitterest issues, not just during the 2016 elections but in the years leading up to it: immigration.

Questions of Fact

In their immigration speeches, both Obama and Trump assume that listeners need to know the truth. They devote a lot of space to answering questions that to them are as verifiable as who won the 2018 World Series.

Obama opens by arguing that immigrants keep America entrepreneurial and that our immigration system is broken, but that because of his efforts, the number of people trying to cross our border illegally is at its lowest level since the 1970s.

> When I took office, I committed to fixing this broken immigration system. And I began by doing what I could to secure our borders. Today, we have more agents and technology deployed to secure our southern border than at any time in our history. And over the past six years, illegal border crossings have been cut by more than half. Although this summer, there was a brief spike in unaccompanied children being apprehended at our border, the number of such children is now actually lower than it's been in nearly two years. Overall, the number of people trying to cross our border illegally is at its lowest level since the 1970s. *Those are the facts.*

Trump says, the truth is, our immigration system is worse than anyone realizes. He too acknowledges the importance of facts but argues the facts aren't known because the media won't report on them:

> In California, a sixty-four-year-old Air Force veteran, Marilyn Pharis, was sexually assaulted and beaten to death with a hammer. Her killer had been arrested on multiple occasions, but was never deported.
> A 2011 report from the Government Accountability Office found that illegal immigrants and other noncitizens in our prisons and jails together had around twenty-five thousand homicide arrests to their names.
> On top of that, illegal immigration costs our country more than $113 billion a year. For the money we are going to spend on illegal immigration over the next ten years, we could provide one million at-risk students with a school voucher.
> While there are many illegal immigrants in our country who are good people, this doesn't change *the fact* that most illegal immigrants are lower-skilled workers with less education who compete directly against vulnerable American workers, and that these illegal workers draw much more out from the system than they will ever pay in.
> *But these facts are never reported.*

We have already said that a fact is something indisputably true, and independently verifiable. Let's assume that Trump and Obama both believe that the information they offer is factual. That doesn't mean listeners should accept it without question. Sometimes speakers are wrong. Sometimes what sounds like a fact is actually an unsupported assertion for which listeners should seek more evidence. "People are entitled to their own opinions," New York senator Daniel Patrick Moynihan once said. "But not their own facts." It is a maxim often observed in the breach.[3]

In Chapter 10, you'll learn more about how to use facts to persuade. Here, it is enough to see that in arguing about immigration, both Trump and Obama begin with them. That makes sense. If Trump wants listeners to believe "illegal workers" are a threat, doesn't it help to tell them that such workers "draw much more out from the system than they will ever pay in"? Despite their differences, in this instance, Obama and Trump both see facts as the foundation for argument.

But facts alone are not enough to persuade listeners.

Questions of Value

Making value judgments means answering questions about what is good or bad, right or wrong, more important or less important. Which do you value most: Family? Career? Education? Religion? National security? Not everyone would answer in exactly the same way.

Values are harder to define than facts. To say "The sun rose this morning" is to utter a fact. We can check whether it's true or false. What about saying we believe in "fairness"? When pollsters ask Americans that question in the abstract, 98 percent say yes. But in 2016 the Pew Research Center polled Americans on whether the American economic system was "fair." Thirty-one percent said yes. Sixty-five percent said no.[4]

Moreover, different segments of Americans gave vastly different answers about fairness. Eighty-eight percent of "solid liberals" said the economic system was unfair. Among "business conservatives," only 31 percent did. Everyone *values* fairness, yes. But can we verify the truth when it comes to what fairness is? Clearly, that is not so easy.

Throughout his speech, Obama tackled the question of values in several ways, reminding listeners of their beliefs in various traditions, expectations, character traits, and what for many Americans is, literally, gospel. Some samples:

> Even as we are a nation of immigrants, we are also a nation of laws. . . . We expect people to play by the rules. We expect that those who cut the line will not be *unfairly* rewarded. . . . Mass deportation would be both impossible and contrary to our character. . . . That's not how our democracy works. Scripture tells us that we shall not oppress a stranger.

Trump also answered the questions of value, using entirely different sentiments—praise for the values of "working people," a reminder of our rights, and the assurance that we will abide by the American traditions of fair play.

> We have to listen to the concerns that working people have over the record pace of immigration and its impact on jobs. These are valid concerns expressed by decent patriotic citizens from all backgrounds. . . . It is our right as a sovereign nation to choose immigrants that we think are the likeliest to thrive and flourish here. . . . We will treat everyone living or residing in our country with dignity. We will be *fair*, just, and compassionate to all. But our greatest compassion must be for American citizens . . .

Both speakers cite fairness as an American value. But that doesn't mean they feel the same about *what* is fair. So while it's fine for politicians to argue that they comport with American values, simply espousing those values and citing facts isn't enough. To be persuaded, audiences want to know how a politician will act.

Questions of Policy

Addressing policy in a speech means answering your listeners' biggest question about the issue you've described: *"What are you going to do about it?"* In 2014, Obama answered by outlining three steps he would take:

> Tonight, I am announcing those actions.
> First, we'll build on our progress at the border with additional resources for our law enforcement personnel so that they can stem the flow of illegal crossings, and speed the return of those who do cross over.
> Second, I'll make it easier and faster for high-skilled immigrants, graduates, and entrepreneurs to stay and contribute to our economy, as so many business leaders have proposed.
> Third, we'll take steps to deal responsibly with the millions of undocumented immigrants who already live in our country.

Trump answered the policy question in the same way, using *we* and *will*.

> Number one: We will build a wall along the southern border.
> Number two: End catch-and-release. Under my administration, anyone who illegally crosses the border will be detained until they are removed out of our country.
> Number three: Zero tolerance for criminal aliens. According to federal data, there are at least two million criminal aliens now inside the country. We will begin moving them out day one, in joint operations with local, state, and federal law enforcement . . .

One might think that since Obama and Trump differ so sharply on policy, they must also disagree on facts and values. In general, they don't. It is only when the two outline their proposed actions that the differences emerge. These two useful speeches differ in structure, language, and use of story. Here, we focus on what the speeches have in common: the need to persuade listeners about the *facts* and assure them that the speakers conform to American *values*. Only then, they believe, will listeners accept the different *policies* each candidate wants.

In most political speeches, you can find some variant of that three-pronged approach. But the polarizing differences now dominating the United States make clear that answering questions of fact or value doesn't necessarily win approval for policy, or in and of itself make a speech persuasive.

What other techniques might? For that question, we do find an answer in Aristotle.

PERSUASION: THE MODES

Of the modes of persuasion furnished by the spoken word there are three kinds. The first kind depends on the personal character of the speaker [ethos]; the second on putting the audience into a certain frame of mind [pathos]; the third on the proof, or apparent proof provided by the words of the speech itself [logos].[5]

Ars Rhetorica

Speechwriters learn early that there is a "rule of three," and that one breaks it at one's peril. The rule applies even to jokes: A rabbi, priest, and minister walk into a bar. Four people walking through that door would make the joke drag; just two would rush it.

Aristotle's rule of three is at the heart of effective persuasion. If you want to persuade listeners about, say, immigration policy, you'll find the tools in the extract above: *logos* (reason), *pathos* (emotion), and *ethos* (character).

To see how politicians use all three, we'll examine speeches from Obama, Trump, and another politician, Arnold Schwarzenegger.

Logos (Reason)

Logos "can produce persuasion," according to the Stanford Encyclopedia of Philosophy, just by using "the argument itself." In other words, by using logical evidence, or reason.[6]

Consider this passage from Schwarzenegger's speech at the 2004 Republican National Convention:

> My fellow immigrants, my fellow Americans, how do you know if you are a Republican? Well, I['ll] tell you how. If you believe that government should be accountable to the people, not the people to the government, then you are a Republican.

Though Democrats might have a hard time accepting it, Schwarzenegger's speech provides a perfect example of how reasoning works in politics.

CHAPTER 2   Persuasion   27

Bear with us as we condense a yearlong logic course into a page. Such courses divide logic into two kinds: deductive and inductive.

Deductive reasoning works from *general* to *specific*:

- General: All humans die.
- Specific: Socrates is human.
- Conclusion: Socrates will die.

Inductive reasoning works from *specific* to *general*:

- Specific: Socrates and everyone we know have died.
- General: All of them are human.
- Conclusion: All humans will die.

This is not the place to review the controversies over whether inductive reasoning exists, or the discussions of what makes a valid syllogism (an argument based on deductive reasoning). For here is the good news: In partisan politics, the embarrassingly simple truth is that almost *all reasoning is deductive*. In fact, it overwhelmingly uses variations of two forms:

- X policy is good.
- Our side has done (or believes in) X.
- We are good.

Or:

- X policy is bad.
- The other side has done X.
- The other side is bad.

Does that seem cynical? Take Schwarzenegger's example. Looked at logically, it would take this form:

- Government accountable to people (X) is good.
- Republicans believe in X (good).
- Believers in X are Republican.

Ah, says the resident Democrat, *but Democrats also believe in accountable government*. Good point. Apparently, Schwarzenegger has taken the first semester of logic, which involves creating a valid syllogism. But he hasn't taken the second semester, which deals with *evidence:* the facts, brief or extended examples, or expert testimony that might make listeners believe.

In Chapter 10, readers will find much more about evidence. Both Obama's and Trump's immigration speeches contain plenty. Here, we draw from Obama's.

He asserts what he believes is fact:

My fellow Americans, we are and always will be a nation of immigrants.

His evidence: the three bodies of water they crossed. Obama believes listeners should accept that as reasonable support.

> We were strangers once, too. And whether our forebears were strangers who crossed the Atlantic, or the Pacific, or the Rio Grande, we are here only because this country welcomed them in, and taught them that to be an American is about something more than what we look like, or what our last names are, or how we worship.

Can a sentence with the words "always will be" be factual? Only if Obama means that because we all descended from somewhere else, our ancestors define us. But as a syllogism, Obama's ideas might look like this:

- Specific: Our families were strangers—just like the immigrants of today.
- General: Others helped our immigrant families.
- Conclusion: We must help the immigrants of today.

If you want to read more about formal logic, consult this book's bibliography. If you want to know enough to write persuasive political speeches responsibly, remember this: for reasons we detail later, paying attention to logic, evidence, reason—*logos*—is worth doing, even in the heat of campaigns.

Pathos (Emotion)

English speakers use the word *pathos* to describe the quality that produces emotion—usually sympathy—in an incident or image they observe, for example, a tear-inducing scene in a movie. Aristotle used pathos to mean an appeal to emotion.

Here is Trump making that appeal in a 2016 speech on immigration:

> Countless Americans who have died in recent years would be alive today if not for the open border policies of this administration. This includes incredible Americans like twenty-one-year-old Sarah Root. The man who killed her arrived at the border, entered federal custody, and then was released into a U.S. community under the policies of this White House. He was released again after the crime, and is now at large.
>
> Sarah had graduated from college with a 4.0, top of her class, the day before.
>
> Also among the victims of the Obama–Clinton open borders policies was Grant Ronnebeck, a twenty-one-year-old convenience store clerk in Mesa, Arizona. He was murdered by an illegal immigrant gang member previously convicted of burglary who had also been released from federal custody.

Root's story offers a way for Trump to use *logos*—an extended example to support his main point. But why include those details about her killer—and the immigrant who killed Grant Ronnebeck? Clearly, Trump wants to elicit *pathos*, too. He has put a human face on tragedy to move listeners. To believe pathos and logos should be isolated from each other is a mistake.

Some listeners hear stories evoking pathos as mawkish and manipulative. Others are just as contemptuous about an overemphasis on logos, considering it dry as dust.

Right or wrong, emotional appeal seems more important in politics than it was in earlier generations. During the 2008 campaign, neuroscientist Antonio Damasio pointed out that the twenty-four-hour online news cycle has supplanted the time voters once had for reflecting on issues. "The amount and speed of information, combined with less time to analyze every new development, pushes us toward the emotion-based decision pathway," he wrote.[7]

The authors aren't sure whether the trend stems so exclusively from technology—nor are we certain how much reflection Americans ever did devote to political issues. But for reasons we discuss more fully in Chapter 8, we believe appeals to reason and emotion both deserve a place in political speech. As does the third—and most misunderstood—of Aristotle's three elements: ethos.

Ethos (Character)

In English, the word seems related to ethics. But ethics makes up only part of what Aristotle meant. While logos and pathos are qualities of the *speech*, ethos refers to the qualities of the *speaker*—that is, the assembly of virtues and flaws that make a speaker trusted, admired, liked, credible, and, ultimately, persuasive.

Some of Aristotle's students and fellow teachers were skeptical of ethos as a concept, maintaining that speakers' personal characteristics should count for nothing in evaluating their argument. He felt compelled to rebut them. "It is not true," he wrote, "that the personal goodness revealed by the speaker contributes nothing to his power of persuasion; his character may . . . be . . . the most effective means of persuasion he possesses."

Note that while his critics argue that ethos should be irrelevant, he argues only that it works.

What Aristotle valued in 350 B.C. voters value today. Politicians demonstrate ethos, or character, by showing that they share the audience's beliefs or by demonstrating virtues not related to belief: intelligence, humility, humor, compassion. In their immigration speeches, Obama and Trump showed humility in a similar way, by praising the virtue of others:

> **OBAMA:** I've seen the courage of students who, except for the circumstances of their birth, are as American as Malia or Sasha; students who bravely come out as undocumented in hopes they could make a difference in the country they love.

> **TRUMP:** I've had a chance to spend time with these incredible law enforcement officers, and I want to take a moment to thank them. The endorsement I've received from the Border Patrol officers means more to me than I can say.

Are the candidates being honest in their praise or making a calculated attempt to seem admirable? One motive doesn't negate the other. But let's return to the objections of Aristotle's critics, who saw evoking emotion or demonstrating virtue as irrelevant to political speech. By tugging at listeners' heartstrings, are you condescending to them as weak? What's wrong with just using evidence?

Fair questions. Clearly, ethical persuasion must involve marshaling evidence, and Chapter 10 explores ways to do that. But the essence of political life is realism. An enormous amount of research confirms that for American audiences, persuasion involves more than logic.

In the 2000 presidential campaign, for instance, researchers found that Americans were more likely to contribute to Bush if their surname began with *B*—and to Gore if their names began with *G*.[8] And a large body of evidence indicates that voters make political choices based not on issues but on whether candidates seem to have "authoritarian" or "antiauthoritarian" personalities.

Who's to say that nonrational reasons are out of bounds when speakers try to persuade? Who's to say that using *logos* is responsible but using *ethos* is not?

In politics, all sides agree: Effective persuasion must include the nonrational. Late in the 2008 presidential campaign, John McCain's campaign manager, Rick Davis, made clear his view about what persuaded voters: "This election is not about issues," he said. "This election is about a composite view of what people take away from these candidates."[9]

In their endorsement of Obama that year, the editors of the *New Yorker* magazine disputed Davis, but only up to a point. "The view that this election is about personalities leaves out policy, complexity, and accountability," they wrote. But they agreed that "what most distinguishes the candidates ... is character."[10]

There is a legitimate place in political speech for all three of Aristotle's elements, or modes. In political speech, they work together with questions of fact, value, and policy, or what in formal rhetoric we call *claims*. Before moving on, we want readers to see how.

To that end, let's analyze the 2016 convention speeches by Donald Trump and Hillary Clinton. Commentators that year focused, rightly, on the huge differences in issues shown by the candidates and their speeches. But while each side heaped contempt upon the way the other side argued, Trump and Clinton each appealed to reason, emotion, and character. And they did that using similar strategies.

APPEALING TO REASON

"Does Evidence Matter?," *Washington Post* columnist E. J. Dionne asked in 2014.[11] He was hopeful, citing a bipartisan effort by Democratic senator Patty Murray (D-WA) and Republican representative Paul Ryan (R-WI) to develop better ways to measure how Congress spends tax dollars.

Evidence refers to the facts, examples, expert testimony, and other techniques that people use in rational thought. In other words, logos.

In 2016, the answer to Dionne's question might have seemed a robust "No!" to some people, including some politicians. Hillary Clinton, in fact, accused Congress of living in an "evidence-free zone."[12] The fact is politicians in both parties still rely on evidence. Again, we have a rule of three.

First, evidence *reinforces*. Even when listeners are friendly, as at a political nominating convention, providing evidence allows the audience to believe more strongly. Listeners think, "I thought that was true, but now I know it!" That reinforcement makes audiences think better of the speaker, as well.

Second, evidence *insulates*. The media covering any major political speech includes plenty of people who are skeptics. In the internal dialogue skeptics carry on with the speaker, they may think: "Oh, really? You expect me to believe that?" Simply using evidence at various points in their speeches shielded Trump and Clinton at least from some of the skeptics who would otherwise have dismissed particular points.

Finally, evidence *convinces*. Whom does it convince? The undecideds, the ones who may be thinking, "I'd like to believe that. But is it really true?" Undecided voters looking for an excuse to commit may not examine the speaker's evidence carefully. "Okay," they think. "The candidate sounds rational. I'll believe." Other voters, however, listen critically; based on what they hear, they evaluate and, believe it or not, make a rational choice.

Thus, when Trump demonstrates a problem, and Clinton a success, each uses one tool of logos: statistics.

> **TRUMP:** These are the facts: Decades of progress made in bringing down crime are now being reversed by this administration's rollback of criminal enforcement. Homicides last year increased by 17 percent in America's fifty largest cities. That's the largest increase in twenty-five years.
>
> **CLINTON:** Our economy is so much stronger than when they took office. Nearly fifteen million new private-sector jobs. Twenty million more Americans with health insurance. And an auto industry that just had its best year ever. That's real progress.

APPEALING TO EMOTION

In the final week of the 2004 presidential campaign, candidate John Kerry published an op-ed in which he contrasted his politics of "hope" with the Republicans' politics of "fear." Four years later, President Obama used his inaugural address to announce that Americans had chosen "hope over fear." Both catered to what voters always tell pollsters: they crave optimism and detest tactics that appeal to their fears, like "negative" ads.

But think about it. Do "negative" appeals actually distort any more than "positive" ones? If you see a bus bearing down on you, you *hope* you can jump out of the way. But you also *fear* what's about to happen. On issues ranging from social justice to nuclear war, appeals to both hope and fear make sense, in the same way that they do in daily life. All politicians aim to appeal to both. As did Trump and Clinton.

Appealing to Fear

Politicians appeal to fear in two ways: first, citing bad things from the past and, second, predicting bad things ahead.

Failures from the Past

TRUMP: And when a Secretary of State illegally stores her emails on a private server, deletes thirty-three thousand of them so the authorities can't see her crime, puts our country at risk, lies about it in every different form, and faces no consequence—I know that corruption has reached a level like never before.

CLINTON: But Trump, he's a businessman. He must know something about the economy. Well, let's take a closer look. In Atlantic City, sixty miles from here, you'll find contractors and small businesses who lost everything because Donald Trump refused to pay his bills. People who did the work and needed the money, and didn't get it—not because he couldn't pay them, but because he wouldn't pay them.

Problems Ahead

TRUMP: Yet Hillary Clinton is proposing mass amnesty, mass immigration, and mass lawlessness. Her plan will overwhelm your schools and hospitals, further reduce your jobs and wages, and make it harder for recent immigrants to escape from poverty.

CLINTON: That sales pitch he's making to be your president? Put your faith in him—and you'll win big? That's the same sales pitch he made to all those small businesses. Then Trump walked away, and left working people holding the bag.

"Fear is easy," one Republican ad-maker told a reporter in 2016. "Fear is the simplest emotion to tweak in a campaign ad. You associate your opponent with terror, with fear, with crime, with causing pain and uncertainty."[13] That may sound cynical. But there is nothing ethically wrong with appeals to fear, either in ads or in speeches. If we cross the street oblivious to the bus barreling down toward us, won't we be grateful to the person who shouts, "Watch out!"?

Still, researchers have found that simply scaring listeners makes them too uncomfortable to keep paying close attention. Listeners also want reasons for optimism.

Appealing to Hope

Taking advantage of the fact that his first hometown was Hope, Arkansas, Bill Clinton made "A Place Called Hope" the slogan of his first presidential campaign. He was smart to do it. In politics, persuasion means not just affixing blame but fixing the problem. So it's strategically vital to adopt the mirror image of an appeal to fear.

Accomplishments from the Past

> **TRUMP:** I have made billions of dollars in business making deals—now I'm going to make our country rich again.

> **CLINTON:** Look at my record. I've worked across the aisle to pass laws and treaties and to launch new programs that help millions of people. And if you give me the chance, that's what I'll do as president.

Solutions Ahead

> **TRUMP:** We are going to build a great border wall to stop illegal immigration, to stop the gangs and the violence, and to stop the drugs from pouring into our communities. By ending catch-and-release on the border, we will stop the cycle of human smuggling and violence. Illegal border crossings will go down. Peace will be restored.

> **CLINTON:** I've laid out my strategy for defeating ISIS. We will strike their sanctuaries from the air, and support local forces taking them out on the ground. We will surge our intelligence so that we detect and prevent attacks before they happen. We will disrupt their efforts online to reach and radicalize young people in our country. It won't be easy or quick, but make no mistake—we will prevail.

Politicians deal with dozens of issues. In major speeches like these, they cover issues without the detail some listeners might want, leaving that for position papers, websites, and speeches to interest groups. Few listeners, they calculate, would absorb nuance at a major event like a party's nominating convention.

It's true that few American voters need to hear every detail in a plan; they just want to know there *is* a plan. But stating proposals and reminding the audience of the other side's unpopular stance aren't the only ways to appeal to hope and fear. If they were, speeches would be too dry to arouse emotion. Stories about "real" people, concrete details, and a variety of rhetorical techniques arouse emotion. But there is a third and final strategy writers and speakers use to appeal to audiences.

APPEALING THROUGH CHARACTERIZATION

Mark Twain once described hearing a sermon in church. At the beginning, he was so enthusiastic that he vowed to put $400 in the collection plate. But the preacher kept talking, the church was hot, and after a while Twain decided to give just $100. At the end, he said, "I stole 10 cents out of it."

Twain's story illustrates what textbooks call the three types of characterization: *initial*, *derived*, and *terminal*, meaning how much the audience trusts or respects a speaker at the start, during, and after a speech.

Some speakers, particularly if an audience doesn't know them, can alter that initial gauge of credibility by giving a good speech. It's harder for politicians. Often, listeners already have opinions about them and their issues. Cognitive dissonance—the discomfort you feel when you hear reasonable-sounding ideas that clash with others you hold—imposes limits on what speakers can do to change those initial views. In 2016, a group of Democrats would have largely distrusted Donald Trump no matter what he said or did, and many Republicans would have felt the same about Hillary Clinton.

Still, politicians can win over some hostile listeners by demonstrating personal virtue. They can demonstrate sympathy to the goals of their listeners by showing they know about their problems and have personal experiences with those problems. Perhaps they have actually tried to solve them, even in partnership with a group. In that way, speakers demonstrate shared values.

Are there ways politicians demonstrate both virtues and values? Yes. Here are five.

Decry Problems to Show Compassion

> **TRUMP:** Only weeks ago, in Orlando, Florida, forty-nine wonderful Americans were savagely murdered by an Islamic terrorist. This time, the terrorist targeted our LGBT community. As your president, I will do everything in my power to protect our LGBT citizens from the violence and oppression of a hateful foreign ideology.

> **CLINTON:** Right now, an awful lot of people feel there is less and less respect for the work they do. And less respect for them, period. . . . My primary mission as president will be to create more opportunity and more good jobs with rising wages right here in the United States.

Tell Stories of Average Folks to Show Understanding

> **TRUMP:** On Monday, we heard from three parents whose children were killed by illegal immigrants. Mary Ann Mendoza, Sabine Durden, and Jamiel Shaw. They are just three brave representatives

of many thousands. Of all my travels in this country, nothing has affected me more deeply than the time I have spent with the mothers and fathers who have lost their children to violence spilling across our border.

CLINTON: Over the last three days, you've seen some of the people who've inspired me. People like Ryan Moore and Lauren Manning. They told their stories Tuesday night. I first met Ryan as a seven-year-old. He was wearing a full body brace that must have weighed forty pounds. Children like Ryan kept me going when our plan for universal health care failed . . . and kept me working with leaders of both parties to help create the Children's Health Insurance Program that covers eight million kids every year.

Reach Out to Demonstrate Belief in Unity

TRUMP: I have seen firsthand how the system is rigged against our citizens, just like it was rigged against Bernie Sanders—he never had a chance. But his supporters will join our movement, because we will fix his biggest issue: trade. Millions of Democrats will join our movement, because we are going to fix the system so it works for all Americans.

CLINTON: Bernie [Sanders], your campaign inspired millions of Americans, particularly the young people who threw their hearts and souls into our primary. You've put economic and social justice issues front and center, where they belong. And to all of your supporters here and around the country: I want you to know, I've heard you. Your cause is our cause. Our country needs your ideas, energy, and passion.

Use First Person to Demonstrate Shared Values

TRUMP: I have embraced crying mothers who have lost their children because our politicians put their personal agendas before the national good. I have no patience for injustice, no tolerance for government incompetence, no sympathy for leaders who fail their citizens.

CLINTON: In this campaign, I've met so many people who motivate me to keep fighting for change. And, with your help, I will carry all of your voices and stories with me to the White House. I will be a president for Democrats, Republicans, and Independents. For the struggling, the striving, and the successful. For those who vote for me and those who don't. For all Americans.

Emphasize Love of Family to Display One Shared Value

TRUMP: My dad, Fred Trump, was the smartest and hardest-working man I ever knew. I wonder sometimes what he'd say if he were here to see this tonight. Then there's my mother, Mary. She was strong, but also warm and fair-minded. She was a truly great mother. She was also one of the most honest and charitable people I have ever known, and a great judge of character.

CLINTON: My grandfather worked in the same Scranton lace mill for fifty years. Because he believed that if he gave everything he had, his children would have a better life than he did. And he was right. My dad, Hugh, made it to college. . . . When the war was over, he started his own small business, printing fabric for draperies. I remember watching him stand for hours over silk screens. He wanted to give my brothers and me opportunities he never had. And he did. My mother, Dorothy, was abandoned by her parents as a young girl. She ended up on her own at fourteen, working as a housemaid.

FINAL WORDS

In his influential book named, appropriately, *Influence*, social scientist Robert Cialdini details the many techniques marketers and salespeople use, dividing them into six categories: reciprocity, social proof, consistency, likability, similarity, and authority.[14] The terms are less important than the question they answer: How does one persuade people to buy a product?

A car salesmen, Cialdini points out, might see golf clubs in your trunk and casually happen to mention their excitement at going out on the links (similarity). They might offer a discount, hoping you will pay them back with an order (reciprocity). Maybe they'll make you worry about the safety of other brands or give you hope with a warranty.

Cialdini doesn't endorse marketers who would, for instance, lie about similarities in order to manipulate potential customers. He doesn't sympathize with deception. Rather, he describes techniques without judging them.

Similarly, we don't necessarily endorse the ways political "marketers," including speechwriters, use the strategies we cover. To describe a gun doesn't mean we endorse a holdup. A speech is a means to an end. The elements and the strategies of political speech can serve the honest politician and the demagogue.

Which is true of the subject we turn to now. Before speechwriters begin the sometimes intuitive and unarticulated process of mapping out strategies, you must learn about your listeners.

Who are these people you hope to persuade? What exactly do they need? How do you find out whether they're concerned about roads, taxes, global warming, war in the Middle East, or jobs in the Midwest?

That's next.

THE SPEECHWRITER'S CHECKLIST: PERSUASION

When Appealing to Reason, Have I:

☐ Tried to persuade about questions of fact, value, and policy?

☐ Varied my approach to include appeals to reason, emotion, and character?

☐ Reinforced views the crowd already holds?

☐ Insulated my boss against hostile questions?

When Appealing to Emotion, Have I:

☐ Addressed both fear and hope?

☐ Demonstrated that the other side has done bad things—and will do more?

☐ Moved the audience with the promise of better days?

When Appealing through Characterization, Will Listeners Feel I:

☐ Share the audience's goals?

☐ Care about its problems—and will work to fix them?

☐ Admire some people the audience admires?

☐ Demonstrated personal virtues the listeners like?

3

Audiences

Two months before Election Day, 2016, Hillary Clinton spoke in New York at the LGBT for Hillary gala. As the name of the event suggests, she thought she faced a friendly crowd.

"You can put half of Trump supporters into what I call the basket of deplorables," Clinton said. "Right? Racist, sexist, homophobic, xenophobic, Islamophobic, you name it. Now, some of those folks—they are irredeemable, but thankfully they are not America."[1]

The live audience laughed, applauded, and cheered. But by the next morning, a storm of outrage had become the real story. What Clinton said not only angered (and motivated) Trump's base but gave Independents another reason to question her.

Did Clinton's "deplorables" quip cost her the election? No one can say for sure. But after the campaign, the Clinton team conducted a review of voter attitudes. After that speech, wrote Clinton consultant Diane Hessan, "All Hell broke loose."[2] The biggest switch from undecided voters to Trump in the entire campaign, they discovered, came right after Clinton's remark.

Whether it changed the outcome of the 2016 election—highly unlikely—the incident demonstrated a couple of key points about political speech. First, clearly, in the smartphone and social media age, few things are truly "off the record."

Second, and the point of this chapter, while most speakers have just one audience, politicians have many. And when it comes to writing and delivering a political speech, it's essential to pay attention to them all.

That means asking four questions:

- Who are your audiences?
- What characteristics make them unique?

- How are they likely to feel about the speaker—friendly, hostile, neutral, or mixed?

- And how do those feelings influence the strategies you use?

WHO ARE YOUR AUDIENCES?

The most obvious is what we call the *primary* audience—the people in the seats.

But politicians also speak to many *secondary* audiences, including reporters; people who read, hear, or see the stories reporters write; lobbyists; or those a political office may alert by a tweet or a text. And what about the audiences segmented within those audiences: legislators, fundraisers, heads of nonprofits, and—oh, yes—voters?

The abundance of audiences sets politicians apart. Teachers in a classroom, lunchtime lecturers at the Rotary Club, or corporate officers talking to their managers rarely face a battery of microphones and cameras. Politicians do. They want to reach some audiences, but not all. Those infuriated by Clinton's gaffe made that clear.

To reach their intended listeners, speakers and their writers must not only be aware of the different audiences but accommodate them. Doing so takes two steps.

First, figure out which audiences will hear, and hear *of*, your remarks. That allows you to determine whether what you say will offend others, and whether that's worth doing.

Second, identify the audiences you *want* to alert. Most voters won't hear speeches politicians deliver—unless you deliberately find a way to reach them. Relatively few voters turn on C-SPAN to watch floor speeches in Congress. If you're in the state legislature or on the city council, the coverage will be smaller still. But tweets, blast emails, newsletters, and direct mail can do what "earned" media—for example, news reports—might not.

Once you've researched the primary audience and the others you want to reach, you have another decision. You may know exactly what the live audience needs. What about including issues listeners won't find as relevant?

Talking to a chamber of commerce doesn't mean you have to ignore the refugees in Syria. Few groups are so narrow that they care only about their own issues. When it comes to speeches, state legislators, mayors, or aldermen should grab every opportunity to demonstrate that they care about more than potholes and stoplights.

In fact, secondary audiences are sometimes so important that they make disagreeing with the live audience worth doing. In the pages to follow, we will see that from John F. Kennedy speaking to Protestant ministers about his

Catholic faith, Bill Clinton speaking to the NAACP about Sister Souljah, and Mitt Romney speaking to the Conservative Political Action Conference.

"You know what the main difference is between your job and mine?" a Clinton speechwriter would remind us when we were working for Al Gore. "You care about the live audience."

He was exaggerating; even a president usually cares most about the people in the seats. But he was right that for someone watched by millions each night, the live audience can be a prop—an excuse to reach the wider audience. For almost all other political speakers, weighing primary and secondary audiences involves a careful balancing act for which identifying them is only a start.

WHAT MAKES EACH AUDIENCE UNIQUE?

No audience is made of people with identical needs. But members of every primary or secondary audience will have some needs in common. A good way to examine those needs: Abraham Maslow's Hierarchy of Needs, shown in Figure 3.1.

Maslow developed it in 1943. His hierarchy, often depicted as the pyramid you see here, ranked needs roughly in the order in which he believed people want to satisfy them. Maslow began at the bottom; people who are starving most likely won't care much about self-actualization.

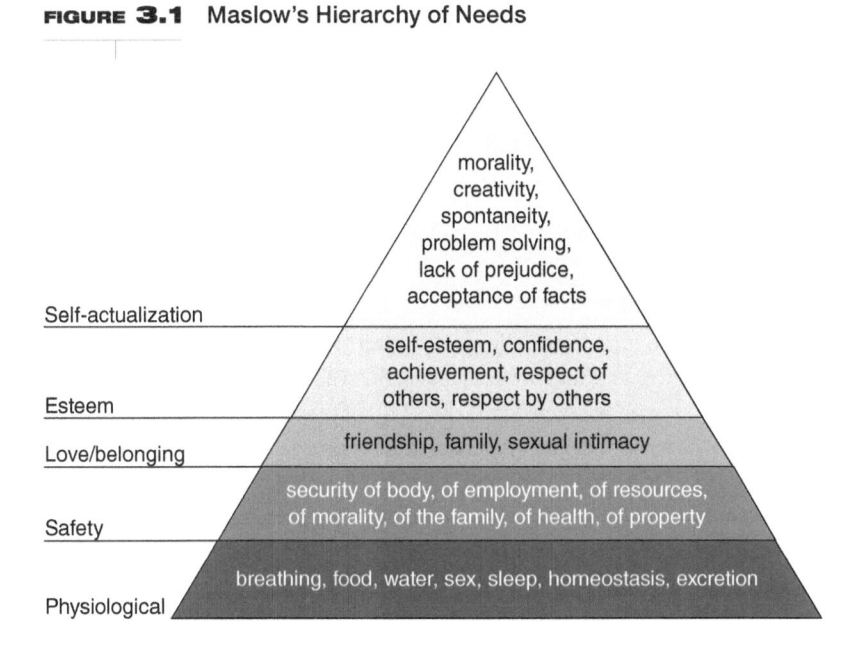

FIGURE 3.1 Maslow's Hierarchy of Needs

Self-actualization: morality, creativity, spontaneity, problem solving, lack of prejudice, acceptance of facts

Esteem: self-esteem, confidence, achievement, respect of others, respect by others

Love/belonging: friendship, family, sexual intimacy

Safety: security of body, of employment, of resources, of morality, of the family, of health, of property

Physiological: breathing, food, water, sex, sleep, homeostasis, excretion

It's easy to dismiss as psychobabble something so symmetrical as the messy business of human psychology. But when you look at political speeches, it's rare *not* to see them appealing to the needs on Maslow's pyramid. Maslow's fifth step of "self-actualization" includes problem solving. Two examples from Hillary Clinton and Donald Trump make one think Maslow was a campaign consultant.

Clinton, in 2016:

> I'd like to bring people from right and left, red, blue, get them into a nice, warm, purple space where everybody is talking and where we're actually trying to solve problems.

Trump, as president, talking about Afghanistan in 2017:

> No one denies that we have inherited a challenging and troubling situation in Afghanistan and South Asia . . . But one way or another, these problems will be solved. I'm a problem solver. And in the end, we will win.

In politics, where speeches are often cobbled together in frantic attempts to beat deadlines, speechwriters sometimes have to make educated guesses about needs. After a while, you get good at guessing correctly. If you're doing a keynote for the ACLU luncheon or panel discussion at the Federalist Society, it doesn't take much to understand what listeners want to hear.

Valuable as Maslow's hierarchy might be, you can't just tape a copy of it to the wall and pick a few elements to include. Sensitive speechwriters try to find out more. For political speakers, the search for what makes a primary audience unique centers on four areas: *beliefs, values, interests,* and *demographics.*

Beliefs

Do audience members believe in God or not? In a literal god? Do they believe life starts at conception or at birth? That government is an instrument for good or an obstacle to markets? All of these beliefs influence how an audience will react to a speaker's views on policy.

In March 2015, Ted Cruz announced his candidacy for president at conservative Liberty University. He would face a very conservative audience there. But a larger, more moderately Republican audience would watch from home. When it came to the role of government, taxes, and health care, the two audiences differed.

Blaming the IRS for high taxes and the deficit, 73 percent of Republicans felt we should balance the budget only or mostly by cutting spending. But 27 percent of Republicans would raise taxes, too.[3]

Conservative and moderate Republicans felt differently about immigration, too. Conservative Republicans were more likely to believe immigrants threatened traditional American customs and values. Many moderates favored keeping borders secure. But they also believed diversity strengthened the United States.

Given all that, here's how Cruz sought to satisfy both audiences:

> Instead of a tax code that crushes innovation, that imposes burdens on families struggling to make ends meet, imagine a simple flat tax . . . that lets every American fill out his or her taxes on a postcard.
> Imagine abolishing the IRS.
> Instead of the lawlessness and the president's unconstitutional executive amnesty, imagine a president that finally, finally, finally secures the borders.
> And imagine a legal immigration system that welcomes and celebrates those who come to achieve the American Dream.

Note that Cruz provides no detail about tax, or immigration policies—the issues on which his various audiences might differ. He appeals almost entirely to the *beliefs* that listeners were likely to have in common: keeping government "out of the way," "abolishing" the IRS, and a president who "finally secures the borders."

Values

In Chapter 2, we discussed questions of value, using the term to include not just beliefs but cultural traits: independence, compassion, democracy, and a sense of fair play. Often Americans precede those ideas with the word *in*, as in "we believe *in* fair play."

It is vital that speechwriters read, research, and talk with their bosses to find out not just which abstract values to mention, but how they apply to listeners. Listeners aren't stupid. They will want to hear not just that speakers value hard work, but what that means in a coal mine.

Of course, talking about values can't please everyone. Ronald Reagan faced a mixed audience in his 1989 farewell address from the Oval Office. His belief that film should reinforce "love of country" and "democratic values" might offend those who believed film should be value neutral—and avoid propaganda. But he and his writers felt differently—and guessed most Americans would, too. They risked offending a few listeners to reach the larger group who would applaud.

> **AS DELIVERED**
>
> ***Ronald Reagan's Farewell Address.*** This is another speech we will examine many times. Aside from education, can you see other areas where Reagan appeals to values?
>
> www.reaganfoundation.org/ronald-reagan/reagan-quotes-speeches/farewell-address-to-the-nation-2/

Expressions like "democratic values" and "patriotism" aren't meaningless. Nor are they controversial. "Some things have changed," Reagan says, carefully leaving out specifics. Yet he risks offense by directly appealing to viewers who believe that schools and entertainment should directly reinforce values, including love of country.

What may seem in Reagan's speech like a random assortment of things we value came from careful choices about what his audience believed.

Interests

Interests in this context doesn't mean what critics sometimes call *special interests*: the powerful groups—like banks, unions, or oil companies—asking for favors. It means the audience's personal interest in issues affecting daily life. Is a company outsourcing and threatening jobs? Do members of the audience have relatives who are ill with cancer? Are they immigrants worried about whether or not their family can stay in the United States? These variables influence audience reactions.

In 2016, for example, any time an audience included some of the estimated eleven million undocumented immigrants in the United States or their sympathizers, speakers needed to know that before writing about immigration policy. Knowing that could make Hillary Clinton, for example, confident about linking those interests to her solutions.

> I believe that when we have millions of hardworking immigrants contributing to our economy [*interests*], it would be self-defeating and inhumane to kick them out [*solution*].
>
> Comprehensive immigration reform will grow our economy and keep our families together [*interests*]—and it's the right thing to do [*solution*].
>
> Whatever party you belong to, or if you belong to no party at all, if you share these beliefs [*interests*], this is your campaign [*solution*].

Knowing the beliefs, values, and interests of your audience helps you map out strategy. But there's one more thing to find out. It's a question that doesn't directly involve beliefs or values, though it is naturally an outgrowth of them all.

Demographics

What's the average age of your listeners? What percentage are male or female? Gay or straight? White, black, or brown? Catholic, Protestant, Jew, Muslim, or atheist? NRA members or ACLU members? Urban or rural? From North or South? These are questions of demographics, quantifiable characteristics of a given group of people. All play a role in determining an audience's rhetorical needs. Demographic data provide clues to what will make listeners cheer or sit on their hands.

To the boisterously adoring crowd at his 2007 NAACP award acceptance, Bono appealed to his audience by lavishly complimenting not only Martin Luther King Jr. but the international influence of the civil rights movement.

> I grew up in Ireland, and when I grew up, Ireland was divided along religious lines, sectarian lines. Young people like me were parched for the vision that poured out of pulpits of black America, and the vision of a black reverend from Atlanta, a man who refused to hate because he knew love would do a better job.
>
> These ideas travel, you know, and they reach me clear as any tune, lodged in my brain like a song. I couldn't shake that. The right to live, period. Those are the stakes in Africa right now.

You've learned about how primary and secondary audiences feel about issues and values. Now you need to know about something personal.

WHAT DO AUDIENCES FEEL ABOUT THE SPEAKER?

While politicians love speaking to friendly crowds, no one can do that all the time. When conservative Republicans avoid talking to the NAACP or liberal Democrats refuse to go on Fox News, they seem weak. Besides, few audiences are monolithic; there are undecideds in most crowds. And what about the most hostile of them; can't you reach *some* people who hate your guts?

Yes, you can. A properly calibrated speech can alter some attitudes in any group, which is why speeches from the Oval Office invariably make approval ratings go up, no matter who is president.

One such smartly calibrated speech: Sarah Palin's at the 2008 Republican National Convention. She faced an overwhelmingly favorable crowd in the seats.

But millions of voters watching a largely unknown nominee on TV included those who ranged from bitterly hostile to completely indifferent. At the end of her speech, written largely before John McCain picked her as his running mate, she won at least initial approval from 53 percent of Independents and 22 percent of Democrats not in the hall—a tribute to writers and researchers who had thought carefully about listeners.

Of course, celebrated speeches with big TV audiences create some unique effects. Robert Cialdini uses the example of television laugh tracks; as a kind of social conformity, audiences laugh more often and longer when others are laughing, too. Applause is similarly contagious. When the favorable crowd leaps to its feet cheering, that has an effect on neutral viewers at home: *Wow! She must be good!* That also happens to be why, on more than a few occasions, it's a speechwriter in the back of the room who starts the applause.

The shrewdest attempts at persuasion won't win over everyone in a hostile crowd, or make partisans out of a neutral one. But politicians who know the three main attitudes they confront can make inroads by following these strategies.

Friendlies: Reinforce Beliefs and Urge Action

Friendly audiences don't need to be persuaded about issues. Speakers *can* make them see the urgency of what they believe. *I knew that*, they'll think, *but I didn't know it was so important.* By mounting a strong case, speakers reinforce beliefs, just as architects reinforce a building to make it impervious to earthquakes. When Cicero spoke, William Jennings Bryan once said, people listened. But, he added, when Demosthenes spoke, people marched. Bryan knew about marching. His 1896 "Cross of Gold" speech ignited the Democratic National Convention. Delegates marched him around on their shoulders and awarded him the presidential nomination.

For friendly crowds: play Demosthenes.

One way to do that is to characterize the speaker. Another is to characterize the audience. In his passionate and skillful speech to the Reform Party, accepting its 2000 nomination for president, Pat Buchanan characterized party members by flattering them: beleaguered people who would stick courageously to principle no matter what.

> Because there has to be one party that has not sold its soul for soft money. There has to be one party that will stand up for our sovereignty and stand by our workers who are being sacrificed on the altar of the Global Economy. There has to be one party that will defend America's history, heritage, and heroes against the Visigoths and Vandals of multiculturalism. There has to be one party willing to drive the money-changers out of the temples of our civilization.

In later chapters, we cover the other techniques Buchanan uses: a litany ("There has to be") that creates power; concrete detail ("drive the money-changers") that paints a picture for listeners, an allusion to Scripture; and alliteration ("history, heritage, and heroes") that makes language memorable. Here we ask only that you see how celebrating shared values and reinforcing common beliefs can make listeners march.

Hostiles: Mitigate Anger

In 1960, with West Virginia's presidential primary approaching, Robert Kennedy visited the heavily Protestant state to meet with organizers and assess his brother's chances. "There's only one problem," a man shouted at him. "He's a Catholic!"[4]

JFK won the primary. But as the general election approached, many hostile Protestants still resented him because of his religion. The National Conference of Citizens for Religious Freedom, an organization of Protestant clergymen, including the well-known Norman Vincent Peale, declared that Kennedy's Catholicism made him unfit for the presidency.

Kennedy knew he had to address the questions people were asking, like whether he believed in the separation of church and state, or whether he would take direction from the Vatican rather than honoring the Constitution.

In September 1960, he got his chance. Addressing the Greater Houston Ministerial Association, an audience of skeptical Protestant clergy, Kennedy began by discussing the country's history of acceptance, using a famous example from Texas to illustrate Americans working together.

> Side by side with Bowie and Crockett died McCafferty and Bailey and Carey. But no one knows whether they were Catholic or not, for there was no religious test at the Alamo.

Then, he tried to make clear that his religion would not interfere with the way he might govern.

> I am not the Catholic candidate for president. I am the Democratic Party's candidate for president, who happens also to be a Catholic. I do not speak for my church on public matters, and the church does not speak for me.

Kennedy couldn't win over all of the Protestant voters hostile to him. It's asking too much to expect speakers to convert a crowd that looks on them as the enemy. That's why researchers who examine audience attitudes suggest a different approach. "If listeners are strongly opposed to your viewpoint, you can consider your speech a success if it leads even a few to re-examine their views," says Stephen Lucas in *The Art of Public Speaking*, a popular textbook.[5]

Speakers can make a hostile audience less angry, or at least less vocal. And that's what Kennedy accomplished. He also succeeded in another way: impressing people not in the room. Taking on the Protestant ministers, his speechwriter Ted Sorensen later wrote, "didn't end the religious controversy . . . but it was widely and enthusiastically applauded . . . all across Texas and the nation."[6]

There are different ways to win support by taking on hostile groups: acknowledging that reasonable people can differ, conceding points to the other side, using self-deprecating humor, and so on. All aim at mitigating anger.

But don't expect miracles.

Neutrals: Seek Incremental Gains

Most listeners are not neutral. And it's not likely that those who are will leap into action the way friendlies will. But undecideds are also less set in their views than hostiles. Speakers may not get them to march. But speakers can at least change some beliefs—what we call "passive persuasion." When folksy, ad-libbing former preacher Mike Huckabee went to the Council on Foreign Relations in 2007, he faced a moderate audience that knew nothing about his views on foreign policy. Huckabee characterized himself as a moderate using two tactics.

Criticize Your Own Side

This administration's bunker mentality has been counterproductive both at home and abroad. They have done as poor a job of communicating and consulting with other countries as they have with the American people.

Take the Middle Ground

We can't export democracy as if it was Coca-Cola . . . but we can nurture native moderate forces in all these countries where al-Qaeda seeks to replace modern evil with medieval evil. . . . My goal in the Muslim world is to correctly calibrate a course between maintaining stability and promoting democracy. We have to support moderates with no favoring of Sunnis or Shiites. . . . It's past time to . . . reach out to moderates with both hands.

Since many undecided listeners are by definition not extremists, they respond well to a strategy of moderation. Huckabee's willingness to take the middle ground, and even concede error, was smart.

Of course, we are examining audiences with three different attitudes. What about the ones who are plain apathetic? What about events where no two people in adjoining seats agree on a single thing? Later we will talk about ways to segment your appeals to reach both. Spoiler alert: nobody has devised a way to persuade everyone.

BEHIND THE SCENES

The President Tweets

It was the first time a President ever *tweeted* from the White House.

In July of 2011, President Obama entered the East Room of the White House, looked down at a silver laptop, adorned with the same presidential seal as the podium it rested on, and typed:

"In order to reduce the deficit, what costs would you cut and what investments would you keep? BO."

"He didn't make news," the *Los Angeles Times* reported, "but that wasn't really the point . . . the goal was to give an online audience an unfiltered dose of Barack Obama."

Obama often gets credit for being the first President of the social media age. It was his successor, though, who showed the power and reach of a tweet.

In 2018 alone, Donald Trump tweeted 2,843 times. He used 1,721 to promote his agenda and accomplishments (the economy, the Wall). The rest, 1,162 tweets, he used to mercilessly attack his opponents (Fake News, Witch Hunt, Crooked Hillary). Each one could reach Trump's audience of more than 58 million followers, not to mention the tens to maybe hundreds of millions more who read and hear the reporting on Trump's tweets. Each one bypassed traditional methods of delivering a message. And each one drove the conversation, communicating instantly the president's mood and thoughts, both impulsive and strategic, with the American people.

It is just the beginning.

At one point during his campaign for president, Trump suggested he would stop the practice if elected. But two years into his term, the allure of reaching so many people so quickly proved too hard to resist.

Speaking at a rally in Cleveland, Dan Scavino Jr., Trump's social media guru, described why: "If things aren't necessarily working out with CNN or somebody, we can put it on his platforms and get more views."

Make that unfiltered views. The tweet is here to stay.

Sources: https://www.youtube.com/watch?v=5cuboYUaUCU; http://articles.latimes.com/2011/jul/07/nation/la-na-obama-twitter-20110707; https://www.politico.com/interactives/2018/interactive_donald-trump-twitter-2018-analysis; https://www.c-span.org/video/?413063-1/donald-trump-accept-endorsement-senator-cruz&live=&vod=

FINAL WORDS

We conclude our chapter on audiences with a question that moves beyond effectiveness to one of ethics. Does learning so much about what an audience wants make it more likely speakers do what voters most distrust about politicians: Pander to them? Tell them only what they want to hear?

The question isn't new. Plato originally disapproved of Aristotle's interest in studying rhetoric for that very reason. He feared that exploring rhetorical technique could make speakers better at deception.

Politicians are more transparent about their views than most people believe. They leave a well-lit trail—speeches, ads, votes, media coverage—making their views known.

Still, deception is not only possible but frequent. It's disappointingly common to hear speakers quote Martin Luther King Jr. or Ronald Reagan just because they're speaking to a group that admires these men.

But knowing to whom you're speaking is not inherently unethical; it's up to speakers to use what they've learned ethically—to make sure statistics are accurate, for example, and "real people" examples actually happened.

Besides, finding out about the beliefs, values, and interests of your listeners only gets you partway home. No matter how sophisticated you are about persuasion, you cannot hope to weave together an effective speech without the dogged, time-consuming, and shrewd effort it takes to collect the threads you'll be weaving.

That is the subject of Chapter 4.

THE SPEECHWRITER'S CHECKLIST: AUDIENCES

- ☐ Who are the audiences for this speech?
- ☐ Which is most important?
- ☐ What makes the primary audience for this speech unique?
  - ☐ Values
  - ☐ Interests
  - ☐ Demographics

- ☐ Who else (secondary audiences) should we alert about the speech?
- ☐ For a friendly audience, what beliefs will the speech reinforce?
- ☐ For a hostile audience, what common ground will the speech help listeners find?
- ☐ For a neutral audience, what specific small gains are possible?
- ☐ If different audiences have conflicting needs, how does the speech acknowledge them?

4

Research

It's 4:30 in the afternoon on a fall day in 1984. At an upstate New York high school football stadium, three people dressed like Bill Murray, Dan Aykroyd, and Harold Ramis are onstage, in front of a giant American flag, warming up the crowd.

They're singing a parody of that summer's box office hit. But instead of "Ghostbusters," they yell "Fritzbusters," poking fun at the Democratic candidate for president, Walter "Fritz" Mondale.

Then comes the main event. To chants of "Four more years! Four more years!" President Ronald Reagan steps onstage and begins his campaign stump speech. He starts this way:

> During our flight into Link Field, Air Force One might have gotten off a little, a little off course. The pilot said he had a little trouble finding Broome County. I told him to radio down and ask a simple question: Which way EJ?

The crowd roars. But one teenager listening to the speech is amazed.

The boy knows his local history—how a Binghamton-area entrepreneur built a shoe factory, Endicott Johnson. EJ. How word of it spread to Europe. How immigrants arriving down at Ellis Island looking for work asked people in the only English they knew, "Which way EJ?"

But how did Reagan know that?

Eric knows now. The answer comes at that moment of truth when speechwriters realize their real title is often "speech researcher."

*Research—what to look for and where to look—*forms the subject of this chapter. Traditional speech texts urge a certain method when it comes

53

to research: select a topic, narrow it, investigate different views, and evaluate every source for VCR (validity, currency, and reliability).

That's great when you have the time. But in politics, you're more likely to experience what Bob did while working for House Majority Whip David Bonior. Once, Bonior walked by Bob's desk at about 11:45 in the morning and said, "I think I want to do a one-minute." One-minutes are the sixty-second speeches any member of Congress can deliver in the half-hour after the House goes into session.

"Great. When do you need it?"

"Noon."

Not much time for research when you're typing as fast as you can, pulling a draft from the printer, and racing up the back stairs of the Capitol and onto the floor just before your boss walks to the lectern.

In politics, one constant is the impossible deadline. That doesn't make research less important. It is essential in political life. Much of what traditional textbooks urge does get done in a political office—by someone, at some point.

There are three key areas, though, that speechwriters should research themselves:

- The event—the logistics about the group, audience, format, and venue
- The ideas—the substantive points you'll make
- The poetry—the stories, examples, and quotes that can enhance the ideas

For each, we begin with the basics: what you need to find and the sources that help.

RESEARCHING THE EVENT

"Hey there."

You look up. Looming over you is a legislative assistant, the LA—or your boss's scheduler; the chief of staff; or, depending on where you work, maybe the boss.

"We've got a speech to some trade group. They put it on the schedule yesterday. Need it by tonight."

The ubiquitous *they*. That's so you know complicating your life isn't their fault.

"No problem," you say, wondering what you'll have to cancel to get it done. Dinner? Certainly the softball game. "You got the invitation?"

And soon you do. It tells you the date, time, place, and maybe a sentence about the group's mission and what it hopes to hear. But you have questions the invitation doesn't answer, starting with one that goes to a steadfast rule of persuasion.

Who is the audience?

How large is it? If the audience is forty people, talking points might be more appropriate than a formal text. If it's a thousand, you might want to use a teleprompter.

Knowing your audience also means answering the questions that fall under the catch-all term we described in Chapter 3: *demographics*. Age, religion, sex, income—knowing this and more about your listeners provides clues to what will make people cheer or sit on their hands.

You'll want to know:

Why did this group invite you or your boss to speak? Are audience members likely to be happy or upset about a vote—and should you write about that?

Has the speaker appeared before this group in the past? If so, when, and what was the context?

Whom does this crowd admire? Will quoting people, mentioning their accomplishments, or recognizing them if they are in attendance have particular resonance?

Does the audience include "influencers"—other legislators and policy makers? Will acknowledging their interests help further yours?

What about members of the media? While these days, it's best to be safe and assume that someone will share whatever is said, you and your speaker will want to know if the event is officially "on the record" or not.

Now you have a clearer picture of the audience. But you need to ask logistical questions, too.

Where is the speech: what town, what building, what room? Did anything significant happen in that spot, recently or in history?

What's the setup of the room: dais with a podium, auditorium style, round tables? Will it be awkward for the speaker to go down into the crowd to shake hands and mingle? Or does the group expect that?

What does the stage look like? Are there screens, and what's on them? Should you use slides or video?

Is there Q&A after the speech? If so, what tough questions are people likely to ask? Do you want to deal with those questions preemptively in the speech, where you can shape an answer the way you want?

Who else is on the program? Who is introducing the speaker; do they know each other?

What time of day is the speech? Audience members are likely to be more focused for a serious policy discussion during a morning keynote than they would be during an after-dinner speech or a reception where everyone is standing and trying to balance a plate of hors d'oeuvres with a glass of wine.

How long is the time slot; how long have the organizers asked your boss to speak? Conference organizers often divide up speakers into 30- to 60-minute segments. That doesn't mean speakers have to talk that long. In fact, we recommend they don't. "Typically," writes educator and researcher Wilbert McKeachie, "attention increases from the beginning of the lecture to 10 minutes into the lecture and decreases after that point."[1] There is a reason TED Talks are 18 minutes or less. As curator Chris Anderson puts it, "18 minutes is short enough to hold people's attention span . . . it's also long enough to say something that matters."[2]

Questions about audience, venue, and format influence what issues to cover, how to cover them, and for how long. That's why many speechwriters, the authors included, start with this list of questions, sometimes taped to the wall next to their computer.

Sources That Work

Other Staffers

Even if your boss is a state legislator, you can be almost certain that someone on staff or at the state party headquarters has worked with the group that issued the speaking invitation. Those people will know about the event—why the invitation came, what the group cares about, and whether it wants a Q&A. Call them. They will also know who can answer the questions they can't. Beyond these specific questions, they will want to be involved, and you will want them to be. They'll add expertise, and the relationship you build will come in handy later.

The Group's Communications Director

Always deal with communications directors. The odds are they can answer a lot of questions themselves, and if they refer you to other people, using their name will get you faster and more candid results. Meanwhile, since communications directors often have an eye for effective detail, you can pick up important information about the event.

The Website

Often the group's website provides important details about the event not included with the invitation: ticket prices, a picture of the hall, info on other speakers. Exploring the website has many other uses as well. Clicking through issues, speeches, the "About" section, or the "Our History" tab for half an hour should give you plenty of useful information.

RESEARCHING THE IDEAS

Like your family doctor, a speechwriter can't know everything about every issue. That's what specialists are for. In politics, all staffers are specialists. Learn to use them. Speeches take a team effort. Even if you are listed on a staff roster as *the* speechwriter, don't think you're on your own. Other staffers should know off the top of their heads what might take you a day to find out. And buried somewhere under the piles of memos, bills, clips, and reports on their desks is material you should read.

Equally important, political speeches shouldn't start from scratch. Whether you're writing a floor speech on a fisheries bill or a convention keynote on children's health, memos and white papers covering these issues already exist. Ask around the office. Explore the research services available for Congress, state legislatures, or executive agencies. Whether you are the sole staffer for a small-town alderman or one of many legislative assistants for a U.S. senator, the times that *nothing* exists for you to use will be very, very rare. Your workload is too great to ignore those who can help.

Sources That Work

Other Staffers

Just as other staffers are vital sources about the event, they also know issues. But like you, your fellow staffers are overworked. That doesn't mean they're too busy to sit down and talk about what should be in the speech. And they'll happily hand you a stack of memos, too.

While you must check for conflict-of-interest problems, you might also ask staffers from cabinet agencies for ideas, or even the media relations staff of the group that sent the invitation. To let them *write* the speech, or even a draft, would be both unethical and fraught with danger. To see what approaches they value or seek out their views on a policy, though, makes good sense.

Just remember that you're consulting people for source material, not for actual writing. Speechwriters sometimes laugh at the clichés and turgid boilerplate that other staffers are known to suggest. We're ashamed to admit we've been known to join the laughter. But who cares about the writing style of a policy expert? *You* know why active verbs are essential to a speech on the stimulus package. Policy wonks know how the stimulus actually works.

Old Speeches

The story you'll find in this chapter's "Behind the Scenes" box is here not just as an interesting bit of historical trivia but as an object lesson for speakers and speechwriters. Like those Martin Luther King Jr.'s aides in 1963, staffers sometimes complain about hearing the same old material. Pay no attention.

First, powerful material doesn't grow on trees. Finding something good, then discarding it, is like throwing out a great recipe for chocolate chip cookies because you've already made a batch.

Second, audiences are most likely hearing material for the first time. They haven't been overexposed the way some staffers have.

Third, even listeners who have heard the speaker want to hear the greatest hits. Nobody goes to a Rolling Stones concert and says, "I hope Mick skips 'Satisfaction.'" In politics, the well-known lines can create a sense of communal anticipation and shared accomplishment. Think about the Bernie Sanders stump speech in 2016.

> Our campaign's financial support comes from more than 1 million Americans who have made more than 3.7 million individual contributions. That is more individual contributions than any candidate in the history of the United States up until this point in an election.
> And, you know what that average contribution was?
> [Crowd yells in response] Twenty-seven dollars!

If Sanders skipped this "call and response," the crowd would have felt deprived. He also would have deprived himself of the chance to remind people why they supported him and bask in the applause. Recycled material allows speakers to recite lines and, like any actor, get good at them. It lets them look out at the crowd and build smoothly toward a climax with the confidence that comes only from knowing the material.

Political speech is one time when familiarity shouldn't breed contempt. Everyone in politics has seen candidates stammer over a stump speech at the start of a campaign—and become powerful before Election Day. Practice makes perfect. As you amass the material you will use in a new speech, begin by looking back at old ones to see what's worth using again.

Journals and Magazines

Serious does not mean dry. The term *magazine* derives from the rooms that used to store ammunition. Today, plenty of magazines hold the ammunition politicians need. The *Atlantic*, the *New Yorker*, the *Economist*, *National Review*, the *New Republic*, and the *Nation*, as well as publications geared toward technology, the workplace, and the economy, like *Inc.*, *Fortune*, *Wired*, and *Fast Company*, all feature interesting articles, full of substantive nuggets to use—or to note and file for later.

Beyond providing ammunition, sources like the ones mentioned have the broadening effect those who speak or write about complex issues need.

And because people in political life can't limit their concerns to narrowly partisan issues, we also suggest including a regular diet of academic journals, whether about global issues like *Foreign Affairs*, or economic issues like *Harvard Business Review*, or specifically politics like the *American Journal of Political Science* or *Presidential Studies Quarterly*, or specifically the intersection of speech and government like *Rhetoric and Public Affairs*.

With so many magazines and academic journals now online, you may need to subscribe. It's worth it. The authors spend some time every day—usually with morning coffee—clicking through our favorite list to see what piques our interest.

You should also make a conscious attempt to read views you oppose. It is sometimes uncomfortable. We are as subject to cognitive dissonance as anyone else. But we all need to escape the limitations of an office or circle of friends where everyone shares the same biases.

Web-Based Research

With so much content online, it's easy for deceptive websites to fool harried researchers. Writers, beware.

It is also easy to overdo web-based research. You don't have to become an expert; for most political speeches, it's a waste to spend hours and hours wading through the tons of position papers you can click through. No matter how important they consider their own issues, most audiences don't expect to hear about them the entire time a speaker is at a podium.

That said, writers should still use the internet to research issues and details, even if they know the topic well. To write from memory about, say, Hurricane Maria or the crowds during the "March for Our Lives" rallies is to deprive yourself of the best details—not to mention to trust your memory more than your memory may deserve.

Go beyond articles and position papers to spend a few minutes clicking through pictures of splintered boats piled on top of one another, or children on their parents' shoulders holding homemade signs. A huge advantage of the internet is that you can essentially return to a time you're writing about and experience the happenings right along with the people who were posting on social media or being covered by reporters. Take advantage of that to bring speeches to life.

The Speech Conference

You may notice that so far, we haven't referred to the way that political staffers, nurtured on stories about Ted Sorensen's long hours spent with John F. Kennedy, or Jon Favreau's partnership with Barack Obama, envision the speechwriting process happening: through meetings with the boss.

Speech conferences can help enormously when they happen. They allow speakers to bless the general thrust of your approach and allow you to get a sense of what the speaker wants. It doesn't hurt that a speech conference also helps the boss appreciate your brainpower. If you come armed with a perceptive comment—even one—it can help your career.

At a meeting in 2005, after Condoleezza Rice became secretary of state, Chris Brose—then a junior writer—raised his hand and asked a thoughtful question. Rice asked her chief of staff, "Who's that skinny, red-haired guy?" Soon Brose was her chief speechwriter, traveling around the world with her and offering advice on policy as well as language.[3]

Such stories are exceptions, and what staffers call "face time" doesn't always produce the best material. Consider these meeting from the point of view of the speaker.

The boss gets off the phone after twenty calls spent winning support for a vote on the floor to see a few people poking their heads in the door. "Speech conference about tomorrow's event. Chamber of Commerce," someone says.

The boss struggles to remember. "How'd that get on the schedule?"

"You approved it."

"Okay. Come in."

You hear the reluctance as you step in the office and take a seat.

The boss suggests a few lines. (*Do something about innovation. You know. Helping entrepreneurs with small business loans.*) There might be fifteen minutes of conversation, during which you can ask a few questions that will help. (*Do you want to be partisan? Do you want to mention your vote on House Bill X?*) You walk off feeling you didn't gain much, while the speaker happily thinks you now have everything you need—except for a bit of what nonwriters like to call wordsmithing.

Occasionally this might even be true. If speechwriters do their jobs, you will transcribe the notes and make sure to include the page of usable material the meeting produced; speakers will see their words and feel they haven't been ignored.

A better approach is to do your homework. Enter the meeting armed with ideas and questions. Expect that a busy schedule has left the boss little time to think about a speech in advance, much less formulate a cohesive argument or outline. Don't expect much from asking, "So, what do you want to say?" Instead, like a good investigative reporter, offer something that could provide a thoughtful response. Ask about things you already know, but haven't heard from the boss's mouth.

"I heard you say once that your parents owned a small business. What was that like? Did your parents talk about business at the dinner table? Did you ever work for the family business?"

A politician may answer, "Well, you would never use this is in a speech, but . . ."

"You'd never use this" is a sign to start typing. Speechwriters find ways to connect personal answers to policy positions in ways that will bring the boss's speech to life. And don't forget: the audience response to that kind of interesting and concrete detail will make the boss more likely to sit through another speech conference.

If you can't get face time with the boss before a particular speech, don't despair. The people who do spend more time with the boss know a lot; it's worth the time to build relationships with them. When the chief of staff returns from an event you didn't attend, ask how it went. Talk to the executive assistant about what the boss said about the event. Call the boss's college roommate, or tennis partner, or spouse.

And, of course, whenever possible, go listen to the boss speak. You'll see for yourself what material worked and what didn't. You'll hear what the boss added while in the car on the way to the event. Then, if there is one, make sure to stay for the Q&A. This is when you will discover the anecdotes you can use again and again.

BEHIND THE SCENES

Wyatt Tee Walker

He has been a theologian, antiapartheid activist, author, and pastor, but Wyatt Tee Walker is best known for being Martin Luther King Jr.'s chief of staff during the days of the March on Washington. In 2008, he told CNN what it was like to be behind the scenes.

It turns out King's staff were distressed that King would use the same old speech. "The inner circle of Dr. King," Walker told CNN reporter Soledad O'Brien, "felt that the 'I have a dream' portion was hackneyed and trite because he used it so many times in other cities."

So, the night before the 1963 speech at the Lincoln Memorial, they decided he should have a new ending. They called it "Normalcy never again."

Wyatt said, "I remember very vividly Andy Young and I going up and down the strips of the hotel taking drafts of what we thought should be a new climax."

King took the new speech with him to the National Mall the next morning. He came to the new ending. And paused.

"I was out in the crowd somewhere," Walker remembered, "and when he swung into 'I have a dream,' I said, 'Oh [expletive deleted]' . . . after all that work.'"

Walker had forgotten what staffers often forget at their peril: what they hear every day, what they find hackneyed and "trite," is fresh to almost everyone else.

Source: This "Behind the Scenes" box is based on Soledad O'Brien's interview for CNN's *Special Investigations Unit* titled "MLK Papers: Words That Changed a Nation," which aired February 24, 2007. The transcript of the program can be found at http://edition.cnn.com/TRANSCRIPTS/0702/24/siu.01.html.

RESEARCHING THE POETRY

"Devote more time to the poetry than substance," Peggy Noonan, columnist and former Ronald Reagan speechwriter, says.[4]

She means that for a speechwriter, more important than the actual points you'll make are the stories, details, examples, quotes—and, yes, sometimes even poetry—that make speeches inspire, excite, and move audiences.

She is absolutely right. Policy people can hand you policy ideas. No one but a speechwriter, though, is likely to suggest the kinds of things that affect an audience: a clever analogy, inspirational story, or genuinely funny joke.

We've been in lots of speech conferences that go something like this: Policy people are asking about nuances in a bill and wondering whether we're using "current numbers."

After a while, the speaker looks at the speechwriter. *What do you need?* her face asks.

"Did you see Trevor Noah last night?" the speechwriter asks. "He said something you could use."

Sometimes other staffers roll their eyes. But as you will see, the "poetry" some view as useless ornament is what audiences remember. It's what moves audiences to march. Because no one else on staff usually cares about that material, the speechwriter must. Because there is no one else to help, it takes the longest time. It's not unusual to spend an entire day finding the right story or detail—and then an hour to write the whole draft. That isn't a mistake; it's a sign you're doing things right.

Sources That Work

Personal Contact

The more time you spend with the boss, the more chance you'll have of uncovering something unexpected.

Once, when Bob worked for Lloyd Bentsen, the senator from Texas, he heard Bentsen tell someone else a story about how his father took him to get his tonsils out.

"Thirty-five dollars," the doctor said.

"Kind of steep," Bentsen's father replied. "If I had five kids, could I get a discount?"

"You don't have five kids."

"My brother does."

The next day, Bentsen remembered, he and his cousins all came in and got their tonsils out, and Bentsen's father got a discount.

Bentsen thought he was telling a funny story. To Bob, the story was funny—and said a lot about the strides the country had made in health care. Furthermore, Bentsen could tell the story well, and it wasn't just surprising for the audience. It had the virtue of being true. That's why the story found its way into a speech about health care—and about ten speeches after that.

Websites

We've already discussed the way web-based research helps with the ideas. It helps with the poetry, too. Speechwriters should search for quotes, quips, and stories that complement the substantive points to make speech memorable. There are infinite ways to do that with web-based research. Below, we offer just a few.

Sites like *history.com* or *onthisday.com* list noteworthy events, famous birthdays, and deaths. Will you find an anniversary or something else interesting that has a direct connection to your speech? The answer is "yes" too frequently to call it serendipity.

Google "political jokes" and you'll see links to cartoons, the best late-night jokes, and a wealth of other items. Many of them are useless. But sometimes, all you need is one.

You can even visit *mentalfloss.com*, *howstuffworks.com*, and other general knowledge sites to discover interesting and usable tidbits.

The authors have gone to websites to find song lyrics, lines from movie scripts, the etymology of words and phrases, the genealogy of speakers, and passenger logs of ships arriving at Ellis Island. All, and many, many other searches, have helped make points more memorable.

Newspapers

Of course, newspapers are sources for ideas. There are great websites that aggregate important stories for economical reading, like *theweek.com*. Others focus specifically on politics, like *Axios*, *Politico*, *Roll Call*, and the *Hill*.

But look at the front page of the *New York Times*, the *Washington Post*, or any local newspaper. You will see as many as half its stories now use anecdotal leads relevant to some public policy issue. They're the issues that matter to voters and elected officials: jobs, health care, education, climate change, poverty, taxes. Use those stories; they are often moving as well as true, making them as valuable as the ideas they illustrate. And cite the paper and the journalist. It will make clear that your boss doesn't just read position papers but—like the audience—reads the newspapers.

TV Late-Night Shows

"I see the Iraqis are writing a constitution," Jay Leno said once, as the Bush administration was beset with news about Abu Ghraib prison, not to mention its own illegal wiretaps. "Why not give them ours? Written by some smart guys, it's lasted for two hundred years—and we're not using it anymore."

Ancient as that seems, one of our clients, who runs a nonprofit that tracks judicial appointments, has been using that joke ever since. "Always gets a laugh," she says.

In Chapter 9, you'll read more about the challenges of using humor in politics: It needs to be edgy—but not raunchy. Politicians love Chris Rock, but they can't quote anything he says. On the other hand, they *can* quote the late-night talk show hosts. And now it's easier than ever to use jokes from Stephen Colbert, Jimmy Fallon, Jimmy Kimmel, or some of the cleaner Trevor Noah or Samantha Bee routines. All are online.

Other Speeches

Speechwriters should make a daily stop at Stephen Lucas's *www.americanrhetoric.com*. There you will find hundreds of great speeches, many with not just text, but audio and video as well. You might find a moving story to suit your immediate needs, and you'll run across stories and memorable lines to save for other days.

Similarly, *TED.com* has speeches that are not only well produced but noteworthy for their use of story, humor, evidence, surprise, and brevity. *Vital Speeches of the Day*, a magazine that has been reprinting speeches since 1934, appears each month with a collection of notable speeches, sometimes about political issues, but always presented without editing.

You can find other political speeches on C-SPAN, in the *Congressional Record* (*www.congress.gov/congressional-record*), or posted on the personal websites of individual members of Congress. Regularly comb through them. Often, when politicians publish speeches, staffers remove the jokes and clean up places that didn't work. They will label speeches "As Prepared" vs. "As Delivered." All versions are useful because they were written for people with the same needs as your boss.

As we were writing this tip, we decided to test whether online speeches do in fact contain usable material. We picked a Democratic senator at random—Dick Durbin of Illinois. One of us went into his website and clicked on a speech from May 21, 2018, about the state of American politics. In it he quotes Franklin Delano Roosevelt:

> In his first inaugural address, in the midst of America's gravest crisis since the Civil War, Franklin Roosevelt acknowledged: "Only a foolish optimist can deny the dark realities of the moment." But he also reassured us that "the only thing we have to fear is fear itself—nameless, unreasoning, unjustified terror which paralyzes needed efforts to convert retreat into advance."

Interesting. Durbin quotes the sound bite we all know, but he includes some of the lesser-known context. Not bad. A Democratic politician could use that. We might find even more of the details about how that line came to be, and make it into a story. We'd certainly put the FDR quote into a file and note it for future use. Test successful.

Books

Books still exist. We googled it.

Despite the wealth of material on the internet, anyone speaking often—or writing speeches often—should amass a library of the immensely useful books of quotes, anecdotes, jokes, and other materials that can bring a speech to life.

Some look down their noses at quote books, arguing that they allow speakers to fake erudition.

Within limits, using such books is ethical and useful. Without quote books, you sacrifice the best way to find the wealth of pithy, insightful, and witty things others have said, or the moving—and often true—accounts of people whose stories can move, inspire, or illustrate your points. Among them: CQ Press's *Respectfully Quoted*; Lewis D. Eigen and Jonathan Siegel's *Macmillan Dictionary of Political Quotations*; the humorous books written by, or the collections edited by, James Humes, such as *Speak like Churchill, Stand like Lincoln* or *Roles Speakers Play*; Clifton Fadiman's *Little, Brown Book of Anecdotes*; Mo Udall's classic, *Too Funny to Be President*; or any of the books published by former senator and presidential candidate Bob Dole.

One particularly useful book: Ralph Keyes's *Quote Verifier*. It's incredible how often the speaker who usually gets credit for a famous line never uttered it. Did Benjamin Franklin say, "An ounce of prevention is worth a pound of cure"? Check Keyes's book.[5] You'll learn that Franklin did, but he didn't claim credit. He would say it was an old saying or a proverb. You can still use the quote. Mentioning who really said it makes listeners see that speakers care about telling the truth.

In addition to quote books, speech anthologies such as William Safire's *Lend Me Your Ears* offer not only a treasure chest of significant speeches but contextual analysis as well.

Biographies and historical accounts—like those by David McCullough (*Truman, The Wright Brothers, 1776*), Ron Chernow (*Hamilton, Grant*), Walter Isaacson (*Benjamin Franklin, Leonardo da Vinci, Steve Jobs*), and Doris Kearns Goodwin (*Team of Rivals, No Ordinary Time*)—offer the kind of detail that can make analogies moving and memorable.

Even books you might find in the business section or under social psychology can be helpful. Malcolm Gladwell (*Tipping Point, Blink, Outliers*) and Dan Pink (*When, Drive, To Sell Is Human*), for instance, each offer loads of interesting findings that can help illustrate your point. That's not surprising. Dan's a former speechwriter, and, full disclosure, Eric shared an office with him.

To be clear: Leafing through a book in the moments just before a speech is due creates a sure way to strike out. At times like that, nothing looks interesting, funny, or remotely usable.

Instead, read books when you have time to think. One of us once gave a book of political jokes to his boss, suggesting he leave it in the bathroom and check off the ones he liked.

He came back a week later. He'd checked off only fifteen jokes. That made it well worth the purchase price.

Podcasts

Podcasts have become an invaluable research tool. Political podcasts like *Pod Save America* (created by former Obama scribes and press aides Jon Favreau, Jon Lovett, Tommy Vietor, and Dan Pfeiffer) and *Slate*'s *Political Gabfest* (run by journalists John Dickerson, Emily Bazelon, and David Plotz) offer sharp commentary. NPR's *Freakonomics Radio,* WNYC's *Radiolab,* and *TED Radio Hour* might be considered general interest but cover ideas essential to anyone in politics. Even the storytelling of the *Moth* has material you can use. Thanks to each, and many others, it's possible to find poetry while exercising on the treadmill or commuting to and from work.

Admittedly, it's difficult to affix a sticky note to a podcast. It's like that old political joke about putting campaign bumper stickers on cars: it's easier when they're parked. When you hear something great on a podcast, make a note in your phone of which episode you heard, or work out some other system to help you remember. It's worth the trouble.

This brings us to a final "source" for research: become your own source.

Personal File

Every time you see, hear, and then use a joke, story, or interesting fact, you have found a bit of material with an important stamp of approval: yours. Whether you are a politician thinking about your own speeches or a staffer writing them for a boss, begin a file. Years ago, this would have meant a cumbersome system of note cards in a file drawer. Now it is easy to copy and paste each joke, quote, interesting litany, startling statistic, or even—it's possible—thoughtful or clever line you have thought up yourself. When you find something great or watch the speaker use it wonderfully, you think you'll remember it forever. In fact, if you don't add it to your inspiration file, you'll forget it next week. Don't let the good ones get away.

FINAL WORDS

Keeping the sources we've talked about in mind, let's return to the 1984 Ronald Reagan speech in Binghamton, New York, that began this chapter.

It wasn't a big event. For the Reagan White House and reelection campaign, it was a *typical* event. Yet Eric has repeated the anecdote for years—not only as an "origin story" for how he became interested in speechwriting, but also for what Reagan's speech teaches other writers. We thought using it could help you see how research affects a speech and its audience—how a narrative helps people remember and, ultimately, act.

Still, for the sake of an academic text, Eric thought he should obey another Reagan lesson: "Trust but verify."

He began by visiting the Reagan Presidential Library's online archive. There he found the transcript. Reagan started talking at 4:34 p.m. Just as Eric remembered, Reagan began and ended by praising the audience members and reminding them that their special story was America's story.

> I know this valley holds a special story—one of hardship overcome, of determination, hard work, family, and faith. And in many ways, your story is America's story.
>
> When those immigrants came to our shores and said "Which way EJ?," they were asking which way opportunity, which way peace, which way freedom.

Check.

A Google image search showed Reagan standing on a stage with an American flag as the backdrop. The entire speech, along with the "Fritzbusters," is on YouTube.[6] The song is more amateurish than Eric remembers. Nevertheless . . .

Check. Check.

Next, he found details in stories from the local Binghamton newspapers. That a high school chorus performed "God Bless America." That the crowd approved. That speechwriter Peter Robinson, a graduate of nearby Vestal High School, wrote the draft.

Wait a second. That's where Eric went.

Soon, thanks to more research that included a visit to LinkedIn, he was on the phone with Robinson, and they discovered they'd shared the same tyrannical soccer coach. But at first, the conversation was disappointing. It turns out "Which way EJ?" didn't exactly validate the purpose of this chapter. Robinson didn't have to research the phrase at all because, like Eric, he'd known about it from childhood. (He did say the White House researchers made sure the story was accurate.)[7]

But then Eric and Robinson began talking about a speechwriter's life. And Robinson happened to mention another speech he'd written—one of Reagan's most famous, actually. The one the president delivered in Berlin in 1984.

Peter Robinson may not have needed research for "Which way EJ?," but the Berlin speech showed that he knew how indispensable research is. For here is guidance he received for the assignment:

"Audience of about 10,000. Length: 20–25 minutes. Subject: foreign policy. Period."[8]

That didn't satisfy Robinson. He flew to Berlin. He visited the embassy. He interviewed diplomats. All he heard was boilerplate, material he could have gotten without crossing the Atlantic—until he had dinner with some Berliners. A woman told him that if Gorbachev was serious, he'd just get rid of the slab of concrete that divided her city, east and west.

That's usable, he thought. The president will respond because it's concrete, literally, and to the point. Robinson scribbled in his notebook. Others had similar ideas, but it was Robinson who, when he returned to Washington, put it in the draft.

"Mr. Gorbachev, tear down this wall."

What should you make of this chapter—this window into the life of a speechwriter? Here are a few things we hope you'll take away.

First, despite what colleagues say about a new speech, it will not "write itself." A speech doesn't research itself either. And no matter how much other staffers know, research and a speechwriter's ability to find compelling details often make the difference for the speaker *and* the audience.

Second, even with robust tools, we can never reduce research to a science. Some days, you take a break, pick up the newspaper, and see the perfect detail jumping off the front page. Other days, you spend hours rejecting one piece of material after another, all for a short, five-minute speech. When your boss calls and asks, "Hey, where's the draft?" you gulp, say, "Forty-five minutes," and go with what you have.

Third, speechwriting can be a lonely exercise, but speech researching shouldn't be. Don't just use other staffers. Cultivate them. Be grateful. Go out of your way to return the favor. Help them if they need advice on how to phrase something. Show your respect. Then, when you need research, they will show theirs for you.

Fourth, don't just rely on an email. Talk to people "on the ground." That's how Peter Robinson came up with a memorable phrase and how, researching for this book, Eric learned about it.

We'll come back to this subject again in Chapter 14. But so far in *The Political Speechwriter's Companion*, we've covered four areas: the special needs of the politician; the ways people have tried to persuade others for almost 2,500 years; the needs of those listening to speakers; and some steps regarding research.

Time now to examine what goes into the speeches themselves, how to *use* all that good stuff you've researched.

Soon we will cover the LAWS of political speech first mentioned in Chapter 1: language, anecdote, wit, and support. They are the elements that can do for a speech what brick, glass, and stone can do for a building: make it beautiful.

You can't have a building without structure. You can't have a good speech without it, either. And while there are many kinds of structure in persuasive rhetoric, Chapter 5 will focus only on one, because of its incredible utility in politics.

THE SPEECHWRITER'S CHECKLIST: RESEARCH

Researching the Event

- ☐ How large is the audience?
- ☐ Who is in the audience, and what do they want to hear?
- ☐ How will the room be set up?
- ☐ Does the speaker want a Q&A session?
- ☐ Will the speaker need a microphone? Teleprompter? Lectern?

Researching Ideas

- ☐ Have I benefited from other staffers' ideas?
- ☐ Have I talked with the communications staff of the group sponsoring the event?
- ☐ Have I looked at the group's website?
- ☐ Have I reviewed old speeches for elements I can recycle?

Researching Poetry

- ☐ Have I talked to my boss specifically about the stories, jokes, quotes, personal reflections, and other elements that add color?
- ☐ Have I looked through recent news stories for anecdotes?
- ☐ Have I asked other staffers for stories they might remember?
- ☐ Have I looked at speeches I admire?
- ☐ Have I checked my personal files and library for quotes, jokes, and anecdotes?
- ☐ Do I *feel* ready to write?

PART II

HOW TO DO IT

5

Structure

People knew Leland Stowe in the 1930s and '40s for being one of the first journalists alerting Americans to the Nazi threat. But one day after World War II was over, Americans heard him speak of a different threat. It was 1948, and Stowe was talking on the radio about what he'd seen on a street corner in Athens. Here's his opening:

> I pray that I'll never have to do it again. Can there be anything much worse than to put only a peanut between a child and death? I hope you'll never have to do it and live with the memory of it afterward. If you had heard their voices and seen their eyes, on that January day in the bomb-scarred workers' district of Athens . . . Yet all I had left was a half-pound can of peanuts.
>
> As I struggled to open it, dozens of ragged kids held me in a vise of frantically clawing bodies. Scores of mothers, with babes in their arms, pushed and fought to get within arm's reach. They held their babies out toward me. Tiny hands of skin and bone stretched convulsively.
>
> I tried to make every peanut count. In their frenzy they nearly swept me off my feet.
>
> Nothing but hundreds of hands, begging hands, clutching hands, despairing hands; all of them pitifully little hands.
>
> One salted peanut here, and one peanut there.
>
> Six peanuts knocked from my fingers and a savage scramble of emaciated bodies at my feet.
>
> Another peanut here and another peanut there.

Hundreds of hands, reaching and pleading: hundreds of eyes with the light of hope flickering out.

I stood there helpless, an empty blue can in my hands . . . Yes, I hope it will never happen to you.[1]

Still powerful, decades later. But relevant to political speechwriting is not just how Stowe began but what he did in the rest of his report. More precisely, it's the structure he used—a five-step sequence designed not just to persuade but to make listeners act.

That structure made Stowe's address a favorite example for Alan Monroe, the rhetoric professor who, while teaching at Purdue University in the 1930s, developed and popularized those five steps you now find in virtually every public speaking text with his name attached: Monroe's Motivated Sequence (MMS).[2]

Maybe because so many professional speechwriters learn on the job, relatively few know Monroe's Motivated Sequence by name. But they understand its power. MMS forms the structure of the two most influential political speeches of the twentieth century: John F. Kennedy's inaugural, and Martin Luther King Jr.'s "I Have a Dream." That's probably one reason why, even without having studied MMS, so many writers use elements of it in their work.

Of all the ways to organize a persuasive speech, none is more tailored to the unique needs of American politics. Thus, it's worth a close and systematic look.

Let's start by describing the steps. In Box 5.1, you will see Monroe's terms first, with some commonly used alternates in parentheses, and how each term applies to political speech.

BOX 5.1
MONROE'S MOTIVATED SEQUENCE

1. **ATTENTION:** Monroe argued that no matter how compelling our ideas, we can't persuade people who aren't paying attention. Listeners are fickle. Grab them as close to the first sentence as possible. After thirty seconds, they should think, *"Wow! This is fascinating. I need to hear more!"*

2. **NEED (*PROBLEM*):** Audiences care most about policy that meets their needs. Monroe's second step: show the audience members not just that they have a need but that it is urgent. This doesn't necessarily mean a personal need, like finding a job. It can mean a need to help others whose situation is so dire that listeners couldn't live with themselves if they didn't try to help solve the problem. *"I had no idea things were this bad,"* you want your

listeners to think after step two. *"How can we fix it?"* Or: *"I knew things were bad. Here's someone else who does! What's the solution?"*

3. **SATISFACTION (*SOLUTION*):** Satisfy that need—in other words, solve the problem. And to Monroe, presenting a solution didn't mean just stating it. Speakers need to provide evidence to show us that the solution works, that it is practical and better than the alternatives. At this stage, listeners should be thinking, *"That just might work!"*

4. **VISUALIZATION:** It's not enough, Monroe said, to persuade listeners with dry evidence and abstractions. To truly motivate them, he suggests letting them visualize success by imagining the future—or showing examples of success in the past to remind listeners what's possible again. Thoughts: *"If that could happen, our lives would be so great!"*

5. **CALL TO ACTION:** Why let your listeners off the hook? If they agree with you, get them to do something about it. Monroe suggested speakers end by urging the crowd to act. Send people out of the room thinking, *"Yes! I want to get involved. I want to do something now!"*

Let's look at the rest of Leland Stowe's short speech. Note how after that (1) *dramatic opening*, Stowe moves into (2) *his description of the problem*, using statistics to show us the scope of it; (3) *presents a solution*, using a variety of ways to persuade us it's a good one; (4) *shows us his vision* of what will happen; and (5) *asks* us directly to *act*.

Who would say that a child's life is worth less than a movie a week, or a lipstick, or a few packs of cigarettes? **Yet, in today's world, there are at least 230 million children who must depend upon the aid of private agencies and individuals.** From Amiens to Athens, from Cairo to Calcutta and Chungking, millions upon millions of waifs of war still hold death barely at arm's length. Their only hope rests in the private relief agencies, which, in turn, depend entirely upon you and me—upon how much we care and what we give.	2. Need/ Problem
A worldwide campaign exists as a demonstration that the people of the United Nations do care. Our own branch of UNAC is American Overseas Aid—United Nations Appeal for Children, with headquarters at 39 Broadway, New York City. In February, American Overseas Aid makes its appeal to raise sixty million dollars from Americans. That's something to put peanuts forever in their place. Something big enough for every American to want to be in on. Every penny contributed to American Overseas Aid will help bring food, medical care, and new life to millions of child war victims.	3. Satisfaction/ Solution

(Continued)

(Continued)

If we could hear their voices and see their eyes, countless ——— 4. Visualization
millions of children, now hungry and diseased or soon to die,
would run and play and laugh once more. It only depends on
how many of us hear and how many see.

Look at their reaching outspread fingers and **send your** ——— 5. Call to Action
contribution to American Overseas Aid, 39 Broadway,
New York.

WHY MONROE WORKS WELL IN POLITICS

Monroe never claimed to have invented his structure. Rather, he codified what he had seen from others—including biblical examples, like Moses's speech to the Israelites before they crossed the River Jordan.

We also see MMS in a short speech by an American president who won *attention* by reminding us of an event "four score and seven years" earlier, then launched into his *problem*—the question of whether "any nation so conceived and so dedicated can long endure."

In that 1863 address at Gettysburg, Abraham Lincoln proposed a *solution*—that the "living be dedicated here to the unfinished work which they who fought here have thus far so nobly advanced"; called for *action* ("we here highly resolve . . ."); and ended with his *visualization* ("that this government, of the people . . ."). In Box 5.2, you can see this nineteenth-century version of MMS at a glance.

BOX 5.2
GETTYSBURG ADDRESS SLIDE

Four score and seven years ago our fathers brought forth ——— 1. Attention
on this continent, a new nation, conceived in Liberty, and
dedicated to the proposition that all men are created equal.
Now we are engaged in a great civil war, testing whether ——— 2. Need
that nation, or any nation so conceived and so dedicated,
can long endure. We are met on a great battle-field of that
war. We have come to dedicate a portion of that field, as a
final resting place for those who here gave their lives that that
nation might live. It is altogether fitting and proper that we
should do this.

But, in a larger sense, we cannot dedicate—we cannot
consecrate—we cannot hallow—this ground. The brave men,
living and dead, who struggled here, have consecrated it, far
above our poor power to add or detract. The world will little
note, nor long remember what we say here, but it can never

CHAPTER 5 Structure 77

forget what they did here. **It is for us the living, rather, to be dedicated here to the unfinished work** which they who fought here have thus far so nobly advanced. It is rather for us to be here dedicated to the great task remaining before us—that from these honored dead we take increased devotion to that cause for which they gave the last full measure of devotion—that **we here highly resolve** that these dead shall not have died in vain—that this nation, under God, shall have a **new birth of freedom**—and that government of the people, by the people, for the people, shall not perish from the earth.	3. Satisfaction 4. Call to Action 5. Visualization

The Gettysburg Address demonstrates that MMS doesn't work just for long speeches. It works just as well for short ones. During the bitter health care debate in the House of Representatives on March 24, 2017, Republican Tom Cole and Democrat Robin Kelly both used MMS.

REPUBLICAN: Congressman Tom Cole (OK-04)

Cole wins attention by describing what President Barack Obama promised—and asserting that this was false. — Attention

> Seven years ago, I was on this floor and I heard that, if you liked your plan, you could keep it.
>
> I heard, if you liked your doctor, you could keep that doctor.
>
> And I heard that health care costs were going to drop by $2,500 per family.
>
> None of it was true.

Cole uses statistics to demonstrate the affordable care problems in his state. — Problem

> I sit here now and look at my state, and I know what is happening next year.
>
> The rates on the Obamacare exchanges are going up by 69 percent. We are down to a single provider.
>
> That is what seven years ago brought us.

Cole outlines the Republican plan and why it will work. — Solution

> Today we have a chance to do something different, and everybody from my state will do something different. They will vote for a plan that actually does what it says it is going to do.
>
> Number one, they will be able to actually have plans that are designed by Oklahomans, not by bureaucrats in Washington, D.C.

(Continued)

(Continued)

> They will be able to have a tax credit, if they are not already insured under Medicaid or Medicare or from their employer.
>
> They will be able to have an individual tax credit to purchase a plan that they design, that they like.
>
> They will be free of the mandates of Obamacare, free to make their own decisions, free of the mandates that require them to buy insurance products that they simply don't need.

Cole describes what lies ahead for voters in his district, and why they will want a "simple choice." ——Visualization

> I have got a lot of people in my district that are in their fifties and sixties. Some of them might like to have children again, but they are not likely to have children again, and they mostly don't want maternity care.
>
> So it is a pretty simple choice for us. It is a choice to be free and make our own decisions. It is a choice to design our own plans. It is a choice to have federal assistance where we need it but to be used under our direction. It is an easy choice.
>
> I urge the passage of this rule, and I urge the passage of the underlying legislation. —— Call to Action

DEMOCRAT: Congresswoman Robin Kelly (IL-02)

Kelly wins attention with a quote from Martin Luther King Jr. —— Attention

> "Of all the forms of inequality, injustice in health care is the most shocking and inhumane."
>
> Dr. King spoke these words because the health of our fellow Americans is a moral imperative.

Kelly offers three problems with the new legislation. —— Problem

> What we have before us today is a morally corrupt bill: morally corrupt because it claws away health insurance from 24 million Americans, morally corrupt because it leaves nearly 1 million of my fellow Illinoisans without health insurance, morally corrupt because 240,000 Illinois kids will no longer have the safety and security of their current coverage.

> Kelly combines, and actually flips, steps three and four. Her solution is to vote for what's best for people, not party. Her visualization reminds colleagues that there are consequences in the "aftermath."
>
>> When you cast your vote today, know that you own its aftermath here, forward. Will you cast your vote for party, or will you cast your vote to do what is best in the lives of the people you represent?
>
> Kelly urges her colleagues to imagine their constituents—and urges them to vote "no."
>
>> Think of the last senior whose hand you shook at a town hall. Think of the last child you hugged at a school visit. Does this bill do right by them? Will they be better off?
>>
>> If you have any doubt, vote "no." Vote "no," and kill this bad bill.

— Solution/Visualization

— Call to Action

In 1964, Monroe explained why he thought this sequence worked.

"Most people seek cognition or balance among cognitions," he wrote. "When confronted with a problem that disturbs their normal orientation, they look for a solution: when they feel a want or need, they search for a way to satisfy it. In short, when anything throws them into a condition of disorganization or dissonance, they are motivated . . . to alter their behavior."[3]

That may seem like a long way of telling us that when people have problems, they look for solutions, which may involve changing behavior. But except for the fact that the problems they solve are societal, isn't that the politician's role? For speechwriters, MMS is invaluable for three practical reasons.

MMS Is Fast

Don't just think about the member of Congress with a bunch of speeches on each day's schedule. Pity the poor writer who has to prepare them all. Because political speeches need to be written fast, there's often no time to wrestle with structure. When you have ten minutes to write a draft, it's a big help to have a reliable structure on speed dial.

MMS Is Compelling

Monroe argued that to persuade audiences, speakers need coherence, order, and a pattern that follows the way listeners think through problems. That makes sense. Of course, smart speakers and speechwriters want to begin by making an audience eager to hear more. Of course, they want to continue by addressing the questions that come naturally to any audience: Why should I listen? Do I care? And, of course, speakers and writers want listeners to agree with their solutions and join the cause.

BOX 5.3
EXERCISE: MONROE, IT'S IN THE BAG

Each semester in our speechwriting class, we put the idea of MMS being intuitive to the test. Actually, we put it in a bag.

We come to our very first class with brown lunch bags, each with an item inside. It might be a pencil, a banana, or a toy from the dollar store.

We divide the students into groups of three or four. Before mentioning Monroe's Motivated Sequence or even introducing the steps, we ask students to look in the bag and spend only five minutes writing a thirty- to sixty-second speech convincing the rest of their class that they can't live without the bag's contents.

It doesn't matter if you're a seasoned speechwriter or a rookie—try it. Pick an item on your desk; how would you sell it? You will see, like we do invariably with every class we teach, these very short speeches demonstrate each step of Monroe.

Here's an example:

"Thinking about that girl you met in speechwriting class?" Attention.

"You want to get her number, but the battery on your phone is dead." Problem.

"Use a pencil!" Solution.

"Your parents will love her." Visualization.

"Buy a pencil. Sharpen your future today." Call to action.

MMS Is Versatile

Think about politicians on the stump. They get our *attention* fast, often with a joke, startling statement, or story. They present a *problem*—usually the other candidate—and a *solution*: electing the speaker. They outline their *vision* of what winning can bring, and *call* for help to get there.

Imagine them after the campaign ends. In speaking, say, to the Sierra Club, they still want to get *attention* fast, and outline a *problem*. In this case, it might be climate change or offshore drilling. The *solution* might be a bill. But a smart politician will also include a *vision* of what can happen once the bill becomes law, and *call* on the group to lobby for it.

Now picture some weekday when the House is in session. Representatives might argue on the floor for a bill like the one on health care. They might rush over to talk to an organization with a special interest—say the pharmaceutical manufacturers. They might detour on the way back to talk to a group of school kids from their home district. Once the House adjourns for the day, they're off to speak at a fundraiser.

Different situations. But in each case, the MMS structure helps by keeping listeners' attention focused on the problems, and on the solutions the politician offers.

Politicians find ways to mention problems and solutions in speeches at all sorts of occasions: toasts, tributes, intros, awards, commencements—even eulogies, as we will see later.

By combining the problem–solution contrast most political speeches need with the inspiration of its vision and call-to-action steps, MMS includes the elements most important to politicians.

MMS is so versatile that it can even accommodate more than one speaker, as in an interesting example, shown in Box 5.4, from one of President Barack Obama's last weekly messages, which he did with the hip-hop star Macklemore.

BOX 5.4
OBAMA AND MACKLEMORE

Remarks of President Barack Obama and Macklemore
The White House
May 14, 2016

Words: 707
Grade level: 8.1
Sentence length: 14.9 words
Passive: 0 percent

ATTENTION: President Obama wins attention by appearing with a celebrity: Macklemore, who recounts his own struggles with addiction.

> **THE PRESIDENT:** Hi, everybody. I've got a special guest with me this week—Macklemore. For those of you who don't share the same love for hip-hop, he's a Grammy-winning artist—but he's also an advocate who's giving voice to a disease we too often just whisper about: the disease of addiction.
>
> **MACKLEMORE:** Hey, everybody. I'm here with President Obama because I take this personally. I abused prescription drugs and battled addiction. If I hadn't gotten the help I needed when I needed it, I might not be here today. And I want to help others facing the same challenges I did.

(Continued)

(Continued)

PROBLEM: Obama uses statistics, examples of how addiction starts, and expert testimony to show the scope of opioid addiction. Macklemore lends urgency to the problem by describing his friend, Kevin.

> **THE PRESIDENT:** Drug overdoses now take more lives every year than traffic accidents. Deaths from opioid overdoses have tripled since 2000. A lot of the time, they're from legal drugs prescribed by a doctor. So addiction doesn't always start in some dark alley—it often starts in a medicine cabinet. In fact, a new study released this month found that 44 percent of Americans know someone who has been addicted to prescription painkillers.
>
> **MACKLEMORE:** I didn't just know someone—I lost someone. My friend Kevin overdosed on painkillers when he was just twenty-one years old. Addiction is like any other disease—it doesn't discriminate. It doesn't care what color you are, whether you're a guy or a girl, rich or poor, whether you live in the inner city, a suburb, or rural America. This doesn't just happen to other people's kids or in some other neighborhood. It can happen to any of us.

SOLUTION: Obama outlines solutions—and examples of them. Macklemore testifies to the effectiveness of one solution: treatment.

> **THE PRESIDENT:** That's why just talking about this crisis isn't enough—we need to get treatment to more people who need it. My administration is working with communities to reduce overdose deaths, including with medication. We're working with law enforcement to help people get into treatment instead of jail. And under Obamacare, health plans in the marketplace have to include coverage for treatment.
>
> **MACKLEMORE:** I know recovery isn't easy or quick, but along with the twelve-step program, treatment has saved my life. Recovery works—and we need our leaders in Washington to fund it and people [need to] know how to find it.
>
> **THE PRESIDENT:** We all need to do more to make that happen. I've asked Congress to expand access to recovery services, and to give first responders the tools they need to treat overdoses before it's too late. This week, the House passed several bills about opioids—but unless they also make actual investments in more treatment, it won't get Americans the help they need. On top of funding, doctors also need more training about the power of the pain medication they prescribe, and the risks they carry. Another way our country can help those suffering in private is to make this conversation public.
>
> **MACKLEMORE:** When you're going through it, it's hard to imagine there could be anything worse than addiction. But shame and the stigma associated with the disease keeps too many people from seeking the help they need. Addiction isn't a personal choice or a personal failing. And sometimes it takes more than a strong will to get better—it takes a strong community and accessible resources.

> **VISUALIZATION:** Obama paints a picture of the future when these solutions become available.
>
> **THE PRESIDENT:** The good news is, there's hope. When we talk about opioid abuse as the public health problem it is, more people will seek the help they need. More people will find the strength to recover, just like Macklemore and millions of Americans have. We'll see fewer preventable deaths and fewer broken families.
>
> **CALL TO ACTION:** Macklemore urges addicts to seek help, and urges listeners to publicize what is available. Obama then urges everyone to take part. Finally, Macklemore closes by urging listeners to watch more on MTV, and call a special number for help.
>
> **MACKLEMORE:** We have to tell people who need help that it's okay to ask for it. We've got to make sure they know where to get it.
>
> **THE PRESIDENT:** We all have a role to play. Even if we haven't fought this battle in our own lives, there's a good chance we know someone who has, or who is.
>
> **MACKLEMORE:** President Obama and I just had a powerful conversation here at the White House about opioid abuse, and what we can do about it. You can catch it this summer on MTV. And to find treatment in your area, call 1-800-662-HELP.
>
> **THE PRESIDENT:** Thanks, and have a great weekend.

OTHER STRUCTURES

Monroe is by no means the only possible structure for persuasive speech. Even in political speechwriting, where goals are well defined and MMS often serves you well, you have many other options for structuring a speech. Here's a brief description of three:

> **Problem-Cause-Solution:** A speech in which a section of background explores the roots of a particular problem as a way of making your solution believable.
>
> **Comparative Advantage:** A format useful when the problem is a given but the audience needs to choose among solutions to decide which work best.
>
> **Refutation:** A four-step format in which you state a solution, refute it at length, outline your different solution, and support it with evidence.

We don't call these "other structures" if writers have added only, say, a few sentences of rebuttal or cause to what is basically the MMS structure. Certainly the ideas above can fit within MMS. But sometimes speeches may be almost entirely rebuttal or ones that describe causes. Those structures deserve different names, as do others, some quite poetic.

When Martin Luther King Jr. went to divinity school, he became enthralled with a variety of speech structures bearing interesting names. Students crowded into chapel to hear him use the "lettuce leaf" (peeling away layers to reveal the truth), the "ladder to heaven" (a series of steps leading to a solution), or the "facet of a diamond" (examining all aspects of a dilemma).[4]

With Monroe, we are less interested in having readers cling rigidly to its five steps, or even their order, and more interested in seeing what they can add.

MONROE PLUS

Simply using MMS doesn't guarantee that you'll write a great speech, any more than a framework of steel girders guarantees a building will be an architectural masterpiece. As a speaker or speechwriter, you'll find yourself wanting to do plenty of things that on the surface don't belong within the MMS structure. But part of the beauty of MMS is that speechwriters can modify and enrich it—especially by adding three things crucial in political life.

Saying Thanks

Part of remaining popular is learning to thank people in the room. Politicians need to praise the people they are addressing, salute past achievements, and find ways to praise themselves without seeming fatuous. Sometimes those thank-yous seem endless, mostly because of the mechanical way they appear, as lists of names at the very beginning. Political audiences often contain people who have knocked themselves out in campaigns, often as volunteers. They want, and deserve, to have their work acknowledged, and politicians need to oblige. Later we show how.

Establishing Credibility

Many political speeches include an *"I'm okay, you're okay"* portion, which in its most hackneyed form goes like this: "It's so great to be at a group that has done so much for [write in issue]. It's my issue too—and I remember working with your president on . . ."

Listeners will certainly find speakers credible when they mention having worked not only on similar issues but in partnership with the audience. There is nothing wrong, though, with waiting for the moment several minutes into a speech when you discuss that issue. At that point, acknowledging partnership becomes relevant.

Part of being credible is also providing background. Particularly in issue-driven speeches, politicians sometimes need to provide context that makes the audience understand the problem or solution better. That can be part of other steps, but sometimes it deserves a section of its own. In fact, it's one way in which politicians can sound thoughtful. Believe it or not, introspection and reflection also help establish credibility and thus belong in political speech. Within limits, political audiences appreciate ideas untrammeled by the need for sharp rhetoric.

In Box 5.5, you will read Ronald Reagan's famous speech from the fortieth anniversary of D-Day. Look closely at the section where he discusses an important question: "What impelled you to put aside the instinct for self-preservation and risk your lives to take these cliffs?"

There is no need for Reagan to discuss that question. But including it offers listeners a portrait of Reagan different than what one writer called his "avuncular style, optimism, and plain-folks demeanor."[5] It makes him seem thoughtful.

Ending Memorably

Who doesn't know instantly where this line came from? *Shall not perish from the earth.* Of course, Lincoln's clincher.

No line has more impact than the *clincher*—the very last lines of a speech. Writers should work hard to end with one listeners will remember.

Later chapters will explore ways to organize each of the MMS steps, including an ending we call the "four-part close." It uses some elements that are new. But Monroe never intended his formula to be all-inclusive. Like a rubber band, it is perfectly capable of expanding to include others.

It is flexible, too. Often, writers reverse steps four and five hoping to end by reminding listeners not just to act, but why they must. Sometimes they may have one section listing all problems before moving to solutions, and in others they will present a solution for each problem.

In political life, we routinely need more than Monroe's five steps. So we suggest a modified version of MMS: Monroe Plus. It would accommodate the need to (1) thank people and praise the audience, (2) provide the background that issue-centered speeches sometimes need, (3) include the kinds of material solution steps need, and (4) end memorably.

Outlined, such a speech might look like this:

1. **Attention**
   - Thank-yous, acknowledgments—and praise for audience
   - Background
2. **Problem**
3. **Solution**
   - Possible rebuttal and comparative advantage
4. **Visualization** (or other way to inspire)
5. **Action**
   - Clincher

MONROE IN PRACTICE: FOUR TIPS

You can use Monroe by adopting the outline intact. But to use Monroe *well* means adapting as much as adopting. It also means avoiding pitfalls. Here are four ways to do that.

Keep Your Balance

MMS works best when you balance each element. You can't devote five minutes to the problem in a seven-minute speech. You can't take half the speech to open with a story, no matter how powerful. Sometimes, you will open with an anecdote you know is too long. Finish the draft, take a deep breath, and pretend you never shared it before. Nerve yourself to cut out some great detail, and remember what Louis Brandeis once said: "There's no great writing. Only great rewriting."

Get Attention Fast

Political offices pressure writers to load up the first few minutes with acknowledgments. Resist. Audiences are fickle. As much as possible, fold in acknowledgments and other bits of rhetorical throat-clearing later in the speech. Don't begin with "It's a pleasure to be here." Your listeners assume it. You're talking to them! Choose the most gripping way to start and get your attention step as close to the first sentence as possible.

Don't Stint on Visualization

One virtue of MMS is that it emphasizes moving an audience; people are more likely to act when they *feel* something. Yet the step that can be most moving—vision—is the one most often neglected. Try to imagine Martin Luther King Jr.'s speech if he hadn't described his dream. You can't. And while visualization doesn't always mean imagining the future, it usually implies hope for the future. There are few audiences who won't be stirred by that if you do it well.

Think Road Maps

Confused readers can go back and reread. Listeners can't. That means speakers have to offer a road map for what's ahead. The next chapter covers transitions—previews, internal summaries, and cuing tips that help audiences follow along.

FINAL WORDS

Great political speech results from a complex interplay of elements that include the event, preparation time, and delivery. As we can't say too often, Monroe's formula alone cannot guarantee a great, or even good, speech. If structure alone could make a speech moving, entertaining, or persuasive, the CliffsNotes of *Hamlet* would be as effective as the play.

If you consider writing the skill that makes you unique, then a voice in your brain may have been protesting throughout this chapter: Wait! Won't relying so much on formula stifle my creativity?

No.

First, even Shakespeare used a formula, a five-act structure, or Freytag's pyramid, for his plays. Second, no blueprint limits your originality. Whatever basic structure you follow, you can still be original in your language and your thinking and the details you choose or juxtapose.

Besides, as we've established, MMS doesn't have to be accepted intact. The Gettysburg Address flips the order of steps four and five. Does that matter? Not at all. In fact, political speechwriters in the Obama years often did the same thing.

Examples fill this book. In the Appendix, you will see a selection of full political speeches illustrating nine kinds: stump, floor, keynote, rally, eulogy, commencement, award, roast, and commemorative. Every one uses most or all of the MMS five steps.

To end this chapter, let's look closely at a speech written by Peggy Noonan for Ronald Reagan. It illustrates the five steps of Monroe and the modifications we suggest.

BOX 5.5
RONALD REAGAN

Remarks of President Ronald Reagan
Fortieth Anniversary of D-Day
Pointe du Hoc, Normandy, France
June 6, 1984

ATTENTION: After a paragraph to set the scene, Reagan wins attention by narrating the story of the Rangers' dangerous attack on the cliffs behind him.

We're here to mark that day in history when the Allied armies joined in battle to reclaim this continent to liberty. For four long years, much of Europe had been under a terrible shadow. Free nations had fallen, Jews cried out in the camps, millions cried out for liberation. Europe was enslaved, and the world prayed for its rescue. Here, in Normandy, the rescue began. Here, the Allies stood and fought against tyranny, in a giant undertaking unparalleled in human history.

We stand on a lonely, windswept point on the northern shore of France. The air is soft, but forty years ago at this moment, the air was dense with smoke and the cries of men, and the air was filled with the crack of rifle fire and the roar of cannon. At dawn, on the morning of the sixth of June, 1944, two hundred and twenty-five Rangers jumped off the British landing craft and ran to the bottom of these cliffs.

Their mission was one of the most difficult and daring of the invasion: to climb these sheer and desolate cliffs and take out the enemy guns. The Allies had been told that some of the mightiest of these guns were here, and they would be trained on the beaches to stop the Allied advance.

The Rangers looked up and saw the enemy soldiers at the edge of the cliffs, shooting down at them with machine guns and throwing grenades. And the American Rangers began to climb. They shot rope ladders over the face of these cliffs and began to pull themselves up. When one Ranger fell, another would take his place. When one rope was cut, a Ranger would grab another and begin his climb again. They climbed, shot back, and held their footing. Soon, one by one, the Rangers pulled themselves over the top, and in seizing the firm land at the top of these cliffs, they began to seize back the continent of Europe. Two hundred and twenty-five came here. After two days of fighting, only ninety could still bear arms.

PRAISE: He brings us back to the present by saluting them.

And behind me is a memorial that symbolizes the Ranger daggers that were thrust into the top of these cliffs. And before me are the men who put them there. These are the boys of Pointe du Hoc. These are the men who took the cliffs. These are the champions who helped free a continent. And these are the heroes who helped end a war. Gentlemen, I look at you and I think of the words of Stephen Spender's poem. You are men who in your "lives fought for life and left the vivid air signed with your honor."

Reagan illustrates their courage with humor—a story painting the soldiers as unassuming in the face of danger.

CHAPTER 5   Structure

I think I know what you may be thinking right now—thinking "we were just part of a bigger effort; everyone was brave that day." Well, everyone was. Do you remember the story of Bill Millin of the Fifty-First Highlanders? Forty years ago today, British troops were pinned down near a bridge, waiting desperately for help. Suddenly, they heard the sound of bagpipes, and some thought they were dreaming. Well, they weren't. They looked up and saw Bill Millin with his bagpipes, leading the reinforcements and ignoring the smack of the bullets into the ground around him.

Lord Lovat was with him—Lord Lovat of Scotland, who calmly announced when he got to the bridge, "Sorry, I'm a few minutes late," as if he'd been delayed by a traffic jam, when in truth he'd just come from the bloody fighting on Sword Beach, which he and his men had just taken.

. . . And now he uses a montage of brief examples to portray the many heroes that day.

There was the impossible valor of the Poles, who threw themselves between the enemy and the rest of Europe as the invasion took hold; and the unsurpassed courage of the Canadians who had already seen the horrors of war on this coast. They knew what awaited them there, but they would not be deterred. And once they hit Juno Beach, they never looked back.

All of these men were part of a roll call of honor with names that spoke of a pride as bright as the colors they bore; the Royal Winnipeg Rifles, Poland's Twenty-Fourth Lancers, the Royal Scots' Fusiliers, the Screaming Eagles, the Yeomen of England's armored divisions, the forces of Free France, the Coast Guard's "Matchbox Fleet," and you, the American Rangers.

PROBLEM I: Reagan raises a problem—but phrased as a question. Why did they show such courage? After all, it's not often that people will show such unselfish willingness to make sacrifices.

Forty summers have passed since the battle that you fought here. You were young the day you took these cliffs; some of you were hardly more than boys, with the deepest joys of life before you. Yet you risked everything here. Why? Why did you do it? What impelled you to put aside the instinct for self-preservation and risk your lives to take these cliffs?

SOLUTION I: Reagan answers his question: it was faith, belief, loyalty and love—and the knowledge that some things are worth dying for.

What inspired all the men of the armies that met here? We look at you, and somehow we know the answer. It was faith and belief. It was loyalty and love.

The men of Normandy had faith that what they were doing was right, faith that they fought for all humanity, faith that a just God would grant them mercy on this beachhead, or on the next. It was the deep knowledge—and pray God we have not lost it—that there is a profound moral difference between the use of force for liberation and the use of force for conquest. You were here to liberate, not to

(Continued)

(Continued)

conquer, and so you and those others did not doubt your cause. And you were right not to doubt.

You all knew that some things are worth dying for. One's country is worth dying for, and democracy is worth dying for, because it's the most deeply honorable form of government ever devised by man. All of you loved liberty. All of you were willing to fight tyranny, and you knew the people of your countries were behind you.

The Americans who fought here that morning knew word of the invasion was spreading through the darkness back home. They fought—or felt in their hearts, though they couldn't know in fact, that in Georgia they were filling the churches at 4:00 a.m. In Kansas they were kneeling on their porches and praying. And in Philadelphia they were ringing the Liberty Bell.

Reagan illustrates his reasoning with a story of Colonel Wolverton's belief in prayer.

Something else helped the men of D-Day; their rock-hard belief that Providence would have a great hand in the events that would unfold here; that God was an ally in this great cause. And so, the night before the invasion, when Colonel Wolverton asked his parachute troops to kneel with him in prayer, he told them: "Do not bow your heads, but look up so you can see God and ask His blessing in what we're about to do." Also, that night, General Matthew Ridgway on his cot, listening in the darkness for the promise God made to Joshua: "I will not fail thee nor forsake thee."

These are the things that impelled them; these are the things that shaped the unity of the Allies.

When the war was over, there were lives to be rebuilt and governments to be returned to the people. There were nations to be reborn. Above all, there was a new peace to be assured. These were huge and daunting tasks. But the Allies summoned strength from the faith, belief, loyalty, and love of those who fell here. They rebuilt a new Europe together. There was first a great reconciliation among those who had been enemies, all of whom had suffered so greatly. The United States did its part, creating the Marshall Plan to help rebuild our allies and our former enemies. The Marshall Plan led to the Atlantic alliance—a great alliance that serves to this day as our shield for freedom, for prosperity, and for peace.

In spite of our great efforts and successes, not all that followed the end of the war was happy or planned. Some liberated countries were lost. The great sadness of this loss echoes down to our own time in the streets of Warsaw, Prague, and East Berlin. The Soviet troops that came to the center of this continent did not leave when peace came. They're still there, uninvited, unwanted, unyielding, almost forty years after the war. Because of this, Allied forces still stand on this continent. Today, as forty years ago, our armies are here for only one purpose: to protect and defend democracy. The only territories we hold are memorials like this one and graveyards where our heroes rest.

PROBLEM II: Now, Reagan raises a second problem: the need to avoid war. His solution: that the Soviet Union gives "up the ways of conquest."

We in America have learned bitter lessons from two world wars. It is better to be here ready to protect the peace than to take blind shelter across the sea, rushing to respond only after freedom is lost. We've learned that isolationism never was and never will be an acceptable response to tyrannical governments with an expansionist intent. But we try always to be prepared for peace, prepared to deter aggression, prepared to negotiate the reduction of arms, and yes, prepared to reach out again in the spirit of reconciliation. In truth, there is no reconciliation we would welcome more than a reconciliation with the Soviet Union, so, together, we can lessen the risks of war, now and forever.

It's fitting to remember here the great losses also suffered by the Russian people during World War II. Twenty million perished, a terrible price that testifies to all the world the necessity of ending war. I tell you from my heart that we in the United States do not want war. We want to wipe from the face of the earth the terrible weapons that man now has in his hands. And I tell you, we are ready to seize that beachhead. We look for some sign from the Soviet Union that they are willing to move forward, that they share our desire and love for peace, and that they will give up the ways of conquest. There must be a changing there that will allow us to turn our hope into action.

SOLUTION II: Reagan offers his solution for now: the alliance that protects us.

We will pray forever that someday that changing will come. But for now, particularly today, it is good and fitting to renew our commitment to each other, to our freedom, and to the alliance that protects it.

We're bound today by what bound us forty years ago, the same loyalties, traditions, and beliefs. We're bound by reality. The strength of America's allies is vital to the United States, and the American security guarantee is essential to the continued freedom of Europe's democracies. We were with you then; we're with you now. Your hopes are our hopes, and your destiny is our destiny.

CALL TO ACTION: He asks us to "stand for the ideals for which they lived and died."

Here, in this place where the West held together, let us make a vow to our dead. Let us show them by our actions that we understand what they died for. Let our actions say to them the words for which Matthew Ridgway listened: "I will not fail thee nor forsake thee."

Strengthened by their courage and heartened by their value [valor] and borne by their memory, let us continue to stand for the ideals for which they lived and died.

Thank you very much, and God bless you all.

Monroe isn't all you'll ever need. Politics isn't that one-dimensional. But MMS can serve as your structure of default. If you think of structure as the skeleton, then *language, anecdote, wit,* and *support* are the flesh, brains, and ligaments that bring your speech to life. They make up the LAWS of political speech. Chapters 6–10 will examine why.

THE SPEECHWRITER'S CHECKLIST: STRUCTURE

- ☐ Does this speech grab listeners' attention from the first sentence?
- ☐ Does it include the listener's road map: a full statement of purpose?
- ☐ Does it use all five MMS steps—Attention, Need, Satisfaction, Visualization, Action?
- ☐ Have I used acknowledgments appropriately?
- ☐ Did I modify Monroe to accommodate important needs—like establishing credibility?
- ☐ Did I balance competing needs?
- ☐ Did I use specifics to persuade about both problem and solution?
- ☐ Did I include the often-overlooked visualization step?

6

Language People Understand

Once, at a news conference back in 1942, President Franklin Delano Roosevelt read reporters aloud a new order submitted for him to approve. The subject: ways to shield government workers during an air raid. It wasn't the policy FDR wanted to highlight, though. It was the language. Here was the first sentence, which he read verbatim:

> Such preparation shall be made as will completely obscure all federal buildings and non-federal buildings occupied by the federal government during an air raid for any period of time from visibility by reason of internal or external illumination.

Reporters started to laugh. FDR went on.

> Such obscuration may be obtained either by blackout construction or by terminating the illumination.[1]

Now—according to the transcript—reporters laughed louder.

Delighted with himself, FDR looked over at Steve Early, his press aide, and issued an order of his own. "Tell them [to write] turn out the lights, and stop there."[2]

Roosevelt made his—and this chapter's—point: In politics, it's crucial to speak so people understand. He also implied another idea that language conveys far more than the literal meanings of words. Full understanding means sensing subtext. The formal first draft of Roosevelt's order carried one message—blackoutswere serious business. Roosevelt's revision carried two others. First, it implied people have to understand the order. Then came a message directed to the reporters: We're not a bunch of pompous bureaucrats.

Just as necklaces are more than strings of beads or pearls, so sentences are more than strings of words. Writers convey many meanings through the seemingly infinite choices of words, sentences, techniques, and strategies we call *style*.

WRITING FOR CLARITY

In one sense, style *is* content—that is, the language and sentence structure you choose become part of your message. To say "I urge you to vote against this bill" is not the same as saying "Vote NO!"—though both statements urge the same step.

Still, we make meaningful distinctions between style and content. If asked about the point of those two sentences—the content—most of us would focus on the step they urged, not the language. But put yourself in the shoes of state senators getting a call from the party whip. To the first version, they might say: "Thanks, I'll consider it." To the second: "Yes, sir!"

The stylistic choices speechwriters face might seem endless. Do you use imagery? How can you vary tone—ironic at times, forceful at others—to suit the event? Do you prefer the informal language of a city council candidate talking to a group of neighbors over coffee, or the lofty diction people refer to as "presidential"?

Such choices convey not just the substance of what speakers say but the kind of people they are—or want people to think they are. Whether Jesse Jackson's rhymes ("Hope in your brain, not dope in your veins!"), Ronald Reagan's "Well . . . ," or Donald Trump's "It's going to be huge," a speaker's style can become a kind of signature.

Such signatures aren't necessarily a virtue. In political life, small examples stereotype speakers. Politicians become known for their penchant for using the wrong words (George W. Bush) or talking too much (Joe Biden). Style isn't always apparent. In his book *Public Speaking: Strategies for Success*, Northwestern University professor David Zarefsky points out that people praise the Gettysburg Address for its absence of style, but fail to see that its brevity and structure also make up elements of style.[3]

Really, politicians don't limit themselves to a single style. Donald Trump is a lot—though not entirely—different at a rally than he was reading from a teleprompter on Inauguration Day. Chapter 7 covers the stylistic choices that make speeches *memorable*. We begin our discussion of language, though, with the stylistic choices writers make among *individual* words to make speeches *clear*. And that begins with one thing that makes a speech unique.

READING VERSUS HEARING

You're on the cell with Uncle Larry, asking for his chili recipe. He recites it, but you don't have a pen and your tablet is upstairs.

Maybe you can just ... remember it all. But after hanging up, you're confused. Those red chili flakes? Two teaspoons or two tablespoons? Garlic or onion? You're embarrassed. But you call him back and ask, "Can you text it to me?" You've done the right thing—and demonstrated a problem for listeners.

They can't reread a speech, at least not while they're listening. That's one reason politicians need to make speeches simpler than, say, an op-ed, even for the same audience. Listeners need repetition, shorter words and sentences, and hints about what's coming next. In speech, we can't ignore this concession to reality.

Well, you might say, George Washington did no such thing. True. But Washington lived in a different America and, for example, didn't actually deliver his famous farewell as a speech. As Robert Schlesinger points out in his entertaining book *White House Ghosts*, Washington's speechwriters, James Madison and Alexander Hamilton, wrote the address, months before he left office, for a Philadelphia newspaper to print.[4] Neither they nor Washington needed to worry about the needs of listeners.

These days, politicians do speak—and, as we hope we have made clear, often. They speak to hairdressers, mechanics, and Uber drivers—as well as nuclear physicists and Silicon Valley entrepreneurs. When the authors of this book worked for Al Gore in the White House, we turned out hundreds of speeches a year—not counting the hundreds of times he spoke off the cuff. Is one style appropriate for every occasion? Of course not. But in politics, you can never forget the difference between language to be read and language to be heard.

The concessions we writers make to the listening audience do not mean nuance has vanished from politics. Those who want to explore political issues in all of their complexity can find that on websites with a few clicks of a mouse. But if you believe Americans who read at a seventh-grade level deserve the chance to understand their president, some concessions are inevitable.

Politicians and those who write their speeches must take pains to be clear. And for those engaged in the partly conscious, partly intuitive, partly imitative way that writers choose words, clarity means making sure six things become as instinctive as breathing.

Short Words

Even for the most formal occasions, short words work best in political speech. Chapter 1 previewed the virtue of using one-syllable words.

Ask not what you can do for your country ...

I have a dream ...

Tear down that wall ...

Yes we can!

Obviously, speakers can't limit simplicity to the occasional lines they hope to see engraved on federal buildings. But we don't need to say "additionally." "Also" will do just fine. English is a rich language. It gives us the tools to make simplicity the rule.

Too often, though, creativity and simplicity are the exception. Politicians don't speak as fatuously as they do in *New Yorker* cartoons, but they are surprisingly willing to tolerate speeches laden with big words and long sentences—profundity by abstraction.

Take this example from a 2017 speech on net neutrality by Utah senator Mike Lee:

> These regulations also have entrenched the market power of large internet service providers while hurting their smaller competitors.
>
> By their very nature, regulations impose conformity on a market. They limit companies' ability to distinguish themselves from their rivals by offering innovative services.

In that forty-two-word passage; twenty-four of the words are two syllables or more. It's written for college sophomores. Why not say it this way?

> What do these regulations do? Help the big internet providers. Hurt the small ones. They make companies conform—not compete. They choke off incentives—and innovation.

That's twenty-six words, only eight more than one syllable. Now 62 percent of Americans would at least understand—including kids in sixth grade.

In politics, that difference creates a big advantage. If politicians find themselves saying "currently" instead of "now," or "utilize" instead of "use," it's time to rewrite.

Concrete Words

Chapter 1 showed how simplicity worked in the "Keep Hope Alive" conclusion to Jesse Jackson's famous 1988 Democratic National Convention speech. But adding to its impact was Jackson's use of concrete detail—the images and language that allow speakers not just to tell, but to show. Jackson didn't just say he grew up in poverty. He put it this way:

> My mother, a working woman. So many of the days she went to work early with runs in her stockings. She knew better, but she wore runs in her stockings so that my brother and I could have matching socks and

> not be laughed at [in] school. . . . At three o'clock on Thanksgiving Day we couldn't eat turkey because Mama was preparing someone else's turkey . . . around six o'clock she would get off the Alta Vista bus, and we would bring up the leftovers and eat our turkey—leftovers, the carcass, the cranberries—around eight o'clock at night.

Jackson could have cut the name of his mother's "Alta Vista bus," a detail almost no one else would remember. But the bus, the runs in his mother's stockings, the turkey carcass—all these real-life details give the passage a ring of truth.

"My task," Joseph Conrad wrote in the preface to one of his most famous novels, "is . . . to make you hear, to make you feel—it is, before all, to make you see."[5] Like readers, listeners also need to see. The convention audience that night could see Jackson's life as a young boy just as, decades later, watching the 2016 Republican National Convention, a single sentence about his childhood allowed listeners to understand more about Marco Rubio.

> I remember the sounds of his keys jingling at the front door of our home, well past midnight, as he returned from another long day at work.

Rubio made the listener not only see, but hear ("keys jingling").

Even the most solemn occasions call for concrete words. During his speech at a prayer vigil in Newtown, Connecticut, soon after the Sandy Hook shooting, President Barack Obama could have recounted the courage and love expressed that day by saying this:

> We know there were brave teachers who protected and comforted their students by telling them help was coming.

Instead, he put it this way:

> We know that there were other teachers who barricaded themselves inside classrooms, and kept steady through it all, and reassured their students by saying "wait for the good guys, they're coming"; "show me your smile."

Obama didn't just say "classrooms." He said "barricaded in classrooms." He didn't say "police." He said "the good guys." He didn't offer an abstract example of a teacher asking a student to stay positive. He quoted a teacher's words to her scared student, "show me your smile."

In Chapter 7, we explore another reason concrete words are so valuable. Here, it is enough to see how detail makes listeners understand a speaker's words, and sometimes—as with Jackson, Rubio, and Obama—the speakers themselves.

Active Verbs

Speaking clearly means conveying who's doing what. In active voice, the subject is the actor (*Republicans created jobs*). In passive, you leave the actor unnamed (*Jobs were created*) or as the object (*Jobs were created by Democrats*).

Passive voice appears in speeches for several reasons. Some academics tolerate it as an academic tradition or think it denotes seriousness. Sometimes speakers don't know who or what caused something, or care more about inciting audiences than restating the nuanced reasons behind a problem, like Bernie Sanders ("The economy is rigged") or Donald Trump ("The entire system is rigged").

But in political speeches, energy is vital. Passive verbs not only sap that energy but confirm voters' suspicions that in politics the chief goal is avoiding blame. Perhaps the most famous example is Press Secretary Ron Ziegler's defense of Richard Nixon during Watergate: "Mistakes were made."

One might think the negative reactions to Ziegler would teach a lesson. But according to other politicians or their spokespeople—Ronald Reagan on sending arms-sale proceeds to the Nicaraguan Contras, Bill Clinton on a fundraising scandal, George W. Bush on the Iraq War—*mistakes were made*.

And here's former New Jersey governor Chris Christie in his 2014 State of the State address:

> The last week has certainly tested this administration. Mistakes were clearly made.

The *Columbia Guide to Standard American English* argues, "If you want your words to seem impersonal, indirect, and noncommittal, passive is the choice."[6] Why create such awful impressions when you can easily convert passive to active? Examine this 2015 joint statement from the twenty-eighth session of the Human Rights Council:

> The Middle East is living in a situation of instability and conflict that recently *have been aggravated*. The consequences are disastrous for the entire population of the region. The existence of many religious communities *is seriously threatened*.[7]

Here's one way to rewrite that passive paragraph to make it active, and clarify the tough situation it describes:

> Rising instability and conflict now aggravate tension in the Middle East. It threatens many religious communities. It spells disaster for everyone in the region.

Passive voice reduced from 100 percent to zero. Understandable to ninth graders instead of twelfth graders. Meaning intact. Energetic. The combination of simple language and active verbs makes a big difference.

Appropriate Words

Now we move to more complicated choices. Simple words, active verbs, and concrete detail are almost always virtues. But language should change as audiences—and situations—change. Audiences expect, or at least tolerate, more complicated diction at a policy conference than a campaign rally. When we worked for Vice President Gore, we experienced that difference firsthand. We illustrate with two examples of our work: the first at a fourth-grade level, the second clocking in at tenth grade:

At a Rally.

> And the same people who opposed Family and Medical Leave and Motor Voter were fighting it tooth and nail.
>
> Did they have a plan of their own?
>
> AUDIENCE: NO!
>
> Did they have a way to get America moving again?
>
> AUDIENCE: NO!
>
> But the president did.

At a Conference about Fatherhood.

> A child does not learn to have an intimate, loving relationship with a father because once a week Dad awkwardly sets out on a walk around the block. Children don't learn from occasional efforts to help with homework or from looking up at the lacrosse game and seeing Dad still in his suit, up in the stands for the final period.
>
> No, fatherhood becomes meaningful from the day-in-day-out experience of being home.
>
> At one point in our culture, such involvement was considered beneath men.

One might quarrel with the notion that choosing appropriate language is an issue of clarity. But examine those two passages again. Words like *intimate* or *loving* convey meaning with a precision that would strike the rally audience as odd. At the conference, they clarified Gore's view. Each speech used language appropriate to the audience and the event.

This does not mean reserving simple words for rallies. The first sentence of Gore's fatherhood speech has more than twice as many one-syllable words as the rally excerpt. In fact, the fatherhood speech, laced with talk about homework and lacrosse games, is actually the more concrete of the two. Certainly, appropriate language can differ from event to event. But speechwriters should look for ways to use simple language for even the densest topics without sacrificing nuance.

Sensitive Words

How do you know this passage didn't come from a recent speech?

In no way have the value and manhood of the American Negro been more fittingly and generously recognized than by the managers of this magnificent exposition . . . when it comes to business, pure and simple, it is in the South that the Negro is given a man's chance . . .

Today, nobody in political life would use *Negro* instead of *black*, or talk about fairness as a "man's chance." It was okay for Booker T. Washington in 1896. Not now.

Politicians can't wait a hundred years to develop sensitivity to race, ethnicity, gender, and orientation. It's not always easy or graceful to find some substitute for *he* as a singular pronoun or settle on terms that can't possibly offend anyone in the audience. Hispanic or Latino? American Indian or Native American? LGBT or LGBTQ?

Critics may believe such questions cater to political correctness. But politicians who ignore the diverse voters in this country can lose votes for each group they offend. Sensitive language not only accurately reflects reality but aids clarity. Speakers use it to make clear to the broader audiences that they embrace diversity and respect groups traditionally excluded from much of American culture.

Colloquial Language

So far, we've examined ways that single-word choices can clarify meaning. But clarity involves more than single words.

Colloquial speech uses the same kinds of words and expressions you might use in everyday conversation. In politics, for example, we might say "kick the can down the road" instead of "we will deliberate and delay our decision until the next legislative session."

Colloquial speech includes a host of devices often discouraged in academic writing: sentence fragments, contractions, and the use of *and* or *but* as transitions instead of *furthermore or however*.

In part, colloquial speech matters to politicians because voters dislike candidates who seem elitist. Anti-intellectualism runs deep in American culture. But it also matters because people understand conversational language instantly. Examine this excerpt from John Kasich, launching his presidential campaign in July 2015:

> We have a little town in Ohio called Wilmington . . .
> Let me tell you about these folks. They played by the rules. Worked every day . . . And one day, an employer said, "We're leaving. We're out of here."
> And thousands of people, thousands of hardworking, God-fearing people like your neighbors, went from getting a paycheck on a Friday afternoon to visiting a food pantry so they could feed their kids.

Kasich opens sentences with words like *and*, *but*, *so*, and *because*. He calls people *folks* and children *kids*. He uses sentence fragments, and common words and expressions ("God-fearing people"), and words you might hear talking to your neighbor over the backyard fence. His listeners understood.

Here's another example, this one from Senator Elizabeth Warren speaking at an economic conference in 2016:

> In the last decade, the number of major U.S. airlines has dropped from nine to four. The four that are left standing—American, Delta, United, and Southwest—control over 80 percent of all domestic airline seats in the country. And man, are they hitting the jackpot now. Last year those four big airlines raked in a record $22 billion in profits.

Even in a passage heavy on statistics, Warren effectively uses colloquial phrases like "left standing," "hitting the jackpot," and "raked in" to make her point.

Should someone like Kasich, who spent nine terms in Congress, or Warren, a former professor at Harvard, use this style? Isn't it manipulative? There is certainly a point at which colloquial speech becomes pandering, hurts precision, or stamps a speaker as insincere. But Harvard professors are people, too. They speak colloquially. Within limits, selecting words Americans understand and use is both sensible and ethical. And in addition to the kinds of words that make speech colloquial, we suggest promoting clarity by taking three more steps.

Keep Sentences and Paragraphs Short. In 2017, Bernie Sanders delivered a commencement address at Brooklyn College containing this thirty-two-word sentence:

> Unbelievably, in many parts of this country today, as a result of hopelessness and despair, life expectancy is actually declining as a frightening number of people experience drug addiction, alcoholism, and suicide.

Readability stats tell us that only about 7 percent of Americans can easily understand what he said. What happens if you use some of the tools this chapter covers: simple words, concrete words, active voice, colloquial language—and sentence fragments?

> Hard to believe. But in parts of our country, where the economy's hurting, people are living shorter lives. Why? Depression. Drugs. Alcohol. And suicide.

We've cut eight words overall, or 25 percent. We went from 7 percent of Americans understanding the first version to 70 percent able to understand the second, mostly because the sentences are shorter and we've used sentence fragments. Most important, the revised version preserves Sanders's meaning.

Ample research demonstrates the trouble listeners have grasping long sentences. Length guarantees neither clarity nor nuance. Short sentences help listeners understand.

They help speakers, too. Even people who speak in public every day have a hard time delivering long sentences, especially in the first few minutes, when nerves might rob them of breath control. Politicians often don't have time to read a draft before getting up to speak. Long sentences and long paragraphs can keep them from spotting the rhetorical devices we cover in Chapter 7. Use of repetition, for example, is easy to spot with single-sentence paragraphs.

Finally, short sentences are fully capable of carrying mature thought. Take this paragraph from Ronald Reagan's famous 1987 speech, annotated in the Appendix and written by Peggy Noonan, after the space shuttle *Challenger* exploded while millions of American children watched in school:

> They wished to serve, and they did. They served all of us. We've grown used to wonders in this century. It's hard to dazzle us. But for twenty-five years the United States space program has been doing just that. We've grown used to the idea of space, and perhaps we forget that we've only just begun. We're still pioneers. They, the members of the *Challenger* crew, were pioneers.

The sentences average about eight words each. Noonan wrote the speech at about a fourth-grade level. The thought that Americans take extraordinary things for granted was hardly childish; Noonan's choice of diction and short sentences allowed Reagan to say something interesting that children and adults could understand.

Eliminate Clutter. Cutting down the word count can improve almost every speech. Once your draft is done, declutter it. Say, "Okay, I'll trim this by 10 percent." Then go to work, sentence by sentence. At first it will seem impossible, but soon you will be amazed by how much you can lose—and how much you gain.

Decluttering doesn't work only for terrible speeches. It makes interesting speeches better. Here's an example from this generally entertaining paragraph in Hillary Clinton's 2001 speech at Yale University's Class Day:

> When I arrived at Yale in 1969, it was the first year that women had been admitted to the college. Some of the students who I had known at Wellesley actually transferred to Yale, and they were on the front lines of integrating Yale. And it was a wonderful adventure for me to look at from the distance of law school. Because I had known that when I had graduated from high school, I and others of my gender could not have applied to Yale. We might have had A averages, but we lacked a Y chromosome. And that was all that mattered in those days.

In our speechwriting class, we use this extract as a class exercise to demonstrate the decluttering step. Here's one result:

> I arrived at Yale in 1969—the first year women were admitted to the college. I had known some of those women at Wellesley. They transferred, and helped integrate this place. That was wonderful to see from the distance of law school. After all, when I had graduated from high school, women could not apply to Yale. We might have had A averages—but we lacked a Y chromosome.

The revised paragraph is 25 percent shorter. It is crisper and less heavy-handed. And just as with a cleaned-up room, every item is easier to see.

Use Transitions. One public speaking text calls transitions the "neurosystem of speeches."[8] It means the system that connects various parts of our speech, just like our nervous system connects different parts of the body. Transitions are vital to speechwriting—and essential for clarity. Remember: Listeners can't reread to figure out what you said. They need to know how one part of a speech connects to the next. Here are some common transitions:

- *Previews.* These warn listeners that the speaker is about to move to a new section or idea. For example, if after this definition we were to examine one preview, one of us might say, "Let's see how that works."

- *Internal Summaries.* Listeners sometimes need to take a brief look back for the rest of a speech to make sense. If we were lecturing on this chapter, one of us might say, "Simple words. Concrete words. Colloquial language. We've covered a lot."

- *Signposts.* Usually, that means the word signals listeners need (*first, second, next, finally*) as speakers move from point to point.

Transitions are not always so mechanical. In fact, they can be quite varied. They compare (*similarly*), contrast (*on the other hand*), or show cause and effect (*as a result*). Important to remember as well: Transitions in speech should be less formal than in writing meant to be read. There, transitions often use full sentences that connect one thought to the next.

Here's an example:

Another way this bill violates the Constitution appears in section X, depriving citizens of habeas corpus.

In a speech, you might write it this way:

Does it violate the Constitution in another big way? Yes. Take habeas corpus rights. Look at section X.

BOX 6.1
EXPERTS TALK: ELVIN LIM

Readers of this book understand that the authors present ways to persuade effectively, urge simple and memorable language, and want students and speakers to use story as a way of moving listeners.

There is another view. We have already mentioned its leading advocate: Elvin Lim, former Wesleyan University professor and now dean of core curriculum and professor of political science at Singapore Management University.

His book, *The Anti-intellectual Presidency*, argues that presidential rhetoric suffers not just from the simplifying language, but from overusing persuasive speech, appealing to emotion, and other tactics.

Professor Lim is a serious, meticulous student of American politics. We want readers to examine his views unfiltered by our biases.

In October 2018, we contacted Professor Lim and asked for an interview. "Great idea!" he said.

This is the result of our conversation, excerpted only for reasons of space.

You say that the "relentless simplification of present presidential rhetoric leads to an impoverishment of presidential rhetoric." Why?

The impoverishment of rhetoric is a concern if we think of rhetoric as the means by which democracy is conducted. If democracy is to be conducted meaningfully, we must be saying substantive things to each other, rather than gesturing with emotional signals and slogans.

Take, for example, the Brett Kavanaugh confirmation hearings. I had to bring him up, right?

Even in a case of "he said she said," it matters exactly and specifically what people said and how they said it.

Now imagine, if we had to conduct these hearings and a wider public conversation in terms of slogans or emotional appeals (which in most quarters we actually have). We would be even further from the truth of what happened.

So my short answer is this: if we care about meaningful deliberative democracy, then rhetoric has to contain the real arguments and the substance of what we're trying to communicate.

Your research makes it clear that the change to simpler language began around the time of Wilson. Was there any noble intent to that? Is it possible that as the country became more democratic, politicians needed to speak simply to make sure listeners understood?

At the top of the book I quote Einstein saying things should be said simply but no simpler. We're now at way too simple.

But would you argue that such simplification comes not from the sincere but misguided belief that average people deserve to understand—but from the intent to deceive?

At one level it is. These are smart guys who fought their way into the White House. They know what they're doing. There is deceit in the sense that there is misrepresentation of who presidents really are. In a way, it is the whole point of speechwriting. It assiduously presents a side of a president rhetorically that would be palatable to an American audience.

And you argue that this stems from the "anti-intellectualism" of modern presidents? In your book, you quote historian Richard Hofstadter's definition of

(Continued)

(Continued)

"anti-intellectualism": "resentment and suspicion of the life of the mind and of those who are considered to represent it." How would you define it?

Beyond my definition in the book, I would say it is a political reflex, the easy rhetorical way out; an abdication of our democratic duty to debate, and engage with one another substantively.

You also say academics would be happier if presidents spoke less like Ford and Carter and more like Washington and Jefferson. Do you mean that literally? Should presidential speech have the level of difficulty of, let's say, Washington's Farewell Address?

No, that would be absolutely inappropriate. That person wouldn't [get past] the first primary debate.

When there's a Rose Garden speech, you see a string of beautiful platitudes, and that's fine—because the occasion calls for it. But there should be variation.

We should at least occasionally [hear] a nuanced argument about a serious subject. Maybe even have the president on prime-time television [discussing] policy with implications that are not immediately obvious to the average citizen. Presidents don't [always] have to be argumentatively nuanced or substantive, but they should at least take on the job as the nation's educator-in-chief occasionally. I would say at this point they never do . . .

Let me come at your question from a different angle: the situation where presidents' normal instinct is to speak at the tenth-grade level but they present themselves as sixth graders. Then someone says, "Well, most Americans speak at that level. What are you prepared to do now?"

I might say back, "If I told you I didn't think you were smart enough to understand me, would you consider that condescending?"

If you said "No," then I'd want to know how far you would allow the discrepancy to go. Maybe from the twelfth-grade to a tenth-grade level, that's fine; but twelve to four or five? Wouldn't that be condescending?

If we write a speech at a seventh-grade level, we get about 65 percent of Americans who can easily understand. You're right. There is a point where simplification becomes oversimplification. But two-thirds doesn't seem that unreasonable, does it?

It depends. Often, when elected representatives think they've got the policy right, they assume it doesn't matter how they get people to agree; only that they do. But getting two-thirds of Americans to understand is not the same as getting the same to agree.

It is easier to accomplish the former than the latter—you see now the strategic value of saying next to nothing. Everyone can agree on platitudes. One of the dangers of presidential anti-intellectualism is that it becomes an excuse not to do the hard work of moderating one's position or educating the citizenry.

So, simplistic rhetoric persuades in a way that improperly influences policy. Which seems to lead into another point you've made. Whatever the problems with oversimplification, you also argue that there's far too much persuasion in American rhetoric. What would you change? No persuasive speech? Less?

I contrast persuasion versus education. Persuasion is a certain kind of violence, because it is unidirectional, and assumes that it is the audience that needs to change their mind, and not the speaker. But presidents aren't just here to sell; they are here also to listen, to facilitate a deliberative democracy. I think it's inevitable in a democracy that rhetoric is deployed mostly for persuasion. But if that's all rhetoric is, then presidents become no different from salesmen.

Salesmen, but not about selling you a car. It's about selling you what they consider a health care policy that might help millions of people right now. Isn't that a virtue?

Persuasion is usually asymmetric. It starts from me being right, and you needing to be converted. Wouldn't persuasion itself be even more edifying for democracy if I were to take your position and logic seriously as starting points of my argument? If so, then rhetoric is more than selling; it is also about deliberation and rational disputation.

What if a president adopted your idea? This president says, "I want to educate—explore problems but not urge any single solution. I don't want to persuade—I just want to give people food for thought." Wouldn't his aides have a fit? Wouldn't they say, "Wait! Remember what Carter did in 1979. He gave this energy speech, and he had no solutions."

I think you're absolutely right. The perils of anti-intellectualism I speak of are embedded in the system. And if the system doesn't change, then it forces us to operate at its margins as mere cogs in a larger wheel. So in many ways my book is a critique of democracy run amok.

You argue that there's far too much reliance on human-interest material—concrete detail, or a moving story. Can't story, a device of pathos, by putting a human face on tragedy or on abstraction, be a legitimate kind of evidence? Do you think it's improper to try to move audiences?

I think two types of rhetoric transpire in any republic. First, there's the sort of democratic persuasive rhetoric that happens almost every day on CNN and Fox News.

There is something else I would call deliberative rhetoric or interbranch deliberation—the rhetoric that happens within the halls of Congress at least when the television cameras are not on. When there are no television cameras, there is very little human-interest story. Very little emotion. Why? Because senators usually will not buy in to someone else's rhetorical trick. They want hard, cold facts. They're trying to get to the bottom of what the policy requires.

(Continued)

(Continued)

What I'm saying is that there is also a time and place for deliberative rhetoric—the framers thought checks and balances really only work when the [legislators] or the representatives of the branches speak frankly to each other and not indirectly via their constituents.

Human-interest rhetoric—story—works for selling to the public, less for making policy within the halls of Congress. For governance, for deliberation, for actual decision-making, we need to go beyond what works rhetorically in the public airwaves.

But don't voters elect modern American presidents to carry out an agenda? Don't they win because of their point of view? Don't presidents need to offer evidence to persuade? Why shouldn't persuasion, including story, become a legitimate way to win over Americans who didn't agree or are in the middle?

That's even more reason for consultative deliberation. More of our elected leaders need to be open to changing their mind. When I've decided I want to persuade you, I have simply decided that I'm right. You only need to be persuaded. That's rather obnoxious. We always think of persuasion as democratic. In some ways, it is autocratic.

Let's talk about ethos. We teach that logos, pathos, and ethos are the three-legged stool of political speech. When we write for politicians, they all want things that characterize themselves: likable, compassionate, and energetic. You say "anti-intellectual presidents are not concerned with signaling their excellence of their character." What do you mean?

The scholarship points out that the early presidents—Washington, Jefferson—did great things. We say therefore their great reputation came from great accomplishments.

Today candidates try to repeat what the patrician presidents did not by action but by words. [We] signal great action by great bragging.

We've been talking about what is wrong with political speech. Let's say you had unlimited power to put things right. To change the way politicians communicate with Americans, what are some concrete changes you'd make?

Moral injunctions or even commandments rarely change behavior. One simple solution? Kill the primary. That would take away at least 30 percent of the pathologies in American politics. Because the length of the campaign would go down, campaign financing imperatives would go down.

Polarization would also be attenuated because primaries reward the loudest and most outlandish partisans whereas the general election draws candidates back to the middle. McGovern–Fraser facilitated the increased polarization of American politics.

NOTE: Lim refers to the 1972 Democratic Party commission run by 1972 Democratic presidential candidate George McGovern and Minnesota congressman Donald Fraser. Its widely adopted recommendation: take the power to select candidates from what supporters called "party bosses," and substitute the primary system.

It is easy to see how seductive is any argument that says take away power from the boss and give it to the people; see how powerfully it works. There are so many [examples] in American history where this was done. Jackson with the decimation of King Caucus and the subsequent introduction of a nominating convention system.

There is something very politically appealing about the argument that the people rule, not the bosses or the elites. True as this may be, all we did in 1972 was to destroy the power of the political bosses—and create a new American aristocracy who could play the new game of primaries as well as the old aristocracy knew how to play the nomination convention system. A new celebrity class consisting of Ronald Reagan, Jesse Ventura, and Donald Trump emerged; so too would anti-intellectualism with a vengeance.

Which brings up another question—one question on everyone's mind here. How does what you argue apply to not the politics of Donald Trump, but his rhetoric? In terms of the anti-intellectual presidency, is he the beginning of the end, or the end of the beginning? Or is it what a lot of his supporters say: he's a breath of fresh air? What's your take on the Trump rhetoric?

The same pattern is playing out. All Trump is doing is out-Palining Bush just like Bush outdid Reagan, and Reagan outdid [Barry] Goldwater. And the role of Twitter has made simplicity even more imperative in modern presidential communication—though I think Trump would have done what he's doing rhetorically with or without Twitter.

Do you think what he does is a conscious anti-intellectual stance, or that's just the way he is?

There are levels of consciousness here. I think he knows what he's doing. He's been on *The Apprentice*. He knows how to work audiences. The reason he won the primaries was that he knew how to cut through the noise. So that part is conscious.

But I think there's also the other part of him that is so natural that it is unconscious and a reflex. This is that part of him that is direct, somewhat abrasive, and in-your-face. In this sense, he and his rhetorical style is simply a product of our system and cultural milieu.

That said, everyone who made it to the presidency is obviously a successful politician, and they would usually have gotten there by going anti-intellectual. So in a way my book can be read as a manual for how, cynically, to succeed in American politics and a simultaneous invitation not to do it via the anti-intellectual way.

FINAL WORDS

Language is your tool for creating clarity. Using short words and sentences, concrete detail, active voice, appropriate words, sensitive language, colloquial speech, and transitions can dramatically increase the numbers of listeners who understand.

But politicians need to be more than clear. They need to be memorable. They must move, inspire, and excite listeners so the experience becomes unforgettable. They also need to be quotable. They need a line journalists will tweet and use in their stories, TV producers will use in their news reports, and listeners will remember.

Creating such lines is the point of Chapter 7.

THE SPEECHWRITER'S CHECKLIST: LANGUAGE PEOPLE UNDERSTAND

- ☐ Have I kept in mind that speeches are meant to be heard, not read?
- ☐ Do I use short words over long ones whenever I can?
- ☐ Am I concrete?
- ☐ Do my readability stats tell me passive verbs are near zero?
- ☐ Is my language appropriate for the event and the audience?
- ☐ Is it colloquial?
- ☐ Have I kept sentences and paragraphs short?
- ☐ Did I declutter without sacrificing meaning?
- ☐ Have I used transitions to signal listeners when my speaker moves to a new subject?
- ☐ Did I listen to Joseph Conrad, and can my listeners see?

7

Language People Remember

He stood up in the Virginia House of Burgesses without a note; spoke, one witness wrote, until "the tendons of his neck stood out white and rigid, like whipcords," and in the end uttered the lines we still learn in school: "I know not what others may do! As for me, give me liberty or give me death!"

Or did he?

The only existing evidence of what Patrick Henry actually said in that famous 1775 speech comes from an account written forty years later.[1] Just try to remember a speech verbatim after four days—not to mention four decades. There's some evidence that the last line was Henry's. The rest was probably fiction.

Whatever the case, though, Henry's line is memorable. If someone quotes its first few words, many Americans can finish the rest.

Chapter 6 emphasized clarity, but being understood isn't enough in politics. If there was a rhetorical lesson in both the 2008 and 2016 presidential campaigns, it was surely the incredible advantage enjoyed by politicians who could use language people remembered, whether "Yes we can" or "Make America great again."

Since the first edition of this book appeared, new platforms have offered even more ways to communicate with voters—perhaps most notably, the tweet. But politicians don't just want people to read or listen. They want to inspire, move, and persuade them. They want people to remember what they say, and even repeat it. The devices of language that make this possible remain largely the same as they were when speakers uttered them in Greek. This chapter covers some, but not all.

For giving them names we credit not just Aristotle but Quintilian, the Roman rhetoric teacher born around the decade Jesus died. Quintilian earned his entry to heaven by cataloging the ways to make speech memorable we call *figures of speech*—forgotten, then rediscovered in the Renaissance. He and a group of his fanatical successors uncovered and listed almost two hundred of them.[2] (Don't worry. In politics, you can make your speeches quotable and exciting with a lot less.)

Much has changed since the days of Patrick Henry. But here's one thing that hasn't. If we believe persuasion is a legitimate goal for political leaders elected to carry out an agenda, and if we believe politicians must make a case for their ideas, then we must know the rhetorical techniques that can inspire, move, and captivate—in other words, that make speech memorable.

This chapter divides those techniques by two effects that make people remember: language that is *vivid*, meaning it appeals to our eyes—what we see—and *rhythmic*, which appeals to the ear.

Here, we begin with what listeners see.

MAKING LANGUAGE VIVID

"If we don't hang together, we'll hang separately," Richard Penn said during the signing of the Declaration of Independence, a clever pun often attributed to Ben Franklin.[3]

Language often becomes memorable—in politics, read "quotable"—when you surprise listeners. In Penn's line, the surprise is obvious: he used the word *hang* in one way, then surprised listeners by using it again with a different meaning.

Surprise marks each of the figures of speech we describe, first defined, and then illustrated.

But after that, we discuss one quality discussed in the last chapter: concrete detail. For while being concrete helps listeners understand, it is essential to becoming memorable.

Figures of Speech

Simile and Metaphor: *Expressions That Compare Two Essentially Unlike Things*

Simile compares unlike things directly, often using *like, as if, more than*, or other explicit words of comparison ("They fought like tigers"). Take this one from 1984 Democratic presidential candidate, Walter Mondale:

> For a working person to vote for Reagan is like a chicken voting for Colonel Sanders.

Mondale used a joke that depended on knowledge. Listeners had to know about both Reagan and Colonel Sanders's Kentucky Fried Chicken. They did, and the line worked well. Of course, similes are not always funny. But when the comparison is concrete and visual, the effect can be electric.

Metaphor doesn't use *like*, so listeners may not realize they have heard a comparison. But the effect can still be powerful. Here is President Donald Trump speaking to the Building Trades Unions Legislative Conference in 2017:

> But really, you're the backbone of America . . . And it's time that we give you the level playing field you deserve.

Trump means builders support America like the spine supports our bodies. By not using *like*, he implies closer similarity than a simile.

Is this original? No. Actually, it is the "mixed metaphor" writers like to mock: a comparison made of two completely unrelated images, in this case, two clichés: "backbone" and "level playing field."

For the record, the authors recommend neither clichés nor mixed metaphors. But the disappointing truth is that metaphors don't have to be original to be effective. In fact, that so many Americans know these platitudes makes them work. No explanation needed. Like similes, they become memorable right away by taking abstractions—like support—and making them visual.

Senator Ed Markey (D-MA), speaking on the floor of the Senate, also used metaphor in 2017, but for a different purpose. He used *crosshairs* and *Godzilla*, not to reassure but to alarm.

> This week we are about to have an incredible battle waged against the Affordable Care Act. Understand this, right in the crosshairs are the hospitals of our country . . . Fentanyl is the Godzilla of opioids.

Markey doesn't mean people literally point rifles at American hospitals. He makes visual the idea that they are a target. What about the fentanyl example? Markey might have used *like*. But that would have weakened the comparison. It would be (like) telling listeners they were too unsophisticated to grasp it. The comparison is at once funny, serious, and far-fetched, and better as metaphor.

Synecdoche and Metonymy: *Two Similar Techniques in Which a Part Stands for the Whole*

Synecdoche and metonymy both surprise the audience with images that are not literally true. How are they different? Technically, metonymy describes something *associated* with the whole. One often-used example: "The pen is mightier than the sword." The pen is not literally part of writing. It is associated with it.

Synecdoche, though, means something that is literally a *part* of the whole. Example: "We counted heads." Usually, that means counting people, most of whom have heads. In this 1960 campaign speech example, Richard Nixon uses two parts of the whole:

> In Europe we gave the cold shoulder to de Gaulle, and now he gives the warm hand to Mao.

Nixon doesn't literally mean a "cold shoulder." He means the United States has demonstrated hostility in a way he doesn't need to spell out. Similarly, the "warm hand" symbolizes Charles de Gaulle's overtures to China.

Finally, from Chapter 5, note Macklemore's use of metonymy as he describes opioid addiction.

> So addiction doesn't always start in some dark alley—it often starts in a medicine cabinet.

Macklemore doesn't literally mean addiction starts in a medicine cabinet. He uses that one detail to stand for the many surprisingly mundane ways addictions begin.

Synecdoche or metonymy? These figures of speech are often hard to tell apart. But let us focus on the most important point. They both visualize the abstract, affect listeners in the same vivid way, and remain useful whether you remember the difference or not.

Pun: *Words That Surprise the Audience by Using a Second Meaning the Audience Hasn't Anticipated*

Audiences often associate puns with the groan-producing one-liners of older comedians ("Politics is like golf: you're trapped in one bad *lie* after another"). But politicians use them often, and effectively.

Puns can use a word in two different ways, like Richard Penn did, or by finding a word that modifies two incongruously different activities, as Ronald Reagan surprised listeners here, in a very visual way, talking about diplomacy in his 1989 Farewell Address:

> If and when they don't, at first pull your punches. If they persist, pull the plug.

In Chapter 2, we discussed ethos—how the character of speakers affects listeners. Reagan here doesn't just draw a laugh. He makes listeners like him.

Understatement: *Words That Seem to Minimize the Significance of What You Say—and Surprise Once the Audience Realizes Their Importance*

Really, understatement is an often-underused kind of humor. The speaker gets credit for dry wit, and the audience can congratulate itself for having the sophistication to appreciate it. It's even effective in serious matters when you normally might shy away from humor, as in these grim lines uttered by George W. Bush in this 2001 CEO dinner in Shanghai:

> I gave Taliban leaders a choice: turn over the terrorists or face your ruin. They chose unwisely.

Bush understands the seriousness of the issue. But he uses understated wit to makes listeners see an image: Taliban leaders realizing the horror of their mistake.

Hyperbole: *Exaggeration, Often for Comic Effect*

Politicians often reserve hyperbole for campaign speeches—with good reason. Red-meat audiences love the mocking exaggeration they would usually acknowledge as untrue. Hyperbole can be risky. In politics, it's common for opponents to quote a hyperbolic remark as if it was meant literally. Here is former vice presidential candidate Sarah Palin's celebrated example during the 2008 campaign:

> Our opponent . . . is someone who sees America, it seems, as being so imperfect that he's palling around with terrorists who would target their own country.

By using the words *palling around*, Palin exaggerates to make a point. Opponents leaped on her phrase as if the important point was whether it was true. A few years later, when Barack Obama told business owners, "You didn't build that," meaning government spending on roads and bridges helped, his hyperbole got a similar reaction.

It's important to realize that hyperbole—as in many of the examples we examine—can also include other techniques. In Senator Markey's reference to opioids, he used metaphor ("Fentanyl is the Godzilla of opioids") in the service of hyperbole.

Rhetorical Questions: *Questions That Need No Answer*

Questions are a staple of political speech. Why? For the reason we have just asked one. Questions, even ones that do not need an answer, surprise by turning what the audience thinks is a monologue into something interactive.

Questions do that in different ways. Take this passage from Richard Nixon's 1952 "Checkers" speech. Under attack for a private slush fund, he describes what he did in a way that will make his audience believe he's innocent:

> Do you think that when I or any other senator makes a political speech, has it printed, [we] should charge the printing of that speech and the mailing of that speech to the taxpayer?

By asking an incredulous question, Nixon lets us know his answer is "No!" And that makes the audience see him as unjustly accused.

In 2016, rhetorical questions made a different speech memorable. Khizr Khan, father of an American soldier who had died in Iraq, was angry at then-candidate Donald Trump's inflammatory rhetoric about Muslims. Pulling a copy of the Constitution from his jacket pocket, he spoke directly to Trump, a device sometimes called "addressing the absent enemy."

> Donald Trump, you are asking Americans to trust you with our future. Let me ask you: *Have you even read the U.S. Constitution?* I will gladly lend you my copy. [*irony*] In this document, look for the words *liberty* and *equal protection of law*. *Have you ever been to Arlington Cemetery?* Go look at the graves of the brave patriots who died defending America—you will see all faiths, genders, and ethnicities.

Note how Khan uses two ways to be visual. First he uses a prop—pulling the Constitution from his pocket. Next, he offers an image. By making listeners imagine the gravesites of those who have sacrificed, he makes memorable his belief that Trump is both ignorant and oblivious to his son's sacrifice. It is an approach that works because Khan knows his audience.

Concrete Detail

Concrete detail is not a figure of speech. Neither is it a device we use only to avoid abstraction and make language understandable. We include it here because it is a way of using details that vividly appeal to our senses. In speech, there are ways to provide images listeners will never forget. Three examples:

Concrete Detail to Inspire Urgency

In 2012, after the Syrian government used nerve gas on civilians, President Obama wanted to convey a sense of how devastating the attack had been. He might have simply told listeners this:

> The attack was devastating. It destroyed families.

Instead, he said this:

> The images from this massacre are sickening: Men, women, children lying in rows, killed by poison gas. Others foaming at the mouth, gasping for breath. A father clutching his dead children, imploring

them to get up and walk. On that terrible night, the world saw in gruesome detail the terrible nature of chemical weapons, and why the overwhelming majority of humanity has declared them off-limits—a crime against humanity, and a violation of the laws of war.

In addition to the physical details, Obama and his writers included one other image: a father unable to admit the truth about his children. Physical details are only one of the ways to make speech unforgettable.

Concrete Detail to Describe Heroism

Sometimes we want listeners to imagine. This differs from story, though they often go hand in hand. What speakers want is an image listeners will not forget. Ronald Reagan, in the D-Day speech you see excerpted here, wanted to describe a scene of heroism.

> We stand on a lonely, windswept point on the northern shore of France. The air is soft, but forty years ago at this moment, the air was dense with smoke and the cries of men, and the air was filled with the crack of rifle fire and the roar of cannon. At dawn, on the morning of the sixth of June, 1944, two hundred and twenty-five Rangers jumped off the British landing craft and ran to the bottom of these cliffs.
>
> Their mission was one of the most difficult and daring of the invasion: to climb these sheer and desolate cliffs and take out the enemy guns. The Allies had been told that some of the mightiest of these guns were here, and they would be trained on the beaches to stop the Allied advance.
>
> The Rangers looked up and saw the enemy soldiers at the edge of the cliffs, shooting down at them with machine guns and throwing grenades. And the American Rangers began to climb.

Note how many images are vivid. The "crack" of rifle fire; the way Rangers "jumped" off the landing craft; the "sheer and desolate" cliffs. Reagan and his writers wanted listeners not just to know what those soldiers went through, but to hear, see, and feel what it was like.

Concrete Detail to Demonstrate Contrast

In the Appendix, you will find Mary Fisher's 1992 Republican National Convention speech about AIDS. Fisher came from a wealthy family. She wanted to make clear that she identified with those who did not.

Though I am female and contracted this disease in marriage and enjoy the warm support of my family, I am one with the lonely gay man sheltering a flickering candle from the cold wind of his family's rejection.

It's not just a candle but a "flickering" one; not just the metaphor of wind but a "cold" wind; not just a gay man but a "lonely" gay man. This sentence works in conjunction with others, but it is the concrete detail that gives it force.

Simile. Metaphor. Synecdoche. Metonymy. Irony. Understatement. Rhetorical questions.

And concrete detail.

In different ways, they each make points more vivid so listeners remember. If you want to compose a sound bite that makes it on the evening news and, sometimes, into the history books, you must uncover the details that give listeners the shock of recognition novels do—or simply evoke shock in a way people will not forget.

Still, an evocative phrase represents only part of what makes audiences remember speeches. After all, each is effective only for the few moments it takes to utter it.

There is another way to make speeches memorable. It is the technique that allows speakers to build in excitement. It is the technique that lends speeches the pulsing beat that make audiences jump to their feet. It is the technique that succeeds because of not a single sentence but all of them.

And as you will see, it is the technique that infuses the paragraph you just read, like it does in songs and poetry, to create rhythm.

MAKING LANGUAGE RHYTHMIC

In elementary school, one of us had a class designed to let us blow off steam. The teacher would hand out cymbals, little drums, triangles, and sticks we could knock against each other. We could bang or shake whatever instrument we had in our hands. We could make as much noise as we wanted. But there was one rule. The teacher would put on a record. We had to bang in time to the music.

They called the class Rhythms. And that's how we learned that all music divides into patterns of repetitive sounds, usually in groups of two or three.

Rhythmic patterns aren't always mechanical successions of twos and threes. Sometimes composers take one rhythmic pattern and use it over and over with different instruments, speeds, and keys. For example: the three short and one long notes opening Beethoven's "Fifth Symphony" (Bu-Bu-Bu-*Baah*). Listeners find repeating those rhythmic patterns—*motifs*, in music—incredibly exciting.

Speakers create excitement in very much the same way, often through repetition.

CHAPTER 7 Language People Remember   119

By *repetition*, we mean the repeated use of grammatical structure, words, or sounds. We have already seen examples: Lincoln's repetition of "people" or Patrick Henry's "give me."

Why is repetition so essential in politics? First, similar sounds are memorable, which is why they are a staple in advertising ("The quicker picker upper"; "Shave time, shave money"). Second, they drive home a point, as any parent knows who has told a toddler who wants ice cream instead of dinner ("No, no, NO!").

We do not tire of reminding readers that repetition is nothing new. We see it in the Gettysburg Address ("of the people, by the people . . ."). And of course we remember it in one speech that lifted the spirits of a frightened nation: Winston Churchill's speech after Dunkirk. He starts his conclusion this way:

We shall fight on the beaches.

By itself, Churchill's audience might not have thought that so memorable. But Churchill continued.

We shall fight on the beaches, we shall fight on the landing grounds, we shall fight in the fields and in the streets, we shall fight in the hills; we shall never surrender.

Imagine British families listening on their radios, hearing Churchill build to his final words until by the end they believe England can beat back the Nazis. Repetition allowed Churchill to create a mounting sense of hope. He affected listeners not just by what his words meant, but by how they sounded.

That is why repetition works in political speech. It allows skilled speakers to raise their pitch, turn up the volume, and accelerate speed. They sound passionate, which creates passion in listeners. It is the reason Martin Luther King Jr. said "I have a dream," not once but five times. That doesn't mean repetition appears in isolation. It allowed King to gain power, but the imagery in each sentence was a vital partner.

I have a dream—that on the red clay hills of Georgia, black children and white children will walk hand in hand.

Sometimes repetition means repeating a sound (alliteration), or repeating words at the beginning of sentences (anaphora), at the end of sentences (epistrophe), or within sentences. Repetition may show contrast (antithesis) or show similarity. In every case, though, an adept speaker can use repetition to gain power. And without it, even the best speakers rarely do.

We begin with seven devices often involving repetition within a single sentence. Next, we move to what this book calls "litany"—ways to use repetition in groups of sentences or phrases.

Finally, we cover three strategies to use repetition well. And while we include the Greek names for each, again, what's most important is not that you remember the strategies' names. What's important is that you use them.

Repetition within Single Sentences

Antimetabole: *Repetition of Words in Reverse Grammatical Structure*

Mankind must put an end to war—or war will put an end to mankind.

> John F. Kennedy, United Nations, 1961

A staple for speakers trying to draw contrast, antimetabole is what some writers call the "reverse raincoat." Like a reversible raincoat, you turn the phrase inside out, like Dumas's *Three Musketeers*. "All for one—and one for all."

Antimetabole can dramatize issues of fairness. JFK did it in 1961, and Barack Obama did it in 2011, speaking to soldiers at Fort Bragg, North Carolina, announcing the end of the Iraq War and emphasizing his view of what Americans owed veterans.

You stood up for America; now America must stand up for you.

Alliteration: *Repetition of Words Beginning with the Same Sound*

We shall not falter; we shall not fail.

> George W. Bush, speech to joint session of Congress after the September 11, 2001, attacks

Just as they know the value of repetition, ad agencies and marketers know the value of alliteration ("pushbutton publishing"). Unlike other devices, they are simple to think up—if you have trouble thinking of two appropriate words, all you have to do is open a small dictionary or go to thesaurus.com and search until you find the right match.

Almost to a fault, alliteration has become one of the most common ways to make listeners remember, whether Donald Trump describing the Empire State Building to construction workers in 2017 ("the big, bold, and daring dream of one man"), or this excerpt from Barack Obama's Fort Hood Memorial that includes an astonishing number of examples in just over one hundred words:

> This generation of soldiers, sailors, airmen, Marines, and Coast Guardsmen have volunteered in the time of certain danger. They are part of the finest fighting force that the world has ever known. They

have served tour after tour of duty in distant, different, and difficult places ... They are men and women; white, black, and brown; of all faiths and all stations—all Americans, serving together to protect our people, while giving others half a world away the chance to lead a better life.... In today's wars, there's not always a simple ceremony that signals our troops' success—no surrender papers to be signed, or capital to be claimed.

Assonance and Consonance: *Similar Techniques That Use the Repetition of Sounds in Nonrhyming Words*

In his inaugural address, President Kennedy used both assonance, repeating vowel sounds:

Both sides overburdened by the cost of modern weapons, both rightly alarmed by the *steady spread* of the *deadly* atom ...

and consonance, repeating consonant sounds within words or ending words:

Let every nation know, whether it wishes us *well* or *ill*, that we *shall* ...

Antithesis: *Parallel Structure, Often Linked by Not to Present Contrast*

Americans expect us to go to Washington for the right reasons, and not just to mingle with the right people.

Sarah Palin, Republican National Convention Keynote, 2008

Antithesis succeeds because such contrast allows speakers, among other things, to urge one course of action and reject another. That's the secret of Patrick Henry's line, whether authentic or not ("Give me liberty or give me death!"). It's also the device President Kennedy used in his famous call to action ("Ask not what your country can do for you—ask what you can do for your country"). Antithesis makes what both Henry and Kennedy accept and reject clear and easy to remember.

In politics, speakers may use antithesis to reject pessimism and embrace optimism. They also use it to contrast their virtues with the other side's shortcomings, as you see in the Palin example. Like sharply contrasting themes in music, the contrast of antithesis becomes memorable partly through rhythm.

Polyptoton: *Repetition of One Word (or Root) Using Different Meanings*

Not as a call to battle, though embattled we are.

John F. Kennedy, Inaugural Address, 1961

Asyndeton: *Omission of the Conjunctions That Ordinarily Join Coordinate Words or Clauses*

Sometimes the repetition of small details creates excitement *because* speakers don't stop for formalities. One example: a passage from Ted Cruz's speech on internet freedom.

> We are entering very dangerous territory, where giant U.S. companies participate in censoring speech because to speak of something like jihad, to speak of the Muslim Brotherhood, to speak of the forcible export of Sharia Law, is deemed inconsistent with political correctness.

Cruz could have broken that sentence into three. Instead, repeating "to speak" so quickly makes his three quick examples achieve critical mass. We often hear politicians use repetition in groups of sentences. You could call this by its formal name: a "scheme of repetition" employing three or more full sentences in parallel construction. Politicians use a shorter one.

"You know the litany," George H. W. Bush told the 1988 Republican National Convention as he accepted the nomination for president, almost as if he was a little embarrassed to be using a rhetorical technique.

And then he used one.

Repetition in Groups of Sentences

Litany: *A Repetitive Recital, in American Politics Usually Involving More Than One Sentence*

Derived from the Greek word meaning "plea," *litany* originally meant the repetitive prayer in which priest and congregation alternate pleas to God.

In politics, litany has become a popular way to refer to any series of repetitive sentences—the "litany of abuses" one scholar uses to refer to the Declaration of Independence, which lists thirteen abuses, each sentence beginning with "He has."

What George H. W. Bush called his "litany"—apparently an ad-lib since the word doesn't appear in his printed text—was one of accomplishment that brought cheers from the crowd:

> Inflation was 13 percent when we came in. We got it down to four.
>   Interest rates were more than 21. We cut them in half.
>   Unemployment was up and climbing, and now it's the lowest in fourteen years.

It's a useful term: brief, imaginatively adapted from religion, and bearing a pedigree (nineteenth-century poet Philip Freneau's most famous poem, "A Political Litany").[4] This book will use the word *litany* for the kind of repetition so common in politics: to excoriate the other side, praise one's own, describe problems, pledge change, rouse the audience to action—or, sometimes, add impact to a quiet passage.

In each instance, litany works. Here's why: First, litany *clarifies*. It demonstrates how much evidence a speaker has. When a speaker launches into a list, moving through two—three, five, ten!—items, each more terrible or wonderful than the last, crowds react: *This threat is dangerous! These solutions can work! This administration has been a success!* The sheer wealth of examples in a skillful litany makes points convincing.

Second, litany *evokes emotion*. It reminds the crowd how urgent the issues are. Let's say Bush had phrased his point this way:

> We reduced inflation and interest rate. They're both way lower than a few years back. And while unemployment was high, it's now the lowest in fourteen years.

That would not have been nearly as effective. Peggy Noonan didn't just want to make the audience remember these three achievements. She wanted to make them see the larger point: that there were lots of them. Bush was not a dynamic speaker, but he needed to sound forceful. Repeating the same grammatical structure, driving home the point again and again, allowed him to do that.

Finally, litany *characterizes*. Speakers get louder. They get faster. *Hey,* the listeners think, *Bush isn't as dull as we thought!* The fact that Bush sounds excited about what the administration did for them makes them excited about backing him.

So, how do you create it? Let's look at two common patterns, anaphora and epistrophe, and a way to organize them.

BOX 7.1
FIGURES OF SPEECH

Sound bites—and their first cousin, applause lines—use a very narrow range of techniques. All involve kinds of parallel construction or imagery discussed either in this chapter or in Chapter 9, on wit. Here are some of the most common figures of speech.

Analogy

> If criminals have a right to a lawyer, then I think working Americans should have the right to a doctor.
>
> Harris Wofford, Pennsylvania Senate Campaign, 1992

(Continued)

(Continued)

Antithesis

It's not a question of being ready on day one. It's a question of being right on day one.

Barack Obama, Rally in Florence, South Carolina, 2008

Alliteration

Sanctimonious, sensitive, supercilious snowflakes.

Jeff Sessions, Speech to Students, 2017

Metaphor

You have a row of dominos set up; you knock over the first one, and what will happen to the last one is the certainty that it will go over very quickly.

Dwight D. Eisenhower, News Conference, 1954

Hyperbole

If Hitler invaded Hell I would make at least a favorable reference to the Devil in the House of Commons.

Winston Churchill, Parliament, 1941

Anaphora: *Deliberate Repetition at the Beginning of Two or More Consecutive Sentences*

Below, note the way President Barack Obama, standing before the Berlin Victory Column in 2008, repeats the phrases "People of the world" and "Look at Berlin."

People of the world—look at Berlin!

Look at Berlin, where Germans and Americans learned to work together and trust each other less than three years after facing each other on the field of battle.

Look at Berlin, where the determination of a people met the generosity of the Marshall Plan and created a German miracle; where a victory over tyranny gave rise to NATO, the greatest alliance ever formed to defend our common security.

Look at Berlin, where the bullet holes in the buildings and the somber stories and pillars near the Brandenburg Gate insist that we never forget our common humanity.

People of the world—look at Berlin, where a wall came down, a continent came together, and history proved that there is no challenge too great for a world that stands as one.

Obama opens the first four words of each sentence the same way, except for the last, where he adds an opening phrase. His examples differ. But repetition allows him to build in excitement about the most important idea: Berlin as a model for the future.

In a very different speech, the March for Life in 2017, Vice President Mike Pence also uses litany.

> And at 1600 Pennsylvania Avenue, we're in the promise-keeping business.
>
> That's why, on Monday, President Trump reinstated the Mexico City policy to prevent foreign aid from funding organizations that [*alliteration*] promote or perform abortions.
>
> That's why this administration will work with Congress to end taxpayer funding for abortion and abortion providers, and we will devote those resources to health care services for women across America.
>
> And that's why, next week, President Donald Trump will announce a Supreme Court nominee who will uphold the God-given liberties enshrined in our Constitution in the tradition of the [*rhyme*] late and great Justice Antonin Scalia.
>
> Life is winning in America. And today is a celebration of the progress that we have made in the cause.

Pence uses a "that's why" repetition to drive home his single main point: that President Trump is keeping his promises to right-to-life voters. As different as the messages are in these two speeches, repetition allows both Obama and Pence to become more forceful at each stage. Pence also uses different devices of repetition—alliteration and rhyme—but by beginning the same way three times, he gains power the other devices can't achieve.

Epistrophe: *Repetition at the End of Two or More Consecutive Sentences*

Repetition at the end of a series of sentences offers an especially useful way to allow speakers to raise their voices, make one point memorable, and signal to listeners that it is time for them to clap. In this 1980 speech, written by Bob Shrum, Ted Kennedy uses repetition to open each sentence, but achieves an emotional effect by repeating his most important idea at the end:

> The same Republicans who are talking about the crisis of unemployment have nominated a man who once said, and I quote, "Unemployment insurance is a prepaid vacation plan for freeloaders." *And that nominee is no friend of labor.*

The same Republicans who are talking about the problems of the inner cities have nominated a man who said, and I quote, "I have included in my morning and evening prayers every day the prayer that the federal government not bail out New York." *And that nominee is no friend of this city and our great urban centers across this nation.*

The same Republicans who are talking about security for the elderly have nominated a man who said just four years ago that "participation in Social Security should be made voluntary." *And that nominee is no friend of the senior citizens of this nation.*

Almost forty years later, Kennedy's great-grandnephew uses the same combination of anaphora and epistrophe in this 2017 health care debate before the U.S. House of Representatives:

The America that I know would never turn its back on a friend or stranger in need. Trumpcare does.

The America that I know doesn't tell the sick or the friend or the elderly that you are on your own. Trumpcare does.

The America that I know doesn't tell the young man struggling through an opioid recovery that your last relapse was one too many. Trumpcare does.

Rep. Joseph Kennedy (D-MA), 2017

Naturally, exciting a crowd doesn't stem from repetition alone. Details and the order in which they come matter, too. In later chapters, we discuss ways you can do that to make language memorable in each section of your speech. Here, we suggest four ways that work for all of them.

1. Climactic Order: Repetition from Least to Most Important

To help increase intensity from beginning to end of a litany, make sure all your examples are urgent for listeners. But make sure, as well, that you build from the least to most urgent—that is, to the examples that matter. Here's a three-part rhetorical question litany, slightly condensed, uttered by President Reagan in 1984:

Who was not embarrassed when the administration handed a major propaganda victory in the United Nations to the enemies of Israel, our staunch Middle East ally for three decades . . . ?

Who does not feel a growing sense of unease as our allies, facing repeated instances of an amateurish and confused administration, reluctantly conclude that America is unwilling or unable to fulfill its obligations as leader of the free world?

> Who does not feel rising alarm when the question in any discussion of foreign policy is no longer "Should we do something?" but "Do we have the capacity to do anything?"
>
> Ronald Reagan Acceptance Speech, Republican National Convention, 1980

Notice the way Reagan moves from "embarrassed" to "unease" to the most extreme emotion: "alarm." Audiences sense when litanies leap to issues of greater and greater importance. It makes the speaker's growing excitement logical—and contagious.

Notice too that in litany speakers may vary the last line, using devices to make endings especially memorable, almost like a punch line. That is true with Obama, who uses three clauses of parallel construction at the end; with Ted Kennedy, whose tone about Reagan becomes noticeably harsher; and with Reagan, who ends with antithesis.

Climactic order is important not just in separate sentences. Here is Ted Cruz, speaking at the 2016 Republican National Convention. He could have repeated "We need" three times. That would have been overkill. Repeating three clauses beginning with "who" in climactic order makes him the passionate speaker too impatient for progress to get his point across with full sentence structures.

> We need a commander-in-chief who will speak the truth, who will address the enemy we face, who will unleash the full force and fury of the American military on defeating ISIS and defeating radical Islamic terrorists.

2. Compare and Contrast: Repetition to Become Quotable

Here, one of Barack Obama's oft-quoted litanies from the 2004 Democratic National Convention that made him famous:

> Well, I say to them tonight, there is not a liberal America and a conservative America—there is the United States of America. There is not a black America and a white America and Latino America and Asian America—there's the United States of America.

Naturally, there are perfectly respectable ways to use terms like *black America*. Obama uses antithesis and anaphora to contrast his view with those he believes segment America along racial or ethnic lines ignoring what they have in common. He had guessed right about his audience. Those lines drew thunderous applause and became perhaps the most often-quoted section of the speech that made him famous.

Similarly, at the 2016 Republican National Convention, Ted Cruz used antithesis to drive home the contrast between his views on terrorism and the views of Democrats:

> You don't defeat terrorism by taking away our guns. You defeat terrorism by using our guns.

Like Obama, Cruz is open to criticism. Like Obama, he caricatures the other side. The fault is not repetition but rather what in Chapter 10 we describe as the "straw man" fallacy.

3. Move from Lists to Litany

Sometimes, speechwriters worry that they overdo the litany. Our advice: relax. Let's say a sentence in your draft reads,

> Freedom means the right to keep and bear arms, to protect your family, that every human life is precious, that Supreme Court justices follow the Constitution—and let states choose policies that reflect local values.

That's not a bad sentence. A skillful speaker could make it more exciting. But lists are boring. Applause comes more easily when it reads the way Ted Cruz or his writer wrote it in 2016.

> Freedom means the right to keep and bear arms and protect your family.
> Freedom means that every human life is precious and must be protected.
> Freedom means Supreme Court justices who do not dictate policy but, instead, follow the Constitution.
> And freedom means recognizing that our Constitution allows states to choose policies that reflect local values.

Whenever you look at a draft and see you have written something like "We must do X, Y, and Z," consider changing that to "We must do X. We must do Y. We must do Z." The difference, when heard, is enormous.

4. Vary Your Approach

Like the holy trinity of Cajun cooking—onion, celery, and bell pepper—combinations produce more than the sum of their parts. This chapter has covered many different ways to use repetition to create power, become quotable, and be remembered. But these do not work only in isolation. Skillful writers must learn to use them in combination.

To see how that works, let's end by examining one section from Hillary Clinton's Democratic National Convention speech, which in one three-minute section uses no fewer than seventeen examples of devices this chapter has covered:

CHAPTER 7 Language People Remember

HILLARY CLINTON
Acceptance Speech, Democratic National Convention, 2016

Polyptoton

When representatives from thirteen unruly colonies met just down the road from here, some wanted to *stick* with the king. Some wanted to *stick it* to the king, and go their own way.

The revolution hung in the balance.

Then somehow they began listening to each other . . .

Alliteration

Compromising . . . finding common purpose.

And by the time they left Philadelphia, they had begun to see themselves as one nation.

Anaphora

That's what made it possible to stand up to a king.

That took courage.

They had courage.

Our founders embraced the enduring truth that we are stronger together.

Anaphora

America is once again at a moment of reckoning.

Powerful forces are threatening to pull us apart.

Bonds of trust and respect are fraying.

And just as with our founders, there are no guarantees.

It truly is up to us.

Antithesis

We have to decide whether we all will work together so we all can rise together.

Our country's motto is e pluribus unum: out of many, we are one.

Rhetorical Question

Will we stay true to that motto?

Well, we heard Donald Trump's answer last week at his convention.

(Continued)

(Continued)

Repetition to Show Contrast

He wants to divide us—from the rest of the world, and from each other.

Alliteration

He's betting that the perils of today's world will blind us to its unlimited promise.

Alliteration and Antithesis

He wants us to fear the future and fear each other.

Well, a great Democratic president, Franklin Delano Roosevelt, came up with the perfect rebuke to Trump more than eighty years ago, during a much more perilous time.

Polyptoton

"The only thing we have to fear is fear itself."

Now we are clear-eyed about what our country is up against.

But we are not afraid.

We will rise to the challenge, just as we always have.

Antithesis

We will not build a wall.

Instead, we will build an economy where everyone who wants a good paying job can get one.

And we'll build a path to citizenship for millions of immigrants who are already contributing to our economy!

Antithesis

We will not ban a religion.

We will work with all Americans and our allies to fight terrorism.

There's a lot of work to do.

Too many people haven't had a pay raise since the crash.

Litany to Show Contrast

There's too much inequality.

Too little social mobility.

Too much paralysis in Washington.

Too many threats at home and abroad.

But just look at the strengths we bring to meet these challenges.

Anaphora

We have the most dynamic and diverse people in the world.

We have the most tolerant and generous young people we've ever had.

We have the most powerful military.

The most innovative entrepreneurs.

The most enduring values.

Freedom and equality, justice and opportunity.

We should be so proud that these words are associated with us. That when people hear them—they hear . . . America.

Anaphora and Epistrophe

So don't let anyone tell you that our country is weak.

We're not.

Don't let anyone tell you we don't have what it takes.

We do.

BOX 7.2

EXERCISE: SOUND BITE WARS

It's a scenario common not just in Washington, D.C., but in state capitals across the country. Intense debate followed by a big vote. But afterward, legislators don't run home. They run to the press gallery. Or maybe to the gaggle of reporters waiting nearby.

We know why. The issue might be settled, but there is still a story to tell. Politicians need publicity, and the speechwriter's orders are clear.

"I want to be quoted," the boss says.

Of course the boss wants to be quoted, but so does every other politician. The competition is on. How do you break through?

In our class, we pick a hot issue. Then, we divide the students evenly, assigning them opposing sides. They have to write three separate sound bites, each using a different rhetorical technique to make language, and their point, memorable. We stop the exercise after ten minutes, asking each student to recite his or her best line. We finish with a survey: who won the sound bite war and why.

(Continued)

> (Continued)
>
> You don't have to be in a classroom to work on using rhetorical devices. Some, like alliteration, may come naturally. Others, like antimetabole, repeating words but reversing the grammatical structure, come only when you consciously try to emulate what you've read or heard. In other words, practice!

FINAL WORDS

"Political language . . . ," said George Orwell in his 1946 essay *"Politics and the English Language,"* "is designed to make lies sound truthful and murder respectable, and to give an appearance of solidity to pure wind."[5]

Before we leave the ways to make speech memorable—and certainly after defending the much-maligned sound bite—we must be careful not to claim too much. Even speechwriters writing for people they admire know there are times when they have oversimplified a complex thought. Sometimes summing up an idea in eight clever words can make audiences believe what they should discard. But that is no reason not to learn how to make memorable the points you believe.

Sound bites are morally neutral—as opposed to the policy they reflect. Politicians and their writers often abuse them. But they communicate substantive thought very well. For evidence, look at Orwell's quote. It contains parallel construction and metaphor: a sound bite if there ever was one.

THE SPEECHWRITER'S CHECKLIST: LANGUAGE PEOPLE REMEMBER

- ☐ Have I consciously worked to make my language vivid, using imagery in a variety of ways?
- ☐ Do I see the virtue of raising questions as a way of engaging listeners?
- ☐ Have I looked for ways to use repetition within single sentences?
- ☐ Have I used litanies of sentences beginning or ending in the same way, allowing speakers to gain power at each step?
- ☐ Do I harness the Monroe structure with the power repetition at each step?
- ☐ Have I used climactic order in a way that creates power?

8
Anecdote

After a few throat-clearing sentences at the 2016 Democratic National Convention, Michelle Obama reminded delegates how in 2008 she had talked about her daughters—and how, since then, she had watched them grow: "a journey," she said, "that started soon after we arrived in Washington when they set off for their first day at their new school."

Then she recounted one moment of that eight-year journey:

> I will never forget that winter morning as I watched our girls, just seven and ten years old, pile into those black SUVs with all those big men with guns.
>
> And I saw their little faces pressed up against the window, and the only thing I could think was "What have we done?"

It was no surprise that listeners laughed and cheered. But Obama, with the help of her speechwriter Sarah Hurwitz (interviewed later in this chapter, in Box 8.1), wasn't finished. She had a point to make.

> See, because at that moment, I realized that our time in the White House would form the foundation for who they would become, and how well we managed this experience could truly make or break them. That is what Barack and I think about every day as we try to guide and protect our girls through the challenges of this unusual life in the spotlight—how we urge them to ignore those who question their father's citizenship or faith.

A few weeks before, Texas senator Ted Cruz opened his speech at the Republican National Convention with a different message—but similar approach.

Just two weeks ago, a nine-year-old girl named Caroline was living a carefree Texas summer. Swimming in the pool, playing with friends, doing all the things a happy child might do. Like most children, she relied upon the love that she received from her mom, Heidi, and her dad, a police sergeant named Michael Smith.

That is until he became one of the five police officers gunned down in Dallas.

The day her father was murdered, Caroline gave him a hug and a kiss as he left for work, but as they parted her dad asked her something he hadn't asked before.

"What if this is the last time you ever kiss or hug me?"

Michael Smith was a former Army Ranger who spent decades with the Dallas Police Department.

I have no idea who he voted for in the last election . . . but his life was a testament to devotion.

What if this right now is our last time? Our last moment to do something for our families, and our country? Did we live up to the values we say we believe? Did we do all we really could?

Like Michelle Obama, Ted Cruz used a moving story to remind listeners of what elections can mean.

AS DELIVERED

Michelle Obama's and Ted Cruz's speeches at the 2016 national political conventions. Having read the stories each uses, take the time to watch them. What makes you think the stories are true? Can you see the effect on the audiences in the hall? What about people watching at home? www.youtube.com/watch?v=4ZNWYqDU948

www.youtube.com/watch?v=XDhqM9ZnVmI

Elvin Lim believes that "applause-rendering . . . human interest appeals" contribute to the "impoverish[ment of] our public deliberative sphere."[1] And yes, both speakers could have delivered their speeches without story. But they would have deprived themselves of the chance to create empathy and win support—not just from the delegates in the hall but from the much larger audience watching at home.

More important, they would have missed the chance to remind listeners that underlying any discussion of policy are the flesh-and-blood human beings who make these policies, and those they affect.

RELEVANT, REMEMBERED, READY TO ACT

Technically, the definitions of *anecdote* and *story* are a little different: An anecdote is entertaining and often biographical; a story usually is a longer narrative that may or may not be true. By those definitions, all anecdotes are stories, but not all stories are anecdotes. This book uses the term *anecdote* because stories in politics are short, often true, and designed to *either* entertain or move.

Whatever use we make of them, anecdotes offer speakers an enormous and legitimate asset. We believe political debate should pay attention to the effects policies have on people. And to win political debates, politicians should use the stories of those people. Sure, there are times when speakers use an anecdote to move listeners in a way that conceals the truth. Anything can be overdone. But as they did for both Obama and Cruz, anecdotes make it more likely that audiences will, in fact, as Joseph Conrad suggested, hear, feel, and see.

The effect story can have isn't just, well, anecdotal. It's backed up by a body of research, seemingly mounting, as "storytelling" has become a popular communications strategy not only for politics and nonprofits but in the private sector as well.

We cite only a few of these studies, beginning with one by Johns Hopkins researcher Keith Quesenberry who wanted to find out which Super Bowl ads viewers liked best. Was it sex appeal? Cute animals?

Actually, it was neither. What the most popular Super Bowl ads had in common, was story. They used the Freytag five-act story structure we mentioned in Chapter 5 as associated with Shakespearean drama. The reason those ads were so effective: "People are attracted to stories," Quesenberry said, "because we're social creatures and we relate to other people."

In other words, the stories in those Super Bowl ads offered ways those watching could see themselves in the characters. In John Steinbeck's 1952 novel, *East of Eden*, one character puts that another way: "If a story is not about the hearer, he [or she] will not listen . . . A great lasting story is about everyone."[2]

Obama and Cruz used stories not just to make a point about themselves or a girl in Dallas. They believed both stories were about emotions and events listeners had experienced. Speaking to different audiences, they used story to reach them in similar ways. The reaction to both showed they guessed right.

But story doesn't just help listeners relate; it makes them remember.

In 1998, three Dutch social scientists tried to measure the effect of anecdote on listeners. They had seen data showing that audiences make up their minds in under a minute about whether a speaker is worth listening to or not. How should speakers best use that first minute?

Testing anecdote against other kinds of openings, the researchers found anecdote "led to significantly higher ratings of... comprehensibility and interest as well as the speaker's credibility. The presence of an anecdote also resulted in higher retention scores."[3]

It didn't even seem to matter what kind of anecdote audiences heard. "Oddly enough," they wrote, "the relevance of the anecdote did not seem to make a difference."

To be clear, the stories you use *should* be relevant to the speech. It is manipulative to elicit emotion only to grab attention rather than help make a point. We share their observation about relevance to show the power of story in persuasion.

That power isn't limited to attention and retention. For speakers seeking to persuade, it is the ability of an anecdote to make listeners act.

There are actually neurological reasons that's true. At one Future of StoryTelling conference, California neuroscientist Paul Zak offered an answer from a different study (https://futureofstorytelling.org/video/paul-zak-empathy-neurochemistry-and-the-dramatic-arc).

He produced a short video about a father whose little boy was dying of cancer. The video told the story of the father's anguish, also using the Freytag model. Using that video, he measured the effect on viewers' brain chemistry.

Specifically, Zak looked at the amounts of cortisol, the powerful chemical associated with distress, and oxytocin, the chemical that influences our ability to feel empathy. Those who watched and were moved by the story produced high levels of both. They were more likely to give. Continuing his research with the Defense Advanced Research Projects Agency (DARPA), Zak discovered not only that this was generally true but that once he knew their distress and empathy levels, he could predict who would give with 80 percent accuracy.

These are just a few of many studies on the effects of storytelling. But the lesson for speechwriters is clear: Anecdote helps listeners relate and believe. It makes listeners remember. It compels people to act. That is especially true when speakers use stories with *on-ramps* and *off-ramps*: the sentences before and after those stories, linking them to the issues they dramatize.

Anecdote is vital for reasons that go beyond moving listeners. Different anecdotes express different ideas. Telling a story about a hero shows listeners you share the hero's values. Telling a story about a victim says to an audience that you understand how others suffer. And telling a story that inspires listeners sends them this message: *If we are both inspired, shouldn't we both act?*

The title of a 2008 *Newsweek* story about audience emotional appeal was "Heard Any Good Stories Lately?" It cited a number of interesting examples in which, wrote science reporter Sharon Begley, "a candidate's personal narrative might sway more voters than experience, positions on issues, and policy proposals."[4]

As we have already pointed out, it is certainly possible to write a great speech without anecdote. Standing in front of the Lincoln Memorial in 1963, Martin Luther King Jr. used none. But to ignore anecdote is to ignore a powerful tool that compels interest from the audience—and respect for the speaker.

Moreover, not every anecdote has to be a full-blown, richly detailed production to move people. In his 2004 Republican National Convention speech, Arnold Schwarzenegger talks about what it was like growing up in divided Austria after World War II under Soviet occupation—how afraid his family was crossing into the Soviet sector, and how he feared Soviet soldiers would take people from their cars to use as "slave labor." Then he tells the audience this:

> My family didn't have a car—but one day we were in my uncle's car. It was near dark as we came to a Soviet checkpoint. I was a little boy. I wasn't an action hero back then, and I remember how scared I was the soldiers would pull my father or my uncle out of the car and I'd never see him again.

Even one who disagrees with his views can see how Schwarzenegger's anecdote prepares the audience for the emotional off-ramp that serves as his punch line:

> My family and so many others lived in fear of the Soviet boot. Today the world no longer fears the Soviet Union—and it is because of the United States of America!

In fewer than one hundred words, Schwarzenegger's narrative compels attention, illustrates a point, and characterizes himself—in this case as a patriot with a sense of humor and an awareness of the difference between fiction and reality ("I wasn't an action hero back then"). Regardless of his views, the speech offers a model for politicians at every level—and every ideological stripe.

Long or short, as current as today or as old as recorded time, stories like Schwarzenegger's enrich speech. Later in this book, we will examine more thoroughly where and how to use them. First, though, let's look at seven types: dramatic, funny, personal, symbolic, illustrative, historical, and parable.

TYPES AND TIPS

Dramatic

Dramatic incidents awaken listeners to the urgency of problems. They can also inspire them by showing stories of courage or sacrifice. In his 2012 speech at the National Peace Officers' Memorial Service, Barack Obama dramatized the issue of police protection with this one—a story not just of heroism, but of the larger point he makes in the final sentence.

> These are officers like Detective John Falcone, of Poughkeepsie, New York. In February, Detective Falcone responded to a shot fired call on Main Street. And when he arrived on the scene, he saw a man holding a gun with one hand, and a small child with the other.
>
> In a situation like that, every instinct pushes us towards self-preservation. But when the suspect fled, still holding the child, Detective Falcone didn't think twice. He took off in pursuit, and tragically, in the struggle that followed, he was shot and killed. He is survived by his parents.
>
> But there's another survivor as well: a three-year-old child who might not be alive today had it not been for the sacrifice of a hero who gave his life for another.
>
> This willingness to risk everything for a complete stranger is extraordinary. And yet, among our nation's law enforcement officers, it is also commonplace.

In 2018, a new president gave his first State of the Union speech, used a powerful story, and drew a conclusion from it in exactly the same way.

> Today is Rare Disease Day, and joining us in the gallery is a rare disease survivor, Megan Crowley. Megan was diagnosed with Pompe disease, a rare and serious illness, when she was fifteen months old. She was not expected to live past five.
>
> On receiving this news, Megan's dad, John, fought with everything he had to save the life of his precious child. He founded a company to look for a cure, and helped develop the drug that saved Megan's life. Today she is twenty years old—and a sophomore at Notre Dame.
>
> Megan's story is about the unbounded power of a father's love for a daughter.

But our slow and burdensome approval process at the Food and Drug Administration keeps too many advances, like the one that saved Megan's life, from reaching those in need.

If we slash the restraints, not just at the FDA but across our government, then we will be blessed with far more miracles like Megan.

Funny

Funny stories characterize speakers not just as having a sense of humor, which might be mean or sarcastic, but as being able to laugh at themselves. They can also illustrate points memorably and provide a change of mood.

At the 2004 Republican National Convention, Laura Bush wanted to show the audience how much her husband valued education. But she also wanted them to see that she and her husband could laugh at themselves. Often, she tells the crowd, people ask her why George W. Bush should be president:

> As you might imagine, I have a lot to say about that. I could talk about my passion: education. At every school we visit, the students are so eager. Last fall, the president and I walked into an elementary school in Hawaii, and a little second grader came out to welcome us and bellowed, "George Washington!"
>
> Close. Just the wrong George W.

In *Hardball*, his witty and useful book about politics, Chris Matthews, now host of the MSNBC program of the same name, tells a no-doubt apocryphal story about Bill Bradley who, shortly after being elected senator from New Jersey, came to speak at a banquet.

> Bradley is sitting at the dais when a waiter puts a pat of butter on his plate.
> Bradley says, "Can I please have another pat of butter?"
> The waiter replies, "One pat per person."
> The emcee overhears this. He rushes over to the waiter and whispers, "Maybe you don't know who that is. Bill Bradley—the All-Pro Knick, Rhodes Scholar, senator from New Jersey!"
> The waiter says, "Well, maybe you don't know who I am."
> "I guess I don't. Who are you?"
> "I'm the guy who controls the butter!"

It's a deservedly popular story among politicians because it allows them to segue neatly into an off-ramp and a point listeners value: the need for partnership. For example:

> No matter how powerful you are, there's always somebody you have to deal with. Nobody—not even the president—will single-handedly decide the matter of X . . .

More memorably than stating the point, Matthews's story and off-ramp work together to stress the importance of working together . . . and the folly of thinking you control everything.

Is it okay to use "old" stories and jokes? Haven't people heard them all? The answer to the first question is "yes." The second answer is "probably no, but it doesn't matter."

First, you can always freshen up an old story with a newer, more relevant transition, or an off-ramp to the next section of the speech. One of Eric's clients once wanted to tell this old joke, popular in business circles:

> Did you hear the one about the chicken who approached his friend the pig and suggested they open a "Ham 'n' Eggs" restaurant together?
>   The pig said, "No way. You only have to invest a few eggs. I have to make a total commitment."

Eric's solution: add the following: "I know what you're thinking: Which came first—the chicken, the egg . . . or that joke?" Good as new.

There is another reason to feel comfortable using old jokes. If you tell listeners "It's like the old joke" or "That reminds me of an old story," the listeners don't focus on the word *old*. They focus on *joke* or *story*. They lift their heads because you've alerted them that something funny lies ahead. Which makes them more likely to listen and laugh.

Personal

Personal stories focus attention, amuse, illustrate, and absorb. But they also have two unique advantages. They demonstrate personal knowledge of an issue, which makes speakers believable. They also let audiences see the private lives of people they usually view from a distance. Such stories make them feel more warmly toward the speaker—as long as they are true. Most are, because these days a made-up story is too checkable to use.

As chairman of the Senate Committee on Veterans' Affairs, Johnny Isakson (R-GA) often used a personal story, reminding audiences to be grateful for the military service and sacrifice of others. Here is one from a speech in May 2018:

> As Memorial Day approaches, I love to tell my favorite story about the great reminder I have of what Memorial Day is all about. It is all about a veteran, Roy C. Irwin, from the state of New Jersey. I have never met Roy; I never knew him.

> When I was in Margraten in the Netherlands at the U.S. cemetery where over eight thousand Americans are buried from the Battle of the Bulge, my wife and I spent an afternoon paying tribute and respect at the graves of our veterans and our soldiers. We walked down the road to look at the Stars of David and the crosses, paused for a minute at each headstone, and gave a prayer of thanks for the veterans who had sacrificed everything so that we could be there.
>
> Then something happened to me that I have never forgotten, and it could happen to any one of you if you ever go to one of those cemeteries and visit. I came upon a headstone, a cross, and I stopped and read it. It said: Roy C. Irwin, New Jersey, private, died, killed in action 12/28/44.
>
> I froze in place; 12/28/44 was not just the day that Roy C. Irwin died in the Battle of the Bulge fighting for us. It was the day I was given birth by my mother in Piedmont Atlanta Hospital in Georgia.
>
> There I was, standing at the foot of someone who had died on the day I was born. He gave his life so that I could enjoy mine.

Isakson not only uses the coincidence of a date to connect his experience to that of a soldier he never met. He uses it to help the audience connect.

Symbolic

It was September 20, 2001, only nine days after hijackers flew three passenger jets into the World Trade Center and the Pentagon and one, on its way to the U.S. Capitol, that crashed in a Pennsylvania field. The terrorist attack killed almost three thousand people. Speaking in front of a joint session of Congress, George W. Bush set out to rally a nation still very much in shock.

He was a president hardly known for soaring speeches, but this one included many of the techniques we discuss. In crystal-clear language, Bush defined what he called for the first time the "war on terror." Though guilty of presenting an "either–or" fallacy ("Either you are with us, or you are with the terrorists"), he used antithesis to unify, parallel construction and alliteration to call people to action ("In our grief and anger, we have found our mission and our moment"), and litany ("We will not tire, we will not falter, and we will not fail") to achieve power.

But Bush also did something else. He used action and a tangible object, a police officer's badge, to symbolize not just one man's bravery, but a nation's resolve.

George W. Bush: Post-9/11 Address to Congress

> We'll go back to our lives and routines, and that is good. Even grief recedes with time and grace. But our resolve must not pass.

It is my hope that in the months and years ahead, life will return almost to normal. Each of us will remember what happened that day, and to whom it happened. We'll remember the moment the news came—where we were and what we were doing. Some will remember an image of a fire, or a story of rescue. Some will carry memories of a face and a voice gone forever.

And I will carry this: It is the police shield of a man named George Howard, who died at the World Trade Center trying to save others. It was given to me by his mom, Arlene, as a proud memorial to her son.

This is my reminder of lives that ended, and a task that does not end. I will not forget this wound to our country or those who inflicted it.

I will not yield; I will not rest; I will not relent in waging this struggle for freedom and security for the American people.

The course of this conflict is not known, yet its outcome is certain. Freedom and fear, justice and cruelty, have always been at war, and we know that God is not neutral between them.

Fellow citizens, we'll meet violence with patient justice—assured of the rightness of our cause, and confident of the victories to come.

In all that lies before us, may God grant us wisdom, and may He watch over the United States of America.

AS DELIVERED

George W. Bush's Address to the Joint Session of Congress after 9/11.
You know why Bush treasures the police officer's shield. Does showing it to his audience make a difference? Is there a moment where Bush reveals personal emotion? Does demonstrating vulnerability actually reveal a strength?

www.youtube.com/watch?v=9vzRMaHCysU

We have already seen the way Michelle Obama opened her 2016 Democratic National Convention keynote. During her years as First Lady, Michelle Obama often used another story, a symbolic one about a five-year-old boy on a family tour of the White House, meeting her husband for the first time. Like every example we have examined, she ends by directly addressing the larger meaning.

> I want you to think about a photo . . . of a young black family visiting the president in the Oval Office . . . In the photo, Barack is bent over

at the waist . . . a little boy, just about five years old—is reaching out his tiny little hand to touch my husband's head.

And it turns out that upon meeting Barack, this little boy gazed up at him longingly, and he said, "I want to know if my hair is just like yours." And Barack replied, "Why don't you touch it and see for yourself?"

So he bent way down so the little boy could feel his hair. And after touching my husband's head, the little boy exclaimed, "Yes, it does feel the same!" . . .

So if you ever wonder whether change is possible, I want you to think about that little black boy in the office—the Oval Office of the White House—touching the head of the first black president.

And as we mark the 150th anniversary of the Emancipation Proclamation, I want you to remember that the house they were standing in—the house my family has the privilege of living in—that house was built in part by slaves.

But today, see, the beauty is children walk through that house and pass by that photo and they think nothing of it, because that's all they've ever known.

In the end, Obama's story becomes not just a heartwarming one about a little boy. The photo symbolizes the significance of her history-making husband, and a country's progress.

BOX 8.1
EXPERTS TALK: SARAH HURWITZ

This chapter includes two excerpts from former first lady Michelle Obama. She didn't just understand the power of story to make points relevant for her audience; she shared and shaped those stories with her talented writer, Sarah Hurwitz. We asked Sarah about her approach to speechwriting and her experiences in Washington, including the rare feat of writing in the White House for the entire eight years of the Obama presidency.

You have a rare perspective—not only working in the White House, but

(Continued)

(Continued)

writing for the same principal for eight years. How do you get fresh material? How do you find new stories?

I think freshness often comes down to the moment and the audience—every moment is new, as is every audience. What's happened in the last few weeks or months that's relevant? How can you celebrate the stories and achievements of people in this particular audience?

What advice would you give to other speechwriters (and politicians or people in public office) on how to build the speaker–builder relationship?

There's no substitute for simply spending time with the speaker so that you can hear the person speaking in their natural cadence. That's how you get someone's voice over time—the more you hear it in person, the more you'll start to hear it in your head as you write. Getting feedback from the speaker is also incredibly important—the more specific and detailed the feedback, the better.

You've made a point about how valuable research and fact-checking were; how did that work?

Fact-checking is extraordinarily important. In the Obama White House, we felt very strongly about always telling the American people the truth, and the thought of inadvertently having a wrong number or incorrect fact in a speech was unbearable. We had a first-rate research team that fact-checked every line of every speech we wrote, and they would produce footnoted versions of our speeches with backup for the facts. They were merciless with their scrutiny, and I am eternally grateful to them.

Audiences often commented on how authentic the First Lady sounded. What's the key to providing the right material for that?

The key was Michelle Obama herself. Michelle Obama knows who she is, and she always knows what she wants to say, and when we met about a speech, she would dictate pages of brilliant, moving, vivid language that I would try to capture verbatim—that language was the basis of the drafts I wrote.

How did speechwriting, or political rhetoric, change over the course of eight years, or even to now?

In recent years, I think we've seen less and less tolerance for the bland, poll-tested language that has been the lingua franca of politics—"we need to support hardworking American middle class family values!" It sounds fake, and it's hard to trust or connect with someone who talks that way. No one speaks like that to their spouse or their friend, and I always tell people: If you wouldn't say something to one person, don't say it to many people—it doesn't get better in front of a crowd. In an era where people watch entire speeches on their iPhones (rather than years ago, when they'd merely see a sound bite or two on the evening news or in the newspaper), it's critical for speakers to talk like human beings—and it's best for them to simply talk like themselves.

Illustrative

Illustrative anecdotes serve as evidence, convincing the audience that a problem is real and urgent, as does this story shared by Facebook's Sheryl Sandberg during a TED Talk.[5] Sandberg wasn't a politician then, but had worked as a political appointee and senior aide at the Treasury Department. She uses story to dramatize an issue with political dimensions—the lack of women in top executive positions.

> A recent study in the U.S. showed that, of married senior managers, two-thirds of the married men had children.
>
> A couple of years ago, I was in New York, and I was pitching a deal, and I was in one of those fancy New York private equity offices you can picture. And I'm in the meeting—it's about a three-hour meeting—and two hours in, there needs to be that bio break, and everyone stands up, and the partner running the meeting starts looking really embarrassed.
>
> And I realized he doesn't know where the women's room is in his office. So I start looking around for moving boxes, figuring they just moved in, but I don't see any. And so I said, "Did you just move into this office?"
>
> And he said, "No, we've been here about a year."
>
> And I said, "Are you telling me that I am the only woman to have pitched a deal in this office in a year?"
>
> And he looked at me, and he said, "Yeah. Or maybe you're the only one who had to go to the bathroom."
>
> So the question is, how are we going to fix this? How do we change these numbers at the top?

Illustrative stories also serve as evidence that the speaker's solution is practical. In this speech, Los Angeles mayor Eric Garcetti used anecdote to persuade listeners that his city was successfully addressing the struggle to find low-income housing:

> Families like the Islam family know that struggle.
>
> Imli Islam works full time as a teacher in Koreatown, preparing the next generation of Angelenos for success. Her husband, Nazrul, also works for Los Angeles Unified School District at an elementary school cafeteria in Silver Lake.
>
> They were raising their three children in a cramped one-bedroom apartment in the center of the city. Every morning, the entire family competed for time in their home's only bathroom.

For three years, Imli and Nazrul scoured the city for a better option, but came up empty-handed. Until they found Selma Community Housing—a project that the city helped fund in partnership with LAUSD, which I was proud to work on as a councilmember.

I was there when Selma opened up sixty-six affordable housing units in the heart of Hollywood last year. And the Islams are some of its newest tenants.

But these stories are rare. Too many still have to choose between making rent and making dinner.

Anecdote helped both Sandberg and Garcetti illustrate their policy points. But it did something else: it helped characterize the speakers.

By sharing a funny story, Sandberg showed a sense of humor. Garcetti's story showed compassion for immigrants and the poor, people from all corners of the large city he leads. He also demonstrated that he values partnership, important for voters put off by bureaucracy or the gridlock of politics.

Historical

Stories about well-remembered historical events inspire audiences, by making them feel like they too are involved in great events. In this 1982 speech to the British Parliament, Ronald Reagan uses a story about Winston Churchill to inspire his audience. In doing so, he allies himself with a legendary British hero. Note the clever one-word switch in the quote when Reagan adapts it:

During the dark days of the Second World War, when this island was incandescent with courage, Winston Churchill exclaimed about Britain's adversaries, "What kind of a people do they think we are?"

Well, Britain's adversaries found out what extraordinary people the British are.

But all the democracies [of that time] paid a terrible price for allowing the dictators to underestimate us. We dare not make that mistake again.

So let us ask ourselves, "What kind of a people do we think we are?"

Parable

Delivered solemnly by speakers, parables can seem pompous. But when Toni Morrison won the Nobel Prize in Literature, she used a somewhat altered version of a parable beloved by litigators. Listeners enjoy hearing how the wise man outwits the prankster. More important, the story fits nicely into a theme politicians like to stress: that the solution to our problems lies in—well, you figure it out.

> There's an ancient story about an old wise man who could answer any riddle of life.
>
> One day a young boy decided to play a trick on the old man.
>
> "I will capture a bird," he told his friends, "hold it cupped in my hands, then ask whether it is dead or alive. If he says 'Dead,' I'll let it fly away. If he says 'Alive,' I'll crush it before opening my hands."
>
> Holding the bird, the boy went to the old man and asked: "Is the bird I have dead or alive?"
>
> The old man replied: "The answer . . . is in your hands."[6]

This chapter doesn't present an exhaustive list of the different ways to use anecdote. We only try to demonstrate the variety of anecdotes and the varied ways politicians can put them to use. And we conclude with three steps that help.

Use Stories with Suspense and Punch Lines

Look back at the parable you just read.

It has a narrative question: Will the boy succeed? It then narrates three connected events: The boy has an idea. He visits the old man. He gives him an ultimatum. Brief as it is, the parable creates suspense. Just like *The Lord of the Rings*, Morrison makes us need to know what happens next. The punch line ("The answer is in your hands") surprises listeners and makes it relevant to Morrison's speech.

In looking for stories, make sure you use that two-pronged approach of suspense and surprise. It will both move your listeners and keep them listening.

Be Truthful

Back in the 1990s, New York Democratic senator Daniel Patrick Moynihan told his home-state audience an old political story as if it had happened to him. It went like this:

> The other day a guy came up to me in the airport.
>> He said, "Anybody ever tell you that you look like Moynihan?"
>> I said, "Yeah."
>> He said, "Don't it make you mad?"

Moynihan left. Ten minutes later, in came New York Republican senator Al D'Amato. He opened like this:

> The other day a guy came up to me in the airport . . .

One of the authors was there. He still remembers the uneasy chuckles, then silence from the embarrassed crowd. Why pretend? In this era of YouTube and cell phones able to record video with excruciating clarity, making things up is risky. But it is senseless, too. Mentioning that a story is apocryphal doesn't make it less effective. Admitting it makes speakers more credible, not less.

Give Stories Room

Sometimes you don't have much time to tell a story. In a three-minute speech, a sixty-second story doesn't allow you enough time to make an argument.

Don't rush things. Concrete detail makes stories believable. Feeling the stories are true makes audiences find them moving. Each detail in Sheryl Sandberg's story contributed to the effect she had. Fight for every second without destroying balance.

BOX 8.2
EXERCISE: THE PIXAR'D PRESS RELEASE

When Emma Coats was a storyboard artist at Pixar, she offered tips for writing a compelling narrative. Her list included what she described as the outline for every Pixar movie. It goes like this:

> Once upon a time, there was ___. Every day, ___. One day, ___. Because of that, ___. Because of that, ___. Until finally, ___.

The outline highlights the difference between *news stories* and *narrative stories*. The former lead with the traditional five *W*s (*who*, *what*, *where*, *when*, and *why*). The latter lead with a character and a challenge, present obstacles to build suspense, and leave the ending for, wait for it, the end.

The five-*W* approach works for a boring press release. It's not so effective when 250 people are in an audience waiting for a speaker to say something interesting.

We say, "Pixar the press release."

Next time you see a press release in your inbox with the note "Here's what the boss is announcing," don't just cut and paste the "news" into your speech. Instead, see if you can rewrite it to conform to the Pixar outline.

Don't just describe the policy. Talk about the people the policy helps. Open with one of their stories. Draw in listeners even more by detailing the obstacles they face. Show how whatever you're announcing will make life better.

Journalists do a version of this all the time. That's why you see so many creative and interesting anecdotal leads, even on the front page of the paper.

Speechwriters should do it, too.

You'll be surprised by how applicable Pixar is for compelling speech.

FINAL WORDS

George Shultz, Reagan's secretary of state, liked to talk about the time he showed Reagan a speech that he'd drafted. Reagan said it was "satisfactory." Then he paused and said, "Of course, if I were giving that speech, it would be different. . . . You've written this so it could be read. I talk to people."

Reagan began editing. He made four or five changes, then put a caret in the margin and wrote "story," Schultz recalled. "He had completely changed the tone of my speech."[7]

It is not surprising that people called Reagan the "great communicator." The reason was not how he said things but his insight into what might move people. His speechwriters rarely talked to him, but had the wisdom to find moving stories. Reagan had the wisdom to use them.

Anyone who writes speeches for a living should know how often the stories you use are the only things people remember, and what it's like to see a listener drift off, glance at his watch, or punch furiously at an iPhone—then snap to attention when the speaker tells an anecdote.

We need to remember what Reagan said to Shultz: "I talk to people."

You do, too.

THE SPEECHWRITER'S CHECKLIST: ANECDOTE

- ☐ Have I used anecdote throughout the draft?
- ☐ Do the stories used in the speech support or illustrate a point? Are they believable?
- ☐ Will the stories inspire, entertain, or move this audience?
- ☐ Have I given the stories room to breathe?
- ☐ Do the stories have punch lines?
- ☐ Have I been honest? Did I attribute quotes or lines if necessary? Have I avoided pretending that imagined stories happened to me or my boss?

9

Wit

October 21, 2016.

Less than three weeks before the election and only twenty-four hours after their third debate, Donald Trump and Hillary Clinton share a stage for the final time as candidates for president. It's the Alfred E. Smith Memorial Foundation Dinner, an annual charity fundraiser held at the Waldorf-Astoria hotel in New York. They will each speak.

But, unlike the night before, they won't try to convince voters their policies are best for America. Instead, this long-standing dinner is about which candidate is *funnier*. They're on stage to show they can tell (and take) a joke.

Trump goes first.

> You know, the president told me to stop whining, but I really have to say, the media is even more biased this year than ever before—ever. You want the proof? Michelle Obama gives a speech, and everyone loves it—it's fantastic. They think she's absolutely great. My wife, Melania, gives the exact same speech . . .

The audience explodes in laughter—so much it interrupts the "punch line."

> And people get on her case.

The laughter keeps going. Trump speaks over it, feigning exasperation.

> And I don't get it. I don't know why.

Trump keeps the laughter going with an aside—that he'll be in big trouble with his wife (she sits just a few seats away) when he goes home. He has the listeners right where he wants them.

Until he doesn't.

Not two minutes later, Trump offers a string of jokes about Hillary that crosses the line. "She is pretending," he says, "she doesn't hate Catholics."

The response is worse than "crickets"—the term comedians use when one of their jokes falls flat and is met by silence. There's a sound this dinner crowd has rarely heard.

Boooooo!

He has lost the crowd, and nobody's coming back.

We recall this event because Trump demonstrated the two "golden rules" of political humor. First, be self-deprecating.

American audiences like leaders who take their jobs seriously—but not themselves. Self-deprecation displays modesty and wit without the harshness associated with making fun of others. Humor, after all, can be a powerful weapon. If you want to be safe, aim it at yourself or your own people. In this case, Trump's wife counts because most reporters leveled the plagiarism charge over Melania's speech not at her, but at the campaign.

Self-deprecation also does something else. Jeff Nussbaum, Eric's Humor Cabinet cofounder who offers more insights later in this chapter (see Box 9.1), says that "having the speaker take themselves down a peg or two—it reduces the power and stature gap between the speaker and the audience, which makes the speaker more relatable and, thus, likable."[1]

Landon Parvin has helped Republican speakers be funny, dating back to Ronald Reagan. He puts it another way. While insulting others can get you in the news, it doesn't "help build . . . the larger persona."[2]

Both explanations lead to the second golden rule of political humor—and mantra of the Gridiron Club—that venerable Washington institution known since 1885 for the roasts it hosts twice a year: "singe, don't burn."[3]

Michelle Wolf, who had no reluctance about burning at the 2018 White House Correspondents' Association Dinner, argued that as a hired comedian, she had license to be mean.[4] Audiences rarely grant that license to people in political life. That was certainly the case with Trump; audience members turned on him as soon as they deemed one of his jokes about Hillary Clinton to be a cheap shot or too personal.

There are other reasons for taking a gentler approach. Listeners believe people charged with providing health care and helping the unemployed should be compassionate. Also, politicians need to work together. Years ago, New Jersey senator Jon Corzine jokingly compared sharing a media market with his Senate colleague Chuck Schumer to sharing a banana with a monkey. The line reportedly ruined their relationship. In politics, today's enemy may be tomorrow's ally. Politicians who make a colleague the target of a joke may discover the next day that their target will provide the deciding vote on a bill.

In this chapter, we provide examples that abide by the two rules—be self-deprecating and singe, don't burn. We'll offer tips on how and where to find funny material. But we must first ask about the risk and the reward.

Politicians, after all, don't train to perform stand-up comedy. Like most people, they dread failure. Humor that doesn't work can damage credibility. At the 2004 Radio and Television Correspondents' Association Dinner, President George W. Bush showed a video of himself looking in between the couch cushions for Saddam Hussein's weapons of mass destruction. He drew enormous criticism for making light of a serious situation.

He wasn't the last politician to get bad press for trying to be funny. In 2014, *Politico* labeled Congresswoman Donna Edwards's awkward attempt at humor "the most painful speech ever."[5]

After a headline like that, is it worth taking the risk?

WRITING TO MAKE THEM LAUGH

Our answer begins with the reason we call this chapter "Wit," not "Humor." Even though we often use the two interchangeably, there is a distinction. We can define humor as the quality that makes something amusing. Wit, however, speaks to mental sharpness and intelligence; it's being resourceful or imaginative in amusing ways.[6]

It's an important distinction. An audience might find humor in a politician slipping on a banana peel, but that might not earn a vote. Demonstrating wit, on the other hand, says more than that a speaker is funny. There are many reasons that make it worth the risk—all crucial to effective speech.

Making a Point

Take this joke, told by Barack Obama during his 2011 State of the Union address. The president was citing examples of waste created by federal agencies with similar responsibilities.

> Then there's my favorite example. The Interior Department is in charge of salmon while they're in freshwater, but the Commerce Department handles them when they're in saltwater. [*pause*] I hear it gets even more complicated once they're smoked.

Obama's punch line reinforced the absurdity of overlapping work in the federal government. But it did more. It made people *remember* that point.

In fact, immediately after the speech, NPR surveyed people about what they had just heard.[7] The speech was close to seven thousand words. The one word most people recalled, regardless of political affiliation: *salmon*.

Changing the Pace

The salmon joke served another purpose, too. Placed in the middle of a very long speech, it made people sit up and take notice.

Sometimes, politicians have been ranting for five minutes about the other party, or wading through some heavy State Department boilerplate about the nettlesome issues of trade. They sense the audience needs variety. They pause. Take a drink of water. Smile to themselves, as if they've just remembered something. And tell a joke.

Listeners need that. Constant hectoring loses its force after a while, even for friendly audiences.

There are other reasons to change pace. Speakers may be approaching a moment where they really want people, including members of the media, to pay attention. They want to alert them that something big is coming. That's what President John F. Kennedy did in his famous speech at Rice University in September 1962, announcing that the United States would send astronauts to the moon.

> But why, some say, the moon? Why choose this as our goal? And they may well ask why climb the highest mountain? Why, thirty-five years ago, fly the Atlantic? Why does Rice play Texas?

Why compare a moon landing with the futility of Rice playing college football powerhouse Texas? Because it both let the audience believe he knew about Rice—and defused the solemnity of speechwriter Ted Sorensen's next line:

> We choose to go to the moon in this decade and do the other things, not because they are easy, but because they are hard . . .

That joke, a change of pace, made the audience laugh so hard that JFK had to restart his "We choose" line over three times. He still came across as serious, but not so serious he couldn't wryly acknowledge the possibility of failure.

Granting Permission (To Say What You Otherwise Can't)

After Donald Trump, it was Hillary Clinton's turn at the Al Smith Dinner. She started with a barb about Trump, who had given a widely publicized interview to Howard Stern where he ranked women with numbers based on appearance.

Clinton's response:

> It's always a special treat for me to be back in New York.
> People look at the Statue of Liberty, and they see a proud symbol of our history as a nation of immigrants, a beacon of hope for people around the world. Donald looks at the Statue of Liberty and sees a "four."
> Maybe a "five" if she loses the torch and tablet and changes her hair.
> You know, come to think of it, you know what would be a good number for a woman? Forty-five.

Some may have deemed that joke too harsh, while others believed Clinton was only firing back. Trump did go first and burned her. She must have been worried, though. In case listeners did disapprove, her joke writers (including one of the authors) had armed Clinton with these two lines allowing her to poke fun at herself:

> But I digress. Now, I'm going to try my best tonight, but I understand I am not known for my sense of humor. That's why it did take a village to write these jokes.

> People say—and I hear them, I know—they say I'm boring compared to Donald. But I'm not boring at all. In fact, I'm the life of every party I attend. I've been to three.

Usually, jokes for these events come from writers. While it's unlikely that they know (and why should they?), both Trump and Clinton have used jokes that work in a way well known to comedy theorists: incongruity.

That's what the novelist Arthur Koestler described in *The Act of Creation*—making audiences laugh by linking two seemingly incompatible frames of reference.[8] In Trump's case, it was Melania's plagiarism and Trump's belief in media bias. For Clinton, it was the Statue of Liberty and Trump's view of women.

The surprise made acceptable something most politicians might prefer not to say outright—that Trump understood his attacks on the press were intended to get more press, and Clinton understood that her opponent was a chauvinist.

Diffusing a Situation

Again, we can look to the partnership of John F. Kennedy and Ted Sorenson. As Kennedy was preparing to run for president, some critics called him a lightweight—or, worse, the pawn his father would use to gain the White House. Reporters wrote about how Joe Kennedy was bankrolling JFK's campaign.

JFK might have responded with anger. Instead, at the 1958 Winter Gridiron Dinner, before anyone could mention it, Kennedy pulled a telegram out of his pocket.

> I just received the following wire from my generous daddy. "Dear Jack, don't buy a single vote more than is necessary. I'll be damned if I'm going to pay for a landslide."

His implied message: "I know what you're thinking. But if I'm willing to laugh at it, how serious can it be?" He diffused the issue—and relieved the natural tension that can exist between speaker and audience when something is unsaid.

Kennedy wasn't the first or last to use humor that way. In 1984, President Reagan, then roughly the same age as Bernie Sanders was in 2016, used the same strategy to deflect the questions of his age and competence while running for reelection against Walter Mondale. Anticipating the question during a debate, he said,

> I will not make age an issue of this campaign. I am not going to exploit for political purposes my opponent's youth and inexperience.

The audience roared. Mondale would later tell moderator Jim Lehrer, "If TV can tell the truth, as you say it can, you will see that I was smiling, but I think if you come in close, you'll see some tears coming down because I knew he had gotten me there."[9]

Characterizing the Speaker

Ultimately, and most importantly, wit *characterizes* a speaker. American audiences aren't looking for a comedian-in-chief. They do, though, like speakers with a sense of humor. And *like* is the operative word. Awhile back, the British comedian Ricky Gervais talked about the difference between British and American humor. Pointing to the changes producers made in the American version of *The Office*, he argued that Americans need less nasty comedy than the British. "Network America," he said, "has to give people a reason to like you—not just a reason to watch you."[10]

And that is why, even in the all-important final days of the presidential campaign, Donald Trump and Hillary Clinton sacrificed an entire evening to sit only a few feet apart, take aim with their best material—and, just as important, force a smile when they were the target.

AS DELIVERED

Trump and Clinton at the 2016 Alfred E. Smith Memorial Foundation Dinner. Look at the entire speech for both candidates. How do they soften the barbs they toss at each other? Among the kinds of wit we examine—one-liners, puns, hyperbole, irony—how many can you find?

www.youtube.com/watch?v=b9n7g8rTiaY

To be sure, Trump's most fervent supporters enjoyed their candidate's no-holds-barred routine, including the use of irony to "say something nice" about Hillary Clinton.

> Hillary has been in Washington a long time. She knows a lot about how government works. And according to her sworn testimony, Hillary has forgotten more things than most of us will ever, ever, ever know . . .

They might even argue it worked. He did win.

But listen for the moments where the audience laughed most. When Trump makes fun of his inability to be, of all things, self-deprecating ("People tell me that modesty is perhaps my best quality"), he is on steadier ground, as is Clinton when she makes fun of the money she made on the speaking circuit ("Usually I charge a lot for speeches like this").

In each of these instances, the speaker comes across as not only self-aware but nice.

Once we establish that humor, or wit, serves many purposes, the next question becomes obvious.

HOW TO DO IT

Sometimes, speakers or their speechwriters despair of their ability to provide this element of speech—even when they know it's what the audience wants.

How, they ask, do comedy writers make up jokes? Here are a few methods they—and Eric—use often. We break them down into process and formula.

The Process

Clustering

It is a staple for those who study creative and/or sketch writing. Clustering allows essayists, or even poets, to explore a lot of ideas before they have a firm concept by brainstorming a word, person, or place, and then listing associations. The idea is to uncover similarity (*The internet gives us a new audience—as did the printing press*). The process for joke writing is much the same with an important distinction.

With humor, the laugh often comes from the surprise of something being out of place.

Imagine, for example, Hillary Clinton's writers preparing for the Al Smith Dinner. They make a list of things commonly associated with New York, where the event takes place—like the Statue of Liberty.

Now imagine them making a list of qualities associated with Donald Trump—say, the way he talks about women. Can you see how these two lists might make comedy writers ask, "Hey! What about a joke where we assume Trump rates all women, including one made of copper 130 years ago?"

That is pretty close to how the process went.

If this is true, what else is true?

"It takes more than three weeks," Mark Twain reportedly said, "to prepare a good impromptu speech."[11]

Brian Agler, whose duties include writing at the speechwriting firm West Wing Writers—and whose hobbies include comedy writing and performing—suggests it works the other way around, too. Improvisation, he says, helps prepare good speeches.[12] Specifically, he cites the Upright Citizens Brigade, a group that has been providing improv comedy from coast to coast for decades. The performers' motto is what they believe is the root of comedy: *Si Haec Insolita Res Vera Est, Quid Exinde Verum Est?* Translation: "If this unusual thing is true, what else is true?"[13]

Using the shorthand "if, then" construct, we start with a known truth or premise and carry it out to its most absurd and exaggerated end. Think about the famous Abbott and Costello bit. *If* the first baseman's name is "Who," *then* what else must be true? Well, the second baseman's name must be "What."

Naturally.

A great example of how that works in politics comes—once again—from the Al Smith Dinner, but this one from Mitt Romney in 2012. Dressed in the traditional attire of white tie and tails, and surrounded by an audience in the same formal attire, Romney said,

A campaign can require a lot of wardrobe changes . . . blue jeans in the morning perhaps, a suit for a lunch fundraiser, sport coat for dinner, but it's nice to finally relax and to wear what Ann and I wear around the house.

If it is true that the Romneys are not just wealthy but super-rich, then it must be true that he wears a tuxedo while relaxing at home.

Former Supreme Court Justice Sandra Day O'Connor also applied the "if, then" joke construct in 2011 at the Alfalfa Club—an exclusive Washington organization that exists only for its annual, off-the-record dinner.

What did she and her gag writers know? The Alfalfa Club's members are mostly old and male, and O'Connor was to be the club's first woman president. So what else could be true? You can find the entire script in the Appendix, but here is one answer:

Today, Alfalfa has gone from an old boys' club . . . to a really old girls' club.

Only at the Alfalfa Club can you simultaneously shatter a glass ceiling . . . and your hip.

Justice O'Connor succeeds by using the "if, then" construct to mix self-deprecation with poking fun at the self-important.

And now we move to one more "process," a way that wit differs from every other element in effective political speech.

Borrowing

In politics, you don't have to make jokes up; you can borrow them.

This approach to humor is completely bipartisan. Here, for example, is a joke popular among Democrats in 2007:

President Bush is out jogging one day, and doesn't notice a bus barreling right toward him. Three boys jump off the sidewalk and push him out of the way, saving his life.

Bush is grateful. "I'm president of the United States," he tells the kids. "You saved my life. I'd like to reward you. What can I give you? Anything at all!"

The kids huddle. One says, "We'd like three plots in Arlington Cemetery."

Bush says, "Funeral plots? Why?"

"We're Democrats. When our dads find out what we did—they'll kill us!"

One of the authors first used that joke in 1988. It was old even then. The same is true of a line that became a staple of the late John McCain's speeches. "Some people ask me how I felt after losing to Barack Obama," he would say. "I've been sleeping like a baby. Sleep two hours, wake up and cry."[14]

No one knows who invented these jokes, but no one expects a source either—and they still work.

Even if you can't invent a joke to save your life, there are many ways to find humor, and many different kinds. There are the arcane literary stories for use on college campuses, like this one about the author of *Gulliver's Travels*, Jonathan Swift—more quote than narrative—from John F. Kennedy's commencement speech at Syracuse University in 1957:

> Dean Swift regarded Oxford . . . as truly a great seat of learning: for all freshmen were required to bring some learning with them in order to meet the standards of admission—but no senior, when he left the university, ever took any learning away; and thus it steadily accumulated.

There are animal stories, campaign stories, sarcastic stories for partisan events, and rueful stories for people who have lost campaigns. Where to find them? Amazon has so many joke books you could go broke buying them. Are most of the jokes useless? Of course. But if you find one joke in a book and use it again and again, you've spent your money wisely. Websites—especially of the late-night talk shows—are useful because they are timely. To say "Stephen Colbert said last night" sends a couple of signals to an audience. First, it says that the speaker recognizes something as funny. Second, rather than implying that a speaker needs to rely on someone else's wit to get attention, it tells the audience to get ready—a joke lies ahead. The speaker gets credit and the laugh. Just make sure you cite the source.

Finally, listen to other political speeches. The jokes in them have the advantage of already being scrubbed for political life. Chances are, they were stolen from someplace else.

FORMULAS

As you explore the wide variety of jokes available online or in books, you will begin to see the formulas behind them. You will also find humor writers who dispute the value of formulas. Of course, formulas cannot ensure success any more than recipes guarantee a good meal. But we still use cookbooks. And here we include three of the formulas writers have used in politics.

The Definition Joke

Hillary Clinton at the Al Smith Dinner:

This dinner brings together a collection of sensible, committed, mainstream Republicans—or, as we now like to call them, Hillary supporters.

The Rule of Three (a rabbi, a priest, and a minister walk into a bar)

Joe Biden during a 2008 debate of Democratic candidates for president:

There's only three things he [Rudy Giuliani] needs in a sentence—a noun, a verb, and 9/11.

Mike Pence comparing himself to Donald Trump at the Conservative Political Action Conference in 2017:

You know, (1) I'm a small-town guy. He's big city. (2) I'm Midwest. He's Manhattan Island. (3) He's known for his bigger than life personality, his charm, and his charisma. And I'm, like, not.

Barack Obama, in 2011, roasting Donald Trump (as an important side note, a few pundits and witnesses believe that Trump's public humiliation played a part in his deciding to run for president a few years later)[15]:

Now, I know that he's taken some flak lately, but no one is happier, no one is prouder to put this birth certificate matter to rest than the Donald. (1) And that's because he can finally get back to focusing on the issues that matter—like, did we fake the moon landing? (2) What really happened in Roswell? (3) And where are Biggie and Tupac? (3)

The Acronym Joke

FEMA—For Emergencies Must Avoid

EPA—Essentially Powerless Agency

Readers should give all of these a try. You might surprise yourself.

TYPES AND TIPS

Finally, we examine the varied number of joke types you will see in political life along with some tips on how to use them.

Quips

These are the asides, sometimes just a sentence fragment long and often delivered as being spontaneous. The aim is to get a mild chuckle. In this example from her 2016 convention speech, Hillary Clinton uses a technique discussed in Chapter 7 (same word, different meaning) to zing Donald Trump about the convention speech he delivered:

> He spoke for seventy-odd minutes . . . and I do mean odd.

One-Liners

Longer than quips, often carefully worked out, designed to be quoted—and not always original. This Ronald Reagan one-liner, from a 1983 speech in New York, is so old he doesn't need to cite a source. Note the strategic value of it. Reagan not only makes the audience laugh but shows that he is skeptical about the ways of Washington, a stance that characterized his entire career:

> I've learned in Washington that that's the only place where sound travels faster than light.

Vice President Mike Pence uses the same technique in this excerpt from his stump speech, describing the need for simpler taxes:

> The tax code is ten times longer than the Bible, without the good news.

Deploying this oldie but goodie is a win-win for Pence. It reaffirms a popular policy position among his base voters. It also characterizes the vice president as someone like the devout audiences he often addresses.

Pop Culture

While they don't always pass the test of time, references to popular culture serve two purposes. First, because of their water cooler prominence, audiences are likely to understand immediately and be "in" on the joke. Second, citing popular culture is another way for politicians to show that they are not only people, too, but hip.

The example below is from the 2014 White House Correspondents' Association Dinner. Barack Obama tells a joke that surprises the audience even though it touches on well-established themes—the president's race and the embattled Speaker of the House's permanent and faux-looking tan. The punch line, of course, is the name of a critically acclaimed television show.

> I'm feeling sorry, believe it or not, for the Speaker of the House as well. These days, the House Republicans actually give John Boehner a harder time than they give me, which means . . . orange really is the new black!

Story-Jokes

In recent years, story-jokes seem to have fallen out of favor in politics. Speakers tend to prefer jokes that get to the point faster and fit in a tweet. Still, these can poke fun at someone or make a point relevant to the speech. They can be long or, like the one below, very short.

> A few nights ago, a thief snuck up behind a man who was about to get into his car.
> The thief had his hand in his pocket as if he had a gun. He said, "Give me your money."
> The man, shocked by the sudden attack, said, "You can't do this. I'm a member of Congress!"
> The thief said, "In that case, give me *my* money!"

It's a popular joke because it plays into the commonly held belief that there is too much government waste and corruption and that the real thieves are in Washington, D.C.

Hyperbole

We've already seen hyperbole in Mike Huckabee's 2008 convention speech. Here's one that doesn't use pop culture. Unlike his earlier joke, George W. Bush's target is his mother, known for being a parent who spoke her mind. But he pokes fun with a light touch (*singe, don't burn*), and the implication that he may be a little intimidated (*self-deprecating*). Either way, the speech was perfectly attuned to this YMCA picnic audience in 2001, making listeners laugh after both the second and third lines:

Part of respect is to respect your mom and dad. So to the campers here, my advice is, listen to your mother.

In my case, I don't have any choice.

Understatement

In Chapter 7, we looked at how George W. Bush used understatement to make a serious point about terrorists vivid and memorable. Here, in his 2012 Democratic National Convention keynote speech, Julián Castro uses the same device to show Republican Mitt Romney as out of touch because most people can't loan their children tens of thousands of dollars.

> Mitt Romney, quite simply, doesn't get it. A few months ago, he visited a university in Ohio and gave the students there a little entrepreneurial advice. "Start a business," he said.
>
> But how? "Borrow money if you have to from your parents," he told them.
>
> Gee, why didn't I think of that?

In this chapter's interview with Jeff Nussbaum (Box 9.1), you can see how the joke came to be.

BOX 9.1

EXPERTS TALK: JEFF NUSSBAUM

Whenever Vice President Al Gore needed jokes for a speech or a roast, he'd bellow, "Assemble the humor cabinet!" Inspired by that, two of his former writers, Eric Schnure and Jeff Nussbaum, created a business by the same name. Since then, Jeff has become one of the most accomplished and sought-after speechwriters in the country.

In the fall of 2018, Eric sat down to interview Jeff Nussbaum, now also a partner at West Wing Writers.

With using humor in speeches, what is the biggest challenge not just for writers but also for speakers?

When speechwriters write humor, they're not writing humor for stand-up comedians. Or an HBO special. They're writing for a different kind of audience. So much of what works is the element of surprise, topicality. Walking up to a line without crossing over it. Getting that right is almost a bigger challenge than getting the joke structure and the punch line.

We often hear: *My bosses won't use humor. My boss isn't funny. I'm not funny.* Is the fear of failure about fear people won't laugh, or is it something else? Like, maybe a joke will come back to bite them?

Two things. Fear of crickets and failure—even though you get credit for just trying to be funny. You get credit for telling a dad joke. You get credit for saying I saw this funny thing the other day.

I also think it's wanting to be safe. How many times does someone say "I want to be funny," and then they're shown jokes that you believe are safe, and they say "I can't say that." Humor triggers that more than anything else.

My rule on jokes is: Does one out of three people think it's funny? Because when one out of three people laughs, people next to them will laugh. It'll feel like the whole room is laughing.

And yet there are times they don't want to be safe. They want to attack. How do you convince a speaker it's better to go soft?

So much political humor now is point scoring. But the ultimate goal is to be liked, even more than making your opponent unliked.

It's sort of first principles. Be liked more than the other person. The right kind of humor can help you do that.

Are roasts still useful?

There is historical usefulness. It shows that in a democracy, politicians can poke fun at their opponents. The press can poke fun at politicians. Politicians can poke fun at the press. I still think that's really valuable.

But I do think these things are losing their utility.

Think about the end of these speeches, where you traditionally would say something patriotic or bipartisan. It almost has no meaning any more, because no one pays attention to it.

I wrote the serious close [to one Al Smith speech]. I kind of hoped that would become the news story. It didn't. Because people listen for insult humor.

What's your approach with an assignment like writing humor for Sandra Day O'Connor?

It starts with identifying things about the speaker *and* audience. What's funny, relevant, and topical about the speaker? How does that relate to this specific audience?

I ask: What insightful, funny things can only this speaker say? Then you kind of match that up with who is in the audience. What does this audience represent collectively? What's their perception of themselves? What's the broader perception of them? Because finding those disconnects is finding the humor.

Take the link between breaking glass ceilings and your hip. We could do that because the audience is old. And they're men. Just those facts were enough. Then you add the speaker being not particularly young and a woman.

(Continued)

(Continued)

Also, O'Connor was a little different. It almost didn't matter what was topical. She was such an iconic individual in that room, everything became relevant.

And that made us think a little about our approach. I mean, I had played basketball in the Supreme Court gym. But I'd never been in chambers. You hadn't either, right?!

But being in this sort of solemn sanctum! Immediately, I started looking at our draft in different ways. She walked in and offered us soup—remember that?—and all I'm thinking is: We're about to pitch the "couple of boobs" joke!

And a drinking joke. And the "I'm so old I broke my hip" joke.

And jokes about what would Sandra Day O'Connor do.

When we first started brainstorming, we went into our joke writing process knowing she was such a trailblazer. The first of firsts. How do we account for that humorously? The humorous concept was just that—there is no comparison. She couldn't ask what would Jesus do. The joke became "What would Sandra Day O'Connor do?" We thought Sandra Day O'Connor repeatedly asking what Sandra Day O'Connor would do in such a circumstance was funny. And it worked.

Sitting in her chambers waiting to pitch that joke, we weren't so sure! I mean, long before Brett Kavanaugh came along, I thought we were the ones who were going to damage the reputation of the Supreme Court!

But giving people choices is all part of the process, right?

Exactly. In the first meeting with people, they tell you what they want. But because they're not joke writers, what they want doesn't really reflect what you need. You want to write your initial round of jokes uninhibited by their expectations. Once someone tells you what they want, you're painting on a pretty narrowly circumscribed canvas.

There are lots of people who come into these processes, and they're maddening. They say I have a setup. Writing a setup is easy. When someone says "I have a setup," that limits what you can do with the punch line. It's best to put everything out there before you meet with anyone.

I'm not sure we would have thought of the "couple of boobs" joke had we been limited by someone else's setup. Of course, that's not to say she accepted everything we did. We had a joke about the football player John Riggins. She rejected that.

NOTE: There was a much-publicized Washington dinner in 1985 where O'Connor and Riggins sat at the same table. The former Redskins star reportedly got drunk, told the Supreme Court justice to "loosen up, Sandy," and then passed out on the floor. (See the Appendix for the full text of O'Connor's speech, including the "couple of boobs" joke.)

I think she thought that was *punching down*.

Yeah, that's right. Or that maybe our joke wasn't that funny.

Always a possibility! Speaking of that, can you tell us about the editing process for a joke?

It's not that different from other writing. We tell our young writers constantly, you don't have to overwrite. Don't overexplain. Less is more. But we're all guilty of that.

Like the joke in Julián Castro's 2012 convention speech. On the trail, a college kid had asked Romney what he should do after he graduates. Romney said, "Start a business." The kid says, "How?" And Romney says, literally, "Borrow some money from your parents."

We knew we were going to use it. We came up with about ten lines. "Mr. Romney, I couldn't do that. My mother made less each year than you spend on care and feeding for your horse."

"When I walked into my kitchen, I didn't see the CEO of American Motors. I saw a woman just scraping by on twenty grand a year."

We had the thoughtful response. The snarky response. The attack response. Ultimately, we realized you don't need to overwrite it. Romney saying "borrow it from your parents" got the laugh. Why step on that?

Castro's punch line was just: "Gee, why didn't I think of that?" Seven words to make people see Romney was out of touch. But it took us awhile.

It's using understatement to get a laugh *and* make a point. Is that something you do consciously?

Yes, because it surprises people. A lot of humor comes from surprise, when people hear a line that arrives in context but when they don't expect it. That's why I like putting jokes in the middle of a speech, not just the beginning. At the beginning of a speech, you're doing it to be liked. When you use it to hammer home a serious point, that surprise is really effective. And since it's done with a smile, it doesn't make you less likable in the process.

What else does humor accomplish?

Well, it can help you deal with controversies. I did a joke for Obama at one of the correspondents' dinners. There were two mini-scandals happening together. Really mini-scandals compared to today. Michelle Obama went sleeveless, which the First Lady hadn't done before. And then, there was the Air Force One flyover of Manhattan.

I wrote a two-joke run, and Obama actually used it. The first was something like "Michelle brought Republicans and Democrats together because we all believe Michelle should have the right to bare arms." Then he said his kids weren't there that night "because I don't care whose kids you are, you can't take Air Force One on a joy ride to Manhattan."

Nobody really talked about the controversies after that.

We know doing those things with a smile is powerful. Can you think of a time when it worked against someone you worked for?

I remember George W. Bush's 2000 convention speech. Gore was saying everything about Bush was a "risky scheme." Bush said, if Gore had been there for the moon mission, it would have been a risky antigravity scheme. If he were there when the light bulb was invented, it would have been a risky anticandle scheme. If Gore had been there when the internet was invented . . . *Oh wait . . .*

Talk about understatement. Bush didn't have to say anything else. It was brutal. Gore didn't use "risky scheme" again for the entire campaign.

(Continued)

> (Continued)
>
> **Let me step back and finish with a question people ask me: When did you know you were funny?**
>
> Great question. I think it's more realizing I could be funny somewhat productively. Remember, we were all doing this before Twitter. You couldn't tweet a snappy one-liner. But for my whole life I'd been making barbed observations about politics. When I got into politics, I realized, "Oh, if I modify these, you know, by a couple clicks, these are things politicians can say."
>
> **And *do* say. That's fulfilling, right?**
>
> Yes, your own snarky observations modified for someone else—they can, actually, serve a goal. Help a cause you believe in.

Irony

A speaker often makes ironic remarks solemnly. Audiences laugh once the real meaning sinks in. In 2008, moderate and right-wing candidates had divided the Republican Party. Governor Mike Huckabee resented reporters who criticized this division, and so did his audience at the 2008 Republican National Convention. So Huckabee uses irony. He pretends to hold the opposite of his view, gratitude, to drive home what the audience knows is his real one.

> I'd like to thank the elite media for doing something that, quite frankly, I wasn't sure could be done, and that's unifying the Republican Party and all of America in support of Senator McCain and Governor Palin.

Analogy

There is more about analogy in the next chapter, as it has its uses in supporting serious points. But it is also a staple of comedy. Republican senator S. I. Hayakawa's analogy to rescue efforts has survived for decades in the speeches of other politicians. Here it is in two versions: the first from Texas senator Lloyd Bentsen on the Senate floor in 1990; the second from Wisconsin representative David Obey, criticizing a 2006 labor bill on the House floor. Both versions demonstrate how you can tailor jokes to the time you have:

BENTSEN: Most of us remember our former colleague Senator Hayakawa's way of summing up the difference between Democrats and Republicans. If Republicans saw a drowning man fifty feet from shore [he said], they'd throw [him] a thirty-foot rope and tell him swimming the rest would build character.

OBEY: Democrats would throw a hundred-foot rope—then walk away looking for other good deeds.

Puns

At the 2009 White House Correspondents' Association Dinner, Barack Obama used his acknowledgment of the First Lady as an opportunity to address, and ultimately quash, a brewing controversy—that Michelle Obama posed in a sleeveless dress for her first official White House photo.

Michelle Obama is here, the First Lady of the United States. She's even begun to bridge the differences that have divided us for so long, because no matter which party you belong to, we can all agree that Michelle has the right to bare arms.

Quotes

The world has gone through centuries in which people have tried to be funny. Some were pretty good at it—like Voltaire, Mark Twain, Winston Churchill, and Bob Hope. And people have made money by compiling these lines in big books in which you can find your very point made with more wit than you can supply, especially during the hectic routine of drafting a political speech.

Quotes can amuse the audience; show that speakers have a literary background, which is not always an advantage; and make your point memorable, as in this rueful and well-known story Adlai Stevenson used after losing his 1952 race for president against Dwight Eisenhower:

Someone asked, as I came in, down on the street, how I felt, and I was reminded of a story that a fellow townsman of ours used to tell—Abraham Lincoln. They asked him how he felt once after an unsuccessful election. He said he felt like a little boy who had stubbed his toe in the dark. He said that he was too old to cry, but it hurt too much to laugh.

BOX 9.2
EXERCISE: THE LATE-NIGHT LAUGH TEST

Here's an exercise created for the classroom but perfect for pros.

Once we introduce processes like clustering and the "if, then" construct, we ask students in our American University class to break into pairs. We tell them to pretend they are writers for their favorite late-night show, and we give them fifteen minutes to write three jokes the host could use in that night's monologue.

Students often groan. "But I'm not funny like that," they say, and "Do we really have to read this aloud to the entire class?" (They do, but our rule is everyone applauds.)

Every year, they amaze themselves and each other with truly creative lines, funny associations that no one saw coming.

But the real surprise is what happens after class, which ends just before 11:00 p.m.

Students go back to their dorms to watch Trevor Noah, Samantha Bee, or Stephen Colbert. And then they email us immediately.

"Professor, did you watch *The Tonight Show*?" They used Miguel's exact same joke!"

It's happened more than once, and it can happen to you. But only if you reject the false premise that you can't write original jokes.

Once you do, see what you come up with. They won't all be winners. Like a photographer, you might take a hundred pictures and keep only one. But share that one with your colleagues. And then, see if it works in a draft you'll deliver to the boss.

Reviewing the types of humor politicians use to demonstrate their wit—there are others, naturally—doesn't tell you how to use them. That's for later in the book. But no matter your purpose or what kind of humor you use, four tips just about always apply.

Use It Throughout

Politicians shouldn't reserve wit for roasts. It's useful in every speech—and every part of a speech. Speakers who open with a joke, then ignore humor for the rest of their speech, seem both obvious and clumsy. It's as if they say, *Okay, I've shown you I can be funny. Don't have to do that anymore.* More important, they ignore a powerful tool that has many uses. Jokes are appropriate at every stage in a speech, including as supporting evidence and even, as we shall see, for the very last line.

Use It with On-Ramps and Off-Ramps

Even if your main goal is to change pace, wit shouldn't appear jammed into a speech. Make it relevant. Audiences will remember the joke—and the point it illustrates. Craft on-ramps and off-ramps, the transitions before and after the joke, with care.

When Senator Joe Lieberman accepted Al Gore's nomination for vice president, he told this story-joke:

> Reminds me of the story about the taxidermist and the veterinarian, who went into business together. They put up a sign saying "Either way you get your dog back."

This joke has been a staple of Republican and Democratic speeches for years. First, there's an edge to it. Second, it fits nicely into a point politicians love to make, which is that it does make a difference how you vote, or what party is in power.

Usually, the on-ramp for this joke is something like "There are those who say there's no difference between Democrats and Republicans." The off-ramp might be "Of course, there is a difference!"

Use It with Taste

There are those who make fun of politicians because, with some exceptions, their jokes are bland. It's true. Raunchy, sexist, or racist jokes are inappropriate for speeches, precisely because characterization is so important.

When Joe Biden was caught on a live mic congratulating President Obama on the Affordable Care Act because it was a "BFD," it created a furor among people who might never object to such language in their own conversations.[16]

In political speech, you must amuse a broad audience, not offend it. Audiences for Chris Rock or Sarah Silverman attend *because* they find them funny. That's not the crowd at a church pancake breakfast.

Use—and Reuse

Sometimes politicians—or their staff—demand new jokes for each speech. *We did that already,* they'll say disdainfully. That's a mistake. Political speakers do need some new material tailored to the event—and there are certainly jokes about current events that have a shelf life of only a few days. But most audiences rarely hear a political speaker; the jokes that bore the speaker and his staff are new to them.

FINAL WORDS

The comedian David Brenner once confessed that he never used a line on *The Tonight Show* unless he'd had it in his act for at least six months. A lot has changed with late-night TV, but the lesson endures. If it takes a professional comedian six months to perfect his timing, inflection, and language, why should a politician think he or she can do it in ten minutes? Politicians constantly on the prowl for new jokes run the risk of stumbling over punch lines, and defeating the very purpose they want to accomplish.

We opened this chapter by calling humor a weapon. Like hand grenades, jokes can win a battle—but they can also explode in your hand. In politics, you can't always say publicly what you would say in private. This makes politicians no different from anybody else who has to swallow an urge to tell off a boss, a parent, a spouse, or an exasperating child.

But sometimes—sometimes—humor allows you to admit truth you can admit in no other way. Mo Udall, still essential reading for political speechwriters, would sometimes end speeches to trade associations with this line: "Well, them's my views. And if you don't like 'em—I'll change 'em."[17]

Udall was always notably unwilling to change any of his views. But by including himself as a participant, he could satirize one of the least savory aspects of politics without offending listeners. Even an audience that devoutly hoped he would change his views could give him credit for wit.

Udall's kind of wit teaches a valuable lesson. His jokes were rarely original, never offensive, and usually funny, and invariably made a serious point. They helped him stay popular during a long career.

THE SPEECHWRITER'S CHECKLIST: WIT

- ☐ Have I followed the political humor rule of thumb: singe, don't burn?
- ☐ Have I given the speaker an opportunity for self-deprecatory humor?
- ☐ Have I avoided offending or insulting listeners?
- ☐ Will the jokes play well in both the room and tomorrow's papers?
- ☐ Do they make a point?
- ☐ Do my off-ramps make those points clearer?
- ☐ Do I use humor throughout?
- ☐ Do I use new jokes only if the speaker practices?

CHAPTER

10

Support

About two weeks after the 2004 elections, while Americans were still debating the results, a Food and Drug Administration scientist named David Graham took his place in front of the Senate Finance Committee and set off a debate about an entirely different set of numbers.

Those concerned Vioxx, Merck's popular anti-inflammatory drug, which by 2004 had been prescribed for over eighty million patients around the world. Graham told the committee that people using Vioxx instead of other drugs were four times as likely to suffer heart attacks and strokes. Did that mean Americans actually had those heart attacks and strokes?

"From 88,000 to 139,000 Americans," said the meticulous Graham. "Of these, 30 to 40 percent probably died."[1]

Those numbers might have been alarming enough. But Graham had also come armed with some eye-popping analogies, including one aimed at the committee chair, Sen. Chuck Grassley (R-IA):

> How many people is one hundred thousand? For Iowa it would be 5 percent; for Maine, 10 percent; for Wyoming, 27 percent. I'm sorry to say, Senator Grassley, but 67 percent of the citizens of Des Moines would be affected, and what's worse, the entire population of every other city in the state of Iowa.

Then Graham used another way to put things in perspective:

> Imagine that instead of a widely used prescription drug, we were talking about jetliners [with] an average of 150 to 200 people on an aircraft. This would be the rough equivalent of 500 to 900 aircraft

dropping from the sky ... 204 aircraft every week, week in and week out, for the past five years. If you were confronted by this situation ... what would you do about it?[2]

Thousands of people testify each year, in Washington and in state capitols across the country. They rarely make news, but Graham did. He had given the senators not only a clinic in the dangers of a popular drug, but also a lesson in how to persuade.

So far, this book has examined ways to reach listeners through understandable and memorable language, anecdote, and humor. When we focus on the more rational side of persuasion, our best ally is evidence. We start with a look at what it is and how to use it.

USING EVIDENCE

In politics, evidence means the information we use to *support* our points. That is why we call this chapter "Support." And it is central to responsible political speech.

Supporting evidence helps people make better decisions—and better speeches. Using evidence responsibly is essential even if it makes speeches a little less conversational, and harder to grasp. And there's no denying the way speakers in both parties neglect that.

A few caveats, though.

First, speakers don't always support every assertion. What support they need depends in part on the audience. Today, in talking to the Chamber of Commerce, speakers don't need to give an elaborate defense for statements like "Cutting taxes creates jobs." They are preaching to the choir.

Second, even the most careful effort to find evidence and use it responsibly doesn't mean we are right. In 2003, American secretary of state Colin Powell gave a much-publicized speech arguing for the United Nations to act against Saddam Hussein because Iraq possessed "weapons of mass destruction." He certainly used the kinds of evidence we recommend.

But Powell was wrong. Later, claiming he had been misled by intelligence officials, he admitted that failure, calling it a "blot" on his career. Whether misled or not, he seems to have tried to find evidence he thought was sound. Sometimes trying hard isn't enough; even a conscientious effort to use sound evidence doesn't mean we are right.

Finally, there is an obstacle to finding good evidence that derails the most conscientious speaker: the limits posed by our own biases.

Researchers have cataloged the long list of ways bias influences how we decide matters: They include stereotyping groups, believing ideas because our friends believe them, and remembering only facts that confirm our own views. A 2018 study by Gallup and the Knight Foundation, for instance, showed how people were often more trusting of news when the name of the media outlet was hidden.[3] And then, of course, there are the ideas we believe without evidence whatsoever, as we freely admit—"I made a leap of faith," religious people often say.

In a country where about 20 percent of the population believes in astrology and 15 percent believes in Bigfoot, audiences include many people for whom evidence is only part of the picture. Political audiences are no different. These audiences also include people, though, who care deeply about information and take seriously the need to hear what their instincts tell them to resist.

Is it possible to write partisan speeches and avoid the biases shaping our own views, and the evidence we choose? Not if we expect perfection. But by being on guard against our own impulses to believe our side is always right, we can become more persuasive, not less. That means building a case using the varied types of evidence most valuable in political life.

In this chapter, we answer three questions:

What types of evidence can we use to convince listeners?

How do we make that evidence interesting?

How can we argue credibly and responsibly, while avoiding the fallacies common in political speech?

TYPES OF EVIDENCE

A list presenting the kinds of evidence common in political speech is not infinite. There are four: statistics, examples, testimony, and, we argue, analogy, a tool of reasoning using fact.

Statistics

The *New Yorker* once ran a cartoon of a politician examining a speech as his speechwriter stands waiting. "It's vague, noncommittal," the politician says. "I like it!"

People often think political speech is vague. "How do politicians talk so much and say nothing?" someone once asked Quora, the website that answers questions for about three hundred million users each month.

The most popular answer: "The goal has to be as noncommittal and nonspecific as possible."

Actually, it is more likely the reverse: speeches far too cluttered with specifics, especially statistics. It's easy to see why we use statistics, the quantified evidence that summarizes, compares, and predicts.

It seems conclusive—how can you argue with a number?

Besides, politicians are comfortable with statistics. They vote on issues involving billions of dollars and people. How much will a road cost? How many people will use it? For politicians determined to argue with integrity, it is hard to muster a persuasive argument about these issues without some numbers.

To see how both sides use statistics to *summarize*, *compare*, and *predict*, let's return to the 2017 U.S. House of Representatives debate over efforts to repeal and replace the Affordable Care Act, first mentioned in Chapter 5.

Summarize

Rep. Phil Roe (R-TN) on the state of the health care market in Tennessee:

> In my district, in the state of Tennessee, over one-third of the counties have no place they can buy insurance; and multiple counties in my state, including the third largest, have no access. Premiums have soared over 60 percent. Eighteen of the twenty-three co-ops went bankrupt, including one in my state, which required people to search for other coverage . . . In my state, and where I practiced medicine for over thirty years, listen to this: 60 to 70 percent of the uncollectible debt now are people with insurance.

Roe uses statistics only to *summarize* conditions in Tennessee. He simply presents numbers to give us scope. He makes no comparison to other states and no prediction about the future.

Compare

His colleague, Rep. Michael Burgess (R-TX), focuses not on one state, but on three.

> In Texas, premiums have jumped 29 percent a year, on average, from 2014 to 2017 . . .
>
> [W]ithin the state of Illinois, there were eight plans in 2015. There are five plans in 2017 with a 57 percent increase in premiums . . .
>
> [I]n the state of Florida, there were ten insurance plans available in the individual market in 2015, down to five plans in 2017, with a 24 percent premium increase . . .

Burgess uses stats to demonstrate that high premiums are a national problem. He *compares* the way these states in different regions have seen their health care markets change since implementation of the law.

Predict

Finally, we see Rep. John Yarmuth (D-KY) using numbers to contrast, a type of comparison, but ultimately to *predict* which groups would be affected by a repeal of the Affordable Care Act.

In this example, pay particular attention not only to how Yarmouth uses these statistics to bolster his argument, but also how he uses devices from Chapter 7: a rhetorical question, litany antithesis. All combine to make his argument forceful and memorable. Evidence doesn't appear in isolation from the techniques we covered earlier. They work together.

> Mr. Speaker, the question every member of Congress should be asking themselves today is: Who in the world is better off because of today's bill?
>
> It is not the twenty-four million people the CBO [Congressional Budget Office] says will lose their health coverage if this bill becomes law.
>
> It is not the seniors who will be priced out of the market by an age tax or the millions of families who will see their health care gutted by the more than $800 billion in cuts to Medicaid.
>
> It is not the 881,000 nonelderly adults in Kentucky with preexisting conditions who would, once again, face staggering health costs with reduced care.
>
> So who is better off? Well, certainly corporations and millionaires who will see nearly $1 trillion in tax cuts from this bill.

Statistics can indicate the scope of a problem—and the likely effects of a solution. The implicit question from both sides in that debate was "Who will be better off with repeal?" Bitterly divided on the answer, both sides used statistics to compare their ideas with the other side. Generally, listeners approve, too, even as they instantly forget the numbers. *She has numbers*, they think. *She must know what she's talking about.*

Whether listeners remember or not, speechwriters must keep four things in mind, central to arguing ethically. Evidence must be accurate, relevant, and up to date. Writers must also be able to cite a source. Since speeches have time limits, especially in debate or on the floor, political speakers can take shortcuts in attribution. Nobody expects the citations we would see in an academic journal. But you can easily attribute numbers using words like "Harvard researchers say" or "A study of five thousand nurses found." Our practice: When a speech is done, we do an annotated or hyperlinked version including every source. We learned that lesson early, after a few instances where we ignored that step, had reporters call, then struggled frantically through our jumbled notes to find an answer before they filed. It also puts speakers at ease knowing you have a source and citation for what they're about to say.

Examples

Overloading a speech with statistics is a mistake not just because listeners can't absorb all those numbers but because listeners expect more. They want politicians to use concrete detail and to see the human side of problems. Thus the importance of examples—factual support that illustrates, clarifies, or describes, with or without numbers. Examples humanize. As James Joyce once described his writing process: "In the particular is contained the universal."[4]

We explore three kinds of example: brief, extended, and hypothetical or imagined, illustrated with excerpts from more than a half-century of political debate.

Brief

Here is Barry Goldwater at the 1964 Republican National Convention, arguing that the Democrats have failed in foreign policy. Note that while Goldwater's examples are concrete, his language is not neutral. Active verbs like *blot*, *infest*, and *haunt* express his contempt for Democratic policy, illustrated by five examples that take up no more than a few words each:

> Now failure cements the wall of shame in Berlin; failures blot the sands of shame at the Bay of Pigs; failures marked the slow death of freedom in Laos; failures infest the jungles of Vietnam; and failures haunt the houses of our once great alliances and undermine the greatest bulwark ever erected by free nations, the NATO [North Atlantic Treaty Organization] community.

Such a catalog is similar to the montage in film: quick cuts from image to image, persuading by the sheer mass of facts, that the speaker is right.

Extended

Sometimes, speakers need more detail than brief examples can provide.

Extended examples include stories, which we examined in Chapter 8. Stories involve a sequence of events—a narrative question and a plot that keeps the action moving. Extended examples also allow us to illustrate points in ways that deal more generally with character but without the conflict-resolution needs of a story. At the Democratic National Convention in 1984, New York governor Mario Cuomo, while using the word *story*, actually used an extended example to illustrate the virtues of ordinary people—in this example, his father:

> That struggle to live with dignity is the real story of the shining city. And it's a story, ladies and gentlemen, that I didn't read in a book, or learn in a classroom. I saw it and lived it, like many of you. I watched a small man with thick calluses on both his hands work fifteen and sixteen hours a day. I saw him once literally bleed from the bottoms of his feet, a man who came here uneducated, alone, unable to speak the language, who taught me all I needed to know about faith and hard work by the simple eloquence of his example. I learned about our kind of democracy from my father.

Nearly thirty-two years later, at the 2016 Republican National Convention, Ivanka Trump took a similar approach:

> My father has a sense of fairness that touches every conviction he's held. I've worked alongside of him for more than a decade now at the Trump Organization, and I've seen how he operates as a leader, making important decisions that shape careers and that change lives. I've learned a lot about the world from walking construction jobs by his side. On every one of his projects, you'll see him talking to the super, the painter, the engineers, the electricians. He'll ask them for their feedback, if they think something should be done differently, or could be done better. When Donald Trump is in charge, all that counts is ability, effort, and excellence.

Both passages carry the power of character, without the "what happened next" suspense that pulls listeners through. Examples put a human face on an abstraction. They help listeners visualize urgent problems, practical solutions, inspirational events, fears, failures, and fairness.

Hypothetical or Imagined

Most people don't think of made-up examples as a kind of evidence, and it's true that hypotheticals don't carry the full force of facts. But sometimes the perfect real-life example doesn't exist or is hard to find. If speakers pick the right details, an imagined example can still be incredibly powerful. Consider this one from a 2017 speech by Mayor Mitch Landrieu about the decision to take down confederate monuments in New Orleans:

Another friend asked me to consider these four monuments from the perspective of an African American mother or father trying to explain to their fifth-grade daughter who Robert E. Lee is and why he stands atop of our beautiful city.

Can you do it? Can you look into that young girl's eyes and convince her that Robert E. Lee is there to encourage her?

Do you think she will feel inspired and hopeful by that story? Do these monuments help her see a future with limitless potential?

Have you ever thought that if her potential is limited, yours and mine are too?

Why use hypothetical examples? After all, they aren't true. But like good fiction, if writers pick evocative detail, they can spark a shock of recognition in listeners. They think, *That's how it is.*

Of course, any time you use something that's not factual, you need to make that clear to your listeners. Often speakers do this with a word like *imagine*—imagine a world where X happens.

Landrieu, for example, telegraphs that he's starting a hypothetical example with the word *consider*. Without that qualification, you risk fabrication—a charge that has damaged the reputation of both speakers and writers.

Whether hypothetical or real, brief or extended, examples can illustrate problems and inspire solutions. Governor Andrew Cuomo, Mario's son, did this at the 2016 Democratic National Convention, using a litany of brief examples to describe the American community coming together:

> Fifteen years ago on September 11, we saw death and destruction—unimaginable horror and cruelty—but we saw something else, my friends. We saw this nation come together like it had never come together before.
>
> We were not Texans, Californians, or New Yorkers. We weren't Democrats, Republicans, or Independents. We weren't Muslims, Christians, or Jews. We were Americans. We weren't black, or white, or brown—we were red, and white, and blue, and those are the only colors that matter in the United States of America. In that moment, we were one.

Cuomo's Freedom Tower example is long. But litany and the number of examples allowed him to express one theme: America's unity.

Testimony

"It's important to note that this range does not depend at all on the data from our Kaiser-FDA study," scientist David Graham said in the Senate testimony that opened this chapter. "Indeed, Dr. Eric Topol at the Cleveland Clinic recently estimated up to 160,000 cases of heart attacks and strokes due to Vioxx."

Graham didn't just cite numbers. He relied on the opinions or firsthand accounts of others we call testimony.

Earlier, we asked why speakers might want story since many great speeches have none. We might ask the same about expertise. Ronald Reagan didn't quote anyone in his farewell address, nor did Lincoln at Gettysburg.

It would certainly have seemed odd if Lincoln had said: "Now we are engaged in what Ulysses S. Grant describes as a 'great civil war.'" Still, the opinions of others, has been essential for political speakers since Demosthenes.

With good reason. A well-chosen quote can align speakers with the expertise, reputation, or status of the source. If you are quoting an opponent who supports your speaker's side, it can be even more powerful. Quotes from others often convey a point with pithiness and wit hard to match; at other times, they evoke powerful emotions that your paraphrase will not.

Quotes also act as direct evidence that an assertion is true and cement alliances, important for anyone who seeks votes or is simply trying to persuade others.

One House of Representatives debate from July 2017 shows how useful quotes can be for both sides.

The debate covered immigration. On this day, representatives were debating "Kate's Law," which took funding away from sanctuary cities and increased penalties for people who returned to the United States after being deported. During the debate, speakers used quotes in each of the ways described above.

Expertise and Status

> John Adams said that we are a government of laws, not of men. As we approach the Fourth of July week, we recognize that America's foundation is that of the rule of law...
>
> Attorney General Sessions has reiterated that federal law enforcement grants are contingent on compliance with existing law, and that the DOJ [Department of Justice] will deny fiscal year 2017 grant funds to jurisdictions that have refused to share information regarding illegal aliens in their custody.
>
> Rep. Doug Collins (R-GA)

Support from Opponents

> While the previous administration frequently flouted immigration laws and, for far too long, took a rain check on holding sanctuary cities accountable, even former Department of Homeland Security

secretary Jeh Johnson agreed that sanctuary cities shouldn't simply be allowed to decline to cooperate with federal government authorities. In fact, he said in 2015 that it is "not acceptable to have no policy of cooperation with immigration enforcement."

Rep. Chris Collins (R-NY)

Evoking Emotion

I also had the misfortune and fortune of having the Root family as my constituents. Sarah Root was tragically killed by an illegal alien on the streets. Her father, Scott Root, testified before the committee. He said this:

"They bailed the killer of my daughter out of jail for less money than it took to bury her, and he was out of this country before we could have the funeral."

Rep. Steve King (R-IA)

Pith

Instead of a wall, we ought to be building opportunity. As Austin mayor Steve Adler said, "Bridges make money, and walls cost money."

Rep. Lloyd Doggett (D-TX)

Direct Evidence

Earlier this year, a Baltimore City Council member introduced a resolution calling on ICE [U.S. Immigration and Customs Enforcement] to arrest only those posing a "serious risk." In discussing this initiative, the council member likened ICE officers to Nazis several times. Such rhetoric is reprehensible.

Rep. Bob Goodlatte (R-VA)

Cementing Alliances

Citing an expert has more than one use. Here, Rep. Jan Schakowsky (D-IL) quotes a city leader in her district, because of his status with her constituents—and maybe because her public shout-out to the mayor enhances the reputation of a political ally:

In jurisdictions within my district, Cook County, cities like Chicago, Evanston, and Skokie, which are immigrant rich, we have adopted sanctuary cities . . .

Skokie mayor George Van Dusen said, "It has taken the village of Skokie years—decades really—to form the bridges that we have of trust with our immigrant community."

One important reason quotations work: They are real. We have already discussed the temptation in political speech to say "Some say . . . ," then caricature what the other side does say. Direct quotations used accurately have impact in part because they avoid what we later discuss: a "straw man" argument.

Analogy

Analogy—inferences or conclusions drawn from things most people know—is a type of reasoning through comparison. Political speeches use two kinds: literal and figurative. We already examined some in Chapter 7: metaphor, simile, and hyperbole. In all cases, analogy must strike listeners as appropriate to be effective.

During the 2016 campaign, Mike Huckabee, interviewed by Megyn Kelly, analogized Hillary Clinton to the shark in *Jaws*—and Donald Trump to Captain Quint:

> Now, Hillary is the shark. She's going to eat your boat, she's gonna have open borders, immigration out the kazoo. Donald Trump is like Captain Quint in *Jaws*. He's vulgar, he's salty, he might even get drunk . . . But hold on here: He's the guy who's gonna save your butt and save your family. And so, at the end of the day, when he kills the shark, you're happy about it.

Analogies need research and thought. If listeners think you are comparing—to use a classic fallacy—apples and oranges, or if your information is wrong, they backfire.

As did that one. "I hate to be the one to tell you this," Kelly said. "Captain Quint got eaten by the shark."[5]

Done right, though, analogies can make issues instantly clear to listeners. *I never thought of it that way!* Let's look more closely at some examples of both kinds.

The Literal Analogy

Literal analogies directly compare one real-life situation with another. Speakers rightly hope that the audience agrees on one and so will agree about the other. In 1996, commenting on a landmark same-sex marriage trial, Sen. Charles Robb (D-VA) said this:

> Until 1967, sixteen states, including my own state of Virginia, had laws banning couples from different races to marry. When the

law was challenged, Virginia argued that interracial marriages were simply immoral. Today we know that the moral discomfort—even revulsion—that citizens then felt about legalizing interracial marriages did not give them the right to discriminate thirty years ago. Just as discomfort over sexual orientation does not give us the right to discriminate against a class of Americans today.

Robb's analogy doesn't prove his case the way factual evidence does. He hoped that the audience might reason something like this:

- We struck down the ban on interracial marriage.
- The ban on same-sex marriage is similar to the ban on interracial marriage.
- We should strike down the ban on same-sex marriage.

More recently, actor and animator Seth MacFarlane used the same type of literal analogy when he waded into politics. Commenting on the Supreme Court's decision to side with a baker who refused to make a wedding cake for a gay couple, he said,

It's a shorter walk than we think, particularly today, from "I won't bake them a cake because they're gay" to "I won't seat him here because he's black."[6]

Politicians use literal analogy to remind their audience of precedent, citing historical events ("Four score and seven years ago"). They use analogy to clarify arguments by demonstrating similarity, as Robb and MacFarlane did. And they use it to ridicule, as Senator Markey did with his analogy about Godzilla in Chapter 7 or as Huckabee attempted to do with his *Jaws* comparison.

Sometimes politicians use literal analogies not to demonstrate that something is wrong but to inspire their listeners with hope. Here, for example, is Barack Obama ending his 2008 inaugural address:

In the year of America's birth, in the coldest of months, a small band of patriots huddled by dying campfires on the shores of an icy river. The capital was abandoned. The enemy was advancing. The snow was stained with blood. At a moment when the outcome of our revolution was most in doubt, the father of our nation ordered these words be read to the people:

"Let it be told to the future world . . . that in the depth of winter, when nothing but hope and virtue could survive . . . that the city and the country, alarmed at one common danger, came forth to meet [it]."

America, in the face of our common dangers, in this winter of our hardship, let us remember these timeless words. With hope and virtue, let us brave once more the icy currents, and endure what storms may come.

The Figurative Analogy

Figurative analogies compare something real to something imagined; they often begin with "It's as if." One noteworthy example: the rich opening of the 1962 John F. Kennedy speech at Rice University urging the country to support the moon mission and known for its famous passage beginning: "We choose to go to the moon!"

The speech opened with an analogy, asking listeners to use their imaginations: "Condense, if you will, the fifty thousand years of man's recorded history in a time span of but half a century."

We know very little about the first forty years, except at the end of them advanced man had learned to use the skins of animals to cover them. Then about ten years ago, under this standard, man emerged from his caves to construct other kinds of shelter. Only five years ago man learned to write and use a cart with wheels. Christianity began less than two years ago.

By appealing to imagination, JFK and speechwriter Ted Sorenson inspired the audience to believe anything is possible. They also accomplished something else, the point of the next section.

AS DELIVERED

President John F. Kennedy at Rice University. Americans endured the spectre of Russian warheads ninety miles off the Florida coast. Now they also faced the indignity of losing the space race. "Sputnik" was circling the Earth, and in 1961, Yuri Gagarin became the first man in space.

How would Kennedy respond? At Rice University, and with Ted Sorenson's help, the answer was by offering a hopeful view, beginning with the skillful analogy showing the speed and possibility of progress.

www.jfklibrary.org/learn/about-jfk/historic-speeches/address-at-rice-university-on-the-nations-space-effort

MAKING EVIDENCE MEMORABLE

In politics, using evidence does not have to clash with a speechwriter's goals of being compelling, inspiring, and exciting. True, nothing makes some people's eyes glaze over faster than a string of facts or numbers. It is hard to bring an audience to its feet when you must explain an idea in all its nuance. But we just showed examples of how using both testimony and analogy can make evidence compelling.

The key is putting evidence in context.

Usually, *context* means all the information we need to understand an event. We use the word in a slightly different way: providing information or changing a frame of reference to help listeners understand how something, like a statistic or abstraction, is relevant and important.

After all, if listeners cannot grasp why what speakers say is important to them, it is unlikely they will remember it at all.

Let's look at some of the ways context works.

Use Statistics in Context

Statistics have power, but they can as easily confuse as clarify. Three out of every two people, the joke goes, don't understand fractions. And in politics, listeners confused by a statistic often suspect they're being misled. "Facts are stubborn things; statistics are pliable," reads a well-known quip often attributed to Mark Twain.

Even understandable statistics can turn off an audience. Hit people over the head with a barrage of statistics, and you'll see why the word *numbers* begins with *numb*.

One rule that makes all the difference: never provide numbers without showing listeners how to put them into human terms.

Here are some ways that work.

Use Analogy for Context

Speaking in 1998, former surgeon general C. Everett Koop tells a Washington, D.C., audience that five hundred million people around the world will die from smoking by 2025. "That's a numbing figure," he says. "So let me put it in other terms for you."

> That's a Vietnam War every day for twenty-seven years. That's a Bhopal every two hours, for twenty-seven years. That's a *Titanic* every forty-three minutes for twenty-seven years.

If we were to build for those tobacco victims a memorial such as the Vietnam Wall, it would stretch from here one thousand miles across seven states to Kansas City.

And, if you want to put it in terms per minute, there's a death every 1.7 seconds, or about 250 to 300 people since I began to speak to you this afternoon.

Koop's strategy here is similar to the one FDA scientist David Graham used in the testimony about drug-related deaths that opened this chapter. Understanding the numbing effect that statistics can have (Koop even used the word *numbing*), both speakers made shocking analogies to provide contexts with which their audiences would be more familiar.

Note how Koop ignored the "rule of three" limit that speakers often impose. He uses no less than six comparisons in this litany of analogies, lining up smoking deaths side by side with great disasters throughout history and around the globe, with the famous memorial not far from where his listeners are sitting, and finally with what has happened during the time they've sat there listening.

Creating this kind of context requires analysis and imagination. But it's not as hard as you think. Start with a statistic and insert it into this formula:

X is the same as Y.

While not using the three magic words—*the same as*—Koop's analogy made listeners see similarity. By calling two different numbers the "same," we don't mean they are identical, of course. Five hundred million is not identical to a twenty-seven-year-long Vietnam War. But analogy clarifies the impact of those deaths in a way the raw number does not.

Analogy isn't the only way to make audiences sit up by adding context to statistics. We offer three others:

Increase Size—Decrease Space

By "increase size," we mean taking a significant number and reframing it for even more impact. Take a look at this excerpt from a 2015 *New York Times* op-ed by Nicholas Kristof, italicized for emphasis:

It's not just occasional mass shootings like the one at an Oregon college on Thursday, but a continuous deluge of gun deaths, *an average of 92 every day in America. Since 1970, more Americans have died from guns than died in all U.S. wars going back to the American Revolution.* The numbers are unarguable: fewer than

1.4 million war deaths since 1775, more than half in the Civil War, versus about 1.45 million gun deaths since 1970 (including suicides, murders and accidents).[7]

In this first passage, Kristof starts with what is already a large number (ninety-two gun deaths every day since 1970). Then he adds context. He tells readers that number is even larger than the total number of American soldiers who have died fighting for their country in every war since 1775. Is that possible? More deaths than all our wars? By comparing gun deaths to what readers imagine must be the larger number, he has created the effect he wants: shock.

Now he continues:

If that doesn't make you flinch, consider this: In America, *more preschoolers are shot dead each year (82 in 2013) than police officers* are in the line of duty (27 in 2013), according to figures from the Centers for Disease Control and Prevention and the FBI.[8]

In the second paragraph, Kristof doesn't increase the size. Instead, he decreases the space, or closes the gap, between the issue and his audience. The mention of preschoolers makes his topic relevant to everyone. You might not be able to wrap your arms around ninety-two deaths each day or something dating back to the American Revolution. But Kristof has used a second way to make a number memorable—because we all know and can hug a child.

The Power of One

There is yet another way to add context: showing what an issue means for just one person.

Wharton business school professor Deborah Small studied the difference between what she calls "statistical victims" and "identifiable victims." She offered subjects two appeals to donate money to Save the Children.[9]

The first started this way: "Any money that you donate will go to Rokia, a seven-year-old girl who lives in Mali in Africa. Rokia is desperately poor and faces a threat of severe hunger, even starvation."

The second began, "Food shortages in Malawi are affecting more than three million children. In Zambia, severe rainfall deficits have resulted in a 42 percent drop in maize production from 2000."

It probably won't surprise you to learn that the first appeal sparked more contributions than the second. Small wanted to find out *why* appealing to the heart worked better than appealing to the head. Participants responded that they felt more enthusiastic about helping one person, the identifiable victim. They knew they could make a difference for a single person; when it came to three million, they weren't so sure. This ability to relate to one identifiable person is just one of the reasons you see presidents pointing to individuals in the balcony during State of the Union speeches.

The "power of one" device can serve speakers talking about not just people but also money or time.

Take a quick look, for example, at the Centers for Disease Control and Prevention's website and you will learn that, "on average, 130 Americans die every day from an opioid overdose."[10] Politicians from both parties use the stat all the time. Why? For the same reason the CDC distilled the number. Because people might have heard stories about opioid addiction without grasping the full scope of the problem. By using the number for just one day, a time span people can grasp, writers and speakers create a sense of urgency.

The Context of Cost

Context does not always involve numbers. At one of his campaign rallies in 2015, Sen. Bernie Sanders (I-VT) didn't use one at all. Instead, he compared the costs of incarceration to the potential costs of paying for a college degree. The argument was particularly appropriate because Sanders was speaking at George Mason University where his comparison would likely resonate with the young college crowd:

> And here's the simple truth: it costs a hell of a lot more money to put somebody in jail than send them to the University of Virginia.[11]

It was not a perfect example; fact-checkers later described it as a "half-truth." One of the biggest changes in speechwriting since the first edition is the ease with which people can both share faulty information online and fact-check it. Among such sites: *www.factcheck.org*, the incredibly useful project of the Annenberg Public Policy Center, which measures the truthfulness of claims and rumors in politics.

Still, the example shows how powerful it can be to put cost in context for an audience.

In Chapter 5 when we first introduced Monroe's Motivated Sequence, we argued that persuasion is about the audience's needs, not your own. Both speakers and writers need examples listeners will find interesting, useful, and memorable.

They are not always the examples that come across your desk. In politics, speechwriters often get a dizzying amount of data from other staffers, pollsters, or even the boss. Naturally, you can't include it all. What goes in, and what stays out?

In his book *Contagious: Why Things Catch On*, marketing professor Jonah Berger suggests several answers.[12] Among other reasons, he argues, ideas stick if they offer practical value for the audience; it's "news they can use." Even if it is not immediately usable, such information has social currency; there's value simply in knowing it. Other ideas stick because they elicit an emotional reaction people consider worth sharing. (The old "Hey, Harvey, listen to *this*!" test.)

All Berger's reasons point to the same conclusion: Speechwriters need to know how to make cases that are interesting and relevant to their audiences. And because different people respond to different types of evidence in different ways, speechwriters should not stick with one but vary the kinds of support they use.

Of course, there is something else speechwriters must do.

ARGUING RESPONSIBLY

Should audiences hold candidates and officeholders to the same rigorous standards that they expect from academics? In the court of public opinion, aren't speeches more like legal briefs, presenting whatever arguments the jury—voters—will accept?

Those aren't dumb questions. It's possible to argue that the other side will do it; that without allowing some hyperbole you can't excite an audience; that knowingly using fallacy creates such a powerful political advantage that it outweighs the need to argue ethically.

We don't want to take the fun out of politics. There are times when the hyperbolic rhetoric at rallies can be acceptable. But writer and former George W. Bush speechwriter David Frum says that political speeches must "stand scrutiny."[13] Standing scrutiny is a virtue. When it comes to policy, we believe that politicians can give up falsehoods, distortions, evasions, and shoddy reasoning without losing a single vote. In the process, they just might increase their own credibility.

Arguing responsibly need not be the death of exciting speech. That's why we close this chapter describing the fallacies common in political speech and arguing against them.

FALLACIES

On June 5, 2005, Secretary of State Condoleezza Rice strode onstage at the Washington meeting of the Organization of American States General Assembly, and, putting in a plug for the virtues of democracy, began this way:

> As recently as 1999, the two million Cubans in the United States earned a combined income of $14 billion. Now compare that with Castro's Cuba, a country of eleven million citizens and a GDP [gross domestic product] only slightly larger than $1 billion.

Already, we have a problem, though not with her reasoning. Rice was using statistics to compare, and the difference certainly seems large. She has her figures wrong; Cuba's GDP was then about $25 billion. But Rice's 14:1 ratio is the same as the per-capita GDP difference between the two countries. Let us assume some staffer got the numbers wrong and no one caught it. Not a big deal.

But then Rice drew this conclusion: "The lesson is clear: When governments champion equality of opportunity, all people can prosper in freedom."

Is that the lesson? It ignores many other reasons like the crippling effects of a decade-long embargo on Cuba, the difference between natural resources available in Cuba and the United States.

Secretary Rice used concrete data. Her last sentence might very well be true, especially with the qualifying word *can*. But she draws her large conclusion from such a small amount of evidence that alert listeners—including the OAS General Assembly—should reject it. Her deduction illustrates "hasty generalization," the fallacy of generalizing with too few facts.

Such fallacies matter because political speech persuades not just by adopting the best qualities of argument, but by avoiding the worst.

Rhetoric scholars usually distinguish between two kinds of fallacy. The first is the fallacy of *matter*, or false statements, which include half-truths, lies, or misstatements, like Rice's about Cuba's GDP. In a class on logic, we'd call that a fallacy of matter, even if it was an honest mistake.

In the first edition of this book, we gave short shrift to the problem of consciously misstating facts—lying. "Few politicians consciously misstate facts," Bob wrote.

That no longer holds true. This book remains resolutely nonpartisan. But the amount and variety of fallacy in 2016's presidential campaign and since seems unprecedented in modern American history, as is the attention paid the sheer volume of misleading statements coming from the White House. That's why in this chapter we expand our discussion of the second kind of fallacy: that of *form*, or invalid reasoning.

We can't cover them all. Consult the bibliography for books that explore fallacies in more detail than this book can afford. In this chapter, we cover twelve. You've seen the one Secretary Rice used in 2005: *hasty generalization*. Now let's look at the others—as well as ways to avoid them.

Straw Man

Straw man carries with it the image of the scarecrow in *The Wizard of Oz*, outfitted with pants and a hat, designed to look formidable to crows or thieves, but really made of straw. In this fallacy, a speaker creates a convincing rebuttal—not to the opponent's muscular, real argument but to a weak, straw-filled one easy to destroy.

One way politicians do that: the inaccurate paraphrase. Instead of rebutting an actual opponent, they rebut their own summary of what the other side believes. It's easy to do. Here, Ted Cruz does exactly that as he addresses small business owners struggling to hire more people while needing to provide health insurance under the Affordable Care Act. He "summarizes" Barack Obama and Democrats' ideas on health care, then dismisses them:

> President Obama said, it's the same thing Democrats have said, which is that you, the small business, you're apparently a bad actor, because you're not allowed to manufacture money . . .

It's a clever idea, but where had Obama ever said that these were his views? Answer: nowhere. No politician in his right mind would say small businesses are "bad actors" because they struggle with health care costs—and certainly they aren't expected to "manufacture money."

This is not a partisan issue. Here, for example, is a passage from Obama himself, defending his tax stimulus package in 2009:

> In recent days, there have been misguided criticisms of this plan that echo the failed theories that helped lead us into this crisis—the notion that tax cuts alone will solve all our problems . . . that we can meet our enormous tests with half-steps and piecemeal measures . . .

Who had argued that "tax cuts alone will solve all our problems," or that "we can meet our enormous tests with half-steps"? Nobody. Obama might have been more responsible by saying something like "Some people suggest *what I feel* are half-steps." Better yet, he could have quoted a real critic and then rebutted what the critic actually said. He did neither.

When we hear speakers say "Some say" or "There are those who say," that is a sure signal distortion is on the way.

Solution: To be credible, go to the trouble of finding an actual quote to rebut.

Ad Hominem

Meaning "to the man"—*ad hominem* involves dismissing people's ideas by attacking them personally.

Keep in mind, attacking an opponent's character isn't always fallacy. Attacks only become ad hominem when you use personal attacks to discredit an opponent's views. Here, for example, is Senator Sanders at a 2017 CNN debate on health care, rebutting opposition to his ideas from Republicans and the health care industry:

> But the bottom line here is, you've got 1,400 well-paid lobbyists right now, and they are working, if I may say this, they're working against you. They're working against your daughter. The only thing they want is more and more profit. And they could care less about the needs of the American people.

Sanders could have rebutted the other side by offering evidence. Instead, he attacks them personally. He asserts that they have an unworthy motive—"profit." He generalizes about their indifference to the "needs" of Americans, including our daughters.

Sanders could have easily made the same points without the personal attack. Let's say he had phrased it this way:

> But the bottom line here is, you've got 1,400 well-paid lobbyists right now, and they are working, if I may say this, they're working for the insurance companies and health care companies. They are not working for you or for your daughter. They are paid to help their companies profit, not to address the needs of the American people.

Solution: Only make assertions about motive when you have the facts to back them up.

False Cause

This tactic labels something as the cause of a problem or solution when it is not. You see this when politicians take credit where they—mostly—don't deserve it, or blame other people for policies they didn't cause.

Again, the CNN debate. Senator Cruz aimed to rebut the idea that he was for big business by noting how the Affordable Care Act had affected the insurance industry:

> In 2008, the ten largest insurance companies in America made just over $8 billion in profit. In 2016—2015, rather—those same ten largest companies made $15 billion in profit. Insurance company profits have doubled under Obamacare. That was the result. Bernie helped write Obamacare.

As reporters quickly noted, Obamacare did not cause the growth cited by Cruz. It came instead from other growing parts of insurers' business. That two events happened at the same time doesn't mean one caused the other. Cruz's "false cause" fallacy came from his implication that Obamacare "doubled" insurance company profits.

Solution: Usually, speakers falling into this trap don't make up lies out of whole cloth. Make sure that your words *and your implications* do not mislead listeners.

Apples and Oranges

People compare apples and oranges all the time—in nutritional value, for example. This kind of comparison becomes *false analogy* when you find similarities between things whose differences are more important, and vice versa. We see the "apples and oranges" fallacy in two instances: (1) when politicians find similarities in an opponent's plan to plans voters don't like, but ignore much more important differences, and (2) when they compare statistics that look the same, but where the context is very different.

Look back at the last example from Cruz.

Cruz compares the insurance industry in 2008—during an economic crisis that crippled the economy—with the insurance industry in 2015, when it enjoyed significant recovery. Refusing to acknowledge this makes Cruz's example incredibly misleading.

Solution: Resist comparing even identical numbers when the context tells a different story.

Non Sequitur

Latin for "it does not follow," a non sequitur is an argument where the conclusion doesn't actually follow from the premise. We see non sequiturs a lot in what politicians call the "pivot." Here's Sen. Tim Kaine's non sequitur as he pivots from a discussion of military policy to Trump's tax returns during the 2016 vice presidential debate:

> Governor Pence just said that Donald Trump will rebuild the military. No, he won't. Donald Trump is avoiding paying taxes. The *New York Times* suggested that he probably didn't pay taxes for about eighteen years starting in 1995. Those years included the years of 9/11.

Donald Trump's taxes do not show us whether or not he would rebuild the military as president. Kaine's pivot to the tax issue doesn't support his argument. It literally "does not follow."

Solution: Make sure evidence is relevant to your point.

Tu Quoque

Tu quoque is Latin for "you also." This fallacy occurs when speakers defend themselves by pointing out that an opponent has done the same thing—or worse. Here is Donald Trump, discussing the infamous *Access Hollywood* tape:

> That was locker room talk. I'm not proud of it . . . If you look at Bill Clinton, far worse. Mine are words, and his was action. His words, what he has done to women. There's never been anybody in the history of politics in this nation that has been so abusive to women.

We don't exonerate a bank robber who argues, "Hey, I'm not the only one who robbed a bank." Trump's emphasis on someone else's bad actions is fallacious because it is irrelevant.

Solution: Two wrongs don't make a right.

Either-Or

This fallacy presents a false choice by ignoring other options. In November 2006, President George W. Bush directed this comment to American allies:

> Over time it's going to be important for nations to know they will be held accountable for inactivity. You're either with us or against us in the fight against terror.

In politics, there are often more than two clear-cut options. Whether or not you sympathize with the president's anger, there were certainly more than two ways to respond to 9/11, not to mention nuances within those options.

One might ask whether Patrick Henry's use of antithesis ("Give me liberty or give me death!"), assuming he said it, was also false choice. It was not. Henry was expressing his personal view. For him, there may have only been two choices.

Bush, though, was not simply expressing a personal opinion. He was urging a policy decision by other countries that would make them active allies of the United States. In fact, by warning them that they would be "held accountable for inactivity," he was close to using a fourth method of persuasion, not mentioned by Aristotle: the "do it or die" technique formally known as persuasion by coercion.

Solution: Don't oversimplify; make sure your arguments reflect the complexity of the issue.

Slippery Slope

The most famous example of this fallacy in American politics is certainly President Dwight D. Eisenhower's 1954 "domino" analogy. Eisenhower used it to argue that if the United States did not defend Vietnam, it would see "the loss of Indochina, of Burma, of Thailand . . . of the Peninsula, and Indonesia."

> You have a row of dominoes set up, you knock over the first one, and what will happen to the last one is the certainty that it will go over very quickly.

Nobody disputes that a domino effect exists—especially anyone who's played with dominoes. To argue that something *might* happen reflects the complexity of world events. To argue that it will, doesn't. The slippery slope, argues rhetoric scholar Stephen Lucas, and almost all historians, is "to assume that all the later steps will occur without proving that they will."[14]

Solution: Qualifiers like *might* or *could* can preserve your point without weakening it.

Ad Absurdum

This fallacy, "reducing to the absurd," is related to slippery slope. It involves taking someone's position and applying it in a way that takes it to a ridiculous extreme.

Here, once again, is Senator Cruz, talking about the Obamacare mandate that Americans must buy insurance or face a penalty:

> Imagine if the federal government mandated that everyone in America must drive a Lamborghini. I've never driven a Lamborghini. I mean, they look kind of fun. But you know what? I'm willing to bet most of us, if that was the mandate—and it would be cool, you sit in a leather seat, you could go two hundred miles an hour—what it would mean for most people is you couldn't afford a car.

There's room for hyperbole in politics. But not at the expense of truth.

Solution: For people to take your arguments seriously, use analogies that reasonably reflect your opponents' views.

Ad Populum

The Latin name is pretty easy to understand: "argument to the people." A speaker commits this fallacy, also called "bandwagon," by arguing a position is right because most people believe it. Consider the following line from Senator Sanders, in one of his Democratic primary debates against Hillary Clinton:

> When this campaign began, I said that we got to end the starvation minimum wage of $7.25, raise it to $15. Secretary Clinton said let's raise it to $12. There's a difference. And, by the way, what has happened is history has outpaced Secretary Clinton, because all over this country, people are standing up and they're saying $12 is not good enough—we need $15 an hour.

Sanders argument here has nothing to do with the relative economic merits of a $15 minimum wage over a $12 one. He doesn't explain why it's a better policy. Instead, he argues only that people believe it is a good policy.

Solution: Popular support is relevant in a democracy, but it doesn't make a position right. Find more evidence.

Fallacy of Definition

In 2008, as Barack Obama was responding to a citizen, he admitted that he would like to "spread the wealth." Republican vice presidential nominee Sarah Palin could have chosen many ways to discredit him. After all, conservative economists had argued in great detail that redistributing wealth was dangerous. She took a different approach:

> Senator Obama said he wants to, quote, "spread the wealth." What that means is he wants government to take your money and dole it out however a politician sees fit. Barack Obama calls it spreading the wealth. But Joe the Plumber and Ed the Dairy Man—I believe that they think that it sounds more like socialism. Friends, now is no time to experiment with socialism.

Palin simply called "spread the wealth" by a word most Americans dislike: *socialism*. She was shrewd—but irresponsible nonetheless.

Let's say someone criticized our book this way:

> Lehrman and Schnure say they want you to avoid fallacy. What that means is avoid any argument they don't like. That sounds like lying to me. Friends, now is no time to experiment with lying.

Solution: Don't use circular reasoning to come up with a definition to suit your needs.

FINAL WORDS

A book covering the basics must omit some complexities—as well as a discussion of other fallacies with colorful names, like "begging the question," "red herring," and "ignoratio elenchi."

One could argue that adopting strict standards for political speech takes the fun out it. After all, politics is filled with examples of arguments with just a germ of truth that make audiences jump to their feet and cheer. Can't we forgive a small rhetorical sin committed out of an excess of passion?

Sorry to be so boring. With a little work, speechwriters could argue more ethically and still have fun. More important, speechwriters have the power to help discourse simply by adding nuance. Use facts and examples that are true, are relevant, and come from unbiased sources. Use real quotes from opponents. Make sure attacks on character do not become the sole way to rebut. Take pleasure every time you see a legitimate argument escape unscathed.

With these final tips, we reach the end not just of our chapter on support, but of our discussion of the five elements basic to speechwriting. We've looked at one kind of structure for the political speech, which contains many of the elements you need. We've looked at the different ways political speeches use language, anecdote, wit, and support. We've also looked at some ways politicians argue that you should try to avoid.

In the preface to this book, we suggested that the LAWS of speechwriting were a little like the strokes in tennis. How do you use them in a match?

Answering that question is the point of Part III.

THE SPEECHWRITER'S CHECKLIST: SUPPORT

- ☐ Have I varied the evidence presented in this speech? Do I include facts, examples, testimony, and analogy?
- ☐ Have I created an effective argument? Does this argument include:
    - ☐ Statistics in context?
    - ☐ Concrete examples?
    - ☐ Pithy quotes?

- ☐ Have I created an ethical argument? Are the facts current, relevant, and responsibly sourced?
- ☐ Are the facts appropriate for this audience?
- ☐ Of the fallacies, have I avoided:
    - ☐ Forming hasty generalizations?
    - ☐ Making an ad hominem attack?
    - ☐ Presenting a false cause?
    - ☐ Constructing a straw man?

PART III

APPLICATIONS

11

Beginnings

Among all the political speeches delivered in the first two weeks of 2018, one—not by a politician but by a billionaire, and not at a rally but at an awards show—decisively grabbed Americans' attention.

Why did Oprah Winfrey's Golden Globes award acceptance provoke such a reaction? As speechwriters, we naturally wish the sole reason had been the writing. In fact, there were many, most of them unique to her and that moment: Winfrey's skill as an actress, the adoration of her audience in the room and her fans watching at home, the importance of the issue she raised and the #MeToo movement—*and* the writing. All helped make one hundred million people watch Winfrey's speech on YouTube, spark calls for her to run for president, and cause a 13 percent increase in the stock of Weight Watchers, where Winfrey sits on the board.[1]

There were many unusual things about her speech. We start this chapter, though, by examining only the way Winfrey's speech began, which in some ways should not be unusual at all.

Skillful politicians, after all, can open by choosing mostly from five structural elements. They can

- **win attention** (to compel people to listen, often with jokes or story),
- **thank listeners** (to seem likable and please those they thank),
- **praise the group** (to establish goodwill),
- **get serious** (to preview a substantive message), or
- **state their purpose** (to offer listeners a verbal GPS for what follows).

You don't have to open with all five elements, or use them in that order. But Winfrey and her writers used them all. Take a look at how effective they are.

Attention through Story

> In 1964, I was a little girl sitting on the linoleum floor of my mother's house in Milwaukee, watching Anne Bancroft present the Oscar for Best Actor at the Thirty-Sixth Academy Awards. She opened the envelope and said five words that literally made history: "The winner is . . . Sidney Poitier."
>
> Up to the stage came the most elegant man I had ever seen. I remember his tie was white and of course his skin was black, and I had never seen a black man being celebrated like that.
>
> And I've tried many many many times to explain what a moment like that means to a little girl, a kid watching from the cheap seats, as my mom came through the door bone tired from cleaning other people's houses.
>
> But all I can do is quote and say that the explanation in Sidney's performance in *Lilies of the Field*—"amen amen, amen amen."
>
> In 1982, Sidney received the Cecil B. DeMille award right here at the Golden Globes, and it is not lost on me that at this moment there are some little girls watching as I become the first black woman to be given this same award.[2]

Many factors make this opening work. Instead of beginning with thank-yous and clichés about what an honor it is to be there, Winfrey surprises us by starting with a story, laced with concrete detail. She wasn't just watching TV. She sat on her mother's *linoleum* floor.

She creates suspense, too. She doesn't just say she watched Sidney Poitier get an award. She first mentions Anne Bancroft who "opened the envelope and said five words."

What words? we wonder. Only then does she tell us.

Winfrey does more to characterize herself. Here is one of the most accomplished women in the world confessing her failure to "explain" what the moment meant to her, describing herself sitting in the "cheap seats." She characterizes her mom, too ("bone tired from cleaning other people's houses").

Finally, she uses a punch line, drawing a parallel with today and reinforcing the significance of the moments. Only then does she move to the second and third building blocks of an opening.

Thank-Yous and Praise

> Dennis Swanson, who took a chance on me for A.M. Chicago. Quincy Jones, who saw me on that show and said to Steven Spielberg, yes, she is Sofia in *The Color Purple*. Gayle, who's been the definition of what a friend is, and Stedman, who's been my rock, just a few to name.
> I'd like to thank the Hollywood Foreign Press Association . . .[3]

We don't include this entire section. Instead, we move to the point where Winfrey switches gears, signaling that she won't be content to simply enjoy her honor.

The Serious Moment

> Because we all know that the press is under siege these days. But we also know that it is the insatiable dedication to uncovering the absolute truth that keeps us from turning a blind eye to corruption and to injustice. To tyrants and victims and secrets and lies.
> I want to say that I value the press more than ever before as we try to navigate these complicated times, which brings me to this: What I know for sure is that speaking your truth is the most powerful tool we all have. And I'm especially proud and inspired by all the women who have felt strong enough and empowered enough to speak up and share their personal stories.[4]

Note how she thanks reporters by introducing an idea that will resonate with a liberal audience ("insatiable dedication to uncovering the absolute truth") and demonstrates humility by saluting women who have shared stories of sexual abuse ("proud and inspired by all the women . . .").

Now, Winfrey moves to the final piece of her opening: the statement of purpose that helps listeners understand what's ahead.

Statement of Purpose

> Each of us in this room are celebrated because of the stories that we tell, and this year we became the story. But it's not just a story affecting the entertainment industry. It's one that transcends any culture, geography, race, religion, politics, or workplace.
> So I want tonight to express gratitude to all the women who have endured years of abuse and assault because they, like my mother, had children to feed and bills to pay and dreams to pursue.[5]

> **AS DELIVERED**
>
> **Oprah Winfrey Accepting the Cecil B. DeMille Award.** There are valuable approaches throughout Winfrey's unusual speech. Do you see the value in delaying the acknowledgments and opting instead to begin by telling a story? How does concrete detail add to that story? How does Winfrey's delivery add to the drama?
>
> www.youtube.com/watch?v=fN5HV79_8B8

Attention through story. Acknowledgments of praise and thanks. A substantive point. Statement of purpose. Winfrey's skillful opening uses them all.

We have said this "should not" be unusual. It is, though. That's partly because one common opening in politics today uses not story or wit, but a boilerplate statement of purpose of the sort uttered thousands of times a day in legislatures around the country ("I rise today to speak of . . . This morning I'd like to discuss . . . I am sad to report . . . It is a pleasure to be here to announce . . .").

Even national politicians often begin with a long list of people to acknowledge, a stale joke, and clichés about how they feel ("I'm honored by your invitation . . . it's a pleasure to be here").

It is possible to find the flat opening perfectly acceptable on the grounds that it characterizes the speaker as a substantive person—too substantive for anecdote.

Those moments do exist. In 2001, in an address to the nation, President George W. Bush thought so:

> Good afternoon. On my orders, the United States military has begun strikes against al-Qaeda training camps and military installations of the Taliban regime in Afghanistan.

In these instances, speakers already have everybody's attention. Bush's opening reflected the gravity of the moment.

Usually, though, writers can do better—even the Gettysburg Address, short and solemn as it is, opens with historical analogy.

If speechwriters feel compelled to use the flat opening, or feel pressed for time—they can still use it artfully, incorporating the techniques of parallel construction or contrast, discussed earlier, as in this example of antithesis from the 2001 Shanghai CEO Summit, again from President Bush:

We meet today with recent memories of great evil—yet great hope for this region and the future.

Politicians have a lot to do in a speech. They must show listeners they support the goals of the audience, acknowledge people in the crowd whose support they need, and finally, like most speakers, discuss issues.

That doesn't mean they must be dull. In what follows, you will see ways to make each opening element exciting, relevant, and interesting.

ATTENTION

Opening with Humor

Mo Udall, whose book *Too Funny to Be President* we recommend, liked the story of a minister who sells a mule to his neighbor. "Now, treat that mule kindly," he tells his neighbor.

A few days later, the minister sees his exasperated neighbor standing with the mule. The mule is hitched to a plow but refusing to move.

"Let me show you how to get him going," the minister says. He picks up a two-by-four and smacks the mule between the eyes. Right away, the mule starts pulling.

"I thought you said to treat him kindly," the farmer says.

"First you have to get his attention."[6]

Lots of politicians know enough about getting attention to start with a joke—just the way this section does. It is practically a tradition.

But speakers do themselves a disservice when they labor through an obligatory opening joke, wait through the polite laughter, then give the audience twenty minutes of unvaried solemnity. The opening only serves to make the rest of the speech seem dull.

Still, why cast aside what works? Opening with a joke usually does. For it sends one message to listeners: *See how likable I am.*

Let's examine a variety of ways to win attention with humor—with examples of evergreens that have worked well.

Poke Fun at Yourself

In 2016, when Mike Pence accepted the Republican nomination for vice president, he talked about his family this way:

Dad ran gas stations in our small town, and he was a great father. If Dad were with us today, I have a feeling he'd enjoy this moment—and probably be pretty surprised.

In Chapter 9, we made clear why self-deprecatory humor is especially useful in politics. Pence follows that rule. But political crowds are not so one-dimensional. Especially during campaigns, partisan crowds want something more.

Insult the Other Side

In 2012, after the routine thank-yous for nominating him, Republican vice-presidential nominee Paul Ryan opened this way:

> I'm the newcomer to this campaign. So let me share a first impression.
>
> I have never seen opponents so silent about their record, and so desperate to keep their power.
>
> They have run out of ideas.
>
> Their moment came and went. Fear and division is all they've got left. With all of their attack ads, the president is just throwing away money.
>
> And he is pretty experienced at that.

Ending with a joke not only insulted an opponent the crowd detested. It made them see Ryan as witty.

Use and Reuse Quips

In addition to making audiences laugh, quips serve other functions. The audience response helps speakers gauge the excitement of the crowd. And if the opening line is one you've used often, it gives you a comfortable, nonnervous way to start.

When the authors worked for Al Gore, we went with him to fundraiser after fundraiser. Imagine the scene: a crowded hotel meeting room, where to squeeze as many people in as possible, staff would remove most of the furniture—and all the chairs.

Gore would walk in and look around. People would start clapping. He would say,

> "Thanks—for the standing ovation."

It worked every time. As he knew it would.

Quote Humorists

Over the centuries, other people have come up with lines too witty to ignore. Using them as openers works for two reasons. First, in a hectic day, you often can't invent anything better. Second, citing someone famous for being funny makes listeners more willing to laugh, as in this favorite of Texas senator and vice-presidential nominee Lloyd Bentsen:

> Washington's a tough place. It reminds me of what Mark Twain once said about Carson City, Nevada, in the early days of the silver boom. "It was no place for a Presbyterian—and I did not long remain one."

Use Analogies to Ridicule

Especially when they use cultural references, analogies are another rhetorical device covered in Chapter 9. Take this hyperbolic example from former governor and presidential candidate Mike Huckabee at the 2008 Republican National Convention, aiming at what he considered inaccurate reporting:

> The reporting of the past few days has been tackier than a costume change at a Madonna concert.

Use a Funny Personal Story

Opening funny doesn't mean unreeling a string of short jokes. Politicians use a vast array of stories to begin speeches on a light note. Some are true. Some are not. Some have existed so long that their origins are forgotten. They are effective, still.

Speaking at Yale, Hillary Clinton once opened with this amusing story about herself to accomplish four things. She won attention, made people laugh, implicitly praised Yale, and characterized herself as someone who knew the sting of discrimination. It was a way to open with humor, yet make a point.

> As Nick was speaking, I thought about how I ended up at Yale Law School. It tells a little bit about how much progress we've made.
>
> I was trying to decide whether to go to Yale Law School or Harvard . . . A young man I knew who was attending Harvard invited me to come to a cocktail reception to meet some of the faculty at Harvard.
>
> I was introduced to a professor who looked as though he just stepped out of the set of *Paper Chase* and . . . my friend said to Professor So-and-So, "This is Hillary Rodham. She's trying to make up her mind between us and our nearest competitor."
>
> And he looked down at me and he said, "First of all we don't have a nearest competitor, and secondly we don't need any more women."
>
> So I decided that Yale was by far the more hospitable place.

Use Stories about Public Speaking

As we say in Chapter 9, story-jokes, less popular now than they once were, are still useful—if they're funny. You'll find them in compendiums of stories like James Humes's *Roles Speakers Play*.[7] Some are corny, some playful, some dated, and some excellent. This one has a slight edge. It's basically about two famous people being mean to each other. That's useful when speakers risk sounding bland. Pay attention to the off-ramp to see how such stories can be made relevant.

> I enjoyed being with you last year. I'm honored that you wanted me back.
>
> You can never take second appearances for granted, you know.
>
> I'm reminded of that story about the time George Bernard Shaw had one of his plays opening up.
>
> He sent Winston Churchill a note, saying, "Here's two tickets to the play. Bring a friend—if you have one."
>
> Churchill wrote back: "Sorry, I'm busy. I'll come for the second performance—if there is one."
>
> So, here I am, back for a second performance. And while I didn't bring a friend, I see a lot of friends, whether it's . . .

Open with Drama

Alfred Hitchcock once claimed, "Drama is life with the dull bits cut out." Using a dramatic story, as Oprah Winfrey did, doesn't guarantee a speech without dull bits. It does, though, provide a variety of uses for speakers and writers who want to open interestingly.

Use Story to Remind Listeners Why They Are There

Celebrating the fiftieth anniversary of the 1963 Selma March, Barack Obama opens with the richly detailed story of one of its leaders on the morning before the march began, signaling that in this speech he will pay tribute to those with a "mission to change America":

> It is a rare honor in this life to follow one of your heroes. And John Lewis is one of my heroes.
>
> Now, I have to imagine that when a younger John Lewis woke up that morning fifty years ago and made his way to Brown Chapel, heroics were not on his mind. A day like this was not on his mind.

Young folks with bedrolls and backpacks were milling about. Veterans of the movement trained newcomers in the tactics of nonviolence—the right way to protect yourself when attacked. A doctor described what tear gas does to the body, while marchers scribbled down instructions for contacting their loved ones. The air was thick with doubt, anticipation, and fear.

And they comforted themselves with the final verse of the final hymn they sung:

"No matter what may be the test, God will take care of you; Lean, weary one, upon His breast, God will take care of you." And then, his knapsack stocked with an apple, a toothbrush, and a book on government—all you need for a night behind bars—John Lewis led them out of the church on a mission to change America.

Use Story to Remind Listeners of a Larger Purpose

At the 2016 Republican National Convention, filled with speeches lambasting Democrats, Sen. Tom Cotton begins with a personal story with one surprising twist. He then uses it to remind delegates, and millions watching, of the principle underlying what they might see as his family's heroism.

> Let me tell you a story about an Arkansas farm boy. When America was at war, he was in school and then in a comfortable job. But he sacrificed that comfort, against the wishes of his father, who himself had served. He volunteered for the Army. He became an infantryman.
>
> That farm boy was my dad. He went to Vietnam in 1969.
>
> Thirty-five years later, I did the same. Against the wishes of my family, I gave up my legal career, and I volunteered for the Army. I became an infantryman. I went to Iraq and Afghanistan. My dad said he felt like God was punishing him for what he did to his dad.
>
> But God wasn't punishing them; God had called us to serve. Just as He calls so many of you.
>
> My family isn't extraordinary; in fact, we're very ordinary. From farms in Arkansas to fire stations in New York, many families could tell the same story.
>
> The defense of this country is a family affair.
>
> We don't fight because we hate our enemies, but because we love our country.

We love its freedom. We love that we are born equal and live free, that no one rules without consent.

Here, too, there is more than one reason to open with story. After the surprise that he is talking about his dad, and that he followed in his footsteps, listeners will admire Cotton as the Democrats did Obama. But Cotton has a point to make: Americans fight not out of hate for the enemy but for love of country.

Use Story to Speak to the Larger Audience

Speakers in the Senate or House often don't bother telling stories, on the theory that there's no one to move when the chamber is practically empty. That unwise decision ignores potential listeners not in the room, the secondary audiences who will watch on C-SPAN or read a speech in a newspaper or on a news website, not to mention staffers and fundraisers.

Opening a Senate hearing in 2018, Sen. Lamar Alexander (R-TN) begins with a story aimed at those wider audiences before getting to the business at hand:

> Sean Lester is, by all accounts, a typical Nashville young adult with a full-time job who also attends college. However, just before his twenty-fifth birthday, he experienced his first schizophrenic experience and has spent ten weeks receiving psychiatric treatment since 2014.
>
> Sean wrote me, saying, "This may seem slightly depressing, but my story does not end there. The doctors and staff I encountered at the hospital and at the Centerstone Clinic taught me to live productively again in society. I have been free of the hospital for a whole year now. During that time, I have taken medication, returned to work, and even paid off a car!"
>
> Sean is one person out of nearly ten million in the United States with a serious mental health condition. Without treatment, his story could have had a very different outcome . . .

PRAISE, THANKS, ACKNOWLEDGMENTS

In September 2016, just a few months before leaving office, President Obama came to the Mall in Washington to dedicate the newly opened National Museum of African American History and Culture. He began this way:

President and Mrs. Bush; President Clinton; Vice President and Dr. Biden; Chief Justice Roberts; Secretary Skorton; Reverend Butts; distinguished guests: Thank you. Thank you for your leadership in making sure this tale is told. We're here in part because of you and because of all those Americans—the Civil War vets, the civil rights foot soldiers, the champions of this effort on Capitol Hill—who, for more than a century, kept the dream of this museum alive.

That includes our leaders in Congress—Paul Ryan and Nancy Pelosi. It includes one of my heroes, John Lewis, who, as he has so often, took the torch from those who came before him and brought us past the finish line. It includes the philanthropists and benefactors and advisory members who have so generously given not only their money but their time. It includes the Americans who offered up all the family keepsakes tucked away in grandma's attic. And of course, it includes a man without whose vision and passion and persistence we would not be here today—Mr. Lonnie Bunch.

This is the eye-glazing ritual of compliments, thank-yous, and praise for the audience that politicians, even skilled orators like Obama, feel they must utter. Though in most of life there's a difference between thanks and praise— one expresses gratitude, the other approval—in politics that is a distinction almost without a difference.

It may seem crazy that you have to pat people on the back so much. But you do. Political speeches attract people too celebrated to ignore, or who have worked hard enough to deserve thanks. Speakers worry that not mentioning them right away will insult friends or influential donors, maybe even voters.

Still, such a long, predictable start makes outside observers laugh at political speech, since it can sound so fatuous. And there's a more important reason to abandon this long tradition. It makes an audience stop listening.

For those who feel compelled to mention people right from the start, we recommend limiting the list. You might simply thank the person who introduces the speaker and the head of the organization hosting. Save other acknowledgments for later in the speech. There are ways to fulfill that obligation without torpedoing your speech's momentum.

Start with a "Howdahell"

Speechwriters used to keep one book close by—*Chase's Calendar of Events*. For each speech, they would consult it for the list of anniversaries, births, and deaths that might be worth mentioning. The reason, as we mention in Chapter 4, was the frequency with which you could find historical events or people with a direct connection to your audience. These days, we no longer need it; we just google a date.

But we can also research the name of popular restaurants and local delicacies. We learn about sports teams and their traditions. Even the state bird. We look for anything that makes an audience sit up.

Here's how that worked when Nancy Pelosi delivered a 2007 campaign speech to the Colorado Democratic Party. The speech was on March 3, the same date back in 1875, Pelosi's researchers discovered, that Congress paved the way for Colorado to enter the Union.

> Democrats are back. And we're getting things done.
> That's not something you could always say about the Congress.
> But on this day—March 3, 1875—Congress did do something.
> Something pretty important.
> They passed a bill allowing Colorado to become a state.
> President Grant signed it—but only because he'd been assured Colorado would be safely Republican.
> He was not the first Republican to guess wrong about Colorado!

Only when the crowd stopped laughing did Pelosi preview what was coming next:

> Still, what would those Republicans back in 1875 think if they were here today?

The value of discovering and citing those connections is more than just coincidence; it makes speakers likable. Where did she find that?" amazed listeners asked, amply justifying the name we had for those moments. The Howdahell.

BEHIND THE SCENES

The Howdahell

Long ago, when the authors were in the White House, Al Gore was speaking in Missoula, Montana. Eric asked the local organizers what was happening there. Nothing, one of them said.

"You want proof that nothing happened here?" the organizer asked. "We're a small town. All people ever talk about is the four-way intersection. Backs up traffic and drives people crazy. We call it 'Malfunction Junction.'"

> Even we were astounded by the reaction when Gore bounded up to the microphone and delivered the line Eric had prepared:
> "Sorry I'm late. The motorcade got stuck at Malfunction Junction."
> "The crowd went nuts. Howdahell did he know that?" someone reported back to us later.
> "You know what? Every speech should have a 'Howdahell,'" Eric said.
> Bob agreed.
> Hence the name.

Make Every Acknowledgment Unique

After her joke about March 3, Pelosi wanted to thank seven people right away. She might have begun as many speakers do, with a list. *Diana DeGette is in the room! Mark Udall is here, too!*

If that opening had won applause, it would have been the applause of ritual, not enthusiasm.

Instead, to this crowd of Democrats, she contrasted 1875 to that night—then linking each of the seven to something concrete, and meaningful. Here are the first two:

> Still, what would those Republicans back in 1875 think if they were here today?
>
> They'd see:
>
> Diana DeGette! The dean of the Colorado delegation! During the first hundred hours of the new Congress, we passed her bill . . . to promote stem cell research . . . and bring hope to America's families. It simply would not have happened without the extraordinary leadership of Diana DeGette! [*applause*]
>
> Mark Udall! He knows we can find the energy America needs and preserve our treasured natural resources. And thanks to him, in the first hundred hours, we rolled back the outrageous subsidies for Big Oil and instead invested in clean, alternative energy resources. [*applause*]
>
> Each won enthusiastic applause, partly because the crowd enjoyed the contrast, and partly because Pelosi mentioned meaningful achievements. Finally, having asked her question, Pelosi won another response by returning to her opening story and making the audience keep listening.

What those Republicans, who voted on March 3, 1875, would see in Colorado today are New Direction Democrats—in fact, New Day Democrats—who are changing the way we meet the needs of the American people.

Harness the Power of *We*

Politicians need to praise others. But they want to celebrate their own achievements, too. The political speechwriting cliché of sentences that begin "That's why I sponsored this bill . . ." can turn off listeners because it sounds like bragging. Changing *I* to *we* gives the audience credit. Here is Ronald Reagan, at a 1994 Republican gala on his eighty-third birthday, reflecting on his years as president. Central to this passage is his use of repetition. But note what he repeats most. *We*. Seven times.

> When we came to Washington on that bright sunny day in January of 1981, we shared a dream for America. It was a time of rampant inflation and crushing interest rates . . . It was a time when cold, ugly walls divided nations and human rights were trampled . . . It was a time when the nuclear arms race was spiraling out of control. We believed that for the future of America and the free world, this could not stand.
>
> So together we got the government off the backs of the American people. We created millions of new jobs for Americans at all income levels. We cut taxes and freed the people from the shackles of too much government . . . brought America back—bigger and better than ever. . . .
>
> The world watched with amazement as we put our house in order and took our rightful place as the most dynamic country in the world. And I firmly believe that history will record our era as one of peace and global prosperity.

Nearly twenty-four years later, speaking to the Conservative Political Action Committee, Donald Trump used the same device:

> Year after year, leaders have stood on this stage to discuss what we can do together to protect our heritage, to promote our culture, and to defend our freedom. . . .
>
> For the last year with your help, we have put more great conservative ideas into use than perhaps ever before in American history.

We have confirmed a record number, so important, of circuit court judges, and we're going to be putting in a lot more.

And they will interpret the law as written, and we have confirmed an incredible new Supreme Court justice, a great man, Neil Gorsuch. Right. We have passed massive, biggest in history, tax cuts and reforms.

Segment Your Audience

At times, you'll want to thank certain subsets of your listeners in individually tailored ways just as Barack Obama did during his 2008 victory speech:

I will never forget who this victory truly belongs to—it belongs to you.

I was never the likeliest candidate for this office. We didn't start with much money or many endorsements. Our campaign was not hatched in the halls of Washington—it began in the backyards of Des Moines and the living rooms of Concord and the front porches of Charleston.

It was built by working men and women who dug into what little savings they had to give $5 and $10 and $20 to the cause.

It grew strength from the young people who rejected the myth of their generation's apathy; who left their homes and their families for jobs that offered little pay and less sleep; it grew strength from the not-so-young people who braved the bitter cold and scorching heat to knock on the doors of perfect strangers; from the millions of Americans who volunteered, and organized, and proved that more than two centuries later, a government of the people, by the people, and for the people has not perished from the Earth.

This is your victory.

Former Republican speechwriter Peggy Noonan singles out the members of one group in her 2017 Catholic University commencement speech. She praises them in a traditional way, then gets a laugh with a line that insulates her from sounding sentimental:

A special and deserved shout-out to the many parents here.

You are hardy, generous souls. This is a special time in your lives too, a golden hour between the time your child graduates from college and the time they move back in with you. So savor these moments.

For you it is the end of a time in which you received phone calls from your student, son or daughter—checking in, catching up, sharing joys, and ending always with those three poignant little words: "I need money."[8]

Praise with a Hypothetical

When Bill Clinton appeared before a group of five thousand black ministers in 1993, standing on the podium where Martin Luther King Jr. gave his last speech before being assassinated, he could have recited a litany of civil rights achievements. Instead, mindful of his audience and the man they revered, Clinton praised the audience by imagining a "report card" for them. Later, he would give lesser grades for things left to do, but here he adds impact with the metaphor of his hypothetical report card from a hero:

> If Martin Luther King were to reappear by my side today and give us a report card on the last twenty-five years, what would he say?
>
> You did a good job, he would say, voting and electing people who formerly were not electable because of the color of their skin.
>
> You did a good job, he would say, letting people who have the ability to do so live wherever they want to live, go wherever they want to go in this great country.
>
> You did a good job, he would say, elevating people of color into the ranks of the United States Armed Forces to the very top or into the very top of our government.
>
> You did a very good job, he would say . . .

Vary Your Approach

Look more closely at the Obama quote that begins this section. Whether or not he really needed to run through so many names, he worked hard to make the list meaningful. He sees four ways to vary his expressions of thanks, each described in Chapter 7 and indicated here:

> That includes our leaders in Congress—Paul Ryan and Nancy Pelosi. It includes one of my heroes, John Lewis, who, as he has so often, took the torch from those who came before him and brought us past the finish line [*metaphor*]. It includes the philanthropists and benefactors and advisory members who have so generously given not only their money but their time [*antithesis*]. It includes the

Americans who offered up all the family keepsakes tucked away in grandma's attic [*concrete detail*]. And of course, it includes a man without whose vision and passion and persistence [*alliteration*] we would not be here today—Mr. Lonnie Bunch.

Use Montage to Praise Those We Don't Name

Sometimes politicians must pay tribute to very large groups. They can't list four hundred million people by name. But speakers have adapted the technique beloved by screenwriters: the cinematic device using very quick shots to show passage of time, or different events.

George W. Bush used montage, along with anaphora, to celebrate heroism after 9/11 in his 2001 address to Congress, mentioned also in Chapter 8.

> We have seen it in the courage of passengers who rushed terrorists to save others on the ground—passengers like an exceptional man named Todd Beamer. And would you please help me to welcome his wife, Lisa Beamer, here tonight.
>
> We have seen the state of our union in the endurance of rescuers, working past exhaustion.
>
> We have seen the unfurling of flags, the lighting of candles, the giving of blood, the saying of prayers—in English, Hebrew, and Arabic.
>
> We have seen the decency of a loving and giving people who have made the grief of strangers their own.

Donald Trump also used this device in his 2018 State of the Union address:

> We saw the volunteers of the "Cajun Navy," racing to the rescue with their fishing boats to save people in the aftermath of a devastating hurricane.
>
> We saw strangers shielding strangers from a hail of gunfire on the Las Vegas Strip.
>
> We heard tales of Americans like Coast Guard petty officer Ashlee Leppert, who is here tonight in the gallery with Melania.
>
> Ashlee was aboard one of the first helicopters on the scene in Houston during Hurricane Harvey. Through eighteen hours of wind and rain, Ashlee braved live power lines and deep water, to help save more than forty lives. Thank you, Ashlee.

So far, each example we have read has something in common. Each asks the audience to pay attention and listen. But sometimes, politicians want and need more. They want people to listen, but also yell. Cheer.

So we end this section on ways to praise and say thank you with a final approach.

Use Praise at Rallies to Win Response from the Crowd

At rallies, inviting listeners to become active, vocal participants is a compliment. In essence, it's a form of implicit praise. It tells the audience, "I know what you're going to say, and I'm with you!"

When Barack Obama visited Ohio State University about a month before the 2012 election, he didn't start with his acknowledgments, or even a story.

Instead, he bounded up to the stage and boomed into the microphone something very familiar to the thousands in attendance. They boomed right back:

OBAMA:	Hello, Buckeyes! [*applause*]
	O-H!
AUDIENCE:	H-I!
OBAMA:	O-H!
AUDIENCE:	H-I!
OBAMA:	O-H!
AUDIENCE:	H-I!

Skillful? Not really. Strategic? Definitely. From the very first sentence, Obama ensures an energetic crowd stays that way. He demonstrates, not surprisingly, that he knows the school nickname, and that this president of the United States has not only learned a favorite cheer but will lead them in it.

Having done that, Obama moves on, and so will we.

Once you've finished your acknowledgments, it's time to remind listeners that your speech is not about thank-yous but about substance. As you move toward your statement of purpose, a serious moment, whether story, example, or expression of belief, can foreshadow what lies ahead.

GETTING SERIOUS AND STATING THE PURPOSE

Just as we combine praise, thanks, and acknowledgments, we here combine getting serious with a statement of purpose, which we will now call SOP to save the life of several trees. It's important to remember what an SOP is—and is not. It is not your message. It is a road map for what lies ahead, usually only a sentence or two long, growing out of the serious material.

It's also important to note that the serious material can take many shapes. While we urge writers to use story in their openings, that is certainly not the only way to signal substance. We examine five speeches that use others before offering listeners the road map they need.

Describe Personal Beliefs to Make Your SOP Relevant

After thanking listeners in his 2017 commencement speech at the University of Pennsylvania, New Jersey senator Cory Booker moves into a summary of beliefs that matter to him, letting the audience know why he chose to discuss what lies ahead before his SOP:

> And so I confessed to you, when I was graduating from college, I felt like I knew a lot and now that I'm about twice your age, I'm not as confident in what I know [*beliefs*]. In fact, I am a person who believes I am in struggle, as we all are. The beautiful thing that I've realized is that we're all in this struggle together.
>
> We perceive that there are differences between us, gaps and gulfs, but we are far more united, far more indivisible, far more involved in a larger common struggle than we know.
>
> And so what I'd like to do very briefly today is confess to you two things I struggle with and it's really two stories, one from someone from history who I've come to admire and the other one is perhaps one of my greatest mentors ever [*SOP*].

Use Concrete Examples to Make Your SOP Memorable

Here, during his visit to Poland in 2017, President Trump, after thanking and praising others, uses concrete detail illustrating the bond between the two countries as a way of justifying his purpose:

> Our two countries share a special bond forged by unique histories and national characters. It's a fellowship that exists only among people who have fought and bled and died for freedom.
>
> The signs of this friendship stand in our nation's capital. Just steps from the White House, we've raised statues of men with names like Pułaski and Kościuszko [*concrete detail*].

The same is true in Warsaw, where street signs carry the name of George Washington, and a monument stands to one of the world's greatest heroes, Ronald Reagan [*concrete detail*].

And so I am here today not just to visit an old ally, but to hold it up as an example for others who seek freedom and who wish to summon the courage and the will to defend our civilization [*SOP*].

Contrast What You Might Say with What You Will

Speaking to a bipartisan group of House of Representatives interns in 2016, House Majority Leader Paul Ryan tells them why they might expect him to talk about the discouraging tenor of politics. Then, he quotes his father to make clear they will hear something else. It surprises the audience and leaves the impression of thoughtfulness.

> Looking around at what's taking place in politics today, it is easy to get disheartened . . . [*what he might say*] Here is what I know now that I want you to know—that you cannot see yourself today . . . Our political discourse—both the kind we see on TV and the kind we experience among each other—did not use to be this bad, and it does not have to be this way . . .
>
> My dad used to say, if you're not a part of the solution, you're a part of the problem. So I have made it a mission of my Speakership to raise our gaze and aim for a brighter horizon.
>
> Instead of talking about what politics is today, I want to talk about what politics can be [*SOP*].

Allow Speakers to Reflect

In the haste to move past the opening to issues, or partisan litanies, we need to remember that sounding thoughtful is a virtue. To most people, politicians exist in a world of wealth and power. Reflective passages allow audiences to see politicians as they should but rarely do.

Ronald Reagan's remarkable 1989 Farewell Address, written by Peggy Noonan, begins with many of the elements this chapter has covered. He thanks listeners and wins attention with an almost wistful acknowledgment of the way presidents can feel isolated—and how he wishes he could "connect." Next, he offers his SOP. "Maybe I can do a little of that tonight."

But then, Reagan describes himself looking quietly out of the window—and reflecting.

His writers know Reagan is comfortable illustrating his thoughts with story. So he sums up the passage by telling us a story and what it means to him. It is a vivid image of where he stands, what he sees, and what he has been thinking.

An effective beginning is more than the sum of its parts. Rich with researched detail, concrete, and thoughtful, the effect of this one is both startling—and reassuring:

> This is the thirty-fourth time I'll speak to you from the Oval Office and the last. We've been together eight years now, and soon it'll be time for me to go. But before I do, I wanted to share some thoughts, some of which I've been saving for a long time.
>
> It's been the honor of my life to be your president [*thank-you*]. So many of you have written the past few weeks to say thanks, but I could say as much to you. Nancy and I are grateful for the opportunity you gave us to serve.
>
> One of the things about the presidency is that you're always somewhat apart. You spent a lot of time going by too fast in a car someone else is driving, and seeing the people through tinted glass—the parents holding up a child, and the wave you saw too late and couldn't return. And so many times I wanted to stop and reach out from behind the glass, and connect [*attention*].
>
> Well, maybe I can do a little of that tonight [*SOP*].
>
> People ask how I feel about leaving [*reflection*]. And the fact is, "parting is such sweet sorrow." The sweet part is California and the ranch and freedom. The sorrow—the goodbyes, of course, and leaving this beautiful place.
>
> You know, down the hall and up the stairs from this office is the part of the White House where the president and his family live. There are a few favorite windows I have up there that I like to stand and look out of early in the morning. The view is over the grounds here to the Washington Monument, and then the Mall and the Jefferson Memorial. But on mornings when the humidity is low, you can see past the Jefferson to the river, the Potomac, and the Virginia shore. Someone said that's the view Lincoln had when he saw the smoke rising from the Battle of Bull Run. Well, I see more prosaic things: the grass on the banks, the morning traffic as people make their way to work, now and then a sailboat on the river.
>
> I've been thinking a bit at that window. I've been reflecting on what the past eight years have meant and mean.

And the image that comes to mind like a refrain is a nautical one—a small story about a big ship, and a refugee, and a sailor. It was back in the early eighties, at the height of the boat people. And the sailor was hard at work on the carrier *Midway*, which was patrolling the South China Sea. The sailor, like most American servicemen, was young, smart, and fiercely observant. The crew spied on the horizon a leaky little boat. And crammed inside were refugees from Indochina hoping to get to America. The *Midway* sent a small launch to bring them to the ship and safety. As the refugees made their way through the choppy seas, one spied the sailor on deck, and stood up, and called out to him. He yelled, "Hello, American sailor. Hello, freedom man."

A small moment with a big meaning, a moment the sailor, who wrote it in a letter, couldn't get out of his mind [*summary*].

BOX 11.1
EXERCISE: EXHUME THE LEAD

You're stuck. You know your draft should conform to Monroe, and that starts with grabbing attention. But you've been looking at an empty screen for more than an hour, and you have to start somewhere. So you type: "Thank you. It's an honor to be here. I'm grateful for the invitation to speak to you tonight."

Three, four drafts later, you have a pretty good speech. Except for one thing. The beginning. It still reads: "Thank you. It's an honor to be here . . ."

You can keep the flat opening, hoping against the odds—and the research—that the audience sticks around until you get to the good stuff. Or, you can look for a better way to win attention. The question is where to look.

How about your own draft?

Here's how it goes:

1. Pick out what you think is the most interesting piece of content in the speech, the one thing that is most likely to get the audience to take notice. Maybe it's a story or a stat. Maybe it's an analogy. Maybe a quote.
2. Next, cut it.
3. Finally, paste it at the top of your text, before anything else, and add a statement of purpose.

Three easy steps to a better beginning.

Yes, there might be speeches where this approach doesn't work. Sometimes you want to construct an argument that builds to a crescendo of what you believe to be your best material. Other times, you want to end with that moving story.

Try it anyway. At the very least, you'll remind yourself how important it is to grab attention immediately. And it'll be the audience who says, "Thank you."

FINAL WORDS

Using wit, story, concrete detail, a statement of purpose, and even reflection offers lots of options to start your speech.

They create different effects for different listeners. But as we implement step one of Monroe's Motivated Sequence, there is one effect openings must have for everyone: making listeners eager to hear what comes next.

Hold onto that goal as you turn the page to examine ways to keep them just as eager through Monroe's second step: presenting the problem.

THE SPEECHWRITER'S CHECKLIST: BEGINNINGS

- ☐ Do I win attention from the very first sentence?
- ☐ Do I build goodwill by praising the audience?
- ☐ Does the praise go beyond generic thanks to cite specific shared beliefs, accomplishments, and personal virtues?
- ☐ Do I try sprinkling acknowledgments throughout the speech? Do I fully preview the message of what's ahead?
- ☐ Where appropriate, have I used humor to enliven the subject and connect with the audience?
- ☐ Do I demonstrate likability through wit and other means of showing humanity?
- ☐ Have I built credibility by demonstrating personal connection to the audience and its issues?
- ☐ Is my opening story both gripping and relevant to the audience's issues? If I didn't use an opening story, what have I done instead, and should I reconsider?
- ☐ Have I chosen quotes for their compelling ideas and wording, not simply because someone famous said them? Does my opening leave listeners primed and eager to hear what follows?

12

Problems

They met in Philadelphia, early in June 1776, and the first order of business was deciding who should write the damn thing.

"You should do it," Thomas Jefferson said.

"I will not," John Adams said.

"Why?"

"Reasons enough."

"What can be your reasons?"

"I am obnoxious, suspected, and unpopular. [And] you can write ten times better than I can."[1]

That's how Adams remembered the conversation, writing it down in a letter to Timothy Pickering almost fifty years afterward. After half a century, he may not have gotten those words exactly right, but there's no question about his reaction a few weeks after that conversation—after Jefferson had finished the final draft of what they would call the Declaration of Independence.

Adams loved it. "I was delighted with its high tone and the flights of oratory with which it abounded," he wrote.[2]

He admitted one reservation. Jefferson had characterized King George as a tyrant. "I thought this too personal," Adams wrote, "for I never believed George to be a tyrant in disposition and in nature; I always believed him to be deceived by his courtiers on both sides of the Atlantic, and in his official capacity, only, cruel."[3]

Adams never asked Jefferson to cut the line, though. He accepted an idea that persists to this day: In politics, it's sometimes necessary to caricature the other side. The Continental Congress approved Jefferson's draft of the document we now see only under glass, and which among other things contains the most famous example of one of the techniques that we discuss in this section—a list of problems, using the kind of repetition we call litany:

> He has obstructed the Administration of Justice, by refusing his Assent to Laws for establishing Judiciary powers.
>
> He has made Judges dependent on his Will alone, for the tenure of their offices and the amount and payment of their salaries.
>
> He has erected a multitude of New Offices, and sent hither swarms of Officers to harass our people, and eat out their substance. . . .

Naturally, *litany* isn't the only word to describe problems. "Litany?" Aristotle might sniff. "It's anaphora." As it is.

But by now readers know our view: *Anaphora* doesn't quite describe such a list any more than *football game* describes the Super Bowl. By *litany*, we mean the traditional sense: repetition allowing speakers to either wail about injustice or urge solutions; we mean sentences marching along in parallel construction, one after the other; we mean the device allowing speakers to build incredible momentum and force. When done well, a litany of problems—or *challenges*, as politicians often prefer to call them, with its implication that the difficulties can be overcome—can arouse anger, fear, sadness, hope for solutions, and above all the urge to act.

Alan Monroe probably didn't know Meredith Willson, but Monroe would have approved of the way Willson had Harold Hill alert townspeople about the problem they had in *The Music Man*:

> Well, either you're closing your eyes
>
> To a situation you do not wish to acknowledge
>
> Or you are not aware of the caliber of disaster indicated
>
> By the presence of a pool table in your community.
>
> Ya got trouble, my friend, right here,
>
> I say, trouble right here in River City. . . .
>
> Trouble with a capital "T"
>
> And that rhymes with "P" and that stands for pool![4]

For listeners already aware of problems they face, hearing them reaffirms their views; for those who don't know, hearing alarms them. But politicians can't stop there. Only when you make people aware of the impending disaster ahead can you make them act.

As speakers outline problems, each of the elements we've reviewed plays a different role. Concrete detail and imagery make points memorable; anecdote makes them relevant, even familiar; wit, and often sarcasm, can unite partisan crowds in their hostility to the other side; and the various ways speechwriters use evidence can turn mildly partisan listeners into followers.

In this chapter, we look at how those strategic needs fuse with each element to make the problem section effective in political speech.

STRUCTURE

There are structural decisions in each part of your speech. For presenting problems, you need to make three:

- How to define the problem
- How to contrast problem and solution
- How to find the clincher—the line that makes audiences clap, cheer, and remember

Defining the Problem: Issue or Culprit

Is the problem climate change or a conservative president who withdraws from the Paris Agreement? Is the problem high crime rates or liberal judges who let criminals go free?

Issues drive all policy speeches. But in campaigns or before highly partisan crowds, politicians identify a culprit. Often, though not always, the culprit is the other party, candidate, or administration. When Mike Pence took the stage to accept his vice-presidential nomination at the 2016 Republican National Convention, he attacked one person with his "it was Hillary Clinton" litany:

> Hillary Clinton's record on foreign affairs gets even worse.
>
> You know, it was Hillary Clinton who helped undo all the gains of the troop surge, a staggering failure of judgment that set ISIS on the loose.
>
> It was Hillary Clinton who instigated the president's disastrous agreement with the radical mullahs in Iran.
>
> And it was Hillary Clinton who left Americans in harm's way in Benghazi and after four Americans fell said, what difference at this point does it make?

> As the proud father of a United States Marine, let me say from my heart, anyone who said that, anyone who did that should be disqualified from ever serving as commander in chief of the armed forces of the United States of America!

Pence focused on one culprit, and the litany of problems he and other Republicans believed she had caused. There's nothing wrong with that. Elections are about the choice voters make between candidates.

Still, even in the heat of campaigns, political speeches are not always so partisan. Candidates speak before plenty of audiences who consider themselves primarily issue-driven, and after a campaign the number of those events climbs.

A little more than a year after the Pence speech, Donald Trump spoke about foreign policy, this time as president of the United States. In that speech, he hoped to demonstrate a broad vision for facing global threats. While he talked about culprits—like terrorists—he used what you might call a *one issue/many examples* litany: a list used to illustrate a single problem, in this case, that freedom and other democratic values were under attack.

> We live in a time of extraordinary opportunity. Breakthroughs in science, technology, and medicine are curing illnesses and solving problems that prior generations thought impossible to solve.
>
> But each day also brings news of growing dangers that threaten everything we cherish and value.
>
> Terrorists and extremists have gathered strength and spread to every region of the planet.
>
> Rogue regimes represented in this body not only support terrorists but threaten other nations and their own people with the most destructive weapons known to humanity.
>
> Authority and authoritarian powers seek to collapse the values, the systems, and alliances that prevented conflict and tilted the world toward freedom since World War II.
>
> International criminal networks traffic drugs, weapons, people; force dislocation and mass migration; threaten our borders; and new forms of aggression exploit technology to menace our citizens.
>
> To put it simply, we meet at a time of both immense promise and great peril. It is entirely up to us whether we lift the world to new heights, or let it fall into a valley of disrepair.

Issue or culprit? Once speakers make that decision they face another—how to group their problems and solutions.

Contrasting Problem and Solution: Direct or Delayed

When Los Angeles mayor Eric Garcetti spoke at the Democratic National Convention, he talked about the shared challenges faced in communities across America:

> We are prepared to confront and solve these problems together, just as we are in my hometown.
>
> In Los Angeles, we looked at America's crumbling infrastructure and started fixing it—putting more than five hundred thousand people and $50 billion to work repairing our roads and building our port, airport, and railways.
>
> In Los Angeles, we saw too many Americans living in poverty, so we became the biggest city in America to raise the minimum wage to $15 an hour, inspiring other cities and states to do the same.
>
> In Los Angeles, we saw too many lives lost to gun violence, so we banned high-capacity magazines and we are taking illegal guns off our streets.
>
> In Los Angeles, we saw too many high school dropouts and too many graduates in debt, so we are making community college free.
>
> We didn't do any of this by finding a common enemy. We found a common purpose.

Garcetti was using the technique of *direct contrast*, immediately offering a solution for each problem he named. Direct contrast can work for speeches about issues that have no clear culprit, or for occasions when speakers want to make sure they come off as able to meet any challenge. In the Garcetti excerpt, which leads to an applause line using antithesis, he chose direct contrast five times in a row, never giving listeners time to forget which problem he was talking about. Time after time, he presented his city as a model and himself as a problem solver.

There is a different advantage to *delayed contrast*. Sometimes, like Jefferson describing King George, speakers wanting to achieve critical mass build toward a culprit responsible for everything. That's what Pence did too. He focused on problems, listing them all before mentioning a solution. Pence's partisan audience hears one problem after another and thinks, "Clinton is awful."

This doesn't always mean using a full list of solutions after your list of problems.

In 2018, Democratic congressman Joe Kennedy used delayed contrast in his response to the president's message to Congress. Using *an* or *a*, he simply listed what he wanted listeners to see as the errors of Republican ways, one after the other:

> We see an economy that makes stocks soar, investor portfolios bulge, and corporate profits climb, but fails to give workers their fair share of the reward.
>
> > A government that struggles to keep itself open.
> > Russia knee-deep in our democracy.
> > An all-out war on environmental protection.
> > A justice department rolling back civil rights by the day.
> > Hatred and supremacy proudly marching in our streets.
> > Bullets tearing through our classrooms, concerts, and congregations,
>
> targeting our safest, sacred places.

Kennedy used a series of parallel sentence fragments to create a staccato effect, making listeners feel Republicans had been wrong a monumental number of times. Then, he offered a "we choose" litany of solutions that responded to none of the problems he had listed:

> As if the parent who lies awake terrified that their transgender son will be beaten and bullied at school is any more or less legitimate than the parent whose heart is shattered by a daughter in the grips of opioid addiction.
>
> > So here is the answer Democrats offer tonight: We choose both. We fight for both. Because the strongest, richest, greatest nation in the world shouldn't leave anyone behind.
> > We choose a better deal for all who call this country home.
> > We choose the living wage, paid leave, and affordable child care your family needs to survive.
> > We choose pensions that are solvent, trade pacts that are fair, roads and bridges that won't rust away, and good education you can afford.
> > We choose a health care system that offers mercy, whether you suffer from cancer or depression or addiction.

Finding the Clincher

Issue or culprit, direct versus delayed—these are decisions about structure. We don't suggest any rigid formula for your choice. The actual event will dictate that decision. But if you truly want audiences to remember, you need a clincher, a memorably worded ending that will ring in their ears.

Here is an example, again from Vice President Pence, from his speech at the 2018 Conservative Political Action Conference, or CPAC. With a billionaire at the top of the ticket, Pence made a strategic decision: remind voters that Republicans aren't all rich. He used delayed contrast—starting with three examples of Nancy Pelosi's elite attitudes:

> But the woman that wants to be Speaker of the House again, Nancy Pelosi, said— [*booing*]
> She said, she actually said, the tax cuts would be Armageddon before they passed.
> Just a few days ago, she said it was unpatriotic to let the American people keep more of what they earned. [*booing*]
> Most amazingly of all, she keeps saying that a $1,000 bonus for working Americans is nothing more than crumbs. [*booing*]

But what can he use for a clincher? He might have landed a broadside evisceration of Pelosi. Instead, he chose a gentler way: self-deprecating humor, as well as colloquial language ("Seriously, folks") to contrast her with himself, an everyday man.

> Let me remind all of you, I come from the Joseph A. Bank wing of the West Wing of the White House.
> Seriously, folks, when our kids were little, we had a term for another $1,000 in our paycheck at the end of the year.
> Christmas. [*applause*]

He mentions a store where neither Trump nor Pelosi would shop. His clincher is a single word, reminding the audience that his was a family of modest means and traditional values.

Direct. Delayed. Clincher. How to start; how to order; how to finish.

It's useful to know those different ways to construct a problem section, in the same way a carpenter needs to know the different types of screws or drill bits. Naturally, though, these decisions are about more than structure. Each example involves decisions about the LAWS of speechwriting.

So next, we'll look further at how language, anecdote, wit, and support can help you craft speeches that show listeners the urgency of problems.

LANGUAGE

Language means more than the words we choose. It includes the ways we combine them. We vary the impact of these devices depending upon our goals.

For clarity, we choose simple words, active verbs, and concrete detail. For memorable language, we choose words in combination that are vivid or rhythmic. By using litany with clauses or sentences in parallel construction, we can make problems memorable. Using concrete detail in example after example of problems can make them urgent.

Note in the examples that follow how speakers can use repetition at the beginning or at the ends of sentences, each allowing them to communicate a different idea.

Note, too, how rhetorical questions add power to problem litanies and, finally, how imagery, similes, or antithesis can sum up a passage, giving the audience new insight into the problems you describe.

Anaphora

Anaphora may be the most common kind of problem litany. As you've seen, it emphasizes similarity by using repetition at the beginning of sentences. In 1995, Hillary Clinton, then First Lady, wanted to make the point that abuse was a problem not just for women but for everyone.

At the Beijing World Conference on Women, she used anaphora for seven different examples of abuse, each sentence starting with the same eight words. The mounting effect ("It is a violation of human rights when . . .") creates suspense. Listeners wonder: *What horrific example comes next?* Clinton builds until the end. Using *antimetabole*, the reverse order we examined in Chapter 7, she, along with her speechwriter Lissa Muscatine, created a clincher that makes the speech memorable. An excerpt:

> It is a violation of *human* rights when a leading cause of death worldwide among women ages fourteen to forty-four is the violence they are subjected to in their own homes by their own relatives.
>
> It is a violation of *human* rights when young girls are brutalized by the painful and degrading practice of genital mutilation.
>
> It is a violation of *human* rights when women are denied the right to plan their own families, and that includes being forced to have abortions or being sterilized against their will.
>
> If there is one message that echoes forth from this conference, let it be that human rights are women's rights and women's rights are human rights once and for *all*.

Epistrophe

You've already seen one classic speech using repetition to end sentences—Ted Kennedy's 1980 convention speech, discussed in Chapter 7. Epistrophe, especially when combined with climactic order, lets speakers comment on the examples they've used.

The most famous example in American history: the "Ain't I a Woman?" speech of Sojourner Truth, which she delivered in 1851. We use it with some hesitation. It is skillful. But historians dispute its accuracy with good reason. Shortly after delivering it, Truth authorized a printed version that included no epistrophe at all. The version we see in anthologies was written in 1863 by a woman who was at the speech but, like the version of Patrick Henry's speech we know, recalled it entirely from memory.

We use it, authentic or not, because it is one of the most famous, and skillful, uses of epistrophe in American rhetoric.

That man over there says that women need to be helped into carriages, and lifted over ditches, and to have the best place everywhere. Nobody ever helps me into carriages, or over mud puddles, or gives me any best place! And ain't I a woman?

Look at me! Look at my arm! I have ploughed and planted, and gathered into barns, and no man could head me! And ain't I a woman?

I could work as much and eat as much as a man—when I could get it—and bear the lash as well! And ain't I a woman?

I have borne thirteen children, and seen most all sold off to slavery, and when I cried out with my mother's grief, none but Jesus heard me! And ain't I a woman?[5]

Finally, we offer a recent example—one that uses repetition at both the beginning and the end to describe and comment on problems. Delivered by teenager Emma González, it combines the two to express outrage after the shooting at her high school in Parkland, Florida, in February 2018:

Politicians who sit in their gilded House and Senate seats funded by the NRA telling us nothing could have been done to prevent this, we call BS.

They say tougher guns laws do not decrease gun violence. We call BS.

They say a good guy with a gun stops a bad guy with a gun. We call BS.

They say guns are just tools like knives and are as dangerous as cars. We call BS.

They say no laws could have prevented the hundreds of senseless tragedies that have occurred. We call BS.

That us kids don't know what we're talking about, that we're too young to understand how the government works. We call BS.[6]

González's litany, watched by millions of people, gave her a memorable way to reveal part of the problem—that she believes the other side's arguments are myths. Her mounting fervor led not just to applause but to the "call and response" reaction between her and the crowd.

Antithesis

In Chapter 7, we looked at ways antithesis can use contrast to make audiences mad. In this example, Senator Chris Murphy of Connecticut, also speaking against gun violence, uses contrast and alliteration to reject different explanations. By rejecting more than one potential reason, his repetition of "not" builds suspense as the audience waits for the real culprit, which turns out to be not inaction of others but our own.

> This epidemic of mass slaughter, this scourge of school shooting after school shooting.
>> It only happens here
>> not because of coincidence . . .
>> not because of bad luck . . .
>> but as a consequence of our inaction.

Concrete Detail

To interest audiences, provide shock of recognition, and evoke anger, be concrete.

At the United Nations in 2017, Ambassador Nikki Haley had two strategic needs: (1) evoke sympathy for the victims of Syria's chemical weapons attack, and (2) prod the international community to respond. She used a series of brief, concrete examples illustrating the horrors of the attack:

> Yesterday morning, we awoke to pictures, to children foaming at the mouth, suffering convulsions, being carried in the arms of desperate parents. We saw rows of lifeless bodies. Some still in diapers . . .

But Haley wasn't finished describing the problem. After sharing those concrete examples, she used another device:

Climactic Order

Her list not only is horrific. It builds to its most important point. Note how that progression allows her to become more passionate and create an undeniable sense of urgency.

Note also three other things. One is structural: delayed juxtaposition to create the mounting sense that Assad's "barbaric regime" was wrong not just once but many times. The two others are decisions of language: the repetition of "We know" to make this more than her own country's idea but one shared by her audience; and the final use of "We know" to surprise listeners with her clincher.

> We cannot close our eyes to those pictures. We cannot close our minds to the responsibility to act . . .
> We know that yesterday's attack bears all the hallmarks of the Assad regime's use of chemical weapons.
> We know that Assad has used these weapons against the Syrian people before. That was confirmed by this council's own independent team of investigators.
> We know that yesterday's attack was a new low, even for the barbaric Assad regime . . . Evidence reported from the scene indicates that Assad is now using even more lethal chemical agents than he did before. The gas that fell out of the sky yesterday was more deadly, leaving men, women, the elderly, and children gasping for their very last breath . . .
> We all also know this: Just a few weeks ago, this council attempted to hold Assad accountable for suffocating his own people to death with toxic chemicals . . .
> There is one more thing we know: We know that if nothing is done, these attacks will continue.

We might call climactic order a decision about structure. Certainly it becomes effective by how we order our examples. We include it here because the language Haley picked, moving from abstract ("responsibility to act") to graphic ("gasping for breath") to the most consequential ("these attacks will continue"), illustrates her point and illustrates the mounting intensity of this device.

Rhetorical Question

You have seen how rhetorical questions pose a choice for listeners. In Chapter 7, we use one of the most famous from John F. Kennedy's inaugural. They are also useful in presenting problems.

In 2014, President Barack Obama used a litany of rhetorical questions, not just to offer a choice but to make clear how serious the *wrong* choices would be:

> Are we a nation that tolerates the hypocrisy of a system where workers who pick our fruit and make our beds never have a chance to get right with the law?

Or are we a nation that gives them a chance to make amends, take responsibility, and give their kids a better future?

Are we a nation that accepts the cruelty of ripping children from their parents' arms, or are we a nation that values families and works together to keep them together?

Are we a nation that educates the world's best and brightest in our universities only to send them home to create businesses in countries that compete against us?

Or are we a nation that encourages them to stay and create jobs here, create businesses here, create industries right here in America?

That's what this debate is all about.

ANECDOTE

"If you need to make an argument about an issue about which you care deeply," wrote one *Harvard Business Review* contributor, "don't use rhetoric. Tell a story."[7]

Technically, story is a rhetorical device. Like any device, it shouldn't be overused. But in this section, you will see how choosing different kinds of stories to illustrate problems produces different effects.

Personal Anecdotes

The problem, she thought, was complacency—young people deciding that national service wasn't worth the sacrifice. At George Washington University's 2017 commencement, Illinois senator Tammy Duckworth used her personal story to persuade listeners otherwise. The graphic detail she uses makes it difficult to stay indifferent. But it is the fact that she is telling her personal story that gives her license to use those details without seeming sensationalistic.

> I was flying high that day over Iraq in my Black Hawk with the best crew out there. Then, without warning, an RPG [rocket-propelled grenade] tore through the cockpit of my aircraft . . .
>
> One of my legs was vaporized, and the other amputated by my instrument panel. The explosion blew off the entire back of my right arm. I was quite literally in pieces.
>
> My pilot-in-command managed to land. They started pulling out the wounded. They thought I was dead at first. But . . . one of my crew members . . . saw that I was still bleeding and thought maybe, just maybe, her heart was still beating.

He did what every troop in combat is willing to do without thinking, even if they hope they never have to do it—he refused treatment for himself to save someone else. My buddies wouldn't give up on me. They refused to leave me behind . . .

They picked me up, covered in my blood and tissue . . . If I didn't make it, they knew they could at least return what was left of me to my family.

But they weren't going to leave me behind in that dusty field in Iraq . . .

The days, weeks, and months that followed were some of the hardest I've ever endured. But in those most challenging moments, my life's mission couldn't have been more clear . . .

I would spend every single day of the rest of my life trying to honor the courage and sacrifice of my buddies who saved me.

Dramatic Anecdotes

In this 2014 immigration speech we mentioned earlier, President Obama gives the story room to develop, adding details that will move and convince his audience that immigration rules cause pain. Again, note how, like Duckworth's, the story he tells works in tandem with two techniques in your rhetorical arsenal: a rhetorical question and a quote (from Scripture).

Astrid [Silva] was brought to America when she was four years old. Her only possessions were a cross, her doll, and the frilly dress she had on.

When she started school, she didn't speak any English. She caught up to other kids by reading newspapers and watching PBS, and she became a good student.

Her father worked in landscaping. Her mom cleaned other people's homes. They wouldn't let Astrid apply to a technology magnet school, not because they didn't love her, but because they were afraid the paperwork would out her as an undocumented immigrant—so she applied behind their back and got in.

Still, she mostly lived in the shadows—until her grandmother, who visited every year from Mexico, passed away, and she couldn't travel to the funeral without risk of being found out and deported . . .

Are we a nation that kicks out a striving, hopeful immigrant like Astrid, or are we a nation that finds a way to welcome her in?

Scripture tells us that we shall not "oppress a stranger, for we know the heart of a stranger—we were strangers once, too."

Historical Anecdotes

Often, political rhetoric tries to demonize the other side. But look at this example from Elie Wiesel, speaking at the White House in 1999 about the lessons of his life, and see how he becomes more credible with this story about Franklin Delano Roosevelt:

> The depressing tale of the *St. Louis* is a case in point.
>
> Sixty years ago, its human cargo—nearly 1,000 Jews—was turned back to Nazi Germany. And that happened after *Kristallnacht*, the first state-sponsored pogrom, with hundreds of Jewish shops destroyed, synagogues burned, thousands of people put in concentration camps. And that ship, which was already in the shores of the United States, was sent back.
> I don't understand.
> Roosevelt was a good man, with a heart. He understood those who needed help.
> Why didn't he allow these refugees to disembark? A thousand people—in America, the great country, the greatest democracy, the most generous of all new nations in modern history.
> What happened?
> I don't understand. Why the indifference, on the highest level, to the suffering of the victims?[8]

We use this story because it illustrates how language—in this case, concrete images and a litany of questions—creates urgency. This speech also does something that we rarely see. He is talking about an enormous problem—indifference. But instead of blaming someone he might demonize, Wiesel picks a president that he and his listeners admire. Instead of castigating FDR, he picks one word to make his problem more compelling. "Why."

He offers no solution. He risks making his audience uncomfortable. But by using that word, and his series of questions with his praise of FDR, Wiesel describes how human beings can be both guilty and good; that evil action comes not just from evil people but from those "with a heart."

WIT

From the profound to the silly.

It's rare in politics to use long story-jokes amid problem sections. Wit often means a quip, aside, pun, quote, analogy, or very short story-joke. Politicians use wit to poke fun at the other side, at the absurdity of a situation—or at themselves to appear likable. Because you don't want to seem to be joking about problems crucial to your listeners, wit in the problem section of speeches is often restricted to sarcasm, hyperbole, and other devices to caricature opponents during campaigns.

In this example from George W. Bush's 2007 State of the Union address, the president needed just six words to get a laugh from a crowd of friends and fierce enemies.

He acknowledges a *problem:* that both sides indulge in secrecy when it comes to spending. He lightens the tone, since the culprits are in his audience. But without the six words at the end, who would remember the problem he cites?

> Next, there is the matter of earmarks. These special interest items are often slipped into bills at the last hour—when not even C-SPAN is watching.

Asides

In theater, an aside means an utterance by an actor heard by the audience but supposedly not heard by the other actors on stage.[9] In political theater, an aside is more of an afterthought revealing an internal musing; it is a brief, often funny, line that might stray from a main subject but still punctuates it—as in this excerpt from a 2011 Mitt Romney speech, a version of which you'll find in the Appendix:

> As he [Barack Obama] watched millions and millions of Americans lose their jobs, lose their homes, and lose their hope, his response was this: It could be worse.
> It could be worse? This is the leader of the free world's answer to the greatest job loss since the Great Depression? What's next? Let them eat cake?
> Oh, excuse me. Organic cake.

Asides in speeches are usually not done off the cuff. Nor should they be. Doing them well takes practice. Because of his wealth, Romney was usually the one defending charges of elitism. "Organic cake," a carefully scripted aside, reminded Romney's Republican base that he shared their values and priorities.

Puns

Truly good puns are rare. The ones that work succeed by surprising audience members with a meaning they didn't anticipate. You won't find many opportunities for puns when talking about serious problems. But if you see one and can lighten the mood without seeming to trivialize the issue, go for it.

Here, speaking before a joint session of Congress, French president Emmanuel Macron uses a pun (as well as a colloquialism) as a clincher in a speech on the dire consequences of ignoring our environment:

> By polluting the oceans, not mitigating fuel emission, and destroying our biodiversity, we're killing our planet. Let us face it. There is no planet B.

SUPPORT

You may have entered speechwriting thinking of evidence as a painful necessity, the rhetorical equivalent of a flu shot. Think again. Backing up your assertions can be the most absorbing element of your argument. In these examples, speakers don't just provide the standard kinds of evidence: brief and extended examples, or testimony, or numbers. They combine them imaginatively with tools of language and structure.

Brief Example

Ronald Reagan's 1987 "tear down this wall" speech, created by Peter Robinson as Chapter 4 describes, uses dramatic examples, organized by geography, to demonstrate how all of Germany suffered.

The heart of that speech is a litany of brief examples. The Berlin Wall, the barbed wire to the south, the guards and checkpoints further south, and Brandenburg Gate.

But as we have done throughout this book, we want readers to see that to give those examples power, Reagan's writers gave them an army of helpers. They included climactic order—Reagan's final example is Berlin, where the speech takes place. They infused concrete detail (the "gash of barbed wire"); inverted traditional grammar ("Behind me stands a wall"); and took a kind of geographic tour using not one or two concrete details but a whole series of small examples to build to and justify his final image.

> Behind me stands a wall that encircles the free sectors of this city, part of a vast system of barriers that divides the entire continent of Europe.
> From the Baltic South, those barriers cut across Germany in a gash of barbed wire, concrete, dog runs, and guard towers.
> Farther south, there may be no visible, no obvious wall. But there remain armed guards and checkpoints all the same—still a restriction

on the right to travel, still an instrument to impose upon ordinary men and women the will of a totalitarian state.

Yet, it is here in Berlin where the wall emerges most clearly; here, cutting across your city, where the news photo and the television screen have imprinted this brutal division of a continent upon the mind of the world.

Standing before the Brandenburg Gate, every man is a German separated from his fellow men.

Every man is a Berliner, forced to look upon a scar.

Extended Example

Sometimes speakers shy away from too much detail about one example, but staying on one for a while can give the audience time to see what you're talking about. And sometimes, speakers use detail those sitting before them find hard to grasp.

That was the case when Rep. Duncan Hunter (R-CA) talked to CPAC in March 2007. He used a single object—his podium—to illustrate the many problems disturbing him about the Chinese economy.

Look closely to see how Hunter uses a variant of the "And there's more!" structure of TV hucksters. Study how he puts a policy into dialogue, as if the Chinese government is a person. But when you are done, ask yourself whether you could repeat Hunter's argument to someone else.

> China is cheating on trade.
>
> And let me tell you how they're doing it.
>
> If this podium was made in China and exported to us here in the United States and it was $100 when it goes down to the water's edge to be exported to us, the government of China walks over and gives its exporter all their taxes back, something we can't do under the trade law we signed, incidentally.
>
> They give them back $17, all their VAT [value-added] taxes. So the cost of this is now down to $83.
>
> When we send the same product over to them, they give us a bill for $17, thereby making us noncompetitive.
>
> And just to make sure that the Americans never win in a competition, they devalue their currency by 40 percent.
>
> And that means that if this product is sitting in a showroom floor somewhere around the world, and sitting next to it is a product made in China, it's the equivalent, and they're both tagged at $100 and somebody's trying to decide which one to buy.

Admittedly, the math is hard to follow. The long sentences add to the complexity. But Hunter knew what he was doing; he included this passage to accomplish what writers need to keep in mind: the lobbyists, reporters, and corporate officers not in the hall.

Testimony

The many varieties of testimony as evidence—quoting opponents, citing experts, using the pithy words of others—lend themselves naturally to defining problems in a speech.

Mary Fisher, an AIDS victim, tries to persuade delegates at the 1992 Republican National Convention to confront the agonizing problem of her disease. Her entire speech is also in the Appendix.

In this passage, Fisher, like Tammy Duckworth, offers her personal testimony. Most striking, though, is her attempt, in 1992, to make her audience believe that AIDS, which many Americans then believed was the fault of its victims, was similar to the Holocaust.

Changing the views of most listeners in a hostile crowd is usually impossible.

But the shift in Fisher's audience is unmistakable. What caused it? Certainly there were a variety of reasons: that she looked like her audience, talked about her children, and had no political axe to grind. But by combining Pastor Niemöller's testimony with her own, and making listeners confront the facts of her agonizing dilemma, Fisher uses the power of the personal example to change their minds.

> Because I was not hemophiliac, I was not at risk. Because I was not gay, I was not at risk. Because I did not inject drugs, I was not at risk.
>
> My father has devoted much of his lifetime guarding against another holocaust.
>
> He is part of the generation who heard Pastor Niemöller come out of the Nazi death camps to say, "They came after the Jews, and I was not a Jew, so, I did not protest. They came after the trade unionists, and I was not a trade unionist, so, I did not protest. Then they came after the Roman Catholics, and I was not a Roman Catholic, so, I did not protest. Then they came after me, and there was no one left to protest."
>
> The lesson history teaches is this: If you believe you are safe, you are at risk.
>
> If you do not see this killer stalking your children, look again.

Also useful is Mitch Landrieu's use of testimony in his speech about taking down Confederate statues, first excerpted in Chapter 10. You've seen how politicians can use a quote to show that an idea is so reasonable even the other side agrees. Here, Landrieu takes the opposite approach. By using the other side's own words, he is looking not to enhance credibility, but rather to express incredulity.

> Should you have further doubt about the true goals of the Confederacy, in the very weeks before the war broke out, the vice president of the Confederacy, Alexander Stephens, made it clear that the Confederate cause was about maintaining slavery and white supremacy.
>
> He said in his now famous "Cornerstone Speech" that the Confederacy's "cornerstone rests upon the great truth, that the negro is not equal to the white man; that slavery—subordination to the superior race—is his natural and normal condition. This, our new government, is the first, in the history of the world, based upon this great physical, philosophical, and moral truth."

Facts/Statistics

Writers and speakers should never be content just to cite a number. A blizzard of numbers can make listeners whip out a phone and start checking their Twitter feed. But in his 1988 Democratic National Convention speech, before smartphones existed, Jesse Jackson won cheers by using stats to make clear the urgency of what he believed were problems facing America.

His first technique was litany. By using repetition ("I just want . . .") at the start of each step, he demonstrated similarity—a lack of common sense. That made him forceful.

He also used antithesis, to contrast what he considered foolish policies with the facts that demonstrated why. That made what he said memorable.

> I just want to take common sense to high places. We're spending $150 billion a year defending Europe and Japan forty-three years after the war is over.
>
> I just want to take common sense to higher places. If we can bail out Europe and Japan, if we can bail out Continental Bank and Chrysler—and [Chrysler CEO Lee] Iacocca makes $8,000 an hour—we can bail out the family farmer.
>
> I just want to make common sense. It does not make sense to close down 650,000 family farms in this country while importing food from abroad subsidized by the U.S. government.

In 2018, Attorney General Jeff Sessions also put statistics in context in this Pittsburgh speech about the opioid epidemic and its connection to violent crime.

He begins by citing a large number of deaths caused by drug overdoses, but then adds perspective and urgency by deducing how often these deaths occur.

Then he makes the problem even more relevant by comparing the number to the population of a Pennsylvania city. Finally, citing a Justice Department study for credibility, he adds even more Pittsburgh-specific statistics while discussing the larger issue of violent crime.

> More Americans are dying because of drugs than ever before. Two thousand and sixteen saw an estimated sixty-four thousand Americans die of drug overdose—one every nine minutes. That's more than the population of Lancaster, Pennsylvania, dead in one year. And in 2017 it appears that the death toll was even higher.
>
> For Americans under the age of fifty, drug overdoses are now the leading cause of death. Millions of Americans are living with the daily struggle of an addiction.
>
> I don't think it was a coincidence that violent crime and drug abuse rose at the same time. I was just reading one of our department-funded studies that found that nearly a quarter of the increase in homicides is the result of the increase in drug-related homicides.
>
> Sadly, Pennsylvania knows this all too well. In 2016 in Pittsburgh, the violent crime rate was double the national average. The murder rate and the robbery rate was triple the national average. Pittsburgh is in the 77th percentile for violent crime overall, the 88th percentile for robbery, and the 90th percentile for murder.

FINAL WORDS

In May 1961, the newly appointed chairman of the Federal Communications Commission stood up in front of the National Association of Broadcasters and the powerful top television executives to deliver his very first speech. He started as you might expect, with some of the elements we discussed in the previous chapter. He thanked his audience for the opportunity. He used wit (describing the way he left his office for the speech as his "maiden station break"). And he offered praise for what he said was a "most honorable profession."

AS DELIVERED

FCC Chairman Newton Minow Speaking to the National Association of Broadcasters. Years later, in an interview he did for the Television Academy Foundation, Newton Minow said he edited the line in his speech that described the problem so vividly and memorably. The draft, he said, included the words "the vast wasteland of junk."

"I crossed off 'of junk' . . . and paid absolutely no attention to it. I was paying attention to two [other] words . . . public interest. I wanted to send a message."[10]

https://www.americanrhetoric.com/speeches/newtonminow.htm

But then, Newton Minow continued to the part of his speech that made it famous: the problem. Television, he said, was not about the public interest; rather, it was a "vast wasteland."

When television is good, nothing—not the theater, not the magazines or newspapers—nothing is better.

But when television is bad, nothing is worse. I invite each of you to sit down in front of your television set when your station goes on the air and stay there, for a day, without a book, without a magazine, without a newspaper, without a profit and loss sheet or a rating book to distract you. Keep your eyes glued to that set until the station signs off. I can assure you that what you will observe is a vast wasteland.

You will see a procession of game shows, formula comedies about totally unbelievable families, blood and thunder, mayhem, violence, sadism, murder, western bad men, western good men, private eyes, gangsters, more violence, and cartoons. And endlessly, commercials—many screaming, cajoling, and offending. And most of all, boredom. True, you'll see a few things you will enjoy. But they will be very, very few. And if you think I exaggerate, I only ask you to try it.

Is there one person in this room who claims that broadcasting can't do better? Well, a glance at next season's proposed programming can give us little heart. Of seventy-three and a half hours of prime evening time, the networks have tentatively scheduled fifty-nine hours of categories of action-adventure, situation comedy, variety, quiz, and movies.

Is there one network president in this room who claims he can't do better? Gentlemen, your trust accounting with your beneficiaries is long overdue. Never have so few owed so much to so many.

Isolating rhetorical techniques is a useful teaching convention. This speech remains known for its vivid analogy. But as we've tried to show you in this chapter and throughout the book, the strength of these techniques comes from the way you combine them to build the effects you want.

Minow starts the section with parallel structure, alerting the audience to the criticism that comes next. He describes a hypothetical situation, asking executives to spend a full day in front of their TVs. That's followed by a litany of "withouts," leading into his analogy.

He doesn't end there, though. He offers brief examples, defying the rule of three to show the scope of the problem. He uses rhetorical devices like consonance (scream*ing*, cajol*ing*, and offend*ing*) and sentence fragments. He offers statistics, asks incredulous rhetorical questions, and ends with a clincher, paraphrasing Winston Churchill.

Each and every technique adds to the urgency of the problem he describes. Not bad for a 264-word excerpt.

We realize that politics is not just, well, politics. There are times when politicians with the help of their writers need to mount a substantive argument that makes few concessions to the audience. Responsible political speech should provide the reasonable, fact-laden problem description that a general audience needs, even if sometimes listeners might have a hard time following. And leadership sometimes demands complexity and nuance.

So critics of "substance-free campaign speeches" have a point. Especially during campaigns, speakers don't detail specific problems and solutions nearly often enough. The more other candidates win attention for keeping speeches flashy and superficial, the more tempting it can be to go there yourself. Resist the temptation. Study speeches, like Newton Minow's, with plenty of substance that still engage listeners through the rhetorical techniques you've examined. It's possible to grab your audience and still feel good about your message.

In many ways, the problem sections of political speeches are the easiest parts to write. Most people agree that poverty, disease, unemployment, and war exist and are not good things. It's when politicians propose solutions that arguments begin. What role should government play? How much should a solution cost?

After all, when it comes to policies, the public expects politicians—helped by staff—to do more than outline problems. They are the fixers. Voters expect them to offer solutions.

This means that after racing through their problem litanies, politicians change pace. They may lower their voice, take a sip of water, and lean over the podium. Then, they may say something as simple as "Terrible problems. How do we fix them?"

Let's see.

THE SPEECHWRITER'S CHECKLIST: PRESENTING THE PROBLEM

- ☐ Have I described problems that are relevant to the audience?
- ☐ Have I used problems in the three ways that are useful in politics: reaffirming beliefs, alerting listeners, and motivating them to act?
- ☐ Have I made a conscious decision between direct and delayed contrast of problem and solution? Does the choice suit my goal?
- ☐ Have I used clinchers for each issue?
- ☐ Have I made good use of litany to do X?
- ☐ Have I described problems concretely, providing statistics as needed?
- ☐ Are problems listed in climactic order?
- ☐ Are problems supported by varying evidence—including story, example, testimony, and fact?
- ☐ If the occasion and audience call for unusual levels of detail, have I crafted a compelling way to provide it? Was I able to find room for humor where appropriate?

13

Solutions

The French Revolution is over. The winners are busy guillotining the corrupt aristocracy. But the priests have ordered them to obey one rule: If the guillotine doesn't work, God has told them the prisoner is innocent. They must set the prisoner free.

First up: a court doctor. He puts his head on the block. The executioner pulls the rope. It's stuck!

"Okay, you're innocent. Go home."

Next: the king's lawyer. The executioner pulls. It's stuck again. Nothing!

"Okay, you're innocent. Get out of here."

Third up: an engineer for the royal palace. The executioner is about to pull the rope.

"Wait!" the engineer cries. "I see the problem!"

*

Politicians love that old joke. Partly that's because people like to laugh at stupidity. But they also laugh because politicians, like that unfortunate engineer, can't help but offer solutions. If, using the tips in Chapter 12, you make listeners see the urgency of problems, you now have a new task: offering solutions.

Offering the wrong solution isn't always fatal; otherwise, officeholders would be out of a job every two years. But offering solutions that listeners dislike—like Jimmy Carter's "wear a sweater" about energy costs, Donald Trump's "arm teachers" after school shootings, or Commerce Secretary Wilbur Ross's "why shouldn't they be able to get a loan" suggestion for furloughed federal employees—can certainly hurt.

Making solutions convincing starts by a return to our questions of fact, values, and policy. You'll answer those for listeners using the same techniques you used for the problem section and highlighted throughout this book: structure and the LAWS of speechwriting: language, anecdote, wit, and, of course, support.

Political speech, though, uses a different approach to solutions than other kinds. General speechwriting guides devote a lot of space to figuring out how to win people over. It makes sense to find out whether listeners are for or against your solutions. Such texts distinguish between what are called "passive agreement" and "immediate action."

But most politicians speak largely to targeted and friendly audiences. They are often less concerned with changing people's minds than putting them to work.

That doesn't always make speeches the place to spell out very detailed solutions. The increasingly rich amount of material online gives politicians plenty of ways to provide substance for those who crave it. Politicians tweet all the time with links to their website and policy proposals. Certainly those proposals should offer enough detail to be credible. In political speeches, though, passive agreement leaves the battle half won. Solutions must sound exciting, and better than the alternatives. In this chapter, we look at two ways to make sure solutions meet that standard—through the language you choose and how you characterize your speaker. And because, as with problems, solutions involve structural decisions, we will look at one particularly effective structure for those as well.

We begin, though, with what is not always obvious. Even when the differences between politicians are dramatically different, they argue in very similar ways.

Consider, for example, the passionate Senate floor debate in January 2018 about what sponsors called the "Pain-Capable Unborn Child Protection Act." It would have prohibited abortions after five months.

It was remarkable for many reasons, not least the sincerity of the speakers and thoroughness of their arguments. Sincerity, though, did not mean civility. The two sides could not have been further apart. For one side, the bill was a brilliant solution to what it considered murder. For the other, the bill was an indefensible assault on what it considered the rights of women. The debate was bitter.

But look at the clash between two Senators on opposite sides that day. Notice the similarity both in the techniques they choose and in what they ignore, while hewing to the triad of fact, value, and policy.

First, an excerpt from a supporter: Sen. Joni Ernst (R-IA).

> Again, I am urging my colleagues to support the Pain-Capable Unborn Child Protection Act. By any measure, at five months of development, an unborn child is a child.
>
> At five months [*statistic*], babies have grown nails on their fingers and on their toes; hair has just begun to grow on their heads; and an ultrasound can tell an expectant mother or father whether their baby is a boy or a girl.

These babies can detect light, hear sounds, they can swallow, and even experience taste as their taste buds grow and develop [*brief examples*].

These unborn babies in all ways are babies [*unsupported assertion*].

There is also significant scientific evidence that at five months of development these babies can feel pain. By five months, babies begin to respond to painful stimulus with distinctive pain response behaviors that are exhibited by older babies. They will scrunch their eyes, they will clench their hands, they pull back their limbs in response to pain, just like any other child experiencing pain [*repetition*]. . . .

As modern medicine has recognized, these babies are humans capable of experiencing pain. Yet there is no federal law protecting these vulnerable humans from abortions. As a result, every year in our country the lives of thousands of babies end painfully through abortion [*dire consequences*]. This is unacceptable [*values*]. . . .

Additionally, multiple states, including my home state of Iowa, have passed legislation that would prohibit abortions after five months of development because these babies are babies [*policy examples*].

There is no way to deny the humanity of these children when you consider stories like that of Micah Pickering.

Micah is from Newton, Iowa. He is a very young friend of mine. He is five years old. Just a few weeks ago on the floor of the Senate I was able to share Micah's story [*story*]. . . .

When I first met Micah, he was about three years old. He and his parents visited my office for the annual March for Life. I had this poster made of these pictures, and they were in my office because I was going to speak on the Senate floor in support of March for Life. Micah is pictured on the right side of the poster board. Micah, a happy, energetic little boy, saw this poster board in my office, and he ran up to it—imagine, this beautiful three-year-old boy—and he pointed not at the picture of himself as he was at three years old, but he pointed to this picture, and he said: Baby. I said:

Yes, Micah, that is a baby.

Now the excerpt from an opponent: Sen. Elizabeth Warren (D-MA).

If it passes, this unconstitutional bill would put women's lives and women's health at risk [*dire consequences*].

Government officials who seek to insert themselves between women and their doctors ought to listen to the women whose lives are on the line and the doctors who care for them. If they were listening right now, we wouldn't be holding this vote.

Only 1 percent of abortions take place at twenty-one weeks or later, and the reasons are heartbreaking [*statistics*]. I have heard from people across Massachusetts who shared their devastating stories. The Senate should hear these stories.

One woman who wrote to me explained that she was ecstatic to have a second child but learned late in her pregnancy that her daughter's brain was severely malformed [*story*]. She said, "Being a grown woman with a husband and daughter, I never imagined that I would need to [get an abortion]. But when I learned that the baby I was carrying suffered from a set of severe brain malformations, I faced a binary choice for her: peace or life. . . . I am deeply grateful that I was able to give her the gift of peace."

She and her husband did what they thought was best for their baby girl. They got an abortion in the third trimester. . . .

But the bill we are voting on today . . . would force women to carry an unviable fetus to term. It would force [*repetition*] women with severe health complications to stay pregnant until their lives were on the line. Whatever you believe about abortion generally, this legislation is dangerous and cruel [*values*].

Devastating fetal abnormalities aren't the only reason women get abortions after twenty weeks. Some women face so many delays when seeking an abortion, like finding a provider, raising money for the procedure, and paying for travel costs—so many delays that a procedure they wanted earlier in pregnancy gets pushed later and later [*brief examples*]. These logistical hurdles fall hardest on young people, on women of color, and on low-income communities.

What is behind some of these delays? State-level abortion restrictions pushed through by Republican legislatures that close down clinics and make it harder for women to get access to the care they need [*unsupported assertion*]. You heard that right. Republican-sponsored abortion restrictions push women to have abortions later and later, and today, Republicans in the Senate push a bill to ban late abortions. It is all connected. . . .

If Mitch McConnell or Paul Ryan or Donald Trump actually wanted to reduce abortions, they could embrace policies that would lessen the economic pressures of pregnancy and of motherhood. They could act to help pregnant women and their babies access health care early and often. They could help young women avoid unwanted pregnancies in the first place [*repetition*]. . . .

It has been forty-five years since *Roe v. Wade*; forty-five years since women gained the constitutional right to a safe, legal abortion; forty-five years since the days of illegal abortions [*examples from the past*]. I have lived in that America. I have lived in the world of back-alley butchers and wrecked lives. And we are not going back—not now, not ever.

The views of each speaker horrify and infuriate the other. Yet both make their case by using brief *examples*. Both use at least one *statistic, story, repetition, values, unsupported assertions*, and *examples*. Both warn of *dire consequences* if the Senate rejects their solutions. Both detail the problems before urging solutions.

But there is no question of their sincerity. Ernst gives listeners evidence that the bill's solution has been tried and worked in her home state, which will satisfy her supporters.

Warren wants to show the opposite: that the bill not only is wrong but ignores solutions that would make things better. She offers an alternative that would meet what she feels are the real needs of "pregnancy and motherhood."

When we examine solutions in political speech, we rarely find speakers wrestling with big philosophical questions. In fact, one could argue that both senators ignore what is at the heart of the debate—the tangled question of whether and when a fetus is a human being. Instead, in politics and as demonstrated by Ernst and Warren, solutions generally focus on four seemingly more practical questions:

Is this solution better than what we have?

Is it better than what the other side offers?

Is it better than doing nothing?

Is it better for most people or just a few?

While it is a weakness in political life that the debate over solutions is so limited, those are not irrelevant questions. And that brings us to the two approaches for how speakers and writers, no matter what their views, can frame solutions to persuade and inspire listeners.

INSPIRE SOLUTIONS WITH LANGUAGE

The point of solutions is not simply to show listeners a speaker has one. It is to make clear that they are listening to speakers who can make things better.

PART III Applications

Better than what? Here we include four examples, making the "better" argument in a different way—and each using a different rhetorical device.

Better Than What We Have

Use Anaphora: A "We Can Do Better" Litany to Suggest Solutions Better Than What Exists

In February 2005 when he was a brand-new senator, Barack Obama used *repetition* and *concrete detail* in a floor speech to rebut supporters of the Bankruptcy Abuse Prevention and Consumer Protection Act of 2005. After a litany of three concrete "we can do better" sentences about problems, contrasting his solution with what existed, he switched to a "we can give" clincher to offer his solution. His solution was vague, but he achieved impact by using repetition again—the two "you may" clauses in his clincher—to argue it was better than what existed.

> But we can do better than one bankruptcy every nineteen seconds.
> We can do better than forcing people to choose between the cost of health care and the cost of college.
> We can do better than big corporations using bankruptcy laws to deny health care and benefits to their employees.
> And we can give people the basic tools and protections they need to believe that in America, your circumstance is no limit to the success you may achieve and the dreams you may fulfill.

Better Than the Other Guy

Use Epistrophe: Repetition at the End to Contrast Your Solution with the Other Side

In George H. W. Bush's 1988 acceptance speech, his clever litany directly contrasts his opponent's solutions to his own. Notice that Bush uses epistrophe to emphasize his view, not Michael Dukakis's. By ending with "I say yes," he ensures the applause line having convinced his audience that his solution was better than that of the other side.

> Should public school teachers be required to lead our children in the Pledge of Allegiance? My opponent says no—and I say yes.
> Should society be allowed to impose the death penalty on those who commit crimes of extraordinary cruelty and violence? My opponent says no—and I say yes.
> And should children have the right to say a voluntary prayer, or even observe a moment of silence in the schools? My opponent says no—and I say yes.

Better Than Doing Nothing

Use Rhetorical Questions to Urge a Better Way with Passion

In the last chapter, we cited the problem section from Federal Communications Commission chair Newton Minow's famous 1961 speech. But it wasn't just the problem section that put in motion change that helped create public television and cable.[1]

It was also the litany of questions Minow used to propose a solution. Each of the six offered a different suggestion for the audience of TV executives. Speakers can deliver questions passionately. By repeating "Is there no room" four times before his call to action, Minow not only used specific images but questions to discredit doing nothing.

> What about your responsibilities? Is there no room on television to teach, to inform, to uplift, to stretch, to enlarge the capacities of our children?
>
> Is there no room for programs deepening their understanding of children in other lands? Is there no room for a children's news show explaining something to them about the world at their level of understanding?
>
> Is there no room for reading the great literature of the past, for teaching them the great traditions of freedom?
>
> There are some fine children's shows, but they are drowned out in the massive doses of cartoons, violence, and more violence. Must these be your trademarks?
>
> Search your consciences and see if you cannot offer more to your young beneficiaries whose future you guide so many hours each and every day.[2]

Better Than What We've Done

Combine "Let Us" with Antithesis to Suggest That Your Solutions Apply to Everyone

In this litany from his inaugural address, John F. Kennedy avoids blaming Russia. Instead, he used the more inclusive "Let us" and "Let both sides," thus paving the way for negotiation.

And while we focus on antithesis, note other language choices in these five sentences: *antimetabole* (the reversal of two words in their different meanings) and *alliteration* (the repetition of initial sounds in neighboring words or syllables).

> So let us begin anew—remembering on both sides that civility is not a sign of weakness, and sincerity is always subject to proof. Let us never negotiate out of fear, but let us never fear to negotiate.

Let both sides explore what problems unite us instead of belaboring those problems which divide us.

Let both sides, for the first time, formulate serious and precise proposals for the inspection and control of arms. . . .

Let both sides seek to invoke the wonders of science instead of its terrors.

To claim that a solution is better than nothing doesn't mean it is. Still, what Minow and JFK offered wasn't meaningless. Listeners knew what Kennedy meant by "fear to negotiate," and what Minow meant by "reading the great literature."

And while the unusually detailed Ernst and Warren floor speeches could grapple more thoughtfully with the issues central to abortion, they demonstrate that even in a small space, it is perfectly possible to use enough evidence, or detail about solutions, to be both credible—and persuasive.

In solutions, litany can be your technique of default. It allows you to set the tone even in the first two words.

- *To create urgency:* We must . . .
- *To bond with listeners:* We need . . .
- *To argue that something can't wait:* Now is [the time] . . .
- *To connect after mentioning a problem:* That's why . . .
- *To evoke the need for partnership:* Let us . . .
- *To reassure those who doubt:* We can . . .

When you combine litany with other techniques we have already discussed, solutions become even more compelling—especially because of another Aristotelian way to persuade: characterizing speakers.

INSPIRE SOLUTIONS THROUGH ETHOS

Imagine yourself in Congress, taking part in the 2018 debate about repealing Obamacare.

If you favor a "single-payer" system—the proposal that government pay all the bills for an individual's health care—you might want listeners to know you will battle for it. If you are pessimistic about the outcome, you might want just to say you believe in it. Or perhaps you simply might open the door to compromise.

You might characterize yourself differently depending on whether you are Democrat or Republican, want to appeal to doctors or a local union, speaking on the floor or back in the district. To sound combative might work well for a partisan crowd but terribly for an audience of clinicians. To promise quick success might appeal to those who don't understand the complicated process of legislation but bring contempt from those who do.

Deciding which approach works is a decision about *ethos*, the Greek word meaning "character" we discuss in Chapter 2. Aristotle argued that in addition to *logos* and *pathos*, speakers could persuade by displaying character audiences admire. None of us likes to be labeled—in theory. Here, though, are five different ways speakers characterize themselves while proposing solutions, each with risks and benefits.

The Achiever

Don't just present solutions—pledge to try your damnedest *to achieve them*.

Pledging to *achieve* success is risky; listeners may admire your boldness but, a year later, ask why you haven't come through.

Pledging to *try* is another matter. In the solutions section from his 1961 inaugural address, John F. Kennedy did not promise success. He offered solutions by segmenting his audience, beginning each section with "To those who," and making a pledge to that group alone.

In this two-sentence excerpt, he uses the repetition of "help" and two skillful examples of antithesis, including the memorable assertion of his "If" clincher.

> To those peoples in the huts and villages of half the globe struggling to break the bonds of mass misery, we pledge our best efforts to help them help themselves, for whatever period is required—not because the Communists may be doing it, not because we seek their votes, but because it is right. . . .
>
> If a free society cannot help the many who are poor, it cannot save the few who are rich.

Note how Kennedy insulates himself against attack by essentially promising to try hard. This is the ethos of realism, common in political life for good reason. Promising to pass a bill—or even introduce one—is too uncertain a proposition to warrant without being sure of the outcome.

The Believer

Demonstrate your belief when you are sure it is one the crowd shares.

While Mike Huckabee did well in the February 5, 2008, "Super Tuesday" primary, he was still a long shot. His victory speech didn't promise success or even command followers to fight. His approach to ethos was simple.

He wanted to remind listeners of what they had in common. He used a "We're here tonight" litany of solutions about family, secure borders, and abortion to do that.

> We're here tonight and winning states across the South because we've stood for the idea that mothers and fathers raise better kids than governments do. And government ought to undergird a family, not undermine a basic family's right to raise their own kids....
>
> We're here tonight because people want to know that the president is going to secure our borders and make it so it's not more difficult to get on an airplane in your hometown than it is to cross the international border....
>
> And we should uphold the sanctity of human life because it is a cornerstone of our culture of life.
>
> And ladies and gentlemen, tonight I believe that one of the things you're seeing across the nation is that people are saying the conservatives do have a choice because the conservatives have a voice.

In one way, stating beliefs seems less risky than the pledge to achieve. You can't be accused of breaking a promise because you have made none. But believers are open to another charge: that in telling listeners what you should do, you are afraid to offer what you would.

The Fighter

Partisan crowds may not be content with speakers who offer beliefs or pledge to do their best. To them, ethos persuades when politicians make it clear they will fight. Fighters should not only offer solutions but characterize themselves as eager to do battle. One way to do that: Challenge the other side with *apostrophe*—which means speaking to the absent enemy.

There are famous examples in real life ("Mr. Gorbachev, tear down this wall"). Here are two others, one from a film, and the other from real life. Note Michael Douglas's approach in the 1995 hit *The American President*. Anaphora, rhetorical question, and sentence fragments all help:

> America isn't easy. America is advanced citizenship. You've gotta want it bad, 'cause it's gonna put up a fight. It's gonna say, "You want free speech? Let's see you acknowledge a man whose words make your blood boil, who's standing center stage and advocating at the top of his lungs that which you would spend a lifetime opposing at the top of yours. You want to claim this land as the land of the free? Then the symbol of your country cannot just be a flag. The

symbol also has to be one of its citizens exercising his right to burn that flag in protest." Now show me that, defend that, celebrate that in your classrooms. Then you can stand up and sing about the land of the free.[3]

Too melodramatic for the real world of politics? Examine the often-cited but rarely quoted 2002 speech by a then-obscure Illinois state senator named Barack Obama, in which he impresses a fiercely antiwar crowd by addressing not the people in front of him, but the president. Note his use of anaphora, rhetorical question, and sentence fragments:

> So for those of us who seek a more just and secure world for our children, let us send a clear message to the president.
>
> You want a fight, President Bush? Let's finish the fight with Bin Laden and al-Qaeda, through effective, coordinated intelligence, and a shutting down of the financial networks that support terrorism, and a homeland security program that involves more than color-coded warnings.
>
> You want a fight, President Bush? Let's fight to make sure that . . . we vigorously enforce a nonproliferation treaty, and that former enemies and current allies like Russia safeguard and ultimately eliminate their stores of nuclear material, and that nations like Pakistan and India never use the terrible weapons already in their possession, and that the arms merchants in our own country stop feeding the countless wars that rage across the globe.
>
> You want a fight, President Bush? Let's fight to wean ourselves off Middle East oil through an energy policy that doesn't simply serve the interests of Exxon and Mobil.
>
> Those are the battles that we need to fight. Those are the battles that we willingly join. The battles against ignorance and intolerance. Corruption and greed. Poverty and despair.

Did Obama consciously or unconsciously imitate Michael Douglas? Who knows? But this should remind you that in the search for models, you shouldn't be above looking to Hollywood.

The Harmonizer

Even in the most partisan environments, you can't ignore a willingness to bring people together using ideas from both sides. Persuasion expert Daniel O'Keefe says it this way: "A communicator is likely to be perceived as more ... trustworthy if the advocated position 'disconfirms' the audience's expectations about the communicator's views." One example he uses: "a life-long Democrat speaking for a Republican candidate."[4]

Seeking a harmonizer has been a consistent refrain in the bitter debates during the Trump administration. To bring harmony means more than criticizing your own side. It can mean acknowledging that the other side's views have merit. That's why in 1996, Bill Clinton, under attack from the right, adopted solutions that allowed him to be, as one aide put it, "more Republican than Republicans" about issues such as welfare reform, free trade, and tax cuts.

In 2009, when Barack Obama gave his controversial commencement speech at the University of Notre Dame, the "pro-choice" president did something similar. Facing an audience that included many "pro-lifers," Obama offered solutions designed to reconcile, or harmonize, the two sides of one of the bitterest debates in American politics, one reflected in the speeches that opened this chapter:

> When we open up our hearts and our minds to those who may not think precisely like we do or believe precisely what we believe—that's when we discover at least the possibility of common ground.
>
> That's when we begin to say, "Maybe we won't agree on abortion, but we can still agree that this heart-wrenching decision for any woman is not made casually, and it has both moral and spiritual dimensions."
>
> So let us work together to reduce the number of women seeking abortions.
>
> Let's reduce unintended pregnancies.
>
> Let's make adoption more available.
>
> Let's—let's provide care and support for women who do carry their children to term.
>
> Let's honor the conscience of those who disagree with abortion, and draft a sensible conscience clause, and make sure that all of our health care policies are grounded not only in sound science, but also in clear ethics, as well as respect for the equality of women.
>
> Those are things we can do.

The Visionary

Politicians can sometimes inspire audiences with the vision of what might happen, even if they cannot promise a timetable. They can't say, "I have a dream"; that approach has been taken. But they can cast solutions as a kind of wish list. In this speech to the nonprofit youth organization Girls Inc., Hillary

Clinton does that with a three-step "I would like to see" litany. It promises nothing, but it shows where her heart is.

> But there is so much more we can do.
> I would like to see us forgive portions of student loans for college students who volunteer as tutors and mentors for children in poor communities.
> I would like to see us try to match every child in foster care, all five hundred thousand of them, with a responsible adult, starting with college students and giving those young people the reward of working with and serving someone else.
> I would like to see us begin to do more through AmeriCorps and national service to help young people navigate through school. We lose too many youngsters too early. By third grade, experienced teachers can tell us who's going to make it and who isn't. We need a little more support, we need a person, a real live person, to be there when someone falters or falls, to send the message that there are those of us behind you—come on, get up, you can keep going . . .
> People say to me all the time, "But isn't that expensive?" Yes, and so are the consequences of not providing that kind of launching pad for children who are otherwise going to be left out and left behind.

While language and ethos can help make solutions persuasive, we have one other way. For in talking about the rhythmic language of repetition, or the ways to characterize oneself, we cannot ignore ways to use evidence, concrete detail, and story. And just as we suggest Monroe's Motivated Sequence as a remarkably effective structure for persuasive speech, so we suggest a structure for offering solutions.

We call it the Three *P*s.

THE THREE Ps: PROPOSAL, PERSUASION, PUNCH LINE

> We've got to do a better job of getting across that America is freedom—freedom of speech, freedom of religion.
> So we've got to teach history based not on what's in fashion but what's important—why the Pilgrims came here, who Jimmy Doolittle was, and what those thirty seconds over Tokyo meant.
> You know, four years ago, on the fortieth anniversary of D-Day, I read a letter from a young woman writing to her late father, who'd fought on Omaha Beach.

Her name was Lisa Zanatta Henn, and she said, "We will always remember, we will never forget what the boys of Normandy did."

Well, let's help her keep her word.

If we forget what we did, we won't know who we are.

What is Ronald Reagan up to in this section about two-thirds of the way through his 1989 farewell address? The departing president was offering a solution to what he saw as a problem with education: that Americans no longer learn patriotism from school and popular culture the way they did in the past. What is his solution?

He offers a proposal, persuasion, and a punch line—the Three *P*s.

You don't have to agree with Reagan's idea to appreciate, and emulate, the way he presents it. Reagan (1) states his *proposal* (a solution with brief examples of how it would work). Then he (2) *persuades* (illustrating with concrete historical examples, a story, and testimony). Finally, Reagan (3) closes with a *punch line* using antithesis, repeating "we" four times to support the idea that his solution would accomplish something Americans value.

All the techniques of language he uses, including colloquial language, repetition, and antithesis, fit within that useful framework. Let's examine that passage again—this time with the elements labeled.

PROPOSAL:
    We've got to do a better job of getting across that **America is freedom—freedom of speech, freedom of religion.** ⎯⎯ Repetition and rule of three

PERSUASION:
    So we've got to teach history based **not on what's in fashion** but what's important—**why the Pilgrims came here, who Jimmy Doolittle was, and what those thirty seconds over Tokyo meant.** ⎯⎯ Antithesis
⎯⎯ Concrete detail and rule of three

    You know, four years ago, on the fortieth anniversary of D-Day, **I read a letter from a young woman** writing to her late father, who'd fought on Omaha Beach. ⎯⎯ Anecdote/quote

    Her name was Lisa Zanatta Henn, and she said, **"We will always remember, we will never forget what the boys of Normandy did."** ⎯⎯ Antithesis and repetition

    Well, let's help her keep her word. ⎯⎯ Deliberately colloquial

PUNCH LINE:
    If we forget what we did, we won't know who we are. ⎯⎯ Antithesis

Like any structure, the Three *P*s can be done well or miserably. Many elements work together to make this passage effective. Note its simplicity—of 122 words, 91 are one syllable. Note, too, the way Reagan uses "You know" and "Well" to create a nonstuffy persona, and the way he includes the woman's name, which convinces the audience that the letter he describes is real.

Maybe you're wondering why the president didn't reject that last line in favor of more elevated language. But think about it. Who would remember the line if Reagan had said, "If we don't understand the nuances of history, we will be confused about what has created the values we share"? Succinct, clear language is memorable, and it works at all levels of politics, not just the presidency.

Such an approach at least makes a stab at nuance, leads into an applause line, and works for many purposes, from a statesmanlike appearance by a president leaving office, to the raucous partisan atmosphere of a campaign rally, to a floor speech.

Here is John McCain, introducing a lobbying reform bill in 2005. McCain is the fighter here, calling for an end to "business as usual." He uses the Three *P* structure: a sarcastic proposal and a "they" litany of brief examples and metaphor, all leading to an "If–then" clincher.

The bill I am introducing today seeks to address business-as-usual in the nation's capitol. ⎯⎯ Proposal

How these lobbyists sought to influence policy and opinion makers is a case study in the ways lobbyists seek to curry favor with legislators and their aides.

For example, they sought to ingratiate themselves with public servants with tickets to plush skyboxes at the MCI Center, FedEx Field, and Camden Yards for sports and entertainment events. ⎯⎯ Persuasion with litany of brief examples

They arranged extravagant getaways to tropical islands, the famed golfing links of St. Andrews, and elsewhere.

They regularly treated people to meals and drinks. Fundraisers and contributions abounded.

This bill **casts some disinfectant on those practices** by simply requiring greater disclosure. ⎯⎯ Metaphor

If there is nothing inherently wrong with such activities, then there is no good reason to hide them from public scrutiny. ⎯⎯ Punch line

The Three *P*s approach works even in wonky, overdetailed, and substantive speech. Hillary Clinton's health care speech, again, is full of traditional support: statistics, background, brief personal example, story, and a punch line using antithesis. All help lift this section above boilerplate.

> In a system of **universal coverage,** insurance companies cannot as easily shift costs through cherry-picking and other means. — Proposal
>
> In fact, **according to a recent McKinsey report, insurance companies in America spend tens of billions a year figuring out how not to cover people**—doing complicated calculations to figure out how to cherry-pick the healthiest persons, and leave everyone else out in the cold. — Persuasion/statistic
>
> **That is how they profit:** by avoiding insuring patients who will be "expensive"—and then trying to avoid paying up once the insured patient actually needs treatment. — Background
>
> **I see this all the time.** — Personal example
>
> **For example, a father called me from northern New York**—his son had a rare illness. Now he and his son were well insured. He'd worked for many years for the same employer who provided a good policy. But when his son needed a special operation—that could only be performed at one place in the country—the insurance company said, sorry, that's out of network, we're not going to send you to have that done. — Story
>
> So my office intervened. And in the end they got permission for the operation.
>
> But I don't think people should have to go to their United States senator to get their insurance company to give them what they've paid for. — Punch line

Finally, let's examine two more passages, one Democrat and one Republican. The first is President Obama addressing Congress. Having contributed to such speeches, we know firsthand the limits of rocketing through solutions in fewer words than a Crest commercial. Here is how he did it, using the Three *P*s—and hewing to the fact–value–policy approach as well.

> We'll take steps to deal responsibly with the millions of undocumented immigrants who already live in our country. — Proposal
>
> I want to say more about this... because it generates the most passion and controversy. Even as we are a nation of immigrants, we're also a nation of laws. Undocumented workers broke our immigration laws, and I believe that they must be held accountable, especially those who may be dangerous.

That's why over the past six years deportations of criminals are up 80 percent, and that's why we're going to keep focusing enforcement resources on actual threats to our security. Felons, not families. Criminals, not children. Gang members, not a mom who's working hard to provide for her kids. We'll prioritize, just like law enforcement does every day.

But even as we focus on deporting criminals, the fact is millions of immigrants in every state, of every race and nationality, still live here illegally. ——— Persuasion (Fact)

And let's be honest, tracking down, rounding up, and deporting millions of people isn't realistic. Anyone who suggests otherwise isn't being straight with you. It's also not who we are as Americans. ——— Persuasion (Values)

After all, most of these immigrants have been here a long time. They work hard, often in tough, low-paying jobs. They support their families. They worship at our churches. Many of the kids are American born or spent most of their lives here. And their hopes, dreams, and patriotism are just like ours.

As my predecessor, President Bush, once put it, they are a part of American life.

Now here is the thing. We expect people who live in this country to play by the rules. We expect those who cut the line will not be unfairly rewarded. So we're going to offer the following deal:

If you've been in America more than five years; if you have children who are American citizens or illegal residents; if you register, pass a criminal background check, and you're willing to pay your fair share of taxes, you'll be able to apply to stay in this country temporarily without fear of deportation. ——— Persuasion (Policy)

You can come out of the shadows and get right with the law. That's what this deal is. ——— Punch Line

The Three *P* structure can accommodate not just differing views but imaginative approaches.

In 2018, Trump administration secretary of labor Alexander Acosta used the Three *P*s in Miami, the city where he grew up. The policy he was speaking about, occupational licensing rules, doesn't sound like an attention grabber. But note how Acosta and his writer infuse the speech with detail that must have mystified his audience—before surprising them with policy.

Reforming occupational licensing requirements could open up new opportunities for Hispanic Americans . . . for all Americans. ——— Proposal

To show you how small business health plans could work, let me take you . . . just for a minute . . . to Little Havana, Miami. ——— Persuasion

You take a walk down Calle Ocho.

You see the barbershop.

You pop into the hardware store.

Then, you smell the Cuban coffee.

You stop and get a cup and a pastelito.

(Continued)

(Continued)

> And then, you continue, and decide you need an ice cream cone from Azucar, too.
> Now you're at the end of Calle Ocho.

You might be surprised at the howdahells and specific, colorful, authentic detail introduced with energetic verbs: *walk . . . see . . . pop . . . smell . . . stop*. But what's he up to?

> And you turn around . . . and face the street.
> And I bring you back to the policy.

What policy? Suddenly Acosta has made listeners understand that he hasn't just been taking them on a walk. He is using each detail to offer concrete ideas that they understand.

> Imagine if all of these small businesses you just visited could band together in one large group association for health insurance.
> Imagine if instead of each one of them having to administer their own health care plan, which comes with plenty of compliance costs, the association could.
> Imagine if that association could benefit from economy of scale, increased purchasing power, and a large, stable risk pool.

Having done that, Acosta uses repetition to deliver his punch line.

> This is the concept behind small business health plans: more access, more choices, more coverage. —— Punch Line

We have now examined the link between problem and solution, described how to inspire through language and character, and looked at one structure that works well for a solution step.

With that, we leave the ways speakers and writers describe solutions to end with what should occur at the beginning.

Simply put, don't go at it alone.

At one point in *What I Saw at the Revolution*, Peggy Noonan describes a "bureaucrat from State," assigned to work with the National Security Council on the annual economic summits. He would refer to himself and his colleagues as "we substantive types," and to the speechwriters as "you wordsmiths."

"He was saying," Noonan writes, "'we do policy and you dance around with the words.' We would smile back. Our smiles said, 'The dancer is the dance.'"[5]

That is an allusion to the William Butler Yeats poem ("How can you know the dancer from the dance?"). Noonan portrays the writer as dancer and dance. But should Noonan or her bureaucrat feel superior to the other? Policy people are not dull, plodding, or unimaginative, and it can certainly take as much imagination to fashion a welfare policy as a speech.

Of course, Noonan was right to resent the "substantive types" for patronizing her—and right to mind something else. The language policy people try to shoehorn into speeches tends to deaden them. People with doctorates in economics have spent years thinking about economics. They're equipped to think up ideas, not package them for people with a seventh-grade reading level. It's somewhat understandable that she calls them "mice," nibbling away at what the truly talented create.

Our view: they aren't mice, and we need them to create the solutions our drafts will advocate. It's not up to speechwriters to decide what solutions the boss should offer, at least not on their own, or to do the research to find out what's likely to pass. And despite the ease with which the word *expertise* is bandied about, our bosses don't have all the answers either. Most politicians are generalists.

In many ways, political life itself works against candor and nuance. Truly nuanced discussion involves careful consideration of the most sophisticated arguments of the other side, of points where the other side may be right, of uncertainty, and of one's own mistakes. No politician can do that in public, especially since solutions are often the results of compromise, supported by a coalition of interests. It's uncomfortable sounding enthusiastic about every part of a bill when your real reason for supporting it is that half a loaf is better than none.

To be sure of your approach with solutions, make other staffers your partners.

FINAL WORDS

Noonan's boss Ronald Reagan always thought his best film was *Kings Row*, the 1942 tearjerker in which a surgeon amputates both his legs.[6] Reagan's character doesn't know the surgeon is going to amputate. He wakes up, looks down the bed, and asks, "Where's the rest of me?"[7]

Reagan later made that the title of his autobiography. It's such an appropriate question in political life, because the public so rarely sees politicians whole. But politicians do more than argue, posture, and speak in sound bites. They have doubts. They have personal experiences that don't lend themselves to two-minute intros. They can be funny, thoughtful, and reflective. If you're a politician, why sacrifice the chance to show listeners the rest of you? Why not put those qualities on display?

You can do that in the *bridge:* the moment between solution and conclusion.

If you have presented a long list of solutions, phrased in a way that gets applause, audiences can use a change of pace. You have time to sound reflective, wise, and funny. You can reminisce, tell a moving story, or reflect on an idea. At this point, you have a chance to show the sides of yourself that audiences rarely see.

Sometimes you can see right away how those more personal passages lead gracefully into the material you've reserved for a conclusion. But the creative process isn't always so cooperative. You may hit on something moving or interesting and not know exactly where it's going. Try it anyway; the odds are you are on the right road.

In George W. Bush's speech to the joint session of Congress after the events of September 11, his writers gave him a long litany ("We will come together to . . ."). Then, before the call to action that would end his speech, urging Americans to stay determined ("We must not lose our resolve"), they gave him this graceful bridge:

> After all that has just passed—all the lives taken, and all the possibilities and hopes that died with them—it is natural to wonder if America's future is one of fear. Some speak of an age of terror. I know there are struggles ahead, and dangers to face. But this country will define our times, not be defined by them.
>
> As long as the United States of America is determined and strong, this will not be an age of terror; this will be an age of liberty, here and across the world. Great harm has been done to us.
>
> We have suffered great loss. And in our grief and anger we have found our mission and our moment. Freedom and fear are at war. The advance of human freedom—the great achievement of our time and the great hope of every time—now depends on us.

One might quarrel about some of the reasoning here; it's a little melodramatic to say that human freedom depends "on us." But, given the moment, that's forgivable. Meanwhile, the reflective tone, enhanced even by the passive verb ("Great harm has been done"), lends the speech, and Bush, a reflective quality the public rarely saw. To us, it was the strongest moment in that speech.

Just as Bush's bridge paved the way for what he would say next, this bridge paves the way for what's next for us: ways to move from persuading listeners to inspiring them.

THE SPEECHWRITER'S CHECKLIST: SOLUTIONS

- ☐ Have I decided on solutions with other staffers or my boss?
- ☐ Are these solutions supported by both speaker and audience? If not, why not? How will I need to adjust the message accordingly?
- ☐ Does the audience want good ideas to fight for—or bad ideas to fight against?
- ☐ Have I presented a middle-ground approach to appeal to undecideds?
- ☐ Have I locked my speaker into a timetable or allowed flexibility in the solution?
- ☐ Have I persuaded as well as presented?
- ☐ Have I showed why the solutions are practical? Better than others?
- ☐ Have I used litany in presenting solutions?
- ☐ Have I used the Three *P*s (list them; it's a review) to build toward applause?
- ☐ Have I supported with varied evidence?
- ☐ Have I created a bridge into the conclusion?

14

Writing Conclusions

He looks down—no teleprompters in those days—and begins the now-familiar final lines. One's eyes shift elsewhere: to Jackie, sitting composed, in a red dress; to Lyndon Johnson, legs crossed, gazing up attentively; to a man in a top hat, looking in contrast to the hatless president like a refugee from another age.

He's gesturing with a closed fist a little above the lectern, looking out at the crowd now but not smiling during the last few words. The applause begins. Johnson, then Nixon, jumps up to grab his hand; the camera pulls back; you see them all in hats and overcoats, clapping and smiling, blissfully unaware of what will happen in the years ahead—or that they've just heard one of the most quotable speeches of the century.

Meanwhile, not on camera, high up and behind them, sitting with his sister, is a staffer who wrote the thing: Ted Sorensen.[1]

Scholars, journalists, and speechwriters have all analyzed John F. Kennedy's inaugural speech in great detail. Here we look only at its conclusion, as full of famous lines as a Shakespeare soliloquy.

It's an ending that has inspired not only listeners but speechwriters. We imitate the way Sorensen relies on Monroe and the devices of language we have reviewed earlier, especially litany and antithesis. We imitate its conclusion, a four-part structure that expands and enriches Monroe's Motivated Sequence.

In politics, conclusions are a time to stir emotions, win applause—and move listeners to act. That's true not only in a floor debate, national convention, or rally but also in delivering a eulogy or commencement address, speaking at a conference, or presenting at a coffee with ten people sitting in a living room.

Yes, politicians need to sound credible, provide varied evidence, define urgent problems, and demonstrate reasonable solutions possibly with some emotion along the way.

But as they move into the conclusion, evoking emotion is not one goal: It is often their chief goal. To get there, you'll want to create the kind of ending used not just by Kennedy but by Lincoln in his Gettysburg Address and Martin Luther King Jr. in "I Have a Dream." We call it the Four-Part Close.

FOUR-PART CLOSE: THE STEPS

In its purest form, it has, naturally, four steps:

- Inspiration
- Lesson Learned
- Call to Action
- Clincher

Step One: Inspiration

Inspiration might come from a quote, story, series of examples, montage, or poem. Aging English majors may remember T. S. Eliot's "objective correlative," the object in a poem that doesn't describe emotion but evokes it.

Often taken from history, the political version of the objective correlative can evoke emotion by featuring sacrifice, or someone succeeding against the odds. For JFK, Sorensen chose an image of sacrifice—the graves of soldiers who fought to keep America free:

> Since this country was founded, each generation of Americans
> has been summoned to give testimony to its national loyalty.
> The graves of young Americans who answered the call to service
> surround the globe.

Step Two: Lesson Learned

Having inspired your listeners, you'll want them to draw a lesson. They should see that example relevant for today. Sometimes your goal will be for listeners to imitate the example (*What they did, we can do!*). You'll pose a question or paint two views of the future, thus creating a moment of suspense (*Will we choose correctly?*).

Kennedy's lesson: the "trumpet" that summoned those soldiers summons "us" to defend freedom.

> Now the trumpet summons us again.

Note that Kennedy doesn't plunge right into the call to action that people remember most vividly.

Instead, he poses a choice. Rather than commanding, he *asks* whether listeners will pick the right path. By offering a choice, speakers can create suspense, paint one option as better than the other, or present an opportunity for listeners to join in and imagine the result. In part, this is a variation on Monroe's visualization step, giving listeners a way to picture the future.

> Can we forge against these enemies a grand and global alliance, North and South, East and West, that can assure a more fruitful life for all mankind? Will you join me in that historic effort?
>
> In the long history of the world, only a few generations have been granted the role of defending freedom in its hour of maximum danger.
>
> The energy, the faith, the devotion which we bring to this endeavor will light our country and all who serve it—and the glow from that fire can truly light the world.

Only after asking whether this is possible does he move on to the next step.

Step Three: Call to Action

Kennedy's call-to-action litany appeals to what alert or obsessive readers will remember formed the highest step in Maslow's pyramid: self-actualization.

> And so, my fellow Americans, ask not what your country can do for you—ask what you can do for your country.
>
> My fellow citizens of the world, ask not what America will do for you, but what together we can do for the freedom of man. . . .
>
> Finally, whether you are citizens of America or citizens of the world, ask of us here the same high standards of strength and sacrifice which we ask of you.

By asking Americans to hold him to those standards, JFK avoids sounding dictatorial. If he had ended the speech there, however, it would have felt abrupt. And so this Four-Part Close involves a final step—the very last line.

Step Four: Clincher

Clinchers usually remind listeners of the larger implications of their actions. By this point in your writing or delivery, you've moved beyond mundane issues of which bills to pass or which candidates to support. It's time to return to the *why*: you're urging your audience to take action because that action will bring a noble end.

But that involves a choice. What is the noble end we choose? In American politics, it is often the choice to ensure freedom, achieve the American Dream, or create a better future for our children. Kennedy's is unusual—he promises only one "sure reward":

> With a good conscience our only sure reward, with history the final
> judge of our deeds, let us go forth to lead the land we love, asking
> his blessing and his help, but knowing that here on earth God's work
> must truly be our own.

The language of Kennedy's clincher is less concrete than other sections, and more hackneyed ("the land we love"). He is careful to hew to the prerequisite of important political speeches by invoking God, whom he refers to as a male.

But his final sentence remains unusual in political speech. First, Kennedy doesn't promise success, nor does he assure his listeners of the rightness of their actions, since "history" is the final judge. Finally, and rare for a politician, he takes sides in one of the great debates of contemporary religion, reminding his listeners that good works, not just faith, will save them.

AS DELIVERED

John F. Kennedy's Inaugural Address. Note the presence of all four steps. And try to imagine how they can be effective in much smaller events.

www.jfklibrary.org/learn/about-jfk/historic-speeches/inaugural-address

By inverting the usual grammatical structure to create suspense, by using alliteration, repetition, and antithesis, JFK's clincher surprises his audience and helped ensure that his entire speech lives on in memories many decades later.

Earlier we showed how the Gettysburg Address conformed to Monroe. Taking another look, you'll now recognize the elements Lincoln put together for his close.

The brave men, living and dead, who struggled here have con- — Inspiration
secrated it far above our poor power to add or detract. The
world will little note nor long remember what we say here, but
it can never forget what they did here.

It is for us the living rather to be dedicated here to the — Lesson learned
unfinished work which they who fought here have thus far so
nobly advanced.

It is rather for us to be here dedicated to the great task — Call to action
remaining before us—that from these honored dead we take
increased devotion to that cause for which they gave the last
full measure of devotion—that we here highly resolve that
these dead shall not have died in vain, that ... this nation
under God shall have a new birth of freedom, and that
government of the people, by the people, for the people shall — Clincher
not perish from the earth.

The Four-Part Close appears in various ways to end many of the most eloquent political speeches of our time.

Using it makes emotional sense. Instead of just moving from solution to visualization to call to action, it inspires listeners with a story, example, or quote that brings a lump to their collective throats—then helps them draw a lesson for their own lives.

And while Lincoln asks listeners to "resolve" that the deaths in a battlefield have meaning, he ends with a memorable last section that reminds them why that choice is worth making.

Just as it worked for Lincoln, it also worked for the famous speech delivered at the memorial honoring him. We've looked at the "I Have a Dream" litany. Here, we see how King uses the words of a famous hymn for inspiration before drawing his lesson ("If America is to become a great nation . . .") and another litany using carefully chosen landmarks for his call to action. Then, he finishes with a series of quotes Americans of all backgrounds know to lend power to his clincher.

This will be the day when all of God's children will be able to
sing with new meaning,
    "My country 'tis of thee — Inspiration
    Sweet land of liberty.
    Of thee I sing:
    Land where my fathers died,
    Land of the pilgrims' pride.
    From every mountainside
    Let freedom ring."

(Continued)

(Continued)

> And if America is to be a great nation this must become true. ⎯⎯ Lesson learned
>
> So let freedom ring from the prodigious hilltops of New Hampshire. Let freedom ring from the mighty mountains of New York. Let freedom ring from the heightening Alleghenies of Pennsylvania. ⎯⎯ Call to action
>
> Let freedom ring from the snowcapped Rockies of Colorado!
>
> Let freedom ring from the curvaceous peaks of California!
>
> But not only that; let freedom ring from Stone Mountain of Georgia!
>
> Let freedom ring from Lookout Mountain of Tennessee!
>
> Let freedom ring from every hill and molehill of Mississippi! From every mountainside, let freedom ring!
>
> And when that happens ... when we let freedom ring, when we let it ring from every village and every hamlet, from every state and every city, we will be able to speed up that day when all of God's children, black men and white men, Jews and Gentiles, Protestants and Catholics, will be able to join hands and sing in ⎯⎯ Clincher the words of the old Negro spiritual, "Free at last! Free at last! Thank God almighty, we are free at last!"

The Four-Part Close is an outline that offers plenty of options. Some speakers will interrupt each step to reflect, or add examples. You might choose to skip using a quote if you don't have a great one. You can decide to do the four parts quickly, or draw them out slowly.

Khizr Khan, the electrifying 2016 Democratic National Convention speaker, used about 130 words to close his speech with these four steps. The Marco Rubio example cited later in this chapter runs more than 600 words.

Finally, while you might think a call to action means commanding listeners to march, that's not always true. Sometimes it will feel more appropriate to leave future action merely implied, or to gently request it.

Limited by space, we cannot include all the sterling examples of political speeches that end this way. But to see the various ways one can use it, we do include two more recent examples: both candidates for president in 2016.

Hillary Clinton: Acceptance Speech, 2016
Democratic National Convention

Personal story inspires in politics because supporters are curious about people who often keep their personal lives hidden. Clinton *inspires* with a story about her mother; draws a *lesson* she learned from her; urges *action*, using her mother's advice to support her own; then returns in her *clincher* to the Founding Fathers and the new "chapter" that lies ahead.

> More than a few times, I've had to pick myself up and get back in the game. ——— Inspiration
>
> Like so much else in my life, I got this from my mother too. She never let me back down from any challenge. When I tried to hide from a neighborhood bully, she literally blocked the door.
>
> "Go back out there," she said.
>
> And she was right. You have to stand up to bullies. ——— Lesson learned
>
> You have to keep working to make things better, even when ——— Call to action
> the odds are long and the opposition is fierce.
>
> We lost our mother a few years ago, but I miss her every day. And I still hear her voice urging me to keep working, keep fighting for right, no matter what.
>
> That's what we need to do together as a nation.
>
> And though "we may not live to see the glory," as the song from the musical *Hamilton* goes, "let us gladly join the fight."
>
> Let our legacy be about "planting seeds in a garden you never get to see."
>
> That's why we're here, not just in this hall, but on this ——— Clincher
> earth.
>
> The founders showed us that, and so have many others since. They were drawn together by love of country, and the selfless passion to build something better for all who follow.
>
> That is the story of America.
>
> And we begin a new chapter tonight.

Clinton clearly aimed her speech at the American left.

President Trump did not. Despite the difference in tone and views, though, his 2018 State of the Union speech ends using the same structure. We abbreviate for length again, encouraging readers to look at the unabridged version.

President Donald Trump: 2018 State of the Union

Far longer than the other conclusions we have seen, the president's closing includes two stories, one of which we reprint below.

> Finally, we are joined by one more witness to the ominous ——— Inspiration
> nature of this regime. His name is Mr. Ji Seong-ho.
>
> In 1996, Seong-ho was a starving boy in North Korea. One day, he tried to steal coal from a railroad car to barter for a few scraps of food. In the process, he passed out on the train tracks exhausted from hunger. He woke up as a train ran over his limbs, then endured multiple amputations without anything to dull the pain.

(Continued)

(Continued)

His brother and sister gave what little food they had to help him recover, and ate dirt themselves—permanently stunting their own growth.

Later, he was tortured by North Korean authorities after returning from a brief visit to China. His tormentors wanted to know if he'd met any Christians. He had—and he resolved to be free. Seong-ho traveled thousands of miles on crutches across China and Southeast Asia to freedom. Most of his family followed. His father was caught trying to escape, and was tortured to death. Today he lives in Seoul, where he rescues other defectors, and broadcasts into North Korea what the regime fears the most—the truth.

Today he has a new leg, but Seong-ho, I understand you still keep those crutches as a reminder of how far you've come.

Your great sacrifice is an inspiration to us all. Seong-ho's story is a testament to the yearning of every human soul to live in freedom. ⎯ Lesson learned

Having told listeners exactly what Ji Seong-ho's example means, Trump does not move right into his call to action. Instead, he now offers more examples of what that yearning means—soldiers who fought around the world, the statue atop the Capitol, and a montage of the American people:

Atop the dome of this Capitol stands the Statue of Freedom. She stands tall and dignified among the monuments to our ancestors who fought and lived and died to protect her. Monuments to Washington and Jefferson, to Lincoln and King. Memorials to the heroes of Yorktown and Saratoga.

To young Americans who shed their blood on the shores of Normandy, and the fields beyond. And others, who went down in the waters of the Pacific, and the skies over Asia.

And freedom stands tall over one more monument: this one. This Capitol—this living monument to the American people.

A people whose heroes live not only in the past, but all around us—defending hope, pride, and the American way. They work in every trade. They sacrifice to raise a family. They care for our children at home. They defend our flag abroad. They are strong moms, and brave kids. They are firefighters, police officers, border agents, medics, and Marines.

But above all else, they are Americans. And this Capitol, this city, this nation, belongs to them.

Trump's call to action is only a sentence long, calling for five things, all beginning with "to."

Our task is to respect them, to listen to them, to serve them, to protect them—and to always be worthy of them. ⎯ Call to action

Finally, Trump offers his clincher, an optimistic vision of what—as long as we choose to be "proud" and "confident of our values"—lies ahead.

The people dreamed this country. The people built this country, and it is the people who are making America great again. ⎯⎯ Clincher

As long as we are proud of who we are, and what we are fighting for—there is nothing we cannot achieve.

As long as we have confidence in our values, faith in our citizens, and trust in our God—we will not fail.

Our families will thrive.

Our people will prosper.

And our nation will forever be safe and strong and proud and mighty and free.

BEHIND THE SCENES

The Lenny Skutnik Story

One afternoon in 1982, a Ronald Reagan speechwriter named Aram Bakshian was sitting at his desk, trying to write part of Reagan's State of the Union speech. Suddenly, he was distracted by the small TV nearby.

An Air Florida plane had crashed into the Potomac. It was February. The water was freezing. Passengers were struggling. Over seventy would die. But as he watched, Bakshian saw a young man pull off his shoes, dive into the water, and pull a woman to safety. It was dramatic, heroic, and moving.

"He has to be in the State of the Union," Bakshian thought. The man, twenty-six-year-old Lenny Skutnik, passed a security check. Bakshian wrote a few paragraphs.

And so it was that a few nights later, Reagan stopped before the end of his speech to talk about American heroes. At the end of that, he said, "Just two weeks ago, in the midst of a terrible tragedy in the Potomac . . . we saw one of our young government employees, Lenny Skutnik."

The cameras swung to Skutnik, up in the gallery beside Nancy Reagan. The entire Congress jumped to its feet. The applause was loud and long. As it died down, a beaming Reagan looked up again—and gave Skutnik a salute. Presidents, including Donald Trump, as you have seen, have used that technique to inspire and draw a lesson almost every year since. Some people call the tactic the "hero in the gallery." Others still call it the "Lenny Skutnik moment."

"I invented the 'hero in the gallery' ploy," Bakshian said later, "which has been milked to death. I almost regret it."

Source: This "Behind the Scenes" box is based on information from Aram Bakshian's oral history. It can be found at https://millercenter.org/the-presidency/presidential-oral-histories/aram-bakshian-jr-oral-history-director-speechwriting.

FOUR-PART CLOSE: STRATEGY

You've now seen speeches covering different issues and offering different views, but ending with the same four steps: inspiration, lesson learned, call to action, and clincher.

The similarities in these endings, from very different politicians, go beyond structure. The *inspiration* may take different forms, but usually it *motivates* with examples of sacrifice for noble ends, like a soldier who died, a refugee who risked it all, or a parent who persevered.

The *lesson learned* defines the task ahead for listeners, as Kennedy does (fighting "these enemies"), emphasizing urgency and leaving little doubt about the right course.

Everyone who does fundraising knows about the "ask"—the moment you explicitly request money. A *call to action* is a different kind of ask. Having heard a speaker define the cause as noble, and inspire by reminding them of their own heroes, how can listeners say no when you ask them to act just as bravely?

Clinchers elevate our gaze and remind us of the larger purpose, animating the call to action.

Like Monroe, the Four-Part Close is simply a structure, a skeleton you can flesh out with your own ideas, in ways that suit each speech's purpose. Success means asking four questions that will differ from audience to audience and from speaker to speaker:

Can we find the stories, examples, or images that will *inspire* this audience?

Can we find the tone, idea, or analogy that will allow listeners to see a *lesson* relevant to their own lives?

Can we find details and language exciting enough so they will listen when we urge *action*?

Can we infuse our clincher with the vivid detail that will make listeners imagine what *choices* lie ahead—and see the promise of choosing wisely?

In the excerpts that follow, those who created or delivered them found strategies that worked for each.

Strategy to Inspire the Audience

Practically unknown when she stepped onto the stage of the Republican National Convention in 2008, Sarah Palin inspires with a *story* rich in detail to bring to life John McCain's heroism as a prisoner of war. She also uses antithesis to contrast McCain with his opponent. She doesn't command action but chooses a more likeable strategy: an ask.

A fellow prisoner of war, a man named Tom Moe of Lancaster, Ohio. Tom Moe recalls looking through a pinhole in his cell door as Lieutenant Commander John McCain was led down the hallway, by the guards, day after day.	Inspiration
And the story is told, "When McCain shuffled back from torturous interrogations, he would turn toward Moe's door and he'd flash a grin and a 'thumbs up'—as if to say, 'We're gonna pull through this.'"	
My fellow Americans, that is the kind of man America needs to see us through the next four years. For a season, a gifted speaker can inspire with his words. But, for a lifetime, John McCain has inspired with his deeds.	Lesson learned
If character is the measure in this election, and hope the theme, and change the goal we share, then I ask you to join our cause.	Call to action
Join our cause and help America elect a great man as the next president of the United States.	Clincher

This next example is not a speech with a national audience, nor is it a speech to a room full of supporters. Rather, here Sen. Robert Menendez of New Jersey is speaking to his home state chamber of commerce.

To inspire, he opens by *quoting* a doctor using the kind of graphic detail most speakers would avoid. But in that week of terrible violence, he has license. By praising doctors as leaders, he makes them feel their actions matter. When he urges action, he uses a slogan adopted by the Parkland, Florida, school shooting survivors. And in his clincher he returns to it, driving home the importance of their choice.

Some of you sit at the helm of New Jersey's health care sector. Well, earlier this week I read a piece by a radiologist who cared for some of the Stoneman Douglas victims.	Inspiration
She described how a typical handgun wound leaves an organ lacerated. But not an AR-15.	
An assault weapon leaves an organ looking like, and I quote, "an overripe melon smashed by a sledgehammer ... nothing was left to repair."	
How can we in a state known for putting patients first sit idly by as children die of these explosive wounds?	

(Continued)

(Continued)

> The reality is no matter what sector you work in, *you* wield — Lesson learned
> enormous influence. Think about the power in this room tonight.
>
> You are innovators. You are investors. You are business owners and industry leaders. When you speak, people listen. When you act, others follow.
>
> It's not enough to have public opinion with us. It's not even enough to have President Trump with us.
>
> We need corporate America with us. We need *you* to help — Call to action
> the students of Parkland turn "once again" into "never again."
>
> Because *never again* do we want children to watch their best friends and beloved teachers die at the hands of a deranged killer armed with weapons of war.
>
> And *never again* do we want to learn of another mass shooting in a school or church or theater or anywhere else!
>
> We can't let that happen.
>
> We must act, and we must do it now—and I'm pleading with — Clincher
> you to use the power of your voice to say with me *never again*.

Strategy to Draw the Lesson

In Chapter 8, we showed how then First Lady Michelle Obama, speaking at the African Methodist Episcopal Church Conference, told a story—and used concrete detail ("a house built by slaves") to dramatize it for her audience.

We include it here, though, for the richness of the lesson she draws. The story she tells is a symbolic one with a little boy representing the change her husband's election meant. Then she uses Scripture to remind her listeners in this churchgoing audience that like Abraham and Sarah they must keep the faith.

Like the earlier Palin example, she does not command. Rather, she implies it by expressing confidence that "we" will succeed. With her clincher, Obama reminds the audience that they can bring "democracy for their children."

> And when you grow weary in this work—and you will— — Inspiration
> when you think about giving up—and you will—I want you to think about a photo that hangs today in the West Wing of the White House. It is a picture of a young black family visiting the president in the Oval Office. The father was a member of the White House staff, and he brought his wife and two young sons to meet my husband. In the photo, Barack is bent over at the waist—way over. And one of the sons, a little boy just five years old, is reaching out his tiny hand to touch my husband's head.

And it turns out that upon meeting Barack, this little boy gazed up at him longingly, and he said, "I want to know if my hair is just like yours." And Barack replied, "Why don't you touch it and see for yourself?"

So he bent way down so the little boy could feel his hair. And after touching my husband's head, the little boy exclaimed, "Yes, it does feel the same!"

And every couple of weeks, the White House photographers change out all the photos that hang in the West Wing—except for that one. See, that one, and that one alone, has hung on that wall for more than three years.

So if you ever wonder whether change is possible in this country, I want you to think about that little black boy in the office—the Oval Office of the White House—touching the head of the first black president. ——— Lesson learned

And I want you to think of the stories in the Bible about folks like Abel and Noah; folks like Abraham and Sarah, and the verse in Hebrews that says, "All these people were still living by faith when they died. They did not receive the things promised. They only saw them and welcomed them from a distance." Through so many heartbreaks and trials, those who came before us kept the faith. They could only see that promised land from a distance, but they never let it out of their sight.

And today, if we're once again willing to work for it, if we're once again willing to sacrifice for it, then I know—I know—we can carry that legacy forward. ——— Implied call to action

I know we can meet our obligations to continue that struggle.

I know we can continue the work of those heroes whose shoulders we all stand on.

And I know we can finish the journey they started and finally fulfill the promise of our democracy for all our children. ——— Clincher

Strategy to Urge Action

At the 2016 Republican National Convention, in front of a partisan audience, Eric Trump has no hesitation about urging action, finishing with an emotional appeal difficult to resist: the appeal of a son whose hero is his father.

Note also how he gets there. Using examples, he amasses incident after incident about Donald Trump. Then he segments his audience so each of six groups can see the relevance: that Eric Trump's father cares about them. He draws a lesson about selflessness, then uses anaphora and epistrophe in the lesson he draws.

Oprah Winfrey once famously asked my father if he envisioned running for the presidency of the United States. His answer? "Only if it got so bad that I had no choice." — Inspiration

Well, ladies and gentlemen, that day has come.

As I travel the world that my dad built, and the greatest golf courses and hotels and real estate projects, I see the unmistakable look in his eyes.

I see in his eyes the indignity and frustration of a domestic infrastructure back at home that is in complete disarray and no longer on par with so many other developed nations.

I see in his eyes the sadness of innocent lives lost, like those of Kate Steinle and Jamiel Shaw and so many others cut short by illegal immigrants in sanctuary cities, victims of a revolving door of government ineptitude and corruption that leaves innocent Americans defenseless.

I see in his eyes the humiliation of an education system ranked thirtieth in the world.

But today I see in his eyes a man who truly loves his country, who is proud of his country, and who wants his country to be great again.

To whom much is given, much will be required. This is the very belief that compelled my father to make this great sacrifice, to run for the most powerful yet unforgiving office in the world. There is no greater calling, there is no more selfless an act. — Lesson learned

To the unemployed voter sitting at home watching me right now, wondering how you're going to make your next mortgage payment, or rent payment, my father is running for you.

To the veteran tuning into this speech from his or her hospital, who has been ignored and disrespected by an ungrateful system for far too long, my father is running for you.

To the schoolteacher forced to walk through metal detectors each and every day into an underfunded school, my father is running for you.

To the laborer who is watching me right now, forced out of a job by undocumented workers, illegal immigrants, my father is running for you.

To the oil and gas industry workers denied a job because of radical regulations from a radical EPA, my father is running for you.

To single mothers, to families with special needs children, to middle class families who can no longer afford medical benefits sufficient to cover their everyday needs, my father is running for you.

This November, I ask you to be true to yourself and vote for the candidate who you know is running for the right reasons. — Call to action

Vote for the candidate who has never been a politician.

Vote for the candidate who has never received a paycheck from our government.

Vote for the candidate who can't be bought, sold, purchased, bribed, coerced, intimidated, or steered from the path that is right and just and true.

And quite frankly, friends, vote for the one candidate who does not need this job.

Never have I been more proud to be a Trump. Never have I been more proud to be my father's son. ⎯⎯ Clincher

I'm incredibly honored to be part of this journey on which he's invited me, Don, Ivanka, Tiffany, Melania, my beautiful wife Lara, our entire family, to play such an integral part.

Dad, you have once again taught us by example, you are my hero, you are my best friend, you are the next president of the United States.

God bless America.

Calls to action aren't always so direct. Yes, to command sounds forceful. To the right crowd it can be exciting. On the other hand, a command sounds bossy. In 1993, President Bill Clinton's Martin Luther King Jr. Day speech did not command, but motivated in a gentler way. He *implied* action.

Here we only include the call-to-action step. But Clinton first inspires his listeners by quoting Scripture; draws his lesson; then, as you see below, calls for action by asking his audience to join him in an unusual series of pledges. That leads directly into his clincher, appropriate for a church audience sitting in the pews.

By using "we," he makes clear he does not exempt himself from such action. By ending with the words "grace of God," he shows his audience he shares belief. By rejecting a litany of commands, he makes his request palatable:

> So in this pulpit, on this day, let me ask all of you in your heart to say we will honor the life and work of Martin Luther King.
> We will honor the meaning of our church.
> We will somehow, by God's grace, we will turn this around.
> We will give these children a future.
> We will take away their guns and give them books.
> We will take away their despair and give them hope.
> We will rebuild the families and the neighborhoods and the communities.

We won't make all the work that has gone on here benefit just a few.

We will do it together by the grace of God.

Strategy to Make the Choice

The clincher is about choosing well. Often, speakers who use the Four-Part Close make that choice explicit and with common themes. For example, in Reagan's Farewell Address, he makes clear the choice between standing still and making progress:

> My friends: We did it. We weren't just marking time. We made a difference. We made the city stronger; we made the city freer; and we left her in good hands. All in all, not bad—not bad at all.

In 1962, during the Cuban Missile Crisis, JFK famously describes another popular choice:

> Our goal is not the victory of might, but the vindication of right—not peace at the expense of freedom but both peace and freedom, here in this hemisphere, and, we hope, around the world.

These aren't the only ways to show contrast and offer a choice, of course. We have already seen clinchers where Kennedy asks listeners to reject those who ask what the country can do for them and accept what they can do for the country; Sarah Palin offers a choice between a candidate of deeds, not one of "words"; and Michelle Obama celebrates the choice of those who did not abandon faith but kept it.

And this example, again from Ronald Reagan, asks us to choose between being the "last best hope" and "darkness." In fact, choice appears in the title of this 1964 speech that put him on the national political map. "A Time for Choosing."

Reagan quotes the enemy, Soviet premier Nikita Khrushchev, to inspire listeners through fear. Then he inspires with another approach—rhetorical questions using historical figures he knows his listeners admire.

Finally, unlike what we have seen so far, he is explicit about the choice listeners face and whose answer to him is clear.

> He [Khrushchev] has told them that we're retreating under the pressure of the Cold War, and someday when the time comes to deliver the final ultimatum, our surrender will be voluntary, because by that time we will have been weakened from within spiritually, morally, and economically. — Inspiration

He believes this because from our side he's heard voices pleading for "peace at any price" or "better red than dead," or as one commentator put it, he'd rather "live on his knees than die on his feet."

And therein lies the road to war, because those voices don't speak for the rest of us.

If nothing in life is worth dying for, when did this begin—just in the face of this enemy? Or should Moses have told the children of Israel to live in slavery under the pharaohs? Should Christ have refused the cross? Should the patriots at Concord Bridge have thrown down their guns and refused to fire the shot heard 'round the world? The martyrs of history were not fools, and our honored dead who gave their lives to stop the advance of the Nazis didn't die in vain.

Where, then, is the road to peace? ——————— Lesson learned
Well, it's a simple answer after all.

You and I have the courage to say to our enemies, "There is a price we will not pay." There is a point beyond which they must not advance.

And this—this is the meaning in the phrase of Barry Goldwater's "peace through strength."

You and I have a rendezvous with destiny. ——————— Call to action
We'll preserve for our children this, the last best hope of man on earth, or we'll sentence them to take the last step into a thousand years of darkness.

We will keep in mind and remember that Barry Goldwater — Clincher
has faith in us. He has faith that you and I have the ability and the dignity and the right to make our own decisions and determine our own destiny.

FINAL WORDS

Like Monroe's Motivated Sequence, the Four-Part Close endures because it works. From speeches delivered over fifty years ago to one delivered as we finish our revisions of this book, from Democrats to Republicans, from political conventions to a chamber of commerce, the speeches we have reviewed show why. It's because far from being cookie-cutter, the Four-Part Close allows for variety, imagination, and ways to end we haven't even considered.

And so we close with two examples from very different politicians who show that variety and imagination: Marco Rubio nominating Mitt Romney at the Republican National Convention in 2012, and Barack Obama speaking on Election Night in 2008.

Why both? Because an idea basic to this book is that techniques do not depend on ideology.

Marco Rubio: Nomination Speech for Mitt Romney, 2012 Republican National Convention

My dad was a bartender. My mom was a cashier, a maid, and a stock clerk at Kmart. They never made it big. They were never rich. And yet they were successful. Because just a few decades removed from hopelessness, they made possible for us all the things that had been impossible for them. ⎯⎯ Inspiration 1

Many nights I heard my father's keys jingling at the door as he came home after another sixteen-hour day. Many mornings, I woke up just as my mother got home from the overnight shift at Kmart.

When you're young, the meaning of moments like these escapes you. But now, as my own children get older, I understand it better.

My dad used to tell us: "En este pais, ustedes van a poder lograr todas las cosas que nosotros no pudimos." "In this country, you will be able to accomplish all the things we never could."

A few years ago during a speech, I noticed a bartender behind a portable bar at the back of the ballroom. I remembered my father who had worked for many years as a banquet bartender.

He was grateful for the work he had, but that's not the life he wanted for us.

He stood behind a bar in the back of the room all those years, so one day I could stand behind a podium in the front of a room.

That journey, from behind that bar to behind this podium, goes to the essence of the American miracle—that we're exceptional not because we have more rich people here.

We're special because dreams that are impossible anywhere else come true here. ⎯⎯ Lesson learned 1

That's not just my story. That's your story. That's our story. ⎯⎯ Inspiration 2

It's the story of your mother who struggled to give you what she never had.

It's the story of your father who worked two jobs so doors closed for him would open for you.

The story of that teacher or that coach who taught you the lessons that shaped who you are today.

And it's the story of a man who was born into an uncertain future in a foreign country. His family came to America to escape revolution.

They struggled through poverty and the Great Depression. And yet he rose to be an admired businessman and public servant.

And in November, his son, Mitt Romney, will be elected president of the United States.

We are all just a generation or two removed from someone who made our future the purpose of their lives. ——— Lesson learned 2

America is the story of everyday people who did extraordinary things. A story woven deep into the fabric of our society.

Their stories may never be famous, but in the lives they lived, you find the living essence of America's greatness. To make sure America is still a place where tomorrow is always better than yesterday, that is what our politics should be about.

And that is what we are deciding in this election.

Do we want our children to inherit our hopes and dreams, or do we want them to inherit our problems?

Mitt Romney believes that if we succeed in changing the direction of our country, our children and grandchildren will be the most prosperous generation ever, and their achievements will astonish the world.

The story of our time will be written by Americans who haven't yet been born.

Let's make sure they write that we did our part. ——— Call to action

That in the early years of this new century, we lived in an uncertain time. But we did not allow fear to cause us to abandon what made us special.

We chose more freedom instead of more government.

We chose the principles of our founding to solve the challenges of our time.

We chose a special man to lead us in a special time.

We chose Mitt Romney to lead our nation.

And because we did, the American miracle lived on for ——— Clincher
another generation to inherit.

Barack Obama: Victory Speech Conclusion, November 2008

This election had many firsts and many stories that will be told ——— Inspiration
for generations. But one that's on my mind tonight's about a woman who cast her ballot in Atlanta. She's a lot like the millions of others who stood in line to make their voice heard in this election, except for one thing: Ann Nixon Cooper is 106 years old.

She was born just a generation past slavery; a time when there were no cars on the road or planes in the sky; when someone like her couldn't vote for two reasons: because she was a woman and because of the color of her skin.

(Continued)

(Continued)

And tonight, I think about all that she's seen throughout her century in America—the heartache and the hope; the struggle and the progress; the times we were told that we can't, and the people who pressed on with that American creed: Yes we can.

At a time when women's voices were silenced and their hopes dismissed, she lived to see them stand up and speak out and reach for the ballot: Yes we can.

When there was despair in the Dust Bowl and depression across the land, she saw a nation conquer fear itself with a New Deal, new jobs, a new sense of common purpose: Yes we can.

When the bombs fell on our harbor and tyranny threatened the world, she was there to witness a generation rise to greatness and a democracy was saved: Yes we can.

She was there for the buses in Montgomery, the hoses in Birmingham, a bridge in Selma, and a preacher from Atlanta who told a people that "we shall overcome": Yes we can.

A man touched down on the moon, a wall came down in Berlin, a world was connected by our own science and imagination.

And this year, in this election, she touched her finger to a screen, and cast her vote, because after 106 years in America, through the best of times and the darkest of hours, she knows how America can change: Yes we can. ⎯ Lesson learned

America, we have come so far. We have seen so much. But there is so much more to do.

So tonight, let us ask ourselves—if our children should live to see the next century; if my daughters should be so lucky to live as long as Ann Nixon Cooper, what change will they see? What progress will we have made? ⎯ Call to action

This is our chance to answer that call.

This is our moment.

This is our time, to put our people back to work and open doors of opportunity for our kids; to restore prosperity and promote the cause of peace; to reclaim the American Dream and reaffirm that fundamental truth, that, out of many, we are one; that while we breathe, we hope.

And where we are met with cynicism and doubt and those who tell us that we can't, we will respond with that timeless creed that sums up the spirit of a people: Yes we can. ⎯ Clincher

You have now looked at the elements of political speech. You have seen how they work in each step of the most common format for persuasion about policy. But a speech is more than a series of steps and combinations of writing techniques. How speakers present the text is key to how listeners perceive them.

So, next up: delivery.

THE SPEECHWRITER'S CHECKLIST: WRITING CONCLUSIONS

- ☐ Have I evoked genuine emotion in this audience?
- ☐ Does the speech demonstrate leadership qualities?
- ☐ Have I broadened my conclusion to include larger themes?
- ☐ Have I offered "choice" or "referral" endings?
- ☐ Have I closed on a note of hope?
- ☐ In using the Four-Part Close, have I:
  - ☐ Found material that will inspire these listeners?
  - ☐ Drawn a parallel they will accept?
  - ☐ Asked, commanded, or implied action in a way that will make them respond?
  - ☐ Made my last line memorable?

CHAPTER 15

Delivery

The reviews could hardly have been more different.

Barack Obama had barely uttered the last words of the 2004 Democratic National Convention speech that made him famous when reporters reacted.

Writing years later, reporter Mark Leibovich called that speech a "touchstone of national unity, a soaring manifesto of hope."[1] In the years since, the criticism of Obama has often centered on how the rest of him doesn't measure up to his ability to speak.

Donald Trump? When it comes to speeches, reporters have been largely critical both during his 2016 campaign and after. In April 2017, writer Olivia Goldhill assembled a group of rhetoric scholars to ponder a mystery: why Trump's "inarticulate speaking style" was so persuasive.[2] Goldhill cited Trump's campaign announcement as a "typical example of his rambling, incoherent speaking style":

> I will build a great wall—and nobody builds walls better than me, believe me—and I'll build them very inexpensively. Our country is in serious trouble. We don't have victories anymore. We used to have victories, but we don't have them. When was the last time anybody saw us beating—let's say China—in a trade deal? I beat China all the time. All the time.

In politics, speaking skills count. They can make a well-written speech dull or a mediocre speech sound terrific. Reporters should pay them attention.

But others watching and listening to Trump, whether at home or in the hall, got a different impression than Goldhill. They saw a speaker standing erect, impeccably dressed in a red tie, white shirt, and blue jacket. They heard him use the techniques we admire in John F. Kennedy and Martin Luther King Jr.: repetition, rhetorical questions, and short sentences.

Incoherent? The readability stats tell us that 80 percent of Americans can understand him easily.

Trump ad-libs. But there is nothing incoherent about that passage. Whatever the substance of their speeches, both Donald Trump and Barack Obama offer strikingly effective ways to deliver them.

Both authors have coached clients, students, and politicians. The stereotype of elected politicians is that most are at least skillful speakers. "Public speaking is an art—and it's one that many great politicians . . . have mastered," writes speech coach John Rydell. "When they step on stage, they seem to draw the audience in from the first word."[3]

The key word is *many*. Many skillful politicians are mediocre speakers. We see that any afternoon of debate in the U.S. House of Representatives as member after member drones through material, eyes wedded to the text, hands gripping the lectern.

It isn't as if they don't understand how to speak well. Some may ignore in practice what they understand in theory. They may rehearse for big speeches but feel too rushed to practice when it's something more routine. In this chapter, we analyze how to deliver material compellingly no matter the occasion.

In a book meant for reading, there are limits to the change we can influence. There is no substitute for teaching delivery face-to-face. But for those who want to improve, we can offer ways that work.

In this chapter, we first cover the three basic elements of effective delivery: appearance, movement, and voice.

Then we'll see how to improve: ways to prepare and practice, first with text, then with extemporaneous speech.

Finally, we'll look at ways speakers can systematically expand their horizons because for those who want to improve, the tools you need are easy to find.

ELEMENTS OF DELIVERY

David Demarest, one of George H. W. Bush's communications directors, once said of his boss that a belief in being a good "orator" just "wasn't in his DNA."[4]

Sorry. To value speaking skills is not genetic, and people whose job entails speaking in public cannot afford to think strong presentation skills are beyond them or practicing beneath them. After years of coaching, teaching public speaking, and speaking ourselves, we know that if the lure of a good grade can turn students into good speakers, the lure of winning elections can, too. All speakers cannot only improve but excel. And that starts before they open their mouths.

Appearance

Appearance counts. Unfortunately. Male candidates with hair do better than bald ones, and better looking ones do better than the less attractive. It is a fact of political life that taller candidates seem to have an advantage over shorter ones—in the United States, men average 5'9" but our last ten presidents included only two at 5'11" and eight at 6' or higher.

We can overrate the significance of these things. Plenty of successful politicians are overweight; the political talk shows are filled with people whose wizened faces would win no beauty contests. Most politicians are in office not because of how they look but for many other factors, including how and what they think.

Still, they need to do the best they can with what they have. In the studiedly cautious words of researcher Shelly Chaiken, physical attractiveness "enhances one's effectiveness as a social influence agent."[5] The research shows that before speakers say anything, audiences have formed some impressions of them. Speakers can't change how tall they are. But they can change how tall they look.

Stand Straight

"Listeners perceive speakers who slouch as being sloppy, unfocused, and even weak," *Speaker's Guidebook* authors Dan O'Hair, Rob Stewart, and Hannah Rubenstein advise.[6]

But while most politicians know enough to stride briskly to the podium and look out at the audience as they start, it's not unusual as the speech progresses to see them slouch, cross their legs at the ankle, lean on the lectern, or commit other sins of body language.

As your mother always said, stand up straight. And whether you move around the stage or stay behind the lectern, keep standing straight for as long as you're up there.

Dress Better Than Your Audience

Over seventy-five years ago, Dale Carnegie, then America's guru of public speaking, in words dripping with contempt put it this way:

> [I]f a speaker has baggy trousers, shapeless coat and footwear, fountain pen and pencils peeping out of his breast pocket, a newspaper or a pipe and can of tobacco bulging out of the sides of his garment, I have noticed that an audience has as little respect for that man as he has for his own appearance. Aren't they very likely to assume that his mind is as sloppy as his unkempt hair and unpolished shoes?[7]

That was then. We no longer worry about fountain pens, and we've moved beyond the days when politicians had to live in a dark suit and dress shoes. On talk shows, you will see male members of Congress willing to take interviews in shirtsleeves. Michelle Obama made news for going sleeveless. But politics still doesn't share the casual vibe of other industries.

Fashion consultant David Wolfe points out that "dressing down" for an interview may imply that an applicant doesn't really need the job.[8] As we never tire of pointing out, every political speech is a job interview. Politicians can't risk that.

Win the Genetic Lottery

Or seem to. It is tempting to argue that the usual remedies for gray hair and bad knees symbolize the posturing of so much of political life. Don't believe it. In 2006, the fourteen women in the U.S. Senate had an average age of fifty-eight, yet only one had gray hair. Audiences don't want their politicians to look twenty-two. But appearance affects more than credibility.

"Speakers who feel attractive are more self-confident," Steven Brydon and Michael Scott argue in their public speaking text *Between One and Many*.[9]

For politicians, this means that within the limits of what culture finds acceptable, you should aggressively attack and mask the effects of aging. Some things don't work: obvious toupees, wretched comb-overs, or a full set of perfectly white implants in a politician over seventy. But age isn't the only issue. Many in the audience thought comedian Joel McHale went too far when he repeatedly made fun of New Jersey governor Chris Christie's weight during his 2014 White House Correspondents' Association Dinner routine. But the speech also reminded people that Christie did not fit the image of the leader of the free world.

Movement

In the 1988 Democratic primary, intelligent, thoughtful Arizona governor Bruce Babbitt knew a lot. Yet he made little headway as a presidential candidate. One small but hard-to-ignore reason: the facial tics he could not control during the early debates, leading one of his consultants to recommend "eyebrow pushups" as a way to stop blinking.

As governor and later secretary of the interior, Babbitt did have a successful career in politics. But in national politics, even a small tic can hurt when cameras zoom in on a face. People in political life can increase their effectiveness as speakers by doing systematic work to eliminate movements that distract—swaying, shifting, jutting out a hip, blinking, licking lips, playing with hair, and a variety of others.

You won't see movement problems much at national conventions, where speech coaches thoroughly rehearse speakers before sending them onstage to a podium flanked by teleprompters. It's more common at coffees or town hall meetings, where politicians sway, slouch, and stick their hands in their pockets; or in rarely rehearsed floor speeches, where they may look down nearly the whole time they're speaking.

In small gatherings like a living room, politicians don't have to stay in one place. But they can learn to limit their movement so it doesn't distract. Don't sway. Don't shift. Such movements signal that a speaker isn't relaxed. That means the audience won't be, either. And while you work on eliminating movements that distract the audience, focus on three areas that help you express your thoughts.

Use Appropriate Facial Expressions

You don't have to smile all the time. When President Trump uses a teleprompter, he often looks almost grim. Certainly in the beginning of a speech, smiles signal that speakers are confident, happy to be speaking, and happy to see the people in front. They may not smile again until the applause after they are done.

But that may be a mistake. Like posture, facial expressions count throughout the speech. It's important not only to watch for inappropriate expressions but to monitor what all your expressions communicate.

One of the authors, Eric, has helped prepare politicians for debates, including vice-presidential candidate Joe Lieberman before his face-off with Dick Cheney in 2000. Two days before that event, they watched the top of the tickets have their first debate. Most agreed that Al Gore knew his material. But they also watched him, unable to hide his exasperation, roll his eyes and sigh as George W. Bush answered questions. The advice to Lieberman, and for any speaker, couldn't be clearer. The camera and mic are on, even when you are not talking.

Maintain Eye Contact

In 1966, during Jimmy Carter's run for governor of Georgia, Atlanta reporter Achsah Nesmith noticed something: Whenever Carter spoke, he would look not at the people in the crowd but above their heads. He seemed to be hunting for an exit.

One day, Carter asked Nesmith her impressions of his speech. She told him. "He looked hurt," she said later, "and I rather regretted it."[10]

But Carter stopped his overhead glances. Ten years later, he'd forgiven Nesmith enough to hire her as a speechwriter.

Americans trust people who look them in the eye. And maybe not just people—in one Cornell University study, researchers used the cartoon rabbit on Trix cereal boxes.[11] They manipulated the rabbit's face, then asked subjects whether they wanted to buy the cereal. The result? Respondents were more likely to choose Trix over others if the rabbit was looking at them instead of somewhere else.

One Cornell professor said, "Making eye contact even with a character on a cereal box inspires powerful feelings of connection."[12]

The reverse is also true; one researcher points out that speakers in the United States who refuse to "establish eye contact are perceived as tentative or ill at ease and may be seen as insincere or dishonest."[13]

This sends an important message to politicians. Before live audiences, looking up allows you to see what listeners are feeling. If speakers see people yawning, checking their phones, or devoting full attention to their cheesecake, it may be time to cut the speech short. It certainly means you should speak less from text.

That is also true during a floor speech. Whether in state capitols or Washington, D.C., legislators give many of them to a sparsely populated chamber. It seems as if no one is watching. But the House of Representatives has televised its sessions since 1979. The audience is not huge. C-SPAN doesn't regularly disclose the precise numbers, though estimates hover around thirty thousand. But that includes staffers, other members, people in D.C., and those who contribute to campaigns. Whether reading from a text, talking points, or a note card, political speakers need to master the art of looking up.

And when you do look up, make sure you also look around. You don't connect with an audience by looking straight ahead; you need to make contact with all corners of the room.

Speakers can vastly improve eye contact by following two rules.

Absorb Groups of Words. Glance at the next two sentences for a moment. Then look up and say what you remember.

> Tonight, we come together to write a new chapter in the American story. Our forebears enshrined the American Dream—life, liberty, and the pursuit of happiness.

Those are the first two sentences from the famous episode in Bill Clinton's administration, when, about to give his 1993 health care address, he realized the wrong speech was in the teleprompter.[14]

He turned to Vice President Gore sitting behind him. Gore raced off stage to tell staffers. While they worked frantically to replace the disc, Clinton had to read from his hard copy until the operators succeeded and scrolled down to catch up.

Clinton was nothing if not resourceful. He first asked for a moment of silence in recognition of a train wreck in Alabama. During that moment, head bowed, he was no doubt practicing.

Then, in the roughly first two minutes of his speech, Clinton looked down fourteen times for the 158 words. That's pretty good. His glances were brief. The ability to take in groups expands with practice.[15]

Try it. Start by reading the first clause in a sentence (*Our forebears enshrined the American Dream*). Then look up, remembering the second part (*life, liberty, and the pursuit of happiness*), and look out as if at an audience. With practice, every one of you reading this chapter should be able to look up for nine out of every ten seconds, just like Clinton.

In front of live audiences, though, it is not enough to look up. That prompts a second rule.

Speak to the Whole Room. In those first two minutes, viewers saw Clinton turning his head each time he looked down. Left, right, right, center, left—even without the teleprompter, he did what public speaking coaches urge clients: to move not just their eyes but their heads.

Imagine yourself speaking not to people but to half a pizza, divided into three slices, the tips pointing toward you. We tell clients and students to divide the audience in thirds, as if they were looking at each slice, moving at pauses from one slice to the next. They can cover the entire room, making eye contact and moving across the room, from left, to center, to right.

In the seven minutes before aides fixed his teleprompter, Clinton still looked up 90 percent of the time. It is a skill any politician can learn.

Use Your Hands and Arms

Whether from undergrads in a public speaking class, corporate officers, or people on the campaign trail, we hear this question again and again:

"What do I do with my hands?"

In political life, it is rare to see speakers with arms pinned to their sides, or gripping the lectern so tightly their white knuckles are visible to the audience. But using hands and arms expressively is not just a matter of appearance. It's well established that American audiences view speakers who use their hands and arms as more open and more believable.

For that reason, some coaches believe speakers should consciously learn and practice gestures that express common emotions. In Box 15.1, you'll find a group of basic gestures once popular among public speaking teachers, but now in disrepute because they sometimes seem so artificial. The authors are agnostic about this issue. We have seen speakers use them robotically and seem almost comic in the attempt. But we have also seen some people use them naturally.

BOX 15.1
DELIVERY: GESTURES

Pointing: finger or hand toward listeners when speaker is addressing them ("You have been courageous . . .")

Giving: both hands outstretched when speaker is indicating support ("I have fought for your issues . . .")

Receiving: one or both hands at chest level, palm(s) turned toward speaker ("I have seen the pain when . . .")

Rejecting: hand up as if taking an oath, palm toward audience, waggling back and forth ("I will not accept . . .")

Counting: finger of one hand tapping fingers of the other, as speaker enumerates ("First, it's wrong. Second, . . .")

Cautioning: index finger up ("But we cannot . . .")

Dividing: one hand chopping down, then the other, to indicate different sides ("On the one hand, X . . . on the other hand, Y")

You can try different gestures by marking where in the text you'd want to use them. Rehearse your speech and check what you look like by setting your smartphone on a nearby shelf. Give these experiments some time. Just like any physical act, gestures will seem awkward at first.

Of course, the movements listed in Box 15.1 are not the only ways to use your hands and arms. President Trump does very well with a few minimal gestures, usually moving his right hand in rhythm to his words, sometimes spreading his arms wide to illustrate great progress. However you decide to use your hands and arms, three rules will help you do it effectively:

Use body movements to express your thoughts. They do more than contribute. Imagine speakers passionate about what they say while their hands stay clasped in front of their chest. The effect is odd, discordant, and distracting.

Use different styles at different events. Your arms should get more of a workout at a rally in a labor hall than a coffee for fifteen people in a New Hampshire living room.

Finally, *use gestures that suit your personality*. What makes one speaker self-conscious might strike another as appropriately expressive. Experiment with gestures as you do with sound. You won't know until you try.

Remember: If you speak forcefully while your hands and arms are motionless, you are sending two different messages. Whatever you feel fits your style, don't rest until you see your body movement help what you say instead of contradicting it.

Voice

The student was smart, hardworking, eager to improve, and full of ideas—which he uttered so fast that he swallowed half his words and spoke the rest in short, machine-gun-like bursts that all of us in the class had to work hard to decipher.

For the first weeks of that semester in 2007, one of us wrote long descriptions of what he sounded like and talked to him about it after class. "Yeahyeahyeah," he would say.

Then, halfway though the course, American University made a great technological advance—the ability to record and watch instantly in the classroom.

The first time we tried it, the student was horrified. "That was gross," he said after class, speaking slowly for the first time. He bought a tape recorder. By next week's speech, he articulated every word.

Now, as a senior congressional aide, that student speaks often. Reminiscing about that horrible moment a decade earlier, he said, "I remember that day. Think about it all the time."

You might be excused for thinking that a decade later all speakers watch themselves. After all, smartphones make that easy. Not true. Even technologically sophisticated students hate the idea. So do older, well-established executives. Recently, Eric coached the CEO of a global corporation, a man in his sixties. He had access to every device imaginable and had *never* watched himself on tape until that first session.

That was a mistake. Watching and listening is the best way to discover if you're speaking too fast. It's also an important tool for what most speech coaches emphasize, vocal variety. That means varying your inflection patterns. It also means varying three qualities that affect the sounds you make—*pitch*, *rate*, and *volume*—and learning to use two techniques for indicating importance or shifts in subject matter: *pauses* and *emphasis*.

Here we examine each, then suggest ways to improve.

Pitch

"Singing is just sustained talking," intones the bass member of *The Music Man*'s barbershop quartet. Like a song, speech has high and low notes. Pitch means how high and low you will go in a speech. The range of highs and lows acceptable in conversation can sound dull in a twenty-minute speech. Announcers consciously learn to extend their pitch range; as an example, listen to any talk show host or weatherperson.

Stand-up comics sometimes parody the pitch range on news shows—especially those delivering the weather—because it sounds unnatural in real life. To sustain interest in their speeches, though, most speakers need to consciously expand their range beyond the highs and lows they use from day to day.

Rate

Normally, people speak at about 125–150 words per minute. In his Berlin speech, Obama took twenty-five minutes to say about 3,000 words; after we subtract several minutes' worth of applause, that is pretty close to average. But these aren't constant rates. For important points, good speakers slow down. At peak moments, they may speed up. Variety is enormously important in maintaining credibility and interest.

Volume

Speech coach Michael Sheehan, who preps speakers for the Democratic conventions, reminds them there's no need to shout. The speakers are using a good sound system, and they have a large TV audience. For folks at home, shouting is as invasive as someone shouting in their living room—which is where the TV may be. Varying volume also helps you shift your tone and convey different emotions. Watch Obama's quiet opening in the Berlin speech, excerpted in Chapter 7, and contrast it with the way he finished. He should not have done it any other way.

AS DELIVERED

Candidate Barack Obama speaks in Berlin, July 24, 2008.
www.youtube.com/watch?v=Q-9ry38AhbU

Pauses

The space *between* words can be an incredibly useful rhetorical tool. A pause can indicate to listeners that you're switching gears, or that you have something important coming up, or that you're searching for the right word because you care about being precise. Watch Ronald Reagan tell the "sailor" story we've cited from his 1989 Farewell. Taken from about two minutes into his speech, watch as a president who began as a radio announcer uses the pause to lend impact to his next words:

> I've been thinking a bit at that window. I've been reflecting on what the past eight years have meant [*pause*] and mean.
>
> And the image that comes to mind like a refrain is [*pause*] a nautical one—a small story [*pause*] about a big ship, and a refugee, and a sailor. It was back in the early eighties, at the height of the boat people. And the sailor was hard at work on the carrier *Midway*, which was patrolling the South China Sea. The sailor, like most American servicemen, was young, smart, and [*pause*] fiercely observant. The crew spied on the horizon a leaky little boat. And crammed inside were refugees from Indochina hoping to get to America. The *Midway* sent a small launch to bring them to the ship and safety. As the refugees made their way through the choppy seas, one spied the sailor on deck, and stood up, and called out to him. He yelled [*pause*], "Hello, American sailor. Hello [*pause*], freedom man."
>
> A small moment with a big meaning, a moment the sailor, who wrote it in a letter, couldn't get out of his mind.
>
> And, when I saw it [*pause*], neither could I.

AS DELIVERED

President Ronald Reagan's Farewell Address.

www.youtube.com/watch?v=UKVsq2daR8Q

We haven't highlighted all the pauses. But note how the ones we include add irony, highlight a compliment, help Reagan make a key word memorable, or just imply emotion.

Emphasis

Read these sentences aloud:

Emphasis makes a big difference.

Emphasis *makes* a big difference.

Emphasis makes a *big* difference.

Now, think back to the Ronald Reagan excerpt, and add another device:

Emphasis [*pause*] makes a big difference.

Emphasis makes [*pause*] a big difference.

Emphasis makes a big [*pause*] difference.

Can you see how pauses and emphasis work in tandem, making a big (*pause*) difference?

Pronunciation

You might think people running for office would know how to pronounce words. Most do. But even a small mistake—like pronouncing *nuclear* as "new-cue-lar"—can erase the good impression of all the words you've pronounced right. To mispronounce a name can be just as damaging.

Once Bob wrote a speech that quoted a Bob Dylan song. His speaker said, "As Bob *Die*-lan put it . . ."

Since then, he includes pronunciation guides in scripts even when he is sure the speaker won't need them. Speakers shouldn't hesitate to seek pronunciation tips, and speechwriters shouldn't recoil at including them. Checking pronunciation is not a sign of ignorance; it's a sign that you want to get things right.

The Articulated Pause

Uh. Ummm. Er. Like. Other ingredients in this list suggest things to improve and ultimately perfect. Here is one to eliminate. Why do speakers lard their speeches with noises, sometimes and descriptively called *disfluencies*, that make them seem unsure of themselves?

Back in 2010, Caroline Kennedy, then angling to be secretary of state, participated in an interview she hoped would show her sophistication.

The *New York Times* focused on something else: that Kennedy used "you know" 142 times in a single interview—12 times in one minute alone.[16]

That's more than twice what most people do. An article in *Harvard Business Review* said that the average speaker uses five "filler" words and sounds per minute, and even that's too much. The optimal number is only one.[17]

People new to speaking tend to feel silence is more awkward than articulation. That makes this a hard habit to break. When we ask students to eliminate the word *like*, they will start, use the word twice, and come to a screeching halt. "I'm, like, saying it again!" one student said during one exercise. "I did it again!" and then sank into silence.

BOX 15.2
EXERCISE: IF YOU WANT TO SAY SOMETHING, SAY NOTHING

Here's an exercise, borrowed from media trainer Brad Phillips.

Brad tells clients to look around the room and pick an object, then begin talking about it for thirty seconds. You can't use "uh" or "um," but you can stop briefly because a silent pause is better than filler. His own thirty-second speech about a printer looked like this:

> I like my printer. I've had it for about two years, and it's been pretty maintenance-free, which I really appreciate as someone who runs his own business. It sits on the corner of my desk in my office in New York City. The best part of my office is the view of the Chrysler Building. It's pretty cool to sit, especially in the winter, and see a Manhattan icon out my office window.[18]

You can practice this anywhere. And you can tape yourself, too, since you may be unaware that you're still doing it.

It's not the only way to get rid of an annoying verbal tic. But it's worth trying. The articulated pause is a sure way to lose credibility.

The basics of delivery may sound simple, but even frequent speakers often neglect to master them. In the next example, Sen. James Inhofe of Oklahoma begins a floor speech on energy. It is still online—a lesson for those who think once they have finished speaking they can relax. We include it not to pick on Inhofe—he's not doing a terrible job—but to examine the way many politicians handle routine speeches.

AS DELIVERED

James Inhofe's Floor Speech on Energy. Watch for ways that his movements distract you, other than the ones noted here. There are plenty.

> [*First articulated pause (AP)*] Uh [*looks down, puts hands in pocket*], thank you, Mr. President. I think, I wanted a chance and I haven't had a chance to do it, to come down [*fixes glasses on nose*] and talk about the Democrat bill [*second AP*] called the Consumer First Energy Act [*scratches nose*], and I—I—you know, we go through this same thing over and over again [*looks up*], and we have an energy bill which has no energy in it. I said this on the floor last [*third AP*], uh, last December. We keep talking about energy, and every time we try to expand energy [*fourth AP*], uh, try to expand the supply [*looks down; fifth AP*], it, it divides right down along party lines.
>
> The Consumer First Energy Act does nothing to increase access to America's extensive oil and natural gas reserves, does nothing to promote [*sixth AP*], uh, nuclear energy, does nothing for, to increase refining capacity, something I've been trying to do for a long period of time, nothing for electricity generation or transmission, and nothing for clean coal technology.
>
> Instead, this act increases taxes by $17 billion [*looks up*] on America's oil and gas producers, which means [*left hand out of pocket to gesture*] you're going to pay more at the pump [*looks down*], that's going to be passed on, we know that [*hand back in pocket*], and it increases government bureaucracy [*hand out of pocket but only to place on podium*].

www.youtube.com/watch?v=5EH1T72hnL8

Nobody expects a politician delivering a dull floor speech to an empty room to compare with a celebrity using a teleprompter to deliver a convention address before ten thousand screaming fans. But Inhofe didn't need to look down almost two-thirds of the time, or use articulated pauses when he tried to ad-lib. With work, he seems perfectly capable of eliminating his many distracting gestures; his rapid, unvarying pace—two hundred words a minute; and his almost complete lack of variation in pitch or volume.

His floor speech, watched by thousands of people, is not the exception in politics, but common. People in political life should try viewing a routine speech not as something to cruise through on autopilot but as a low-stakes occasion for practicing delivery skills. To become better speakers, politicians need do only what college students do in public speaking classes every semester: practice.

DELIVERY'S BEST PRACTICE: PRACTICE

Naturally, not all speeches need the same kind of practice. In the world of public speaking, there are four methods of delivery. Two of them, *impromptu* and *memorized* speeches, don't count—or shouldn't. Memorized speeches take a prodigious amount of time and aren't worth the effort. Impromptu speeches are too risky.

Two others dominate political speech. The first is *manuscript* or *text*, when you're reading a speech that's been entirely written out. The second is *extemporaneous*—the carefully prepared and practiced but not memorized speech, usually from talking points or some other form of notes.

Speaking from text may seem easy. But why did listeners interrupt Barack Obama sixteen times for applause in the last five minutes of his 2004 speech—against five for John Kerry?

It was not just the language. Neither was it the coaching they got; like tennis, a coach can suggest, but the player has to be willing to hit a million balls and learn from each one.

Here, in a chapter aimed at speakers but offering ways to involve staffers, we offer seven tips that over time will help both:

> **Use every speech as a chance to get better.** It's common in politics to think that some speeches don't matter. Our suggestion: Every speech gives speakers the chance to practice. But that means practicing, performing, and reviewing the right way. Like running, eating breakfast, or playing guitar, make this part of your day.

> **Don't just rehearse—record.** It used to be hard to see yourself. You needed a camera, a VHS tape, and someone to work the camera. That might scare speakers off—even senators don't like the idea of other people watching them stumble through a first try.

> Today, the smartphone gives speakers no excuse. You can set it up in private, speak, and then watch. Our suggestion: Resist the temptation to just sit at your desk and run through the draft. You want to see exactly how you will look and sound when you deliver.

> **Don't just watch—correct.** Each time you watch yourself, watch for specific things to change. Arms at your side? Voice a monotone? Next time work on that, and watch to see whether you look or sound different.

Are you standing straight? Varying your voice? Do you use your hands expressively? Look up most of the time? Look around? Deliver your speech again, working on the things that bother you most. Check your phone again. Repeat as needed.

Set specific goals. It shouldn't take long for you to know what gives you trouble. Take voice. Do you need more variety? Do rehearsals where you work only on that.

Rely on the kindness of others. In general, speakers are their severest critics. But nobody has a corner on insight. Politicians cannot be inhibited about asking staffers for advice. Create a climate of candor. Once staffers know you want honesty, they will be eager to give it.

Debrief. Have someone record the actual speech, then hold a session to review it. Politicians can't depend on asking people how things went. The impulse to flatter you is too great. Much better: a session in which the speaker and communication people watch together, knowing that the goal is to get better.

Finally:

Don't expect miracles. Practice is one habit you cannot abandon. But like most things, genuine improvement takes time.

And while you wait, we have some tips—in this case aimed mostly at those giving the speech—on rehearsing the two types you will use most.

Practicing with Text

During the 2004 presidential campaign, one of us walked into a friend's office to see that he had pasted the pages of a speech around his walls, in two different colors of ink. Black was the text he had written. Blue were the ad-libs his boss had delivered. The pages were about 80 percent blue—and almost 100 percent terrible. "He hates being scripted," the friend said, mournfully.

It is an occupational hazard. Most politicians need to speak fluently about dozens of subjects, and a lot rides on avoiding errors. That means, like it or not, they often need a text. Speeches read word for word might sound stiff in front of small groups, but for bigger crowds, a formal text allows politicians to speak effectively about issues only staffers should know.

There is often no way around having to read, whether with a teleprompter or without one. Besides, it's always good to have a text to distribute to reporters.

We have heard speakers practice by droning through a text and, with preparation, inspire. But usually just sitting at a desk mumbling through the script, occasionally stopping to change a word, does not work. Here are some ways to rehearse that can make you better:

Rehearse like you mean it. That means standing at the podium and practicing exactly the voice and tone and gestures you will use. Only in that way will you be able to time the speech accurately and judge what works in your nonverbal language.

Mark up your drafts. Just because you have the text in front of you doesn't mean you remember everything you need. Do you use anaphora three times in a row? Underline each so you remember to get a little louder each time. Racing through sentences? Write "slow down" in the margin. Especially important: pause and emphasis. Don't hesitate to write "pause" or some symbol that reminds you to pause. Underline or use italics to emphasize.

Rehearse not just for what's there—but to add what isn't. The best speechwriters in the world cannot guess exactly what you want. Use at least one rehearsal to figure out what you want and don't want. Revise. Then mark up the manuscript and start again.

Cut. Every draft ever written can be cut. After you have a revised draft, use one rehearsal to cut 10 percent—including words for ideas that could just as easily be conveyed by a gesture alone. Some examples: *It's a great honor . . . I want to make it clear that . . .*

Extend eye contact. Even a rehearsal or two will allow you to remember larger groups of words each time, so you can preserve the eye contact so vital to persuasion.

It may be tempting to skimp on rehearsal and practice with a text already done. But in addition to sacrificing the chance to work on overall speech goals, even a single rehearsal can make speakers more effective.

Record and review. You may take a few hours to go to a conference, speak, and come back. It's worth thirty minutes to see how you did.

Did you stand up straight? Use your arms expressively? Vary your voice? Rise in pitch approaching an applause line? Be tough on yourself. Invite staff—and family—to watch and comment. Tell your kids you want them to be honest. They will oblige.

Practicing the Extemporaneous Speech

To give an extended speech without notes, or with only a few talking points, takes careful preparation and many, many hours of rehearsal. But if speakers prepare, learn, and deliver an extemporaneous speech well, they can create the same impact they would with a teleprompter. They will seem to know a lot, sound relaxed and conversational, and be able to make eye contact the entire time. That, of course, includes delivering the stump speech, the most difficult and most valuable speech in politics.

At the local level, state legislators or small-town mayors should rarely rely on prepared texts; the audiences are too small, and the things they need to say are not that different from one event to the next. But even at the national level, politicians should speak extemporaneously much more often than they do. Yes, text speeches make an event easy. You can eat, schmooze with the guests, and not give a thought to the speech until you pull it out of your inside jacket pocket.

But if you want to be really effective, use a stump not just during the campaign but as often as possible. Remember, even if staffers and reporters have heard the stump speech a hundred times, most audiences haven't. Also, why sacrifice the chance to exhibit all the skills that make listeners say, "Let's march!"? That includes the polished delivery—constant eye contact, expressive gestures, pause, and emphasis—that comes from using material that you've planned and practiced.

When we teach public speaking, largely about extemporaneous speech, we tell students they should think of the new assignment not as one speech but as fifteen. Even once they have created an outline that works, it will take them at least that many rehearsals to deliver a three-minute speech well.

Even for speakers who have used stumps often, we suggest ten steps that should allow you to deliver one well:

1. Create a detailed outline of your stump—but not a full speech—with careful attention to themes that work everywhere.

2. Limit it to ten to twelve minutes, or about 1,500 to 1,800 words.

3. Practice first with your outline, then with fewer notes, and then with none.

4. Record and watch yourself, each time, noting what needs improvement whether appearance, movement, or voice. Work to correct.

5. Now speak in front of staff. Solicit comments. Pay special attention to elements of delivery contained in this chapter: pitch, rate, volume, emphasis, pause, and articulation. Resist annoyance at comments by junior staffers.

6. Revise. Strengthen weak sections and practice intensely.
7. Try out with less-important groups. Deliver the speech you've prepared; do not vary or digress.
8. Make sure stories and jokes remain intact.
9. Begin using the speech before groups for whom you might previously have used a text.
10. Monitor constantly for creeping length.

Like an antibiotic, stumps take time to work. You need that time to become fluent, to become confident, to experiment with new material, and to learn from failure. But as you do, remember that this kind of practice can get you only so far. To really become good, keep assessing your progress. Questions to ask yourself—mostly about delivery—appear at the end of this chapter.

Practicing the Q & A

It is almost axiomatic that politicians follow a stump by taking questions. There are good reasons for that. Listeners often like to hear themselves talk, and also have some important questions.

Most elected officials feel comfortable answering questions. If they don't know the answers, they can say, "I don't know—but I'll get back to you." If it is one they want to evade, they can say, "I don't want to comment on that."

But that doesn't mean they answer questions well. What works well in a presidential campaign debate prep session works just as well for a city council member in a small town.

Here are four tips:

1. Have a briefing book filled with thought-out, crisp answers to the questions most likely to come up.
2. Rehearse regularly—while walking the dog, driving home, or taking a shower.
3. Hold sessions with aides, answering the questions they hurl. Encourage them to ask them in an obnoxious way, the better to prepare you for what lies ahead. They will think that's a lot of fun.
4. Learn to pivot, carefully.

That's the kind of answer beginning something like this:
"Great question, Joe. Yes, I'd like to do X. But Joe, the real question is . . ."

Sometimes, the impossible demands of public life make the pivot necessary. But it is an evasion. In our view, constant preparation with aides can almost always arm speakers with a persuasive answer. The pivot should be plan B.

So far, we have focused on improving techniques, speaking skills. But there are other ways to improve delivery.

EXPANDING YOUR HORIZONS

Learn How Speeches Are Made

Often, elected officials don't systematically examine the questions of structure or language. But delivery cannot be totally divorced from content. If, say, House members or state senators don't know how repetition or parallel construction can increase power, why would they use them?

For those of you reading this book as you run for office, you're learning just the kinds of things that will help you. But check the web links and watch every example. Look at some of the books listed in this book's bibliography—even *The Political Speechwriter's Companion* doesn't have a corner on ideas. The more you read, the more you listen, the more ideas you'll have for your own speeches.

Watch Other Speakers

Not everyone should deliver a speech the same way. But whether you are a state representative in Illinois or a ten-term member of Congress, you've noticed which of your colleagues speak well. Imitating the things they do is a permissible form of plagiarism. In our classes, we see that happen every semester. ("Oh! *That's* how litany sounds. Let me try!") If twenty-year-olds can learn by imitating, so should their parents.

Why don't more politicians learn from one another? We learn how to speak French by listening to people who know how. We learn how to play tennis from a coach. We learn how to dance from—well, okay, some people never do learn. We can learn to speak by copying others.

If you need evidence, look at the role model admired by so many politicians: the Rev. Martin Luther King Jr.. Taylor Branch's biography describes King at Morehouse College, having decided to become a minister, in the balcony of Wheat Street Baptist with some friends to study the speaking style of William Borders, a minister whose style they admired.[19]

Later, at Crozer Theological Seminary, King studied oratory: the "proven" sermon structures (the Ladder, the Jewel, the Twin, and others) and how to apply the Crozer version of the Three *Ps*. That version included proving, painting, and persuasion "to win over successively the mind, imagination, and heart."[20] Soon, his fellow students were crowding into a chapel to hear King deliver the Thursday morning student sermon.

You can make a case that King was a better speaker than writer. But he wasn't born that way.

Expose Yourself to Ridicule

Constantly. Video has made observation much easier for us than it was for King. Any friend or staffer with a camcorder can unobtrusively provide a tape of every appearance. But don't just watch. Watch critically, watch with friends or staff, and watch with the checklist you will find at the end of this chapter. Meanwhile, when someone points out a flaw, work on it. And keep working on it. Not overnight, but over time, you will not just improve but revolutionize your delivery. And you will make that task easier with another step:

Rely on the Advice of Others

This chapter has already urged reviewing speeches with staff. We have not explored how difficult that can be.

Politicians and candidates surround themselves with deferential aides. For a young midlevel staffer to tell them about their bad posture is uncomfortable for both. Neither can you count on an honest critique from the people who invited you to speak. Take the advice of longtime congressional management consultant Rick Shapiro, whose interview appears in Chapter 17. "These people need you. They'll always say, 'Great speech.'"

Still, and here we speak not to staffers but to those they work for, politicians cannot rely only on their own evaluation of their abilities. You may be reluctant to face the truth—or too harsh on yourself. You must subject yourself to the honest evaluation of others. Because our voices come to us altered by the thickness of our own skulls, we do not sound to ourselves the way we do to others. We don't know when we're slumping, swaying, or droning. Only exasperating and sometimes humiliating practice can help, aided by video and the frank assessment of people who care about their goals and know what they're talking about. For politicians used to fawning praise, honest criticism can be tough to take.

Our advice: Get over it. You have hired bright people. Now make sure you create an atmosphere that fosters good feedback.

If you encourage honest assessment, deal with it maturely when it comes, and then act on it in ways everyone can see, eventually you will get plenty of useful advice—even from someone who looks younger than your kids. After all, if, say, U.S. senators feel comfortable delegating to a twenty-three-year-old the job of deciding how to vote on a $100 million appropriation, they should feel equally comfortable hearing that person's judgments about eye contact.

Make the Teleprompter Your Friend

We leave this suggestion for last because not everyone has access to one. Also, in front of a small audience, a teleprompter looks out of place, like a crutch for someone who is walking well.

Still, it can make a world of difference.

Television audiences in 2008 felt Barack Obama was speaking to them. He was looking up and out at them, after all. No one could see his eyes moving. They were amazed to learn that his speech was scrolling down teleprompter screens just out of camera range.

Sixty years after Dwight Eisenhower became the first American president to use one, most people still do not know how common this device is in politics.

Bob once gave a workshop in Hanoi for Vietnamese diplomats. He showed a clip of Obama. "How does he memorize speeches so fast?" one of the students asked when it was over.

Bob was confused. "He's using a teleprompter."

It turned out that not a single diplomat had ever heard the word.

Teleprompters come in for a lot of criticism, some of it reasonable. At one rally, Donald Trump started with a teleprompter, then admitted to the crowd it had broken. Then he knocked one of the screens to the floor. "I like it better without the teleprompter," he said.

The fact is, when, like Trump, you are saying the same thing from event to event, that's true. But now he uses one. Naturally, teleprompters are an illusion—one of the things that make voters distrust politics. To us, the solution is to stop pretending they don't exist. Without them, not only would speakers sound inarticulate. Listeners would be less informed.

Meanwhile, there are ways to improve that involve no technology.

FINAL WORDS

In *White House Ghosts*, Robert Schlesinger's engaging and useful book about presidential speechwriters, he paints two very different portraits of presidents through the eyes of the people who worked for them.[21]

The first is George H. W. Bush, one of whose speechwriters once asked the president if he ever read his speeches out loud before delivering them.

No, Bush said.

He didn't think about "how he wanted a speech to sound when he delivered it?" the speechwriter asked.

No, Bush said. That would take too long.

Later in the book, Schlesinger describes how Bush's "unwillingness to practice and habit of ad-libbing continued to dog him." In the words of a staffer writing about one speech,

> He ad-libbed significantly—embracing some lines verbatim, but mostly opening his arms to his own words . . . When he did look down to the lines on the cards, it sounded like bumper car met bumper car; lines ran head on into other lines, paragraphs into paragraphs. Transitions in almost every case were lost.[22]

Oratory did not decide the 1992 election. But it may have been the deciding factor in 2008. George H. W. Bush wasn't a terrible speaker. But who knows how good a speaker he could have become if he'd tried? When politicians limit their own aspirations, they deprive themselves of what's possible.

We say to those running: raise your sights. It should be clear from this chapter that the key to becoming an exciting speaker is what you do not at the podium—but away from it. Those sessions pay off for a skill often vital to your career. For except for the clergy, no field other than politics puts such a premium on speaking well.

And it allows you to express qualities uniquely yours. Speakers don't have to imitate Barack Obama or Donald Trump to be good. In the 2016 campaign, Ted Cruz, Marco Rubio, Carly Fiorina, Hillary Clinton, Michelle Obama, and Bernie Sanders all moved audiences in different ways. This chapter should give speakers confidence about the elements of delivery, the way to practice, and the way to lift your game to a new level.

Audiences may still not remember much of what you say. But if you speak well, they will remember you.

THE SPEECHWRITER'S CHECKLIST: DELIVERY

Appearance

- ☐ Am I standing straight?
- ☐ Did I take time to get a haircut and check my wardrobe?
- ☐ Do I try to stay reasonably physically fit?

(Continued)

(Continued)

Movement

- ☐ Have I refrained from swaying or other distracting movements?
- ☐ Do my facial expressions resemble those I'd use in conversation?
- ☐ Am I using my hands appropriately and expressively?

Eye Contact

- ☐ Have I rehearsed enough so I can look at the audience at least two-thirds of the time?
- ☐ Am I following the "three slices of pizza" rule?

Voice

- ☐ Am I using a good range of high and low notes?
- ☐ Have I varied my inflections and speaking rate to suit the material?
- ☐ Do I articulate clearly and pronounce everything perfectly?

Preparation

Do I:

- ☐ Routinely mark up speeches?
- ☐ Rehearse to cut and reshape?
- ☐ Practice extending eye contact?
- ☐ Systematically prepare my stump?
- ☐ Listen to other speakers?
- ☐ Investigate ways speeches are made?
- ☐ Watch other speakers?
- ☐ Study my own performance?
- ☐ Rely on the advice of others?

16

Ethics

Lie? Falsehood? What to call the president's words.[1]

That question headlined a Pete Vernon article in Columbia University's May 29, 2018, *Columbia Journalism Review*, examining an issue that, in its detail, tone, passion, and national attention, had never before faced any American president.

Note the word *falsehood*. During the 2016 campaign and after Donald Trump's inauguration, reporters didn't know quite what to call the clearly incorrect statements that characterized much of his remarks. They were quick to point out statements where the president got the facts wrong.

But were they falsehoods? Innocent mistakes? Ignorance?

Or lies?

Reporters weren't splitting hairs. A lie is not just something false, but a conscious, deliberate decision to utter something false about a matter of fact. How could they know whether that was the case? At first, it seemed like calling the president a liar meant reporters would have to be deep inside his brain.[2]

A year and a half into his presidency, the debate about what to call Trump's assertions shifted. Whatever reporters call them, the president's claims—whether factually incorrect or unsupported; whether in speeches, tweets, or shouted comments on the way to his helicopter—have made journalists, even those known for being rigorously nonpartisan, use the *L* word.

Telling lies is certainly not the province of one party or one politician. We understand that, in a book written by two people who come out of Democratic politics, readers may want to take our views with a grain of salt.

But it would be naive to treat President Trump's attitude toward the truth as just another example of politics as usual.

It is distressing that in February 2019 *PolitiFact*, the Pulitzer Prize–winning fact-check site, characterized 70 percent of President Trump's statements as "mostly false," "false," or "pants on fire."[3]

Citing a rally speech in Tampa, Florida, *Washington Post* fact-checker Glenn Kessler wrote this:

> [T]he President made 35 false or misleading claims, including some of his greatest hits: He passed the biggest tax cuts in U.S. history (it ranks eighth); his promised wall along the Mexican border is being built (Congress has not appropriated the funds); the MS-13 gang is occupying towns and cities (it is not); U.S. Steel has announced the opening of six steel mills (the company has only restarted two blast furnaces); and that the trade deficit is $500 billion (it is $375 billion). . . . [T]he president also retweeted his false claim that "the most popular person in the history of the Republican Party is Trump . . ." [suggesting] that his approval rating was higher than even that of "honest Abe Lincoln," even though public opinion didn't exist then.[4]

A few weeks later, Kessler went further. He wrote that though his column had documented 4,229[5] "false or misleading claims" from the president, he had been reluctant to use the *L* word. But after that week's guilty plea by long-time Trump personal lawyer Michael Cohen, the truth was "indisputable." The president, he said, "was deliberately dishonest." So he was willing to attach that word for the first time.

His headline: "Not just misleading. Not merely false. A lie."[6]

In our political experience, totaling about seventy-five years, we have never seen anything like it: the President's endless repetition of falsehoods on matters of fact, whether comical, like the attendance at his inauguration, or vital, like unemployment figures; the denials of his Stormy Daniels payoff, even when contradicted by his own lawyers; and his repetition of unsupported claims at rallies months after reporters had presented material impossible to refute. Whether they stem from ignorance or the deliberate intent to deceive, we find this shocking, dangerous, and, yes, unethical.

There are many ethical issues in political life that have nothing to do with speech. But in the years since the first edition of this book appeared, particularly since 2016, the ethics of rhetoric has dominated the news, about many issues other than the bald-faced lie. We thus expand this chapter far beyond its original role.

Not that ethical issues are new. They were important to the Greeks; in the dialogue illuminating rhetorical issues he wrote around 370 BC, Plato had one character, Phaedrus, argue that a good speaker needed to know not the truth but only how to persuade others.[7] Today, we can examine codes of ethics from groups like the National Communication Association and the Professional Speechwriters Association, professors of communication, and many public speaking textbooks.

They distinguish among a speaker's intent, means, and ends. They urge readers to respect diversity; avoid hate speech and sexism; be courageous in expressing views; be truthful, fair, and responsible; tolerate dissent; and promote a "climate of caring."[8] Other suggestions: cite sources in your text, avoid exaggeration or half-truths, and refrain from "unnecessarily tapping into emotion rather than logic."[9] At least one code of ethics focuses on the decisions professional speechwriters face—whether or not, for example, to tell a client about conflicts of interest. Some are clearly aimed at informative speech, urging speakers to respectfully present both sides of an issue. For the record, the authors oppose "half-truths," and in our classrooms try hard to promote a climate of caring. In informative speech, we agree: respectfully present "both sides."

But these are not relevant to that part of American culture assigned the struggle over the bitterest disagreements of our time.

Is it reasonable to expect a "climate of caring" and "respect for dissent" when politicians argue about a bill to ban abortion or support a declaration of war? We think that's unrealistic.

At some political events, listeners expect a certain amount of "exaggeration." We call it "hyperbole." Audiences at rallies relish it.

Neither do we agree with the concern over "unnecessarily" tapping into emotion. Any time a speaker spends one hundred words on a moving story, it substitutes for one hundred words that might offer, say, statistics. Actually, story—technically an extended example—is a kind of evidence. It puts the human face on tragedy and moves listeners by offering a kind of evidence statistics cannot provide. In political speech, "tapping into emotion" becomes invaluable. In fact, by now, readers of this book know the authors believe it would be unethical *not* to tap "into emotion" when talking about issues of, say, war and peace.

What about citing information within the speech? Speakers should have sources. But in building toward a climax, was Martin Luther King Jr. unethical by not citing a single source during his "Dream" speech ("Mississippi, a state sweltering with injustice as two Harvard professors amply demonstrated in their 1962 report . . .")?

Discounting these well-meaning suggestions by no means exempts politicians from behaving ethically. Plato was right. Ethical questions remain central to the art of writing and delivering political speeches. The give-and-take of politics does not mean anything goes. We believe the ethical violations of political speech combined with the technology that can promote them are dangerous to democracy.

In this book we don't focus on issues like confidentiality or conflict of interest. Instead, we concentrate on the issues most relevant to political speechwriting.

In this chapter, we examine four. Three influence the actual texts of what politicians and their writers produce, and are the responsibility of both:

- Plagiarism
- Misleading listeners
- Lying

The fourth involves a broader ethical issue about the speechwriting profession as a whole.

PLAGIARISM

To *plagiarize* is "to steal and pass off (the ideas or words of another) as one's own," and comes from the Latin *plagiarius*, or "kidnapper."[10]

The first reaction was to deny that it was plagiarism at all. But the evidence seemed clear.

At the 2016 Democratic National Convention, Michelle Obama said this:

You work hard for what you want in life; that your word is your bond, and you do what you say you're going to do, and keep your promise; that you treat people with dignity and respect.

A few weeks later, at the Republican National Convention, Melania Trump said this:

You work hard for what you want in life; that your word is your bond and you do what you say and keep your promises; that you treat people with respect.

Her sentences rolled on, sixty words in all, different by only a word or two from Obama's. TV reporters had a field day playing the two speakers back-to-back, sentence by sentence.

It's not plagiarism, said New Jersey governor Chris Christie, because "93% of the speech is completely different than Michelle Obama's."[11]

As a former prosecutor, Christie should have known better. If you rob only 7 percent of a bank's money, you have still robbed a bank. And sure enough, two days later, the campaign explained: Apparently Melania Trump had copied those words down, and told her speechwriter those were the kinds of things she wanted to say. Her speechwriter, Meredith McIver, hearing them over the phone, just used them verbatim.

It wasn't the first time plagiarism had surfaced in a presidential campaign. During 2008, for example, there was another issue, involving another Obama.

At the time, it had become clear that the Democratic primary race would be between Barack Obama and Hillary Clinton. Obama had begun attracting attention for how much better than Clinton's were both his speeches and his ability to deliver them.

For someone speaking ten times a day, it must hurt to walk onstage imagining everyone is comparing every line to your rival ("*So* stiff!"). As John McCain would do later, an exasperated Clinton had begun criticizing Obama in ads and speeches for offering "speeches, not solutions."

"When there's work to be done," one of her ads argued, "talk doesn't cut it." Obama had to hit back.

Here's how he put it one night shortly before the Wisconsin primary:

Don't tell me words don't matter! "I have a dream." Just words? "We hold these truths to be self-evident, that all men are created equal." Just words! "We have nothing to fear but fear itself." Just words— just speeches!

It was effective, dramatic, and moving.

But as the opposition research people in the Clinton campaign soon discovered, Obama's words were almost identical to what Massachusetts governor Deval Patrick had said, answering a similar charge in his campaign two years earlier against Republican candidate Kerry Healey:

But her dismissive point, and I hear it a lot from her staff, is that all I have to offer is words—just words. "We hold these truths to be self-evident, that all men are created equal." Just words—just words! "We have nothing to fear but fear itself." Just words! Just words!

"When an author plagiarizes from another author there is damage done," Clinton's spokesman said.[12]

At first, the Obama team pretended this was nothing at all like plagiarism. One staffer put it this way: "They're friends who share similar views and talk and trade good lines all the time." Eventually, Obama quietly admitted error.

Plagiarism is less common in political speech than you might think. But it happens. For decades, critics of Martin Luther King Jr. have pointed to the similarity of the ending of his "Dream" speech and that of Archibald Carey, a black minister speaking at the 1952 Republican National Convention.[13]

Plagiarism or not? Ethical or not? And what should the penalties be?

A political speech is not a doctoral dissertation. That was one of Rand Paul's defenses when several instances of plagiarism dogged him in 2015–2016; he claimed the speeches were different and that he was a victim of the "footnote police."[14]

Paul was trying to excuse what seems to be his speechwriter's ethical lapse, including the decision to lift two paragraphs word for word from Wikipedia.

We believe *Webster*'s definition makes things clear. Even when the speakers believed otherwise, each of these examples involved plagiarism.

Each instance was also easily preventable. Obama might have said, "Deval Patrick once heard the same charge. He put it this way." He could still have gotten his applause line.

There are those who argue that using words written by a speechwriter is also plagiarism. Isn't what speechwriters do performed by others without attribution? Later in this chapter, unsurprisingly, we examine why that view, though a serious argument, doesn't hold up. But presenting the words of others as if they are one's own, even in the heat of a rousing litany, doesn't qualify for the speechwriter exemption.

Normally—whether with Martin Luther King Jr., Melania Trump, Barack Obama, or Rand Paul—the penalties are light. There are exceptions, including the plagiarism charge that torpedoed Joe Biden's 1988 presidential run.

Does that make plagiarism just an academic question? In one way, it is. Both authors teach on college campuses, including the course they teach together at American University. There and at virtually every other college, schools punish plagiarism with penalties that can ultimately include expulsion. And AU leaves no doubt about what it means by the word. Here is its official definition:

> Plagiarism is the representation of someone else's writing, ideas, or work as one's own without attribution. Plagiarism may involve using someone else's wording without using quotation marks—a distinctive name, a phrase, a sentence or an entire passage or essay. Misrepresenting sources is another form of plagiarism. The issue of plagiarism applies to any type of work.[15]

Even one sentence? A phrase? Not just others' words, but their ideas? By that standard, Trump's "word is your bond" passage, Obama's "just words" section, and Paul's recitation from Wikipedia were wrong for the same reason students are wrong on a college campus. Plagiarism can make teachers believe students are more eloquent, thoughtful, and knowledgeable than they really are; and it can deceive those listening to politicians in exactly the same way. Paul said his writer was sloppy, not dishonest. It was both.

But what should the penalty be?

At our school, officials take this seriously. They ask us to report offenders. The school does an investigation. If it finds that the language was not that of the student, it was lifted on purpose, and the student knew what plagiarism was, he or she will flunk the course—and even face expulsion.

Is it possible that we ask less of a presidential candidate than a naive college freshman? Do we kick students out of school for something that normally gets a presidential candidate a slap on the wrist?

Compounding that issue is what has steadily become a richer research tool in political life and what can be summed up by the public service advertising tagline from a few years back that warned about what's online: Beware What You Share.[16]

Everything is online, and it stays there. Has it been said before? All you need to do is google it.

Google, for instance, allowed one reporter to discover that the first four words of the very distinctive opening litany in Democratic candidate for president John Edwards's stump speech in 2008—"Somewhere in America tonight"—were identical to the opening of the 1996 Democratic National Convention speech by his campaign chair—and Bob's former boss—David Bonior. By AU standards, that would require an inquiry.

Bob had had no involvement in either speech. But when reporters asked about this, he saw that Google made something else possible. It gave him no fewer than 380,000 sites where others used the same phrase, including a song by The Outfield[17] and a New York Central Railroad ad from 1943 addressed to mothers with sons in the army ("Somewhere in America tonight . . . a young man sits in a railway car bound for a destination unknown").

It's possible that Edwards's speechwriter did lift the phrase from Bonior. But it is also possible that the phrase came from a song lodged deep in the brains of both, and popped onto the computer screen as if it were original. Or maybe they had *never* heard it. Maybe they really made it up.

In the case of Trump or Obama, there was little doubt surrounding the origins. But with the existence of sophisticated research tools, the mere use of "someone else's words" can't be proof of "knowing misrepresentation." Not anymore. Today, it is possible, even easy, to suspect plagiarism when there is none.

But technology also makes possible exposing the unethical examples of King, Biden, and Obama, and probably Trump.

All four speakers knew the source. Politicians may be reluctant to let an audience know they didn't think up a great line. But like the fallacies we reviewed in Chapter 10, you can cite sources without killing your ability to soar. Three suggestions:

If you have consciously borrowed material of at least one sentence, find an economical way of acknowledging that you have a source. Who thinks Obama's audience wouldn't have cheered if he had done what we suggest: added "As Deval Patrick put it" in that litany? Neither is this the only way. Phrases like "I'm not the first to say" signal to reporters that you're not claiming originality.

Keep an annotated record of your sources. In fact, keep a record of anything you've gotten from somewhere else. Why? Because you're going to forget. You have twenty minutes to finish a draft. You find something on a website that looks perfect. You add it in, careful to say "I'm not the first to say." A month later, a reporter calls to ask who was the first. You've completely forgotten.

Use the same tool opposition research is using on you. Many universities offer students access to services like Turnitin, a commercial, internet-based plagiarism-detection tool; according to the site, there are about thirty million education users and a database of more than five hundred million submissions.[18] There are similar services for those outside of the education sector; some, like www.grammarly.com/plagiarism-checker, allow you to check the originality of your work for free. Of course, you can always just search your latest pithy phrase, too. And you should.

We make one exception to this rule: jokes. If it's, say, a quip where speakers know the source, they should cite it ("Mark Twain put it this way . . ."). But so much political humor consists of old jokes with no known author. Preface those jokes by saying "There's an old joke . . . ," and nobody should accuse you of plagiarism.

Other than that, politicians should hold themselves to the standards they learned in college. It's worth fighting for. And to speechwriters, if your bosses want to pretend a quote originated with them, tell them it's a practice sites like Google have made too dangerous to ignore.

MISLEADING LISTENERS

To *mislead* is (1) "to lead in a wrong direction or into a mistaken action or belief often by deliberate deceit" and (2) "to lead astray: give a wrong impression."[19]

Lawyers are like cab drivers, a well-known member of the Bar once argued. They take you where you want to go. In other words, regardless of what they personally believe, lawyers should make whatever argument can persuade a jury, as long as the client is paying the bill.

Not all lawyers agree. A sign on the Yale Law School walls once said, "A LAWYER IS NOT A TAXI!" Even lawyers, they argue, have ethical choices. But while they certainly do, American society basically accepts the idea that lawyers are not obligated to point out weaknesses in their own arguments—or facts the other side failed to uncover.

Just ask anybody who hires one. What about in political speech? Far more often than plagiarism—far, far more often than the bald-faced lie—is the frequency with which political speakers mislead listeners.

Readers have already examined this issue briefly in Chapter 10, where we discuss fallacies. Here we cover it in more detail, not just because it happens so often but because speakers and writers can avoid it so easily, even at rallies where there is a tradition of permissible hyperbole. It is not naive to believe that truth matters. Politicians value integrity. They frown at outright fabrication of facts—and not just because it's too easy to get caught.

But what about moments when it seems easy to rationalize an ethical lapse? Here are four common examples, and the rationale speakers and speechwriters use:

> **Caricaturing the other side.** *What's wrong with a satiric thrust? I'm talking to friends. They hate the other side.*
>
> **Made-up quotes.** *Yes, let's quote the other side. But who wants to spend hours looking up an actual quote? Just say "Some say . . ." or "There are those who say . . ." We'll get it right. At least the sentiment.*
>
> **Not citing sources.** *A source for this? I know I read it someplace. Besides, isn't it the other side's responsibility to catch us if we're wrong?*
>
> **Correcting the boss.** *Why fight the boss on every little thing? It'll just make him mad.*

If you question whether or not speakers and writers rationalize in this way, we offer one example, taken from a speech highly praised when it took on Republicans:

> The radical right . . . the purveyors of the politics of hate and division . . . had some real success. They dismantled enforcement at the Department of Justice.
>
> They filled the federal courts with those who saw no need to redress the inequities of the past.
>
> Want to end unlawful school segregation? They blocked it. Want to prohibit federal funding of discrimination? They opposed it.

Want justices on the Supreme Court who understood what discrimination had meant for Americans of color? They sent nominee after nominee who didn't have a clue.

You wanted to bring Americans together. They wanted to keep us apart.

It is skillful enough, with its three-part "want" litany, repetition of "they," and a punch line using antithesis, bringing forth the applause line its writers wanted.

But look more closely.

The radical right . . . the purveyors of the politics of hate and division . . . had some real success. They dismantled enforcement at the Department of Justice. (*Hasty generalization:* They abolished some regulations but not all. The evidence was far too slim to justify a word like *dismantled*.)

They filled the federal courts with those who saw no need to redress the inequities of the past. (*Ad hominem:* The speechwriters could not possibly know such judges enough to attack them on the grounds that when it came to correcting past injustice, they "saw no need.")

Want to end unlawful school segregation? They blocked it. (*Ad hominem:* To accuse judges of letting defendants get away with actions they knew were unlawful slanders them. The writers had no way to know whether judges felt that way.)

Want to prohibit federal funding of discrimination? They opposed it. (*Apples and oranges:* The speechwriters certainly knew the data about federal money for specific programs, but the amounts did not support the idea that "they" believed those programs caused discrimination.)

Want justices on the Supreme Court who understood what discrimination had meant for Americans of color? They sent nominee after nominee who didn't have a clue. (*Ad hominem:* The speechwriters knew only about their rulings—not whether they were "clueless.")

You wanted to bring Americans together. They wanted to keep us apart. (*Ad hominem:* Did the speechwriters have evidence that "they" wanted to cause division? Probably, they wanted everyone to agree. They certainly had no reason to assert the opposite.)

Each of these six examples distorted the reasons and motives of the other side in an unethical way. Who were the deceitful people creating this wholesale violation of ethics? And how are the authors of this book so confident about what those writers did not know?

We are sorry to tell readers that we were the ones who created these unethical passages in writing a speech to the Memphis, Tennessee, chapter of the NAACP, on March 30, 1994, by the vice president of the United States.

Looking back, it is clear that we went too far. Did we have any idea that someday we would have to repudiate our work? Memories are vague. We doubt it.

But we include it not just as a *mea culpa* but to help readers see how easily speechwriters can remove misleading language without destroying applause lines. For as we study that speech, we wish we had written this:

> The radical right . . . the purveyors of the politics of hate and division . . . had some real success. They *crippled* enforcement at the Department of Justice.
>
> They filled the federal courts with those whose *verdicts blocked those of us* who would redress the inequities of the past.
>
> Want to end school segregation? They blocked that, too. Want to prohibit federal funding of discrimination? They *allowed* it.
>
> Want justices on the Supreme Court who understood what discrimination had meant for Americans of color? They sent nominee after nominee who didn't *seem to have* a clue.
>
> You wanted to bring Americans together. *Those rulings* kept us apart.

It is never too late to repent.

So in the spirit of urging higher standards, we turn to another much-criticized rally speech by President Trump.

It was four months before the 2018 midterms.

The president went to Montana, a state he had carried easily in 2016, to endorse a Senate candidate running against Democratic senator Jon Tester. It was a week where the media was filled with assessments of the president's truthfulness. "Anatomy of a Trump rally: 76% of claims are false," said the *Washington Post*.[20]

Three out of every four claims false? There was a lot of distortion, to be sure. We don't want to soft-pedal our outrage at how often Donald Trump's speeches violate even the ethical norms of politics.

But let's say the president's writers were determined to act ethically.

To show what is possible, we offer three examples of *fallacies* in Trump's speech. We follow each with the *facts*, rebuttals from the *Toronto Star*, whose rigorous Washington bureau chief Daniel Dale has been monitoring the president's "falsehoods" for over two years.[21]

Finally, because the point is not whether the president consciously misled his audience but how easy it would be to correct, we offer the easy *fix*.

THREE EXAMPLES OF FALLACIES

FALLACY 1 (False Facts/Unsupported Assertion): "Wages, for the first time in eighteen years, are rising again. People can go out, they can actually choose a job, and they have wages that are rising."

FACTS: Wages have been rising since 2014. In June, the month before Trump spoke, average hourly earnings rose by 2.7 percent, the same as in Obama's last month in office, December 2016.

FIX: To win applause, one small cut to eliminate the "eighteen years" falsehood: "Here's what you see since Inauguration Day. Wages, up! Unemployment, down! Less people getting pink slips! More people getting good jobs!"

FALLACY 2 (Exaggeration/Impermissible Hyperbole): "And yet, I see Jon Tester saying such nice things about me. I say, yes, but he never votes for me."

FACTS: Tester, the Democratic senator from Montana, had voted with Trump 37 percent of the time on the day Trump spoke, according to analysis by the website FiveThirtyEight. Among other things, Tester supported Trump's push to loosen bank regulations.

FIX: Stick with the truth: "I see Jon Tester saying such nice things about me. He voted against us on tax cuts! Voted against us on Obamacare! Voted against us on Justice Gorsuch! Forget the compliments, Jon! Remember the people of Montana!"

FALLACY 3 (Hasty Generalization): "Jon Tester voted no on cutting the estate tax or the death tax for your farms, your farmers, and your small businesses. Think of that one. But you got it anyway because we got it passed. . . . For the most part, you will have no estate tax or death tax to pay. You can leave your farm, you can leave your small business to your children or whoever you want to leave them . . . We saved family farms."

FACTS: According to the Tax Policy Center's Daniel Berger,

> Realistically North Dakota family farmers probably should worry more about being hit by lightning than paying the estate tax. In the entire

> US, only about 80 small farms and businesses will pay the estate tax this year and only 44 estates of any kind in North Dakota paid any amount of estate tax in 2015.[22]
>
> (Author's note: The United States includes roughly 190,000 farms in the category of "family farms.")
>
> **FIX:** Again, don't pretend a law affects everyone: "Jon Tester voted no on cutting the estate tax or the death tax for farms, for small businesses. Anybody here worried about the death tax? Don't. For the most part, you will have no estate tax or death tax to pay. Leave your kids the farm! Leave them that small business you built from nothing. Leave them to whomever you want! That's the law!"

We don't argue that these passages are now perfect. We only point out that the language that misleads listeners is easy to correct—if the speaker is willing.

As a practical matter, it is impossible for speechwriters to put up a fight each time their bosses or other staffers insist on using what we think distorts the truth. The reality of speechwriting is that most first drafts get written by one person sitting at a computer, armed with memos, partial drafts and emails from other staffers—and the power to make small changes. Here are some different approaches you can use during that stage of speechwriting:

Don't use facts or arguments you don't trust. If in your own research you find a fact that seems too good to be true, check further. You don't want to be responsible for inaccuracies alert reporters will catch. If other staffers suggest an approach you think is unethical, simply leave it out of the draft. The odds are that the people who suggested it knew it was inaccurate. They may not insist on it in a speech conference ("Why don't I see that half-truth I gave you?"). If they do, you can explain why; even if you're overruled, they usually won't be angry. And you will have done the right thing.

Insert caveats. There are times when what's unethical about an argument is not a false fact, but the failure to add nuance. *Caveats*—Latin for "beware"—are handy devices to use. Examples: *The argument is more complicated than we have time for, but . . . It's not either–or, but . . .* Speakers, who don't like distortions themselves, sometimes appreciate these ways to plant clues to the listener that the speaker is willing to acknowledge what has been left out.

Create a fact-checking department within the speechwriting office. The Obama administration was not the first to have official fact-checkers in the White House. But in 2017, Michelle Obama's speechwriter Sarah Hurwitz, whose interview we include in Chapter 8, offered this description of the effect it had:

> One of the most important and time-consuming parts of our jobs in the Obama White House, as in all recent administrations, was also the least glamorous: fact-checking.
>
> Every speech my colleagues and I wrote for the president or First Lady was subjected to a painstaking review by the White House Research Department. And those folks were merciless.
>
> If a speech contained a statistic they couldn't independently verify, they would ask us to produce the source—and if they deemed that source insufficiently reputable, we cut the statistic from the speech.
>
> If language in a speech seemed to contradict something the president or First Lady had said elsewhere, they would point out the discrepancy so we could reconcile it.[23]

The reality of politics, and every other industry, is that there are times when your boss doesn't care about the niceties of truth telling and orders you to insert something you detest.

In politics, as carefully as you choose whom to write for, you may not escape the need to write arguments reflecting different values from your own.

That in itself raises a serious ethical question. In every area of human life, we see ourselves accepting things we oppose without objection: a sexist remark, or maybe a rude comment to a bus driver. As partisan as politics is, nobody agrees with the boss all the time. When someone who opposes abortion must write a speech supporting "choice," or when one who opposes the death penalty must support it, can writers draw the line?

Both authors have seen and been through such situations. It would be presumptuous to offer solutions that work for everyone.

Except this. In really disturbing moments, remember: Bosses are human. Often nice. In situations where you feel they have asked you to write something you deeply oppose or think is false, we make two suggestions:

Discuss it with them. If you explain your view in a mature way, politicians will sometimes see the light.

Accept limited disagreement. You have had an impact. See if you can live with it. For if you need perfect agreement, political speechwriting may not be for you.

LYING

To *lie* is "to make an untrue statement with intent to deceive."[24]

In 1956, Arkansas Democratic senator J. William Fulbright faced a dilemma. He personally approved of the Supreme Court decision, *Brown v. Board of Education*, integrating schools. But if he admitted it, Arkansas voters would vote him out of office. There was no doubt about it. And so he signed the so-called Southern Manifesto—the document opposing it that was signed by every southern senator except three.[25]

This preserved his career, allowing him to later lead opposition to the Vietnam War, confounding antiwar activists who didn't want a racist on their side.

Was this wrong? If so, few people in political life are not similarly guilty. There are some issues that are so charged, particularly in their districts, that politicians must pretend to feel otherwise to survive. They and their speechwriters—who often know the truth—essentially agree to lie.

There is an argument that in politics, not all lies deserve the same level of contempt. After all, there are the lies that preserve compromise. Any time politicians announce support for a bill, their speeches must contain glowing expressions of support. They disguise the mixed feelings they have in order to preserve a coalition.

We certainly believe intentional lies about substantive matters have no place in the rhetoric of politics. We can also see issues where the answers are less clear.

Donald Trump is not the only president who has lied. The history of modern politics is full of examples: Dwight Eisenhower about U.S. spy planes; John F. Kennedy about Cuba ("The U.S. plans no military intervention in Cuba"); Lyndon Johnson about the Gulf of Tonkin; Ronald Reagan about trading arms for hostages with Iran.

Still, in 2018, the sheer number of falsehoods coming from the White House—which, because they are repeated so often, cross the line between what is misleading and what is a lie—is staggering.

What is the role of the writer, and what role does one have in the remedy?

For an administration interested in ethical speech, the remedies are not hard. It should be routine to fact-check carefully before a speech, as the authors have. And there is nothing hard about what to do when a statement proves false:

- Correct the record, with a candid explanation of how it happened.
- Don't repeat it.

The Trump administration does not show interest in such steps. The publicity surrounding such lies has had some effect; 65 percent of Americans characterize the president as "dishonest." But that has not been enough to bring change.[26]

To us as teachers, one of the distressing results of the last few years has been the number of students who approach us after class to ask, hesitantly—they don't want to insult us—"Is this the way politics works?"

Our answer is usually something like "Not usually."

It is some consolation that the question of dishonesty, amply publicized by aggressive reporters, has clearly eroded the president's popularity. But in the imperfect and ethically fraught world of politics, the personal decisions speechwriters face don't always lend themselves to easy answers. We leave this discussion of the ethical dimension of lying, uneasy that we have no better answer. But we agree with those who believe that politics—and a political speech—is a moral act.

BOX 16.1
EXPERTS TALK: CLARK JUDGE

Long-time speechwriter and Founder and Managing Partner of White House Writers Group, Clark Judge has spent decades writing for conservative causes and Republican candidates. As a speechwriter for President Ronald Reagan and Vice President George H. W. Bush, Clark has first-hand familiarity with the needs of presidential speech.

To explore the views of those who vigorously support the policies and defend the rhetoric of President Trump, we interviewed Clark. Here are his answers, informed by his experience and candor.

Let's start with the elephant in the White House. President Trump gives a speech and reporters immediately cite the distortions, or even the lies. Do the vast number of inaccuracies from President Trump concern you?

I am not as bothered by the president's supposed inaccuracies as you. But then again, I am in there, as often as not, cheering on his charges of "Fake News."

I remember when the Washington press corps jumped all over Ronald Reagan after he talked about real poverty going up in the wake of the Great Society. Ignorant fool if not brazen liar was their verdict, as it was so often on so many matters. Except that Mr. Reagan had read the cutting edge research of Charles Murray, recently published in *The Public Interest*, hardly an obscure publication at the time. Some Reagan media critics may have apologized later, past midnight, in back alley, in a whisper. If so, I don't recall it.

I also remember in the 1988 campaign *Newsweek's* slurring of George H. W. Bush, with that cover, "The Wimp Factor." I gather the editor did subsequently say he regretted the Fake News hit –– decades later.

I think of Dan Rather and the hoax letter about the National Guard and George W. Bush. Wasn't his excuse for pumping the allegation on air with little or no checking for authenticity more or less that, even if the story was not true in fact, it was true in essence? Close enough for television work, I guess.

Do you really think the press so hostile to President Trump that they can't be objective?

Perhaps you remember the early months of the 2016 campaign. As Trump was gaining traction, a lively debate sprang up in the ranks of the Fourth Estate about whether he posed such a danger to the Republic that it was time to jettison objective reporting. It was time to freeze out the Trump message and leave no room for the American people to think anything other than what every good journalist thought – that this man must be stopped. Many in the media took that road and many are still on it. So far as I can tell, their only regret is that, come the election, it didn't work.

So it's fair, then, to say that you think it's all Fake News? What about those who admit Trump plays fast and loose with the facts? What about those like Salena Zito who said Trumps' supporters take him "seriously but not literally"? We take that to mean that his facts are wrong, but his larger points make sense.

You can't dismiss Donald Trump's readiness to speak truth to power – even if it is a tonal truth. You could ask, isn't that like Dan Rather all those years ago? They might reply, what goes around comes around, baby.

There is a serious point here. Many Republican and Republican leaning voters came into the 2016 election feeling toward the media in particular much like that guy in the movie *Network*, "I'm mad as Hell and I'm not going to take it any more." Donald Trump channeled their anger and disgust. Then and now many of those people heard the unending sanctimony that flowed from the liberal media and Democrats in Congress – the rote charges of racism, sexism and every conceivable repulsive –ism, except socialism, to cut off all serious attempts at serious discussions of serious issues facing the country. They heard that *mierda del toro* and they said, it's about time someone had the *cojones* to give it back to those self-righteous hypocrites and give it to them good.

(Continued)

(Continued)

Okay, but does that excuse the errors? Our politics might be different, but we're all speechwriters who care about ethical rhetoric, right? What effect do you see Trump's approach to rhetoric having on future presidents?

I would say that future presidents—and their speechwriters—could take a page from Donald Trump's use of language, anecdote, wit, story and all the other things that go into great speeches. That would go for his addresses to Congress, his overseas speeches and other major policy speeches, too. Take a particularly close look at how in the last two joint session addresses he matched a guest with each program or point he was making. Ask also how, with a Congress as hostile as this one, he had the entire Congress singing "Happy Birthday" as one.

Likewise, his rally speeches are great theater – perhaps more accurately performance art. What other American figure in generations could regularly hold audiences enthralled for well over an hour? And if he misspeaks because he is speaking extemporaneously, so be it.

He has a particular skill. I don't see others duplicating him in that. But keep in mind that during the campaign, as reported by *The Atlantic*, the tweeting was coordinated with the rally remarks. As he rambled through what were seemingly stream of conscious remarks, his social media people had pre-prepared tweets reinforcing his points that they fired off when he hit the cues. There is much more art in the Trump style than our ever-so-astute media has yet grasped. I do feel that some of that will become a perpetual part of the presidential pretenders' playbooks.

You mentioned the tweets; what about the tweets now that he's president?

Count me a fan. Early morning Tweeting has enable the President to take control of the news cycle away from the *New York Times* and the *Washington Post*. It used to be that between them the two papers set the agenda for the morning television shows – *Today; Good Morning, America* – which then carried through the day to the evening news. Now the President fires off a tweet at 6am just as the currently six morning shows are going on air, and the news cycle becomes his. Particularly with a mainstream media as pathologically hostile as the one he faces, you should not underestimate the value of tweeting as a tool for keeping his program on track.

I see the Trump communication style as an astute response to contemporary realities, including the rise of new media. It is a mistake to think of the Trump tweet as a communications tool in isolation. In and of itself, that he tweets is not all that big an event. What makes his tweeting so powerful is that the television, radio and cable news operations pick up his tweets and build their coverage for the day around them.

In his use of Twitter he is like earlier presidents who dominated public discussion. He has understood how to make new use of a new communications medium. There is a rhythm to these innovations. Lincoln discovered the mass circulation newspaper (that made him a national figure by printing transcripts of the Lincoln-Douglas Debates and key speeches). TR, building on Lincoln, discovered Monday (dominating the weekly news cycle by making the front page of the slow-news Monday papers). Woodrow

> Wilson was the first president to use radio; FDR, like TR with newspapers, mastered it with his fireside chats. JFK made use of television with his Oval office addresses and charming televised press conference performances; Reagan was to television what TR and FDR had been to the new media of their time, with events like that at the Berlin Wall that became mini-dramas conveying far more than was said. Obama discovered the web, but used it as if it were a communications vehicle like any other. Trump is the first to see how it could drive coverage in all other established media.
>
> **Let's finish by returning to the question of facts: you seem to believe much of the media fact-checking obsession looks designed to avoid the larger and often important truth Trump is making. How would you back that up?**
>
> Is the state of the Mexico-US border dangerous? People down there were telling me that as long ago as George W. Bush's administration.
>
> Has the Trump program brought job and wage growth in areas and to people that were left out for decades? Every new economic report says so.
>
> After decades of flailing, has our national security policy been engaging with threats like ISIS and North Korea that had been drifting for nearly a decade? We will see the outcome, but the age of denial is over.
>
> I could go on, but you get the point. Whether you agree with him or not – and I appreciate that you do not – Donald Trump and his administration have been calling attention to and confronting in words and actions serious national challenges that had not been effectively addressed for years.
>
> That is not Fake News. Literally and seriously, it is a core truth of our time.

And now, we close with an ethical issue broader than what we have covered so far. It involves the question people are too diplomatic to mention to speechwriters—but that journalists and academics write about often. For aside from questions about plagiarism, attempts to mislead, and even lying, we need to examine another view. That involves the belief that no matter how meticulous speechwriters are in their work—no matter how much we fact-check, work for nuance, resist the temptation to distort, and head off the unequivocal lie—we should call into question the entire business of writing for others.

Or, to give it the full flavor of what disturbs critics:

SPEECHWRITING: UNETHICAL BY DEFINITION?

Eric once joked that an *Onion* headline would read, "Speechwriters Seek Ghostwriter to Write Code of Ethics." But that raises a serious question about the profession itself.

For almost all of American history, politicians have rarely acknowledged the speechwriters who write their speeches. Isn't it deceitful and thus unethical to let audiences believe that the eloquence and information—even the wit—in political speeches came from the speakers themselves?

It is not as if nobody notices. In 1986, Wayne State professor Matthew Seeger described the case for calling most speechwriting unethical. Seeger was talking about corporate speechwriting, not as an advocate but as one simply describing a variety of views in a paper called "Ethical Issues in Corporate Speechwriting." Here's what he wrote, slightly condensed:

> According to this view, executive speechwriting circumvents the process of developing ethos or credibility during the speech. The appeals, arguments and language employed do not arise from the executive speaker. Rather they are the product of some others who are kept hidden from the audience. The audience's ability to make judgments about the speaker, including the validity of arguments, sincerity of purpose and general character is short-circuited. Just as the student plagiarizing a term paper might be judged as deceitful so too we would judge the executive who employs a ghostwriter as intentionally deceiving the audience. In judging speakers according to their traditional standards, it is necessary to examine the degree to which the speech is a product of the speaker. . . . [It] may be entirely the product of the ghostwriter with the speaker having little or no input into its preparation.
>
> The situation may be compounded further with the use of devices such as teleprompters or delivery coaches, public opinion pollsters, makeup and even video-tape technology used to portray the speaker as fluent, articulate, thoughtful, and attuned to audience interests and needs.[27]

There is no question about it. Seeger has described the way many speechwriters work, whether in corporate or political life. Despite the romantic picture of Ted Sorensen and JFK working together over every line, speechwriters often produce speeches with hardly any contact with the speaker. They supply not just language but rhetorical techniques the speaker could not possibly know. The ideas as well come from other aides in a political office—speechwriters usually don't know enough about, say, the environment to produce a twenty-minute keynote about global warming or to make a nuanced argument for how tariffs affect free trade. And yes, add a teleprompter, and mediocre speakers can seem articulate, informed, and thoughtful.

Meanwhile, politicians have kept their speechwriters hidden in a different way than they have other staffers. When the first edition of this book came out, only seventeen of a hundred U.S. senators listed their speechwriters in the Senate staff directory. In 2017, twenty-nine did.[28] Yes, sometimes writers have different titles and a number of roles. The labels aren't always meant to hide what they do. At other times, though, the reason they have been kept under wraps is hard to defend. When politicians tell a joke or a moving story—or analyze a complicated point about global warming—it would embarrass them if the audience knew they were reading something composed by some twenty-six-year-old slaving away in a cubicle.

Compounding that deception is the notion even political junkies have of speechwriter as confidante—a constant presence at the boss's side sharing lofty ideas—the "alter ego," as many of Sorensen's obituaries described his relationship with JFK.[29]

The truth is that has become the exception. These days, speechwriters get little face time; at the higher levels, speakers often head for the floor or up to the podium looking for the first time at a draft 100 percent produced by staff.

No wonder academics see an ethical problem. Didn't Aristotle say that demonstrating character (*ethos*) was one of the three ways we persuade? When speechwriters funnel eloquence, or wit, or just well-researched paragraphs to politicians, aren't they fooling an audience into seeing virtues these speakers really don't have?

Defenders of the speechwriters' role raise a number of arguments on their behalf. Let's examine three.

1. Getting help is no different from what we do in our home.

When the roof collapses, we don't fix it ourselves. That would be a disaster. We call a roofer to get expert advice, and a skillful repair job. Why should anyone expect politicians to do any less?

Actually, later in his piece, Seeger summarized that argument, too. He cites one expert who argues that "a responsible executive" *should* "draw on the best advice available in all their activities, including speechwriting."[30]

But even Seeger's expert recommends that the "ghostwriter work in close collaboration with the speaker . . . and be publicly recognized for participating."

Not only does that almost never happen; it ignores the unique needs political audiences have. They don't just listen for "advice." They size up the speaker. Judging a politician's views, intellect, and eloquence determines how they vote. Listening to a member of Congress has consequences more important than listening to the roofer.

2. Speechwriting is ethical if the speaker possesses speechwriting skills.

This is the argument of Thomas Bivins, author of the well-respected *Public Relations Writing*. It is wrong, Bivins argues, to "impart eloquence, wit, coherence, and incisive ideas to a communicator who might not possess these qualities otherwise."[31]

He cites an ethicist, who argues that one test of "ethicality" is whether or not "the communicator uses ghostwriters to make himself or herself appear to possess personal qualities that he or she really does not have."

Bivins's solution: speechwriting is ethical only if the speaker can write a speech as well as his or her speechwriter.

He's not the only one who feels that way. After the plagiarism issue arose with Barack Obama, James Fallows, once a White House speechwriter himself, defended Obama's use of speechwriters on the grounds that in his books Obama had shown that he was skilled enough to have written his speeches.

But Fallows admitted that he didn't believe this was always true. "If a public figure's basic quality of mind or ability to express himself is in question," Fallows wrote, "as frankly is the case with President George W. Bush, then it might be worth investigating whether the words he is uttering actually reflect his underlying outlook and comprehension."[32]

To us, this argument—basically that speechwriters only produce what the politician could write—makes no sense.

There are plenty of principled, smart, thoughtful politicians who can't write to save themselves. Politicians need to move, inspire, and persuade—the skills we have taken hundreds of pages to try to teach. After 9/11, President Bush felt it was urgent to unite and reassure the country. Would it have been more ethical to insist that he write his own speech instead of the talented Michael Gerson and Matt Scully?

The idea of giving politicians only what they themselves could produce would make speechwriters the only people in the entire workforce hired on the condition that they *not* try their best. Neither speechwriters nor politicians could accept that.

3. Speechwriting is ethical if the speaker has given instructions about what should be in a speech.

This was Sorensen's view; he insisted that JFK was the "author" of *Profiles in Courage* because he "decided the substance, structure, and theme of the book; read and revised each draft, inspired, constructed, and improved the work."[33]

No. None of these steps substitutes for a writer, sitting at a desk for hours or days, and these days hopping from website to website, before writing a single word. If it did, producers wouldn't need to list screenwriters in the list of credits. Our view is that JFK produced and directed. Sorensen wrote the book.

There is another reason to question that view. There are times when a speechwriter gets explicit directions from his or her boss, and they are the opposite of what the speechwriter believes.

During the confirmation hearings for Justice Brett Kavanaugh, Stephen Rodrick wrote an op-ed for the *Washington Post* about his experience during the Clarence Thomas hearings in 1991. Rodrick, now a writer for *Rolling Stone*, remembers the directions from his boss, then Illinois senator Alan Dixon. He expected Dixon would defend one witness, the courageous Anita Hill.

Instead, Rodrick's assignment was to write the floor statement explaining why his boss would not change his vote.

"I wrote some gibberish about the long, storied presumption of innocence . . . I went home and threw up." He eventually left politics. "If you stay and write words you don't believe in, it'll haunt you."[34]

How far should speechwriters go in writing views they don't share?

So far, we have examined arguments defending speechwriting if done right.

There is also the view vented during the 2008 vice-presidential debates by David McGrath, a college English professor from Alabama:

We shouldn't accept ghostwritten speeches at all

McGrath made this analogy: "Today, selling term papers to students to use as their own is still illegal, but selling speeches to politicians to use as their own remains a legitimate enterprise. How can that be?"[35]

"Presidents should write their own speeches," a *Post* reporter told one of us, once, barely concealing his distaste for our chosen career.

Those making this argument often point to presidents who wrote their own. In fact, though, presidents have often had writers; Alexander Hamilton wrote Washington's Farewell Address, and the revered "better angels of our nature" section in Lincoln's second inaugural came mostly from his secretary of the interior.

Still, asking politicians to write their own speeches ignores the profound change in political speech since Washington's time—that presidents speak often. When the authors worked for Vice President Al Gore, we wrote about one each day—and that didn't include times he spoke from a few talking points.

The fact is, the public speech, whether on the floor, on the stump, or on TV, has become a major tool of governing, and not just because it can inspire a nation. For every speech from the Oval Office, elected officials deliver thousands of speeches each day at Rotary Club lunches, Sierra Club dinners, statehouse floors, or just coffees in living rooms. They stimulate discussion, promote ideas, and add to knowledge.

Should politicians write their own? Nobody in his or her right mind should want such a thing. Yes, Lincoln wrote his speech on the train heading up to Gettysburg, but he only had a page to write—and without a smartphone, no distractions. If he had three hundred speeches a year, he would have had a few speechwriters, too. Politicians should spend their days deciding whether to make war or peace. Someone else should write the announcement.

But given what we have described about the speechwriter's life, the question isn't so crazy. How do we satisfy the yawning maw in politics for speeches without the charade that accompanies it?

Readers of this book know we believe that when we describe a problem, a solution must follow.

We have one.

Don't Dismiss. Disclose

For the heart of the ethical problem is not that one person writes for another. That's too common in American life. Joke writers invent quips for Trevor Noah. Clerks write rulings for Supreme Court justices. Fundraisers write the letters college presidents send to alums. Most never get credit.

The difference between them and the political speechwriter is that Americans think the character of a politician is important. But character includes honesty. No speechwriter wants the boss to give credit from the podium ("And in conclusion . . . I thank my writer, Joe, who . . ."). And not all speechwriters want credit; some are content to be heard and not seen.

But wouldn't it be more ethical to acknowledge the truth? Eric once wrote a roast for Bill Richardson, then governor of New Mexico. The speech went well. As he left the room, someone asked him the secret of his success. According to the *Washington Post*, Richardson answered, "I hired a couple of jokesters and prepared extensively. You can't bomb in a big speech like this."

It didn't seem to hurt him any, and Eric didn't mind being called a jokester. He kind of enjoyed it. If others followed suit, such honesty might even help.

If that seems unrealistic, we can still acknowledge speechwriters to the same degree Hollywood does screenwriters. That doesn't mean scrolling credits, but politicians can list speechwriters openly in staff directories and stop pretending they only "provide research."

Doing that would accelerate a change already under way. The secrecy surrounding political speechwriters seems to be on the decline. Since *What I Saw at the Revolution*, Peggy Noonan's entertaining book about writing for Ronald Reagan, speechwriters for Bill Clinton, George W. Bush, and Barack Obama have written about their experiences. Bush gave credit to his writers. During the Obama years, reporters had access to his writers; Jon Favreau and others got plenty of publicity, and two have already written books. Their bosses seem to have survived.

FINAL WORDS

Because the authors confront the issues surrounding speechwriters every day, we are aware of how much this chapter leaves out. But the issues of plagiarism, distortion, and lying—whether by writers or their bosses—and the broader issue of secrecy are central to the purpose of this book.

Once, back in 1998, Eric was writing speeches for the NASA administrator when John Glenn, America's first astronaut to orbit Earth, decided that, at seventy-seven, he was going back into space. It was a sensational event, attended by thousands, including many of his Senate colleagues, and watched by millions.

As usual, NASA had an announcer who did the countdown and described the event ("Three . . . Two . . . One . . . blastoff! Thirty mice go into space testing the effects of weightlessness!").

But this time, the announcer was terrified. She raced off to Eric and asked, "What should I say?"

"How about," Eric said, "'six Astronaut heroes and one American legend'?"[36]

That is what she said. The phrase made headlines. The clip ran all weekend, including at the beginning of ESPN's *SportsCenter*. And a couple of days later, the NASA launch commentator was a guest on Rosie O'Donnell, who asked, "How did you think of that?"

"It just came to me," she said.

We hope one lesson of this book is that eloquence rarely just "comes" to people. It takes discipline, talent, and, like any sport, training, whether in how to research, write, or rewrite.

So maybe we should ask: Where is the evidence anywhere that acknowledging a speechwriter cost anyone a single vote? Disclosure should be an easy step. It would make speechwriting more ethical. It would mean American politics has taken one step toward the honesty voters would like to see.

THE SPEECHWRITER'S CHECKLIST: ETHICS

- ☐ Do I cite or imply a source for all words, terms, or phrases I have appropriated from someone else's work?
- ☐ Have I kept a record of what those sources were?
- ☐ Have I investigated information or arguments I don't trust?
- ☐ Have I avoided them if I believe they are false or misleading?
- ☐ Have I used caveats to fairly indicate to listeners complications the speaker cannot explore?
- ☐ If I'm uncomfortable writing about issues of personal concern, have I discussed my concerns with my boss?
- ☐ If asked to lie or conceal illegal actions, have I refused?
- ☐ If convinced that my boss is lying about issues that are not illegal—personal beliefs or behavior, for example—have I tried to avoid them in my draft?
- ☐ If ordered to lie about such issues, have I explored every other alternative?
- ☐ If asked to conceal my role in writing speeches—such as accepting a misleading title—have I suggested other options?
- ☐ Have I accepted the idea that in writing speeches I must write the very best drafts I can, regardless of my boss's abilities?
- ☐ Am I comfortable with the compromises I'm asked to accept concerning the ethical issues of political speechwriting?

17

The Uneasy Partnership
ADVICE FOR SPEAKERS AND WRITERS

They were similar in many ways.

Both John F. Kennedy's 1961 inaugural speech and Franklin Delano Roosevelt's twenty-eight years earlier included memorable lines that helped define the eras that followed ("Ask not . . ."; "The only thing we have to fear . . ."). When rhetoric scholars rated the top hundred speeches of the twentieth century, both finished in the top three, behind only Martin Luther King Jr.'s "I Have a Dream."[1]

But both had something else in common—the lengths each speaker went to conceal who wrote the speech.

Days before Kennedy's inauguration, the president-elect sat on a flight to Washington with reporter Hugh Sidey. In front of him lay a yellow legal pad filled with unreadable notes and paragraphs. The drafting process was tough, JFK said. Sidey reported how amazed he was that the speech was still so rough.[2]

Except it wasn't. In fact, Ted Sorenson's almost complete and fully typed draft was waiting for JFK to land.

In FDR's case, Raymond Moley wrote the speech—though not the most famous "fear" line later inserted by FDR strategist Louis Howe.

After they reviewed the draft together at Hyde Park, FDR told Moley he would copy the speech by hand so people would think he actually wrote it. "This is your speech now," Moley said.[3] He crumpled up his draft and tossed it into the roaring fireplace.

Today, audiences are more aware that speechwriters exist. But not everything has changed.

On January 18, 2017, Donald Trump tweeted a picture of himself behind a desk with a stack of paper and pen in hand. "Writing my inaugural address at the Winter White House, Mar-a-Lago, three weeks ago."[4] Before Barack Obama's second inaugural, the Obama White House released photos of a page of speech text filled with the president's cross-outs, arrows, and new passages rewritten by hand.[5]

This is not just true for presidents. Ask dedicated Senate staffers about a speech they wrote, and often they'll reflexively tell you "the boss wrote most of it." You might also hear this popular nonanswer answer: "the boss is the best writer on the staff."

Sometimes that's true. Most of the time, it's not.

In the last chapter, we discussed the ethics of such deception. We asked if it's right to expect listeners to judge speakers delivering a speech written by someone else. In this chapter, we examine not the ethics of the partnership between a speaker and the writer, but the partnership itself. We offer tips to keep that relationship professional and productive. And we begin by asking you to imagine this scenario:

The senator rides in the back of a black sedan. The speechwriter is back at the office. Beside the senator sits the chief of staff. They are headed for the Hilton to deliver a keynote. The speech draft looks great: crisp pages stacked neatly inside a folder with an embossed seal. There's only one problem. The politician hates it.

"These aren't my ideas," she says. "I hate the joke. I've already used it five times—when do I get something new? And these health care facts? Are they even right—what if someone asks me about them? He mentions my family, Jack's broken arm! He doesn't *know* my kid! Who gave him the right to—where's a pen? How long do I have?"

"Seven minutes."

"Seven—get Sara on the phone. She knows the bill. Why wasn't *she* involved?"

Now imagine the writer. It's a few hours later. The chief of staff has delivered a version of the senator's assessment—sanitized, but not too sanitized.

The writer feels sick, and furious. "How can I know what she wants?" the writer says. "She *canceled* the speech meeting! And those facts? They *came* from Sara. She said I *had* to use them. And her son? She tells me to make the speeches sound personal, but she won't give me any stories."

It happens often. Once Eric heard his boss's wife playfully teasing her husband about his receding hairline. Eric included a self-deprecating joke about male-pattern baldness in the next speech. The boss looked up. "Why would you ever think that's something I'd joke about?"

In July 2018, one news story offered a reason for Philippines president Rodrigo Duterte's rambling, off-message speeches: "Duterte usually discards his prepared speeches during public engagements, saying they do not reflect his sentiments and his concerns."[6]

These aren't stories of poor, victimized speechwriters blamed for everything by insensitive bosses. And these aren't challenges always solved by doing what President Duterte's spokesman suggested—looking for better speechwriters.[7] Instead, they reflect tension—often unspoken—between speakers and speechwriters.

The authors have written for governors, for members of the House including those in leadership, for senators, and at the White House. We've seen enough offices to know that the basic tenor of any political staff comes from the boss. Corporate CEOs have thousands of people on the payroll who never lay eyes on the boss. Even senators only have about fifty. When they are in a bad mood, nobody escapes.

And exacerbating their moods are the emotional highs and lows of an office where every day seems to bring a new crisis. Every job has its pressures. Most don't involve deciding whether to send troops into harm's way, who gets health care and who doesn't, or how much aid to send to a community where a hurricane has left piles of twigs and turned over cars where homes once stood.

Not all members of Congress get to decide these issues. They feel like they might—and so do the staff. Such stakes make people work seventy hours a week for little money and still feel disappointed if they're not asked to stay for a midnight strategy session. Complicating such tensions are the kinds of people politics attracts: those ambitious and willing to fight others for promotions and face time—or to argue about every word in a sentence.

Meanwhile, though politicians often complain about the sacrifices of their jobs, most of them love what they do. But *because* they love their work, each day brings more worries. Will they get reelected? Should they think about leaving the House and running for that open Senate seat? What will this bill—or this speech—do to make that possible? And it's not just the important question of what comes next in their career; it's the urgent matter of what comes next on their schedule. They have committee meetings and hearings, followed by votes. They have ribbon cuttings, photo ops, and fundraising dinners. Each of those means time spent away from their families.

In other words, they are busy. Every politician has a hundred claims on his or her attention that seem at least as important as meeting with a writer for a speech conference. David Murray, editor of *Vital Speeches of the Day* and executive director of the Professional Speechwriters Association, rightly reminds writers, "Good Speechwriting Client" is not a core competency for being a leader.[8]

All this can make life tough for the speechwriter, often the sole staffer who understands how hard a job writing is. It's stressful to have a constant stream of people ducking their heads into your office and shouting, "Got it? Got it? He needs it in *five minutes! Five!*"

Tight deadlines. High stakes. The inevitable clashes of personalities and egos. And one other thing. Political speechwriting is tense because while to the limited extent that most people imagine speechwriters at all—the stereotype is the Ted Sorensen model: the trusted aide meeting every day with the boss—the reality is very different.

These days, even full-time speechwriters are often midlevel staffers who get material filtered to them through a communications director. Speechwriters aren't the only ones fighting for access and influence. They have to fight for time to ask the questions policy people won't ask (*When Jimmy broke his arm, did you go to the hospital? How long were you in the waiting room?*).

When they do, they may meet resistance. Even people in the public eye can be intensely private. They may shrink from the idea of using their personal lives to affect an audience. They may feel embarrassed *because* the media and their audience know or assume a speechwriter had a hand in something so personal. At other times, they think of staff, especially speechwriters, as a necessary evil. *He's my kid's age! He's scripting me?*

In one interview, Barton Swaim, author of *The Speechwriter: A Brief Education in Politics*, described the challenge in writing for Mark Sanford, then the Republican governor of South Carolina:

> A politician's only real weapon is words. And if he's not good at it, he needs to hire someone who can do it for him, at least in the written form. But a lot of politicians think that they actually are good writers . . . They don't hire you because they think you are better at putting words together than they. They hire you to put together the words that they would have put together if they had had time. That's a dicey situation.[9]

The result: Politicians cancel speech conferences, maybe without even articulating the reasons to themselves. That leaves speechwriters having to obey higher-ranking staffers whose expertise is policy, not persuasion. It's a wonder these awkward but necessary relationships work at all.

But they can.

Just as speechwriters and their bosses must think about the needs of an audience, they must consider each other's needs, too.

FOR SPEAKERS: WHAT SPEECHWRITERS NEED FROM YOU

The more you clarify what you want from staff, the more likely it is that you will get what you want from them. Here's what that advice means when it comes to using speechwriters.

Clearly Define the Speechwriter's Role

Do you want to review drafts of all speeches, or just the big ones? How much time do you need? How much turnaround time do you think is fair for incorporating your suggestions? Do you want a speechwriter who handles just text, or one responsible for the list of acknowledgments and thank-yous? What about slides or other props? How long should your speeches be? How comfortable are you taking Q&A?

Not even your communications director can answer all of these questions, and dozens more, in ways that a speechwriter needs. Only you. So make sure your chief of staff, communications director, *and* speechwriter know what makes you comfortable. Spell everything out in writing.

Include in the job description these elements: the need to make changes quickly, to understand that criticism is inevitable but not personal, to provide sources for data, to work with the rest of your staff, and to learn about not just the issues but the politics surrounding them.

But then, do what is rare in our experience and the experience of dozens of other speechwriters in politics; talk about this with your speechwriter there, making clear that you welcome comments.

As noted consultant Rick Shapiro, who has spent decades advising congressional offices, points out (see Box 17.1), confusion about what you need is a constant source of tension on both sides. The problem is neither that you are insensitive nor that they are disobedient. It is the catch-as-catch-can culture of political life. Clarity is an asset in speeches *and* in producing them.

Provide Training

Even if speechwriters come to your office with a portfolio of professional work, the odds are great that they learned on the fly in someone else's office rather than through any kind of formal training. It's not unusual for people in government to attend management workshops or seminars in the legislative process; speechwriters could benefit from them, too.

There is another obstacle to making speeches work. Many writers believe speechwriting is whatever it was in the last place they worked. Different politicians, though, have different needs. Some hate stories. Others love them. Some want colloquial speech. Others want a more lawyerly approach.

If you want speechwriters who share your standards, perspectives, and ideas, some training should come directly from you. Even before new writers give you their first speech, talk to them directly about what you want. Show them the formatting you like—and tell them why. Go over the kind of research you expect. We've had clients who want 20-point type triple-spaced, leaving the bottom third of the page empty. That way, you keep your chin away from your chest. Another speaker wanted every page to end with a period. He didn't want to shuffle papers in the middle of a thought. That was useful to know.

Another personal example. One of us worked in an office where a consultant put staffers in a circle and played the "telephone" game, where a staffer at one point in the circle whispers an idea to the next one, who passes it on. The last person says the idea out loud. The two versions were very different. The consultant was delighted. He made his point, and ours. If speechwriters are to know exactly what you need, they need to hear it directly from you.

Learn More about What Makes Speeches Good

Some aspects of giving a good speech are up to you, not your writers.

Anyone who's walked into a bookstore to pick up a book on investing strategy or done an internet search on how to fix a leaky faucet shouldn't look askance at learning more about persuasive speech. There are many good resources besides the one you hold.

When you train your writer, be specific. Don't say "I want it to be like a TED Talk." Identify the elements that make TED Talks interesting to you. Read systematically about the role that concrete detail or story can play in moving audiences, or why research matters, or why Monroe's Motivated Sequence is so effective.

Make time to speak about these issues with your writer, not just when you have a speech to give, but when you have an empty slot on your schedule. Without pressure, you will articulate more clearly to your writers exactly what you want—and see drafts coming in that reflect your advice.

Involve Yourself in Finding Content

For many officeholders, speech conferences—if they happen at all—can feel like a waste of time. You are busy right up until the minute your staffers file in to talk. Your mind's a blank. You barely remember what event they're talking about. You're grateful that someone seems to have ideas, because right now you don't.

But five minutes' advance work on your part could make that conference valuable. Spend those minutes jotting down points that reflect your thinking, including material from your personal life. Think about what you want to convey. Staffers who hear what you think will be eager to include your language. That will make you feel more comfortable delivering the speech they hand you.

Better still, don't wait for a speech conference to think about material. Issues are relatively easy for your staff to research, but only you can tell them what has been happening in your life. Have you heard a joke you liked recently? Read a moving letter from a constituent? Yes, writers can provide you with jokes, and most speeches should have them—but only you know what you find compelling.

In the old days, sharing ideas with staff was cumbersome; you had to clip and copy articles and send them around. Now things are simpler. Bombard your speechwriters with texts and emails (*Check this health article in the* Post *... Good stuff... Heard a joke I like the other day . . .*). They would have to be idiots not to include them in the next draft.

And if they don't, ask them why not. Even idiots should know enough to change.

Encourage Recycling

If you have read this entire book, skip these paragraphs. If you haven't, we encourage you to find our advice on recycling. To find something good and then discard it is like closing down a hit show after opening night. Besides, recycled material lets you look out at the crowd and build fluently toward a climax with the confidence that comes only from familiarity. Everyone running for office should see the difference between the stump speech at the start of a campaign—and what it is like just before Election Day. Practice makes perfect, especially when you want to be dramatic.

For Delivery, Practice (Maybe Even Hire a Consultant)

Chapter 15 of this book, "Delivery," asks you to gird yourself, watch and listen to yourself on tape, then solicit honest advice.

Here, we suggest something else: ask for that advice from someone outside the office, or maybe even hire a consultant. C'mon. Admit it. Don't you sometimes think staffers are too young or inexperienced to know how to train you? Would you rather have someone you know has worked well with your colleagues? Or just a fresh opinion?

Go outside. You are a celebrity, often with enormous power. Staffers may be afraid to be entirely candid. When you were, say, twenty-five, would you have felt comfortable telling your bosses that they slumped over the podium, swallowed words, and ad-libbed a tasteless joke?

Consultants can speak candidly, and hiring them doesn't have to mean spending a fortune. You can find, say, public speaking teachers at a community college who would be happy to volunteer their time or work for a modest fee. The important part is not just their advice but their freedom to be honest.

But don't stop there. During those sessions, involve the millennials who write for you. They won't just learn a lot; they will add a lot. No one else in the office knows more about what you need or can spot problems faster. It might take time for staffers to believe that you really want candor about the things consultants point out. But over time, they will see you're really listening. Then, even a twenty-five-year-old may relax and start telling you the truth.

Give Speechwriters Face Time

So far, this chapter has encouraged you to resist the belief that you can deal with speechwriters through other staffers, be it the chief of staff or the communications director.

Yes, speechwriters can get statistics, ideas, and acknowledgments from other staffers. But they need personal contact with you even more than do some staffers who outrank them.

It is because of the questions they need to ask. *Did the caseworkers send you anything moving this week? Do you have a favorite story about this? Did your kids say anything funny this week? Did you read anything in the papers that made you mad?*

Other staffers rightly focus on policy ("Can it get out of Committee?"). But only speechwriters will ask the questions whose answers make your speeches personal in a way that audiences love.

In fact, that is why it's sometimes useful to include speechwriters in meetings for which they have no official role. You may say something as an aside that staffers concerned with policy will ignore. Good speechwriters will hear that aside as something important to you and take it down verbatim. Then they can find a way to include it in the draft, phrased in a way that makes you comfortable. That's good for you, good for the speechwriter, and good for the speech.

Don't Expect Perfect First Drafts

Even if you hire the best speechwriters and follow every tip in this chapter, a perfect draft can't possibly appear on your desk every time. First drafts are never perfect in any kind of writing; speechwriting in particular calls for give-and-take.

Instead of just scribbling out some changes, accept that working with speechwriters means learning to read analytically and give concrete feedback on a draft's virtues and problems. *I hate it; do it over* doesn't help anyone. Even a compliment works better if it's specific (*Love this part about the [fill in the blank]; can you do more like that?*). And scolding writers for guessing wrong is a sure way to make them give you only the safest—and blandest—material.

BOX 17.1
EXPERTS TALK: RICK SHAPIRO

Few people can pinpoint the problems congressional offices face better than Rick Shapiro. A management consultant and former director of the Congressional Management Foundation, the nonprofit that provides management guidance to congressional offices, Rick has spent three decades helping Democrats and Republicans make their offices work better.

In the first edition of this book, Bob asked Rick for ways political offices could make the speechwriting process effective. He outlined four steps: training, coaching, debriefing, and creating templates—establishing clear operating procedures on how the speechwriting process should work.

For this edition, Bob asked him to give advice again. Here is what he said:

It's been ten years since we talked about this. What's changed?
Well, one thing. Speechwriters and press secretaries used to be the primary messengers in the office. Now they are competing with other messengers in enlarged media shops that now include staff who oversee the office's website. They also do social media, including Twitter. These are a number of new ways of delivering messages. And new staff to produce them.

What about the change in technology? Important?
Websites and social media have become incredibly valuable in getting out the message. Members used to worry about doing enough speeches back in the District. Now people in the District don't need to hear a speech or attend a town hall meeting to know where their member stands. But a speechwriter should remember something else. The new technology means the speeches they write can have more value. They go on YouTube or on the office website. The people reading and viewing them are a much larger group than the people attending the event.

In addition to what makes speeches effective, are there specific areas the new speechwriter must learn?
You need to learn about policy *and* politics. You can't just know the substance of an issue; you have to also understand the politics of an issue—both the national or inside-the-beltway politics as well as the unique politics of the District.

Second, you need to learn about the boss. If you are a speechwriter, you can't miss a speech conference. Those are ideal opportunities to develop rapport with the

(Continued)

(Continued)

boss and demonstrate that you have good ideas and can be trusted. Meanwhile, you need to go to every speech you can. How else will you learn the boss's voice? Or develop the confidence and trust to be able to say to your boss, say, "Your jokes aren't working. We need to work on that."

But we hear speechwriters say there are limits to how much they can push back. Is that right?
Sure. You have to pick your battles. But many politicians are fonts of ideas. They generate and propose new ideas every day. Good staffers understand that they like to think out loud and most members understand that not all of their ideas are good. A speechwriter's job, implicitly, is to assess the ideas and try to separate the wheat from the chaff. That means discussing these ideas with the boss and pushing back or creating the dialogue that allows for the selection of the best ideas

Are there other suggestions you have for promoting the professional development of speechwriters?
I'll give you two.

First, cultivate relationships with more seasoned speechwriters. Pick their brains and seek their guidance on all aspects of speechwriting, including how to give and solicit feedback from the boss. Use them as sounding boards. This year, in the House, speechwriters from one party met every Friday. This is an ideal opportunity to learn and find mentors.

Second, work to create what in the military they call "after-action reviews." Organize a group of staff who participated in the speech preparation to assess speeches right after every speech to figure out what worked and what you would change in future speeches. Your boss may not always have time to participate in these discussions, but speechwriters can receive valuable feedback and insights from this ongoing process that provide ongoing data to continually improve the effectiveness of the speeches.

Is that the kind of advice they will hear when you provide management advice?
In part. Usually, I organize a retreat for the office. But what works in a retreat is only part of what a speechwriter needs. Retreats aren't aimed at problems involving a small group of staffers. Speechwriters need to know a few people well. Like the legislative assistants. That work happens in the office. It happens at lunch. If you are doing a speech on public health, you should know the health care LA well.

Final question. If you have one piece of advice for a new speechwriter—what would it be?
Build a strong, trusting relationship with your boss. That is often not easy to do. There are very real barriers. Members are often 20 to 30 years older than their speechwriter. Members also have very little down time to relax and hang out with their staff.

So, make the most of the time you have in speech conferences or traveling with the boss to a speech. Write down the questions you want to ask ahead of time rather than winging it. Seek candid feedback on your work and use the feedback to improve your speeches. Find interesting ways of engaging your boss in thinking about and reflecting on his or her speeches and how to improve them. There is not much that bosses like more than staff who seek feedback and use the feedback to enhance their skills.

But enhancing skills takes more than just good listening and good intentions. It takes hard work, diligence and a commitment to pushing yourself hard to continually improve a wide range of skills. Because great speechwriters are much more than great writers. They are skilled researchers, effective collaborators and consensus-builders, creative thinkers and good at both receiving and providing feedback, often to bosses who don't really want to hear it. So put in the time. Do your homework and, if possible, seek to develop a personal rapport with your boss that promotes honest and comfortable communications between the two of you.

FOR SPEECHWRITERS: WHAT SPEAKERS NEED FROM YOU

In *Thanks, Obama*, his entertaining—and reflective—book about being a speechwriter for Barack Obama, David Litt sums up his experience this way:

> For eight formative years, often against my will, I was forced to act like an adult. Children strive for pleasure; adults for fulfillment. Children demand adoration; adults earn respect. Children find worth in what they acquire; adults find worth in the responsibilities they bear.[10]

Even if you are twenty-two, your job is one for adults. How do you find fulfillment, respect, and worth in your enormous responsibility?

Yes, the boss owes you feedback. You owe the boss and everyone else in the office not just your best efforts but your respect. Writing may be a solitary occupation, but winning respect means working as part of what is at best a cohesive political team.

Here are some ways to help that team work together so you can better handle the responsibilities you bear.

Be Realistic

In the beginning, even Ted Sorensen wasn't Ted Sorensen. Relationships and trust with your boss develop over time, not overnight. But from your boss's perspective, you are one midlevel staffer who will probably leave in two or three years. It might not seem at first that you're worth investing the time and thought you crave. Give it time.

Meanwhile, just as relationships take time, so do skills. Being a good writer isn't all you need. You will have to listen carefully and work hard to become great at writing speeches for politicians. How long do they like to speak? What kinds of stories will they tell? Do they want to rehearse? There are dozens of questions that you'll answer only through trial and error or bad mistakes—like the old man renowned for his good judgment who said, "I learned good judgment . . . through bad judgment."

Learn More about What Makes a Good Speech

Yes, you.

The authors run workshops for speechwriters each year, all working full time, only a handful of whom have ever heard of Monroe, the classic and most appropriate structure for writing persuasive policy speeches.

That's not surprising. Speechwriting, even today, is often an accidental career; people come to it from journalism, law, or other areas, for reasons that include simply being the staffer who writes the best. Very few have systematically explored the variety of techniques taught in most college public speaking courses.

You should. Books like the one you hold aren't the only way. Journalists learn by reading journalism. Screenwriters learn by watching movies. You should read and listen to speeches. With YouTube, TED.com, or even C-SPAN .org, you can do this slouched in your chair, switching from speech to speech literally by moving one finger. Find the ones you admire most. What makes them great? How can you apply those ideas to your own drafts?

Later in this book, you will read Sen. John Kerry's Kenyon College commencement speech in which he tells the story of one speechwriter. The lesson: every meeting you have, and every draft you write, offers the chance to show what you have learned—and will do.

Research before (and More Than) You Write

If we ever needed help remembering this, the daily work on *Political Speechwriter* would remind us.

Take the beginning of this chapter. Drafting the general points on the partnership between writers and speakers, in the first draft, didn't take long. But to find and delineate precise examples to illustrate points in this chapter and throughout the book? Sifting through different possibilities, locating them, and deciding which details were vital took a full day.

Even then, neither of us knew the story about JFK and Hugh Sidey. It wasn't until several drafts later, and the persistent questions of a brilliant editor, that we did even more research to produce the detail that satisfied us both.

That opening section took you about five minutes to read. It took about a morning of writing time to create. But finding the material we needed took almost two days of research.

This is not unusual. A few years ago, one of us had to write an award speech an actress would deliver in a two-minute video.

Researching took about five hours. Writing the script? About twenty minutes.

It was worth it. One sure way to write a bad speech is to think you need only what is in your head.

Before you are a speechwriter, you must be a speech researcher. No matter how thorough your speech conference was, only your own research can uncover the stories, wit, pithy quotes, concrete detail, and instantly persuasive examples that will keep people listening, even with topics you've written about before.

It may take hours looking at horrible jokes to uncover the one that's perfect, or the concrete detail that puts a dry statistic into startling context. But remember: it can be more memorable for an audience than all of the draft's policy ideas put together.

Work for More Face Time

Often, the reality of speechwriting is about not access, but "lack-cess."

Like children, staffers compete for the attention of their boss. Even your friends may try to cut you out of speech conferences. You'll know this is happening when you hear telltale sentences like "Oh, you don't have to come"; or "I'll get you everything you need"; or the classic "We'll just be talking about logistics."

After the 1986 *Challenger* disaster, Peggy Noonan wasn't in the meeting when Ronald Reagan shared his initial reaction. After it, Reagan's chief of staff decided the speech had to be emotional. "Get the girl," he said.[11]

Noonan asked participants what the president said, learned that he wanted to speak directly to the children who watched, and got to work.

Not all of the most moving moments came from what the staff relayed. The closing was a poem she knew.[12] She hoped Reagan knew the poem. As luck would have it, he did.[13]

So yes, you can write great speeches without face time. But there is still no replacing it. The best way to learn about personal feelings is in person, talking face-to-face about an upcoming speech.

When people say "You don't have to come," smile and tell them you need to know about logistics, too. Then try to go to the meeting. If you can't get permission, try again next time. Otherwise, the boss won't identify you with the draft. He or she won't call you with ideas. And you won't get the chance to ask the questions that no one else will ask.

Learn How to Handle Speech Conferences

At some point, like Alexander Hamilton, you will be "in the room where it happens." When you get there, don't throw away your shot.

First, prepare. Go to the other staffers and find out what they're going to say so you'll know how to head them off if they're wrong or support them if they make sense. Read some old speeches to see what's been done for similar groups. Write out the questions you need to ask—not just to sound smart, but because in the heat of discussion and the distraction of note-taking you're unlikely to remember the questions that occurred to you during the quiet moments at your desk.

If you ask the boss "Got any stories about that?" you're likely to only get back a blank look. But if you've done your homework, you can ask specific questions that lend themselves to anecdotal answers:

In the Q&A the other day, I heard you mention your mom worked as a teacher. Did she teach in your school? What was that like?

Or: *I read a profile piece from your first campaign; did you really drive around in a pickup truck?*

Or: *Can you tell me about a soldier you met when you visited the military hospital?*

You can retell what you've learned, but with details only the boss knows.

Second, take voluminous notes—and certainly record every word your boss says. You need the information for yourself, and if questions come up later, you want to be the smart one who knows exactly what each person said.

Third, whatever you do, make sure the ideas the boss comes up with appear in some form in your draft. Bosses mention ideas because they want to see them in the speech. They may not ask why you ignored them. But they will notice—and remember.

Speech conferences will never give you all you need. But they will tell you what you need to find.

Cultivate Relationships

No speechwriter is an island. You need other staffers—and to enjoy that relationship. If you go to them for advice and take it, you will find they undercut you less in meetings and support you more. They'll shoot you an email saying something like "Liked what you said about X. Did you see this article about that?"

We have heard other writers tell us about the fights in their office. "I fight with Joe," they'll say, "but the boss likes me."

Not even speechwriters are immune from self-deception. You can't always tell who likes you, and you won't always hear about complaints. One excellent writer we know said that a few weeks before the chief of staff fired him. It turned out his boss didn't like him after all.

One danger for speechwriters: making fun of policy wonks. The wonks may not write well. But they think well and know more about their area than you could ever learn. Work to make them like you, too.

Do this for staffers at every level. Eric was once hired to write a speech for a senator. He didn't know that the senator had asked a personal friend—we'll call him Fred—to do a competing draft, then picked Fred's draft without reading Eric's.

As the senator was leaving for the day, his receptionist said, "You took Fred's? The other one is much better."

The senator was so startled, he sat down and read both—and changed his mind. The lesson: in a political office, everyone is smart, and everyone might be part of the process.

Work Hard on the Cover Memo

Yes, you can send a quick email or write a sticky note reading, *Here's the draft. Tell me what you think.*

That would be a colossal mistake. Speakers and other staffers are busy. They can't pore over your draft to appreciate each fine point you want them to notice. Instead, write a cover memo that directs their attention by including three sections:

Section 1: *I've done what you asked.*

- Make sure your memo says something like "You will see your ideas incorporated throughout the draft. For example . . ." And list each example.

Section 2: *Here's what I didn't change, and why.*

- Some suggestions made in brainstorming sessions just don't work when you get to the computer. Highlight them. "One change I didn't make was X, because . . ." Usually, the boss will agree. Even if they don't, at least it won't seem like you were trying to hide something. Warning: if you haven't incorporated far more of the boss's ideas than you've ignored, think again.

Section 3: *Here's how you can check everything I did.*

- Keep and carry a draft with tracked changes. Bosses may never look at the tracked version, but they will appreciate your openness. They'll know you value their views, and that will make them value you.

Go to Every Speech

That means *every* speech. At least the local ones. Two reasons.

First, hearing your speeches delivered is in your boss's interest. You will hear the applause line delivered just right. But you will see—and cringe at—each mistake you've made: a clumsy sentence, a joke that gets no reaction, a story that goes on too long. Seeing your boss come to the punch line, look up, and hear only silence will make you more careful about what you hand in next time.

Second, you will see what speakers can and can't do. Are they too inhibited to be forceful? Too animated telling a story? Unable to expand from sketchy talking points? You will be able to use ad-libbed anecdotes, answers from the Q&A, and other material in later drafts.

Taking the boss's strengths and limitations into account is your job, too.

Equally important is what happens afterward. That's the best time to get feedback on how the speaker felt about the speech. Even a few minutes in the elevator or car can give you insights you'll get no other way.

Notice we say "get feedback," not necessarily "give feedback." You have to pick your spots. When Eric worked at General Electric, sometimes when he was still in the crowd, just after a speech, his phone would vibrate. It was a text from his boss.

It looked like this: "That went well. What did you think? Sent from my iPad."

Eric knew this was not the time for constructive criticism.

But Eric also knew something else. The boss noticed he was at the event.

You want your bosses to identify you with these drafts that appear on their desks. Sometimes—especially when speakers are in the expansive mood that comes after a speech is done—they'll include you in the relaxed conversations that lift you at least temporarily above your current rank. And—not a small point—if things go well, you can bask in the high-fives.

Take Responsibility for More Than the Drafts

Keep an anecdote file. Include every story, joke, and quote your boss ever uses. It will prove invaluable.

Also build an archive of video. If no one is recording an event, you or another staffer can use your phone. There's no better way for bosses to see what's not working than to watch themselves. They may start watching with no one else in the room. When you've shown yourself as someone to trust, you might get invited to sit in. Then you can advise on delivery—with the evidence right there, you can be more candid—and find one more way of making yourself indispensable.

Recycle

For all the reasons we mentioned earlier, this is good advice for speakers *and* writers. And for writers, there is one more, essential just to them.

Most political speechwriters are incredibly rushed. Anyone producing a short speech for House members ten minutes before they speak, or finishing a speech conference and beginning revisions a half-hour before Air Force Two touches down, or producing sixty speeches in a single month, will understand how useful it is to pull up an old draft, insert a few small changes to make it current, and hit Send before your deadline.

Do More Than Capture Your Boss's Voice

It is the classic advice for writers: "find your speaker's voice." It contains a germ of truth. Not all speakers use exactly the same diction or tone, or tell a joke or story the same way, or feel the same about how partisan to be. As a speechwriter, you need to listen and learn how your boss thinks and speaks.

But that isn't all you need. It's not even close. You may never hear some elements of a good speech—simple, concrete, uncluttered language; storytelling and wit—in your boss's conversations or see them in the drafts of the writers who preceded you. Use all the best techniques in your drafts whether you've heard the speaker use them or not.

Because the job of a speechwriter isn't just finding the speaker's voice. It's helping speakers find their own—then making it better.

Don't Expect to Hear Your Material Word for Word

It's common for a speechwriter to start out thinking that the fun of speechwriting will be hearing a famous and powerful person mouth the words you have created.

Think again.

Any speaker with a brain will want to change some things you've written. Sometimes speakers will have a thought up on the podium and want to digress. Sometimes they'll deliver your lines well. Sometimes they'll butcher them.

Sometimes they will make them better.

And sometimes, hearing your lines, you'll wish you had done one more rewrite. If your only idea of a reward is hearing someone say exactly what you wrote, you're destined to have a miserable time.

Instead, look for the things you've done that make a contribution: the joke you found, the line that got applause, the story that moved an audience, the dry stat you put into context, and the sound bite everybody's talking about when it makes the evening news.

A speechwriter is part of a team. You don't always score the only run.

FINAL WORDS

Of the countless times Al Gore introduced President Clinton, Eric remembers one in particular. It was at a White House event, and part of the speech touting the strong economy referenced retirement plans. Eric wanted to be safe, so he included a phonetic pronunciation key:

401-K (FOUR-OH-ONE-KAY).

Eric didn't twice think about it until his friend Dave, who was in the briefing, called him laughing hysterically.

"You won't believe this. The VP just showed your draft to POTUS and said, 'Look how stupid my speechwriter thinks I am!'"

You might think Eric was distraught. He was—and exhilarated. He had made the leader of the free world laugh!

The uneasy partnership in politics means that it is inevitable your bosses won't always recognize what you do for them, just as you won't always recognize what they need or want.

The partnership may never be perfect. Or easy. But in the end, there are steps each side can take to make both the partnership and the speeches it produces better.

THE SPEECHWRITER'S CHECKLIST: THE UNEASY PARTNERSHIP—ADVICE FOR SPEAKERS AND WRITERS

For the Speaker

- ☐ Have I clearly defined in writing the speechwriter's role, making clear important issues that include:
  - ☐ Workload?
  - ☐ Deadlines?
  - ☐ Process?
  - ☐ Sources for data?
  - ☐ Appropriate staff to consult?
  - ☐ Issues to know?
  - ☐ Political context?

- ☐ Have I offered the speechwriter opportunities for training, including conferences, coursework, and mentoring?
- ☐ For delivery issues, do I understand the difficulties of achieving candor from staff?
- ☐ Have I explored hiring outside consultants for help with delivery?
- ☐ Do I understand the need for recycled material both for me and for those writing drafts?
- ☐ Do I give speechwriters the face time they need?
- ☐ Do I include the speechwriter in discussions of the political needs of an appearance?
- ☐ Do I provide candid feedback?

For the Speechwriter

- ☐ Am I realistic about the relationship I can expect with my boss?
- ☐ Have I explored ways to educate myself about speech, including:
  - ☐ Reading?
  - ☐ Courses?
  - ☐ Conferences?
  - ☐ Consulting with others?
  - ☐ Regular exploration of speeches by others and old speeches by my boss?
- ☐ To the extent possible, do I research more than I write?
- ☐ Do I make an effort to work well with staff?
- ☐ Do I attend every speech possible?
- ☐ Do I prepare well for speech conferences?
- ☐ Does my cover memo fairly explain how I tried to achieve my boss's goals?
- ☐ Do I take responsibility for more than drafts, including files of jokes, quotes, and other material that worked well?
- ☐ Do I urge recycling?
- ☐ Do I solicit candid feedback and try to apply what I have heard?

CHAPTER 18

Final, Final Words

At the beginning of each semester, as American University students file into our classroom for the first time wondering how much work it will take to get an A and if we'll keep them until the class's listed end time of 10:50 p.m., I ask a basic question:

How many of you want to become speechwriters?

About 75 percent raise their hand.

Maybe that shouldn't be surprising, even for an elective. We teach in Washington, D.C. Our students are political junkies and policy wonks. They intern on Capitol Hill and in the executive branch. They quote episodes of *The West Wing*. They have intense debates on what's a bigger score, a selfie with Chuck Todd or Jake Tapper.

Still, I often joke with Bob that with so many wannabe speechwriters, our primary responsibility should be spending the next fifteen weeks together dissuading them. Like many jokes, that one contains a kernel of truth. Budding speechwriters should be under no illusions about the romance of the job. It has its frustrations, many of which we've already discussed: Meeting unreasonable deadlines. Seeing bad editors wreck good drafts. Listening to writers hold you in contempt for writing under someone else's name. Having to give voice to unpalatable views. Trying to produce intellectually coherent arguments about policies produced by compromise. Hearing speakers who say they're grateful for your work but try to disguise your role; wishing other speakers would disguise your role a little bit more because their monotonous delivery does it no service.

Why do it?

To begin, speeches matter. That's not always obvious. When politicians can launch a bid for the presidency on Stephen Colbert, introduce themselves with a Hollywood-produced YouTube video, or announce a new policy with a tweet that instantly reaches more than fifty-five million followers, it's fair to ask if speeches have the same utility they once did.

As you reach the end of this book, our view won't surprise you. All the technology in the world can't replace a speaker in front of an audience holding forth on issues, making an appeal, trying to inform and maybe even inspire. And in politics, the subjects of the speeches—issues and people—are not abstract concepts. In ways large and small, they are relevant to our own lives.

When politicians speak to us about going to war, we think of our neighbor in the Marines. When they try to explain the budget, we wonder what will happen to our child's music program at school or the Medicaid program our parents need. When they talk about tax breaks for a new commercial development, we worry about the rent going up and the traffic driving home from work. The issues politicians talk about affect us all. So watching and hearing their speeches, whether politicians exceed our expectations or fall short, is as valuable as ever.

If speeches matter, it only follows that speech*writing* and speech*writers* matter, too.

I've been writing speeches for more than twenty-five years. For many of those years, I never thought of myself as a writer. In fact, in 1993 when I first walked into Al Gore's speechwriting office in what's now the Eisenhower Executive Office Building, I only had two qualifications. I told Gore's chief speechwriter, Bob Lehrman, that in college and grad school I preferred writing papers to taking tests, and that, at least for a little while, I would work for free.

I had little choice about the latter. A week earlier I had an interview in the office of my home state senator, the late Daniel Patrick Moynihan. The person who interviewed me walked into the room where I was waiting, holding my résumé. He glanced at it, put it down on the table, and said, before even a hello: "You're the worst kind. You have a graduate degree and no experience. You won't take an entry-level job, and you're not qualified to do anything else." (It was a short interview.)

Bob had studied with Kurt Vonnegut. He had published novels. He's a writer, I'd say to myself, not me. The way Bob marked up the first speeches I drafted only confirmed my belief.

So what changed? When did I realize that speechwriters do more than "turn a phrase," and that, as we've said earlier in this book, speeches don't write themselves?

Over the last fifteen years, sharing a classroom, we've both seen how the satisfaction of teaching speechwriting fully equals the best moments of writing speeches. It's incredibly gratifying to work out ways to put into words what speechwriters do intuitively and see how quickly twenty-two-year-olds in a college lecture hall, as well as established writers at a professional development workshop, learn to do what sophisticated White House speechwriters have done.

Our "charity contest" is a great example. Each year, near the end of our class, we ask students to put $5 each in a pot—then write speeches designed to persuade the group to donate that pot to their favorite charity. We match the dollar amount and make a contribution to the winning cause.

The assignment has a profound effect. Some students have links between a charity and their own lives: a mother with breast cancer; a friend who attempted suicide after being bullied for being gay; or, in one case, a student who had been told he was dying granted a last wish by the Make-A-Wish Foundation. Others just admire the work a charity does, whether caring for Syrian refugees, mentoring inner-city kids, or even saving the manatees.

They use techniques they've learned as homework. But because they care deeply, they harness them to speeches so compelling we sometimes call a recess to recover. They have learned how to take something that matters to them, and make it matter to us.

That, of course, is what I try to do when I write a speech: when I realized that, I finally started to think of myself as a writer.

In the introduction to this book, we shared the story of how uneasy I was receiving credit for the first speech I wrote in the White House. It's true—I was slightly embarrassed. But there was also the rush of adrenaline that comes from hearing someone powerful recite the words you put to paper. There was elation when the crowd laughed at the joke. There was relief when people clapped at the end.

Mostly, though, there was pride. And not only in the job I did. The pride came from what many think is the romance of speechwriting itself: writing the actual words for people you believe in, accomplishing things you believe are worth doing, whether it is a U.S. president or a city councilman pushing for a stop sign.

This book, now in its second edition, exists for that reason. If something is worth doing, it's worth doing well. Does that mean you really have to understand parallel construction or know the five steps of Monroe? Didn't we point out that Abraham Lincoln used those steps before Monroe was born? Well, if you've read it from beginning to end—not a requirement—you know that while the book does introduce some new concepts, it focuses on examining techniques common to successful speeches. Systematic, formal teaching seems to help most people become at least competent, whether at piano or golf. (Okay, maybe not golf.) Why not speechwriting?

As Bob and I have seen over and over again, speechwriters find this approach especially valuable. Even though more and more people set out to become speechwriters, most still learn on the job. Except for the Gettysburg Address, King's "Dream" speech, and a few others, most speechwriters start paying attention to speeches only when they have to write one.

Of course, speechwriting has changed since those famous speeches. It's even changed since the first edition of this book. For example: We write sound bites for Twitter and not TV; we are much more robust about checking the facts, even as a president ignores them; we can reach a lot more people; and, with viral video, we think of every speech as written and delivered for posterity.

To see what we mean, just look on YouTube for Howard Dean's scream or Phil Davison who delivered a memorable speech in 2010 while running for local office. They are both still a click away and will be forever.

But here's what hasn't changed.

Political speeches are as important as ever because they exist to further ideas—ideas that people believe in deeply and passionately. Meanwhile, structure, imaginative language, moving anecdote, wit, and support are still the tools that persuade audiences to believe, too.

Whether Bob and I are writing for others or, as in this book, writing for readers, what we do grows out of the same passion for ideas.

Are our ideas right? It is entirely possible that we are as wrong as the Cardinals who believed they were right as they excommunicated Galileo.

But when it comes to the material in this book—how we build arguments, how we make points memorable, how we appeal to audiences, how we write those speeches—those are important for people of every ideological stripe.

We once had a student, argumentative, aggressive, and highly partisan when it came to politics.

A few years later, one of us saw his name on the staff list of someone completely against everything he had said in class.

One of us emailed him. "Tony! Why are you working for her?"

The email came back. "Because of what I used to say? That was a youthful aberration!"

People may change their views. But politics, in the end, is not about whether a president had an affair or took a bribe. It is about whether people can find work, see a doctor, go to a good school, or get sent to fight a war. These issues endure.

And because of that, artfully composed, persuasive speeches remain an enduring custom of American political life.

Our students are not wrong to raise their hands on these first days of each semester. No matter their views, we want them to not just learn how to write good speeches, but believe they are worth the trouble.

As our students have taught us, since speeches matter so much to others, doing them well should matter to them, whether they do it for a year or a lifetime, for themselves or for others, to further ideas or stir emotion.

And that is why the privilege of writing this book means so much to us.

Eric Schnure

Appendix

A Speech for *Almost* Every Occasion

Almost every occasion?

So far, we've examined ways to use structures, language, anecdote, wit, or support in almost all political speeches. Still, each type of event has elements that make it unique. So here we examine some of the most common, equally balanced between Republicans and Democrats: stump; floor, including a short floor speech; rally; two kinds of keynotes, political and issue; commemorative; commencement; eulogy; awards; and roast.

Naturally, there are others. Politicians speak at hearings, fundraisers, and prayer breakfasts. They declare victory and concede defeat. They deliver inaugural addresses and speeches assessing the state of the union, state, or city. Most of what this book suggests can apply to those events as well.

Our purpose in this appendix is not to offer perfect speeches. Most have flaws. Neither is it to urge readers to slavishly follow these examples—not even the two your authors wrote.

But we offer them because they offer models writers new to these types can use.

For each kind, you will find a general discussion, along with some tips, including outlines, and a full-length example complete with Flesch-Kincaid stats.

We have also annotated each speech so you can see the techniques we suggest at a glance. Read them with an eye for what you can imitate—and what you can improve.

THE STUMP

The first record of this term appeared in 1840, but it was already a political tradition. Politicians would travel on horseback from town to town, jump up on a tree stump, and deliver their campaign speech. Then, back on the horse, they'd travel to the next town, find another stump, and give the same speech again.

Today, it means the speech politicians use over and over. Many resent it. How can you deliver the same speech four hundred times without getting bored? Sometimes, speakers suspect audiences may have heard it before, and they're bored too.

But politicians need stumps. Like rehearsing a play, endless repetition is precisely what allows them to deliver lines without thinking—and thus to concentrate on being expressive.

Sometimes people think stump speeches exist only for campaigns. Not true. Elected officials need them *in* office too. Plenty of appearances call for the same material. They also call for the modified version of Monroe's Motivated Sequence (MMS) detailed in Chapter 5. Winning *attention* through opening jokes, *acknowledging* local politicians, detailing *problem* and *solution*, using the inspirational example to *visualize* success, and *calling to action*—each meets needs that remain whether you're in a race or in office. Some tips:

- **Prepare with care.** Often, politicians allow stumps to develop haphazardly. That's a mistake. Finding the most compelling way to start, the most inspirational way to close, and the best examples for every point takes sitting down at a computer, thinking, talking, writing, and rehearsing. Stumps evolve, just as do all our plans. But let them evolve from a plan.

- **Work for audience response.** Stumps should be interactive. There is nothing that makes a speaker feel worse than a rally where the audience sits on its hands. Stumps are for times you want the crowd to interrupt. Whether in a campaign or at a keynote, speakers are energized by applause. Use the ways to make applause lines effective, yes. But even the most unimaginative applause line (*Isn't Joe great?*) works better than nothing.

- **Take advantage of audience anger.** If schedulers have done their job, politicians will almost always talk to friendly crowds. Political audiences are animated not just by love of their side but by hostility to the other. Applause lines come not just from what you're for, but from sarcasm and other ways to excoriate what you're against.

- **Leave one section—preferably at the end of the Solution section—for the special issues of this crowd.** Your basic issues should stay the same from group to group. But every group and every town has its own pet issue. Make sure you cover it, and in a way that leads to an applause line. It may be the loudest and longest of the night.

- **Customize.** Even if 90 percent of the speech stays the same, tailor it a little for every event. Howdahells are crucial; mentioning examples and real people important to the group carries weight. Don't make the audience think you're dialing the speech in.

Stump Speech Outline

Introduction

Opening joke (Often something barbed about the other side.)

Acknowledgments (The perfect place for crowd response.)

Howdahells

Serious attention-getter

Praise for the group (Remember to work for audience response.)

Statement of purpose (Reason you're there.)

Body

Record of accomplishment by party (The reminder of principles shared, accomplishments won. Common litany: *We're the party that* . . .)

Problems (Both failures by the other side and social problems. Common litany: *How can we be satisfied when . . . ?*)

Transition to solutions (*We have a different idea.*)

Solutions (Bills and policies you support, laced with startling statistics, anecdote, humor—and applause lines. Remember the special needs of the group. Common litanies: *We can . . . We must . . . We will . . .*)

Conclusion

Reflective section

Inspiration/vision of success

Lesson learned (A litany of things we can do if everyone works together. Common litany: *I believe we can . . .*)

Call to action (Another chance for audience response.)

Clincher (Remember referral endings and antithesis.)

MITT ROMNEY, NEW HAMPSHIRE STUMP, DECEMBER 20, 2011

Words: 2,079
Grade level: 8.6
Sentence length: 15.6 words
Passive: 4 percent

Thanks, you guys. Thank you so much for being here this evening.
I appreciate your coming out on a cold winter night as what seems like finally the beginning of winter in New Hampshire.

— Romney opens traditionally: thank-yous, a local reference—as governor of a neighboring state, he shows he understands about New Hampshire slopes.

(Continued)

(Continued)

They're going to start making snow at the ski resorts and get people from Massachusetts across the border to come up and ski on the slopes in New Hampshire.	
And I appreciate your willingness to spend a little time with me this evening.	
I want to talk about the choice that I think America is presented in the election of 2012.	Romney quickly gets to his statement of purpose: he will talk about choice.
And I want to have you give some thought to it, and we'll get a chance to talk more about this as the campaign goes on.	
Six months ago, as you know, I launched my campaign for the presidency not terribly far from here on a perfect day, **a** beautiful New Hampshire summer day.	
I spoke of an America in peril, under a president who had disappointed even his own supporters and was clearly failing.	He reminds listeners that his campaign started in their state and he was perceptive enough to see Barack Obama's failures: unemployment, poverty, lost homes.
Since then, as you know, the unemployment rate has remained stubbornly high.	
More Americans have lost their homes, and more Americans have slipped from the middle class into a world of poverty they never imagined they'd see.	
Our soldiers return from war unable to find a decent job.	
Over the last six months, I've traveled up and down New Hampshire and across the country.	
I've listened to anxious voices in town meetings, visited with students who are frightened by the magnitude of their college loans, but even more frightened by the lack of jobs.	
From break rooms to back offices, I've heard stories of The Great Obama Recession. Of families getting by on less, of long planned-for retirements replaced by two jobs at minimum wage.	Romney doesn't tell those stories. But he praises Americans for not giving up hope. He uses skillful antithesis ("yesterday" versus "tomorrow" . . . "long unemployment lines" versus "small dreams") to blame Obama.
It's a long litany of dreams deferred and economic stress that quickly become family stress. I've heard stories that frankly break my heart.	

But let me tell you what I rarely heard—hopelessness.
Even in these very difficult times, the worst economy since the Great Depression, I've found Americans refusing to believe that these troubled days are our destiny. Sometimes with pride, often with anger, I've heard time and again, a constant refrain: This is not the America we love.
This is not the America we deserve.
This is the America of yesterday, and we will not allow it to become the America of tomorrow.
We are Americans. And we will not surrender our dreams to the failures of this president. We are bigger than the misguided policies and weak leadership of one man. America is bigger than Barack Obama's failures.
This America of long unemployment lines and small dreams is not the America you and I love.
It is not a Live Free or Die America. These troubled years are President Obama's legacy, but they are not our future.

This is an election not to replace a president but to save a vision of America. It's a choice between two very different destinies.
Four years ago, many Americans trusted candidate Barack Obama when he promised to bring Americans together.
But now we've learned that President Obama's idea of bringing us together is not to lift us up but instead to use the invisible boot of government to bring us all down.
I have a vision of a very different America, an America united not by our limits but by our ambitions, our hopes, our shared dreams.
I am tired of a president who wakes up every day, looks out across America, and is proud to announce, "It could be worse."

He quotes the New Hampshire State motto, antithesis again (Obama's legacy vs. "our future," to return to his theme of choice).

Note Romney's skill with imagery. He doesn't just quote Obama but imagines him waking up, looking out across America, and announcing "It could be worse." While skillful, it is false. (Obama did ask listeners to imagine the alternative to his economic plans, but this description came from his critics.)

(Continued)

(Continued)

It could be worse? Is that what it means to be an American? It could be worse?

Of course not.

If I am president, I will wake up every day and remind Americans that not only must we do better but also that we can do better, because I believe in America.

President Obama boasts that he will "fundamentally transform" America. I want to restore America to our founding principles.

I believe that our founding principles are what made America the greatest nation in the history of the earth.

Among those core principles is what the founders called the "pursuit of happiness." We call that opportunity, or the freedom to choose our course in life. That principle is the foundation of a society that is based on ability, not birthright.

— Here, Romney moves to what he calls the central difference between him and Obama: a belief in merit versus entitlement. The speech would be better if he had direct quotes. He might have found a direct quote where Obama called for "equal outcomes." But notice the skill with which he uses parallel repetition ("equal opportunities" and "equal outcomes").

In a merit-based society, people achieve their dreams through hard work, education, risk-taking, and even a little luck. An opportunity society produces pioneers and inventors; it inspires its citizens to build and create. And these people exert effort and take risks, and when they do so, they employ and lift others and create prosperity. Their success does not make others poorer. It makes all of us better off.

President Obama sees America differently. He believes in an entitlement society.

Once we thought that "entitlement" meant that Americans were entitled to the privilege of trying to succeed in the greatest nation in the world. Americans fought and died to earn and protect that entitlement. But today, the new entitlement battle of this president is over the size of the check you get from Washington.

— In three short paragraphs, Romney mocks what he says is Obama's belief in ways popular with his audience: the size of government handouts; a play on JFK's famous line; and what he calls Obama's difference from Teddy Roosevelt.

President Obama has reversed John Kennedy's call for sacrifice. He would have Americans ask, "What can the country do for you?"

Just a couple of weeks ago in Kansas, President Obama lectured us about Teddy Roosevelt's philosophy of government. But he failed to mention the important difference between Teddy Roosevelt and himself. Roosevelt believed that government should level the playing field to create equal opportunities. President Obama believes that government should create equal outcomes.

In an entitlement society, everyone receives the same or similar rewards, regardless of education, effort, and willingness to take risk. That which is earned by some is redistributed to others. And the only people who truly enjoy real rewards are those who do the redistributing—government.

The truth is that everyone may get the same rewards under that kind of system, but virtually everyone will be worse off. President Obama's entitlement society would demand a massive growth of government. To preserve opportunity, however, we have to shrink government, not grow it.

Last month, I laid out specific solutions to the spending crisis we are facing, including the need to reform fundamentally Medicare for the coming generations. I'm very pleased to see that Wisconsin's congressman Paul Ryan got together with Democratic senator Ron Wyden of Oregon and pushed a similar Medicare reform package that I hope will save this very important and critical program.

— To demonstrate his own solutions, Romney mentions his view on Medicare reform and describes what he feels is bipartisan support for it.

But this is more than a spending crisis that we face. Even if we could afford the ever-expanding payments of an "entitlement society," it is a fundamental corruption of the American spirit.

The battle we face today is more than a fight over our budget; it's a battle for America's soul.

We can't begin to answer the question of who should be our next president until we start asking ourselves, "Who are we as Americans, and what kind of America do we want for our children?"

(Continued)

(Continued)

I know that my answers to those questions are very different than the current president of the United States.
President Obama has spent the last thirty-five months building a government so large that feeding it will consume a greater and greater share of our paychecks. And does anybody believe in America that they are better off than they were four years ago?
He pushed through Obamacare, an entitlement program we didn't want and we can't afford.

He's refused to advance a responsible plan to strengthen existing entitlements. Instead of fostering competition and choice, he's cultivating government dependence. President Obama talks about a country where everyone plays by the same rules, but when it comes to his favorite friends, he makes sure the rules don't apply.
He's given his supporters waivers exempting them from the burden of Obamacare. His NLRB [National Labor Relations Board] bullies businesses when they don't bow to union demands.
In the energy industry, he's picked winners—who by the way turned out to be the losers—like Solyndra.
That's how an entitlement society works, by the way—those in government control, those that have the resources and make the rules get to take care of their friends. And while the rest of us stand still, they make sure that their friends get ahead.
The result of President Obama's approach is a staggering list of failures.
It took eighteen tax increases just to get Obamacare off the ground.
Our growing welfare state is slated to cost $10.3 trillion over the next ten years—that's $72,000 a household. I will take a different path.

— He now he returns to Obama's failure and takes off the gloves using repetition—a litany of five "he's" to describe six specific examples of failure.

— A traditional stump speech approach first presents the other side's failures, then ticks off one's own plan. Whatever one thinks of Romney's ideas, don't ignore the skill with language: short sentences, language an eighth grader can understand, anaphora and a return to his mockery of "it could be worse."

First, I will repeal Obamacare. And you heard me say this before, on the first day as president, I will issue waivers from Obamacare to all fifty states.

And, I will strengthen Medicare by empowering the next generation of seniors to choose the solutions that are right for them. And I'll send Medicaid back to the states because the states know best how to serve their own citizens. My administration will create an environment where the private sector can thrive and where American businesses can reach their full potential. I'll reduce federal regulation, open up new markets to our goods, and fully exploit our energy resources. I'll cut taxes, cap spending, and finally, finally get America on track to balance our budget.

Now, this time next year, all the yard signs will have come down, hopefully. Town hall meetings will be about local budgets, not the defense budget or Medicare. It'll be safe to watch television again, at least for a little while. Americans will have made their choice. The path I lay out is not one paved with ever-increasing government checks and cradle-to-grave assurances that government will always be the solution. If this election is a bidding war for who can promise more benefits, that's a battle I'm not going to join.

This will be a campaign about the soul of America, about American greatness. I'm confident that Americans won't settle for an excuse like this: "it could be worse." I'm confident that Americans will refuse to be bought off by cheap promises that turn into never-ending debts for our children and grandchildren.

This is a time when we look beyond who we are today and ask who we will become tomorrow. — Another skillful use of antithesis, contrasting "today" with "tomorrow."

Not far from here, an idea called America was born. — In a state proud of its Revolutionary War history, Romney starts his Four Part Close by reminding listeners of that history and what it created.

(Continued)

(Continued)

It came in a moment when a peaceful people realized they could not continue on the same path. Those farmers and merchants, aristocrats, blacksmiths, they put aside their fears to take up arms against the greatest power in the world. There was not a single rational reason to believe they could succeed.

But they believed in God and they believed in themselves. They believed that the guiding force in their lives should not be fear, but rather a strong belief that life without freedom is slow death and an abiding conviction that they could build a better world.

That world is America.

Here in New Hampshire, in Iowa, South Carolina, Florida, Michigan—across the country—we are at the beginning of a democratic process that those early patriots risked all to secure for us. This is the moment when we reject failure and commit to make the disappointments of the past few years only a detour, not a destiny.

We believe in America.

We believe America can do better, because we believe in America.

And tonight, I ask each of you to remember how special it is to be an American. ——— He uses that inspirational example to draw a lesson for today.

I want you to remember what it was like to be hopeful and excited about the future, not to dread each new headline. When you spent more time looking for a house to buy than searching for a new job; when you spent more time thinking about a vacation with your family than how to make it to the end of the next paycheck.

That America is still out there. An America when you weren't afraid to look at your retirement savings or the price at the pump. An America when you never had to wake up to hear a president apologizing for America.

I say let's fight for that America. The America that brings out the best in each of us, that challenges us to be better and bigger than ourselves. ——— Having opened by telling them he has seen Americans willing to fight, he now asks his audience to fight . . .

This election, let's fight for the America we love.
Because we believe in America. ——— And ends memorably, stating the belief they share and the future they want.

Thank you so much. Great to be with you tonight. Thank you. Thanks, you guys.

THE FLOOR SPEECH

For 185 years, Americans had only one way to watch their representatives speak on the floor of the House and Senate: go in person, and sit in the gallery. But in 1977, House Speaker Tip O'Neill had an idea. Why not televise the sessions?

It wasn't popular with members. But after a three-month tryout, the House agreed to try. The Senate followed suit in 1986. And since then, anyone who wants to watch can tune in on C-SPAN.

It is not the most popular show on the air. The daily audience seems to be about thirty thousand. And no wonder. What happens is not exactly like the Jimmy Stewart histrionics in *Mr. Smith Goes to Washington*. Americans are more likely to see members milling around waiting to vote ("Clerk will call the role"). And the speeches are often, well, terrible.

Written in haste, floor speeches are the orphan children of the political speech world, and it is clear why.

First, floor speeches often deal with a specific solution—a bill, often long, written in the arcane language of legislation. Who writes them? Often staff aides whose strength is not language. It might seem like the only audience is legislators presumably familiar with the bill.

No. Actually, legislators can be the least important listeners. Floor speeches rarely change votes. By the time a bill is on the floor, both parties know almost to a person what the vote will be.

But floor speeches carry weight with secondary audiences: staffers who might pay attention to a neglected issue or interesting approach, reporters, and trade associations.

Floor speeches aren't all the same. There's a big difference between writing the short, often angry speeches that pass for debate in the House of Representatives and the longer, more measured addresses in a body whose members have to win support throughout an entire state. They differ too because they reflect the different personalities of the speaker and the importance of the issue.

That said, well-written and well-rehearsed floor speeches of every variety can attract attention and win influence far beyond their minimal effect on switching votes. Tips:

- **Make them brief.** Well, of course. Aren't we limited by debate? When that happens, everything gets compressed. A two-minute floor speech means you don't have room for story-jokes or detailed anecdote—though you can look for quips, quotes, and headlines to win attention. Not every speech has time limits, though. But even in the longer ones—permitted by special orders, for example—resist rambling on the floor for a long time; you can still get all the benefits you need in a short speech.

- **Fit them to an overall strategy.** Work with the leadership to create an approach not duplicated by everyone else on your side.

- **Make them quotable.** Too often, speakers think they've discharged their duty by appearing in the well and handing in the text for the *Congressional Record*. Resist! Reporters are listening.

- **Deliver them well!** Because politicians often speak to an empty chamber, they think they can read their speech without ever looking up. But people watch members of Congress on C-SPAN. Reporters are in the gallery. Even one or two rehearsals will make speakers able to look up so members of the TV audience think they're speaking to them.

- **Get mileage from them.** Put them in newsletters; quote the best lines in other speeches; and mail them to the reporters, supporters, and lobbyists who will like them.

Floor Speech Outline

Introduction

Attention step (*Brief* story illustrating the problem, solved by the bill up for a vote.)

Statement of purpose (What the general problem is and how the bill helps or hurts.)

Body

Problems (Both failures by the other side and social problems. Common litany: *How can we be satisfied when . . . ?*)

Solution (Bills and policies you support, laced with startling statistics, anecdote, humor—and applause lines. Remember the special needs of the group. Common litanies: *We can . . . We must . . . We will . . .*)

Conclusion (forty-five seconds)

Inspiration

Lesson learned (A litany of things we can do if everyone works together. Common litany: *I believe we can...*)

Call to action (Address to members.)

Clincher (Remember referral endings and antithesis.)

Finally, floor speeches done well do not have to be bombastic, arcane, or dull.

In January 2018, the House considered a bill about "partial birth abortion"—one that would have limited abortions to the first twenty weeks of pregnancy, on the grounds that at that point a fetus can feel pain.

Whatever one thinks about the merit of that bill, there is no question about the passion and sincerity of those who spoke. In this book, we have used excerpts from that debate. Here, we present the full version of two speeches to demonstrate how floor speeches create impact. Readers should notice how well the Monroe structure works for both, how concrete their language is, the effect of story, and many other techniques covered in this book.

SEN. JONI ERNST AND SEN. ELIZABETH WARREN ON PARTIAL BIRTH ABORTION, JANUARY 29, 2018

Words: 1,202
Grade level: 8.7
Sentence length: 17.3 words
Passive: 0 percent

Joni Ernst

Mr. President, I rise to urge each of my colleagues to support the Pain-Capable Unborn Child Protection Act. This critical legislation would prohibit a child from being aborted at five months of development.

Senator Ernst begins in the traditional way: a flat statement of purpose. But she has already won attention by coming to the well of the Senate with a visual aide: photos of fetuses at about twenty weeks.

For those we have watching today, I would like you to focus a little bit on these photos, and I will return to them in a moment.

Again, I am urging my colleagues to support the Pain-Capable Unborn Child Protection Act. By any measure, at five months of development, an unborn child is a child.

(Continued)

(Continued)

At five months, babies have grown nails on their fingers and on their toes; hair has just begun to grow on their heads; and an ultrasound can tell an expectant mother or father whether their baby is a boy or a girl.	Ernst begins describing the problem through concrete detail, trying to make listeners see an "unborn child." Note that Ernst calls them "babies." By being so visual, she hopes listeners will find it impossible to avoid seeing their human traits.
These babies can detect light, hear sounds, they can swallow, and even experience taste as their taste buds grow and develop.	
These unborn babies in all ways are babies.	Having used eight details, she draws her conclusion: these are no less "babies" than they will be after delivery.
There is also significant scientific evidence that at five months **of** development these babies can feel pain. By five months, babies begin to respond to painful stimulus with distinctive pain response behaviors that are exhibited by older babies. They will scrunch their eyes, they will clench their hands, they pull back their limbs in response to pain, just like any other child experiencing pain.	Note the use of repetition; Ernst uses "they" three times and "these babies" three times, too. Now she shows the evidence that they can feel pain, using not just the physical, but expert testimony with a direct quote from a medical text. And do listeners think she is mistaken? Ernst offers a fact about what doctors actually do—and repeats herself.
There is also a great deal of evidence that stress hormone levels rise substantially when babies at this age are exposed to pain. In 2015, a Cambridge University Press medical textbook acknowledged that a "fetus . . . becomes capable of experiencing pain between twenty and thirty weeks of gestation."	
In fact, fetal surgeons routinely administer pain medications for babies after only four months of development. Doctors are giving babies pain medication after four months of development. As modern medicine has recognized, these babies are humans capable of experiencing pain. Yet there is no federal law protecting these vulnerable humans from abortions. As a result, every year in our country the lives of thousands of babies end painfully through abortion. This is unacceptable.	And now, having established what she believes—that these are no different from any infant, Ernst comes to the crux of the problem: we kill them.

The majority of men and women across the nation agree with this premise. According to a recent Marist poll, 6 out of 10 Americans surveyed support a law prohibiting abortion after five months of pregnancy.	As she moves to her solution, Ernst's structure is straight Monroe. She uses statistics taken from a poll; precedent, citing states that have prohibited abortions; and a story of a boy born at twenty weeks and now healthy.
Additionally, multiple states, including my home state of Iowa, have passed legislation that would prohibit abortions after five months of development because these babies are babies.	
There is no way to deny the humanity of these children when you consider stories like that of Micah Pickering.	Now, going into her Four-Part Close, she uses Micah, illustrating with pictures.
Micah is from Newton, Iowa. He is a very young friend of mine. He is five years old. Just a few weeks ago on the floor of the Senate I was able to share Micah's story. As you may recall, Micah was born at just twenty weeks postfertilization—the very point at which the Pain-Capable Unborn Child Protection Act would begin to protect these young lives.	
Today, Micah is a very happy, very energetic little five-year-old. Now, I would like to go back to these pictures.	
When I first met Micah, he was about three years old. He and his parents visited my office for the annual March for Life. I had this poster made of these pictures, and they were in my office because I was going to speak on the Senate floor in support of March for Life. Micah is pictured on the right side of the poster board. Micah, a happy, energetic little boy, saw this poster board in my office, and he ran up to it—imagine, this beautiful three-year-old boy—and he pointed not at the picture of himself as he was at three years old, but he pointed to this picture, and he said: Baby. I said:	
Yes, Micah, that is a baby.	
This is Micah when he was born. Micah at three years old understood that this was a baby. He didn't understand that was him when he was born, but he understood that was a baby.	

(Continued)

384   The Political Speechwriter's Companion

(Continued)

If you look at the picture, you will see Micah is grasping his mama and daddy's hands with five perfectly formed little fingers on each hand. It is a baby, folks. Micah knew that. While he might not have known that was him when he was born, he knew that was a baby—five months of gestation. Today, Micah is a happy, extraordinarily healthy young boy. I got to see him again this last year. Again, he was running around my office, just full of energy and life.

Yes, Micah, this is a baby. I agree.

Micah's story is not an isolated incident. Extraordinary stories of babies who are surviving after just five months of development can be found all around the world.   — Having moved listeners with story, Ernst wants to make sure we know this isn't an isolated incident. She gives us more examples, bolstering it with statistics. So far, she has used statistics, story, and expert testimony.

A little over a year ago, Dakota Harris was born in Ohio at nineteen weeks of development—even younger than Micah. Last May, she left the hospital with her family as a healthy seven-pound baby.

In 2016, Baby Aharon was born at twenty weeks of development, becoming the youngest premature baby to survive in Israel. After five months of care at a hospital in Tel Aviv, he was able to go home, again, as a healthy baby.

In 2010, Frieda Mangold, who was born in Germany at just under twenty weeks of development, became Europe's youngest premature baby to survive. After receiving intensive care, she too was able to go home with her family as a happy seven-pound baby.

Babies have been on record as surviving birth after just five months of development for three decades now—three decades.

What greater evidence do you need that at five months of development, an unborn child in every way is a child?   — Ernst draws the lesson she has learned.

Despite the clear evidence of the humanity of these children, the United States is one of only seven countries in the world to allow abortions after five months of development. That means   — Evidence that the United States is isolated from the rest of the world.
that while an overwhelming majority of the world recognizes and protects the humanity of these vulnerable children, the United States keeps the company of countries like China and North Korea. They deny unborn children the most basic of protections. This is not who we are as a nation.

It is time we listen to the scientific evidence, the men and women across America, and a majority of the rest of the world. There should be no disagreement when it comes to protecting the life of an unborn child who can feel pain and, as the inspiring stories of Micah Pickering and others show, survive outside of the womb. ——— Important to realize is that there is actually furious disagreement about this issue. By using "should" in her call to action, Ernst does not distort her argument.

It is up to us to ensure these children have the chance to grow up and lead the happy, healthy lives that God has granted them.

As a mother and a grandmother, I am urging my colleagues to support the Pain-Capable Unborn Child Protection Act, which recognizes these unborn babies as the children they are and provides them the same protection from pain and suffering that all of our children deserve.

For my dear little friend Micah, I would say: ——— Her clincher, in which she tries to move us by speaking to Micah, is a skillful use of the referral ending discussed in this book.
Yes, Micah, this is a baby, and we are glad to have you here. God bless him.

I yield the floor.

Elizabeth Warren

Words: 1,262
Grade level: 9.5
Sentence length: 16.7 words
Passive: 0 percent

Mr. President, I want to thank the senior senator from Washington for her leadership on this important issue and for gathering women to come to the floor today to talk about the Republican bill that has been proposed and that we will be voting on soon.

——— Note that Senator Warren is thanking not Ernst but Senator Murray (D-WA) before winning attention.

When I was a girl growing up in Oklahoma, women got abortions. Make no mistake, abortions were illegal back then, but women got them. Desperate women turned to back-alley ——— butchers, and some even tried the procedure on their own, using coat hangers or drinking turpentine. Some were lucky, but some weren't. Some women bled to death. Some died of infection. Some were poisoned. And they all went through hell.

Like Ernst, Warren uses a series of short sentences using concrete detail. Unlike Ernst, she describes not a fetus but women who got abortions when it was available. Still, her method is very similar: six separate images of abortions using coat hangers or turpentine, and three sentences using repetition beginning with "Some." Her language is grittier, and the tone, bitter ("they all went through hell").

(Continued)

Appendix 385

(Continued)

In 1973, the Supreme Court stepped in. Forty-five years after *Roe v. Wade*, abortions are safer than getting your tonsils out. A lot of women are alive today because of *Roe*. Nearly 70 percent of Americans agree, *Roe v. Wade* is worth celebrating.

I wish I were here today to acknowledge the impact of *Roe*. Instead, I am here to defend it from attack.

Last week President Trump marked the anniversary of *Roe v. Wade* by calling for a ban on a rare category of abortions—ones that take place after twenty weeks of pregnancy. So today, the Senate is voting on a bill to do exactly that.

Let's be honest about why this vote is happening now. Today's vote is happening because politicians who have never been pregnant, who have never had an abortion, who have never had to make a wrenching decision after learning that the child they are carrying will not survive childbirth—those politicians want to score political points at the expense of women and their families.

We are having this vote today because President Trump asked for it.

If it passes, this unconstitutional bill would put women's lives and women's health at risk.

Government officials who seek to insert themselves between women and their doctors ought to listen to the women whose lives are on the line and the doctors who care for them. If they were listening right now, we wouldn't be holding this vote.

Only 1 percent of abortions take place at twenty-one weeks or later, and the reasons are heartbreaking. I have heard from people across Massachusetts who shared their devastating stories. The Senate should hear these stories.

One woman who wrote to me explained that she was ecstatic to have a second child but learned late in her pregnancy that her daughter's brain was severely malformed. She said,

---

Like Ernst, Warren is not content with generalities. She uses statistics (unsourced) before a statement of purpose.

Like Ernst, Warren states her problem. But while Ernst is content to simply assert these "babies" have no protection, Warren attacks the motives and ignorance of those on the other side, accusing them of trying to "score political points." She also suggests supporters of the bill should listen to those "whose lives are on the line."

And now, like Ernst, Warren uses story to put the human face on tragedy. She uses direct quotes, and many examples.

> Being a grown woman with a husband and daughter, I never imagined that I would need to [get an abortion]. But when I learned that the baby I was carrying suffered from a set of severe brain malformations, I faced a binary choice for her: peace or life. . . . I am deeply grateful that I was able to give her the gift of peace.

She and her husband did what they thought was best for their baby girl. They got an abortion in the third trimester.

Another couple chose to get an abortion at twenty-two weeks, after learning that their son's heart would never fully develop. The husband wrote to me:

> His pulmonary veins did not connect to his heart in the right place. He had ventricular septal defect, an atrial septal defect . . . and the left side of his heart was smaller than his right. . . . We hoped to be eligible for in-utero heart surgery, but our fetal cardiologists told us that our son's heart could not be fixed. Our little boy—our miracle—wasn't going to make it.

He described their choice as an act of mercy. He said:

> My wife and I are both pro-life, and we would never encourage an abortion. [But] there isn't a day that I regret what we did because we both believe our child is watching over us from a safer place. There also isn't a day I wonder who else could possibly understand what we went through. No law can save my child from his complex congenital heart disease, or save my wife from her suffering.

But the bill we are voting on today says that the government should have been part of that decision—no, not just part of that decision. It would have allowed the government to make that decision, instead of leaving the choice to these brokenhearted parents.

(Continued)

(Continued)

The bill we are considering today would ban all abortions after twenty weeks, with only limited exceptions. It would force women to carry an unviable fetus to term. It would force women with severe health complications to stay pregnant until their lives were on the line. Whatever you believe about abortion generally, this legislation is dangerous and cruel. Devastating fetal abnormalities aren't the only reason women get abortions after twenty weeks. Some women face so many delays when seeking an abortion, like finding a provider, raising money for the procedure, and paying for travel costs—so many delays that a procedure they wanted earlier in pregnancy gets pushed later and later. These logistical hurdles fall hardest on young people, on women of color, and on low-income communities.

What is behind some of these delays? State-level abortion restrictions pushed through by Republican legislatures that close down clinics and make it harder for women to get access to the care they need. You heard that right. Republican-sponsored abortion restrictions push women to have abortions later and later, and today, Republicans in the Senate push a bill to ban late abortions. It is all connected. This bill is only one part of a broad and sustained assault by Republican politicians on women's rights to make decisions about their own bodies. Through repeated efforts to limit birth control access, to defund Planned Parenthood, and to restrict abortions, Republicans are chipping away at women's health, women's safety, and women's economic independence.

> So far, Warren and Ernst have used very similar approaches, each skillful. But now, Warren turns personal and partisan, calling the bill part of "a broad and sustained assault" by Republican politicians.

If Mitch McConnell or Paul Ryan or Donald Trump actually wanted to reduce abortions, they could embrace policies that would lessen the economic pressures of pregnancy and of motherhood. They could act to help pregnant women and their babies access health care early and often. They could help young women avoid unwanted pregnancies in the first place.

> And as she moves to the solution, she presents solutions she wishes Republicans would embrace. Note that just as Ernst never rebuts the arguments that pro-choice people believe—that a fetus does not have the same rights as a baby will after birth—Warren does not rebut the assertions Ernst has made: that they have an equal claim to life.

Instead, they have spent the last year doing exactly the opposite. They have held vote after vote to try to gut the Affordable Care Act and Medicaid, when we should be expanding those programs. Affordable health care, accessible contraceptives, and other programs that support working women and families are all under attack. And today, Republican politicians want to distract from their hypocrisy with an unconstitutional twenty-week abortion ban—one that will not pass, that ignores the actual experiences of women, and would cause enormous harm if it were signed into law. Today's vote, which we all know will fail, isn't about policy; it is about political theater. But women don't get abortions to prove a political point. Reproductive rights are about health. They are about safety. And this particular vote about banning abortions at twenty weeks is about a bunch of politicians intruding on one of the most wrenching decisions that a woman will ever make.

It has been forty-five years since *Roe v. Wade*; forty-five years since women gained the constitutional right to a safe, legal abortion; forty-five years since the days of illegal abortions. I have lived in that America. I have lived in the world of back-alley butchers and wrecked lives. And we are not going back—not now, not ever.

Thank you. I yield the floor.

> Warren does not use the Four-Part Close. She does, though, use a referral ending—and a call to action.

The Short Floor Speech

Floor speeches are not all alike. They can be as short as a minute and as long as a filibuster. We opened with two midsize ones that took place in the passionate debate early in 2018. We end with one from twenty years earlier, 1998, illustrating the role of short speeches.

This one, by then congressman Dick Durbin (D-IL), is not part of the long-standing U.S. House of Representatives tradition that allows one-minute speeches just after the House goes into session. It is forty-five seconds longer. Nor is it about a policy being debated in Congress. It's about, of all things, wooden baseball bats.

But we include it here for several reasons. First, it demonstrates an important principle: Effectiveness is by no means limited to a slavish imitation of Monroe. There is always room for creativity. Second, even if on first glance the speech doesn't conform exactly to Monroe, it does follow the common format of floor speeches, including many of the elements covered in the previous pages. Third and finally, if a speech is so skillful and witty that people still talk about it twenty years later, we think it's worth sharing.

DICK DURBIN, 2010

Words: 260
Grade level: 7.7
Sentence length: 16.2 words
Passive: 0 percent

Mr. Speaker, I rise to condemn the desecration of a great American symbol. No, I am not referring to flag burning; I am referring to the baseball bat.	Durbin grabs attention by using antithesis (not this, but that) and parallelism (referring to), as well as the element of surprise. He evokes a sense of urgency talking about a "great American symbol," and then states his purpose when he reveals what that symbol is, "the baseball bat."
Several experts tell us that the wooden baseball bat is doomed to extinction, that major league baseball players will soon be standing at home plate with aluminum bats in their hands. Baseball fans have been forced to endure countless indignities by those who just cannot leave well enough alone.	Now, Durbin introduces the problem—the threat posed by modernization to wooden baseball bats.
Designated hitters, plastic grass, uniforms that look like pajamas, chicken clowns dancing on the baselines, and of course the most heinous sacrilege, lights in Wrigley Field.	Durbin uses brief but concrete examples to illustrate the indignities mentioned above.
Are we willing to hear the crack of a bat replaced by the dinky ping? Are we ready to see the Louisville Slugger replaced by the aluminum ping dinger? Is nothing sacred?	He asks a litany of witty, rhetorical questions that Durbin complements with vivid ("crack of the bat") and colloquial ("ping dinger") language.
Please, do not tell me that wooden bats are too expensive when players who cannot hit their weight are being paid more money than the president of the United States.	Durbin uses repetition, but this time to refute the other side. He also uses irony to makes his point—that millionaire athletes, or those who pay them, shouldn't cry poor.
Please, do not try to sell me on the notion that these metal clubs will make better hitters.	

What is next? Teflon baseballs? Radar-enhanced gloves? I ask you.	Durbin begins his visualization by rhetorically asking the audience to consider failure, a sport so changed by technology it becomes unrecognizable. In a more serious speech, we might consider this an example of the Slippery Slope fallacy. In this instance, it elicits a laugh and only reinforces the speaker's love of the game.
I do not want to hear about saving trees. Any tree in America would gladly give its life for the glory of a day at home plate.	Having presented what might happen if we don't act, Durbin now imaginatively contrasts that with the more traditional visualization step of showing success. The idea of a tree proud (personification) because it will one day be a bat is absurd, witty—and memorable.
I do not know if it will take a constitutional amendment to keep the baseball traditions alive, but if we forsake the great Americana of broken-bat singles and pine tar, we will have certainly lost our way as a nation.	Throughout the speech, the solution, save wooden bats, is implied. In his clincher, Durbin kiddingly suggests one however unlikely call to action. He also, in a referral to his opening, makes a bigger point: that this is not only about baseball bats but a way of life.

THE RALLY

Martin Luther King Jr.'s "Dream," probably the most celebrated speech of the twentieth century, was written for a rally: the 1963 March on Washington. But, of course, its influence makes it transcend any one category.

What gives it that stature?

It certainly wasn't language alone, some of which is ponderous. It wasn't just the moment: a rally dramatizing—King's word—the racism of American life; there were dozens of speakers that day. Hardly anyone remembers what they said. Originality? We have already pointed out how much came from others.

Was it King's sonorous voice? His national reputation? We resist the temptation to answer. More important is to look at the speech analytically. For those who look for ways to write a rally speech, such a step offers a lot. Some suggestions:

> **Rally speeches should be interactive.** Thousands of people massed in a stadium or on the Washington Mall don't want to stand there, silent. King used about twelve minutes of text—he got applause about twenty-five times adding about four minutes to the speech.

They thrive on repetition. The device that allows speakers to build toward applause. One way to look at King's approach: while the speech is classic Monroe, he builds it around six moments that use extraordinary litanies of what readers know is anaphora.

They are meant for urgent situations. Organizers don't hold rallies about pork-barrel legislation. Rallies are passionate.

The King speech meets those tests. It uses many of the devices that evoke response in addition to repetition: structure, imagery, and familiar quotations. For those who watch this speech, note King's unrushed effectiveness at both pause and emphasis.

We can look at this speech for why we watch it after a half-century. Here we look at it for the ways it uses rhetoric we can use in rally speeches of our own. Some tips for those:

- **Acknowledgments.** The fewer, the better. Rallies have many speakers. The quicker speakers get to the point, the happier listeners will be. King uses none.

- **Praise.** Appropriate for those who are there—and for the solutions that rally speakers will urge, hoping for applause.

- **A problem section.** Vital. Whether racial injustice, immigration, sexual abuse, or presidential campaigns, rallies draw crowds not only to support good things but because listeners are angry at what's wrong. The cliché in politics is that rally crowds want red meat. Rally speakers should provide it.

- **Solutions.** Yes, and not only in one section. It's common for rally speeches to have several alternating sections of problem and solution.

- **A call to action.** Yes, often stressing partnership, since a crowd may include people who don't agree on everything.

- **Simple language.** Barack Obama would normally speak at about an eighth-grade level. For rallies? Fifth grade. Other points about language:

  o **Use concrete detail.** Don't describe problems in general terms, like "injustice." Note King's approach: signs that say "For Whites Only."

  o **Use repetition.** From the moment King begins four sentences in a row with "Now," repetition is essential to response.

○ **Rhetorical questions.** Do you want an audience to respond? Questions do that. King uses only one. But it allows him to answer in one of his most memorable ways.

Outline

Not every rally has the dimensions faced by King in 1963. This outline includes elements he didn't need. But you might.

Attention

Win immediate attention and, if with story, make it brief. Aim for applause with the first sentence.

Move swiftly to your statement of purpose, aiming for applause again.

Praise

Salute the record of accomplishment by party or group, aiming for applause. That might include the reminder of principles shared or accomplishments won. (One common litany: *We're the party that* . . . [for political]; *You're the ones who* . . . [for nonpolitical].)

Problems

Use failures by the other side and social problems with no one cause. Be concrete. Don't say, "We have seen families separated by executive order." Say, "We have seen children ripped from a mother's arms and sent to prison cells alone. Is that what we want?"

Solutions

Don't be satisfied with the abstract ("We need comprehensive immigration reform"). Tie solutions to startling statistics, anecdote, and memorable language ("We need to protect our borders and a path to citizenship"). Remember the special needs of the group. (Common litanies: *We can . . . We must . . . We will . . .*)

Conclusion

Inspiration. Use a litany of brief examples, aiming for applause each time.

Lesson learned. Litany of things we can do if everyone works together. (Common litany: *I believe we can . . .*)

Call to action. Don't stop with three. Let the applause build.

Clincher. Make it the line everyone will remember most.

MARTIN LUTHER KING JR., 1963 MARCH ON WASHINGTON

Words: 1,668
Grade level: 8.6
Sentence length: 18.5 words
Passive: 8 percent

I am happy to join with you today in what will go down in history as the greatest demonstration for freedom in the history of our nation.

Five score years ago, a great American, in whose symbolic shadow we stand today, signed the Emancipation Proclamation.

> King wins attention with a historical reference (Lincoln signing the Emancipation Proclamation), then four images: "beacon light ... seared in the flames" and antithesis contrasting "daybreak" and "night."

This momentous decree came as a great beacon light of hope to millions of Negro slaves who had been seared in the flames of withering injustice. It came as a joyous daybreak to end the long night of their captivity.

But one hundred years later, the Negro still is not free.

One hundred years later, the life of the Negro is still sadly crippled by the manacles of segregation and the chains of discrimination.

One hundred years later, the Negro lives on a lonely island of poverty in the midst of a vast ocean of material prosperity.

One hundred years later, the Negro is still languished in the corners of American society and finds himself an exile in his own land.

> He then quickly uses imagery again to tell listeners the Negro is not free: "manacles ... chains ... the lonely island of poverty," and "exile in his own land."

And so we've come here today to dramatize a shameful condition.

> Statement of purpose: Note his key word. He has not come to inform or persuade. The crowd has come to "dramatize."

In a sense, we've come to our nation's capital to cash a check. When the architects of our republic wrote the magnificent words of the Constitution and the Declaration of Independence, they were signing a promissory note to which every American was to fall heir.

> Drawing no applause, this is an image critics have called one of the weaker moments in the speech. King uses a metaphor comparing the Constitution to a promissory note.

This note was a promise that all men, yes, black men as well as white men, would be guaranteed the "unalienable Rights" of "Life, Liberty and the pursuit of Happiness." It is obvious today that America has defaulted on this promissory note, insofar as her citizens of color are concerned. Instead of honoring this sacred obligation, America has given the Negro people a bad check, a check which has come back marked "insufficient funds."
But we refuse to believe that the bank of justice is bankrupt.
We refuse to believe that there are insufficient funds in the great vaults of opportunity of this nation. And so, we've come to cash this check, a check that will give us upon demand the riches of freedom and the security of justice.

> Here, King begins using one of the six sections using repetition. Two sentences open with "We refuse." In the next paragraph, four begin with "Now." Listeners have applauded before. Here, they interrupt with applause, three times before he is done.

We have also come to this hallowed spot to remind America of the fierce urgency of Now. This is no time to engage in the luxury of cooling off or to take the tranquilizing drug of gradualism.
Now is the time to make real the promises of democracy.
Now is the time to rise from the dark and desolate valley of segregation to the sunlit path of racial justice.
Now is the time to lift our nation from the quicksands of racial injustice to the solid rock of brotherhood.
Now is the time to make justice a reality for all of God's children.
It would be fatal for the nation to overlook the urgency of the moment. This sweltering summer of the Negro's legitimate discontent will not pass until there is an invigorating autumn of freedom and equality. Nineteen sixty-three is not an end, but a beginning. And those who hope that the Negro needed to blow off steam and will now be content will have a rude awakening if the nation returns to business as usual. And there will be neither rest nor tranquility in America until the Negro is granted his citizenship rights.

> Note that in addition to repetition—alliteration and antithesis—King uses metaphor, as he does through the speech.

(Continued)

(Continued)

The whirlwinds of revolt will continue to shake the foundations of our nation until the bright day of justice emerges.

But there is something that I must say to my people, who stand on the warm threshold which leads into the palace of justice:

> Why does King feel this is so important? At a time when white Americans were angered by African American militants, King felt it necessary to emphasize his call for nonviolence in this *second* use of repetition.

In the process of gaining our rightful place, we must not be guilty of wrongful deeds. Let us not seek to satisfy our thirst for freedom by drinking from the cup of bitterness and hatred. We must forever conduct our struggle on the high plane of dignity and discipline.

We must not allow our creative protest to degenerate into physical violence.

Again and again, we must rise to the majestic heights of meeting physical force with soul force.

The marvelous new militancy which has engulfed the Negro community must not lead us to a distrust of all white people, for many of our white brothers, as evidenced by their presence here today, have come to realize that their destiny is tied up with our destiny. And they have come to realize that their freedom is inextricably bound to our freedom.

We cannot walk alone.

And as we walk, we must make the pledge that we shall always march ahead.

We cannot turn back.

There are those who are asking the devotees of civil rights, "When will you be satisfied?"

> Note how King uses a question he can answer with his "satisfied" litany, the third use of extended repetition, finishing with a quotation from Scripture.

We can never be satisfied as long as the Negro is the victim of the unspeakable horrors of police brutality.

We can never be satisfied as long as our bodies, heavy with the fatigue of travel, cannot gain lodging in the motels of the highways and the hotels of the cities.

We cannot be satisfied as long as the Negro's basic mobility is from a smaller ghetto to a larger one.

We can never be satisfied as long as our children are stripped of their self-hood and robbed of their dignity by signs stating "For Whites Only." We cannot be satisfied as long as a Negro in Mississippi cannot vote and a Negro in New York believes he has nothing for which to vote. No, no, we are not satisfied, and we will not be satisfied until "justice rolls down like waters, and righteousness like a mighty stream."

I am not unmindful that some of you have come here out of great trials and tribulations. Some of you have come fresh from narrow jail cells.

And some of you have come from areas where your quest—quest for freedom left you battered by the storms of persecution and staggered by the winds of police brutality. You have been the veterans of creative suffering. Continue to work with the faith that unearned suffering is redemptive.

Go back to Mississippi, go back to Alabama, go back to South Carolina, go back to Georgia, go back to Louisiana, go back to the slums and ghettos of our northern cities, knowing that somehow this situation can and will be changed.

Let us not wallow in the valley of despair, I say to you today, my friends.

— Fourth example. Again, no rule of three here. He might have been content to urge this return in a sentence, but King says "go back" no fewer than six times, speaking to African Americans in North and South.

— Visualization: We have already mentioned the fact that King's staff had prepared him a new ending for this speech. This is the moment where he discards their work, and returns in this fifth section using anaphora—and epistrophe—to the vision of the future he has performed often—and is the moment Americans remember most.

And so even though we face the difficulties of today and tomorrow, I still have a dream. It is a dream deeply rooted in the American Dream. I have a dream that one day this nation will rise up and live out the true meaning of its creed: "We hold these truths to be self-evident, that all men are created equal."

I have a dream that one day on the red hills of Georgia, the sons of former slaves and the sons of former slave owners will be able to sit down together at the table of brotherhood.

— Inspiration.

(Continued)

(Continued)

I have a dream that one day even the state of Mississippi, a state sweltering with the heat of injustice, sweltering with the heat of oppression, will be transformed into an oasis of freedom and justice.

I have a dream that my four little children will one day live in a nation where they will not be judged by the color of their skin but by the content of their character.

I have a *dream* today!

I have a dream that one day, down in Alabama, with its vicious racists, with its governor having his lips dripping with the words of "interposition" and "nullification"—one day right there in Alabama little black boys and black girls will be able to join hands with little white boys and white girls as sisters and brothers.

I have a *dream* today!

I have a dream that one day every valley shall be exalted, and every hill and mountain shall be made low, the rough places will be made plain, and the crooked places will be made straight; "and the glory of the Lord shall be revealed and all flesh shall see it together."

This is our hope, and this is the faith that I go back to the South with. ——— Lesson learned.

With this faith, we will be able to hew out of the mountain of despair a stone of hope.

With this faith, we will be able to transform the jangling discords of our nation into a beautiful symphony of brotherhood.

With this faith, we will be able to work together, to pray together, to struggle together, to go to jail together, to stand up for freedom together, knowing that we will be free one day.

And this will be the day—this will be the day when all of God's children will be able to sing with new meaning:

> My country 'tis of thee, sweet land of liberty, of thee I sing.
> Land where my fathers died, land of the Pilgrims' pride,
> From every mountainside, let freedom ring! ———

Call to action: Do we think King is done? It is the sixth of his key repetitive sections. Using the last three words of that hymn, he calls Americans to act eight times, harnessing each to a different place before moving into his clincher.

And if America is to be a great nation, this must become true.
And so let freedom ring from the prodigious hilltops of New Hampshire.
Let freedom ring from the mighty mountains of New York.
Let freedom ring from the heightening Alleghenies of Pennsylvania.
Let freedom ring from the snow-capped Rockies of Colorado.
Let freedom ring from the curvaceous slopes of California.
But not only that:
Let freedom ring from Stone Mountain of Georgia.
Let freedom ring from Lookout Mountain of Tennessee.
Let freedom ring from every hill and molehill of Mississippi.
From every mountainside, let freedom ring.
And when this happens, when we let freedom ring, when we let it ring from every village and every hamlet, from every state and every city, we will be able to speed up that day when *all* of God's children, black men and white men, Jews and Gentiles, Protestants and Catholics, will be able to join hands and sing in the words of the old Negro spiritual: *Free at last! Free at last! Thank God almighty, we are free at last!*

— Clincher: Almost shouting now, King tells us the result: freedom not just for African Americans but for "all God's children."

THE KEYNOTE

Musicians know that the key note—or ruling note—is a note in a piece of tonal music they play. In Bach's C Major Prelude, the key note is C.

In politics, a keynote speech strikes the ruling theme of the event, and there are mainly two types: political and issue-driven keynotes. For politicians, both kinds are essentially political. Whether speaking at a meeting of county Republicans or talking to the local business roundtable, politicians offer or imply the same message: vote for me.

That is not to say they are without their differences. Here we start with the basic elements of a political keynote.

The Political Keynote

Basically, a political keynote follows the format of an expanded stump. In addition to the Monroe steps, someone keynoting the big political dinners—

Jefferson–Jackson Day dinners for Democrats or Lincoln–Reagan Day dinners for Republicans—or, as printed here, a national political convention will include these elements:

- **Acknowledgments.** Sometimes called shout-outs, because you shout out each name, hoping to generate applause. (*And isn't it great to see Janet Smith, who has fought so hard for . . . ?*)
- **Praise.** For the party and for the achievements of people in the audience.
- **A problem section.** Consisting of an extensive list of failures of the other party over a wide range of subjects.
- **Solutions.** Ending memorably enough to generate applause.
- **A call to action that ends in specific action.** Writing checks, taking yard signs, or working on Election Day.
- **Audience interaction.** Questions designed to elicit reaction. (*Has there ever been an administration more unwilling to face X?* Audience: *No!*) Remember: these are often red-meat affairs.

Political Keynote Speech Outline

Introduction

Opening joke (Often something barbed about the other side.)

Acknowledgments

Howdahells

Praise for the group

Serious attention-getter

Statement of purpose

Body

Record of accomplishment by candidate, party, or group (The reminder of principles shared, accomplishments won. Common litany: *We're the party that . . .* [for political]; *You're the ones who . . .* [for nonpolitical].)

Problems (Both failures by the other side and social problems. Common litany: *How can we be satisfied when . . . ?*)

Solutions (Bills, policies. Candidates you support, laced with startling statistics, anecdote, and humor-and-applause lines. Remember the special needs of the group. Common litanies: *We can . . . We must . . . We will . . .*)

Conclusion

Reflective section

Inspiration

Lesson learned (Litany of things we can do if everyone works together. Common litany: *I believe we can . . .*)

Call to action (Another chance for audience response.)

Clincher

In this 2016 Democratic National Convention speech, penned by her longtime speechwriter Sarah Hurwitz, Michelle Obama conforms to the Monroe Motivated Sequence (attention, need, satisfaction, visualization, and call to action) with two differences from the classic model.

First, she merges her problem and solution steps, offering two problems: (1) choosing the right president and (2) choosing the nominee who would best help children. In both cases, her solution is the same: Hillary Clinton.

Second, rather than simply moving into visualization and call to action, Obama does what has become increasingly popular in politics, a Four-Part Close: she stops for an inspirational example—and the lesson we should learn from that—before moving to her call to action and clincher.

MICHELLE OBAMA, 2016 DEMOCRATIC NATIONAL CONVENTION

Words: 1,555
Grade level: 9.4
Sentence length: 23.2 words
Passive: 1 percent

Thank you all. Thank you so much.
You know, it's hard to believe that it has been eight years since I first came to this convention to talk with you about why I thought my husband should be president. Remember how I told you about his character and conviction, his decency and his grace—the traits that we've seen every day that he's served our country in the White House.

Michelle Obama begins her attention step not only by thanking the audience members but by praising them (and her husband). She does so by talking about a shared journey—reminiscing

(Continued)

(Continued)

I also told you about our daughters—how they are the heart of our hearts, the center of our world. And during our time in the White House, we've had the joy of watching them grow from bubbly little girls into poised young women—a journey that started soon after we arrived in Washington, when they set off for their first day at their new school.

I will never forget that winter morning as I watched our girls, just seven and ten years old, pile into those black SUVs with all those big men with guns.

about her speech eight years ago and implying what was possible because of the audience's support.

Obama then moves into a story about her daughters. She uses concrete detail, self-deprecating humor, and colloquial language to provide an image and win attention.

And I saw their little faces pressed up against the window, and the only thing I could think was "What have we done?"

See, because at that moment, I realized that our time in the White House would form the foundation for who they would become, and how well we managed this experience could truly make or break them. That is what Barack and I think about every day as we try to guide and protect our girls through the challenges of this unusual life in the spotlight—how we urge them to ignore those who question their father's citizenship or faith. How we insist that the hateful language they hear from public figures on TV does not represent the true spirit of this country. How we explain that when someone is cruel, or acts like a bully, you don't stoop to their level—no, our motto is, when they go low, we go high.

With every word we utter, with every action we take, we know our kids are watching us. We as parents are their most important role models. And let me tell you, Barack and I take that same approach to our jobs as President and First Lady, because we know that our words and actions matter not just to our girls, but to children across this country—kids who tell us, "I saw you on TV; I wrote a report on you for school." Kids like the little black boy who looked up at my husband, his eyes wide with hope, and he wondered, is my hair like yours?

And make no mistake about it, this November, when we go to the polls, that is what we're deciding—not Democrat or Republican, not left or right. No, this election, and every election, is about who will have the power to shape our children for the next four or eight years of their lives. And I am here tonight because in this election, there is only one person who I trust with that responsibility, only one person who I believe is truly qualified to be president of the United States, and that is our friend, Hillary Clinton.

See, I trust Hillary to lead this country because I've seen her lifelong devotion to our nation's children—not just her own daughter, who she has raised to perfection—but every child who needs a champion: Kids who take the long way to school to avoid the gangs. Kids who wonder how they'll ever afford college. Kids whose parents don't speak a word of English but dream of a better life. Kids who look to us to determine who and what they can be.

Obama tells us why her solution will work. But she also uses sentence fragments (each beginning with "Kids") to offer more concrete detail about the problem.

You see, Hillary has spent decades doing the relentless, thankless work to actually make a difference in their lives—advocating for kids with disabilities as a young lawyer. Fighting for children's health care as First Lady and for quality child care in the Senate. And when she didn't win the nomination eight years ago, she didn't get angry or disillusioned. Hillary did not pack up and go home. Because as a true public servant, Hillary knows that this is so much bigger than her own desires and disappointments. So she proudly stepped up to serve our country once again as secretary of state, traveling the globe to keep our kids safe.

As evidence on why Hillary Clinton is the solution, Obama shares with the audience examples of not just Clinton's experience, but her character.

And look, there were plenty of moments when Hillary could have decided that this work was too hard, that the price of public service was too high, that she was tired of being picked apart for how she looks or how she talks or even how she laughs. But here's the thing—what I admire most about Hillary is that she never buckles under pressure. She never takes the easy way out. And Hillary Clinton has never quit on anything in her life.

And when I think about the kind of president that I want for my girls and all our children, that's what I want. I want someone with the proven strength to persevere. Someone who knows this job and takes it seriously. Someone who understands that the issues a president faces are not black and white and cannot be boiled down to 140 characters. Because when you have the nuclear codes at your fingertips and the military in your command, you can't make snap decisions. You can't have a thin skin or a tendency to lash out. You need to be steady, and measured, and well informed.

Obama now starts to define another problem. Using repetition ("Someone"), she shares what traits listeners should want to avoid in their next president.

(Continued)

(Continued)

I want a president with a record of public service, someone whose life's work shows our children that we don't chase fame and fortune for ourselves; we fight to give everyone a chance to succeed—and we give back, even when we're struggling ourselves, because we know that there is always someone worse off, and there but for the grace of God go I.	Then, using the litany of "I want," she describes the values a president should have.
I want a president who will teach our children that everyone in this country matters—a president who truly believes in the vision that our founders put forth all those years ago: that we are all created equal, each a beloved part of the great American story. And when crisis hits, we don't turn against each other—no, we listen to each other. We lean on each other. Because we are always stronger together.	
And I am here tonight because I know that that is the kind of president that Hillary Clinton will be. And that's why, in this election, I'm with her.	
You see, Hillary understands that the president is about one thing and one thing only—it's about leaving something better for our kids. That's how we've always moved this country forward, by all of us coming together on behalf of our children—folks who volunteer to coach that team, to teach that Sunday School class because they know it takes a village. Heroes of every color and creed who wear the uniform and risk their lives to keep passing down those blessings of liberty. Police officers and protesters in Dallas who all desperately want to keep our children safe.	To support this point, Obama asserts that (1) Clinton understands what's at stake: our children; and (2) we've always done right by our children.
People who lined up in Orlando to donate blood because it could have been their son, their daughter in that club.	
Leaders like Tim Kaine—who show our kids what decency and devotion look like.	A montage of examples, followed by a shout-out.
Leaders like Hillary Clinton, who has the guts and the grace to keep coming back and putting those cracks in that highest and hardest glass ceiling until she finally breaks through, lifting all of us along with her.	Obama ends the section with Hillary. But she includes more repetition, alliteration, and detail.
That is the story of this country, the story that has brought me to this stage tonight, the story of generations of people who felt the lash of bondage, the shame of servitude, the sting of segregation, but who kept on striving and hoping and doing what needed to be done so that today, I wake up every morning in a house that was built by slaves.	Rather than simply moving into visualization and call to action, Obama uses a Four-Part Close. She reflects with an inspirational example, using alliteration again to summarize the history of African Americans—including a startling example of her own life and that of her daughters.

And I watch my daughters—two beautiful, intelligent, black young women—playing with their dogs on the White House lawn. And because of Hillary Clinton, my daughters—and all our sons and daughters—now take for granted that a woman can be president of the United States.

So don't let anyone ever tell you that this country isn't great, that somehow we need to make it great again. Because this, right now, is the greatest country on earth. And as my daughters prepare to set out into the world, I want a leader who is worthy of that truth, a leader who is worthy of my girls' promise and all our kids' promise, a leader who will be guided every day by the love and hope and impossibly big dreams that we all have for our children.

So in this election, we cannot sit back and hope that everything works out for the best. We cannot afford to be tired, or frustrated, or cynical. No, hear me— between now and November, we need to do what we did eight years ago and four years ago: We need to knock on every door. We need to get out every vote. We need to pour every last ounce of our passion and our strength and our love for this country into electing Hillary Clinton as president of the United States of America.

Let's get to work. Thank you all, and God bless.

Then she tries to persuade by showing how Hillary Clinton and her candidacy fit into this story.

Lesson learned: listeners should have faith in America.

Now, she moves into her visualization step using a creative device that she and her husband have used before: imagining the world their daughter will grow up in.

Call to action: Obama uses a "we need" litany, urging listeners to reject cynicism and work for Clinton.

Clincher.

The Issues Keynote

In August 1992, a woman almost nobody knew came onstage at the Houston Astrodome during the Republican National Convention, and announced something nobody expected.

"I want your attention, not your applause," she said, without a smile. Then, she launched into a speech that—at first—made many listeners squirm.

The woman was Mary Fisher, daughter of a wealthy Republican fundraiser. At a time when Americans were horrified and repulsed by the AIDS epidemic, Fisher, married, with two young children, had the virus.

"Less than three months ago at platform hearings in Salt Lake City," she said, "I asked the Republican Party to lift the shroud of silence which has been draped over the issue of HIV and AIDS. I have come tonight to bring our silence to an end."

Major speeches at political conventions are always partisan—and always upbeat. Her speech dealt with an issue.

In deciding which speech to illustrate the "issues" keynote, we might have chosen from an infinite array of speeches aimed at more traditional groups: the Sierra Club, the Urban League, the NRA, or the NAACP.

We chose hers because it illustrates so much of what we urge about keynotes in the last few pages.

The main reason we chose it, though, is that, sensational as it was that night, it also illustrates something else: what is possible in politics when partisanship takes a back seat. Within a conventional structure—Monroe with a Four-Part Close—writing below a seventh-grade level, Fisher shows what speeches can do even with a hostile audience, using story, concrete detail, and statistics to both move and persuade.

She taught her audience a lesson. The way she and her writers did that carries lessons for us.

Issue Keynote Speech Outline

While the six elements we list here are the same as they are for a political keynote, here's what often looks different in the draft for an issue-driven one:

- **Acknowledgments.** Generally fewer, since politicians are less worried about insulting anyone. Since the atmosphere is a little less circuslike at conferences, they often aren't done as shout-outs.

- **Praise.** Here it is for the group, and sometimes the larger movement of which it's a part—as well as those in the audience.

- **A problem section.** Might involve a discussion of the issue itself, more background, and only a hint at the other party's failures in this one area.

- **Solutions.** Should still end memorably enough to generate applause—but about a much narrower range of issues. They often include a discussion of legislative prospects and announce support for a particular bill.

- **A call to action.** Much more likely to stress the theme of partnership—since the group may not agree with everything the speaker has done.

- **Audience interaction.** Less likely, but not unheard of, particularly for the crowd at nonprofit events who basically fall in one political camp—the Federalist Society for Republicans, for example, and Alliance for Justice for Democrats.

MARY FISHER, THE SHROUD OF SILENCE, 1992 REPUBLICAN NATIONAL CONVENTION

Words: 1,484
Grade level: 6.2
Sentence length: 15.2 words
Passive: 8 percent

Less than three months ago at platform hearings in Salt Lake City, I asked the Republican Party to lift the shroud of silence which has been draped over the issue of HIV and AIDS. I have come tonight to bring our silence to an end. I bear a message of challenge, not self-congratulation. I want your attention, not your applause.

I would never have asked to be HIV positive, but I believe that in all things there is a purpose; and I stand before you and before the nation gladly. The reality of AIDS is brutally clear. Two hundred thousand Americans are dead or dying. A million more are infected. Worldwide, forty million, sixty million, or a hundred million infections will be counted in the coming few years. But despite science and research, White House meetings, and congressional hearings, despite good intentions and bold initiatives, campaign slogans, and hopeful promises, it is—despite it all—the epidemic which is winning tonight.

— Fisher defies convention here: a blizzard of statistics without context. But she wins attention with the warning/problem most listeners would not yet know.

In the context of an election year, I ask you, here in this great hall, or listening in the quiet of your home, to recognize that AIDS virus is not a political creature. It does not care whether you are Democrat or Republican; it does not ask whether you are black or white, male or female, gay or straight, young or old.

Note two literary touches rare in politics but signaling seriousness: the contrast between the "great" hall and "quiet" homes; and the way she personifies a disease.

Tonight, I represent an AIDS community whose members have been reluctantly drafted from every segment of American society. Though I am white and a mother, I am one with a black infant struggling with tubes in a Philadelphia hospital. Though I am female and contracted this disease in marriage and enjoy the warm support of my family, I am one with the lonely gay man sheltering a flickering candle from the cold wind of his family's rejection.

Knowing how unsympathetic listeners were then to those with AIDS, Fisher rejects the notion that she is unique with two concrete images—not just an infant but one with tubes in a "Philadelphia" hospital; not just a lonely gay man but one "sheltering a flickering candle."

(Continued)

(Continued)

This is not a distant threat. It is a present danger. The rate of infection is increasing fastest among women and children. Largely unknown a decade ago, AIDS is the third leading killer of young adult Americans today. But it won't be third for long, because unlike other diseases, this one travels. Adolescents don't give each other cancer or heart disease because they believe they are in love, but HIV is different; and we have helped it along. We have killed each other with our ignorance, our prejudice, and our silence.

— And here Fisher breaks another rule of persuasion: praise your audience. Instead she blames her audience, not exempting herself ("our ignorance, our prejudice . . . ").

We may take refuge in our stereotypes, but we cannot hide there long, because HIV asks only one thing of those it attacks. Are you human? And this is the right question. Are you human? Because people with HIV have not entered some alien state of being. They are human. They have not earned cruelty, and they do not deserve meanness. They don't benefit from being isolated or treated as outcasts. Each of them is exactly what God made: a person; not evil, deserving of our judgment; not victims, longing for our pity—people, ready for support and worthy of compassion.

— Finally, note how Fisher uses repetition to remind listeners that AIDS victims are "not evil." Surveys during that period showed almost 30 percent of Americans were "angry" or disgusted" by victims, over 35 percent were afraid of them, and 20 percent of white Americans believed they got "what they deserved."

My call to you, my party, is to take a public stand, no less compassionate than that of the president and Mrs. Bush. They have embraced me and my family in memorable ways. In the place of judgment, they have shown affection. In difficult moments, they have raised our spirits. In the darkest hours, I have seen them reaching not only to me, but also to my parents, armed with that stunning grief and special grace that comes only to parents who have themselves leaned too long over the bedside of a dying child. With the president's leadership, much good has been done. Much of the good has gone unheralded, and as the president has insisted, much remains to be done. But we do the president's cause no good if we praise the American family but ignore a virus that destroys it.

— Fisher's solution does not involve detailed policy. Recognizing that she is at an RNC convention, she wins sympathy by reminding listeners she is a loyal Republican, admiring the views of President Bush.

We must be consistent if we are to be believed. We cannot love justice and ignore prejudice, love our children and fear to teach them. Whatever our role as parent or policy maker, we must act as eloquently as we speak—else we have no integrity. My call to the nation is a plea for awareness.

— Perhaps recognizing the folly of a specific proposal ("Support NIH research!"), she asks only for "awareness."

If you believe you are safe, you are in danger. Because I was not hemophiliac, I was not at risk. Because I was not gay, I was not at risk. Because I did not inject drugs, I was not at risk.	Awareness means awareness of the threat. Fisher uses repetition to remind listeners that the wealthy are not immune ...
My father has devoted much of his lifetime guarding against another holocaust.	
He is part of the generation who heard Pastor Niemöller come out of the Nazi death camps to say, "They came after the Jews, and I was not a Jew, so, I did not protest. They came after the trade unionists, and I was not a trade unionist, so, I did not protest. Then they came after the Roman Catholics, and I was not a Roman Catholic, so, I did not protest. Then they came after me, and there was no one left to protest."	... and a famous quote to remind them about the risk of staying silent.
The lesson history teaches is this: If you believe you are safe, you are at risk.	
If you do not see this killer stalking your children, look again. There is no family or community, no race or religion, no place left in America that is safe. Until we genuinely embrace this message, we are a nation at risk.	
Tonight, HIV marches resolutely toward AIDS in more than a million American homes, littering its pathway with the bodies of the young—young men, young women, young parents, and young children. One of the families is mine. If it is true that HIV inevitably turns to AIDS, then my children will inevitably turn to orphans. My family has been a rock of support.	
My eighty-four-year-old father, who has pursued the healing of the nations, will not accept the premise that he cannot heal his daughter. My mother refuses to be broken. She still calls at midnight to tell wonderful jokes that make me laugh. Sisters and friends, and my brother Phillip, whose birthday is today, all have helped carry me over the hardest places. I am blessed, richly and deeply blessed, to have such a family.	
But not all of you—but not all of you have been so blessed. You are HIV positive, but dare not say it. You have lost loved ones, but you dare not whisper the word *AIDS*. You weep silently. You grieve alone. I have a message for you. It is not you who should feel shame. It is we—we who tolerate ignorance and practice prejudice, we who have taught you to fear. We must lift our shroud of silence, making it safe for you to reach out for compassion.	At this point, people begin to pay attention. But now comes one of the most unusual passages in this speech: Fisher's willingness to sympathize with victims and criticize those many listeners who think people affected by HIV/AIDS "got what was coming to them."

(Continued)

(Continued)

It is our task to seek safety for our children, not in quiet denial, but in effective action.

Someday our children will be grown. My son Max, now four, will take the measure of his mother. My son Zachary, now two, will sort through his memories. I may not be here to hear their judgments, but I know already what I hope they are. I want my children to know that their mother was not a victim. She was a messenger. I do not want them to think, as I once did, that courage is the absence of fear. I want them to know that courage is the strength to act wisely when most we are afraid. I want them to have the courage to step forward when called by their nation or their party and give leadership, no matter what the personal cost.

— In one way, Fisher's approach is conventional: a Four-Part Close. The inspiration: her children. She names Max and Zachary and tells us about her hopes for them.

I ask no more of you than I ask of myself or of my children.

— Her lesson: what she asks of her children is what she asks listeners.

To the millions of you who are grieving, who are frightened, who have suffered the ravages of AIDS firsthand: have courage, and you will find support.

— Moving toward the end, she segments her audience—as JFK did in his inaugural—repeating "To" four times in a way that lets her build to her final sentence—a "referral" ending returning to the word she used in her very first sentence.

To the millions who are strong, I issue the plea: set aside prejudice and politics to make room for compassion and sound policy.

To my children, I make this pledge: I will not give in, Zachary, because I draw my courage from you. Your silly giggle gives me hope; your gentle prayers give me strength; and you, my child, give me the reason to say to America, "You are at risk." And I will not rest, Max, until I have done all I can to make your world safe. I will seek a place where intimacy is not the prelude to suffering. I will not hurry to leave you, my children, but when I go, I pray that you will not suffer shame on my account.

To all within the sound of my voice, I appeal: learn with me the lessons of history and of grace, so my children will not be afraid to say the word *AIDS* when I am gone.

Then, their children and yours may not need to whisper it at all.

— Fisher's powerful clincher doubles as an equally powerful visualization step.

God bless the children, and God bless us all. Good night.

THE COMMEMORATIVE SPEECH

It's a myth.

Abraham Lincoln did not scribble the Gettysburg Address on the back of an envelope. Schoolchildren don't commit to memory some last-second jolt of inspiration thought of in its entirety as Lincoln's train rolled north from Washington.

According to Pulitzer Prize–winning biographer David Herbert Donald, Lincoln "carefully reflected on his words," and thought about them for weeks.[1]

It worked. And it is worth dispelling another myth—that Americans ignored Lincoln's words. In fact, they got a fair amount of attention, though mostly along partisan lines. "The dedicatory remarks by President Lincoln will live among the annals of man," reported the *Chicago Tribune* in a review that must have seemed like hyperbole but turned out to be prophetic.

We leave others to determine where the Gettysburg Address ranks. Here, we offer it to introduce the elements of the commemorative speeches (tributes, memorials, anniversaries) that have become so commonplace in modern-day political life that we often refer to the job of president as consoler-in-chief.

Readers accustomed to seeing politicians delivering tributes in tragic moments—like a school shooting in Florida or a hurricane in Louisiana—might wonder how these speeches differ from eulogies. But politicians often pay tribute to people alive, sometimes sitting right onstage.

Such speeches help us remember historic events. Two examples: President Obama's speech in Selma, Alabama, on the fiftieth anniversary of Bloody Sunday (discussed in Chapter 11), and Ronald Reagan's speech on the fortieth anniversary of D-Day (discussed in Chapter 5). Readers will see that, yes, they console. But they also congratulate. Ultimately, they offer important context, sometimes making that explicit. As President Obama said in his "Bloody Sunday" speech, "There are places, and moments in America, where this nation's destiny has been decided . . . Selma is such a place."

Writing commemorative speeches begins with questions.

What does the speaking program look like? As with all events, we need to know who else is speaking and how long a speech should be.

What can we say that won't duplicate what anyone else says? That means coordinating remarks with others.

What does the honoree, if present, want said? Or want avoided? Speakers should not write a tribute in isolation.

But we must be practical. When Peggy Noonan set out to write the tribute we examine, she had no time to consult with anyone. There are other questions to ask:

What should we admire about the honoree?

What accomplishments do we want to include?

Is there a larger lesson from his or her work?

Whatever the answers, commemorative speeches should include a number of elements:

Anecdote: These speeches are about people and actual events. They are not the place for abstractions.

Concrete detail: This may mean stories about the person or people you celebrate. But it might also mean the detail we find in historical examples.

Colloquial speech: To move listeners, speakers need them to be understood.

Poetry: For centuries, writers have said moving things about others. Why ignore the great repository of eloquence?

Wit: Not always. But we encourage readers to look at others—the award speeches by Vice President Biden and Senator McCain at the Liberty Medal awards, which basically involve a tribute to each from the other, laced with wit.

The larger significance: Look for deeds that have broad significance and meaning and achievements that—even symbolically—have relevance to the audience.

The Commemorative Outline

Introduction: Often anecdotal to involve listeners right away. Story does that, and helps with what comes next.

   a. Characterize your subject, which might involve quotes from others, the speaker's own experience, or details from your subject's life.

Statement of purpose: A way to describe the importance of this tribute, often no more than a sentence.

Achievements: In a sense, this is a problem section. Often we honor those who have overcome obstacles. What were they?

Sadness: There are times, like the one we examine, where speakers are talking about a tragic death. If in a noble cause, that is worth talking about.

The larger point: Often speakers pay tribute not just to a life well lived but to an example set. What is the broader point your speaker might want to make?

The inspirational close: This is the moment when you want to make a point with eloquence.

Now we turn to a tribute more recent than Gettysburg: President Ronald Reagan's televised address to the nation after the Space Shuttle *Challenger* exploded shortly after launch in January 1986.

Written in just a matter of hours by Peggy Noonan, and mentioned in Chapter 17, the speech's intent is to reassure. It offers comfort in the aftermath of a horrifying event witnessed by millions. But Noonan and Reagan don't stop there. They provide an argument for why exploration matters and why it must continue. As the best commemorative speeches do, Reagan speaks about the event itself and offers condolences to those directly affected. But he also describes the larger context that helps people find meaning.

RONALD REAGAN, SPEECH AFTER THE *CHALLENGER* TRAGEDY

Words: 652
Grade level: 5.7
Sentence length: 13.1 words
Passive: 2 percent

Ladies and gentlemen, I'd planned to speak to you tonight to report on the state of the union, but the events of earlier today have led me to change those plans. Today is a day for mourning and remembering. Nancy and I are pained to the core by the tragedy of the shuttle *Challenger*. We know we share this pain with all of the people of our country. This is truly a national loss.

Nineteen years ago, almost to the day, we lost three astronauts in a terrible accident on the ground. But we've never lost an astronaut in flight. We've never had a tragedy like this.

Reagan grabs attention by reminding people that he was scheduled to deliver a different speech. The understatement that he had to "change those plans" creates suspense, even though the audience is well aware of the tragedy.

(Continued)

(Continued)

And perhaps we've forgotten the courage it took for the crew of the shuttle. But they, the *Challenger* Seven, were aware of the dangers, but overcame them and did their jobs brilliantly. We mourn seven heroes: Michael Smith, Dick Scobee, Judith Resnik, Ronald McNair, Ellison Onizuka, Gregory Jarvis, and Christa McAuliffe.

We mourn their loss as a nation together.

For the families of the seven, we cannot bear, as you do, the full impact of this tragedy. But we feel the loss, and we're thinking about you so very much. Your loved ones were daring and brave, and they had that special grace, that special spirit that says, "Give me a challenge, and I'll meet it with joy." They had a hunger to explore the universe and discover its truths. They wished to serve, and they did. They served all of us.

— As he speaks directly to the families who lost their loved ones, Reagan uses repetition ("that special grace, that special spirit") and litany ("They had . . . They wished . . . They served").

We've grown used to wonders in this century. It's hard to dazzle us. But for twenty-five years, the United States space program has been doing just that. We've grown used to the idea of space, and perhaps we forget that we've only just begun. We're still pioneers. They, the members of the *Challenger* crew, were pioneers.

— Here Reagan puts this tragedy into the larger context of scientific discovery. By doing that, he goes beyond consolation to introduce a "problem": the need to explore, and thus need what the *Challenger* crew were: "pioneers."

And I want to say something to the schoolchildren of America who were watching the live coverage of the shuttle's takeoff. I know it's hard to understand, but sometimes painful things like this happen. It's all part of the process of exploration and discovery. It's all part of taking a chance and expanding man's horizons. The future doesn't belong to the fainthearted; it belongs to the brave. The *Challenger* crew was pulling us into the future, and we'll continue to follow them.

— As speechwriter Peggy Noonan rushed to start her draft, she heard that the president was worried about all the schoolchildren who had watched and that he wanted to speak to them. Here, using alliteration and antithesis ("future . . . fainthearted," "belongs . . . brave"), she makes those children part of the solution—that we must continue and "follow" the crew "into the future."

I've always had great faith in and respect for our space program. And what happened today does nothing to diminish it. We don't hide our space program. We don't keep secrets and cover things up. We do it all up front and in public. That's the way freedom is, and we wouldn't change it for a minute.

— Even in a tribute, Reagan can make a political statement. Reagan sees American openness as part of the way Americans can cope with the Challenger tragedy.

We'll continue our quest in space. There will be more shuttle flights and more shuttle crews and, yes, more volunteers, more civilians, more teachers in space. Nothing ends here; our hopes and our journeys continue. — Visualization.

I want to add that I wish I could talk to every man and woman who works for NASA, or who worked on this mission, and tell them: "Your dedication and professionalism have moved and impressed us for decades. And we know of your anguish. We share it."

There's a coincidence today. On this day three hundred and ninety years ago, the great explorer Sir Francis Drake died aboard ship off the coast of Panama. In his lifetime, the great frontiers were the oceans, and a historian later said, "He lived by the sea, died on it, and was buried in it." Well, today, we can say of the *Challenger* crew: Their dedication was, like Drake's, complete. — Reagan begins a Four-Part Close, using Sir Francis Drake as the inspiration.

Lesson learned. full and complete dedication to greatness.

The crew of the space shuttle *Challenger* honored us by the manner in which they lived their lives. We will never forget them, nor the last time we saw them, this morning, as they prepared for their journey and waved goodbye and "slipped the surly bonds of earth" to "touch the face of God." — Call to action.

Clincher. Speechwriter Peggy Noonan, while not conferring with Reagan about whether or not he knew the poem (she found out later that he did), included the final lines from a poem by World War II aviator John McGee.

Thank you.

THE COMMENCEMENT

Political life is contentious. One person's president is another's war criminal. We expect argument in political speeches. Commencements, though, are celebrations, where people who may disagree about politics celebrate together. They don't want to hear views that set their teeth on edge.

Does that mean speakers have to be bland? Not at all.

First of all, not all campuses are alike. Some schools may overwhelmingly share a speaker's views. Sometimes that's why the school invites them. What might be controversial elsewhere becomes the right approach there.

Most campuses, though, are mixed. When politicians speak at commencements, they should at least think about soft-pedaling views offensive to people who want to feel comfortable. Once in a while, it's possible to be celebratory and insightful without controversy.

And whether speakers are controversial or not, they usually conform to the traditional things commencement speakers are expected to do:

- Express thanks for the invitation and honorary degree (if there is one).
- Talk about some personal connection to the school, no matter how tenuous.
- Applaud the students and the school—and parents.
- Make a few serious points about something for which the school is known.
- Challenge the students to make the world better.
- Acknowledge the sadness of leaving the campus, but inspire them with a vision of what lies ahead.

Is there one reason commencement speeches are so unmemorable? Not really. These are the elements graduates need. What makes them unmemorable is that so many are abstract—the kinds of statements that could work on any campus. Five suggestions:

1. **Personalize.** Don't just mouth general words of praise. Look on the school's website to find some genuine accomplishments and people who illustrate them—especially in the graduating class. This will make it clear that the speaker cares about the event.

2. **Talk to people on campus.** Find out what's really going on. It will help make the draft relevant.

3. **Include stories involving classmates.** That is, if you talk about intellectual growth, relate it to a class others have taken, or to an event others have experienced.

4. **Provide a shock of recognition.** Find the concrete details graduates will recognize from their own experiences to make them feel your speech represents them too.

5. **Do all that in about ten minutes.** Students are listening. They—and certainly their parents—can be moved. But they're also eager to have the ceremony end.

Commencement Speech Outline

Introduction

Brief opening joke

Express thanks for invitation

Praise the students and parents

Attention step (Story or description of some personal connection with campus.)

Praise the school, using concrete examples

Statement of purpose (Often, the speaker will demonstrate conviction that these graduates can help solve what the speaker sees as the challenge of our time.)

Body

Problem (Graphic litany of some problems the world faces, including stories to illustrate.)

Solution (Specific support for the idea that these graduates can make a difference. As in any persuasive speech, lace this section with story, startling statistics, anecdote, and humor—and applause lines—but with examples from the school and student body.)

Conclusion

Inspiration (Again, often one that involves a connection to this campus.)

Lesson learned (A litany of things we can do if everyone works together.)

Call to action (Paint your vision of what these students can do.)

Clincher (Again, revolve your final sentence around something relevant to this campus.)

SEN. JOHN KERRY, KENYON COLLEGE, MAY 20, 2006

Words: 2,579
Grade level: 6.1
Sentence length: 12.8 words
Passive: 4 percent

Ohio was the last state to count ballots in the 2004 presidential election. Meanwhile, Kenyon, a small Ohio college, had only two voting machines for the campus. A campus that strongly supported Kerry, its students had waited in line to vote for hours. They and Kerry waited tensely for the results—which, when they came in, meant George W. Bush had won.

Thank you, Hayes. (Maybe afterward you can tell me what the dork bell is.)
Thank you, President Nugent.
President! Some people would do a lot for that title.

After his question for the student speaker introducing him, Kerry opens with a joke referring to the election result that brought him there.

Class of 2006—fellow survivors of November 2, 2004.

I'm happy to be here at this beautiful school ... which had my admiration long before that night when the country wondered whether I would win—and whether you would vote.

Your website has a profile of a very smart math major in the class of 2006. Joe Neilson. He said that once, after a statistics course here, he realized "the probability of any event in our lives is about zero."

"I probably spent a week," Joe said, "annoying my friends by saying: 'What are the odds?'"

Joe, what were the odds that we'd be linked by those long hours—not that I keep track —560 days ago?

And note that his next joke is self-deprecating. And rather than just saying he and Teresa were honored, he tries to make it meaningful by tying it to the political events in her life.

Like everyone that night, I admired the tenacity of Kenyon students.
But what you did went far beyond tenacity.

Appendix

My wife, Teresa, is honored by the degree you grant her, today. But she's also here because when you grow up in a dictatorship as she did . . . when you don't get a chance to vote until you're thirty-one . . . when you see your father voting for the first time in his seventies . . . you know what a privilege it is to cast a ballot. Through that long night, we in Massachusetts watched you in Gambier. We were honored. We were inspired. We were determined not to concede until our team had checked every possibility.

If you could stay up all night to vote, we could certainly stay up that next day to make sure your vote would count.

> He reassures the largely Democratic campus that he was aware of the effort the students had made.

We couldn't close the gap. I say to my supporters: I would have given anything to have fulfilled your hopes. Thank you for your faith in our campaign. . . .

And I thank those who cast a ballot for my opponent.

> But now he takes another, and necessary, step. He compliments Republicans. This is a crowd that includes both sides. It would be insensitive to slight either. Commencements are not the place to be partisan. While he can give them a mild dig, his tone is rueful.

I say to them: I wish all Republicans had been just like you at Kenyon—informed, willing to stand up for your views . . . and only 10 percent of the vote.

Actually, all of you, through your patience and good humor, showed Americans that politics matters to young people. I really do thank every student here.

And I want to thank someone who *isn't* a student.

> So far, he has said things listeners might expect him to know. Here, though, he surprises them—and a popular coach—with something they wouldn't expect.

Because at the meeting Hayes was kind enough to mention—and I did take notes—the alums made it clear how much they'd been influenced by great friends, great teachers.

(Continued)

(Continued)

Or a great coach. — The student introducing him mentioned that Kerry had assembled a group of ex-Kenyon students in D.C. to find out more about the school—and that he took his own notes.

I happen to know what it's like to be on a team before an important game. I know how crucial that last practice can be.

For the field hockey team, that November 2 was the last day before the Oberlin game. Winning meant getting into the league championship—and from there to the NCAAs.

So I can understand why players were upset after hours waiting in line at the polling place that afternoon. When Maggie Hill called her coach to ask if she should come back to practice—you'd expect the coach to say yes.

This coach had a different reaction. "I'll cancel practice," she said, "and I'm sending the whole team to vote."

In that one moment, she became a hero to me. It takes a big coach to know there are more important things than a big game.

So I'd like a *huge* round of applause for Robin Cash.

(Note: If applause goes on a long time, you — It did continue for a long time—and *might add: "Maybe I should stop here.")* started again when he included the Oberlin score.

Her values are the values of Kenyon. By the way, for parents who may not remember, Kenyon played brilliantly— and won that Oberlin game 3–zip.

Now—it's not as if seeing brilliance here is a surprise. Like everybody, I know that when you look at a résumé and see a Kenyon degree, you think, "Smart. Committed. Good writer."

And maybe, "Likes to see a lot of stars at night."

But there's more. The Kenyon alums were — Praising a school is a cliché in so eloquent about what it meant to be here, commencement speeches. By actually where all your friends live, study, and play quoting students, Kerry makes more along a one-mile path in a town surrounded of an impression—a lesson about the by **cornfields**. — importance of research.

"I came here on a cold, rainy October [day]," one of them said, "but after my interview I saw professors having coffee at the deli, and heard everybody so excited about the Tom Stoppard play they were putting on—and fell in love with the place."
"Intelligent conversation permeates the whole campus," someone else said.
Another one said—I don't think he was kidding—"Nobody gets drunk at Commencement."
We talked till I got dragged into an intelligence briefing from the White House. Believe me, I learned more at the Kenyon meeting.

Stories mean more in commencements than policy discussion. Students liked his next one because it describes a student putting down his dad—and because it bridges the opening to his problem section.

What they said sounded very familiar. And wonderful. Because there are other places where you can find a small community—where the bonds you forge will never dissolve. You can find it on a tiny boat in Vietnam's Cam Ranh Bay.
You can even find it in the Senate.
Someone described to me what it's like walking into Gund for dinner after your girlfriend breaks up with you. You see every single person staring to make sure you're all right. I thought, "Sounds like walking into the Democratic Caucus after that first New Hampshire poll."
The Kenyon grads in Washington didn't agree on everything. But they agreed that Kenyon is a place where you have the luxury of examining an issue not for whether it sounds good but for whether it is good.
Actually, one Kenyon parent told me something that bothered him. His son took Quest for Justice his first semester at Kenyon. That's not what bothered him. But, the class met early in the morning—and his son made every class. After years of pushing this kid to get out of bed, the father wanted to know, "What changed?"
His son said, "Dad, I could disappoint you. But not Professor Baumann."

(Continued)

(Continued)

And that brings up one of the things I want to talk about.

For the Election Day event that united us was a disappointment. There's no way around it. Even as we flew in over Columbus this morning, I was looking down at the Ohio landscape, thinking: we came so close. So what.

You cannot go through life without disappointment. No team, no politician, no writer, no scientist—*no* one avoids defeat. The question is: What do you do next? Here's what I think. —————— In campaigns, a problem section might be long, and deal with policy. Kerry wanted his to be more personal: coping with disappointment.

You pick yourself up and keep on fighting. Losing a battle doesn't mean you've lost the war. Whether it's a term paper, an experiment... or a race for president... you will learn from experience, and experience success.

That's important, because there are so many things to fight for. —————— He did not, though, want his solution to be abstract. He also had a competing need: reassuring students that though Kenyon is small he knows the achievements of its graduates. He mentions some—and suggests others that might lie ahead.

By that, I don't just mean the things we fight over in the halls of Congress. Kenyon produces graduates that produce our literature and drama—like E. L. Doctorow did with *The March*, fifty-four years after leaving Gambier. Or Allison Janney did on *West Wing*—the first show ever to portray politics with something approaching the complexity it deserves. Your challenge is to produce and perform the rich imaginative works that move and illuminate your time. Kenyon has vastly expanded its science programs. And your challenge is to fight in laboratories against enemies like the tiny HIV virus that has created the most devastating epidemic in human history—killing more people every two hours than there are in this graduating class.

At a time when we read about the high-tech jobs of a globalized world, your challenge is to find a way to educate the millions of Americans who can't get those jobs—because they can't read well enough to understand how to get online.	
And now, we are engaged in a misguided war.	And now comes the controversial part. At the height of the Iraq War, Kerry felt he should discuss that, though we knew there were those in the audience who believed in it. To ignore that issue seemed evasive. But how to discuss it without angering some people in the crowd?
Like the war of my generation, it began with an official deception.	
It's a war that in addition to the human cost—the tragedy of tens of thousands of Iraqis and Americans dead and wounded—will cost a trillion dollars.	
Enough to endow ten thousand Kenyons.	
Money that could fight poverty, disease, and hunger.	
To me, we cannot stand by and watch our troops sacrificed for a policy that isn't working.	
We cannot tolerate those who brand unpatriotic dissenters who ask tough questions.	
As it was with Vietnam, it is again right to make clear that the best way to support the troops is to oppose a course that squanders their lives.	The solution: make clear he is speaking for himself. But while most people listening agreed, not everyone did.
And so, your challenge is also to find a way to reclaim America's conscience.	
I have no doubt you will.	Kerry keeps the problem section brief, moving back to more traditional commencement themes: like saluting the parents there.
For one thing, you have great role models. Like your parents, sitting out there under the trees.	Kerry inspires by saluting parents.
You may laugh looking at the old photos of your dad in a ponytail, and your mom in bellbottoms and that crazy, tie-dyed shirt. But their generation too faced the task of ending a war. And they did.	

(Continued)

(Continued)

And went on to invent Earth Day, march against racism, bring women into the workplace, and become the first generation to usher in an acceptance for people regardless of sexual preference.

They honored democracy by making government face issues of conscience—and I ask you to applaud them for making the world better *before* they made it better by making you what you are!

[*Reaction*]

And of course, in addition to those sitting behind you . . . you have great role models sitting *among* you. Students from this class who had a dream, took a chance, and have already achieved great things. — And by saluting more students.

I know, because sitting here is a student who dreamed of being published, and felt ambitious enough to send a poem he'd written for class to the *Chautauqua* literary journal. And so Sam Anderson became a published poet at the age of twenty-one.

I know, because sitting here is a student who, watching a cousin struggle with Duchenne muscular dystrophy, dreamed of finding a way to help—and designed a project that involved her with the leading DMD researcher in the world. Now Amy Aloe's been invited to work in his groundbreaking lab.

I know, because sitting here is a student who dreamed of returning to the country of her birth, the country that shaped much of my life. And in Vietnam, Nhu Truong could examine not just issues, but the more difficult job of examining herself.

They all took a chance. If you ever despair of making a difference, you'll have Kenyon people to remind you of what's possible if *you* take a chance.

And not just from the class of '06.

One of the alums mentioned that every week, a group of them meet to talk about issues. They don't think alike about every idea, he said. But they share a *passion* for ideas they learned here.

Another asked me to tell those of you suspicious of government that "it's made up of people like us, trying to make things better."

The group included one alum who's well known here—and getting well known in Washington.

But awhile back he was just a nervous twenty-four-year old, sitting silently in a meeting with a new secretary of state. Until he got up the nerve to raise his hand and make a point.

"Who's that young, red-haired kid?" Condoleezza Rice said afterward, to an aide. "Keep your eye on him."

No, she didn't mean he was a security risk. He'd said something that, as a *Washington Post* reporter put it, "crystallized her thoughts about foreign policy."

And now Chris Brose, Kenyon 2002, travels everywhere with Secretary Rice, not just crafting her speeches but talking about policy.

I wish the policies were a little different . . . But he's making a mark. He's making a difference.

"I whimsically tripped into political science," Chris said, "and it changed my life." He has no doubt that every day he uses in Washington what he learned in Gambier.

You know, during World War II, my father was flying planes in the Army Air Corps. While he was away on duty, my mother was volunteering at home. She sent him a letter about **it**.

"You have no idea of the ways in which one can be useful right now," she wrote. "There's something for everyone to do."

She was right about her time. What she wrote is right about yours. —— Having saluted Chris Brose, Kerry returns to the personal to make clear the lesson learned.

In a few minutes, you will walk across this stage for your diploma. You'll line up on the steps of Rosse Hall to sing for the last time. You'll turn in your hoods, go back and finish packing. Maybe sell that ratty sofa to somebody from the class of 2007. And then you'll watch the cars pull away.

I know you've heard the old saying that commencement is not an end but a beginning. The truth is, it's both.

It is a day to feel sad about leaving Gambier. It's a day to feel eager about what lies ahead.

(Continued)

(Continued)

Because you have a special mission.	Kerry reverses the visualization step and call to action. He uses a referral ending: bringing back the student with whom he began, the coach, and his "quest for justice story" to make memorable his fine, clinching point.
Those who worked to end a war long ago now ask you to help end new wars.	
Those who worked to end poverty ask you to finish what we have left undone.	
We ask you to take a chance.	
We ask you to work for change.	
Promise yourselves, promise your parents, promise your teachers that you will use what you have learned.	
Don't doubt that you can.	
Only doubt those pessimists who say you can't.	
For all along the way, I promise, that while you leave the campus, Kenyon will never leave you.	
You will be linked by the experiences vividly brought to life today by Hayes Wong, who experienced them with you.	
As you fight for justice in this world, you will be linked by the insights you all had in courses like Quest for Justice.	
You will be linked to classmates whose success you predict will take the world by storm—and to some whose success takes you by surprise.	
You will be linked by the times you sat on a bench in Middle Path and argued about politics with people whose views you opposed—and learned you could be friends, anyway.	
At some point, you'll see that this small campus that changed you has produced enormous change in the world.	
And you will see that it came from what you learned here: from a class so compelling you were awake at the crack of dawn . . . from that night Teresa and I will never forget when you waited patiently till 4:15 at a polling place in Gambier . . . or from a coach who knew that her mission was to teach you how to win on and off the field.	

THE EULOGY

One odd thing about political life is that people you don't know well ask you to speak at funerals. Bob once wrote a eulogy for his boss to deliver. It was about the mother of someone his boss knew. Bob put in the requisite compliments to the dead woman of whom he knew nothing. In a spasm of hubris, he wrote that she had "inculcated" high moral values to her children.

"Clearly," said the boss, "you don't know the family."

Then he went out and delivered it anyway.

To steal a line from Wilford Brimley, it was the right thing to do.

You don't speak ill of the dead—at least not at the funeral. Eulogies are not events at which you note the complexities of the dead person's life or character, or the tensions, rivalries, and disappointments of family life. People at a funeral service are usually saddened, some bereft, and even those present merely out of obligation will weep, even if only because they have confronted the idea of their own mortality.

For people in public life, eulogies should do more than express grief. Often, speakers are talking about colleagues. By celebrating their achievements, they remind listeners about the importance of the causes they cared about. Since audiences usually have worked for the same causes, this drives home another useful point: that the speaker admires not just the dead person, but them.

"We don't just mourn a loss," eulogizers often say, "but celebrate a life." *Eulogy* actually comes from the Greek word meaning "praise." *Euphemism* comes from the same root. Even in the most tragic circumstances, listeners need to feel the dead person's life had lasting value. Some tips:

- **Use anecdote.** Abstractions cannot hold an audience's attention and—more important—won't move it.

- **Be funny.** Mourners need the relief. Stories that make gentle fun of the dead person can work well as long as they are gentle. One way to tell: ask yourself if the dead person would be upset if he or she could hear.

- **Try poetry.** This is a time when lines that might seem too literary for politics can sum up feeling. Peggy Noonan's reputation comes mostly from a poem she found, which President Reagan used at the end of his eulogy for the *Challenger* astronauts.

- **Use phrases that bond the group.** (*All of us who cared for . . .*) It makes those not speaking feel their views have been heard.

- **Give the loss a larger significance.** In mentioning that the dead person will be mourned by his or her family *and* those sharing his or her concerns, you further those causes and please the audience, who will usually share them.
- **Talk little about yourself.** Unless it's to express gratitude for the dead person's influence. Audiences want to hear about the person they mourn, not the speaker.
- **Don't feel you have to mask grief.** It's natural to choke up. Nobody will be offended.

Eulogy Outline

Introduction

Attention step (Story or description of the dead person relating to your theme.)

Statement of purpose (Often, that we're here not just to mourn a loss but to celebrate a life; religious mourners may take comfort by asserting that the dead have joined their maker, or are free of earthly cares.)

Body

Praise general qualities of person (Use concrete examples.)

Describe the larger context (The causes the person fought for, the successes he or she achieved.)

Return to individual (More stories illustrating different qualities.)

Conclusion

Inspiration (Here is a chance to be moving with poetry or other literary allusions—or something the deceased once said.)

Lesson learned (Why the example sums up the deceased.)

Call to action (Ask the audience to remember the person in the way he or she would want.)

Clincher (Yes, even here. Remember referral endings and antithesis.)

There have been many effective eulogies in political life since the first edition appeared. We write this the week Senator McCain died, and the family announced that former presidents George W. Bush and Barack Obama would deliver eulogies.

We were struck, though, by one more personal eulogy: that written after former First Lady Barbara Bush died, and delivered by her son, Jeb Bush. One might think that the outline you have just read through was written after studying Jeb Bush's draft. Actually, it is exactly what appeared here in 2009.

Just seven minutes long, Jeb Bush's speech is a role model for writers wanting to blend humor with sadness, use story and conversational language, and convey love, all in the traditional structure we suggest.

We also include another. In the Foreword of this book, Sen. Lamar Alexander describes as "near perfect" historian Jon Meacham's eulogy of Barbara Bush's husband, the forty-first president of the United States, George H. W. Bush. With its use of story, concrete detail, memorable language, and wit and a powerful referral ending, we agree. But we want readers to see that what makes Meacham's eulogy so exceptional is not the techniques alone. It's how he uses them together to create a rich portrait of a man he admired.

EULOGY FOR FORMER FIRST LADY BARBARA BUSH, DELIVERED BY HER SON JEB: APRIL 21, 2018

Words: 1,044
Grade level: 6.0
Sentence length: 14 words
Passive: 0 percent

As I stand here today to share a few words about my mom, I feel her looming presence behind me.	Opening with humor, Jeb's use of "looming" conveys the attitude her children had toward their mother, and makes plain his theme: her "unconditional but tough love."
And I know exactly what she's thinking right now. "Jeb, keep it short. Don't drag this out. People have already heard enough remarks already, and most of all, don't get weepy. Remember, I've spent decades laughing and living a life with these people!"	He supports that by imagining what she would say, then moves quickly to praise her general qualities.
And that is true. Barbara Bush filled our lives with laughter and joy, and in the case of her family, she was our teacher and role model on how to live a life of purpose and meaning.	
On behalf of our family, we want to thank the thousands and thousands of expressions of condolence and love for our precious mother.	He gets the obligatory thank-yous out of the way, lacing even this often routine duty with humor, making fun of Jon Meacham who had spoken before.

(Continued)

(Continued)

We want to thank Mom's caregivers for their compassionate care in the last months of her life. I want to thank Neil and Maria for their next-door family love of our parents and thank John and Suzanne for their eloquent words. Meacham, you might have been a little long, but it was beautiful. We want to thank Russ and Laura for their friendship and pastoral care of our parents, and we want to thank all that are here to celebrate the life of Barbara Bush.

Now, it is appropriate to express gratitude because we learned to do that at a very early age. ——— Now, Bush is free to fulfill his main task: characterizing Barbara Bush. Note that he characterizes her in two ways: first, in the stern way a mother would lecture young kids and, second, in ways that show her as wise and compassionate ("Be kind").

You see, our mom was our first and most important teacher.

"Sit up, look people in the eye, say please and thank you, do your homework, quit whining and stop complaining, eat your broccoli."

Yes, Dad, she said that.

The little things we learned became habits, and they led to bigger things like "Be kind. Always tell the truth. Never disparage anyone. Serve others."

"Treat everyone as you would want to be treated, and love your God with your heart and soul."

What a blessing to have a teacher like that 24/7. Now to be clear, her students weren't perfect. That's an understatement.

Mom got us through our difficult times with consistent, take-it-to-the-bank, unconditional but tough love.

She called her style a benevolent dictatorship. But honestly, it wasn't always benevolent.

When our children got a little older, they would spend more time visiting their Gampy and ——— And note here how grateful he is for how she treated his own children, and how concrete and visual is his language.

All it would take would be one week, and when they came home, all of a sudden they were pitching in around the house. They didn't fight as much, and they were actually nice to be with.

I attribute this to the unbridled fear of the Ganny lecture and the habit-forming effects of better behavior taking hold. Even in her nineties, Mom could strike fear into her grandchildren, nephews, nieces, and her children, if someone didn't behave.

There were no safe spaces or microaggressions allowed with Barbara Pierce Bush.

But in the end, every grandchild knew their Ganny loved them. We learned a lot more from our mom and our Ganny. We learned not to take ourselves too seriously.

We learned that humor is a joy that should be shared. Some of my greatest memories are participating in our family dinners when Mom would get into it, most of the time with George W., as you might imagine, and having us all laughing to tears.

We learned to strive to be genuine and authentic by the best role model in the world.

Her authentic, plastic pearls. Her not coloring her hair—by the way, she was beautiful till the day she died.

Her hugging of an HIV/AIDS patient at a time when her own mother wouldn't do it.

Her standing by her man with a little rhyming poetry in the 1984 election. And a thousand other ways. Barbara Pierce Bush was real, and that's why people admired her and loved her so.

Finally, our family has had front-row seats for the most amazing love story.

Through a multitude of moves, from New Haven to Odessa to Ventura, to Bakersfield, to Compton, to Midland, to Houston, to D.C., to New York, to D.C., to Beijing, to D.C., to Houston, to D.C., back to Houston and Kennebunkport, their love was a constant in our lives.

My dad is a phenomenal letter writer, and he would write Mom on their wedding anniversaries, which totaled an amazing seventy-three years.

Here's one of them written on January 6, 1994:

Barbara Bush's husband, ill himself, sits in the front row. To move his audience, Jeb Bush quotes from a letter written by George H. W. Bush.

(Continued)

(Continued)

Will you marry me? Oops, I forgot we did that 49 years ago. I was very happy on that day in 1945 but I am even happier today.

You have given me joy that few men know. You have made our boys into men by balling them out and then, right away, by loving them.

You've helped Doro be the sweetest, greatest daughter in the whole wide world.

I have climbed perhaps the highest mountain in the world but even that cannot hold a candle to being Barbara's husband.

Mom used to tell me, "Now, George, don't walk ahead." Little did she know I was only trying to keep up, keep up with Barbara Pierce from Rye, New York.

I love you.

The last time mom went in to the hospital, I think Dad got sick on purpose so that he could be with her.

That's my theory, at least, 'cause literally a day later he showed up with an illness. He came into a room when she was sleeping and held her hand. His hair was standing straight up. He was wearing a mask to improve his breathing. He was wearing a hospital gown. In other words, he looked like hell.

Mom opened her eyes and said, "My god, George, you are devastatingly handsome!"

Every nurse, doctor, staffer had to run to the hallway because they all started crying.

I hope you can see why we think our mom and our dad are teachers and models for our entire family and for many others.

Finally, the last time I was with her, I asked her about dying. Was she ready to go? Was she sad? Without missing a beat, she said, "Jeb, I believe in Jesus, and he is my savior.

"I don't want to leave your dad, but I know I will be in a beautiful place."

Mom, we look forward to being with you and Robyn and all of God's children.

We love you.

> Jeb finishes with a final story blending humor with sadness before moving to his last line.

EULOGY FOR PRESIDENT GEORGE HERBERT WALKER BUSH, DELIVERED BY BIOGRAPHER JON MEACHAM: DECEMBER 5, 2018

Words: 1,215
Grade level: 6.9
Sentence length: 15.1 words
Passive: 0 percent

The story was almost over even before it had fully begun. Shortly after dawn on Saturday, September 2, 1944, Lieutenant Junior Grade George Herbert Walker Bush joined by two crewmates took off from the *USS San Jacinto* to attack a radio tower on Chichijima. As they approached the target, the air was heavy with flack. The plane was hit. Smoke filled the cockpit. Flames raced across the wings. "My god," Lieutenant Bush thought, "this thing's going to go down." Yet he kept the plane in its 35-degree dive, dropped his bombs, and then roared off out to sea telling his crewmates to hit the silk.

— Meacham's first sentence creates suspense before he even begins to tell the story.

Following protocol, Lieutenant Bush turned the plane so they could bail out. Only then did Bush parachute from the cockpit. The wind propelled him backward, and he gashed his head on the tail of the plane as he flew through the sky. He plunged deep into the ocean, bobbed to the surface, and flopped onto a tiny raft. His head bleeding, his eyes burning, his mouth and throat raw from saltwater, the future forty-first president of the United States was alone. Sensing that his men had not made it, he was overcome. He felt the weight of responsibility as a nearly physical burden, and he wept. Then, at four minutes shy of noon, a submarine emerged to rescue the downed pilot. George Herbert Walker Bush was safe.

— Meacham's use of concrete detail allows the audience to experience what Bush experienced.

The story, his story and ours, would go on by God's grace. Through the ensuing decades, President Bush would frequently ask, nearly daily, he'd ask himself why me? Why was I spared? And in a sense, the rest of his life was a perennial effort to prove himself worthy of his salvation on that distant morning.

— Meacham skillfully uses the question Bush asked of himself to serve as his statement of purpose for the eulogy. The rest of the speech is the answer to that question.

To him, his life was no longer his own. There were always more missions to undertake, more lives to touch, and more love to give. And what a headlong grace he made of it all. He never slowed down. On the primary campaign trail in New Hampshire once, he grabbed the hand of a department store mannequin asking for votes. When he realized his mistake, he said, "Never know. Got to ask."

— Meacham uses humor here not only to characterize Bush as funny and humble but to change the pace after such a powerful opening.

(Continued)

Appendix 433

The Political Speechwriter's Companion

(Continued)

You can hear the voice, can't you? As Dana Carvey said, the key to a Bush 41 impersonation is Mr. Rogers trying to be John Wayne.

George Herbert Walker Bush was America's last great soldier statesman, a twentieth-century founding father. He governed with virtues that most closely resembled those of Washington and of Adams, of TR and of FDR, of Truman and Eisenhower, of men who believed in causes larger than themselves. Six foot two, handsome, dominant in person, President Bush spoke with those big strong hands making fists to underscore points.

A master of what Franklin Roosevelt called the science of human relationships, he believed that to whom much is given, much is expected. And because life gave him so much, he gave back again and again and again.

He stood in the breach in the Cold War against totalitarianism. — Here Meacham uses litany to list accomplishments, ending with a segue to a more personal section.

He stood in the breach in Washington against unthinking partisanship.

He stood in the breach against tyranny and discrimination, and on his watch a wall fell in Berlin, a dictator's aggression did not stand, and doors across America opened to those with disabilities.

And in his personal life, he stood in the breach against heartbreak and hurt, always offering an outstretched hand, a warm word, a sympathetic tear.

If you were down, he would rush to lift you up, and if you were soaring, he would rush to savor your success. Strong and gracious, comforting and charming, loving and loyal, he was our shield in dangers hour.

Now, of course, there was ambition too. Loads of that. To serve, he had to succeed; to preside he had to prevail. Politics, he once admitted, isn't a pure undertaking. Not if you want to win it's not. — Parallel construction and alliteration.

— Another imaginative use of repetition.

An imperfect man, he left us a more perfect union.

It must be said that for a keenly intelligent statesman of stirring almost unparalleled private eloquence, public speaking was not exactly a strong suit. "Fluency in English," President Bush once remarked, "is something that I'm often not accused of." — Once again Meacham uses humor, in this instance to present a full picture of the man.

Looking ahead to the '88 election, he observed, "Inarguably it's no exaggeration to say that the undecideds could go one way or the other."

And late in his presidency, he allowed that "we're enjoying sluggish times, but we're not enjoying them very much."

His tongue may have run amok at moments, but his heart was steadfast. His life code, as he said, was tell the truth, don't blame people. Be strong, do your best, try hard, forgive, stay the course. And that was and is the most American of creeds. Abraham Lincoln's Better Angels of Our Nature and George H. W. Bush's Thousand Points of Light are companion verses in America's national hymn, for Lincoln and Bush both called on us to choose the right over the convenient, to hope rather than to fear, and to heed not our worst impulses, but our best instincts. — Antithesis.

In this work, he had the most wonderful of allies in Barbara Pierce Bush, his wife of seventy-three years. He called her Barb, the silver fox and, when the situation warranted, the enforcer. He was the only boy she ever kissed. Her children, Mrs. Bush liked to say, always wanted to throw up when they heard that. In a letter to Barbara during the war, young George H. W. Bush had written, "I love you, precious, with all my heart and to know that you love me means my life. How lucky our children will be to have a mother like you." And as they will tell you, they surely were.

As vice president, Bush once visited a children's leukemia ward in Krakow. Thirty-five years before, he and Barbara had lost a daughter, Robin, to the disease. In Krakow, a small boy wanted to greet the American vice president. Learning that the child was sick with the cancer that had taken Robin, Bush began to cry. To his diary later that day, the vice president said this. "My eyes flooded with tears and behind me was a bank of television cameras and I thought I can't turn around. I can't dissolve because of personal tragedy in the face of the nurses that give of themselves every day. So I stood there looking at this little guy tears running down my cheek hoping he wouldn't see. But if he did, hoping he'd feel that I loved him." — Meacham uses another story—this time to convey not courage but compassion and humanity.

That was the real George H. W. Bush, a loving man with a big, vibrant, all-enveloping heart. And so we ask as we commend his soul to God, and has he did, why him? Why was he spared? The workings of Providence are mysterious, but this much is clear, that George Herbert Walker Bush, who survived that fiery fall into the waters of the Pacific three-quarters of a century ago, made our lives and the lives of nations freer, better, warmer, and nobler. That was his mission. That was his heartbeat. And if we listen closely enough, we can hear that heartbeat even now, for it's the heartbeat of a lion, a lion who not only led us, but who loved us. That's why him. That's why he was spared. — The referral to the opening story serves as a thematic framing device for the conclusion.

— Meacham's clincher combines vivid language, metaphor, antithesis, alliteration, and repetition.

AWARDS

"Winning may not be everything," Democratic senator Dianne Feinstein once quipped, "but losing has little to recommend it."[2]

It is not surprising she'd feel that way. Victory speeches are more fun than concessions. For politicians, winning means job security. We measure their abilities by their achievements—their name attached to legislation that becomes law and, of course, on a ballot on Election Day. But they also—often—"win" in other ways.

Quite often, actually. And not just Nobel Peace Prizes. Arkansas senator Tom Cotton won the Heritage Foundation's first "Distinguished Intern Alumni Award."[3] Emily's List honored Sen. Patty Murray with its We Are Emily Award.[4] Congressmen Will Hurd (R) and Beto O'Rourke (D) together received the Allegheny College Prize for Civility in Public Life.[5] Still other politicians are routinely honored for their public service, for their work on any given issue, or for being the "Legislator of the Year." They are even inducted into their high school's Hall of Fame.

We have already analyzed an awards presentation speech, even if not by a politician—Oprah Winfrey's receiving the Cecil B. DeMille Award.

But politicians don't just accept awards; they present awards, as well. They honor the "Teacher of the Year," small business owners for their charitable work, the soldier from their district who is returning home after her second tour of duty. So here, we examine President Barack Obama's speech presenting at the Kennedy Center Honors Reception.

The Kennedy Center Honors, given each year since 1978, include a series of events usually honoring five or six people from theater, music, and popular entertainment. The Reception is given at the White House; it is when the president actually confers the awards.

There is no rigid formula for presenting awards. But there are a variety of elements presenters often use. The 2016 Reception, an excellent model, included three sections: (1) opening remarks thanking and welcoming the crowd, and general remarks about the arts and the event; (2) separate presentations honoring each artist; and (3) summing up with a brief ending including the names of each honoree—and a final call for applause.

On that night, Obama introduced six people or groups. We include Obama's opening and final remarks, as well as his presentation to the first honoree, singer Mavis Maples, and the last, the surviving members of The Eagles.

Elements Often Forming Part of Presentation

- Opening story illustrating character of recipient
- Background: history and importance of award

- Brief account of achievement and the larger meaning
- Testimonials by others
- Anecdotes and concrete examples that reinforce the credibility of the recipient by making us see why he or she is special

Elements That Often Form Part of Acceptances

- Acknowledgment of purpose of award and group responsible for it
- Acknowledgment of others working in same cause
- Expression of gratitude
- Pledge to carry on work
- Anecdote that speaks to the work in a concrete way

BARACK OBAMA, PRESENTING THE KENNEDY CENTER HONORS, 2016 (EXCERPT)

Words: 1,294
Grade level: 6.3
Sentence length: 12.8 words
Passive: 5 percent

Thank you so much, everybody. Thank you. Thank you very much. Everybody please have a seat. Thank you.

Well, good evening, everybody. On behalf of Michelle and myself, welcome to the White House. Over the past eight years, this has always been one of our favorite nights. And this year, I was especially looking forward to seeing how Joe Walsh cleans up—pretty good.

Obama immediately signals his familiarity with pop culture and willingness to be edgy by showing he knows about Walsh, originally considered too "wild" to fit in with The Eagles.

I want to begin by once again thanking everybody who makes this wonderful evening possible, including David Rubenstein, the Kennedy Center trustees—I'm getting a big echo back there—and the Kennedy Center president, Deborah Rutter. Give them a big round of applause.

We have some outstanding members of Congress here tonight. And we are honored also to have Vicki Kennedy and three of President Kennedy's grandchildren with us here—Rose, Tatiana, and Jack.

JFK did not found the awards, but the Center was named after him and Obama will pay tribute to the Kennedys who were proponents of the arts during their years in the White House.

(Continued)

(Continued)

So the arts have always been part of life at the White House, because the arts are always central to American life.	The first time Obama uses what we will see often: repetition to draw the parallel between the importance of the arts to Americans and to the Obamas.
And that's why, over the past eight years, Michelle and I have invited some of the best writers and musicians, actors, dancers to share their gifts with the American people, and to help tell the story of who we are, and to inspire what's best in all of us. Along the way, we've enjoyed some unbelievable performances—this is one of the perks of the job that I will miss. Thanks to Michelle's efforts, we've brought the arts to more young people—from hosting workshops where they learn firsthand from accomplished artists, to bringing *Hamilton* to students who wouldn't normally get a ticket to Broadway.	An Obama trademark: the importance of good works, backed up by concrete detail and wit.
And on behalf of all of us, I want to say thanks to my wife for having done simply—yes. And she's always looked really good doing it. She does. This is part of how we've tried to honor the legacy of President and Mrs. Kennedy. They understood just how vital art is to our democracy—that we need song and cinema and paintings and performance to help us challenge our assumptions, to question the way things are, and maybe inspire us to think about how things might be.	And here, the decision to remind listeners of the Kennedy legacy.
The arts help us celebrate our triumphs, but also hold up a mirror to our flaws.	Finally, note how Obama uses repetition ("It helps," a quote from JFK, and a final sentence echoing the JFK lines).
And all of that deepens our understanding of the human condition. It helps us to see ourselves in each other. It helps to bind us together as a people. As President Kennedy once said, "In serving his vision of the truth, the artist best serves his nation." Tonight, we honor five amazing artists who have dedicated their lives to telling their truth, and helping us to see our own . . .	

At eight years old, Mavis Staples climbed onto a chair in church, leaned into the microphone, raised her eyes upwards, and belted out the gospel.	Obama opens with anecdote as an attention step, including mention of family to make sure listeners know of the family's early role.
When people heard that deep, old soul coming out of that little girl, they wept—which, understandably, concerned her. But her mother told her, "Mavis, they're happy. Your singing makes them cry happy tears." It was those early appearances on the South Side of Chicago—South Side!—with Mavis, her siblings, their father, Roebuck "Pops" Staples, that launched the legendary Staple Singers. Theirs was gospel with just a touch of country, a twist of the blues, little bit of funk. There was a little bit of sin with the salvation. And driven by Pops's reverbed guitar, Mavis's powerhouse vocals and the harmonies that only family can make, the Staple Singers broke new ground with songs like "Uncloudy Day." They had some truths to tell. Inspired by Dr. King, Pops would tell his kids, "If he can preach it, we can sing it."	Here, Obama uses a second traditional element: the Staple Singers pioneering "new ground" and the meaning—truths—in their lyrics.
And so they wrote anthems like "Freedom Highway" and "When Will We Be Paid"—which became the soundtrack of the civil rights movement. As a solo artist, Mavis has done it all and worked with just about everybody from Bob Dylan to Prince to Jeff Tweedy.	Element number 3: specific songs, and the collaborations her fans remember.
On albums like *We'll Never Turn Back* and *One True Vine*, she still is singing for justice and equality, and influencing a new generation of musicians and fans. And each soulful note—even in heartbreak and even in despair—is grounded in faith, and in hope, and the belief that there are better days yet to come.	The reminder of Mavis Staples's philosophy—faith, and hope—that makes her more than a musician.
"These aren't just songs I'm singing to be moving my lips," she says. "I mean this."	A final anecdote, allowing Obama to close with a serious note: that she has meant what she sang, an ending that leads into applause.

(Continued)

(Continued)

And we mean it too. Six decades on, nobody makes us feel "the weight" like Mavis Staples. Give her a big round of applause.

And finally, there have been some interesting things said about this next group, including being called "one of rock's most contentiously dysfunctional families."

So, yeah, it was so unlikely that they'd ever get back together and that they called their reunion tour "Hell Freezes Over." — *We might expect Obama to make note of The Eagles' contentious history.*

I love that.

But here's the thing—when you listen to The Eagles, you hear the exact opposite story, and that is perfect harmony. — *But note how he turns that opening into a compliment. An award should make honorees feel good. There is a limit to how much fun to poke.*

You hear it in the crisp, overpowering a cappella chords of "Seven Bridges Road"; dueling guitar solos in "Hotel California"; complex, funky riffs opening "Life in the Fast Lane."

It's the sound not just of a California band, but one of America's signature bands—a supergroup whose greatest hits sold more copies in the United States than any other record in the 20th century. — *Again, a reminder of their specific achievements.*

And the 20th century had some pretty good music.

So, here tonight, we have three of The Eagles: Don Henley, the meticulous, introspective songwriter with an unmistakable voice that soars above his drum set.

Timothy Schmit, the bass player and topline of many of those harmonies.

And Joe Walsh, who's as rowdy with a guitar lick as I'm told he once was in a hotel room.

Twice.

This is the White House, though.

And Michelle and I are about to leave. — *Obama is careful to mention each Eagle—as well as the sober inclusion of the founding member no longer alive.*

As I've said before, we want to get our security deposit back.

But, of course, the Eagles are also the one and only Glenn Frey. And we all wish Glenn was still here with us.

THE ROAST

Each year, in our American University speechwriting class, when it comes time to teach "wit," we have the students participate in two exercises. The first is to bring a joke—any joke—to class. The surprise is when they come in the door and learn they have to deliver it in front of their professors and thirty-five of their peers. Inevitably, someone always comes with an off-color joke, and the lesson is obvious: telling a joke isn't so easy.

The second exercise, shared in Chapter 9, gives them fifteen minutes to write jokes for one of the late-night talk shows. It teaches them that while telling a joke can be difficult, *writing* jokes isn't always as hard as it seems.

When Eric started writing jokes with Jeff Nussbaum, now a partner at West Wing Writers, they were as surprised as anyone at how good they turned out to be. Since then, Eric and Jeff cofounded The Humor Cabinet and have written countless roasts for leading politicians of both parties, including the Sandra Day O'Connor speech reprinted here.

Roasts are popular for two reasons. They are fun for the audience, and they are great for political careers. Like any other political speech, roasts characterize the speaker. Speakers need to be likable. Does that mean they can't poke fun at others? Of course not. But they should make sure that at the end they've reassured the audience the jokes were all in good fun, and even served a larger purpose: bringing people together.

While we don't provide a detailed outline for roasts here, sometimes they are nothing more than a string of loosely connected jokes, similar to a monologue. What follows, though, is a checklist of what's often included in political roasts:

- Make fun of the emcee and acknowledge the group.

- Make fun of other guests.

- Make fun of yourself.

- Reassure the audience that it's all in good fun.

- Make a serious point.

- Close with a final zinger.

Political roasts resemble only in format the Friars Club and Comedy Central roasts, which actually do burn while the targets pretend to enjoy it. The Gridiron Club's motto, "Singe, don't burn," is still the mantra for political roast scriptwriters. Self-deprecating humor is still the rule.

That's what you will see in the speech that follows. In 2011, Sandra Day O'Connor became the first woman president of the Alfalfa Club, an exclusive social club. Founded in 1913, Alfalfa's sole purpose is to host its annual dinner held on the last Saturday in January. The Gridiron membership consists of journalists. Alfalfans, so named because the plant's roots will go to great lengths for a drink, come from business and politics; they are united by their wealth and influence.

In the O'Connor example, you'll see the elements we suggest. And while political humor is supposed to be often topical—making it obsolete in days—a surprising number remain funny.

As you read, note a few things:

- **The skit.** The O'Connor roast isn't a series of unconnected jokes. Instead, while filled with one-liners, it forms a narrative. This gives her jokes continuity and, as each joke tops the last, allows the laughter to build.

- **The pun.** While far from being a wallflower, the conservative O'Connor still takes the audience by surprise with a pun.

- **The story joke.** *Where's she going, and what did she do next?* the audience asks as O'Connor describes a typical day on the court, or what she's been doing in retirement.

- **Untraditional self-mockery.** O'Connor pokes fun at not just her age but her frailty. She also willingly makes fun of how the court decides its cases.

- **Misdirection.** Using a staple of political humor, O'Connor lets us think she was fully supportive of the second woman on the court, even giving Ruth Bader Ginsburg a "hug." We're fooled—and surprised into laughter when she territorially says, "Remember who got here first!"

There isn't enough space in this book to include other scripts showing the many ways humor works in politics. But you should try it. You might surprise yourself.

SANDRA DAY O'CONNOR, PRESIDENT OF THE ALFALFA CLUB, 2011

Words: 1,242
Grade level: 6.6
Sentence length: 13.7 words
Passive: 7 percent

The Alfalfa Club is a special place. It's a place where Republicans can be very happy that tax cuts for the wealthy got extended. And a place where Democrats like Senator Warner can be secretly happy that the tax cuts for the wealthy got extended.

— O'Connor begins, as speeches often do, by praising the audience. Here, though, she does it with a joke that acknowledges what connects everyone in the room—power and wealth.

But seriously, thank you, Mark, for your service to this club.
I'd also like to thank our vice president, Representative Steny Hoyer. It's like the old saying goes: "behind every successful man stands a woman." And behind every *really* successful woman . . . waits Steny Hoyer.
This is such a special moment for me, I promised myself I wouldn't cry . . . at least until that part of the evening when I do my John Boehner impersonation.
It is a huge honor to be the first woman president of Alfalfa.

— After a couple of lines that single out others in the room, O'Connor quickly moves to self-deprecating material, first by exaggerating self-importance.

And it calls to mind another woman pioneer: Sandra Day O'Connor, the first woman justice on the Supreme Court. As I lead the Alfalfa Club, I promise to always ask myself: what would Sandra Day O'Connor do in this situation?
This, my fellow Alfalfans, is progress. It is a populist victory.
Today, Alfalfa has gone from an old boys club . . . to a really old girls' club.
Only at the Alfalfa Club can you simultaneously shatter a glass ceiling . . . and your hip.

— Rule of three.

— As discussed in Chapter 9, this joke follows the "If this is true (Alfalfa is dominated by old men, and O'Connor is a woman), what else is true?" (you can break both a glass ceiling and your hip).

(Continued)

Appendix 443

(Continued)

As you know, the last person to have held the titles of both Supreme Court justice and president is William Howard Taft. Taft and I have more than that in common. Both of us needed help getting out of the bathtub.

In any event, it is long past time for a woman leader. After ninety years of male Alfalfa presidents who haven't accomplished a single thing, isn't it time for a woman president who can do anything a man can do? And although I am the first woman president of Alfalfa, I hasten to add that this is actually in keeping with Alfalfa tradition . . . we're once again being led by a couple of boobs. —— O'Connor surprises her audience not only with a pun, but with her willingness to say something edgy.

[*Pause*]

Being the first of anything is never easy.

I do remember how relieved I was when Ruth Bader Ginsburg joined the court.

I remember walking into her chambers, giving her a hug, welcoming her . . . and then whispering in her ear: "always remember who got here first." —— O'Connor surprises with a classic misdirection

Of course, I'm joking. I love Ruth, and now Sonia and Elena.

[*Pause*]

So much has changed.

When I got my law degree in 1952, it was very hard for a woman to get hired as a lawyer. You were lucky if you could get work as a criminal.

This is true: when I graduated from law school, the only job offer I got from a private firm was a legal secretarial position. I turned it down. It was an insult to my intelligence.

Which all begs the question—now why did I accept *this* job?

(Well, sometimes in life, you just don't figure things out until it's too late—kind of like some of our —— An aside. Supreme Court cases.)

When President Reagan appointed me to the Supreme Court, there were men who thought women were too emotional to serve on the Supreme Court . . . now we have a Speaker of the House who has to be held and comforted every time he watches *Toy Story*.

Maybe it was the early prejudice I experienced that made me so against discrimination based on gender. In the case *Mississippi University for Women v. Hogan*, I wrote that it was unconstitutional for a state nursing school to refuse to admit men.

Appendix

I'm proud to say that once these men got comfortable in their dresses and learned to sit with their legs together, they proved to be invaluable to the medical profession.

— In addition to furthering the narrative of taking on a man's world, these two jokes include concrete detail (*Toy Story* as a sad movie, and naming the actual case). They also allow the audience to visualize the absurd punch lines.

**

It was the highlight of my life to serve on the Supreme Court. Such a heady experience.

— This "day in the life" structure helps change the pace by allowing O'Connor to speak as if she's telling a story. Also, similar to a Top Ten list, the construct allows for more than one punch line. Of course, her willingness to poke fun at a fellow justice's independence also surprised the audience.

We'd arrive each morning and immediately begin deliberating the great questions of the day.
And then one minute later, we'd start looking through take-out menus for what we were going to have for lunch.
Interesting fact: Clarence Thomas had the same thing for lunch every day: whatever Nino Scalia was having. I shouldn't admit this, but sometimes we'd actually rule based on what we ate that day. For example, *Hamdan v. Rumsfeld*?
We made that decision after some really good falafel. And we had other ways of making other decisions. [*Holding up a Magic 8-Ball*]
This is a Magic 8-Ball, or as those of us on the Court nicknamed it, "the tenth justice."
Was the Eighteenth Amendment the worst thing to happen to the Alfalfa Club? [*Shakes ball*] It is decidedly so!

— O'Connor uses a prop to set up hyperbole—that Prohibition was the worst thing to ever happen to the audience.

[*Pause*]
But ultimately it came time for me to retire. Like Donovan McNabb, I had been on the bench a long time.
**

(Continued)

(Continued)

I'd be lying if I didn't say that after twenty-five years on the Court I was looking for a little time off. Unfortunately, two days after hanging up my robe, I was called for jury duty. — This is a take on observational humor. An actual event, embellished with a one liner.

Luckily, they let me off when I said that the defendant just "had a guilty look about him."

I guess the defendant got off, too, because he's right over there!

But it's hard to find something meaningful to do after you've been on the Supreme Court. For a while I worked as a notary at a Kinko's.

**

But now, here at Alfalfa, I've finally found my calling. And I have some ideas for how things should be run. For starters, as president, I am going to make the rules for this club. And I also will decide whether they're constitutional.

Next, I will require every Alfalfan to read the Constitution. Or, if you don't have time for that, you can just read the House of Representatives version. — Here O'Connor uses the Rule of three again. But she also uses climactic order, ending on the edgiest of the jokes.

And I will continue to make sure that our dinner includes the steak *and* the lobster. After all, this is a matter of precedent, and because I believe in choice.

**

Back in Texas where I was born, we have a saying that an old judge is like an old shoe—everything is worn out except the tongue. — Simile.

So I do want to take advantage of this powerful and captive audience—and my new bully pulpit—to make a serious point. — The serious close, referencing the mass shooting that severely injured Congresswoman Gabby Giffords and left six dead, and calling for less division and more cooperation.

It's been a tough time not just for my home state of Arizona, but for our country. What happened in Tucson was devastating.

I so appreciated the president's visit, both because it was heartfelt, and because it reminded us that this wasn't just a tragedy in one city, and one state—it was a national tragedy.

And the president's call has meaning for us as well. If Alfalfa plants can grow together—so too can Alfalfa members.

So let us pledge to leave here with the same spirit of
fellowship that brings us together here every year.
In closing, I do wish my late husband, John, could
have been here tonight. He passed away a year and a
half ago. He would have loved this event.
In his absence, I wanted to leave you with his
advice—advice you have heard from me before.
"Now you don't have to drink to have a good time, but — For the clincher, O'Connor
why take a chance?" borrows with attribution.
Thank you.

Notes

INTRODUCTION

1. Elvin Lim, *The Anti-intellectual Presidency: The Decline of Presidential Rhetoric from George Washington to George W. Bush* (New York: Oxford University Press, 2008), Preface, x.

CHAPTER 1

1. Ann Devroy, "Clinton: 'There Is Room' to Pray in Public School; White House Conciliatory toward GOP," *The Washington Post*, November 16, 1994.
2. Jeffrey K. Tulis, *The Rhetorical Presidency* (Princeton, NJ: Princeton University Press, 1987).
3. Chris Sittenfeld, "What Michelle Obama Would Bring to the White House," *Time*, September 27, 2008.
4. Stephen Lucas, *The Art of Public Speaking*, 9th ed. (New York: McGraw-Hill, 2007), 372.
5. Ibid., 400.
6. Lou Cannon, "Obama and Reagan: The Likeability Factor," *RealClear Politics*, September 14, 2012.
7. Chris Cillizza, "Four Poll Numbers That Should Really Unnerve Hillary Clinton," *The Washington Post*, July 27, 2015.
8. Emily Peck, "Why Hillary Clinton Is Really Unpopular—Again," *HuffPost*, July 18, 2017.
9. Matt Lewis, "I'll Say It: Elizabeth Warren Isn't Likeable," *Daily Beast*, January 4, 2019.
10. Patrick Anderson, *Electing Jimmy Carter: The Campaign of 1976* (Baton Rouge: Louisiana State University Press, 1976), 167.
11. Ibid., 167.
12. Cited in Daniel Goleman, "Gauging the Election by Nominee's Outlook," *The New York Times*, August 21, 1988.
13. Elvin Lim, *The Anti-intellectual Presidency: The Decline of Presidential Rhetoric from George Washington to George W. Bush* (New York: Oxford University Press, 2008).
14. Quoted in William Safire, "On Language; Sound Bite, Define Yourself!," *The New York Times Magazine*, November 13, 1988.
15. Shanto Iyengar, *Media Politics: A Citizen's Guide* (New York: Norton, 2007), 211.

CHAPTER 2

1. William Goldman, *William Goldman: Four Screenplays with Essays* (Milwaukee, WI: Applause Theatre & Cinema Books, 2000), 317.
2. Aristotle, *Rhetoric*, translated by W. Rhys Roberts, http://classics.mit.edu/Aristotle/rhetoric.1.i.html.
3. Steven R. Weisman, ed., *Daniel Patrick Moynihan: A Portrait in Letters of an American Visionary* (New York: Public Affairs, 2010), 2.
4. Hannah Fingerhut, "Most Americans Say U.S. Economic System Is Unfair, but High-Income Republicans Disagree," *Pew Research Center*, February 10, 2016, http://www.pewresearch.org/fact-tank/2016/02/10/most-americans-say-u-s-economic-system-is-unfair-but-high-income-republicans-disagree/.
5. Aristotle, *Rhetoric*.
6. Stanford Encyclopedia of Philosophy, "Aristotle's *Rhetoric*," https://plato.stanford.edu/entries/aristotle-rhetoric/.
7. Sharon Begley, "Heard Any Good Stories Lately?," *Newsweek*, September 22, 2008.
8. Stephanie Rosenbloom, "Names That Match Forge a Bond on the Internet," *The New York Times*, April 10, 2008.
9. *Fox News Sunday* transcript, September 7, 2008.
10. "The Choice: Comment," *The New Yorker*, October 13, 2008.
11. E. J. Dionne, "In Politics, Does Evidence Matter?," *The Washington Post*, December 7, 2014.
12. Sean Sullivan, "Hillary Clinton: Congress Living in an 'Evidence-Free Zone,'" *The Washington Post*, September 18, 2014.
13. Molly Ball, "Donald Trump and the Politics of Fear," *The Atlantic*, September 2, 2016.
14. Robert B. Cialdini, *Influence: The Psychology of Persuasion*, rev. ed. (New York: Harper Business, 2006).

CHAPTER 3

1. Abby Phillip, "Clinton: Half of Trump's Supporters Fit in 'Basket of Deplorables,'" *The Washington Post*, September 9, 2016.
2. Diane Hessan, "Understanding the Undecided Voters," *The Boston Globe*, November 21, 2016.
3. Jeffrey M. Jones, "Americans Are More Positive about Their Taxes This Year," *Gallup*, April 13, 2017, news.gallup.com/poll/208511/americans-positive-taxes-year.aspx.

4. Craig Allen Smith, *Presidential Campaign Communication: The Quest for the White House* (Cambridge: Polity Press, March 2010), 84–85.

5. Stephen Lucas, *The Art of Public Speaking*, 9th ed. (New York: McGraw-Hill, 2007), 402.

6. Ted Sorensen, *Kennedy* (First Harper Perennial Political Classics Edition, 2009), 193.

CHAPTER 4

1. Wilbert J. McKeachie, *Teaching Tips: Strategies, Research, and Theory for College and University Teachers*, 10th ed. (Lexington, MA: Heath, 1999), 62.

2. Carmine Gallo, "Neuroscience Proves You Should Follow TED's 18-Minute Rule to Win Your Pitch," *Inc.*, February 21, 2017, https://www.inc.com/carmine-gallo/why-your-next-pitch-should-follow-teds-18-minute-rule.html.

3. Glenn Kessler, "The Young Speechwriter Who Captured Rice's Voice," *The Washington Post*, March 14, 2006.

4. Peggy Noonan, *What I Saw at the Revolution* (New York: Random House, 1990), 229.

5. Ralph Keyes, *The Quote Verifier: Who Said What, Where, and When* (New York: St. Martin's Griffin, 2006), 69.

6. Reagan Library, "President Reagan's Remarks at a Reagan-Bush '84 Rally in Endicott, New York, on September 12, 1984," posted August 15, 2017, https://www.youtube.com/watch?v=9qJChlT_D1E&t=606s.

7. Personal conversation, January 19, 2018.

8. Tunku Varadarajan, "Speechwriter Who Helped Reagan 'Tear Down That Wall,'" *Politico Europe*, June 12, 2017.

CHAPTER 5

1. Alan H. Monroe and Douglas Ehninger, *Principles of Speech Communication*, Sixth Brief Edition (Scott Foresman and Company, 1969), 263–264.

2. Ibid.

3. Ibid.

4. Taylor Branch, *Parting the Waters: America in the King Years 1954–63* (New York: Simon and Schuster, 2008), 76–77.

5. Peter Dreier, "Don't Add Reagan's Face to Mount Rushmore," *Fredricksburg.com*, April 3, 2011, https://www.fredericksburg.com/opinionop-ed/don-t-add-reagan-s-face-to-mount-rushmore/article_9a329ef8-6d41-5a80-80b5-085a28f07316.html.

CHAPTER 6

1. Franklin D. Roosevelt, "Excerpts from the Press Conference," March 10, 1942, https://www.presidency.ucsb.edu/documents/excerpts-from-the-press-conference-57.
2. Ibid.
3. David Zarefsky, *Strategies for Success*, 3rd ed. (New York: Allyn and Bacon, 2002), 261.
4. Robert Schlesinger, *White House Ghosts* (New York: Simon and Schuster, 2008).
5. Joseph Conrad, *The Nigger of the "Narcissus"* (London: Heinemann, 1897).
6. Kenneth G. Wilson, *The Columbia Guide to Standard American English* (New York: Columbia University Press, 1996), 457.
7. *Joint Statement on "Supporting the Human Rights of Christians and Other Communities, particularly in the Middle East" at the 28th Session of the Human Rights Council* (Geneva, March 13, 2015), https://press.vatican.va/content/salastampa/it/bollettino/pubblico/2015/03/13/0186/00415.html.
8. Dan O'Hair, Rob Stewart, and Hannah Rubenstein, *A Speaker's Guidebook: Text and Reference*, 4th ed. (Boston: Bedford/St. Martin's, 2008), 198.

CHAPTER 7

1. Aaron J. Palmer, *Dictionary of American History* (Farmington Hills, MI: Gale Cengage Learning, 2003).
2. Edward P. J. Corbett, *Classical Rhetoric for the Modern Student*, 2nd ed. (Oxford: Oxford University Press, 1971), 459.
3. Ralph Keyes, *The Quote Verifier* (New York: St. Martin's Griffin, 2006), 88.
4. Scott Horton, "Freneau—A Political Litany," *Harper's*, August 16, 2009, https://harpers.org/blog/2009/08/freneau-a-political-litany/.
5. George Orwell, "Politics and the English Language," *Horizon*, April 1946.

CHAPTER 8

1. Elvin Lim, *The Anti-intellectual Presidency: The Decline of Presidential Rhetoric from George Washington to George W. Bush* (New York: Oxford University Press, 2008), 4, 6.
2. John Steinbeck, *East of Eden*, reissue ed. (New York: Penguin Classics, 1952), 268.
3. Bas Andeweg, Hans Hoeken, and Jaap de Jong, "'May I Have Your Attention?': Exordial Techniques in Informative Oral Presentations," *Technical Communication Quarterly*, June 1998, 271–284.
4. Sharon Begley, "Heard Any Good Stories Lately?," *Newsweek*, September 22, 2008.

5. Sheryl Sandberg, "Why We Have Too Few Women Leaders," *TEDWomen 2010*, https://www.ted.com/talks/sheryl_sandberg_why_we_have_too_few_women_leaders.

6. Toni Morrison, "Nobel Lecture," December 7, 1993, https://www.nobelprize.org/prizes/literature/1993/morrison/lecture/.

7. Fred Barnes, "The Complete Package," *The Weekly Standard*, February 18, 2013, https://www.weeklystandard.com/fred-barnes/the-complete-package.

CHAPTER 9

1. Jeff Nussbaum, "Voters Like Pols Who Can Laugh at Themselves. Why Can't These Candidates Pull It Off?," *The Washington Post*, March 4, 2016, https://www.washingtonpost.com/posteverything/wp/2016/03/04/voters-like-pols-who-can-laugh-at-themselves-why-cant-these-candidates-pull-it-off/?utm_term=.87824c160e37.

2. Ibid.

3. C-SPAN, "Gridiron Club President Clarence Page Interview," March 14, 2015, https://www.c-span.org/video/?324808-4/gridiron-club-president-clarence-page-interview.

4. Daniel Kreps, "Michelle Wolf Defends Controversial White House Correspondent's Dinner Speech," *Rolling Stone*, May 1, 2018.

5. Rachael Bade, "The Most Painful Speech Ever," *Politico*, February 6, 2014, https://www.politico.com/story/2014/02/donna-edwards-speech-103238.

6. "Wit," *Merriam-Webster*, https://www.merriam-webster.com/dictionary/wit.

7. "The State of the Union, in Your Words," *NPR*, January 25, 2011, https://www.npr.org/2011/01/28/133211131/the-state-of-the-union-in-your-words.

8. Arthur Koestler, *The Act of Creation*, rev. ed. (New York: Penguin Books, 1990).

9. "Walter Mondale Interview," May 25, 1990, https://www.pbs.org/newshour/spc/debatingourdestiny/interviews/mondale.html.

10. Ricky Gervais, "The Difference between American and British Humour," *Time*, November 9, 2011.

11. "Mark Twain Quotes," *ThinkExist.com*, http://thinkexist.com/quotation/it_usually_takes_more_than_three_weeks_to_prepare/216612.html.

12. Personal conversation, September 4, 2018.

13. Emma Allen, "How the Upright Citizens Brigade Improvised a Comedy Empire," *The New Yorker*, November 5, 2016.

14. "Transcript of McCain on 'The Tonight Show,'" *Politico*, November 11, 2008, https://www.politico.com/story/2008/11/transcript-of-mccain-on-the-tonight-show-015542.

15. Emily Heil, "Is Obama's 2011 White House Correspondents' Dinner Burn to Blame for Trump's Campaign?," *The Washington Post*, February 10, 2016, https://www.washingtonpost.com/news/reliable-source/wp/2016/02/10/is-obamas-2011-white-house-correspondents-dinner-burn-to-blame-for-trumps-campaign/?utm_term=.a01ce21e827c.

16. Rachel Weiner, "Biden to Obama: 'A Big [Expletive] Deal,'" *The Washington Post*, March 23, 2010, http://voices.washingtonpost.com/44/2010/03/did-biden-tell-obama-signing-w.html.

17. Morris K. Udall, with Bob Neuman and Randy Udall, *Too Funny to Be President* (New York: Henry Holt, 1987).

CHAPTER 10

1. "Testimony of David J. Graham, MD, MPH," November 18, 2004, https://www.finance.senate.gov/imo/media/doc/111804dgtest.pdf.

2. Ibid.

3. Knight Foundation, "An Online Experimental Platform to Assess Trust in the Media," July 18, 2018, https://knightfoundation.org/reports/an-online-experimental-platform-to-assess-trust-in-the-media/.

4. Richard Ellmann, *James Joyce: The First Revision of the 1959 Classic* (New York: Oxford University Press, 1982), 505.

5. Maxwell Strachan, "This 'Jaws' Analogy Did Not Go Well for Mike Huckabee," *HuffPost*, October 11, 2016, https://www.huffingtonpost.com/entry/mike-huckabee-jaws-megyn-kelly_us_57fd3eb9e4b07b9b8752f352.

6. Jenna Amatulli, "Seth MacFarlane Links Not Baking Gay Wedding Cake to Not Seating Black People," *HuffPost*, June 4, 2018, https://www.huffingtonpost.com/entry/seth-macfarlane-not-baking-gay-wedding-cake-not-seating-black-people_us_5b156a96e4b010565aae77b6.

7. Nicholas Kristof, "A New Way to Tackle Gun Deaths," *The New York Times*, October 3, 2015, https://www.nytimes.com/2015/10/04/opinion/sunday/nicholas-kristof-a-new-way-to-tackle-gun-deaths.html.

8. Ibid.

9. "To Increase Charitable Donations, Appeal to the Heart—Not the Head," *Knowledge @ Wharton*, June 27, 2007, http://knowledge.wharton.upenn.edu/article/to-increase-charitable-donations-appeal-to-the-heart-not-the-head/.

10. Centers for Disease Control and Prevention, "Opioid Overdose: Understanding the Epidemic," December 19, 2018, https://www.cdc.gov/drugoverdose/epidemic/.

11. "Debate Night in America: Bernie Sanders vs Ted Cruz," *CNN*, February 7, 2017, https://archive.org/details/CNNW_20170208_020000_Debate_Night_In_America_Bernie_Sanders_vs_Ted_Cruz.

12. Jonah Berger, *Contagious: Why Things Catch On* (New York: Simon & Schuster, 2013).

13. Interview with Bob Lehrman, included in *The Political Speechwriter's Companion* (Washington, DC: CQ Press, 2009), 133.
14. Stephen Lucas, *The Art of Public Speaking*, 11th ed. (New York: McGraw-Hill, 2011), 341.

CHAPTER 11

1. Laura Sanicola, "Oprah's Golden Globes Speech Sends Weight Watchers Stock Soaring," *CNN Business*, January 8, 2018, https://money.cnn.com/2018/01/08/news/companies/weight-watchers-stock-oprah/index.html.
2. Jackie Strause, "Golden Globes: Oprah Calls for Day When Women Never Have to Say 'Me Too' Again," *The Hollywood Reporter*, January 7, 2018, https://www.hollywoodreporter.com/news/oprah-winfrey-golden-globes-2018-speech-1072351.
3. Ibid.
4. Ibid.
5. Ibid.
6. Morris K. Udall, with Bob Neuman and Randy Udall, *Too Funny to Be President* (New York: Henry Holt, 1987).
7. James C. Humes, *Roles Speakers Play* (New York: Harper and Row, 1976).
8. Peggy Noonan, "128th Annual Commencement Remarks," *The Catholic University of America*, May 13, 2017, https://www.catholic.edu/speeches-and-homilies/2017/commencement-2017.html.

CHAPTER 12

1. EyeWitness to History.com, "Writing the Declaration of Independence, 1776," http://eyewitnesstohistory.com/jefferson.htm.
2. Ibid.
3. Ibid.
4. Meredith Willson, "*Music Man*, the Lyrics," www.allmusicals.com/m/musicmanthe.htm.
5. William Safire, ed., *Lend Me Your Ears: Great Speeches in History*, updated and expanded ed. (New York: Norton, 2004), 685.
6. Christal Hayes, "Emma Gonzalez Survived the Florida Shooting. Now She's Taking on Trump and the NRA," *USA Today*, February 17, 2018, https://www.usatoday.com/story/news/2018/02/17/student-emma-gonzalez-school-shooting-gives-passionate-speech-against-g/348357002/.
7. John Baldoni, "Using Stories to Persuade," *Harvard Business Review*, March 24, 2011, https://hbr.org/2011/03/using-stories-as-a-tool-of-per.

8. Elie Wiesel, "The Perils of Indifference," delivered April 12, 1999, https://www.americanrhetoric.com/speeches/ewieselperilsofindifference.html.

9. "Aside," *Merriam-Webster*, https://www.merriam-webster.com/dictionary/aside.

10. Newton N. Minow, "Full Interview," Television Academy Foundation, https://interviews.televisionacademy.com/interviews/newton-n-minow#interview-clips.

CHAPTER 13

1. Lily Rothman, "The Scathing Speech That Made Television History," *Time*, May 9, 2016, http://time.com/4315217/newton-minow-vast-wasteland-1961-speech/.

2. Newton N. Minow, "Television and the Public Interest," delivered May 9, 1961, https://www.americanrhetoric.com/speeches/newtonminow.htm.

3. Aaron Sorkin, *The American President* (screenplay), http://www.dailyscript.com/scripts/american_president.html.

4. Daniel J. O'Keefe, *Persuasion: Theory and Research* (Thousand Oaks, CA: Sage, 2002), 187.

5. Peggy Noonan, *What I Saw at the Revolution* (New York: Random House, 1990), 229.

6. Ronald Reagan, *Where's the Rest of Me?* (New York: Duell, Sloan, and Pearce, 1965).

7. Hollywood's Golden Age, "*Kings Row* (1942)," http://www.hollywoodsgoldenage.com/movies/kings-row.html.

CHAPTER 14

1. Ted Sorensen, *Counselor: A Life at the Edge of History* (New York: Harper Perennial, 2009).

CHAPTER 15

1. Mark Leibovich, "The Speech That Made Obama," *The New York Times*, July 27, 2016, https://www.nytimes.com/2016/07/27/magazine/the-speech-that-made-obama.html.

2. Olivia Goldhill, "Rhetoric Scholars Pinpoint Why Trump's Inarticulate Speaking Style Is So Persuasive," *Quartz*, April 22, 2017, https://qz.com/965004/rhetoric-scholars-pinpoint-why-trumps-inarticulate-speaking-style-is-so-persuasive/.

3. John L. Rydell, "Public Speaking Tips You Can Learn from Politicians," *MeetingBurner*, February 25, 2016, https://www.meetingburner.com/blog/4-public-speaking-tips-you-can-learn-from-politicians/.

4. Robert Schlesinger, *White House Ghosts* (New York: Simon and Schuster, 2008), 364.
5. Shelly Chaiken, "Physical Appearance and Social Influence," in *Physical Appearance, Stigma, and Social Behavior: The Ontario Symposium*, vol. 3, ed. Peter Herman, Mark P. Zanna, and E. Tory Higgins (Hillsdale, NJ: Erlbaum, 1986), 143–147.
6. Dan O'Hair, Rob Stewart, and Hannah Rubenstein, *A Speaker's Guidebook* with *The Essential Guide to Rhetoric* (Boston: Bedford, 2012), 274.
7. Dale Carnegie, *Public Speaking and Influencing Men in Business* (Whitefish, MT: Kessinger, 2003), 131.
8. Francine Parnes, "In Business; From Dressing Down to Suiting Up," *The New York Times*, July 15, 2001, https://www.nytimes.com/2001/07/15/nyregion/in-business-from-dressing-down-to-suiting-up.html?pagewanted=all.
9. Steven Brydon and Michael Scott, *Between One and Many: The Art and Science of Public Speaking* (Mountain View, CA: Mayfield, 2007), 272.
10. Schlesinger, *White House Ghosts*, 271.
11. Justin Caba, "Cereal Box Psychology: Consumers More Likely to Buy Cereal If Character on Box Is Staring Directly at Them," *Medical Daily*, April 2, 2014, https://www.medicaldaily.com/cereal-box-psychology-consumers-more-likely-buy-cereal-if-character-box-staring-directly-them-274042.
12. Kate Murphy, "Psst. Look over Here," *The New York Times*, May 16, 2014, https://www.nytimes.com/2014/05/17/sunday-review/the-eyes-have-it.html.
13. Stephen Lucas, *The Art of Public Speaking*, 8th ed. (New York: McGraw-Hill, 2004), 372.
14. Peter Baker, "The (Very) Scripted President," *The New York Times*, March 5, 2009, https://www.nytimes.com/2009/03/05/world/americas/05iht-prompt.4.20623004.html.
15. "Pres. Clinton's Address to Congress on Health Care (1993)," https://www.youtube.com/watch?v=3K1d3E-BoUw.
16. Toby Harnden, "Caroline Kennedy Repeats 'You Know' 142 Times in Interview," *The Telegraph*, December 29, 2008, https://www.telegraph.co.uk/news/world news/northamerica/usa/4015918/Caroline-Kennedy-repeats-you-know-142-times-in-interview.html.
17. Noah Zandan, "How to Stop Saying 'Um,' 'Ah,' and 'You Know,'" *Harvard Business Review*, August 1, 2018, https://hbr.org/2018/08/how-to-stop-saying-um-ah-and-you-know.
18. Brad Phillips, "Are a Few 'Umms' Really That Bad?," *Mr. Media Training*, October 31, 2013, http://www.mrmediatraining.com/2013/10/31/are-a-few-ummms-really-that-bad/.
19. Taylor Branch, *Parting the Waters: America in the King Years, 1954–63* (New York: Simon and Schuster), 64.

20. Ibid., 76.

21. Robert Schlesinger, *White House Ghosts*, (Simon and Schuster, 2008), 365.

22. Ibid., 395.

CHAPTER 16

1. Pete Vernon, "Lie? Falsehood? What to Call the President's Words," *Columbia Journalism Review*, May 29, 2018, https://www.cjr.org/the_media_today/trump-lie-falsehood.php.

2. Bulletin Board, "Lies? False Claims? When Trump's Statements Aren't True," *The New York Times*, June 25, 2018, https://www.nytimes.com/2018/06/25/reader-center/donald-trump-lies-falsehoods.html.

3. "Donald Trump's File," *PolitiFact*, https://www.politifact.com/personalities/donald-trump/.

4. Glenn Kessler, Salvador Rizzo, and Meg Kelly, "As President Digs In, Falsehoods Fly," *The Washington Post*, August 2, 2018, https://www.pressreader.com/usa/the-washington-post/20180802/281500752062844.

5. Glenn Kessler, Salvador Rizzo, and Meg Kelly, "The Fact Checker: President Trump Has Made 4,229 False or Misleading Claims in 558 Days," *The Washington Post*, August 1, 2018, https://www.washingtonpost.com/news/fact-checker/wp/2018/08/01/president-trump-has-made-4229-false-or-misleading-claims-in-558-days/?utm_term=.bc17b67cbecf.

6. Glenn Kessler, "Not Just Misleading. Not Merely False. A Lie," *The Washington Post*, August 22, 2018, https://www.washingtonpost.com/politics/2018/08/23/not-just-misleading-not-merely-false-lie/?utm_term=.124a149c5062.

7. Plato, "Phaedrus," translated by Benjamin Jowett, http://classics.mit.edu/Plato/phaedrus.html.

8. National Communication Association Credo for Ethical Communication, http://open.lib.umn.edu/publicspeaking/chapter/2-2-ethics-in-public-speaking/.

9. "Understanding the Ethics of Public Speaking," https://press.rebus.community/uwmpublicspeaking/chapter/ethics-matters-understanding-the-ethics-of-public-speaking/.

10. "Plagiarize," *Merriam-Webster*, https://www.merriam-webster.com/dictionary/plagiarize.

11. Aaron Blake, "93 Percent Different: The Trump Team's Brazenly Bad Defenses of Melania's Alleged Plagiarism," *The Washington Post*, July 19, 2016, https://www.washingtonpost.com/news/the-fix/wp/2016/07/19/the-trump-campaigns-brazen-attempts-to-defend-melania-trumps-alleged-plagiarism/?utm_term=.a520489e127a.

12. Mike Allen, "Clinton Aide Accuses Obama of Plagiarism," *Politico*, February 18, 2008.

13. Mark Memmott, "LISTEN: Rare Recording of '52 Speech That King Drew From," *NPR*, August 28, 2013, https://www.npr.org/sections/thetwo-way/2013/08/28/216466421/listen-rare-recording-of-52-speech-that-king-drew-from.

14. Aaron Blake, "Rand Paul's Plagiarism Allegations, and Why They Matter," *The Washington Post*, November 4, 2013, https://www.washingtonpost.com/news/the-fix/wp/2013/11/04/rand-pauls-plagiarism-allegations-and-why-they-matter/.

15. American University, "Academic Integrity Code," https://american.edu/academics/integrity/code.cfm.

16. Leslie Horn, "Ad Council Teams with Google, AT&T for Internet Safety Coalition," *PC Magazine*, November 4, 2010, https://www.pcmag.com/article2/0,2817,2372135,00.asp.

17. The Outfield, "Somewhere in America" lyrics, https://www.azlyrics.com/lyrics/outfield/somewhereinamerica.html.

18. Turnitin, https://www.turnitin.com.

19. "Mislead," *Merriam-Webster*, https://www.merriam-webster.com/dictionary/mislead.

20. Salvador Rizzo and Meg Kelly, "Anatomy of a Trump Rally: 76 Percent of Claims Are False, Misleading or Lacking Evidence," *The Washington Post*, July 10, 2018, https://www.washingtonpost.com/news/fact-checker/wp/2018/07/10/anatomy-of-a-trump-rally-76-percent-of-claims-are-false-misleading-or-lacking-evidence/?utm_term=.826a9545aecf.

21. "Daniel Dale's Trump Checks," *Toronto Star*, https://www.thestar.com/news/donald-trump-fact-check.html.

22. Daniel Berger, "The Unintended Consequences of Killing the Estate Tax," *TaxVox*, October 9, 2017, https://www.taxpolicycenter.org/taxvox/unintended-consequences-killing-estate-tax.

23. Sara Hurwitz, "Fact-Checking Is Job 1 for Any White House: Speechwriter," *USA Today*, January 26, 2017, https://www.usatoday.com/story/opinion/2017/01/26/fact-checking-job-one-for-any-white-house-speechwriter-column/97001236/.

24. "Lie," *Merriam-Webster*, https://www.merriam-webster.com/dictionary/lie.

25. John Mueller, "The Democratic Party Fights to Save 'Jim Crow' and Restore Segregation," *Armored Column*, February 11, 2017, http://armored-column.com/the-democratic-party-fights-to-save-jim-crow-and-restore-segregation/; Randall Bennett Woods, *Fulbright: A Biography* (New York: Cambridge University Press, 1998).

26. "Trump Is Intelligent, but Not Fit or Level-Headed," *Quinnipac University Poll*, January 10, 2018, https://poll.qu.edu/national/release-detail?ReleaseID=2511.

27. Matthew Seeger, "Ethical Issues in Corporate Speechwriting," *Journal of Business Ethics* 11, no. 7 (July 1992): 501–504.

28. Counted by Bob Lehrman, U.S. Senate Telephone Directory 2017, compiled by the Sergeant at Arms, U.S. Senate.

29. Tim Weiner, "Theodore C. Sorensen, 82, Kennedy Counselor, Dies," *The New York Times*, October 31, 2010, https://www.nytimes.com/2010/11/01/us/01sorensen.html.

30. Seeger, "Ethical Issues," 501–504.

31. Thomas H. Bivins, *Public Relations Writing: The Essentials of Style and Format* (Lincolnwood, IL: NTC/Contemporary Publishing Group), 46.

32. James Fallows, "More on Speechwriting and Obama's Wesleyan Address," *The Atlantic*, May 26, 2008, https://www.theatlantic.com/technology/archive 2008/05/more-on-speechwriting-and-obama-apos-s-wesleyan-address-updated/8061/.

33. Ted Sorensen, *Counselor: A Life at the Edge of History* (New York: Harper Perennial, 2009), 151.

34. Stephen Rodrick, "I Helped Write a Speech Defending a Vote for Clarence Thomas. I Regret It Still," *The Washington Post*, September 21, 2018, https://www.washingtonpost.com/outlook/i-helped-write-a-speech-defending-a-vote-for-clarence-thomas-i-regret-it-still/2018/09/21/d60b3300-bcee-11e8-8792-78719177250f_story.html?utm_term=.7e726c55c8ff.

35. David McGrath, "In the Words of My Speechwriter," *The Washington Post*, September 4, 2008.

36. "Astronaut John Glenn Laid to Rest at Arlington National Cemetery," *Reuters*, April 6, 2017, https://www.reuters.com/article/us-people-johnglenn/astronaut-john-glenn-laid-to-rest-at-arlington-national-cemetery-idUSKBN17828L.

CHAPTER 17

1. American Rhetoric, "Top 100 Speeches," https://www.americanrhetoric.com/newtop100speeches.htm.

2. Robert Schlesinger, "JFK, FDR, and the Secret History of How a Great Inaugural Address Is Written," *U.S. News & World Report*, January 15, 2009, https://www.usnews.com/opinion/articles/2009/01/15/jfk-fdr-and-the-secret-history-of-how-a-great-inaugural-address-is-written.

3. Ibid.

4. Donald J. Trump (@realDonaldTrump), "Writing my inaugural address," *Twitter*, January 18, 2017, 9:33 a.m., https://twitter.com/realDonaldTrump/status/821772494864580614.

5. "Photo: Obama's Handwritten Notes," *CNN Politics*, February 19, 2013, http://politicalticker.blogs.cnn.com/2013/02/19/photo-obamas-handwritten-notes/.

6. "Roque Wants 'Better' Speechwriters for Duterte," *PhilStar*, July 19, 2018, https://www.philstar.com/headlines/2018/07/19/1834965/roque-wants-better-speechwriters-duterte.

7. Ibid.
8. Personal conversation, July 10, 2018.
9. Albert Mohler, "Lessons from a Speechwriter: A Conversation with Barton Swaim," *Thinking in Public*, March 27, 2017, https://albertmohler.com/2017/03/27/speechwriter-conversation-barton-swaim/.
10. David Litt, *Thanks, Obama: My Hopey, Changey White House Years* (New York: HarperCollins, 2017), 304.
11. Peter Grier, "Challenger Explosion: How President Reagan Responded," *The Christian Science Monitor*, January 28, 2011, https://www.csmonitor.com/USA/Politics/The-Vote/2011/0128/Challenger-explosion-How-President-Reagan-responded.
12. HWASpeakersBureau, "Peggy Noonan: A Poem, Ronald Reagan, and the Challenger Speech," November 13, 2017, https://www.youtube.com/watch?v=KfXQ8yto2DI.
13. Ibid.

APPENDIX

1. David Herbert Donald, *Lincoln* (New York: Simon and Schuster, 1995), 460–466.
2. Barbara Mikulski et al., *Nine and Counting: The Women of the Senate* (New York: HarperCollins, 2001), https://www.goodreads.com/work/quotes/128818.
3. James Sherk, "The Heritage Foundation Honors Alumnus, Senator Tom Cotton," *The Heritage Foundation*, December 9, 2016, https://www.heritage.org/conservatism/report/the-heritage-foundation-honors-alumnus-senator-tom-cotton.
4. Emily's List, "2018 We Are Family Conference and Gala," https://emilyslist.org/2018.
5. Allegheny College, "Prize for Civility in Public Life," https://sites.allegheny.edu/civilityaward/2018-allegheny-college-prize-for-civility-in-public-life/.

Bibliography

The Political Speechwriter's Companion might be unique in its focus on how to write and deliver political speeches. But there exist many books about speech that include the political: scholarly books on rhetoric or persuasion, public speaking textbooks, anthologies, quote books, joke and anecdote compendiums, histories, memoirs, biographies, and how-to books on humor or argument, among others.

Since the 2016 campaign when rhetoric emerged as an important issue, journalists and other writers have produced hundreds of useful articles about the candidates' speeches.

Meanwhile, since the first edition of this book appeared, we have seen an explosion of new websites dealing with politics. Not all political websites are useful for speechwriters—some don't meet the standards for scholarship that would allow us to cite them here. But there's no questioning how helpful Wikipedia and others are for the practical work of getting a speech done.

In this bibliography, you'll find many of the books, articles, and websites cited in this book—as well as others we've found useful. We've listed them in each section with a brief guide to what you might find useful about them.

In no way is this a complete list; it's a sampling of the kinds of books and websites harried speechwriters in politics use. Spending some time with these can lead you to many others.

Final note: Some of the items on this list are out of print. Even ten years ago, it would have been pointless to list them, even if they contained valuable insights. Now, however, Google and Amazon make it easy to track them down, place an order, and for a few dollars find them on your doorstep within days. Don't be put off by books published 20—or 2,500—years ago. We include them because they remain useful today.

BOOKS ON RHETORIC OR PERSUASION

Aristotle. *Ars Rhetorica*. New York: Oxford University Press, 1959.

Berger, Jonah. *Contagious: Why Things Catch On*. New York: Simon and Schuster, 2013.

Cialdini, Robert B. *Influence: The Psychology of Persuasion*. Rev. ed. New York: Harper Business, 2006.

Corbitt, Edward P. J., and Robert Connors. *Classical Rhetoric for the Modern Student*. 4th ed. New York: Oxford University Press, 1998.

Gottschall, Jonathan. *The Storytelling Animal: How Stories Make Us Human.* Boston: Houghton Mifflin Harcourt, 2012.

Heath, Chip, and Dan Heath. *Made to Stick: Why Some Ideas Survive and Others Die.* New York: Random House, 2007.

Jowett, Garth S., and Victoria O'Donnell. *Propaganda and Persuasion.* Thousand Oaks, CA: Sage, 2006.

O'Keefe, Daniel J. *Persuasion, Theory, and Research.* 2nd ed. Thousand Oaks, CA: Sage, 2002.

Pink, Daniel H. *To Sell Is Human: The Surprising Truth about Motivating Others.* New York: Riverhead Books, 2012.

Toulmin, Stephen, Richard Rieke, and Allen Janik. *An Introduction to Reasoning.* New York: Macmillan, 1979.

Wheelan, Charles. *Naked Statistics: Stripping Dread from Data.* New York: Norton, 2013.

Each is interesting for different reasons: Aristotle to amaze you with how many ideas are still useful after 2,300 years; Berger for his ideas on what makes ideas go viral; Cialdini because of the research he uses and the interesting examples he cites; Corbitt because it still provides a complete overview of rhetorical techniques only touched on in this book; Gottschall because he (and others) focuses on the power of narrative; Jowett and O'Donnell for its insights into the ethics of persuasion; O'Keefe because it gives you confidence that meticulous research lies beyond the tips on persuasion covered here; Pink because in the colloquial voice of a former speechwriter, he makes the science of persuasion accessible and relevant; Toulmin et al. for its surprisingly readable way of making us see that techniques of persuasion in politics aren't much different from what we do in the rest of our lives; and Wheelan for the many ways he helps even data-deficient writers understand numbers.

PUBLIC SPEAKING TEXTBOOKS

Gamble, Michael, and Teri Kwal Gamble. *The Public Speaking Playbook.* 2nd ed. Thousand Oaks, CA: Sage, 2017.

Lucas, Stephen E. *The Art of Public Speaking.* 12th ed. New York: McGraw-Hill, 2009.

Monroe, Alan H., and Douglas Ehninger. *Principles of Speech.* 5th brief ed. Glenview, IL: Scott, Foresman, 1964.

O'Hair, Daniel, Rob Stewart, and Hannah Rubenstein. *Speaker's Guidebook: Text and Reference.* 3rd ed. Boston: Bedford/St. Martins, 2007.

Zarefsky, David. *Public Speaking: Strategies for Success.* 8th ed. Boston: Pearson, 2016.

Lucas remains the best-selling public speaking book now in print, for many good reasons. Gamble and Gamble provides useful interactive and collaborative exercises; O'Hair et al. is an excellent resource for its handy yet not simplistic way of approaching every part of speechmaking; and Zarefsky is valuable for its emphasis on the strategic decision involved in speech. While there are more current editions of Monroe, we include this one out of sentiment, and because there should be some readers interested in what Monroe, whose ideas so influenced this book, wrote on his own fifty years ago.

BOOKS ON POLITICAL SPEECH

Heinrichs, Jay. *Thank You for Arguing: What Aristotle, Lincoln, and Homer Simpson Can Teach Us about the Art of Persuasion*. New York: Three Rivers Press, 2007.

Jamieson, Kathleen Hall. *Eloquence in an Electronic Age: The Transformation of Political Speechmaking*. New York: Oxford University Press, 1988.

Jamieson, Kathleen Hall, and Karlyn Kohrs Campbell. *The Interplay of Influence: News Advertising, Politics, and the Mass Media*. 4th ed. Belmont, CA: Wadsworth, 1997.

Kusnet, David. *Speaking American: How the Democrats Can Win in the Nineties*. New York: Thunder's Mouth Press, 1992.

Lakoff, George. *Don't Think of an Elephant*. White River Junction, VT: Chelsea Green, 2004.

Lim, Elvin. *The Anti-intellectual Presidency: The Decline of Presidential Rhetoric from George Washington to George W. Bush*. New York: Oxford University Press, 2008.

Luntz, Frank. *Words That Work: It's Not What You Say, It's What People Hear*. New York: Hyperion, 2007.

Nelson, Michael, and Russell L. Riley, eds. *The President's Words: Speeches and Speechwriting in the Modern White House*. Lawrence: University of Kansas Press, 2010.

Schlesinger, Robert. *White House Ghosts: Presidents and Their Speechwriters*. New York: Simon and Schuster, 2008.

Thompson, Mark. *Enough Said: What's Gone Wrong with the Language of Politics*. New York: St. Martin's Press, 2016.

Tulis, Jeffrey K. *The Rhetorical Presidency*. Princeton, NJ: Princeton University Press, 1988.

It shouldn't surprise you that not everyone agrees with every idea in *The Political Speechwriter's Companion*. You don't have to completely share Jamieson and Lim's alarm about the trends in political speech to profit from the substance, nuance, and insight with which the authors make their case. Heinrichs manages to take Aristotle and show you how what he said is as contemporary as yesterday's argument with your kid. Luntz and Lakoff have become famous for the way politicians use their insights. Kusnet was written for a specific campaign but remains relevant. Nelson and Riley offer analysis not just of speeches, but from speechwriters. Schlesinger will give you an anecdotal look at presidential speechwriting that both could and should influence the way you work. Thompson provides a stingingly critical look at the role language plays in modern politics. And Tulis offers you historical context, covering two centuries that can explain the way political speeches get written in this one.

ANTHOLOGIES

Dionne, E. J., and Joy-Ann Reid, eds. *We Are the Change We Seek: The Speeches of Barack Obama*. New York: Bloomsbury USA, 2017.

MacArthur, Brian, ed. *The Penguin Book of Historic Speeches*. London: Penguin, 1996.

Safire, William, ed. *Lend Me Your Ears: Great Speeches in History*. Updated and expanded ed. New York: Norton, 2004.

Widmer, Ted, ed. *American Speeches: Political Oratory from Patrick Henry to Barack Obama*. New York: Library of America, 2011.

No one would try writing a novel or screenplay without first reading hundreds of them. Why should speechwriting be any different? There are hundreds of speech anthologies. Here are a few, useful for different reasons. Dionne and Reid gives us a look at a president whose speeches were central to his appeal; the Penguin anthology teaches us that there are many famous speeches effective for a single line while not particularly effective elsewhere; Safire, justifiably a classic, should interest readers not just because of the selections or how Safire groups them, but for his interesting introductions to each one; and Widmer, a historian and former speechwriter, offers a compilation that shows how speech can capture not only our politics but our identity.

QUOTATIONS, HUMOR, AND ANECDOTES

Quotations

Eigen, Lewis D., and Jonathan P. Siegel, eds. *The Macmillan Dictionary of Political Quotations*. New York: Macmillan, 1993.

Goldstein, Sharon, ed. *Langenscheidt's Pocket Merriam-Webster Guide to Quotations*. New York: Langescheidt, 2002.

Grothe, Mardy. *Never Let a Fool Kiss You or a Kiss Fool You*. New York: Penguin Group, 2002.

Humes, James C. *The Wit and Wisdom of Winston Churchill*. New York: Harper Perennial, 1995.

Jay, Antony. *The Oxford Dictionary of Political Quotations*. New York: Oxford University Press, 2001.

Keyes, Ralph. *The Quote Verifier: Who Said What, Where, and When*. New York: St. Martin's Griffin, 2006.

O'Brien, Geoffrey. *Bartlett's Familiar Quotations*. 18th ed. Boston: Little Brown, 2012.

Petros, Ross, and Kathryn Petros. *The Stupidest Things Ever Said by Politicians*. New York: Pocket Books, 1999.

Platt, Suzy. *Respectfully Quoted: A Dictionary of Quotations from the Library of Congress*. Washington, DC: Congressional Quarterly, 1992.

Shapiro, Fred, ed. *The Yale Book of Quotations*. New Haven, CT: Yale University Press, 2006.

Torricelli, Robert G., ed. *Quotations for Public Speakers: A Historical, Literary, and Political Anthology*. New Brunswick, NJ: Rutgers University Press, 2000.

Humor

Dole, Bob. *Great Political Wit*. New York: Nan Talese/Doubleday, 1998.

Udall, Morris. *Too Funny to Be President*. New York: Holt, 1987.

Anecdotes

Fadiman, Clifton, ed. *The Little, Brown Book of Anecdotes*. Boston: Little, Brown, 1985.

Fuller, Edmund, ed. *2500 Anecdotes for All Occasions*. New York: Avenel Books, 1980.

Such books come in for biting criticism, and not without reason. Listeners who hear speakers quote Mark Twain often don't know they are reading a line picked out by some staffer from a book. In the best of all worlds, quotes might be ones speakers remember themselves. On the other hand, there is no simple way to find the variety of pithy ways people have expressed the ideas you'd like to include. The quote books here all emphasize subjects suited to politics: Grothe is full of interesting examples about a figure of speech only touched on in this book; *The Quote Verifier* not only helps you avoid making embarrassing mistakes, but provides material you can actually include because its nuggets of information are so interesting; Dole and Udall offer the advantage of jokes that the authors actually used in politics; and the anecdote books, especially Fadiman, provide stories you can use at any stage in your speech.

REFERENCE

The American Heritage Dictionary. 5th ed. Boston: Houghton Mifflin, 2015.

Burns, Christopher, ed. *The Seashell Anthology of Great Poetry*. Edgartown, MA: Seashell Press, 2011.

Chase's Calendar of Events. New York: McGraw-Hill Professional. Annual.

It goes without saying that speechwriters need a dictionary. Actually, you need several; *American Heritage* is good because it reflects common usage—and the paperback version is little enough to carry around with you. We include Burns because we could all use more poetry. And why *Chase's Calendar*? Because we have learned how often it helps make speeches interesting, and moving—as it does in President Reagan's *Challenger* speech found in this book's appendix ("There's a coincidence today"). Most events throughout history remain useful. And while there are plenty of internet sites offering famous events for every day of the year, we include this one because its creators update it annually.

BOOKS ABOUT POLITICS

Conrad, Jessamyn. *What You Should Know about Politics ... but Don't: A Nonpartisan Guide to the Issues That Matter*. New York: Arcade, 2016.

Greenfield, Jeff. *Playing to Win: An Insider's Guide to Politics*. New York: Simon and Schuster, 1980.

Iyengar, Shanto. *Media Politics: A Citizen's Guide*. 3rd ed. New York: Norton, 2016.

Matthews, Christopher. *Hardball: How Politics Is Played, Told by One Who Knows the Game*. Rev. ed. New York: Touchstone, 1999.

Meacham, Jon. *The Soul of America: The Battle for Our Better Angels*. New York: Random House, 2018.

A variety of books about how politics really works. Conrad offers context not only for recent elections but for perennial issues. Greenfield, long out of print, is easy to find online: look for the parody of the political stump speech. Matthews's insight into politics, on display each day by the former Carter speechwriter, includes a lot that's relevant for speechwriters today. Meacham looks at the politics of division with a historical lens. Iyengar gives readers a well-researched and sometimes fascinating look at how political campaigns cope with the changes in news media coverage.

MEMOIRS

Anderson, Patrick. *Electing Jimmy Carter*. Baton Rouge: Louisiana State University Press, 1994.

Litt, David. *Thanks Obama: My Hopey, Changey White House Years.* New York: HarperCollins, 2017.

Noonan, Peggy. *What I Saw at the Revolution: A Political Life in the Reagan Era.* New York: Random House, 1990.

Shrum, Robert. *No Excuses: Concessions of a Serial Campaigner.* New York: Simon and Schuster, 2007.

Sorensen, Ted. *Counselor.* New York: HarperCollins, 2008.

Swaim, Barton. *The Speechwriter: A Brief Education in Politics.* New York: Simon and Schuster, 2015.

Waldman, Michael. *POTUS Speaks: Finding the Words That Defined the Clinton Presidency.* New York: Simon and Schuster, 2000.

Each of these, candid and detailed, presents portraits of the different ways speakers and writers interact. The liveliest are Noonan's and Litt's. Noonan's reads as if the former Reagan speechwriter were keeping a daily journal; Litt, who in addition to working on serious policy speeches was often the lead writer on Obama's humor speeches, provides a coming-of-age story that is funny yet earnest. Shrum covers far more than speech issues: the former McGovern speechwriter provides a candid look at over three decades of presidential campaigns. Despite some evasions about his role in speeches, Sorensen's book is indispensable for those wanting to know about the decade that has influenced political speech for over fifty years. Swaim's account is equal parts cynical, funny, and detailed. Waldman's slim book is reasonably candid about how the speeches worked during the Clinton administration with a particularly detailed account of how an administration puts together a State of the Union address.

HOW-TO BOOKS

Anderson, Chris. *TED Talks: The Official TED Guide to Public Speaking.* Boston: Mariner Books, 2017.

Clark, Roy Peter. *Writing Tools: Fifty Essential Strategies for Every Writer.* Washington, DC: CQ Press, 2008.

Cook, Jeff Scott. *The Elements of Speechwriting and Public Speaking.* New York: Macmillan, 1988.

Grebanier, Bernard. *Playwriting: How to Write for the Theater.* Apollo ed. New York: Crowell, 1965.

Humes, James C. *Speak like Churchill, Stand like Lincoln: 21 Powerful Secrets of History's Greatest Speakers.* New York: Three Rivers Press, 2009.

Noonan, Peggy. *On Speaking Well: How to Give a Speech with Style, Substance, and Clarity.* New York: Harper Perennial, 1999.

Strunk, William, Jr., and E. B. White. *The Elements of Style.* 4th ed. London: Longman, 1995.

Anderson is the curator of the TED franchise, and we put this resource in this section (and not Public Speaking) because of its insight on a specific but very popular and emulated format. While not just about politics, Noonan and Cook are useful and succinct. The E. B. White revision of Strunk may have first appeared fifty years ago, but various editors have revised it, and it still has useful suggestions for writers—though not more than Clark's less well-known but graceful and sensible book. Humes unlocks the speaking secrets of great leaders. And Grebanier? Cited in this book, it reminds us that speechwriting isn't the only kind of writing for which systematic study helps.

ARTICLES

Scholarly

Allcott, Hunt, and Matthew Gentzkow. "Social Media and Fake News in the 2016 Election." *Journal of Economic Perspectives* 31, no. 2 (Spring 2017): 211–236. https://web.stanford.edu/~gentzkow/research/fakenews.pdf.

Bhattacharjee, Yudhijit. "Why We Lie: The Science Behind Our Deceptive Ways." *National Geographic*, June 2017. www.nationalgeographic.com/magazine/2017/06/lying-hoax-false-fibs-science/.

Frobish, Todd S. "Jamieson Meets Lucas: Eloquence and Pedagogical Model(s) in the Art of Public Speaking." *Communication Education* 49 (July 2000): 239–252.

Lucas, Stephen E. "Speechmaking, Pedagogy, and Civic Responsibility." *American Communication Journal* 5, no. 2 (Winter 2002). http://ac-journal.org/journal/vol5/iss2/special/lucas.pdf.

On Speechwriting

McGrath, David. "In the Words of my Speechwriter . . ." *The Washington Post*, September 4, 2008. www.washingtonpost.com/wp-dyn/content/article/2008/09/03/AR2008090303133.html.

Scully, Matthew. "Present at the Creation." *The Atlantic* (September 2007). www.theatlantic.com/doc/200709/michael-gerson.

Shesol, Jeff. "Five Myths about Speechwriting." *The Washington Post*, July 22, 2016.

Allcott and Gentzkow, as well as Bhattacharjee, helped provide context for the chapter on ethics. Frobish and Lucas are useful for readers interested in the scholarly differences about rhetoric that are relevant to political speeches. Scully provides the kind of candid discussion almost unheard of in the field.

Shesol lifts the curtain on the perception of speechwriting. McGrath suggests politicians credit their writers.

WEBSITES

The internet has revolutionized the way speechwriters approach speechwriting—they can access transcripts instantly, live stream events, or even watch a speech on YouTube years after it has been given. It has also dramatically changed the way we research, even since the first edition was released ten years ago.

The sites below barely scratch the surface. But they will help you diversify your speechwriting resources.

American Rhetoric (www.americanrhetoric.com). Of all the sites whose URLs should be at your fingertips, Stephen Lucas's might be the most useful. Its enormous bank of political speeches, usually providing both video and transcript, is indispensable for anyone seriously interested in seeing what has been done. The speech bank generally organizes speeches alphabetically by speaker's *first* name.

Bartleby (www.bartleby.com). A great source for quotes and inspirational material.

Congressional Record **(www.congress.gov/congressional-record).** This has a transcript of every speech delivered on the House and Senate floors in Washington. (You can also watch the proceedings here: **www.houselive.gov** and **www.senate.gov/floor**.)

C-SPAN. On **www.c-span.org**, you can watch floor proceedings as well as press conferences and a host of other public policy and political events.

Democratic National Committee (www.democrats.org) and **Republican National Committee (www.gop.com).** The websites of the DNC and RNC are good for a quick look at what your party urges on every issue.

Dictionary.com. As mentioned, speechwriters should have more than one dictionary. This online version is easy to access. Its sister site, **Thesaurus.com**, is particularly useful when you, as the authors have, need to find alliterative words in a hurry.

Etymonline.com, an online etymology dictionary, is a great resource when you need more than just a definition.

FactCheck.org and others (**www.politfact.com**). Consult these for their rigorous analysis of whether politicians are telling the truth.

Harris Poll (www.harrisinteractive.com/harris_poll) and **Pew Research Center (www.pewresearch.org).** With the incredible Harris and Pew archives of American attitudes on specific issues, political and cultural, uncovering credible information quickly has become much easier for speechwriters.

History.com. Like *Chase's Calendar*, **www.history.com/this-day-in-history** is a great resource, showing how serendipity can be a speechwriter's best friend.

Ragan Communications (www.ragan.com). This publisher puts on conferences for speechwriters and also provides useful content about different speech issues.

TED.com, with its library of interesting presentations, has become a must for any speechwriter whose boss has said, "I'd like to make this like a TED Talk." (In other words, every speechwriter.)

Vital Speeches of the Day has published noteworthy oratory since 1934. Today, mainly through its website **VSOTD.com**, it's an invaluable resource because it offers not only an archive of important speeches but other resources, including white papers and a link to the Professional Speechwriters Association.

Index

Acceptance speeches, elements, 437
Access Hollywood, 195
Accomplishments from past,
    examples, 34
Achiever character, inspire solutions, 259
Acknowledgements:
    compliments, 419
    ending speeches memorably, 86
    examples, 213, 371, 425
    problem, 241
    saluting, 423–424
    thank-yous, praise and, 205, 206
    unique, make each, 215–216
    See also Praise; Thank-yous
ACLU, 42
Acosta, Alexander, 267–268
Acronym joke, 161
Active verbs, 98–99
Ad absurdum fallacy, 196
Adams, John, 227
Addressing the absent enemy, 116
Ad hominem fallacy, 192–193, 328
Ad-libbing, 317
Ad populum fallacy, 196–197
Advertising, as stories, 87. *See also*
    Marketing techniques
Agler, Brian, xix, 158
"Ain't I a Woman?" (Truth), 235
Alexander, Lamar (Senator),
    xxi–xxiii, 212
Alfalfa Club roasts, 159, 165–166,
    442–447
Alliances, cementing, 182–183
Alliteration:
    examples, 1, 124, 129, 219, 257–258,
        395, 404, 414, 434, 435
    in litany, 125

purpose of, 47
repetition and, 119–121, 130
American Journal of Political
    Science, 59
American President, The (film),
    260–261
Americanrhetoric.com, 64–65
Ammerman, Colleen, 14–15
Analogy:
    context, evidence and, 186–187
    domino, 195–196
    as evidence, 183
    example, 123–124
    figurative, 185
    literal, 183–185
    ridicule and, 209
    wit and, 168–169
Analogy resources, 66
Anaphora:
    examples, 2, 124–125, 129,
        131, 376, 397
    litany *v.,* 228
    repetition and, 119
    "we can do better" litany and, 256
Anderson, Chris, 56
Anderson, Patrick (Carter
    speechwriter), 15
Anecdote:
    archive file of, 360
    books on, 467
    defining, 135
    delivery, take your time, 148
    dramatic, 138–139, 239
    examples, 133–134, 439
    exercise, 148
    funny, 139–140
    historical, 146, 240

illustrative, 145–146
neurology and, 136
parable, 146–147
personal, 140–141, 238–239
persuasion and, 136
problems and, 238–240
punch lines, 147
research on, 136
speechwriter's checklist, 149
story structures, 135
storytelling and, 136–137
symbolic, 141–143
truthfulness and, 147
"An or a" litany, 231–232
Anthologies, of speeches, 466
Anti-intellectualism, 101, 104–109
Anti-intellectual Presidency, The (Lim), 4, 104–109
Antimetabole, 120, 234, 257–258
Antithesis, 121
    contrast, problems, 236
    examples, 124, 129, 130, 218, 372, 377, 395, 414, 435
    "let us" solutions and, 257–258
Apostrophe, 260–261
Appeals:
    characterization (ethos), 35–37
    emotion (pathos), 28–29
    reason (logos), 31–32
Appearance:
    attractiveness, age and, 298
    delivery and, 297
    dress better than audience, 297–298
    posture, stand straight, 297
Applause:
    contagious, 46
    human interest appeals and, 134
    ritual of, 215
    solutions and, 270
Applause lines, 123, 127, 231, 256, 265
Apples and oranges, false analogy, 194, 328

Argue responsibly, 190, 385
Arguing responsibly, 190
Arguments:
    ad hominem, 192–193, 328
    ad populum, 196–197
    apples and oranges, 194
    either-or, 195
    false cause, 193–194
    slippery slope, 195–196, 391
    straw man, 191–192
    See also Fallacies
Aristotle:
    Ars Rhetorica, 21, 26
    ethos (character), 29–31
    logos (reasoning), 31–32
    pathos (emotions) and, 28
    persuasive speech and, 13
    quote, 30
    rhetoric and, 21
    rule of three, 26–31
Arm movement, speech delivery, 301–303
Ars Rhetorica (Aristotle), 21, 26
Articulated phrase (uh, ummm, er), speech delivery and, 306–309
Art of Confession, The (Koestler), 155
Art of Public Speaking, The (Lucas), 48
Asides:
    example, 444
    problems and, 241
Assertions:
    motives and, 193
    unsupported, 253
Assonance, 121
Asyndeton, 122
Atlantic, magazine, 59
Attention:
    analogy, use for ridicule, 209
    drama, open with, 210–211
    examples, 88, 223, 390, 394, 401–402, 407, 413
    exercise, exhume the lead, 224

Index

humor, opening with, 207
insult the other side, 208
listeners, remind purpose, 210–212
Monroe's Motivated Sequence and, 74–79, 86
personal story, open with funny, 209
poke fun at yourself, 207–208
public speaking stories, 210
quips, 208
quote humorists, 208–209
storytelling and, 204
See also Beginning speeches
Attribution, 447
Audiences:
 accommodating different, 40
 appeals to. *See* Appeals
 beliefs of, 42–43
 crowd response, praise and, 220
 demographics of, 45
 dress better than your, 297–298
 feelings about speaker, 45–46
 friendly, 46–47
 identifying, 40–41
 inspire, strategy to, 282–284
 interests of, 44–45
 laughter and, 46
 live, 18, 41, 301
 MMS and praising, 86
 needs of each unique, 41–42
 neutrals, incremental gains and, 48
 partisan, 231, 285
 passive persuasion, 48
 praising, 443
 primary/secondary, 40
 questions to ask about, 39–40
 research event demographics, 55
 segment, 217–218, 410
 speechwriter's checklist, 50–51
 story to speak to larger, 212
 uniqueness of, 41–45
 values of, 43–44
 See also Demographics; Listeners

Average folk, stories about, 35
Awards speeches:
 elements of, 436–437
 example, 437–440
 types of, 436
Awareness, 408–409
Axios (political news aggregate), 64

Background, credibility and, 85
Baker, Howard, Jr., xxii
Bakshian, Aram (Reagan speechwriter), 281
Balance speech elements, MMS, 86
Bazelon, Emily, 67
Bee, Samantha, 64, 170
Beginning speeches:
 attention through story, 204
 dramatic, 210–211
 flat opening, 206
 "howdahell" opening, 213–215
 humorous opening with, 207
 personal story, open with funny, 209
 praise, thanks acknowledgements, 212–220
 speechwriter's checklist, 225
 thank-yous and praise, 205
 See also Attention; Structure, speech
Begley, Sharon, 137
Beliefs, audience:
 persuasive speech, 42–43
 reinforce, urge action, 46–47
Believer character, inspire solutions, 259–260
Benjamin Franklin (Isaacson), 66
Bentsen, Lloyd (Senator), 168, 169, 209
Better than doing nothing, 257
Better than the other guy, 256
Better than what exists, 256
Better than what we've done, 257–258
Between One and Many (Brydon & Scott), 298
Biases, avoiding, 175

Biden, Joe, 94, 161, 171
Biographies, as research source, 66
Bivens, Thomas, 340
Blink (Gladwell), 66
Body language, 297. *See also* Gestures, speech delivery and; Movement, speech delivery and
Bonior, David, 54, 323
Bono, 45
Booker, Corey (Senator), 221
Books (resource), 65–66
  anecdotes, 467
  anthologies, 466
  how-to, 469–470
  humor, 467
  memoirs, 468–469
  political speech, 465–644
  politics, 468
  quotations, 466–467
  reference, 468
Books (resource)—specific
  Anti-intellectual Presidency, The (Lim), 4, 104–109
  Art of Public Speaking, The (Lucas), 48
  Benjamin Franklin (Isaacson), 66
  Blink (Gladwell), 66
  Chase's Calendar of Events, 213
  Columbia Guide to Standard English, 98
  Contagious: Why Things Catch On (Berger), 189–190
  Drive (Pink), 66
  Grant (Chernow), 66
  Hamilton (Chernow), 66
  Influence (Cialdini), 37
  Lend Me Your Ears (Safire), 66
  Leonardo da Vinci (Isaacson), 66
  Little, Brown Book of Anecdotes (Fadiman), 66
  Macmillan Dictionary of Political Quotations (Eigen & Siegel), 66
  Media Politics: A Citizen's Guide (Iyengar), 20
  No Ordinary Time (Goodwin), 66
  Between One and Many (Brydon & Scott), 298
  Outliers (Gladwell), 66
  Political Speechwriter's Companion, The, 314
  Public Speaking: Strategies for Success (Zarefsky), 94
  Quote Verifier (Keyes), 66
  Respectfully Quoted (CQ Press), 66
  Rhetorical Presidency, The (Tulis), 11
  Roles Speakers Play (Humes), 66, 210
  To Sell Is Human (Pink), 66
  1776 (McCullough), 66
  Speaker's Guidebook (O'Hair, Stewart & Rubenstein), 297
  Speak Like Churchill, Stand Like Lincoln (Humes), 66
  Speechwriter, The: A Brief Education in Politics (Swaim), 348
  Steve Jobs (Isaacson), 66
  Team of Rivals (Goodwin), 66
  Thanks Obama (Litt), 355
  Tipping Point (Gladwell), 66
  Too Funny to Be President (Udall), 66, 207
  Truman (McCullough), 66
  Twilight of the Presidency, The (Reedy), xxii
  What I Saw at the Revolution (Noonan), 268–269
  When (Pink), 66
  White House Ghosts (Schlesinger), 95, 316–317
  Wright Brothers, The (McCullough), 66
Borrowing, jokes, 159–160
Bradley, Bill, 139

Branch, Taylor, 314
Brandeis, Louis, 86
Brenner, David, 171
Bridge, 269
Brief examples, 242–243, 253, 254, 390
Briefing book, 6
Broder, David, xxiii
Brose, Chris, 60
Brown v. Board of Education, 333
Bryan, William Jennings, 46
Brydon, Steven, 298
Buchanan, Pat, 46, 47
Burgess, Michael (R-TX), 176
Bush, Barbara, xxii, 429–432
Bush, George H. W., xxii, 122, 256
Bush, George W.:
   failed humor, 153
   quotes, 115, 120, 195, 206
   speeches, as delivered (weblink), 142
   speech excerpts, 141–142, 164, 207,
      219, 241, 270
   wrong word usage, 94
Bush, Jeb, 429–432
Bush, Laura, 139

Caddell, Pat (Carter pollster), 15
Calibrated speech, 45–46
Call to action:
   closing and, 275, 285–286
   examples, 389, 398–399, 405, 415, 426
   Monroe's Motivated Sequence and,
      75–79, 86, 91
Carey, Archibald, 324
Carnegie, Dale, 297
Carter, Jimmy, 4, 15, 299
Castro, Julián, 164, 167
Caveats, using, 331
Chaiken, Shelly, 297
Character/characterization (ethos),
      29–31
   appeals to, 35–37
   example, 430

litany and, 123
speaker, wit and, 156–157
speechwriter's checklist, 38
types of, 35
Chase's Calendar of Events, 213
Chernow, Ron, 66
Chicago Tribune, 411
Children's Health Insurance Program
   (CHIP), 36
Choice, closing strategy, 288–289
Christie, Chris, , 98, 298
Churchill, Winston, 119, 124
Cialdini, Robert, 37, 46
Cicero, 47
Circular reasoning, 197
Clarity:
   language and, 234
   litany and, 123
   write for, 94
Classic misdirection, 444
Clients, what speechwriters need from:
   content, involvement in finding,
      350–351
   define role, 349
   encourage recycling, 351
   first drafts, 352
   learn elements, good speeches, 350
   practice delivery/hire consultant,
      351–352
   talk to writer directly, 352
   training, provide, 349–350
Climatic order, problem and, 236–237
Clincher:
   closing strategy, 288–289
   examples, 385, 399, 405, 415,
      435, 447
   four-part close and, 275–276
   memorable, 232–233
   MMS and, 86
   we can give, 256
   "we know," 237
   "you may" clause, 256

Clinton, Bill, 41
  "A Place Called Hope," 34
  Shesol, Jeff, speechwriter, 3
  speech excerpts, 218, 287–288
Clinton, Hillary:
  "basket of deplorables," 39
  likeability, 14
  quote, 162
  speech as delivered (weblink), 157
  speech excerpts, 1–3, 19, 32–37, 39, 42, 44, 103, 129–131, 155, 161, 209, 234, 263, 266, 279–280
Close:
  call to action, 275, 285–286
  clincher, 275–276, 288–289
  four-part, steps, 274–281
  inspiration, 274, 282–284
  lesson learned, 274–275, 284–285
  referral ending, 389
  serious, 446
  See also Conclusions; Four-part close
Clustering, writing wit and, 158
Coats, Emma, 148
Cohen, Michael, 320
Colbert, Stephen, 64, 170
Cole, Tom (R-OK), 77–78
Collins, Chris (R-NY), 181–182
Collins, Doug (R-GA), 181
Colloquialism, 242
Colloquial speech, 100–101
  clutter, eliminate, 103
  sentences, short, 101–103
  transitions, use, 103–104
Columbia Guide to Standard English, 98
Columbia Journalism Review, 319
Comedy Central roasts, 441
Commemorative speech:
  consoling, 411
  elements of, 412
  example 413–415
  outline, 412–413
  questions before writing, 411–412
  tips for writing, 411–411
Commencement speech:
  defining purpose, 415
  expectations, 416
  outline, 417
  tips for, 416
Communications director, 57
Comparative-advantage speech structure, 83
Compare and contrast:
  apples and oranges (false analogy), 194
  evidence, statistics and, 176
  repetition and, 120, 127–128
  See also Contrast
Compassion, decry problems to show, 35
Compliment, example, 440
Conclusions:
  draw, 382
  example, 432
  famous inspirational, 273
  four-part close, steps/strategy, 274–289
  inspiration, 274
  lesson learned, 274–275
  memorable, 379
  speechwriter's checklist, 293
  See also Close; Four-part close
Concrete detail:
  contrast, demonstrate, 117–118
  examples, 219, 433, 438
  heroism and, 117
  problems and, 236
  statement of purpose and, 221–222
  urgency and, 116–117
Concrete words, 96–97
Confident speech, 15–16
Congressional Record, 5, 65
Consistency, 37
Consonance, 121
Contagious: Why Things Catch On (Berger), 189–190

Context:
　analogy for, 186–187
　cost and, 189–190
　increase size, decrease space, 187–188
　power of one, 188–189
Contrast:
　antithesis and, 236
　concrete detail, 117–118
　example, 222
　litany and, 129, 130–131
　problem/solution, direct/delayed, 231–232
　See also Compare and contrast
Convention, defy, 407
Convince, evidence and, 32
Corporations, political speech and, 10–11
Corzine, Jon (Senator), 152
Cost, context of, 189–190
Cotton, Tom (Senator), 211–212
Council of Jewish Federations, 9–10
Council on Foreign Relations, 48
Cover memo, 359
CQ Press, 66
Credibility speech, establish (MMS), 84–85
Criticize your own side, 48
Critique speeches, 310, 315
"Cross of Gold" 1886 speech (Bryan, W. J.), 46
Crozer Theological Seminary, 314–315
Cruz, Ted:
　quotes, 42, 43, 122, 127, 128, 133–132, 192, 196
　speech (as delivered, weblink), 134
　speech excerpt, 193–194
C-SPAN, 40, 65
Culprits, defining, 229–230
Cuomo, Andrew, 180
Cuomo, Mario, 179

Daily Beast, 15
Dale, Daniel, 330
Damasio, Antonio, 29
D'Amato, Al (Senator), 147
Davis, John (McCain campaign manager), 31
Davison, Phil, 368
"Day in the life" structure, 445
Dean, Howard, 368
Deception, 37
Declaration of Independence, 227–228
Deductive reasoning, 27
Defense Advanced Research Projects Agency (DARPA), 136
Definition, fallacy of, 197
Definition joke, 161
Delayed contrast, 231–232
Delayed juxtaposition, 237
Delivery:
　advice, listen to, 315–316
　anecdotes, 148
　appearance and, 297–298
　articulated pause/disfluencies (exercise), 307
　critique your, 315
　importance of, xxii
　movement and, 298–303
　practice goals, 308–310
　speakers, study others, 314–315
　speechwriter's checklist, 317–318
　teleprompters and, 316
　voice, 303–309
　See also individual entries
Demarest, David, 296
Democratic values, (Reagan), 43–44
Demographics:
　audience, 45
　research event audience, 55
　See also Audiences
Demosthenes, 46
Derived characterization, 35
Dickerson, John, 67

Dionne, E. J., 31
Dire consequences, 253, 254
Direct contrast, 231–232
Direct evidence, 183
Dirksen, Everett, xxii
Disfluencies, articulated pause, 306–309
Dixon, Alan, 340
"Does Evidence Matter?" (Dionne), 31
Doggett, Lloyd (D-TX), 183
Dole, Bob, 66
Domino analogy, 195–196
Donald, David Herbert, 411
Douglas, Michael, movie speech excerpt, 260–261
Drafts:
　cover memos and, 359
　recycle speeches, 361
Dramatic anecdote, 138–139, 239
Dramatic story, 210–211
Drive (Pink), 66
Duckworth, Tammy (Senator), 238–239
Dumas, Alexander, 120
Durbin, Dick (Senator), 4, 65, 390–391
Durden, Sabine, 35
Dylan, Bob, 306

Early, Steve, 93
East of Eden (Steinbeck), 87
Economist, 59
Edwards, Donna (Congresswoman), 153
Edwards, John, 325
Eigen, Lewis D., 66
Eisenhower, Dwight D., 124, 195–196
Either-or fallacy, 195
Eliot, T. S., 274
Elitist language, 101
Emotions (pathos), 28–29
　appeals to, 32–34
　fear and, 33

hope, 34
litany and, 123
negative appeals, 32
persuasive speech and, 13
speechwriter's checklist, 38
Emphasis, speech delivery and, 306
Endings. *See* Close; Conclusions; Four-part close
Ending speeches memorably, MMS and, 85–86
Epistrophe:
　examples, 125–126, 131, 397
　presidential campaign, use of, 2
　problem litany, 235
　repetition at the end, solutions, 256
Ernst, Joni (R-IA), 252–253, 381–385
"Ethical Issues in Corporate Speechwriting" (Seeger), 338
Ethics:
　disclosure and, 342–343
　discuss falsehoods with boss, 332
　distorting the truth, 331
　fact checking and, 320
　ghostwriting and, 341–342
　interview (Judge), 334–337
　lying and, 333–334
　misleading listeners, 326–332
　plagiarism, 322–326
　political speeches and, 2
　rationalizing lapses of, 327
　speechwriter's checklist, 344
　speechwriting, inherently unethical, 337–343
Ethos (character), 13
　appeals through, 35–37
　persuasive speech and, 29–31
　solutions, inspire with, 258–263
　speechwriter's checklist, 38
Eulogy:
　Alexander rule for, xxiii
　defining, 427

examples, 429–432, 433–435
outline, 428–429
tips, 427–428
Event, research, 54–56
audience demographics, 55
ideas for, 57–62
logistics, format and venue, 55–56
poetry, moving the audience, 62–67
Evidence, facts and, 28
convinces, 32
defining, 31
"Does Evidence Matter?" (Dionne), 31
examples, 382, 384
insulates, 32
problems, 245–246
reinforcing, 31
See also Evidence, supporting
Evidence, supporting:
ad absurdum, 196
ad hominem, 192–193
ad populum, 196–197
analogy as, 183
argue responsibly, 190
arguing responsibly, 190
brief, examples, 178
cementing alliances, 182–183
compare, 176
context, analogy for, 186–187
cost, context of, 189–190
direct, 183
emotion, evoke, 182
example, 404
expertise/status, 181–182
extended example, 178–179
fallacies, 190–197
fallacy of definition, 197
false cause, 193–194
false choice, 195
figurative analogy, 185
hypothetical/imagined example, 179–180

increase size, decrease space, 187–188
literal analogy, 183–185
memorable, 186–190
non sequitur and, 194
pith and, 183
power of one, 188–189
predict with, 177
relevance of, 194
slippery slope, 195–196
speechwriter's checklist, 198–199
statistics as, 175–178
straw man, 191–192
summarize, 176
support from opponents, 181–182
testimony, 180–181
tu quoque, 194–195
use of, 174–175
See also Evidence, facts and
Examples, evidence and:
brief, 178, 242–243, 253, 254, 390
defined, 178
extended, 178–179, 243–244
hypothetical/imagined, 179–180
inspirational, 378
from the past, 255
Exercises:
anecdote, 148
disfluencies, articulated pause, 307
exhume the lead, 224
late-night laugh test, 170
Monroe's Motivated Sequence, 80
sound bites, 131–132
Expertise, evidence and, 181–182
Extemporaneous speech, practice, 311–313
Extended examples, 243–244
Extended repetition, 396
Eye contact, speech delivery and maintain, 299–300

read ahead, 300–301
speak to the whole room, 301
See also Gestures, speech delivery and; Movement, speech delivery and

"Facet of a diamond" speech structure, 84
Facial expressions, speech delivery and, 299
Fact checking, 320, 332
Facts:
    checking, 320, 332
    evidence and. *See* Evidence, facts and; Evidence, supporting
    logos and, 28
    problems and, 245–246
    questions of, persuasive speech and, 22–23
    syllogism and, 28
    using trustworthy, 331
Fadiman, Clifton, 66
Failures from the past, 33
Fairness, as American value, 24–25
Fallacies, 190–191
    ad absurdum, 196
    ad hominem, 192–193
    ad populum, 196–197
    apples and oranges, 194
    correcting, 330–331
    fallacy of definition, 197
    false cause, 193–194
    false choice, 195
    non sequitur, 194
    slippery slope, 195–196
    straw man, 191–192
    tu quoque, 194–195
    See also Arguments
Fallon, Jimmy, 64
Fallows, James, 340
False cause fallacy, 193–194
False choice fallacy, 195

Falsehoods, 319
Family values:
    appeals to love of, 37
    2016 presidential campaign, use of, 2
Fanburg, Julie, 9
Fast Company, 59
Favreau, Jon (Obama speechwriter), 12, 60, 67
Fear:
    appeals to, 33
    inspire through, 288
    See also Pathos (emotion)
Federalist Society, 42
Feedback, speechwriters and, 355
Feinstein, Diane, 436
Fighter character, inspire solutions, 260–261
Figurative analogy, 185
Figures of speech, 111–112, 123–124
Fisher, Mary, 118, 407–410
Five-*W* approach, 148
Flat opening, 206, 381
Flesch, Rudolf, 16
Flesch-Kincaid Readability Test, 16
    award speech, 437
    commemorative speech, 413
    commencement, 417
    eulogy, 429, 433
    floor speech, 385
    issues keynote, 407
    rally speech (King, Jr.), 394
    roast, 442
    short floor (Durbin), 390–391
    stump speech, 371
Floor speech:
    defining/uses of, 379
    examples, 381–385, 385–389
    outline for, 380–381
    tips for, 379–380
    See also Short floor speech
Foreign Affairs, journal, 59
Formal logic, 28

Formulas, writing humor, 160–161
Fortune, 59
Four-part close:
   choice, 288
   steps of, 274–281
   strategy, 282–289
   See also Close; Conclusions
Four-part close, examples:
   "A Time for Choosing" (Reagan), 288–289
   Challenger Tragedy (Reagan, 415
   Gettysburg Address (Lincoln), 277
   "I Have a Dream" (King), 277–278
   Kennedy Inaugural Speech, 274–276
   1992 RNC (Fisher), 410
   1993 Martin Luther King Jr. Day speech (Clinton, B.), 287–288
   NJ state chamber of commerce (Menendez), 283–284
   partial birth abortion (Ernst), 383–385
   2008 election victory speech, excerpt (Obama, B.), 291–292
   2008 RNC (Palin), 282–283
   2012 African Methodist Church (Obama, M.), 284–285
   2016 DNC (Obama, M.), 404–405
   2016 DNC nomination acceptance speech (Clinton, H.), 278–279
   2016 RNC, Trump, Eric, 285–287
   2012 RNC nomination speech (Rubio), 290–291
   2018 State of the Union (Trump), 279–281
Freakonomics Radio (NPR podcast), 67
Freneau, Philip, 122
Freytag five-act story structure, 87, 135, 136
Friars Club roasts, 441
Frum, David, 190
Fulbright, J. William (Senator), 333
Future of Storytelling conference, 136

Gallup, 175
Garcetti, Eric, 145–146, 231
Gender, likeability and, 14–15
Gerson, Michael, 340
Gestures, 301–303
Gettysburg Address (Lincoln), 76–77, 276–277
Ghostwriting, ethics and, 341–342
Gibbs, Robert, 12
Gladwell, Malcolm, 66
Glenn, John, 343
Goldhill, Olivia, 295
Goldman, William, 21
Goldwater, Barry, 178
González, Emma, 235
Goodlatte, Bob (R-VA), 183
Goodwin, Doris Kearns, 66
Gore, Al (Vice President), 4, 41, 95
   appropriate words, rally *v.* conference, 99–100
   jokes of, 9–10
   quotes, 6, 208, 214–215
   speech excerpt, 328
Graham, David, speech excerpts, 173–174, 181
Grant (Chernow), 66
Graphic detail, 238–239
Gridiron Club, roasts, 152, 156, 442
Gulliver's Travels (Swift), 160

Haley, Alex, xxi
Haley, Nikki (Ambassador), 236–237
Hamilton, Alexander, 95, 341
Hamilton (Chernow), 66
Hamlet, 87
Hand movement, speech delivery, 301–303
Hardball (Matthews), 139
Harmonizer character, inspire solutions, 261–262
Harvard Business Review, 59, 238, 307

Harvard Business School Gender Initiative, 14
Hasty generalization, 191, 328
Hayakawa, S. I. (Senator), 168
Healthcare Roundtable, 12
"Heard Any Good Stories Lately?" (Begley), 137
Hearing, reading v., 94–95. *See also* Language
Henry, Patrick, 111, 121, 195
Heroism, concrete detail and, 117
Hessan, Diane, 39
Hierarchy of Needs, 41f
Hill, Anita, 340
Hill (political news aggregate), 64
Historical accounts, as research source, 66
Historical anecdotes, 146, 240
Historical references, openings, 394
Hope, appealing to, 34
Hopkins, John, 135
"Howdahell" as opener, 213–215
How-to, speechwriting books, 469–470
Howstuffworks.com, 64
Huckabee, Mike:
  Council on Foreign Relations speech (2007), 48
  interview, 183
  speech excerpts, 168, 209, 260
HuffPost, 14–15
Human Rights Council, 98
Hume, David, 22
Humes, James, 66, 210
Humor
  books for research, 467
  examples, 433–434, 434, 437
  funny anecdotes, 139–140
  hyperbole and, 115
  Nussbaum interview on writing, 164–168
  observational, 446
  opening with, 207, 429
  personal story, use funny, 209
  political, self-depreciating 152
  puns, 114
  Reagan and, 88–89
  self-depreciating, 207–208
  understatement, 114–115
  as weapon, 152, 172
  wit v. *See* Wit
  writing for laughter, 153–157
  See also Jokes; Laughter; Political humor; Wit
Humor Cabinet, 441
Hunter, Duncan (R-CA), speech excerpt, 243
Hurd, Will, 436
Hurwitz, Sarah (Obama speechwriter), 133, 143–144, 332
Hyperbole, 115, 124, 445
Hypothetical, praise with, 218
Hypothetical example, 179–180

Ideas, researching, 57–62
  journals magazines, 59
  speeches, refer to old, 58–59
  staffers, 57–58
"If, then" construct, wit and, 158–159
Illustrative anecdotes, 145–146
Imagery:
  concrete detail and, 229, 407
  examples, 385, 394
Imagined example, 179–180
Immigration speeches, 22–23, 28–30
Impromptu speech, 309
Inaccurate paraphrase, 192
Inaugural speeches, 16–17
Inc., magazine, 59
Inductive reasoning, 27
Influence (Cialdini), 37
Informative speech, politics and, 13
Inhofe, James (Senator), speech as delivered (weblink), 308

Initial characterization, 35
Inspiration:
    example, 378
    four-part close, 274
    MMS and, 86
Insulate, evidence and, 32
Insult the other side, 208
Interest, of audiences, 44–45
Internal summaries, transition, 104
Internet research, 59–60
Interviews:
    Hurwitz, Sarah, 143–144
    Nussbaum, Jeff, 164–168
    Shapiro, Rick, 353–355
    Walker, Wyatt Tee, 62
Irony, 168
Isaacson, Walter, 66
Isakson, Johnny (R-GA), 140–141
Issues:
    one issue, many examples, 230
    problems and, 229–230
Issues keynote speech:
    example, 407–410
    outline, 406–407
    as partisan, upbeat, 405–406
Iyengar, Shanto, 20

Jackson, Jesse, 17, 96–97, 245
Jefferson, Thomas, 17, 227–228
Jokes:
    acronym, 161
    definition, 161
    example, 443, 445
    funny anecdotes, 139–140
    Gore, Al and, 9–10
    Nussbaum interview on writing, 164–168
    Obama, 153
    opening and, 418
    quoting late night television, 64
    similes and, 112–113
    See also Humor; Wit

Journals, as research source, 59
Joyce, James, 178
Judge, Clark (interview), 334–337

Kaine, Tim, 194
Kasich, John, 101
Kavanaugh, Brett, 340
Kelly, Megyn, 183
Kelly, Robin (D-IL), 78–79
Kennedy, Caroline, 306–307
Kennedy, Joe (D-MA), 126, 232
Kennedy, John F.:
    addressing his religion, 47–48
    Inaugural Address, as delivered (weblink), 276
    press conferences and, 19
    quotes, 120, 121, 288
    Rice University, as delivered (weblink), 185
    speech excerpts, 154, 156, 257–258, 259, 274–276
Kennedy, Robert, 47
Kennedy, Ted, 125–126
Kerry, John:
    2006 Kenyon College commencement, 418–426
    2014 op-ed, 32
Kessler, Glenn, 320
Keyes, Ralph, 66
Keynote speech, tips/outline/examples:
    issues, 405–410
    political, 399–405
    See also Issues keynote speech; Political keynote speech
Khan, Khizr, 116
Kimmel, Jimmy, 64
Kincaid, John, 16
King, Martin Luther, Jr.:
    Bono, 2007 NAACP awards acceptance speech and, 45
    "I Have a Dream," 119, 277–278

rally speech, March on Washington, 394–399
speech structures of, 84
Walker, Wyatt Tee and, 62
King, Pee Wee, xxiii
King, Steve (R-IA), 182
Kings Row (film), 269
Knight Foundation, 175
Koestler, Arthur, 155
Koop, C. Everett, 186–187
Kristof, Nicholas, 187–188
Khrushchev, Nikita, 288

"Ladder to heaven" speech structure, 84
"Lamar Alexander's Little Plaid Book" (Alexander), xxiii
Landrieu, Mitch (NOLA Mayor), 179, 180, 245
Language:
　active verbs, 98–99
　anaphora, problem litany, 234
　appropriate words, 99–100
　clarity and, 94
　clutter, eliminate, 103
　colloquial, 100–101
　concrete words, 96–97
　Flesch-Kincaid test and, 17
　gritty details, 385
　"human English," xxii
　memorable. *See* Memorable language
　political, 1
　problems and, 233–238
　pronunciation, speech delivery and, 306
　reading, hearing *v.*, 94–95
　rhythmic, 118–132. *See also* Rhythmic language
　sensitive words, 100
　sentences, keep short, 101–103
　short words, 95–96
　skillful use, 376
　solutions, inspire with, 255–258
　sound bite exercise, 131–132
　speechwriter's checklist, 110
　style and, 94
　transitions, use, 103–104
　vivid, 435
　See also Word Choice
Late-night television shows, 64
Laughter:
　audiences and, 46
　writing for, 153–157
　See also Humor; Jokes; Wit
LAWS (language, anecdote, wit, support), 20
Lee, Mike (UT-Senator), speech excerpt, 96
Lee, Robert E., 180
Lehrer, Jim, 156
Lehrman, Robert, xxi, xxii
Leibovich, Mark, 295
Lend Me Your Ears (Safire), 66
Leno, Jay, 64
Leonardo da Vinci (Isaacson), 66
Lesson learned:
　conclusions and, 274–275, 284–285, 384
　examples, 405, 415, 425
"Lettuce leaf" speech structure, 84
Lewis, Matt, 15
Liberman, Joe, 171
Liberty University, 42
Likeability, 14–15, 37
Lim, Elvin, 4, 16, 104–109, 134
Lincoln, Abraham, 76–77, 181, 276–277
Listeners:
　anecdotes and, 136
　appeals to reason, reinforcing evidence, 31
　facts/evidence and, 23, 31
　influencing, 18
　learn about, 37–38

misleading, ethics and, 326–332
optimism and, 33
repetition and, 95
story, remind purpose, 210–212
surprise, 237
See also Audience
Litany, 122–123
   anaphora and, 125, 234
   "an or a," 231
   contrast and, 129
   culprit and, 229–230
   epistrophe, solutions and, 256
   examples, 376, 390, 404, 405, 434
   from lists to, 128
   one issue, many examples, 230
   presidential campaign, use of, 2
   repetition, 228
   rhetorical questions, 237–238
   solutions and, 258
   we can do better, 256
   we choose, 232
   we're here tonight, solutions, 260
Literal analogy, 183–185
Literary speech, 407
Litt, David (Obama speechwriter), 355
Little, Brown Book of Anecdotes (Fadiman), 66
Live audiences, speech delivery and, 301
Logic. *See* Logos (reason); Reason (logos)
Logistics, research event format/venue, 55–56
Logos (reasoning), 13
   appeals to, 31–32
   persuasive speech, 26–27
   speechwriter's checklist, 38
   statistics and, 32
Lord of the Rings, 147
Lovett, Jon, 67
Lucas, Stephen, 48, 64–65
Lying, 333–334

MacFarlane, Seth, 184
Macklemore, Obama, drug addiction speech, 81–83, 114
Macmillan Dictionary of Political Quotations (Eigen & Siegel), 66
Macron, Emmanuel, 242
Madison, James, 95
Magazines, as research source, 59
"Malaise" speech, 1979 (Carter), 15
Mandela, Nelson, 4
Manning, Lauren, 36
Manuscript political speech, 309
Marcus, Ruth, xxiii
Marketing techniques, 37
Markey, Ed (D-MA), 113
Maslow, Abraham, 41–42
Maslow's Hierarchy of Needs, 41*f*–42
Matthews, Chris, 139
McCain, John:
   campaign manager (Davis), 31
   Palin, Sarah and, 46
   speech excerpt, 265
McConnell, Mitch, xxi
McCullough, David, 66
McGrath, David, 341
McHale, Joel, 298
McKeachie, Wilbert, 56
McLuhan, Marshall, xxii
Meacham, Jon, 433–435
Media:
   late-night television, 64
   speech dissemination and, 18
   twenty-four-hour online news cycle, 29
Media Politics: A Citizen's Guide (Iyengar), 20
Memoirs, books for research, 468–469
Memorable clincher, 232–233, 379
Memorable ending, MMS and, 85–86
Memorable evidence, using, 186–190
Memorable language:
   addressing the absent enemy, 116
   concrete detail, 116–118

contrast, demonstrate, 117–118
figures of speech, 111–112, 123–124
hyperbole, 115
metaphor, 124
puns, 114
rhetorical questions, 115–116
simile/metaphor, 112–113
sound bite exercise, 131–132
speechwriter's checklist for, 132
synecdoche/metonymy, 113–114
understatement, 114–115
vivid, 112–118
See also Language; Word choice
Memorized speech, 309
Mendoza, Mary Ann, 35
Menendez, Robert, speech excerpt, 283–284
Mentalfloss.com, 64
Metaphor, 112–113, 218
  examples, 124, 218, 394, 395, 435
Metonymy, 113–114
Middle ground, take the, 48
Minow, Newton (FCC chair), 247–248, 257
Misdirection, 444
Misleading listeners, 326–332
Mistakes were made, passive voice, 98
Mixed metaphors, 113
"MLK Papers: Words That Changed a Nation," 62
MMS. *See* Monroe's Motivated Sequence (MMS)
Mondale, Walter, 112
Monroe, Alan, 74
Monroe's Motivated Sequence (MMS):
  attention, gripping open, 86, 88
  balance elements, 86
  call to action and, 91
  compelling, 79–80
  credibility, establish, 84–85
  ending speeches memorably, 85–86
  examples, 81–83, 76–79, 276–277
  exercise for, 80
  fast technique, 79
  humor and, 88–89
  map out future, 87
  outlining speech, 86
  politics and, 76
  praise and, 88–89
  presidential campaign and, 1
  problems and, 89, 90–91
  saying thanks with, 84
  solution and, 89–90, 91
  speech excerpt (Stowe), 75–76
  speech structures, additional, 83–84
  speechwriter's checklist, 92
  steps of, 74–75
  versatility of, 80–81
  visualization, stir audience, 87
  See also Persuasive speech; Political speech
Montage, praise large group, 219–220
Moore, Ryan, 36
Morrison, Toni, 146–147
Moth podcast, 67
Movement, speech delivery and:
  eye contact, 299–301
  facial expressions, use appropriate, 299
  gestures, use hands/arms, 301–303
Moyer, Bill, xxiii
Moynihan, Daniel Patrick (Senator), 23, 147
Murphy, Chris (Senator), 236
Murray, David, 347
Murray, Patty (D-WA), 31
Music Man, The (musical), 228, 304
Muskie, Ed, 4

NAACP awards, 45
Nation, magazine, 59
National Communication Association, 321
National Governors Association, 11–12
National Review, 59

Index

Need, Monroe's Motivated Sequence and, 74–79
Needs, audiences and Maslow's hierarchy of, 41f
Negative appeals, 32–33
Nesmith, Achsah, 299
New Republic, 59
Newspapers, research and, 64
Newsweek, 137
New Yorker, 31, 59
New York Times, 64, 187–188, 307
Nixon, Richard M., 98, 114–116
Noah, Trevor, 63, 64, 170
Nomination acceptance speeches, 16
"No Name Waltz, The," xxiii
Nonrational speech, 31
Non sequitur, fallacy, 194
Noonan, Peggy, 343
   Bush speechwriter, 123
   Reagan speechwriter, 62, 88–91, 102–103, 222–224, 357, 413
   speech excerpts, 217–218
No Ordinary Time (Goodwin), 66
NSNBC, 139
Nussbaum, Jeff, 441, 164–168

Obama, Barack:
   Berlin speech, as delivered (weblink), 304
   likeability, 14
   Macklemore speech, addiction treatment, 81–83
   New Yorker endorsement, 31
   quotes, 115, 120, 124
   Sandy Hook speech, 97
   speaking style of, 295–296
   speech excerpts, 15, 22–25, 28, 30, 32, 116–117, 120–121, 127, 138, 153, 161, 163, 169, 184–185, 192, 210–211, 213, 217, 218–219, 220, 237–238, 239, 256, 261, 262, 266–267, 290–291, 437–440
   speechwriter of, 12
   Twitter and, 49
Obama, Michelle:
   anecdote, 142–143
   as delivered (weblink), 134
   political keynote speech, 401–405
   on repetition, 11
   speech excerpts, 133, 284–285
Obey, David, 168, 169
Objective correlation, 274
Observational humor, 446
O'Connor, Sandra Day, 159, 165–166, 443–447
Office, The (television), 156
Off-ramps, 170–171, 210
O'Hair, Dan, 297
O'Keefe, Daniel, 261–262
One issue/many examples, 230
One-liners, 162, 446
On-ramps, 170–171
Opening. *See* Beginning speeches
Opinions, facts v., 23
Optimism, 16, 32
O'Rourke, Robert (Beto), 436
Orwell, George, 132
Outliers (Gladwell), 66
Outline speech:
   commencement, 417
   floor speech, 380–381
   issues keynote, 406–407
   MMS and, 86
   political keynote, 400–401
   rally, 393
   stump, 370–371
Oversimplification, 195

Pace, change with wit, 154
Palin, Sarah:
   calibrated speech and, 45–46
   quotes, 115, 121, 197
   speech excerpts, 282–283

Parable, anecdote, 146–147
Parallel construction, 434
Parallelism, 390
Parallel repetition, 374
Parallel sentence fragments, 232
Partisanship, 231, 285, 388, 405–406
Parvin, Landon, 152
Passive persuasion, 48
Passive voice, 98
Past accomplishments, appeals to hope, 34
Past failures, 33
Pathos (emotion), 13
  appeals to, 32–34
  fear and, 33
  hope, 34
  negative appeals, 32
  persuasive speech and, 28–29
  speechwriter's checklist, 38
Patrick, Deval, 323, 324
Patriotism, (Reagan), 43–44
Patterns, rhythmic. *See* Rhythmic language
Paul, Rand, 324
Pelosi, Nancy, 214–216
Pence, Mike (Vice President):
  quotes, 124, 161, 162, 207
  speech excerpts, 11–12, 229–230, 233
Penn, Richard, 114
Personal anecdote, 140–141, 238–239
Personal files, research resource, 67
Personality, likeability and, 14–15
Personal story, use funny, 209
Personification, 391, 407
Persuasive speech:
  breaking rules of, 408
  defined, 21
  education *v.*, 107
  ethos (character), 29–31
  example, 405

  facts and, 22–23
  LAWS of writing, 20
  logos (reasoning), 26–27
  Monroe's Motivated Sequence and, 74–83
  nonrational, 31
  passive, 48
  pathos (emotion), 28–29
  policy, addressing, 25–26
  politicians and, 13–14
  proposal, punch lines, solutions and, 263–269
  questions central to, 13
  rule of three, 26–31
  speaker's job, xxii
  speechwriter's checklist, 38
  value judgments, 24–25
  See also Political speech; specific types of persuasive speech
Pessimism, Roosevelt and, 16
Pew Research Center, 24
Pfeiffer, Dan, 67
Phaedrus, 320
Pharis, Marilyn, 23
Phillips, Brad, 307
Physical attractiveness, 297
Pickering, Timothy, 227
Pink, Dan, 66
Pitch, speech delivery and voice, 304
Pith, evidence and, 183
Pixar, 148
Plagiarism:
  defined, 324
  ethics and, 322–326
  knowing misrepresentation, proof, 325
  penalty for, 325
  search engines to find, 325
  sources, citing, 326
  Turnitin plagiary detection tool, 326
Plato, 50
Pledging, 259

Index 491

Plotz, David, 67
Podcasts, research and, 67
Poetry, moving the audience, 62–67
Policy:
   examples, 253
   political speech and, 11
   questions of, persuasive speech and, 25–26
Political humor:
   self-depreciating, 152
   singe don't burn, 152, 443
   See also Humor; Jokes; Laughter; Wit
Political keynote speech:
   elements of, 400
   example, 401–405
   outline, 400–401
Political life, speechwriting and, 5–6
Political podcasts, 67
Political roasts, 441
Political speech:
   books, research source, 465–644
   corporations and, 10–11
   energy and, 98
   importance of, 368
   manuscript/text, 309
   Monroe's Motivated Sequence and, 74–83
   as persuasion, 21–22. *See also* Persuasive speech
   plagiarism and, 323–324
   problem-cause-solution, 83
   solutions and, 252. *See also* Solutions
   stumps, 11
   See also Monroe's Motivated Sequence (MMS); Persuasive speech; Political humor; Political keynote speech; *speech entries*
Political Speechwriter's Companion, The, 314

Political statement, 414
Politicians:
   appeal to average people, 16–18
   confident/upbeat, 15–16
   likeability of, 14–15
   persuasive speech and, 13–14
   sound bites/quotes, 18–19
   speaking more, 10–12
   See also Political speech
Politico (political news aggregate), 64, 153
Politics, books for research on, 468
"Politics and the English Language" (Orwell), 132
PolitiFact, 320
Polyptoton, 121, 129, 130
Pop culture, jokes and, 162–163
Positive appeals, 32
Posture, speaking and, 297
Powell, Colin, 174
Practice delivery:
   extemporaneous speech, 311–313
   goals, 310
   Q & A, 313–314
   record, 309
   rehearsal tips, 311
   stump speeches, 312–313
   text, using to speak from, 308–311
   text speeches, 310–311
   tips, 308–310
Praise:
   audience and, 443
   examples, 401–402, 420, 429, 443
   hypothetical, use to, 218
   MMS and, 88–89
   montage, for large groups, 219–220
   response, use to win crowd, 220
   segment audience, 217–218
   thank-yous, 205
   "we" harness power of, 216–217
   See also Acknowledgements; Thank-yous

Predict, supporting evidence, 177
President, job of, xxii
Presidential campaigns:
 atmosphere (2016), 1–3
 political choices of voters (2000), 30
Presidential rhetoric, anti-intellectualism and, 104–109
Presidential Studies Quarterly, 59
Press conferences, presidential, 19
Previews, transition, 104
Primary audience, 40
Princess Bride (film), 21
Problem-cause-solution speech structure, 83
 examples, 386, 390–391, 403, 421–423
 floor speech and, 382
 See also Problem(s); Problem-solving; Solutions
Problem(s):
 alert to, 228–229
 anaphora, litany, 234
 anecdotes and, 238–240
 antithesis contrast, 236
 climatic order, 236–237
 clincher, find memorable, 232–233
 concrete detail and, 236
 contrasting/solution, 231–232
 defining culprit/issue as, 229–230
 examples, 89–91
 language and, 233–238
 MMS and, 74–79, 86
 rhetorical questions and, 237–238
 speechwriter's checklist, 249
 support, backing up assertions, 242–246
 wit and, 240–242
 See also Problem-cause-solution speech structure; Problem-solving; Solutions
Problems ahead, 33

Problem-solving:
 compassion, decry problems to show, 35
 fear, appeals to, 33
 logos, statistics and, 32
 political speech and, 13
 self-actualization, 42
 See also Problem-cause-solution speech structure; Problem(s); Solutions
Professional Speechwriters Association, 321
Profiles in Courage (Kennedy & Sorensen), 340
Pronunciation, speech delivery and, 306
Props, 445
Proposal, solutions, persuasion, punch lines and, 263–269
Public Affairs, journal, 59
Public Relations Writing (Bivins), 340
Public speaking, storytelling and, 210
Public Speaking: Strategies for Success (Zarefsky), 94
Punch lines, 147
 example, 445
 memorable, 153–154
 solutions, persuasion, proposal and, 263–269
Puns:
 example, 444
 use of humor and, 114
 wit and, 169
Purpose:
 remind listeners of, 210–212
 statement of, 205, 206
 statement of. *See* Statement of purpose (SOP)
 story defines, xxi

Qualifiers, 196
Quesenberry, Keith, 135

Question and answer period, practice, 313–314
Questions, identify audience, 39–40
Questions, persuasive speech and:
    facts, 22–23
    policy, 25–26
    values, 24–25
Quintilian, 111–112
Quips, 162, 208
Quotations:
    examples, 373, 409, 431–432
    humorists, 208–209
    humor/wit and, 169
    importance of, sound bites and, 18
    resource books, 65–66, 466–467
    testimony as evidence, 180–181
    See also entries for individual speakers
Quote Verifier (Keyes), 66

Radiolab (WNYC podcast), 67
Rally speech:
    example, 394–399
    outline, 393
    rhetoric tips, 392–393
    writing tips, 391–392
Rate of speech, 304
Readability gauges:
    Flesch-Kincaid Readability Test, 16
    presidential campaign and (2016), 1
    short sentences, 102
    See also Flesch-Kincaid Readability Test
Read ahead, speech delivery and, 300–301
Reading, hearing *v.*, 94–95. *See also* Language
Reagan, Ronald:
    Farewell Address (weblink), 44, 305
    "Lenny Skutnik moment," 281
    Noonan, speechwriter, 62
    quotes, 114, 162, 269, 288
    speech excerpts, 43–44, 67–69, 88–91, 102, 117, 126–127, 146, 156, 216, 222–224, 242–243, 263–264, 288–289, 305, 413–415
Reason (logos):
    appealing to, 31–32
    deductive/inductive, 27
    persuasive speech, 26–27
    speechwriter's checklist, 38
Rebuttal, MMS and, 86
Reciprocity, 37
Recycle speeches, 361
Reedy, George, xxii
Reference books, list, 468
Referral ending, 389
Reflection, speaker, 222–224
Reform Party, Buchanan acceptance speech to (2000), 46
Refutation speech structure, 83
Rehearsal tips, 311
Religion, politicians and, 47–48
Repetition:
    anaphora, 124–125, 129, 131
    antimetabole, 120
    assonance/consonance, 121
    climatic order, 126–127
    compare and contrast, 127–128
    at the end, epistrophe and, 256
    epistrophe, 125–126, 131, 256
    examples, 228, 253, 254, 382, 385, 390, 395, 396, 397, 404, 408, 409, 414, 434, 435, 438
    extended, 396
    groups of sentences, 122–126
    listeners and, 95
    litany and, 122–123
    parallel, 374
    presidential campaign and, 1
    problems, 235
    as rhythmic language, 118–120

single sentences, 120–122
stumps and, 11–12
"that's why," 124
Research:
anecdotes, listeners and, 136
archive, anecdotes/videos, 360
books, 65–66. *See also* Books (resource)
communications director and, 57
event, 54–56
ideas, event speeches and, 57–62
local history, 53
newspapers, 64
personal contact, 63
personal files and, 67
podcasts, 67
sources of information, 56
speech conference, 60–61
speeches, as resource, 64
speechwriter's checklist, 70
talk to people, 69
television, late-night shows, 64
three key areas of, 54
web-based, 59–60, 63–64
website, group's "About" section, 57
before writing, 356–357
Resources, lack of speechwriting, 5
Respectfully Quoted (CQ Press), 66
Retail Advocates Summit, 11
Rhatican, Bill, 18
Rhetoric, 17
anti-intellectualism and, 104–109
devices of, 248
epistrophic litany and, 235–236
presidential, anti-intellectualism and, 104–109
sound bite exercise, 131–132
techniques, 247–248
See also Rhetorical questions
Rhetoric, journal, 59
Rhetorical Presidency, The (Tulis), 11

Rhetorical questions, 115–116, 129, 239
examples, 391, 433–434
problems and, 237–238
solutions, better than doing nothing, 257
See also Rhetoric
Rhythmic language, 120
alliteration, 120–121, 124, 129, 130
anaphora, 124–125, 129, 131
antimetabole, 120
antithesis, 121, 124, 129, 130
assonance/consonance, 121
asyndeton, 122
climatic order, repetition and, 126–127
defining, repetition and, 118–120
epistrophe, 125–126, 131
lists, move to litany from, 128
litany, 122–123
polyptoton, 121, 129, 130
sound bit exercise, 131–132
vary approach to, 128
Rice, Condoleezza, 60, 190–191
Richards, Ann, 4
Richardson, Bill (Gov. NM), 342–343
Ridicule, analogy for, 209
Road map, MMS and, 87
Roast(s):
checklist, 441
defined, 441
elements of, 442
example, 443–447
Nussbaum on writing for, 165–166
Robb, Charles (D-VA), 183–184
Robinson, Peter, 68–69, 242
Rock, Chris, 64, 171
Rodrick, Stephen, 340
Roe, Phil (R-TN), 176
Roles Speakers Play (Humes), 66, 210
Roll Call (political news aggregate), 64
Rolling Stone, 340

Romney, Mitt, 41
    likeability factor and, 14
    speech excerpts, 158–159, 241
    stump speech, complete, 371–379
Ronnebeck, Grant, 29
Roosevelt, Franklin Delano, 16, 65, 93
Root, Sarah, 29
Rose, Wesley, xxiii
Rubenstein, Hannah, 297
Rubio, Marco (Senator), 97, 290–291
Rule of three:
    ethos (character), 29–31
    evidence and, 31–32
    examples, 443, 446
    joke and, 161
    logos (reason), 26–27
    pathos (emotion), 28–29
Ryan, Paul (R-WI), xxi, 31, 208, 222
Rydell, John, 296

Safire, William, 66
Sandberg, Sheryl, TED Talk, 145
Sanders, Bernie (I-VT):
    quotes, 189, 197
    speech excerpts, 102, 192–193
    stump speech, 2016, 58
Sanford, Mark (Gov. SC), 348
Satiric thrusts, 327
Satisfaction (solution), Monroe's
    Motivated Sequence and, 75–79
Savage, Becky, xxi
Scavino, Dan, Jr., 49
Schakowsky, Jan (D-IL), 182–183
Schlesinger, Robert, 95
Schnure, Eric, xxi, xxii
Schultz, George, 149
Schumer, Chuck (Senator), 152
Schwarzenegger, Arnold, 26–28, 137
Scott, Michael, 298
Scully, Matt, 340
Secondary audience, 40
Seeger, Matthew, 338

Segment audience, 410
Self-actualization, 42
Self-awareness, wit and, 156–157
Self-deprecation:
    examples, 418, 443
    humor and, 207–208
    wit/humor and, 152–153
Seligman, Martin, 15–16
Sensitive words, 100
Sentences:
    repetition in groups, 122–126
    repetition within single, 120–122
Serious moment, 205
Sessions, Jeff:
    alliteration quote, 124
    speech excerpts, 246
1776 (McCullough), 66
Shakespeare, 87
Shapiro, Rick, 315, 349, 353–355
Shared values, 36
Shaw, Jamiel, 35
Sheehan, Michael, 304
Shesol, Jeff (Bill Clinton speechwriter), 3
Shout-out, 182–183, 404
Shrum, Bob (Ted Kennedy
    speechwriter), 125–126
Siegel, Jonathan, 66
Siegenthaler, John, xxii
Signposts, transition, 104
Silverman, Sarah, 171
Simile, 112–113, 446
"Singe not burn," 152–153, 443
Sister Souljah, 41
Skutnik, Lenny, 281
Slate's Political Gabfest (podcast), 67
Slippery slope fallacy, 195–196, 391
Small Deborah, 188
Smiling, 167
Social proof, 37
Solutions:
    achiever character to inspire, 259
    appeals to hope, 34

audience interests and, 44
believer character to inspire, 259–260
better than doing nothing, 257
better than the other guy, 256
better than what exists, 256
better than what we've done, 257–258
contrasting problem and, 231–232
ethos, inspire with, 258–263
examples, 89–90, 91, 375, 383, 403, 408, 422, 423
fighter character to inspire, 260–261
harmonizer character to inspire, 261–262
litany and, 258
MMS and, 75–79, 86
proposal, persuasion, punch line, three Ps, 263–269
speechwriter's checklist, 271
types of, 13
visionary character, inspire, 262–263
"we choose," 232
See also Problem(s); Problem-solving; Problem-cause-solution speech structure; Problem(s); Solutions
Sorensen, Ted (JFK speechwriter), 60, 154, 155–156, 185
Sound bites:
  exercise, 131–132
  importance of, 18–19, 123–124
Sources:
  citing, ethics and, 327
  credible, 3
  event research and, 56
  journals/magazines, 59
  newspapers, 64
  personal contact, 63
  speeches as, 64–65
  staffers, event information and, 56
  web-based research, 59–60, 63–64
  websites, 57

Southern Manifesto, 333
Speakers:
  audience feelings about, 45–46
  ethos (character) and, 29–31, 35–37
Speaker's Guidebook (O'Hair, Stewart & Rubenstein), 297
Speaking rate, 304
Speak Like Churchill, Stand Like Lincoln (Humes), 66
Special interests:
  audiences and, 44–45
  solutions and, 44
Speech:
  colloquial, 100–101
  See also Language; Political speech; *speech entries*
Speech conference, 60–61, 358
Speeches:
  criticize your own side, 48
  edits to, expect, 361
  ethics and political, 2
  five necessary elements, 18–19
  humor and, interview, 164–168. *See also* Humor; Jokes; Wit
  importance of, 20
  inaugural, readability scores and, 16–17
  old, as event research source, 58–59
  outlined, MMS and, 85–86
  as research source, 64–65
  resources for, lack of, 5
  stump delivery, 11–12, 312–313
  types of, 309
  See also Political speech; *speech entries*
Speeches, as delivered (weblinks):
  Cecil B. DeMille Award acceptance (Winfry), 206
  Farewell Address (Reagan), 44, 305
  floor speech on energy (Inhofe), 308
  Inaugural Address (Kennedy, J. F.), 276

Joint Session of Congress, 9/11 (Bush, G. W.), 142
National Association of Broadcasters, FCC (Minow), 247
Rice University (Kennedy, J.F.), 185
2008 Berlin speech (Obama), 304
2016 Alfred E. Smith Memorial Foundation Dinner (Trump & Clinton, H.), 157
2016 DNC (Obama, M.), 134
2016 RNC (Cruz), 134
Speeches, complete:
   1963 March on Washington (King Jr.), 394–399
   1986 Challenger memorial (Reagan), 413–415
   1992 RNC issues keynote (Fisher), 407–410
   2006 Kenyon College commencement (Kerry), 418–426
   2010 short floor (Durbin), 390–391
   2011 Alfalfa Club (O'Connor), 443–447
   2011 stump speech, (Romney), 371–379
   2016 DNC keynote (Obama, M.), 401–405
   2018 Bush, Barbara, eulogy (Bush, Jeb), 429–432
   2018 Bush, G. H. W., eulogy (Meacham), 433–435
   2018 floor speech (Ernst), 381–385
   2018 floor speech (Warren), 385–389
Speeches, excerpts (1800–1899):
   1851 abolitionist (Truth), 235
   1863 Gettysburg Address (Lincoln), 76–77, 276–277
   1886 "Cross of Gold" (Bryan)
Speeches, excerpts (1900–1999):
   1942 Roosevelt, F.D. air raid speech, 93
   1948 Stowe, Leland, 73–74, 75–76
   1960 Greater Houston Ministerial Association (Kennedy, J.F.), 47
   1961 inaugural address (Kennedy, J.F.), 257–258, 259
   1961 National Association of Broadcasters, (Minow), 257
   1962 Rice University moon (Kennedy), 154
   1964 campaign (Reagan), 288–289
   1964 RNC (Goldwater), 178
   1967 maiden speech to U.S. Senate (Baker), xxii
   1980 RNC nomination acceptance speech (Reagan), 126–127
   1984 D-Day Anniversary (Reagan), 88–91
   1984 D-Day anniversary (Reagan), 117
   1984 DNC (Cuomo), 179
   1984 re-election campaign, (Reagan), 53, 68–69
   1988 DNC (Jackson), 245
   1988 RNC nomination acceptance speech (Bush, G. H. W.), 256
   1989 Farewell Address (Reagan), 222–224, 254
   1992 Martin Luther King Jr. Day (Clinton, B.), 287–288
   1993 black ministers (Clinton, B.), 218
   1994 NAACP (Gore), 328
   1994 Republican gala (Reagan), 216
   1995 Beijing World Conference on Women (Clinton, H.), 234
   1996 presidential campaign (Alexander), xxi
   1996 same-sex marriage trial (Robb), 183–184
Speeches, excerpts (2000–2018):
   1988 DNC (Jackson), 96–97
   2000 Reform Party acceptance (Buchanan), 46

2001 Joint Session of Congress, 9/11 (Bush, G. W.), 141–142, 219, 270
2001 Shanghai CEO Summit (Bush, G. W.), 207
2001 Yale Class Day speech (Clinton, H.), 103, 209
2001 YMC picnic (Bush, G. W.), 164
2002 antiwar (Obama), 261
2003 Selma March Anniversary (Obama), 210–211, 218–219
2004 DNC (Obama), 127
2004 RNC (Schwarzenegger), 26, 137
2004 Senate Finance Committee Vioxx testimony (Graham, D.), 173–174
2005 floor speech on bankruptcy (Obama), 256
2005 Organization of American States, GA (Rice), 190–191
2007 Council on Foreign Relations (Huckabee), 48
2007 CPAC trade (Hunter), 243
2007 NAACP awards (Bono), 45
2007 State of the Union (Bush, G. W.), 241
2008 election victory speech (Obama), 217, 290–291
2008 inaugural address (Obama), 184–185
2008 inaugural speech (Obama), 22–23, 28, 30
2008 RNC (Huckabee), 168, 209
2008 RNC (Palin), 282–283
2008 Super Tuesday (Huckabee), 260
2009 Berlin Victory (Obama), 124
2009 Notre Dame commencement speech (Obama), 262
2009 White House Correspondents' Association Dinner (Obama), 169
2011 Alfalfa Club speech (O'Connor), 159
2011 State of the Union (Obama), 153
2012 African Methodist Church (Obama, M.), 284–285
2012 Alfred E. Smith Memorial Dinner (Romney), 158–159
2012 DNC keynote (Castro), 164
2012 National Peace Officers' Memorial Service (Obama), 138
2012 RNC nomination speech (Rubio for Romney), 290–291
2012 Syrian nerve gas (Obama), 116–117
2014 immigration (Obama), 22, 24–25, 28, 30, 239, 266–267
2014 White House Correspondents' Association Dinner (Obama), 163
2015 presidential campaign launch (Kasich), 101
2015 presidential candidacy announcement (Cruz), 43
2016 addiction treatment (Obama/Macklemore), 81–83
2016 Alfred E. Smith Memorial Dinner (Clinton, H.), 155
2016 Alfred E. Smith Memorial Dinner (Trump), 151–152, 157
2016 campaign (Clinton), 33, 42
2016 campaign (Trump), 33
2016 campaign stump (Sanders), 58
2016 Democratic Party nomination acceptance (Clinton, H.), 1–3
2016 DNC (Clinton, H.), 32–34, 36–37, 44, 279–280
2016 DNC (Cuomo), 180
2016 DNC (Garcetti), 231
2016 DNC (Obama, M.), 133
2016 DNC nomination acceptance speech (Clinton, H.), 129–131
2016 economic conference (Warren), 101
2016 healthcare (Clinton, H.), 266
2016 immigration (Trump), 29, 30

Index | 499

2016 Kennedy Center Honors (Obama), 437–440
2016 National Museum of African American History and Culture (Obama), 213
2016 Republican Party nomination acceptance (Trump), 1–3
2016 RNC (Cotton), 211–212
2016 RNC (Cruz), 127, 128, 133–134
2016 RNC (Rubio), 97
2016 RNC (Trump), 32–36, 37
2016 RNC (Trump, E.), 285–287
2016 RNC (Trump, I.), 179
2016 RNC nomination acceptance (Pence), 229–230
2017 Afghanistan (Trump), 42
2017 Building Trades Union Legislative Conference (Trump), 113
2017 Catholic University commencement (Noonan), 217–218
2017 commencement address, (Sanders), 102
2017 confederate monument removal (Landrieu), 180, 245
2017 George Washington University commencement (Duckworth), 238–239
2017 Girls Inc. (Clinton, H.), 263
2017 health care debate (Cole), 77–78
2017 healthcare debate speech (Kelly), 78–79
2017 Healthcare Roundtable (Pence), 12
2017 house immigration debate (Collins, D.), 182
2017 house immigration debate (Collins, S.), 182–183
2017 house immigration debate (Doggett), 183
2017 house immigration debate (Goodlatte), 183
2017 house immigration debate (King), 183
2017 house immigration debate (Schakowsky), 182–183
2017 immigration (Trump), 23–25
2017 March for Life (Pence), 124
2017 National Governors Association (Pence), 11–12
2017 net neutrality speech (Lee), 96
2017 Polish visit (Trump), 221–222
2017 Retail Advocates Summit (Pence), 11
2017 U.S. House of Representatives, AAC repeal debate (Burgess), 176
2017 U.S. House of Representatives, AAC repeal debate (Roe), 176
2017 U.S. House of Representatives, AAC repeal debate (Yarmuth), 177
2017 UN Assembly address (Trump), 230
2017 University of PA commencement speech (Booker), 221
2018 abortion, senate floor debate (Ernst), 252–253
2018 abortion, senate floor debate (Warren), 253–254
2018 Conservative Action Committee (Trump), 216–217
2018 Conservative Political Action Conferences(Pence), 233
2018 Democratic response (Kennedy), 232
2018 Senate hearing (Alexander), 212
2018 State of the Union (Trump), 138–139, 219–220, 279–281

Speeches, excerpts (by name):
    "Ain't I a Woman?" 1851 (Truth), 235
    "A Place Called Hope" (Clinton, B.), 34
    "A Time for Choosing" (Reagan), 288–289
    "Checkers" 1952 (Nixon), 115
    "Cross of Gold" 1886 (Bryan) 46
    "I Have a Dream" (King), 119, 277–278
    "Keep Hope Alive" 1988 (Jackson), 17
    "malaise" speech, 1979 (Carter), 15
    "Tear Down this Wall" (Reagan), 242–243

Speeches, tips/outline/example:
    acceptance speeches, elements, 437
    awards, 436–440
    commemorative speech, 411–415
    commencement, 413–426
    eulogies, 427–432, 433–435
    floor speech, 379–389
    issues keynote, 405–410
    keynote, 405–410
    political keynote, 399–405
    rally speech, 391–399
    roast, 441–447
    short floor speech, 389–391
    stump speech, 369–379
    See also entries for individual speech types

Speechwriter, The: A Brief Education in Politics (Swaim), 348

Speechwriters:
    advice for, expert interview, 353–355
    anecdote checklist, 149
    archive research, anecdotes/videos, 360
    attend speeches, boss, 360
    audiences, checklist, 50–51
    beginnings checklist, 225
    clients of. Clients, what speechwriters need from
    codes of ethics and, 321
    conclusions, checklist, 293
    conferences, learn to handle speech, 358
    cover memos, 359
    defending role of, 339–341
    delivery checklist, 317–318
    ethics checklist, 344
    expect changes to work, 361
    face time with boss, 357
    memorable language checklist, 132
    partnership checklist, 362
    persuasion checklist, 38
    pressures/stress of, 347–348
    problem, checklist, 249
    public awareness of, 345–347
    recycle speeches, 361
    relationship, build with employer, 355–356
    reliance on, politicians and, 12
    research, before writing, 356–357
    research checklist, 70
    rule of three and, 26
    solutions checklist, 271
    staff, cultivate relationship with, 358–359
    structure checklist, MMS, 92
    study great speeches, 356
    support evidence, checklist, 198–199
    voice, find boss's, 361
    wit and humor checklist, 172
    work, finding as, 366
    See also Speeches, tips/outline/example; Speechwriting

Speechwriting:
    disclosure, ethics and, 342–343
    does it matter?, 3–5
    ethical conditions of, 339–341
    how-to books, 469–470
    importance of, 1–3
    political life as focus of, 5–6
    rule of three and, 26–31

speaking skills, ethics and, 340
unethical by definition?, 337–343
See also Speechwriters
Spencer, Stuart, 14
Staccato effect, 232
Staffers:
  cultivate relationships with, 358–359
  event research sources and, 56
Stanford Encyclopedia of Philosophy, 26
Statement of purpose (SOP), 205, 206
  concrete examples, memorable, 221–222
  contrast, what you might say, what you will say *v.*, 222
  examples, 372, 386, 394
  flat, 381
  get serious, 220–221
  reflect, 222–224
Statistics:
  compare evidence, 176
  context, use in, 186–187
  cost, context of, 189–190
  evidence, 175–178
  examples, 252, 254, 386, 407
  increase size, decrease space, 187–188
  logos and, 32
  power of one, 188–189
  predict with, 177
  problems and, 245–246
  scope of problem and, 177
  summarize evidence, 176
Status, evidence and, 181–182
Steinbeck, John, 87
Stern, Howard, 155
Steve Jobs (Isaacson), 66
Stevenson, Adlai, 169
Stewart, Redd, xxiii
Stewart, Rob, 297
Story:
  anecdotes as, 238
  attention through, 204
  dramatic, 210–212
  examples, 253, 254, 402, 421, 433, 435
  human face on tragedy, 386–388
  larger audience, 212
  moving listeners with, 384
  personal, open with funny, 209
  public speaking, use, 210
  purpose and, 210–212
  See also Story-jokes; Storytelling
Story-jokes, 163
Storytelling:
  advertising as, 135
  anecdotes and. *See* Anecdotes
  five-*W* approach, 148
  jokes/humor, 160
  podcasts and, 67
  See also Story; Story-jokes
Stowe, Leland, 73–76
Strategy, closing to inspire, 282–284
Straw man fallacy, 191–192
Structure, speech:
  attention through story, 204
  delay juxtaposition, 237
  Monroe's Motivated Sequence (MMS) and. *See* Monroe's Motivated Sequence (MMS)
  problem, defining, 229
  serious moment, 205
  statement of purpose, 205–206
  thank-yous and praise, 205–206
Stump speech:
  examples, 11–12, 58, 371–379
  outline, 370–371
  practice delivery, 312–313
  tips for writing, 370
  uses of, 369–370
Style as content, 94
Summarize evidence, statistics, 176
Summary, 224
Sumner, Charles, 13
Support evidence. *See* Evidence, supporting

Supporting assertions, problems:
    brief example, 242–243
    extended example, 243–244
    facts/statistics, 245–246
    testimony, 244–245
    See also Evidence, facts and; Evidence, supporting
Supporting points, using evidence, 174–175
Swaim, Barton, 348
Swift, Jonathan, 160
Syllogism, 28–28
Symbolic anecdote, 141–143
Synecdoche, 113–114

Team of Rivals (Goodwin), 66
Technology:
    Flesch-Kincaid Readability Test, Microsoft, 16
    information dissemination and, 20
    speech dissemination and, 18
    speechwriting and, 353
    Twitter, presidents and, 49
TED.com, 65
TED Radio Hour (podcast), 67
TED Talk, (Sandberg), 145
Teleprompters, use of, 316
Tennessean, The, xxii
"Tennessee Waltz" (King & Stewart), xxiii
Terminal characterization, 35
Testimony, as evidence, 244–245
    expertise/status, 181–182
    quotes and, 180–181
    support from opponents, 181–182
Text:
    political speech, 309, 310–311
    reading from, delivery 308-311
Thanks, Obama (Litt), 355
Thank-yous:
    examples, 213, 215–216, 223, 372, 385, 401–402, 429–430
    segment audience, 217–218
    use of, 205
    vary approach to, 218–219
    See also Acknowledgements; Praise
Thank you speech, MMS and, 84, 86
Thatcher, Margaret, xxii
Thematic framing, 435
Theweek.com, 64
Thomas, Clarence, 340
Three Musketeers (Dumas), 120
Three *Ps* speech (proposal, persuasion, punch line), 263–269
Tipping Point (Gladwell), 66
Tone, set with litany, 258
Tonight Show, 170, 171
Too Funny to Be President (Udall), 66, 207
Top Ten list, 445
Toronto Star, 330
To Sell Is Human (Pink), 66
Toy Story (film), 445
Transitions, using, 103–104
Truman (McCullough), 66
Trump, Donald:
    Access Hollywood, 195
    Clark Judge interview on, 334–337
    press conferences and, 19
    quotes, 19, 120
    speaking style of, 295–296
    speech as delivered (weblink), 157
    speech excerpts, 1–3, 16, 23–25, 29–30, 32–37, 42, 113, 138–139, 151–152, 157, 216–217, 219–220, 221–222, 230, 279–281, 295
    style of, 94
    Twitter and, 49, 336–337
Trump, Eric, speech excerpt, 285–287
Trump, Fred, 2, 37
Trump, Ivanka, 179
Trump, Mary, 27
Trump, Melania, 322
Truth, Sojourner, speech excerpt, 235
Truth, techniques for telling, 3

Truthfulness, anecdotes and, 147
Tulis, Jeffrey K., 11
Tu quoque, fallacy, 194–195
Turnitin, plagiary detection tool, 326
Twain, Mark, 35
Twilight of the Presidency, The (Reedy), xxii
Twitter:
   presidential tweets, 49
   Trump and, 336–337

Udall, Mo, 66, 172, 207
Understanding, "average folk" stories to show, 35–36
Understatement:
   example, 413
   use of, 114–115
   wit and, 164
Uniqueness of audience, 41–45
Unity, reaching out to demonstrate belief in, 36
Unsupported assertion, 253–254
Upright Citizens Brigade, improv comedy, 158
Urgency, concrete detail and, 116–117

Valid syllogism, 27, 28
Values:
   audiences and, 43–44
   examples, 253, 254
   family, 2, 37
   questions of, persuasive speech and, 24–25
   shared, 36
Video your speech, critique, 315
Vietor, Tommy, 67
Visionary character, inspire solutions, 262–263
Visualization:
   examples, 275, 391, 397, 405, 415, 430–431
   Monroe's Motivated Sequence and, 75–79, 86

Vital Speeches of the Day, magazine, 65, 347
Vivid language, 112–118
Voice, capture more than boss's, 361
Voice, speech delivery and:
   articulated pause, disfluencies, 306–309
   emphasis, 306
   pauses, 305
   pitch, 304
   pronunciation, 306
   rate, 304
   volume, 304
Voles, Lorraine, 4
Volume, speech delivery and, 304

Walker, Wyatt Tee (interview), 62
Warren, Elizabeth:
   floor speech, complete, 385–389
   likeability, 15
   quote, 101
   speech excerpts, 253–254
Washington, Booker T., 100
Washington, George, 95
Washington Post, The, xxiii, 9, 14, 18, 31, 64, 329, 340, 342
"We," power of, 216–217
Web-based research, 59–60
Websites:
   americanrhetoric.com, Bakshian, Aram, oral history, 281
   congress.gov/congressional-record, 65
   event research, groups and, 57
   futureofstorytelling.org, 136
   howstuffworks.com, 64
   mentalfloss.com, 64
   "MLK Papers: Words That Changed a Nation," 62
   poetry research and, 63–64
   political information/discussions, 20
   political news aggregates, 64
   presidential twitter analysis, 49

reference list, 471–472
TED.com, 65
theweek.com, 64
64–65
See also Speeches, as delivered (weblinks)
Webster's, 324
"We Can Do Better" litany, 256
"We can give" clincher, 256
"We choose" solutions, 232
"We know" clincher, 237
West Wing, The (television), 365
West Wing Writers, 158, 164, 441
What I Saw at the Revolution (Noonan), 268, 343
When (Pink), 66
White House Ghosts (Schlesinger), 95, 316–317
Wiesel, Eliezer, 240
Wilson, Woodrow, 19
Winfrey, Oprah, 203, 205, 206
Wired, 59
Wit:
   acronym joke, 161
   asides, 241
   borrowing, old jokes, 159–160
   brainstorming/clustering, 158
   characterizing the speaker, 156–157
   definition joke, 161
   diffusing a situation, 155–156
   example, 438
   exercise, late-night laugh test, 169
   formulas, 160–161
   humor *v*., 153
   hyperbole and, 163–164
   if this is true, what else is true?, 158–159
   irony, 168
   making a point and, 153–154
   Nussbaum interview on writing, 164–168
   one-liners, 162
   on-ramps/off-ramps for use, 170–171
   pace, changing with, 154
   pop culture and, 162–163
   problems and, 240–242
   puns, 241–242
   quips, 162
   quotes, 169
   saying things you can't say without, 154–155
   speechwriter's checklist, 172
   story-jokes, 163
   tasteful, 171
   understatement, 164
   use/reuse, 171
   use throughout speech, 170
   See also Humor; Jokes; Laughter; Political humor
Wizard of Oz, The (film), 191
Wofford, Harris, 123
Wolf, Michelle, 152
Wolfe, David, 297
Word choice:
   active verbs, 98–99
   colloquial, 100–101
   concrete, 96–97
   sensitive, 100
   short, 95–96
   See also Language; Memorable language
Word count, cut, 103
Wright Brothers, The (McCullough), 66

Yarmuth, John (D-KY), 177
Yeats, William Butler, 268
"You may" clause, clincher, 256

Zak, Paul, 136
Zarefsky, David, 94
Ziegler, Ron, 98
Zullow, Harold, 15–16

Index of Speakers

Acosta, Alexander, 267–268
Alexander, Lamar, 212
Ammerman, Colleen, 14–15
Anderson, Chris, 56
Aristotle, 21, 26, 30

Baker, Howard, Jr., xxii
Bentsen, Lloyd, 168, 169, 209
Biden, Joe, 161, 171
Bonior, David, 54
Bono, 45
Booker, Corey, 221
Bradley, Bill, 139
Brandeis, Louis, 86
Broder, David, xxiii
Bryan, William Jennings, 46
Buchanan, Pat, 46
Burgess, Michael, 176
Bush, Barbara, xxii
Bush, George H. W., xxii, 122, 256
Bush, George W., 94, 115, 120, 141–142, 164, 195, 206, 207, 219, 241, 270
Bush, Jeb, 429–432
Bush, Laura, 139

Carnegie, Dale, 297
Carter, Jimmy, 15
Castro, Julián, 164, 167
Christie, Chris, 98
Churchill, Winston, 119, 124
Clinton, Bill, 34, 218, 287–288
Clinton, Hillary, 1–3, 19, 32–37, 39, 42, 44, 103, 129–131, 155, 157, 161, 162, 209, 234, 263, 266, 279–280
Cole, Tom, 77–78
Collins, Chris, 181–182
Collins, Doug, 181

Cotton, Tom, 211–212
Cruz, Ted, 42, 43, 122, 127, 128, 133–132, 134, 192, 193–194, 196
Cuomo, Andrew, 180
Cuomo, Mario, 179

Damasio, Antonio, 29
D'Amato, Al, 147
Doggett, Lloyd, 183
Duckworth, Tammy, 238–239
Durbin, Dick, 4, 65, 390–391

Edwards, John, 325
Eisenhower, Dwight D., 124, 195–196
Ernst, Joni, 252–253, 381–385

Fisher, Mary, 118, 407–410
Frum, David, 190

Garcetti, Eric, 145–146, 231
Goldwater, Barry, 178
González, Emma, 235
Goodlatte, Bob, 183
Gore, Al, 4, 6, 9–10, 41, 95, 99–100, 208, 214–215, 328
Graham, David, 173–174, 181

Haley, Nikki, 236–237
Henry, Patrick, 111, 121, 195
Hessan, Diane, 39
Huckabee, Mike, 48, 168, 183, 209, 260
Hunter, Duncan, 243
Hurwitz, Sarah, 143–144, 332

Inhofe, James, 308
Isakson, Johnny (R-GA), 140–141

Jackson, Jesse, 17, 96–97, 245
Jefferson, Thomas, 17
Judge, Clark, 334–337

Kaine, Tim, 194
Kasich, John, 101
Kelly, Robin, 78–79
Kennedy, Joe, 126, 232
Kennedy, John F., 47–48, 120, 121, 154, 156, 185, 257–258, 259, 274–276, 276, 288
Kennedy, Ted, 125–126
Kerry, John, 418–426
Khan, Khizr, 116
King, Martin Luther, Jr., 119, 277–278, 394–399
King, Steve, 182
Koop, C. Everett, 186–187
Kristof, Nicholas, 187–188

Landrieu, Mitch, 180, 245
Lee, Mike, 96
Leno, Jay, 64
Liberman, Joe, 171
Lim, Elvin, 104–109, 134
Lincoln, Abraham, 76–77, 181, 276–277
Litt, David, 355

MacFarlane, Seth, 184
Macklemore, 81–83, 114
Macron, Emmanuel, 242
Markey, Ed, 113
McCain, John, 265
McKeachie, Wilbert, 56
Meacham, Jon, 433–435
Minow, Newton, 247–248, 257
Mondale, Walter, 112
Morrison, Toni, 146–147
Moynihan, Daniel Patrick, 23, 147
Murphy, Chris, 236
Muskie, Ed, 4

Nixon, Richard M., 98, 114, 115–116
Noonan, Peggy, 217–218
Nussbaum, Jeff, 164–168

Obama, Barack, 15, 22–25, 28, 30, 32, 81–83, 97, 115, 116–117, 120–121, 124, 127, 138, 153, 161, 163, 169, 184–185, 192, 210–211, 213, 217, 218–219, 220, 237–238, 239, 256, 261, 262, 266–267, 290–291, 304, 437–440
Obama, Michelle, 133, 134, 142–143, 284–285, 401–405
Obey, David, 168, 169
O'Connor, Sandra Day, 159, 443–447
O'Keefe, Daniel, 261–262

Palin, Sarah, 45–46, 115, 121, 197, 282–283
Patrick, Deval, 323, 324
Parvin, Landon, 152
Pelosi, Nancy, 214, 215–216
Pence, Mike, 11–12, 124, 161, 162, 207, 229–230, 233
Powell, Colin, 174

Quintilian, 111–112

Reagan, Ronald, 43–44, 53, 67–69, 88–91, 102, 114, 117, 126–127, 146, 156, 162, 216, 222–224, 242–243, 263–264, 269, 281, 288–289, 305, 413–415
Rhatican, Bill, 18
Rice, Condoleezza, 190–191
Robb, Charles, 183–184
Roe, Phil, 176
Romney, Mitt, 41, 158–159, 241, 371–379
Roosevelt, Franklin Delano, 16, 65, 93
Rubio, Marco, 97, 290–291
Ryan, Paul, 208, 222

Index of Speakers

Sandberg, Sheryl, 145
Sanders, Bernie, 58, 102, 189, 192–193, 197
Schakowsky, Jan, 182–183
Schultz, George, 149
Schwarzenegger, Arnold, 26–28, 137
Seeger, Matthew, 338
Sessions, Jeff, 124, 246
Shapiro, Rick, 353–355
Small Deborah, 188
Spencer, Stuart, 14
Stevenson, Adlai, 169
Stowe, Leland, 73–74, 75–76

Thatcher, Margaret, xxii
Trump, Donald, 1–3, 16, 19, 23–25, 29–30, 32–37, 42, 113, 120, 138–139, 151–152, 157, 216–217, 219–220, 221–222, 230, 279–281, 295
Trump, Eric, 285–287
Trump, Ivanka, 179
Trump, Melania, 322
Truth, Sojourner, 235

Udall, Mo, 172

Warren, Elizabeth, 101, 253–254, 385–389
Washington, Booker T., 100
Wiesel, Eliezer, 240
Wilson, Woodrow, 19
Winfrey, Oprah, 204, 205, 206
Wofford, Harris, 123

Yarmuth, John, 177

About the Authors

Novelist, journalist, and teacher **Robert A. Lehrman** served as chief speechwriter to Vice President Al Gore and, in 2004, as chief speechwriter for the Democratic National Committee during his long speechwriting career.

He has written for political figures, celebrities, heads of nonprofits, and corporate CEOs, including two governors, Senator Lloyd Bentsen (D-TX), and two members of the Democratic leadership in the House of Representatives, as well as the CEOs of Texaco, Fannie Mae, and Pfizer.

Shortly after leaving the White House, Lehrman started Lehrman Communications. In 2005 he created and, with Professor Schnure, now co-teaches the political speechwriting course at American University, where he was awarded the 2010 University Faculty Award for Outstanding Teaching in an Adjunct Appointment.

Lehrman speaks often at other campuses, conferences, and associations, on the topic of political speech, and has conducted workshops for diplomats in many places, including Vietnam, South Korea, and Australia.

Author of a number of award-winning novels, coauthor of a highly acclaimed nonfiction book for young adults, and coauthor of *Democratic Orators from JFK to Barack Obama* (Palgrave Macmillan, 2016), Lehrman also frequently writes political analysis under his own name and offers commentary on a variety of news programs. Lehrman earned a BA from Tufts University where he played soccer, and an MFA from the University of Iowa Writers' Workshop, where he studied with Kurt Vonnegut and Richard Yates.

Lehrman is married to Dr. Susan Thaul. They have two children both in the film and TV business in Los Angeles, and two grandchildren, Theo and Miles. When he's not writing or teaching, Lehrman is playing table tennis where he loses regularly in tournaments. He does, however, hold his own against the table tennis robot installed in his garage.

For twenty-five years, former White House speechwriter **Eric Schnure** has written speeches for politicians, Fortune 100 executives, and other leaders, helping make their messages more memorable, their words more effective, and their delivery more powerful.

He began his career in 1993 as a speechwriter for Vice President Al Gore. Since then, he has worked in both public and private sectors, including his role leading executive communications at General Electric. He now runs his own firm and has helped clients from some of the most well-known companies in the world: Google, UPS, American Express, Marriott, HP, and Airbus, as well as global institutions such as the European Commission. He lectures regularly and runs workshops in the United States and internationally specializing in speechwriting, storytelling, leadership communications, and the art and science of persuasion.

Schnure also teaches as an adjunct at Johns Hopkins University and American University; the AU speechwriting course he and Professor Lehrman teach together has produced dozens of graduates writing for politicians of both parties.

In 2004, Schnure cofounded the communications consulting firm The Humor Cabinet and is known in Washington for incorporating humor into speeches. He is a Friend of the Gridiron, the venerable club of journalists famous for its annual roast, and *Roll Call* even described him as one of Washington's "go-to guys" for political humor.

Schnure graduated from Hobart College, and holds a master's degree in international history from the London School of Economics. He lives in Chevy Chase, Maryland, with his wife, Nancy, and their two sons, Benjamin and Daniel.

A native of upstate New York, Schnure was skating almost as early as he was walking. He remains an avid, though often-injured, hockey player. As of publication, he still had all of his own teeth.